MW00787328

Private Wilson Farner, Company C, Third Ohio Cavalry.

HISTORY OF THE SERVICE

OF

THE THIRD OHIO VETERAN VOLUNTEER CAVALRY

IN THE

WAR FOR THE PRESERVATION OF THE UNION
FROM 1861-1865

COMPILED FROM THE OFFICIAL RECORDS AND FROM
DIARIES OF MEMBERS OF THE REGIMENT BY
SERG'T. THOS. CROFTS, COMPANY C,
REGIMENTAL HISTORIAN

———

MEMBERS OF THE HISTORY COMMITTEE:

COL. CHAS. B. SEIDEL   LIEUT.-COL. D. E. LIVERMORE
DR. CHAS. O. BROWN   SERGEANT D. W. WOOD

———

TOLEDO, OHIO
1910

THE STONEMAN PRESS, COLUMBUS, O.

Reprinted by

BLUE ACORN PRESS
P.O. Box 2684
Huntington, WV 25726

New Material Copyright 1997 Blue Acorn Press

ISBN 1-885033-18-4

Manufactured in the United States

Acknowledgments.

Blue Acorn Press is indebted deeply to Larry M. Strayer of Dayton, Ohio, for making available his large collection of Third Ohio Cavalry photographs for this new edition of the regiment's history.

Sincere gratitude also is extended to the Follett House Museum in Sandusky, Ohio; Nan Card of Elmore, Ohio; Richard F. Carlile of Dayton, Ohio; Brad Pruden of Marietta, Georgia; Ron Chojnacki of Medina, Ohio; Roger D. Hunt of Rockville, Maryland; Dale R. Niesen of South Rockwood, Michigan; Thelma Shope of Toledo, Ohio; and Richard A. Baumgartner of Huntington, West Virginia.

The portraits of Colonels Lewis Zahm and Horace N. Howland are from the photographic collections of the Massachusetts Commandery, Military Order of the Loyal Legion of the United States, U.S. Army Military History Institute, Carlisle, Pennsylvania.

General Eli Long's portrait is from *The Story of the Fourth Regiment Ohio Veteran Volunteer Cavalry* by Lucien Wulsin, Cincinnati, 1912.

The engraving of Lieutenant Colonel Douglas A. Murray came from Joseph G. Vale's *Minty and the Cavalry: A History of Cavalry Campaigns in the Western Armies,* Harrisburg: Edwin K. Meyers, 1886.

Contents

To the Members of the Third Ohio Veteran Volunteer Cavalry Memorial Association:

Comrades—Three years ago at your annual reunion in Toledo, Ohio, you selected me to write a history of the service of our grand old regiment.

It was with many misgivings on the part of your historian that he accepted the trust and undertook the work. Knowing something of the many difficulties in the way that must be overcome before the work could be completed in anything like a satisfactory manner.

Many incidents and details are from necessity left out of the history that would have tended to make it both cumbersome and monotonous.

Your historian having an earnest desire to serve you to the best of his ability, has tried in all things to be entirely fair and impartial. He now submits to you the result of his labors, hoping for your kindly approval. To all those comrades who have so kindly encouraged and assisted me in the work I tender my most grateful thanks, and in an especial manner are these due to Colonel Seidel, Captain Howland, Lieutenant Skillman, Sergeant D. J. Prickitt, Philip Henley, William Smith and Dr. G. B. Spencer, for diaries and papers furnished.

Very sincerely your comrade,
Thomas Crofts, Regimental Historian.

BOODY HOUSE

TOLEDO, OHIO, March 8, 1910.

The History Committee of the Third Ohio Cavalry, in all-day session with the Historian, Comrade Thomas Crofts, held at the Boody House, has this day completed its work, which has been mainly to listen, as at previous sessions, to the reading and approve of the thrilling story which tells in faithful detail the marches and battles of our noble regiment.

Our Historian has done his work with painstaking fidelity. We doubt if there exists elsewhere a regimental history which so completely covers the ground.

As the reading progressed we lived again amid the stirring scenes of that greatest epoch of our history. The story moved on and the hours passed almost unnoticed. Sometimes we laughed and sometimes the tears came, but all the time it was as if we were once more in camp or field, marching "by fours," or lined up for the charge, every nerve quivering at the order to be off and with sabres flashing in the southern sun.

Old Kenesaw loomed fortress-like and threatening and the campaign was as real as though "Uncle Billy" were again the inspiration of his mighty army and Atlanta our goal. Gravelly Springs—ah! We starved again at the mention. Selma—we heard again the shout of the battle and "bombs bursting in air." Macon—we wept again for joy as the flag of truce from the Confederate commander brought the news to our battle front that the war was over.

The clank of sabre, the click of carbine, the incidents of foraging squads, the riotous shout and joy of victory, the remembered music of bugle and regimental band, the hearty comradeship of voices, long silenced in the grave, that came back to us through the mists and vapors of half a century; the glory of great days when heroic decoration was the dust of the march and the grime of the battle with old glory over all, when liberty and the nation were coming to their new birth, these are items in the inventory of heroic wealth, not told "on charge" or balanced by the clearing house, but perpetuated for us by this history of the old Third.

You will read it, comrades, and forget that you are grandfathers. You will say, "I, too, was there," and 'mid the glow of such memories you will not care that you are old or that you may be poor. You will say: "The memories of these deeds are my riches and Old Glory is worth all that it cost,"

A younger generation, enjoying to the full the heritage that our sufferings purchased, may pass the story with little note and short remembrance; but could they hear as we hear the undying voices of the past,

5

could they see as we see the glory of deeds that saved the Union, they, too, would forget the clamor of commerce and the jargon of political strife and heed the story that illustrates an epoch that made present greatness possible.

For the Committee,

CHARLES O. BROWN,
Formerly Regimental Bugler.

COL. C. B. SEIDEL,
DR. CHARLES O. BROWN,
SERGT. DE WILTON WOOD,
Committee.

Sergeant Thomas Crofts
Regimental Historian.

Members of the Regimental History Committee.

Colonel Charles B. Seidel

Sergeant D. Wilton Wood

Doctor Charles O. Brown

The History of the Third Ohio Veteran Volunteer Cavalry

BY THOMAS CROFTS

CHAPTER I.

CAMP WORCESTER

On the 6th day of August, 1861, Lewis Zahm of Norwalk, was commissioned by the Governor of the State of Ohio to raise a regiment of volunteer cavalry for the United States service, for three years or during the war. The campaign of 1861 had demonstrated that the war was to be no small affair; that the leaders of the South had determined to divide the country, and would exhaust every resource in their mad efforts to do so. The terms of the first volunteers called out for three months had expired, they had been discharged, and President Lincoln had issued a proclamation calling for 500,000 volunteers for three years' service, and the response rang back from factory and farm, from store and school house, "We are coming, Father Abraham, 500,000 more." The whole North became one vast recruiting camp, and in every town and city and village the sound of fife and drum was heard, banners were everywhere flung out and in the midst of it all were bodies of marching men, forming by companies and regiments, getting ready to go to the front to fight for the Union. As soon as Colonel Zahm had received his commission he set men to work recruiting in all the towns of northwestern Ohio, and before the end of August a goodly number of volunteers had signed the muster rolls and were ready to go into camp for instruction. Monroeville, a prosperous town on the Lake Shore Railroad, fifty-three miles east of Toledo, had been selected as the point where the camp should be located. August 28 the first detachment of recruits for the new regiment arrived from Toledo. It consisted of some sixty men under command of Horace N. Howland. As neither tents, camp equipage nor cooking utensils had arrived, we were assigned to quarters in an old warehouse. It stood a little back from the main street with a vacant lot in front, in the center of which stood a flagstaff from the top of which waved our"Star Spangled Banner"—we had not learned to call it "Old Glory" yet—that came later, after we had seen it waving in the smoke of battle. We had no blankets, although some of the boys had foresight enough to bring along bed quilts from home, but the weather was warm, and we had plenty of clean straw, so that we considered ourselves very comfortably situated. It was late in the afternoon when we arrived, and soon after we were ordered to fall in and march to supper. We found our commissary department established in a building near the center of the town with the dining hall on the second floor, and here we ate our first army meal, and this continued to be our boarding place as long as we were quartered in Monroeville.

There was considerable dissatisfaction manifested at various times in regard to the manner of cooking and serving the meals. There was an abundance, but not much variety; and it was not always well cooked and seasoned or served in a cleanly manner. The coffee was not always "like mother used to make." The beans and soup were frequently scorched; the pork was fat, the beef was tough, and the pie, and pudding and cake, and sauce that we had been used to were conspicuous by their absence. But what the men grumbled about was the dirty, slovenly manner in which the cooking and serving was done. The dissatisfaction of the men finally culminated in a riot during the latter half of September. One morning at breakfast the tables were turned over and wrecked and dishes and food tramped under the feet of the angry men in an indiscriminate mess. The quartermaster was appealed to, but after examining the kitchen and cooking utensils, he discharged the cooks and waiters. A detail of two men from each company was made to serve in their places. The tables were set up, new dishes bought, kettles and cooking utensils cleaned, and everything put in first class shape. It was 4 o'clock in the afternoon before dinner was ready, but it was clean and appetizing, and the men showed their appreciation by giving three cheers for the cooks. Occasionally one of the boys who happened not to be giving strict attention to the matter in hand would find on taking a drink of coffee that some obliging comrade had seasoned it with salt, just for a joke; and it was generally taken in good part, which was by far the best way to take jokes in the army. After the arrival of the first detachment there were fresh arrivals of recruits almost daily—the men being quartered in different buildings about town. The days were spent in drilling on foot, learning different evolutions—keeping step, forming and marching in line, etc. The evenings were passed in singing songs, telling stories and playing various games. There were many good singers among the men, and it was very enjoyable to sit outside the quarters in the quiet evenings and listen to the songs—patriotic or sentimental. Sometimes a foot race would create some excitement among the men. The writer recalls one race in which James H. Zedicher of Company C was one of the contestants. Zedicher did not look like much of a sprinter, but some of the men who knew him said he could run. He had all confidence in himself, and after he had prepared himself he told the boys they need not be afraid to bet their nickels on him. When the men toed the scratch no one would have picked Zedicher for the winner—but the way he shot forward when the word was given was a revelation. The other fellow never finished—Zedicher got so far ahead he gave it up. After that everybody conceded that Zedicher was in a class by himself. "You can't always tell from the looks of a toad just how far he'll jump." By the tenth of September the regiment had been designated as the Third Ohio Volunteer Cavalry to consist of twelve companies of 100 men each. While we were still quartered in the town an incident occurred that made a deep impression on the men. Two men belonging to the Marine Corps visited Monroeville and succeeded in getting a member of Company C intoxicated, and persuaded him that the navy was the only place for a man to be, with the result that he went with them to Sandusky. The orderly sergeant of his company was sent after him to put him under arrest and bring him back. The sergeant succeeded in locating him and brought him back to camp. He was court martialed for desertion, found guilty, and sentenced to be confined in the guard house for three days on bread and water and to stand on a barrel six hours each day bearing a placard containing the word "Deserter." There was considerable difference of opinion in the regiment regarding the punishment in this case, most of the men thinking it was entirely too severe under the circumstances. But no doubt the officers composing the court believed it best to make an example in this case that would deter any others from a like offense. The writer was well acquainted with this comrade and there is no doubt but that he felt his disgrace keenly, although we do not think that any of his comrades ever reminded him of it. He continued to do his duty as a soldier until he was taken prisoner at Lexington, in October, 1862. He did not return to the regiment after he was exchanged and as far as we know was never afterwards heard from.

About the last of September a lot of axes, hatchets, spades, shovels, and pickaxes arrived and were distributed among the different companies, and the next day details were sent out to the place selected for our camp, and commenced clearing the ground of logs, underbrush and rubbish, and putting it in shape for our tents. On the fourth of October we pitched our tents, and the next day moved with our traps and calamities out to camp. Our first camp was named "Worcester," and was located about half a mile south of Monroeville. The ground was admirably adapted for the purpose on a piece of high, well drained land on the east side of the road—parade ground in front next to the road backed by woods, where our tents were pitched. The Huron river furnished an abundance of good water. The camp was laid out with the streets running east and west, officers tents next to the parade ground. The officers had wall tents, while those of the men were known as Bell tents. Whether they were so named after the man that designed them or because of their resemblance to an old cow bell we were never able to determine. Each tent was supposed to accommodate twelve men. The only place where a man could stand upright was near the center. We slept on the ground, feet toward the center of the tent, no room for table or chairs, a low box for a seat or table was all that could be utilized. There were no stoves nor fires in the tents, and here we were destined to remain until the middle of January. For more than three months this was our only shelter from rain and snow, storm and sleet, and cold, and all the rigor of a winter in Northern Ohio. Our cooking was all done over open fires built outside the tents. There was no shelter whatever for our cooking arrangements. Each mess was provided with two iron camp kettles, one for making coffee, and the other for meat and vegetables. They also had a skillet for frying meat. Each mess made arrangements for its own cooking, either by changing off or by hiring one of their number to cook all the time. Cooks were excused from most duties in camp. Each company had a strong picket rope stretched the length of the company street, to which the horses were tied when we were in camp. But after we got into active service we had no use for a picket rope. Our horses were tied to the first thing that came handy—fences, trees or buildings. When we moved to camp each man received a knife, fork, spoon, tin plate and cup, canteen and haversack. The day we moved it rained and everything was damp, chilly and disagreeable in the tents, and wet outside.

In addition to the articles mentioned relating to his commissary or subsistence department, the cavalryman when fully equipped had a uniform consisting of change of underclothing, socks and shirts, one pair of trousers, jacket, blouse, overcoat, hat, boots and spurs and double blanket, arms consisting of carbine and sling, saber and belt, revolver and holster, cartridge and cap boxes and screw drivers. Horse and equipments consisting of saddle and saddle blanket, bridle, halter and watering bit, saddlebags, nosebag, lariet rope, and pin, surcingle, currycomb and brush. So, taking it all together, we had many things to look after, some of which we found in the latter years of the war we could dispense with to advantage. The boys that went out in 1861 were the pioneers of the service, and had to learn many things in the bitter school of experience—an experience by which the volunteers who came after were enabled in a large measure to profit. After we moved to Camp Worcester the boundaries of the camp were established, guards posted, and neither officers nor men allowed outside without passes. When our camp equipage came there was a bunch of muskets and bayonets for the camp guard. They came down to us from the Revolution or some other remote period, but they went to the scrap pile when we were through with them, for as the weather grew cold the guards were allowed to have fires on their beats, and the bayonets and gun barrels came handy to poke the burning embers together.

Colonel Lewis Zahm, the regiment's first commander, was born in Zweibrücken, Bavaria, in 1820 and died at the age of 70 in Seneca, Kansas. He received a brigadier general's brevet in March 1865 for meritorious service.

CAVALRY!

YOUNG MEN & MIDDLE AGED MEN!
YOUR COUNTRY CALLS YOU!

She has need of your services, shall she call in vain? or will you rush to do her bidding as of yore your fathers rushed to vindicate their rights? Now is the time to manifest your patriotism! Unite then under the lead of

COL. ZAHM !

Of Monroeville, to do battle for your country.

Col. ZAHM has been disappointed by one of the Companies that was to go into his Regiment, and therefore is under the necessity of raising one more company. The Regiment is full with the exception of this one Company. Come, then, to the rescue, and fill it up at once. We have now nearly 800 horses in Camp and will soon be ready to drill on horse back.

I have been authorized by the Governor of Ohio, as a Lieutenant to recruit volunteers for Col. Zahm's Regiment, and subsist them until ready to go into camp at Monroeville. Soldiers to receive pay from date of enrollment.

Then fill up the ranks, advance the Column, and on to the rescue of our common country.

Lieut. JOEL MORSE,

Headquarters at Vermillion, Erie Co. O.   *Recruiting Officer.*

A PUBLIC MEETING WILL BE HELD

At ....

On ....

Good Speakers will be in attendance.

Camp life now commenced in earnest. The bugles sounded the reveille at 5:30 and in a short time the assembly for roll call, when each man must fall in and answer to his name. Then came stable call, when horses must be fed and groomed, then breakfast call. After breakfast the water call would blow and all horses must be taken to water; then came sick call, guard mounting, and then drill, either on foot or mounted. If it was mounted drill, boots and saddles would sound, followed by the assembly— and thus the days passed from reveille in the morning until taps sounded at night. That bugle was constantly calling the men to duty, and we thought its notes seemed to echo with fiendish joy as they broke in on our pleasure and comfort. A story is told of one old trooper who after he had come home from the war paid a bugler $5 to come and blow the reveille under his bedroom window every morning for a week at 3 o'clock. A friend said to him, "You must think a great deal of those bugle calls." "No," he said, "it's not that, but I just want to have the satisfaction of telling the d—d bugler to go to the d—l and then turning over and going to sleep again." We know that most of the boys will think that he got a lot of satisfaction for a little money. And now a word about the drill: It was the one thing that we always had plenty of. It commenced when we first went to Monroeville and ended with the close of the war. And while we shall have very little, if anything, to say about drilling, after we cross the Ohio into Dixie, yet we wish the reader to understand that it did not stop there, for we never laid in camp at any time during the war for any length of time but the drill was taken up. And this was necessary, not only for our own efficiency, but after the first year in service we were constantly receiving fresh recruits in the regiment, and it was absolutely necessary on their account. The efficiency of a regiment hinges on its drill and discipline. The great majority of the men realized this, and submitted gracefully and cheerfully to the officers placed over them, and the rules governing camp life. And yet it was not always easy to get along without friction. There were some officers that were not always tactful, and there were some men that were difficult to restrain, but we have no doubt that matters progressed as smoothly in the Third Ohio as they did in any other regiment. It was not an easy lesson for the Union volunteers to learn—that obedience to orders is the first duty of a soldier; that it was

> "Their's not to make reply,
> Their's not to reason why,
> Their's but to do, and die,"

and that they learned their lesson well was attested on hundreds of battlefields, where they fought and died to uphold the integrity of our nation.

October 8th Captain Flanagan, who had had some experience in the army, drilled the non-commissioned officers of the regiment in cavalry tactics, which we found were entirely different from infantry. On the tenth our first installment of horses was received and from that time forth they continued to arrive almost daily. As they were unbroken and we had no bridles, and in many cases no halters, simply a rope around the horse's neck, they were sometimes rather difficult to control by the rider, but they did not stay in camp very long until they were ridden. The men made bits out of pieces of wood, or rope, and after fixing a sort of bridle would mount the most unruly of them. Sometimes the horse would bolt with his rider and after a wild run come to a sudden stop in front of some ditch or mud hole, pitching his rider head first into it. The boys got no end of fun out of breaking colts. By the middle of October many of the men were badly in need of clothing. The regiment was very much in the same condition as was the army of Washington at Valley Forge. Some were almost barefooted, and taken all together, it presented a rather dilapidated appearance; but on the fifteenth the first installment of clothing arrived and was issued. It consisted of drawers, shirts, boots, caps, and one blanket to each two men. We at once commenced to put on airs, and the next day held our first dress parade, orders being for the men to parade in their shirt sleeves. So we were in uniform, and made a very creditable appearance. The music for the parade was furnished by the Monroeville band. The next Sabbath, October 20, we had dress parade at 10 a. m. and preaching in camp by Chaplain Warner. October 22 our lieutenant colonel, Douglas A. Murray, joined the regiment, promoted from the Second United States Cavalry. A man of fine appearance, he was to be our authority on cavalry tactics. As his name indicates, he was a Scotchman and had a very peculiar brogue, rolling his r's in a wonderful fashion. He gave his commands in a sharp, crisp way, and while it was difficult to understand his words, the men soon learned to know what he meant, although that singular accent afforded us infinite amusement. He conducted our dress parade at 4 p. m., the music being furnished by a drum corps composed of three drummer boys and two Mexican veterans as fifers. The latter part of October the Norwalk band in fine new uniforms visited our camp and gave us an excellent concert which was very much appreciated by the men. It furnished a very agreeable change to the ordinary routine of camp life. Early in November the men began to manifest a great deal of impatience because our uniforms did not come, many of them were suffering from the lack of clothing and were wishing they had gone into the infantry.

On November 6th the good ladies of the surrounding country visited our camp and gladdened our hearts with their presence and with the abundance of good things they had brought with them to give us a picnic dinner. Our cooks prepared coffee, and each company erected tables. We had dress parade at 2:30 and marched from the parade ground to the tables. And what we did to that dinner was plenty. In a case of that kind the Third Ohio was always equal to the occasion. We expressed our thanks to the ladies by giving them three rousing cheers. A few days after the picnic our uniforms commenced coming and we received jackets, pants and blouses, halters, watering bits, saddle blankets, surcingles, currycombs and brushes.

November 12th horses were assigned, each company receiving horses of the same color. The horses were already branded "U. S." on the left shoulder, and the company blacksmiths branded them with the letter of the company above the "U. S." The horses were assigned to the men by the company officers. Our saddles were being made in Monroeville, and very naturally the men were taking a lively interest in that part of the work and in watching its progress, and we began to realize something in regard to the immense amount of material required to fit out a cavalry regiment.

On November 15th a consignment of overcoats came, and as there were not enough to go around, they were issued to the men who had no blankets.

November 20th another picnic dinner was given by the ladies of the near-by towns and we had an enjoyable time. A number of the officers made patriotic speeches, and music, sweet music, was furnished by the Monroeville band. There were many visitors in camp. We showed our appreciation by eating the dinner and giving three cheers for the ladies, and also for the band.

Yet, notwithstanding these variations, camp life was getting to be very irksome and monotonous. Our drilling was simply the dismounted drill. Until we got our saddles we could make no headway with mounted drill. We were simply learning to keep step, to march in column, and from column into line and from line into column, learning the facings, etc., day after day and week after week, until many of the men became impatient, saying we did not enlist to do this; we enlisted to put down the rebellion. The 1200 men who composed the Third Ohio Cavalry were just a plain average lot of American citizens, who had enlisted from patriotic motives to put down the rebellion, and they wanted to get at it, to get it done and get home again. They could not see the necessity of so much drilling—but they saw it later.

December 16th we marched to Monroeville, one company at a time, to get our saddles—and it began to look as if we would get there after a while. And the next day we had our first mounted inspection and review, at which orders were read notifying the regiment to be ready to march on the morrow at 9 a. m. to Norwalk and receive our regimental colors.

December 18th we marched out at 9 a. m. in column of fours and went through Monroeville. When near Camp McClellan we were joined by the Fifty-fifth Infantry Regiment, and escorted by the Norwalk and Fifty-fifth bands, we marched to the grounds where the presentation exercises were to be held. The Third formed on three sides of a hollow square, in four ranks open order, the infantry occupying the fourth side. Speeches of presentation were made, Colonel Zahm responding for the Third, thanking the ladies and citizens of Norwalk for the beautiful flag and banner and pledging the regiment to guard and protect them with their life's blood and bring them back with honor. The color sergeant and guards then marched to the center and received the colors from Colonel Zahm. Company F was selected for the color company. The presentation exercises lasted about two hours, during which time we sat on our horses, after which we formed columns of platoons, with the infantry in advance, and passed in review, saluting the colors, and after some further evolutions we broke into column of fours and marched through Norwalk, after which we returned to our camp just at dark. The next day we drew our spurs. The cavalry drill in 1861 and 1862 was a double rank drill, and it was a cumbersome and unwieldy affair. In forming the company the men led their horses into ranks, and standing holding the reins of their horses in the right hand near the bit, counted off by fours, and at the command, "Prepare to mount," numbers one and three in the front rank led forward a horse's length, and in the rear rank numbers two and four reined back, and all grasping the reins in the left hand near the pommel of the saddle and placing the left foot in the stirrup, with the left hand on the pommel and the right on the rear of the saddle. At the command, "Mount!" all sprang into the saddle as one man, numbers two and four in both ranks riding forward into place at once without further orders. In dismounting the same maneuvers had to be gone through. In 1863 the drill was changed to single rank, which simplified matters. Mounted drill in sections of four or in platoons of eight was simple and easily learned and executed, but when it came to marching and wheeling in sections of twenty-four or in company front it was different. Then if the men on the wheeling flank did not allow proper distance as they came around on a trot the men in the center would get the legs almost crushed off them between the horses, and we soon learned why it was necessary for cavalrymen to wear boots—we thought sometimes that we needed castiron ones.

The citizens of Bellevue had extended an invitation to the regiment to pay them a visit, and December 20th we started out at 9 a. m. It was a fine day, and the people of Bellevue gave us a most cordial welcome. The town was decorated with flags, and everybody was out on the streets to greet the cavalry. Tables had been spread and they were loaded down with good things. We did ample justice to the dinner, after which the assembly sounded. We fell in line, and after an hour's drill, marched back to camp, where we arrived just at dusk, everybody in excellent spirits, having enjoyed the day. We had not yet received our cavalry bridles, but mounted drill was now the order of the day. Mounted drill by companies, by battalions and regimental, besides mounted inspection and dress parade.

On January 3d we received our cavalry bridles, and on the 5th at dress parade marching orders were read. The regiment was ordered to Camp Dennison, and the movement was to commence on the 13th—two companies to go each day. We were to march to Shelby and there load our horses on the cars. On the 8th we went to a new drill ground near Cook's Corners, north of Monroeville, drilling from 10 a. m. untl 3 p. m., making charges and evolutions, by companies, squadrons, battalions, and by the entire regiment. There was some wild riding. One horse was killed, one man's leg broken, one officer's horse bolted with him and ran wildly all the way back to camp, his rider hatless, coat tails streaming out behind, and bounding in the saddle like a rubber ball at every jump of the horse. The next day we went to the same ground and for five hours practiced the same evolutions, with no mishaps. We returned to camp, men and horses covered with mud. The regiment was organized into three battalions—the First, composed of Companies B, H, L and M, under Major Foster; the Second, Companies A, D, E and F, under Major Parmore; the Third, Companies C, G, I and K, under Major Seidel.

In the latter part of the war the battalions were composed of companies arranged in regular alphabetical order. While we lay at Monroeville some of the men began to develop a fine ability as foragers, mainly in the chicken line, and it has been charged that the country was so thoroughly cleaned up that the people had to import new stock the next spring. Colonel Zahm had a fine flock of turkeys, and he made the boast that the boys would not be able to get them—they roosted too high. Some of the boys heard of the boast, which just put them on their mettle, and after spying out the roosting place, they determined to make an attempt to get the turkeys. It is needless to say they captured the flock, and invited the Colonel to dinner. After dinner the cigars were passed and everybody was in a first rate humor. The Colonel praised the dinner and thanked the boys for the good time he had had. One of the boys replied that he need not feel under any great obligations, as they were his own turkeys. The Colonel enjoyed the joke immensely, and never tired of telling it to his friends.

After the regiment got into active service there were many times when foraging was absolutely necessary to its existence. When men and horses were compelled to live off the country, and while individual foraging was disapproved of by the commanding officers, yet there were always daring spirits who were willing to take any risk when rations were short. Organized foraging parties were sent out through the country both between the lines and on the flanks and rear of the army, gathering up horses, cattle, hogs, and provisions and forage of every kind. Sometimes these foraging parties were compelled to go long distances and under strong escort, and many skirmishes were the result.

January 13th the advance guard of the regiment, Companies B and H, struck their tents and took up the line of march Southward. So we moved out from Camp Worcester, two companies each day during the week. There were several small towns between Monroeville and Shelby, and each squadron as it passed through was entertained at dinner at one or another of them. That day's march was long remembered by the boys. It was Wednesday, the 15th, when our squadron made the trip. The day was clear and cold, the ground was covered with a thin coat of snow which flashed and sparkled in the sunlight—an ideal winter day. We were to eat dinner at Plymouth, but the entire population of the country were out to cheer us on and bid us God speed. Houses were decorated with flags and bunting, and all along that line of march, at every farm house and every cross-road, men, women and children were waiting for us with hot coffee, sandwiches, doughnuts, apples, etc., etc. We ate all we could, and then filled our haversacks—but there is a limit to the amount of stuff that even a cavalryman can stow away. At Plymouth tables were set down the center of the main street loaded down with a splendid dinner, to which we were made welcome by the people of the town, who treated us with the most cordial hospitality and bade us good-bye with best wishes for the success of our cause. As we resumed our journey Southward, at one of the little red school houses that we passed the teacher had his pupils in line by the roadside and they were singing "Dixie for the Union," and just as the writer was passing, these words caught his ear: "And should your courage falter, boys, remember Bunker Hill, hurrah!" In the months and years that followed, in the camp, on the march, on the lonely picket, in the skirmish, or fierce conflict, when opposing armies were put in battle array, or in the wild charge, where squadrons met, mid rifle shot and bursting shell, how often did memory recur to the school children by the wayside singing "Remember Bunker Hill"! Yes, we often needed to remember everything that would inspire courage, patriotism, endurance. We reached Shelby just at nightfall, and after unsaddling and feeding our horses, we lay down to rest by the roadside under the shining stars. The night was clear and cold. In the morning we made coffee and ate of the luxuries left over from yesterday for breakfast. During the forenoon we loaded our horses on the cars and continued our journey toward the Sunny South, passed through Columbus in the evening and arrived at Camp Dennison on the 17th about 10 a. m. The last squadron of the regiment arrived on the 20th, it having taken the largest and best equipped railroad in Ohio just one week to transport the regiment across the state. There were a number of boys who came out with the regiment as servants for the officers. The writer wishes he knew something of the history of those boys so that he could record it. There are only two, however, that he can give any account of. One of these was known as Little Johnny Mitch. When we lay at Monroeville Johnny came to Captain Howland of Company C and wanted to enlist in the cavalry. The Captain looked the lad over, then shook his head and said, "No, my boy, you are too young to go into the army." But Johnny was persistent, and it resulted in the Captain hiring him to take care of his horse for six months. Everybody that knew Johnny learned to like him. He was short in stature, but a blocky little fellow—a good natured, obliging little Dutch boy. Well, when Johnny's six months expired we were at Jeffersonville, Ind., and he wanted Captain Howland to enlist him. But the Captain thought him too young and small for the service, so Johnny went across the river to Louisville and enlisted in the Fourth Kentucky Infantry, and when he came back to bid us good-bye he was dressed in the army blue, and oh, so proud to be a soldier! We of Company C always took a great interest in Johnny, and he visited us whenever we were near each other. Johnny looked more of a boy than ever when in the ranks of those tall Kentuckians; and yet what he lacked in stature he made up in pluck and endurance. His Lieutenant said of him, on that forced march to Shiloh : "Some nights when we stacked arms there would not be more than fifteen or twenty men in the ranks; the rest of them were played out by the wayside; but Johnny was always up with the company." Well, Johnny soon came under the notice of his Colonel, who took him for his orderly. The Colonel afterwards got command of the brigade, but he kept Johnny with him, and thus things went on until the autumn of 1863. In the terriffic Battle of Chickamauga, Johnny, finding that the sore need was for men in the ranks, picked up the rifle that had fallen from the grasp of a dying comrade, got some cartridges, and moving up to the firing line, went to work loading and firing steady as a clock. It was while thus engaged that he was struck with a spent ball. Entering his mouth it lodged in his neck, inflicting a dangerous and painful wound. Our men were driven back, and Johnny was left on the field—dead, it was supposed. He lay on the battlefield for four days, when he was picked up by the enemy and exchanged. He finally recovered, but his speech was somewhat impaired. The latest reports we had in regard to him were to the effect that his Colonel sent him North to school.

One other of the boys that were with us when we left Monroeville was the son of Lieutenant Brown of Company C. He went with the regiment as his father's servant—he was then thirteen years old. Charley learned to blow the bugle, and when the regiment veteranized he was enlisted as a bugler, and in August, 1864, was appointed regimental bugler by Colonel Seidel and served in that capacity until the close of the war. He then went to school and afterwards entered the ministry, becoming famous as a platform speaker, and at our annual reunions the eloquent addresses of Dr. Charles O. Brown of Chicago are the feature of the occasion.

CHAPTER II.

CAMP DENNISON

Camp Dennison was located on the west bank of the Little Miami River about twelve miles north of Cincinnati. It was specially fitted up for a permanent camp, with barracks for the men and stables for the horses, and during all our service the only time when shelter and protection were provided for our horses was during the few weeks we remained at Camp Dennison. In the heat of summer or the cold blasts of winter, in snow and hail and rain and sleet, our faithful horses had no shelter whatever. The service was hard on the men, but on the horses it was simply terrific. Often they were ridden to the utmost point of endurance for days and nights together with very little food and less care. It is not to be wondered at that they succumbed to hardship and privation and were left by the wayside by scores and by hundreds. Each one of the barrack buildings at Dennison was fitted up to accommodate 100 men— three tiers of bunks on each side and tables down the center—cooking facilities in one end. While here we had company cooking and company mess. Our recollections of Camp Dennison were not pleasant. The season was just changing from winter to spring—consequently we had a great amount of rain, and the parade ground was a perfect sea of mud, in which we paraded, marching and countermarching and charging day after day.

January 20th we received our sabers and belts, cap and cartridge boxes, and commenced to learn the saber drill—drilling in barracks when it was too stormy for drill outside. Our first saber drill was something to be remembered. Methinks that could the hosts of rebeldom have seen the way in which we cut great gashes in the atmosphere they would have realized that their cause was hopeless, and would at once have given up the conflict. The saber drill was by far the hardest to master, and the real value of the saber as an arm of the cavalry service has always been a mooted question, and while there is no disputing the fact that in a hand

Unidentified group from Company H, photographed during the regiment's early-war stay at Camp Worcester near Monroeville, Ohio.

Bugler Charles O. Brown, Company C, was 13 years old
when this portrait was made at Monroeville, Ohio, in December 1861.

**Bugler Charles O. Brown, photographed here by W.A. Smith
in Plymouth, Ohio, was the youngest member of the regiment.**

Unknown first lieutenant (possibly Richard B. Wood, Company D) posed
at Norwalk, Ohio's Denham Gallery with a Wesson carbine and Savage revolver.

**Captain William B. Amsden, Company D,
died June 19, 1862 at Fremont, Ohio.**

Unidentified trooper from Company B.
Note inverted cavalry insignia on hat.

Private Hezekiah Edwards, Company D, was discharged for disability in August 1862. During the summer of 1864 he served in the 100-day 139th O.V.I., guarding Confederate prisoners at Point Lookout, Maryland.

Private Rose J. Parks, Company M, posed well armed with saber and
Remington revolver. He was discharged for disability in March 1863,
and later served in Company C, 144th O.V.I. for 100 days in 1864.

to hand conflict it is a very effective weapon, is always loaded and never misses fire, yet during the latter years of the war when much of the fighting was done on foot, we often found it very much in the way. In advancing at a double quick it had a most disagreeable habit of getting entangled in a fellow's legs and sending him forward on his nose in a very undignified manner; and an observant person would have noted that it was the cause of a vast amount of profanity. While at Dennison we also received our revolvers and a part of our carbines. The carbines were of three different makes, the Sharps, Burnside and Remington, all single shot breech-loaders. With the Burnside and Remington there was more or less difficulty in extracting the empty shell after firing, and while the Sharps was a good single-shot gun, yet it was not to be compared with the Spencer, with which we were armed in the latter years of the war. Notwithstanding the fact that everything was being done to get us ready for the front as rapidly as possible, yet many of the men were impatient of delay, and the fear was frequently expressed that the war would be over before we got to the field. The camp was always full of rumors, either that we were to be disbanded or that the end of the war was close at hand. and in any case we would never get to see any fighting. Colonel Zahm heard of the rumors, and one day at dress parade he made a brief speech to the regiment, saying in substance: "Poys, I hear that some of you pe afraid that the war will pe over pefore we get to the front, and that we won't see any fighting. I tells you don't pe afraid! You get your pellies full of fighting yet!" Future events proved that the Colonel was a true prophet. General Wright and Attorney General Wade inspected and reviewed the regiment while we were at Dennison, and commended us for our fine military appearance.

The recreations in the barracks in the evenings were manifold. There were songs and stories. Company B organized a literary society, with Lieutenant Culver at its head. They had a number of lectures, debates, etc., that were largely attended and enjoyed by the men. Company L organized a minstrel troupe and gave some performances which drew crowded houses and furnished a lot of amusement. There were games of different kinds—cards, checkers, chess. On the Sabbath there was preaching in some of the company barracks, to which all might go who wished, and there were prayer meetings held in some of the officers quarters. While there was not much difference between the Sabbath and other days in the duties of the soldier in the field, yet when in camp there was no drill on the Sabbath day. We would generally clean up and have inspection about 9 o'clock, then preaching in the open air if the weather was fair, and sometimes dress parade in the afternoon.

February 9th three days rations were issued and we were ordered to be ready to move. The next morning the general call sounded, and after breakfast boots and saddles, and forming into line at 8 a. m., we marched out of Camp Dennison and, headed by the Fifth Regiment band, started for Cincinnati.

CHAPTER III.

DOWN THE OHIO

The Third Ohio Cavalry never made a finer appearance than it did on the morning of February 10, 1862, when it marched out of Camp Dennison and took up its line of march for Cincinnati to embark on steamers for a journey down the Ohio River. A regiment 1200 strong, well mounted, with bright, new uniforms and arms, with banners flying and with martial music, it took its way, the silvery notes of the bugles echoing and re-echoing among the hills and valleys. We left Dennison at 8 o'clock in the morning, but it was 3 o'clock in the afternoon before we were in line on the levee in Cincinnati, and it was midnight before all our horses and baggage were loaded on the boats. It took six large steamers to carry the regiment.

February 11th, when morning dawned, we were steaming down the river, which was at its flood, and was a grand sight to many of us, who were looking on it for the first time. The current was very strong, and the boats made rapid progress. There was a great amount of driftwood, and on some of the logs mud turtles had taken passage. Some of the boys tried their revolvers on them and sometimes they would drop off into the river. Our destination was Jeffersonville, Ind., which place we reached at 3 o'clock in the afternoon, and went into camp in the mud. Our stopping place was named Camp Wright, and was on the farm of Jessie D. Bright, an opposition senator from Indiana. The river was in full view from our camp, and very soon after our arrival an almost continuous procession of steamboats loaded with our gallant boys in blue passed on down the river with banners waving, bands playing and men cheering. It was an inspiring sight and there was no doubt in our minds but that the war would soon be over and we would be marching home again.

Fort Henry had surrendered to General Grant while we were at Camp Dennison, and on the sixteenth of February the news came that the forces at Fort Donelson had surrendered, opening up the Cumberland River, and forcing the rebels to leave Bowling Green and Nashville and take a line of defense further south. There was much rejoicing in the Union camps over the news. Battery G of the First Ohio Light Artillery celebrated the event by firing 100 guns in honor of the victory. While we lay at Camp Wright we received Sibley tents in exchange for the old Bell tents we had used at Camp Worcester. They were a great improvement when we were in camp, but of little use in active field service. It was necessary to haul them in wagons, which very often did not get to camp in time, and were altogether too cumbersome to use when on the march, (as we very soon found out). We also received another installment of carbines and revolvers. On the twenty-fourth of February the prisoners taken at Fort Donelson passed through on their way North. They were the first rebel soldiers we had seen. On the 27th the United States paymaster visited us and we received two months pay—$26—in greenbacks. Many of us had been in the service six months, yet there were no complaints at the small amount received. We knew the government was doing the best it could for us. Forage for our horses was very short at Camp Wright. In fact, very many times during the war our horses were on short rations of musty corn. On Saturday, March 1st, marching orders came, rations were issued, also ammunition for carbines and revolvers. Sunday, March 2d, general call sounded at 8 a. m. It was a disagreeable, cold, rainy morning, but we were all elated at the thought of getting into service. Our tents and baggage were soon packed and loaded into wagons, but it was slow business ferrying the regiment over the river, and it was the middle of the afternoon before we stood in line in the City of Louisville, soaked to the skin and chilled to the marrow. We took up the march southward, going into camp in a low piece of meadow land about four miles from the city.

Our camp was soon converted into a mud hole under the tramping feet of men and horses, and by the time we had our Sibley tents pitched the ground was in such a condition that we were compelled to carry in rails for floors to keep our bodies out of the mud; and there, lying on the sharp edges of those rails in our wet clothing and blankets, we passed one of the most miserably disagreeable nights of our lives.

During the night the rain changed to snow and in the morning a sharp, frosty wind was blowing, but we got our fires started and made coffee. The sun came out clear and bright, and as we took up the line of march southward our surroundings appeared much more bright and cheerful. We marched about twenty-five miles and camped near Salt River. March 4th we resumed the march at 8 a. m. and camped about three miles south of Bardstown. The scenery along the way was very fine—high hills, deep ravines and fine springs of clear water. We remained in camp on the 5th. (No forage for our horses, weather very cold; snowed during the night.) We were compelled to use fence rails for our fires. The orders were that we should take only the top rail, and it is needless to say that the order was obeyed to the letter—when a man wanted a rail he invariably took the top one.

During the next three days we continued our march southward. The roads were very bad, the country rough. The wagons were unable to keep up with the column, so we had no tents or cooking utensils. March 9th we crossed Green river on the railroad bridge at Mumfordsville.

Here we saw the first signs of conflict. There had been a skirmish, and some of the horses killed in the fight were still unburied. Some of the houses in the town showed marks of shot and shell. Upon a hill were a number of graves, each marked with a wooden headboard with name, regiment and company carved by the hand of a comrade. They were soldiers of the Union who had fallen in the fight; with their blankets tenderly wrapped about them, they had been laid to rest; taps had sounded, a volley had been fired over their graves, and their comrades had marched on at duty's call. No sadder duty than this falls to the lot of a soldier. We remained at Mumfordsville one day. The weather was wet and disagreeable. Thus far on our march we had had very little pleasant weather.

On the 11th we resumed the march over a rough, broken country, camped about half a mile from Mammoth Cave, and many of the boys spent most of the night in exploring that famous cavern.

The next morning we continued our march southward, arriving at Bowling Green on the 13th. We remained in camp one day and then moved on toward Nashville.

On the 17th we camped about nine miles from Nashville, and on the 18th we arrived at the Cumberland river about noon. The bridges had been destroyed. Crossing on ferryboats, we marched through Nashville and camped about two miles south of the city, near General Buell's headquarters. Here we were assigned to General T. J. Wood's, Sixth Division, Army of the Ohio. The next day the regiment was inspected by the inspector of General Wood's division. March 20th, about noon, general call sounded, and we packed up and moved out about one mile south on the Nolensville pike. The camp was laid out and tents put up as if we were going to stay awhile. The next day we had inspection of arms by the company officers, after which the regiment was formed and inspected by Colonel Zahm. At retreat orders were read for three roll calls each day, at reveille, retreat and tattoo, the men to fall in with their arms at each roll call. Dress parade and inspection each day at 3 p. m.

March 26th the regiment was inspected by General Wood, who complimented it highly on its appearance and drill.

CHAPTER IV.

SHILOH

March 29th—Drew three days rations, broke camp and started south-ward at 6 a. m. on the Franklin pike, the regiment at the head of the division. Camped at 3 p. m. in a piece of woods near a stream of good water.

March 30th—Started at 6 o'clock, passed through Franklin and went into camp. The day was hot, the roads dusty, and many men in the infantry were overcome and compelled to fall out by the wayside. Oh, how they did envy the cavalrymen!

March 31st—Started at 5:30; weather hot and roads dusty. Crossed Rutherford Creek and camped.

April 1st—Did not move until 10 a. m. Passed the division of General Thomas; forded Duck River at Columbia and went into camp about three miles south of the town, near the plantation of General Pillow.

April 2d and 3d—Still on the march. Nothing out of the ordinary occurred. On the 2d we passed through Mt. Pleasant. On the even-ing of the 3d we camped near General Buell's headquarters. On the morning of April 4th, six companies of the regiment, under command of Lieutenant Colonel Murray, left the main column and started for Law-renceburg, the county seat of Lawrence County, about fifteen miles to the southeast, where it was reported that a small force of rebel cavalry was stationed. We were accompanied by two regiments of infantry, General Milo S. Hascall commanding the expedition. After marching about half the distance the infantry halted while we went on to the town. There had been a small force of cavalry at the place, but nearly all had gone before we got there. Our advance got sight of a few of them as they charged into the town, and fired a few shots at long range as they ran; but as their horses were fresh, our men were unable to overtake them. We camped near the town. The rain came down in torrents, and the night was very dark. We found a lot of pork in the place, to which we helped ourselves, as we were on short rations of meat at the time. The following is Brigadier General Hascall's report of the expedition:

HDQRS. FIFTEENTH BRIGADE, ARMY OF THE OHIO,

FIELD OF SHILOH, April 12, 1862.

Agreeably to the order of General Wood, I proceeded on the morn-ing of the 4th instant from our camp, 23 miles beyond Waynesborough and about 60 miles from this place, with two regiments of my brigade, to wit: the Twenty-sixth Ohio and the Seventeenth Indiana, together with a detachment of about 600 of the Third Ohio Cavalry, under Lieu-tenant-Colonel Murray, of that regiment, and marched for Lawrenceburg.

The general had been informed that about 500 of the enemy's cavalry were at that point, with the intention of making a descent upon our train after the troops had passed. My instructions were to proceed cautiously to Lawrenceburg, a distance of about 14 miles from our camp, and capture the enemy, if possible and to disperse him at all events. It happened that the day was very rainy and exceedingly bad for the infantry to make the march, on account of the swollen streams and mud. I proceeded very cautiously, leaving a couple of cavalry at every house we passed, to prevent any one taking information to Lawrenceburg of our approach, but when getting about two miles from there we had to pass over a succession of hills, in full view of the town, so that further precaution in this respect was useless.

By this time I had learned that there were not more than from 50 to 100 cavalry there at furthest, and being desirous of saving the infantry as much as possible for the forced march that was still before them, before reaching this point I ordered the infantry to halt, and after getting their dinner, to return to the camp they left in the morning and join the other two regiments of my brigade. I then proceeded with the cavalry as fast as the roads would permit, and when getting within about one-fourth of a mile from town, ordered a charge upon the town, which was splendidly executed by Lieutenant-Colonel Murray at the head of his men. I learned that there were 50 to 75 cavalry in town, but as soon as they observed our approach put themselves in readiness to leave. They left principally in the direction of Florence and Mount Pleasant, and, their horses being fresh, but few could be overtaken, though they were pursued some eight miles in both directions by our cavalry. Two of the enemy were severely wounded, as evidenced by the blood upon their horses which fell into our hands. The result of the expedition was the breaking up of the secession rendezvous at that point, the capture of six cavalry horses and saddles, about 4000 pounds of fine bacon, a dozen or two shotguns and squirrel rifles, and two drums.

I take great pleasure in reporting that a strong Union sentiment seemed to pervade the whole country through which we passed going and returning, my command being everywhere received (except at Lawrenceburg) with every demonstration of joy and treated with the utmost kindness and consideration.

Fearing that that portion of the rebel cavalry that fled toward Mount Pleasant might be part of a larger band in that direction, and might seriously embarrass, if not capture, portions of our train, I dispatched Major Foster, of the cavalry, with two companies, to scout the country as far as Mount Pleasant, and then to join his regiment at Savannah; since which time I have received no tidings from him, but presume he has joined his regiment some time since.

The remainder of the cavalry, with myself and staff, bivouacked near Lawrenceburg the night of the 4th, and having procured wagons in the neighborhood with which to transport the captured bacon, started early the next morning, and about noon overtook the infantry of my brigade, who were *en route* for this place.

All of which is respectfully submitted,

MILO S. HASCALL, Brig. Gen.,

Commanding Fifteenth Brigade.

April 5th—We Started early to rejoin the column. Marched by the way of Waynesboro; camped in a piece of woods. The day was wet and very disagreeable.

April 6th—We were on the march early. We had not gone far, however, before rumors of a battle in progress reached us. The roads were in terrible condition—ammunition wagons and artillery struggling through the heavy mud; infantry and cavalry marching along the sides. We received an order to leave our baggage and wagons and hurry up all troops as fast as possible. And so we marched through the rain and mud all that fateful Sunday, our hearts filled with forebodings of impending disaster, all the rumors indicating that our comrades on the banks of the Tennessee were sore pressed and badly in need of reinforcements. Toward night we halted and fed our horses and took a few hours rest.

April 7th—Bugles sounded just after midnight, and we moved out at 1:30. What a night it was! No one who passed through that experience will ever forget it. The rain poured down in torrents. So intense was the darkness that it was impossible even to see our hands held before our faces. The thunder was terrific, the lightning flashes blinding in their intensity, revealing for an instant the whole scene of struggling men and horses, and followed by darkness that could be felt, and through it all the constant, steady boom! boom! boom! of the cannon on the gunboats, telling us that the battle was not yet over; that the struggle would be renewed when morning came. Our progress during the night was necessarily slow, but when day dawned we went forward more rapidly. As we neared Savannah the sounds of battle could be heard more distinctly. To the booming of the cannon was added the rattle of musketry, which could be plainly heard. We reached Savannah about noon, where we found the remainder of the regiment halted by the roadside awaiting orders. Our infantry was embarking on boats going to the battlefield, while at the landing was a sight never to be forgotten. Wounded men by scores and hundreds lay side by side on the wet, blood-stained ground, waiting until they could be cared for in the buildings and tents that were being converted into hospitals. Many had died during the brief passage down the river, and were laid in rows and covered with blankets until they could be buried. All day long each boat coming down the river brought its load of wounded, and as soon as they were landed the command, "Forward!" would be given and a regiment of boys in blue, with steady step, marched on board and were off for the battlefield. What a picture of war in all its aspects was presented that day at Savannah! Men pressing forward with banners flying and drums beating in all the pomp and pride of military display, coming back bearing all the signs of conflict—bruised and bleeding, dying and dead. We knew then that Sherman's definition was right when he said, "War is hell." We remained at Savannah helping care for the wounded until the 9th, when the regiment was stationed by companies about three miles apart along the road between Waynesboro and Savannah, to protect the wagon trains and guard the telegraph line. We were engaged in this work and in picket patrol and scouting duty until April 23d, when the regiment was united at Savannah.

April 25th—Moved up the river to a point opposite Pittsburg; crossed on ferryboats and camped on the battlefield near the landing.

April 26th—Moved out about four miles and joined the division camping near General Wood's headquarters. Orders for drill every day that we lay in camp. Hot weather and poor water caused much sickness among the men. Camp diarrhœa, fevers, etc., incident to change of climate became very prevalent and continued until after the capture of Corinth.

CHAPTER V.

THE SIEGE OF CORINTH

April 28th—A general movement of the whole army toward Corinth commenced. It was an immense army. General Halleck was on the field in person, commanding the entire force.

April 29th—Moved forward five or six miles in the direction of Corinth.

April 30th—The paymaster visited us and distributed a few greenbacks among the men. His visits were always welcome. There was some cannonading in the direction of Corinth. The general advance appeared to us to be very slow.

May 2d—A part of the regiment went out four or five miles in the direction of Monterey. We had a little skirmish at long range with no apparent results.

May 6th—Went as escort for Colonel Innes looking up roads at the front.

May 9th—Two squadrons of the regiment under command of Major Foster and Major Paramore, while on outpost picket in front of Corinth, had a skirmish with the enemy. As there was some criticism of the manner in which the officers handled their men, we publish their official reports in full:

Report of Major John H. Foster, Third Ohio Cavalry, of Skirmish Near Corinth, Miss., May 9th.

HDQRS. THIRD REGT. OHIO VOLUNTEER CAVALRY,
CAMP NEAR CORINTH, May 9, 1862.

SIR: In compliance with your orders of May 8th, 1862, I proceeded with two companies (L and M) of the Third Regiment Ohio Volunteer Cavalry to relieve two companies of the same regiment on picket duty on the Corinth road, about five miles from Corinth. On coming up to the companies on duty I inquired of Captain D. C. Doane, the officer in command, for instructions where to place my pickets. He said he was instructed to place them across the mud-hole, as he called it, the other side or south side of the woods, but had not done so, not considering it safe to do so. I then went across the branch and mud-hole, and discovered four men in an open field near the house. I rode up, and found two men of General Buell's staff and two of General Nelson's staff. I went on to a Mr. Lee's, half a mile beyond there, and ascertained from Mr. and Mrs. Lee where the enemy's pickets had been, and that they had drawn them in that day. I returned to the Shoeff house, where I first saw the officers of General Nelson's staff. They requested me to accompany them to General Nelson. I did so. He informed me he should occupy the Farmington road with a regiment of infantry, which road was in my front, and left of the Shoeff house and part of the farm, which I was told was the place where Captain Doane was ordered to place his pickets. General Nelson also said he should place his pickets from the Farmington road to the left side of the Corinth road, half a mile in advance of the Shoeff farm, where, I was informed, was my place to put out my pickets. He suggested that I continue on his right my line of pickets to the Purdy road across the Lee farm, which I did.

At 1 o'clock next morning I was informed that General Nelson was drawing in his pickets. I sent out and drew in mine from the Purdy road and placed them on the Farmington and Corinth roads, and they remained there until driven in by the enemy.

About 9 o'clock on the 9th instant two companies of the Third Ohio Volunteer Cavalry came up to relieve us, under the command of Major James W. Paramore, and before I gave him orders in regard to placing his pickets that I had received, our pickets were fired on. I sent a squad of men to ascertain the position and strength of the enemy. They reported about 350 men near Lee's house, across the branch and mud-hole, firing at our pickets. We were then four companies strong (or parts of companies) of cavalry, and at that moment Colonel Innes, of the Mechanics and Engineers, came up and a company of his men. He sent them on the Corinth road toward Mr. Lee's house, and I sent one company of cavalry, (Company L, Third Regiment, Ohio Volunteer Cavalry) and soon the skirmishing commenced. Three companies of infantry came up, and in the meantime Major Paramore had ordered his two companies across the mud-hole, half a mile in the rear. I ordered them back to Shoeff's farm, formed a line, and prepared to sustain the men who had gone forward. Colonel Innes took his men (three companies) to the right and toward the Purdy road, to prevent the enemy from flanking us and to get in their rear if possible. I was to remain on the Shoeff field, and to give support to the two companies fighting. If they fell back, I was to fall back to the lower side of the field to draw out the enemy from the woods and then charge on them in open field, allowing Colonel Innes to come in their rear. Such was our position and arrangement when Major Paramore ordered his two companies to retreat. I ordered them to halt. At this I sent 25 men to sustain Colonel Innes on the right and guard a road that led through the woods on my right.

At this time Captain William M. Flanagan, of Company L, came out of the woods, and said the bushes were so thick his men could not fight to advantage, and asked to dismount his men. I ordered his men to dismount and lead their horses to the rear; also ten men of each company to dismount and act as infantry, under the command of Captain Flanagan. At this moment Major Paramore ordered the men to retreat, and our men fell back to the lower part of the field before I was aware of their intentions. I rode in front, and ordered them to halt and rightabout wheel and form line. Major Paramore again ordered his men to retreat, saying he would command his own men and I might mine. His men commenced a left wheel to move off, and I deeming it imprudent to hold my two companies, consisting of 70 men, after he had ordered his to retreat, saying he would command his own men, there could be no concert of action between us, and I ordered my men across the branch and mud-hole.

I have the honor to be your obedient servant,

JOHN H. FOSTER,
Major Third Regiment, Ohio Volunteer Cavalry.
COLONEL L. ZAHM.

*Report of Major James W. Paramore, Third Ohio Cavalry, of Skirmish
Near Corinth, Miss., May 9th.*

CAMP THIRD OHIO VOLUNTEER CAVALRY,

May 10, 1862.

SIR: I have the honor to submit the following report of the part
taken by my command in the skirmish in front of General Wood's division
on Friday, May 9, 1862:

I left camp at 7 o'clock of said day, in command of the Third Squadron of the Third Ohio Volunteer Cavalry, composed of Companies E,
Captain T. D. McClelland, and F, Captain O. G. Smith, with orders to
report to General Wood. I did so, and received verbal instructions from
him to proceed to the outpost of his division and relieve the two companies sent out on the 8th instant, in command of Major J. H. Foster,
also of our regiment, and station my vedettes the same as his, and await
further orders. I proceeded accordingly to the outpost, and found the
reserve of the squadron, under Major Foster, stationed at an old deserted
house on the left of the road, through the open space shown in the
diagram. I halted my command, and was informed by Captain Flanagan
that Major Foster, with a detachment of his command, had gone down
the Corinth road to take a reconnaissance. I waited until he returned,
when I informed him that I had come with my command to relieve him,
and asked him where his vedettes were stationed and for instructions, etc.
He informed me that he had just been down within two miles of Corinth,
and had "waked up the gentlemen in force, and thought we would see
some fun, and that he would not return till he saw the result." He then
sent back a small patrol on the road to watch their movements. They
had not been gone long before they were fired upon and returned the
fire, and sent back for reinforcements. Major Foster then assumed command of all the forces, and sent out Company L and a part of Company M
and five or six of Company E, in command of Captain Flanagan, as
skirmishers, to reinforce the patrol. I then asked him for permission to
station the two companies under my command in the edge of the woods
on the north side of the open field, in a position to command that in case
our men should be driven back and the enemy follow them. "No," he
replied, "that would not do, for, in case they were obliged to retreat, they
could not cross the marsh below," but for me to fall back with them to
some point on the road and station them as a reserve. Accordingly I
took them back across the bridge where the slough crossed the road, and
stationed them in line of battle at the side of the road, in a position to
command it.

About this time a sharp fire was opened up in the woods along our
whole line of skirmishers with the enemy, who appeared to be in force,
with infantry. Major Foster, who was then stationed near the barn in the

open field with a small reserve of Company M, Captain Marvin, sent down and ordered my command forward into the open field, and stationed it to the right and front of his reserve, on the high ground, and within twenty or twenty-five rods of the upper edge of the woods, with a small detachment of Company E on another rise of ground at the farther end of the field. We remained in that position without any command to forward or retreat, until a small party of infantry (which had come up from a working party in General McCook's division, and deployed in the woods to assist our cavalry) had all retreated and left the woods, some in the direction from which they came and others to the woods in rear of us; and the cavalry skirmishers, under Captain Flanagan also, with great coolness and good order, were compelled to retire from the woods before a superior force of infantry, which, with all the advantage of thick woods, had fallen back to our right and rear, thus leaving no force whatever between us and the enemy, who were rapidly advancing to the endge of the woods and sending their leaden messengers thickly around and among us, and reported by our skirmishers to be a much superior force. Then seeing the danger of our position, where the enemy could advance, under cover of thick woods, within twenty or twenty-five rods of us without our being able to see them and they could us, I took the responsibility of ordering my squadron to about wheel and retreat down to the lower side of the field, which they did on a walk. I then ordered them to halt and about wheel again in line of battle. Captain Flanagan, with his company, had formed on my right, and also brought his men down to the woods, and at the same time faced about in line on my right, which brought us in position to command the open field. Almost simultaneously Major Foster came down with his reserve of Company M and ordered us to retreat across the swale or slough, which order was obeyed, and he led the column across the swale to the rising ground, where he formed his squadron in line on the left of the road and I formed mine on the right.

General Wagner, who was in command of a reserve of infantry and section of artillery, a short distance to the rear of us, then came up and inquired who was in command of that cavalry. I told him that I had been sent to relieve Major Foster, which I was ready to do. He then ordered me to station vedettes to connect with those of General McCook, and extend across to the Purdy road. Accordingly I immediately took Company F and went back across the swale to the north side of that open field, and there stationed them as vedettes in the edge of the woods, where they could view the field, and extended them across to the Purdy road, which position I held till regularly relieved today, the 10th instant. This skirmish occurred between 10:30 and 11:30 o'clock of the 9th instant. The enemy did not advance farther than the edge of the woods on the south side of the field, where they remained a short time, and then fell back to their old position.

The casualties were one man of Company L slightly wounded. All the officers and men of the command behaved with uncommon coolness and bravery, executing and obeying every order given with promptness and good order.

All of which is respectfully submitted.

J. W. PARAMORE,
Major Third Ohio Volunteer Cavalry.

COLONEL L. ZAHM,

During the entire month of May in the advance on Corinth, we were constantly engaged in picket and scout duty. Skirmishes with the enemy were of almost daily occurrence, but the casualties were light, as both sides were very cautious about exposing themselves when in range. Sometimes the picket lines were in close proximity, but were cautioned not to expose themselves. May 21st moved camp within about six miles of Corinth. On May 27th we went with a force of cavalry and infantry to the left and rear of the Rebel lines—did not find the enemy in much force.

May 29th, during the night, we heard many explosions in the direction of Corinth, and the illumination of the sky was more than ordinarily bright, indicating that something unusual was going on. We were early in the saddle and moving toward the town. We came to the outer line of works and found them abandoned. The works were very strong. At every point where artillery could be advantageously posted forts had been constructed. The woods in front of their fortifications had been cut down, and all the branches trimmed so that they pointed toward the front. In places where there was no timber they had constructed abatis, using for that purpose everything available—telegraph poles, sharpened stakes, small trees, fastened together with telegraph wire, and a net-work of wire woven through the fallen timber, so that it would have been almost impossible for the infantry to get through. But they had concluded not to risk a battle.

We marched into Corinth and found the town practically abandoned by the white population. Only the old men, the women and the children were left. Most of the people we saw were negroes. Not an armed foe was in sight anywhere. They had not stopped to tell us why—they had not stopped to say good-bye. They evidently thought the country was getting too thickly settled and they moved out. A large amount of army supplies had been destroyed, the fires being still burning when we entered the town. Among the relics was a large pile of home-made butcher knives, the handles having been burned off. They had started out with the intention of using them to carve up the "Yanks," but after their experience at Pittsburg Landing, they came to the conclusion that they didn't want to get near enough to the Yanks to use knives. It did not take our leaders long to find out that Beauregard had shown them a clean pair of heels and it was no use to give chase. We were sent on picket to the south of the town and remained until the evening of the 31st, when we returned to our camp north of Corinth. Beauregard had retreated to Tupelo, about fifty miles south, on the Mobile and Ohio Railroad. We held Corinth. It was an important point, but somehow we were not greatly impressed with the fruits of the victory. We had had a great lesson in the strategy and the art of war, but we didn't think much of that kind of strategy. The Union commander had more than one hundred thousand men marking time for thirty days, between Pittsburg Landing and Corinth. With that kind of strategy the war would not have been ended yet. If the same conditions that existed at Pittsburg Landing on the morning of April 8th, 1862, had existed in 1864, and General Sherman had been in command, his army would have been in battle array in front of Corinth the next day, and there would have been another battle fought, and Corinth would have been won by the Union arms.

During the three months that had elapsed since we crossed the Ohio river our regiment had suffered the loss of a large number of men, mainly through diseases incident to camp life, change of water and climate. The water between Pittsburg Landing and Corinth was generally very bad, so that during the month of May our ranks had thinned rapidly.

CHAPTER VI.

NORTHERN ALABAMA

June 2d the regiment went on a scout out on the Memphis & Charleston Railroad. On the 3d we returned to camp and joined General Wood's division near Bear Creek.

June 4th the Third Battalion, under Major Seidel, was attached temporarily to General Nelson's division as he had no cavalry, the balance of the regiment remaining with Wood's division, the Army of the Ohio were moving east on the Memphis & Charleston Railroad, with orders to repair it. Chattanooga was the next objective at which the army under General Buel was directed.

June 5th Wood's division moved to Iuka and the First and Second Battalions camped about a mile east of the town, where they remained until the 11th of the month.

June 11th, Companies A and D went on a scout and captured some rebel officers. Nelson's Division came up and Major Seidel reported to

Colonel Zahm that during the seven days the Third Battalion had been with General Nelson's Division they had been on scout or picket every day and on picket six nights out of the seven. That he (Seidel) had reported to Nelson and asked to have his men relieved by some of the infantry.

Nelson cursed him and told him he could take his men off as he had three of them under arrest and was going to have them shot for sleeping on post. When the matter was reported to General Wood he ordered the Third Battalion back to the regiment and the three men were not shot, either.

June 12th, 13th and 14th—On the march going east along the railroad. On the 14th reveille at 3 a. m. Started at 4 o'clock. Camped in a piece of woods northwest of Tuscumbia. The wagons did not come up until next morning. Tuscumbia is noted for its famous spring of splendid water large enough to supply an army. It gushes from the rock by the roadside. Our camp was located on the east bank of a large creek, of which the great spring is the head and from thence flowing in a northwest direction, it empties into the Tennessee river below Florence. The health of the men was much improved since leaving Corinth. We had found an abundance of good water after coming into Alabama, which added materially to the health and comfort of the men while here. A ripple of excitement was caused by a slave escaping and coming into our camp, closely pursued by his master, armed with an order from headquarters giving him authority to take his property. Meanwhile Lieutenant Brown of Company C, who, by the way was an ardent abolitionist and earnest defender of the rights of the colored race, having been a conductor on the underground railroad at East Toledo, Ohio, during the days of the "Fugitive Slave Law," guiding many a hunted slave on his way to Canada, had taken this one under his protection and hidden him in his tent.

When the slave master came to claim his man, Brown stood defiantly in front of his tent and refused to allow a search to be made, or to recognize the order from headquarters. During the altercation that was going on in front of the tent, the slave inside was an eager and anxious listener. Becoming satisfied that eventually he would be given up to his master, he sprang out of the tent, made a dash for the creek, and at one bound leaped almost to the middle of the stream, then struck out boldly and swam to the opposite shore, climbed up the bank and was lost to our sight in the woods, going like a streak of lightning. He was a magnificent specimen of physical manhood. We had stood in silent admiration watching the fugitive make his dash for liberty. He was greeted with a cheer as he ascended the bank and disappeared into the woods. An officer turning to the slave hunter said, "There's your man, catch him." With a look of disgust he replied, "Catch the devil; the fleetest horse you have got couldn't catch that d—d nigger." And as far as most of the men were concerned, the fugitive had their sympathy and they hoped he never would be caught. Lieutenant Brown was ordered under arrest, but nothing more ever came of it.

June 16th—A report was brought in that a wagon train had been attacked and the regiment went out to the rescue, but it proved to be a false alarm.

June 17th—Orders came for us to pack all extra clothing and send it to Florence. We turned over all except one suit, a change of underclothing and a single blanket for each man.

It was reported that it was loaded on an old barge which afterwards sank in the Ohio river. At least we never saw it again, and were never reimbursed by the government for its loss.

June 18th—Six companies of the regiment went on a scout to Russellville and Frankfort, but found no rebs. We camped at Frankfort and the next day returned to Tuscumbia .

June 20th—Company C was sent to Russellville to remain as an outpost watching the movements of the enemy in that direction. It was eighteen miles south of Tuscumbia, which was our nearest support in case of attack. It was after dark when we arrived at Russellville. Company I came out to reinforce us about midnight. We remained at Russellville ten days, during which time we sent in a large number of prisoners—most of them deserters from the rebel army who were tired of the war.

All the time we were at Russellville we were constantly on scout and picket. It took one company to picket the roads leading to our camp, the companies taking alternate nights on picket, and when not on picket we were engaged patroling the roads leading out from the town. We never felt very secure while at this place. It was certain that sooner or later the enemy would attack the post, and when they did it was sure to result disastrously to the few men holding it. We were too far from our supports for such a small force.

June 29th—We were relieved by two companies from the First Ohio Cavalry, and returning to Tuscumbia found it occupied by General Thomas' division, our division and regiment having gone on east to Decatur.

June 30th—Companies C and I left Tuscumbia at daylight and marched to Courtland, about twenty-five miles east. We arrived about noon. The day was very hot and eight of our horses died from the effects of the march in the hot sun.

July 1st—Companies C and I left Courtland early in the morning. Marched to Decatur; arrived about 11 a. m., where we rejoined the regiment.

The men of the First Ohio, who had relieved Companies C and I, were attacked July 1st and in the fight which ensued they lost two men killed and the Captain of Company G mortally wounded.

We now resume the movements of the balance of the regiment during the time Companies C and I were at Russellville. We left them encamped at Tuscumbia.

June 20th—The regiment started on a scout at 5 a. m.; camped near Courtland, and the next day marched to Decatur and camped, returning to Courtland on the 22d.

June 24th—Part of the regiment went to Moulton, arriving at 10 a. m. Captured a lot of tents belonging to "secesh" cavalry; burned them and returned to camp at Courtland.

June 26th—Started early. Marched to Elliot Place, about eight miles from Decatur, and went into camp. A terrific wind and rainstorm came on in the evening, lasting for several hours.

June 27th—The regiment on the march early, arriving at Decatur during the forenoon.

June 28th—Part of the regiment crossed the Tennessee river and Company H went to Mooresville. Saw some rebs on the south side of the river.

July 3d—Corporal Jacob Bauman of Company A was killed by guerrillas and stripped of all his clothing as he was returning to camp. Late in the afternoon Companies C and G ferried over the river and bivouacked on the north bank.

July 4th—Marched to Mooresville, eleven miles by wagon road. Had a celebration in the afternoon—patrotic speeches and a national salute of thirty-four guns—the last a volley from the entire battery.

July 5th—The rest of the regiment arrived from Decatur. For the next four days we were engaged foraging and guarding wagon trains.

July 9th—The Second and Third Battalions left the division. Camped at night eleven miles west of Huntsville.

July 10th—We passed through Huntsville and camped on Flint river, eight miles east of the town. Huntsville was by far the prettiest town we had seen thus far in the entire South—finely located, many handsome residences, the homes of wealthy people before the war. It has a very large spring of good, pure, cold water from which the town is supplied.

July 11th—Marched to Woodville and pitched our tents. We were to remain here for some time, guarding the railroad, foraging, scouting among the hills and chasing guerrillas. Woodville, Alabama, was an insignificant town on the railroad some thirty-five miles southwest of Stevenson. It was situated in a rough, mountainous country. The hills and mountains were infested by a gang of guerrillas headed by a man named Frank Gurley. These men knew every road and bridle path through all that region, and it was the most difficult thing in the world to locate them and convict them of any crime. There was no doubt in our minds that the people living throughout that region acted as spies on our men, furnishing the enemy with information in regard to our movements, and as they very seldom traveled on the main roads, but used bridle paths across the mountains, it was impossible to follow them. They took no chances in an open fight, no matter what their numbers. They would lay in ambush for our men and it was very seldom that they missed their aim. For a while our pickets were fired on almost every night, until we were compelled to change their location after dark, to prevent their being ambushed. Our duties at Woodville were most arduous. When not on camp guard or picket we were scouting, foraging, or patroling the roads. We had very little time for recreation in camp. We were compelled to get all our forage for the horses in the country.

July 14th—Companies C and I started on a scout at 8 a. m. with three days rations. Marched all day over the rough mountain roads; camped at night on the mountains about twenty-five miles out.

July 15th—Passed through New Market. Camped at night at Maysville. Plenty of rumors of rebels, but none to be found.

July 16th—Returned to Woodville, having marched about 100 miles in the three days.

July 21st—Companies C and I started out at 3 a. m. with the wagon train for Stevenson. Camped at Larkinsville, and the next day started at 4 a. m. Camped on Crow creek, four miles from Stevenson.

July 23d—Marched to Stevenson, left the wagon train and started back for Woodville. Camped at Larkinsville. Heard rumor that a force of rebels had crossed the river to make an attack on Woodville, but as there were so many rumors always in the air we did not place much confidence in them.

July 24th—Left Larkinsville at 3:30. Arrived at Woodville at 8 a. m. Found that an attack on the place was expected. Moved camp to the bridge at Paint Rock. Strong pickets sent out. Orders to keep the horses saddled and ready to fall in at a moment's notice, but as usual our friends the enemy did not call on us.

July 25th—Moved camp back to Woodville, but changed the location to one that could be more easily defended in case of attack.

July 27th—A regiment of infantry and a section of artillery came up from Huntsville and, accompanied by the Third Battalion, started for Gunter's Landing on the Tennesse river, some twenty miles south of Woodville. It was reported that there was a force of rebel cavalry in the town of Guntersville on the south side of the river, and the object of the expedition was to capture and destroy the ferry-boats on the river in that locality. We left Woodville in the afternoon and arrived in the vicinity of the landing about midnight. We dismounted in a piece of woods about half a mile from the river, and leaving our horses, moved up to the river above and below the landing. The orders were to keep under cover and not make any noise, as we hoped to remain undiscovered until they came over with one of the boats, when we were to charge down to the landing and capture it. As the day dawned and it became light enough for us to see across the river from our hiding places in the bushes on the north side, we saw a number of rebels come down to the river on the opposite side, and it was very evident that they were suspicious. They stood in groups talking and looking across toward our hiding place. Just then a darkey came down the road in plain view from the opposite bank and went to a spring near the landing for a pail of water. As soon as the rebs saw him they hailed him from the opposite shore, "Hello, Sam, are there any Yanks over there?" and Sam answered, "Lawd, yes; heaps on 'em," and our sneak game wasn't worth the candle. Our cake was dough, and as we came out from our hiding we could hear them say, "Oh, yes, I see 'em"—and then they opened fire on us, but their shots fell short, most of them dropping in the river. We raised the sights on our Sharps carbines and commenced firing, when they quickly ran for cover and did not expose themselves again during the day. There was an island in the river opposite the town. It was covered with a heavy growth of timber and underbrush so that it was impossible to see anything behind or on the island. We could see nothing of the boats. The artillery was brought up and commenced shelling the town, setting fire to a number of buildings. A raft was constructed and an attempt made to land men on the island under cover of the fire from the artillery. But the rebs had possession of the island, and as our raft neared the shore and the artillery had to cease firing for fear of hitting our own men, the rebs opened on them from the woods, and our officers seeing that they could not make a landing, the recall was sounded and the party came back. In attempting to cross the men placed their guns on the raft and, swimming beside it, pushed it over. It was now late in the afternoon, and we got orders to return to our horses, when we moved back two miles and went into camp.

July 29th—Got up early, fed our horses, and a number of squads were sent up and down the river to different landings and succeeded in destroying three flat boats. While we were on the march James Weldon of Company K was shot and instantly killed by some one in ambush. He and Corporal Frank Allen of Company C had gone ahead of the advance guard, and the shot was fired from a piece of woods some distance from the road. We were unable to get any trace of the party who fired the shot. The records of our regiment are very incomplete. No record of the wounded was ever kept. And in this case the Ohio Roster says that James Weldon died August 15th, 1862, in hospital at Woodville, Alabama. The writer has a very vivid recollection of the incident. He was with the advance guard at the time, and saw Comrade Weldon a few moments after he was killed. Major Paramore in his report of the expedition says the man was instantly killed, which report is here published in full.

We returned to our camp at Woodville and the infantry and artillery left us at Vienna and returned to Huntsville by another road.

JULY 27-30, 1862.—Expedition from Woodville to Guntersville, Ala., and skirmishes (28th) at Guntersville and Law's Landing, and (29th) at Old Deposit Ferry.

Report of Major James W. Paramore, Third Ohio Cavalry.

WOODVILLE, ALA., *July* 31, 1862.

SIR: I have the honor to report the entire success of the expedition sent out under my command on the 27th instant for the purpose of destroying the ferries on the Tennessee river from Law's Landing down to Whitesburg.

In accordance with instructions, the expedition—consisting of the Fifteenth Kentucky Infantry, commanded by Major Campbell, and a section of Loomis' battery, commanded by Lieutenant Chandler—left Huntsville on the morning of the 27th and proceeded by rail to Woodville, where we were joined by the Third Battalion of the Third Ohio Cavalry, in command of Major Charles B. Seidel, from which place I proceeded with the whole command, as above stated, for the Tennessee River, which we reached about 8 o'clock the same day, and encamped opposite Matthew's Landing, a distance of about twenty miles from Woodville, and over a rough, mountainous road. This was the first point on the route where we could get forage and water for our animals, and although it was a fatiguing march, it was accomplished without a murmur, so eager were the officers and men for the accomplishment of the purpose for which they were sent. I sent out the same evening of our arrival a strong picket, consisting of infantry and cavalry, to each of the ferries at Law's and Matthews' Landings, and also a squadron of cavalry, in command of Major Seidel, down to Guntersville, to watch the movements of the enemy, guard the boats, and prevent any one from crossing to give information of our approach. A courier from Major Seidel informed me that he was apprehensive that they would move their boats from Guntersville unless prevented by our artillery.

Accordingly I left the guards at Matthews' and Law's Ferries and proceeded with the command by daylight the next morning to Guntersville. I found the town strongly garrisoned by Forrest's cavalry and some independent companies of guerrillas and bushwhackers raised in the vicinity, with a heavy picket guard down at the landing guarding their boats and a warehouse filled with forage and commissary stores. I concealed most of my forces and artillery in a wood a short distance back from the landing, and deployed two companies of infantry as skirmishers to reconnoiter the position and ascertain the whereabouts of the enemy at the landing. True to their bushwhacking mode of warfare, the enemy soon fired on them from their concealed positions behind trees and the old buildings on the opposite side of the river. The fire was returned by our skirmishers and cavalry pickets and continued for a short time sharply on both sides, when I ordered one piece of artillery to be placed on the high bluff above the landing in a position to command their camp and the town and the other so as to command the landing and buildings opposite.

At about 7 a. m. we commenced a simultaneous shelling of their camp and the woods on the island above the landing with an occasional round of canister, which soon scattered the astonished rebels in every direction and set them to riding and running in the utmost confusion, and with the assistance of our carbines and long-range rifles soon cleared the opposite shore. The enemy having taken all their boats and skiffs to the opposite shore and concealed them in the creek between the town and the island (as shown in the accompanying diagram*) it was necessary that we should cross the river to destroy them.

Accordingly I set some men to work constructing a raft with such material as we had at our command for the purpose of crossing the river to destroy their boats. The enemy, perceiving our object, gathered in the old buildings opposite and commenced firing on the workmen. I then directed Lieutenant Chandler to shell those buildings, which he did, and they were soon discovered to be on fire, and the flames spread rapidly and consumed that part of the town.

As soon as the raft was completed Captain Allen of the Fifteenth Kentucky and ten men volunteered for the daring feat of crossing the river in search of the boats, and the raft not being large enough to carry more, one brave fellow swam the river to assist them. The party crossed safely to the island, and proceeded under cover of our guns up along the bank of the creek, and found that their boats had just been destroyed and sunk in the creek, all except one large one, which laid near the mouth of the creek partially sunk, but not destroyed. This they tried to raise and bring across, but the fire of the enemy's sharpshooters rendered it too hazardous, and Captain Allen abandoned it, and returned safely with his men to the command. I then ordered one of the guns down to a position below the landing, where the boat could be seen, and a few well-directed shells totally destroyed it. A vigorous fire was kept up on both sides from about 7 a. m. till 12 m., when the well-directed fire of our artillery had driven them from their camp and town to the mountains for safety, and the firing gradually subsided into an irregular skirmish of sharpshooters with long-range guns from concealed positions. This was continued until about 6 o'clock in the evening, when, having completed the destruction of their boats, and having no sufficient means of crossing my command to pursue the enemy further, I withdrew all the command except one company of cavalry and one of infantry (which I left on picket at that place to hold and watch the movements of the enemy) back to our old camp near Matthews' Landing.

All this was accomplished without any loss on our side except one man of the artillery slightly wounded in the foot. The loss of the enemy we could not ascertain definitely, but learned from a citizen who crossed the river the next day that their loss was about thirty killed and wounded, besides their camp and town badly damaged by our shells and about ten buildings, including the warehouse, filled with forage and commissary stores, burned.

Their force at that point and Law's and Matthews' Landings was variously estimated at from 600 to 1200, all mounted, with no artillery, and is said to consist of a battalion of Forrest's cavalry, a battalion of Adams' cavalry and two or three companies of guerillas and bushwhackers raised in that vicinity.

During that night (Monday, 28th) the boat from Matthews' Ferry was moved up to Law's Landing and an attempt was made to cross under cover of night and get in our rear, but by the vigilance of Captain Spaulding, of the Fifteenth Kentucky, and his company, who were on picket guard at that place, they were prevented from crossing, and compelled to leave their boat, with a loss of two killed and several wounded.

The next morning I took a part of my forces, consisting of one company of cavalry and one of infantry and one gun, and went to that point and destroyed their boat, also giving them a farewell salute of a few shells in their camp, about a mile distant, but with what effect we could not ascertain. Having previously sent out scouting parties and thoroughly canvassed the shore for boats and ascertained that there were none, at least that could be found between that point and Guntersville, we returned to camp and collected our forces and proceeded down the river toward Whitesburg and encamped at Cottonville, near the Old Deposit Ferry. Then I sent a small force, consisting of one company of cavalry and one gun, under command of Major Seidel, down to the ferry to destroy the boat at that point. On their approach the rebel pickets cut the boat loose and it floated down the stream over a mile before it was discovered, when the first shot from the artillery struck and sunk it. Having accomplished their object they returned to camp.

The next morning I sent Major Seidel with a detachment of cavalry on a scout to Ferrin's Landing, about four miles below Deposit, to ascertain if there were any boats at that place, and report if necessary to destroy them. I then left one piece of artillery and one company of cavalry and one of infantry at the road leading to this point to assist in destroying the boats, if necessary, and proceeded with the balance of the command to Vienna, and there awaited their arrival. When they came up Major Seidel reported that he found one large boat on this side of the river at that point and another on the opposite side. He dismounted a part of his cavalry and crossed in the boat lying on this side, and procured the other and brought them both to this shore, and totally destroyed and sunk them without the aid of the other forces. They then pushed on and joined us at Vienna, where our command separated, Major Campbell, with the infantry and artillery, proceeding toward Whitesburg, and I returned with the cavalry the same evening (Wednesday, 30th) to our camp at Woodville.

I regret to record that while proceeding with the command near Vienna one of my men—James Weldon, of Company K, Third Ohio Volunteer Cavalry—was shot and instantly killed by a villain concealed in the thick woods near the road. I immediately sent out scouting parties in all directions, with instructions to shoot down all persons found in arms and arrest all male citizens found in the vicinity. Only one was found and arrested—McDonald, living in sight of where the man was shot. He denies all connection with or knowledge of the murder, but I think it almost impossible that he could not know something about it, if he was not actually engaged in it. I therefore send him to your headquarters for such punishment as you may think proper, fully satisfied that to put down bushwhacking vigorous and severe measures must be used, and all the citizens in the vicinity where these outrages are committed must be held responsible for them.

It would be injustice to close this report without speaking more particularly of the bravery and gallant conduct of all the officers and men composing the expedition. Without mentioning their names, I would say that all are entitled to great credit for the promptness with which they obeyed and executed all orders given and the energy they evinced in accomplishing the object for which they were sent; and I would particularly mention the names of Major Campbell, commanding the infantry; Lieutenant Chandler, commanding the artillery, and Major Seidel, commanding cavalry; also Captains Spaulding and Allen, of the Fifteenth Kentucky, and Lieutenant Heflebower, of Company G, Third Ohio Volunteer Cavalry, for their co-operation and valuable services rendered in the expedition.

During the route we destroyed seven boats, viz: one at Law's Landing, three at Guntersville, one at Deposit, and two at Ferrin's Landing; but I was hardly satisfied with our operations at Guntersville. I think that nest of treason and rendezvous of guerrillas and bushwhackers should be entirely destroyed and purified by fire, for as long as it is permitted to remain their facilities for reconstructing their boats and its proximity to the railroad will make it a dangerous place for the safety of our trains and railroad bridges and require it to be closely watched.

All of which is respectfully submitted.

J. W. Paramore,
Major, Third Ohio Volunteer Cavalry, Comdg. Expedition.

Lieutenant-Colonel Murray,
Commanding Third Ohio Cavalry.

———

August 4th—Sergeant Patrick and four men of Company G while returning from a little scouting expedition and only a short distance from the pickets were fired on by bushwhackers from ambush. Sergeant Patrick and one man were killed and two of the men were wounded. One man escaped. The shots were plainly heard in camp. Company C was already mounted ready to go on picket. Captain Howland gave the command, "Forward!" and the company was off at a gallop. We met the man who had escaped, coming in, and a short distance beyond the picket post, found his companions lying on the rocks dead and wounded, but no trace of the men who had so cruelly murdered them. It was an ideal spot for such an ambush—a wild, lonely place. On one side the mountain rose abruptly from the roadside. The thick undergrowth afforded a complete shelter, so that the men in hiding might almost touch those riding by with their guns, and still remain undiscovered. If a small party was seen by these people going out, the bushwhackers would lie in ambush until they came back, and without any warning fire their shots at close range, and they very seldom missed their man. They would then betake themselves to their hiding places in the mountains, and it was the next thing to impossible to find them. The people living in the vicinity were either friendly to them or afraid to give information against them. There was a family living in a house near where these men were ambushed. We could get no information from any of them, and believing that it was a nest for spies, the house was burned. We scoured the country for miles in every direction and gathered up and brought in five men on suspicion. They were sent to headquarters at Huntsville and I believe were let go, as it was claimed there was no evidence that they were bushwhackers. The following is Lieutenant Colonel Murray's official report of the affair:

AUGUST 4-7, 1862.—Attack on Union pickets near Woodville, Ala (4th), and reconnaissance from Woodville to Guntersville, Ala. (5th-7th).

Reports of Lieut. Col. Douglas A. Murray, Third Ohio Cavalry.

COLONEL: I have the honor to inform you that between the hours of 3 and 4 our outward pickets on the Guntersville road were fired at from the bushes by a party of ten guerrillas or bushwhackers. One of the men was shot dead—the sergeant, a most worthy, good man, mortally wounded through the head, who died shortly afterward; the two other men were both dangerously wounded, only one of five escaping uninjured, who, being driven by the murderers, was forced to fall back. He describes the scene above as follows:

"The party, consisting of a sergeant and four privates, belonging to Company G, Third Ohio Cavalry, who were in the advance of the rest of the company at the outpost of the line of pickets on the road, about a mile and one-fourth distant from the camp, between the hours of 3 and 4 o'clock p. m., were fired on by a party of ten or twelve armed men. The first intimation they had of their approach was a volley of ball and buckshot. He, being the only one of the party who escaped its fatal effects, fired his carbine and revolver upon the party, but being so hardly pressed by the entire number had to retire. All this was so quickly done that the other pickets had not time to come to the assistance of the unfortunate men. The murderers turned into the bushes, which just at that place were thick, the mountain steep and rocky. Lieutenant Heflebower, the officer in charge of the picket, dismounted some of the men and searched all over for them without success."

Hearing the firing in camp from the line of pickets I immediately sent out a squadron to scour the country in the neighborhood of the scene. After much trouble, found the tracks of the murderers up and across the mountain; taking a circuitous route to some houses about one and one-half miles from where the firing took place, finding four men who could not account for themselves and from their contradictory statements were arrested. Finding any further efforts to make discoveries fruitless the command returned to camp. I brought each of the prisoners separately before the wounded men, then in the regimental hospital, one of whom, N. J. Fletcher, was identified immediately by Private Lewis H. Palmer, who is positive that he is the man that fired on him. Private Steckel, the only one of the party uninjured, also identified him, Fletcher, and one other, John Peters, jr., as being two of the men of the party of ten. The other two state that they were in company with Fletcher and Peters all day, and further their statements are both contradictory and changeable, and I have no doubt that each and all of them are guilty of the murders committed.

I had to use, assisted by the other officers of the regiment, the most strenuous efforts to prevent the men from lynching them, their guilt being so palpable. I hear from good authority that three of the ten men that are now in this vicinity bushwhacking are of those I have sent down to headquarters and who have been recently released, and are now boasting of being Union men.

Very respectfully, I have the honor to be, your obedient servant,

D. A. Murray,
Lieutenant-Colonel Third Ohio Cavalry, Commanding.

P. S.—Since writing the above Private Steckel has recognized Lewis Turner, another of the prisoners, also John Peters, as being two that were of the party. Private William Smith, Company C, recognizes one of the prisoners, Fletcher, as being one that fired upon him a few days since; Private Smith is now lying in hospital from wounds received, he states, by his hands.

Respectfully, yours,

D. A. Murray,
Lieutenant-Colonel Third Ohio Cavalry, Commanding.

Col. J. B. Fry, *Chief of Staff, Army of the Ohio.*

————

Headquarters Third Ohio Cavalry,
In Camp, Woodville, Ala., *August 7*, 1862.

Colonel: I have the honor to report for your information that the squadron of the Third Ohio Cavalry that left these headquarters on the morning of the 5th instant on a reconnaissance to the river opposite to Guntersville returned this day at noon.

The officer in command of the squadron reports that the encampment of the enemy has been moved back from the river about two miles, and there appears to be a larger force there now than when our troops, accompanied by artillery and infantry, were there. The enemy have dug rifle pits, and have also mounted two pieces of artillery to command the old ferries at that point. The ferry-boats destroyed by our troops are being repaired, and I have heard from good authority will be ready for use this day or tomorrow. It is rumored that they, the enemy, will cross with the intention of destroying the bridges on the railroad as soon as they possibly can. If not too great a liberty, might I suggest that two pieces of artillery may be sent to this point or the bridge near by. I have no doubt if artillery were here and could be spared they would render good service. The country being so miserably adapted for cavalry being as effectual as they otherwise would be on more suitable ground might be obviated by having the assistance of artillery. If artillery cannot be

Lieutenant Colonel Douglas A. Murray
was appointed to the Third Ohio Cavalry from the Regular Army.
He resigned his commission in June 1863.

Colonel Horace N. Howland, the regiment's final commander,
was brevetted brigadier general to date from March 13, 1865.

Larry M. Strayer collection

**Lieutenant Colonel Darius E. Livermore advanced from the rank
of first lieutenant of Company K. He was taken prisoner briefly
at the battle of Lexington, Kentucky, in October 1862.**

**Surgeon Marion C. Cuykendall served as the regiment's
chief medical officer until his muster-out in November 1864.**

Surgeon William B. Boyd was promoted from assistant surgeon when Surgeon Cuykendall's term of service expired.

The Reverend Benjamin F.W. Cozier was the Third Ohio Cavalry's second and last chaplain, joining the regiment during the Atlanta Campaign.

Sergeant Boston Lidruff, Company A, posed in front of a painted backdrop at the firm of R.E. Weeks in Sandusky, Ohio.

**Commissary Sergeant William H.H. Green, Company A,
also served as a quartermaster sergeant in 1865.**

**Sergeant Eugene A. Osborn, Company A,
photographed during veteran furlough in Norwalk, Ohio.**

Private John H. Kendall, Company A, joined the regiment in February 1864.

spared, two companies of infantry would, I have no doubt, prevent any damage being done to railroad in our vicinity.

The squadron arrested Mr. Hornbuckle, a noted bushwhacker, who attempted after his arrest to escape, and did succeed in getting off some distance; would have made good his escape but for the steps taken to prevent it.

Very respectfully, I have the honor to be, your obedient servant,

D. A. MURRAY,
Lieutenant-Colonel Third Ohio Cavalry, Commanding.
COL. J. B. FRY, *Chief of Staff.*

————

August 5th—Albert D. Noble of Company F was killed and John Cannon of Company C wounded by guerrillas. Companies C and K went in pursuit of the marauders but found nothing of them. Three houses were burned in obedience to orders to burn all houses near the scene of these outrages.

August 6th—Pickets fired on at midnight, and the command turned out. A patrol was sent out, but found no enemy. It was no doubt guerrillas.

August 9th—A report was brought to camp that General Robert McCook had been murdered by guerrillas while sick and riding in an ambulance near New Market.

August 10th—We started out with three days rations and a guide on a hunt for Gurley and his band of bushwhackers, the murderers of General McCook. We went in the direction of New Market. Camped at night at Paint Rock river. Arrested a number of men on suspicion that they might be implicated or might be able to give some information.

August 11th—Arrived at New Market about midnight after a rough march over the mountains. The rebs had been there but had left before we arrived.

August 12th—Started south from New Market; found where the guerrillas had camped the night before. We took up the trail and followed all day over the mountain roads, camping on the trail at nightfall when it became too dark to follow.

August 13th—We were in the saddle as soon as it was light. The trail led us into a narrow defile in the mountains, which ended in a pocket with no outlet, and here we came upon the band which we had been pursuing.

They were compelled to abandon their horses and take to the mountains on foot, where they fired upon us from the shelter of the rocks and trees, as they retreated up the mountain sides. We captured eighteen horses, one of them a splendid gray which had belonged to General McCook. We also wounded one of their men. We found a number of very good horses at a place a few miles away. The same night we marched to Huntsville and camped.

August 14th—Officers and men from the different companies started North to recruit men to fill up our ranks. The command started back to Woodville at 1 p. m. Camped at Flint river.

August 15th—Started on the march at 6 a. m. We heard that Gurley had gone to his plantation, and a detachment was sent back to catch him if possible, but a thorough search failed to reveal any trace of him. Reached camp at Woodville in the evening.

August 20th—The dismounted men started at 5 a. m. for Decherd for horses, going by the way of Stevenson, arriving at Decherd on the 21st, where they remained until the balance of the Second and Third Battalions came up.

August 26th—The Second and Third Battalions having marched through from Woodville, arrived at Decherd and camped near the station. Rumors that Bragg had crossed the river at Chattanooga, and there was a general movement of our army to be ready to check his advance as soon as his plans could be discovered.

CHAPTER VII.

BACK INTO KENTUCKY

After the evacuation of Corinth and the withdrawal of the rebel army to Tupelo, General Beauregard was removed and General Bragg placed in command. His army moving east, parallel to that of General Buell, occupied Chattanooga, which was well known to be the objective of the Union army. By the latter part of July it became evident to our leaders that General Bragg had planned a campaign of his own and for a time at least we should dance to his music. On August 19th Bragg commenced to cross the Tennesse river at Chattanooga and points above, and by the 22d his army was all on the north side; but for several days our leaders were in doubt as to his intentions. Was it northern Alabama? Was it Nashville, or was it East Tennessee and Kentucky? It proved to be the last. General Bragg had conceived the bold plan of a concentrated movement of all the troops he could control in a rapid movement into Kentucky. General Kirby Smith was sent from Knoxville by the way of Cumberland Gap to join General Morgan. Forrest was to move on our communications in middle Tennessee, and then northward into Kentucky. Generals Price and VanDorn were to keep Generals Grant and Rosecrans busy, or follow them if they undertook to reinforce Buell, while Bragg himself, moving rapidly by the way of Sparta, crossed the Cumberland river at Carthage, marched by the way of Scottsboro and Glasgow, striking the Louisville & Nashville Railroad north of Bowling Green, intended to form a junction with Kirby Smith, Morgan and Forrest and take Louisville before Buell's army could intercept him. It was a bold plan and had a fair prospect of success, his hopes being based largely on the expected recruits that his armies would get as they marched through Kentucky, but the people failed to respond to his appeals.

On the 22d of August General Buell was at Decherd gathering in his army, General Thomas with his division was at McMinnville and General Wood's division was near Manchester. As soon as General Buell learned that Bragg was moving east of McMinnville he put his army in motion for Nashville, by the way of Murfreesboro.

August 28th—The Second and Third Battalions left Decherd guarding Buell's army wagon train on its way north, and as the guarding of this wagon train was a new experience to us, a few words about wagon trains in general, and this one in particular, may not be out of place.

Of all the duties that fell to a cavalryman's lot the one that he disliked above all others was guarding wagon trains. For if you knew where you were going you never knew when you would get there, and when it moved you didn't know how soon it would stop. And if it stopped you didn't know how long it would be before it would start again. And if at a halt you sat on your horse awhile expecting it to move, until both you and your horse were tired and you dismounted for a rest, it would at once move forward, and you could mount and move along at a snail's pace. And so it was halt and move forward, halt and move forward, interspersed with helping the wagons over the mountains, across the streams, over bad places in the roads, from morning until night, and often far into the night, and sometimes all night, before you reached camp and could get your cup of coffee and lie down to rest. Buell's army train when stretched on the road was almost twenty miles long. And when it was on the march the rear of the train never got to camp until after the advance had started out next day. We camped that night at Shelbyville.

August 29th—Moved out at 7 a. m. and camped at Murfreesboro at night. We remained here until Sept. 7th. While at Murfreesboro we were routed out one night soon after midnight and saddled up expecting an attack.

September 7th—We left Murfreesboro for Nashville, Company C as rear guard. About noon some rebels came in sight, but did not attack us. We marched all night. The heavens were bright with fires of burning stores and buildings. Camped in the morning about 4 o'clock, three miles south of Nashville.

September 8th—All sorts of rumors in camp. Reported that Cincinnati had been taken by Kirby Smith. Reported that General Forrest was near here with 3000 cavalry. We were saddled up ready to move at a moment's notice.

September 10th—We left our camp at 3 a. m. Started north with the wagon train. Went into camp Sept. 11th at 3 a. m., having made eleven miles in twenty-four hours. After four hours rest in camp we moved out at 7 a. m. Camped at Three Springs, twenty-four miles north of Nashville. The advance found some rebs here and had a skirmish.

September 12th—Our regiment was rear guard today. We marched fifteen miles.

September 13th—Passed through Franklin, Ky., and camped.

September 14th—Left camp at 2 a. m. Reached Bowling Green before noon. One man and four mules drowned in Cave river.

September 16th—Ordered to saddle up and be ready to move at 1 p. m. Did not leave camp until 5. Marched sixteen miles; ran onto some rebs and had a little skirmish near where we camped.

September 17th—Drove in the rebel pickets; took some prisoners.

September 18th—Met Mitchell's forces and went back with them to Glasgow. Captured about 200 prisoners and five wagons loaded with flour and meat, and some whisky.

September 20th—Left Glasgow going in a northerly direction. As we were coming in toward Cave City after dark, Company C in the advance, we were fired on by the cavalry pickets of Rouseau's division. They were from the Second Kentucky. They fired one volley and galloped into camp. We followed them right in and gave them the merry ha! ha! as we met them going back to their post. We camped at 11 p. m.

September 22—Marched north, forded Green river at Mumfordsville, the bridge being burned. Camped about two miles north of the town.

September 23d—Marched from Mumfordsville to Elizabethtown, forty miles. Late when we went into camp; the rebels one day's march ahead of us.

September 25th—Started out with the Fourth Ohio and Fifth Kentucky Cavalry Regiments. Marched to Millerstown, some thirty-five miles, and camped.

September 26th—Marched in a southeast direction; roads very bad.

September 27th—Got to Bowling Green turnpike and followed it to Green river and camped.

September 28th—Marched to Brownsville and found our old friends of the wagon train waiting for us to escort them to the Ohio river.

September 29th—We lay at Brownsville waiting until the wagon train crossed Green river. For the next four days and nights we were engaged in escorting the train to the Ohio river at West Point, at which place we arrived in the afternoon of October 3d. In coming through we had avoided the main pike, keeping to the west, as the wagon train would have been a valuable prize for the enemy, and it was thought best to keep it as much as possible out of his way.

Colonel Zahm's report on bringing General Buell's army train from Brownsville to the Ohio river:

HEADQUARTERS SECOND CAVALRY BRIGADE,
Salt River, October 3, 1862—9 a. m.

COL. J. B. FRY,
Chief of Staff, Army of the Ohio:

I have the honor to report the arrival of the head of the train at this place at 7:30 this a. m. I found your instructions here. In accordance therewith I immediately had the train move forward for Louisville. They are proceeding finely; some 150 teams have crossed the river at this time. I had divided the train into three sections. The first section will arrive at Louisville tonight; the second section will reach half way to Louisville; the third section will perhaps cross the river yet tonight.

This morning everything was in order throughout the train; we had not lost a dollar's worth of property, with the exception of a few broken-down wagons, which we had to abandon.

I reached Hancher's Ferry on the morning of the 27th; found no wagons there. My courier arrived in the evening; reported that the wagons would cross at Brownsville. On the 28th I proceeded to Mooresville. On arrival there I found the head of the train in the act of crossing; some 100 teams had crossed. I found the coming up on the bank of the river very bad and very slow getting up.

We crossed some 500 teams yet on the 28th. On the 29th worked with a will; kept repairing the roads; kept two gangs of men ready with a long rope and hook to help the teams up. By 6 o'clock we had the teams all across, some 1700 in number, all told. On the morning of the 30th I set the train in motion in three different sections, with escort properly distributed. We continued our march without any interruption worth mentioning up to this time, over very rough, some places rocky and hilly, roads. It was not possible to have made twenty-five miles per day over the roads we had to come without breaking down one-half the teams. We worked busily all the while; kept going as far as the mules could stand it to go. We managed to find plenty of feed and water at our camping places for our stock; in fact everything appeared to move off as well as could be wished for. I shall feel very thankful when the rear of the train gets up, of which I think there will not be much doubt. I do not ask it as a favor to shoulder such a responsibility very soon again. I have never heard of a train moving of this large proportion. At 50 feet to the team, which is a small space for them to travel, it made a column of over seventeen miles in length, besides the brigade of cavalry occupying nearly another mile. On the pike I could have made twenty-five miles per day easier than fifteen miles per day the way I came. Up to this point I averaged a daily march of twenty miles and over.

On my arrival here I received your instructions to move to Shepherdsville with my brigade, and to let the train proceed on to Louisville without an escort. As the rear of the train will not be up before night, I shall not be able to move to Shepherdsville before tomorrow morning. I was in hopes that we would be allowed to move on to Louisville to give us a little rest, as both men and horses are very much worked down from hard labor performed for four weeks back, and to give us an opportunity to fit out the command in good shape again. As we are now we are in a poor condition to move against the enemy.

At least one-third of my men (Third Ohio) are dismounted, the horses having sore backs and given out otherwise on these long, hard trips of late. The horses we have on hand are very much jaded and fatigued. Then the command is without haversacks and canteens; in a great measure many out of clothing. We likewise need more horse equipments of all kinds and arms, as owing to the want of transportation we had to turn over these articles, as fast as they accumulated, at Savannah, Pittsburg Landing, Tuscumbia, etc., having a good many more sick in Nashville, Savannah, before Corinth who had entered the hospitals or were sent home on sick leave who had to leave their arms with the command. A large number of these convalescents have returned and are without arms, horses, or horse equipments. With the other two regiments, the Fourth Ohio and Fifth Kentucky, it is about the same thing. On the whole, as stated above, we are rather in a bad shape to make a forced march. Another thing which I hoped to have brought about: My regiment has now seven months' pay due them; both officers and men need money very much, which I had hoped would be paid them on arrival at Louisville, where they would have forwarded it to their families.

As for myself I am about worn-out and nearly down sick from the hard labors and exposures subjected to for the past month. Our transportation needs repairing very much before going on again with it. The same is scattered. One part of it, which was left at Nashville, is now moving with this train to Louisville; one part of it, which we left at Elizabethtown before going southward, I am not aware of its whereabouts; each part of the same has men and horses with it. Our property is scattered throughout the three parts of our transportation. Then again my men ought to have their overcoats, which they had to pack up at Tuscumbia; where they were sent to I know not. Nights are getting wet and cool, and men doing picket duty need their overcoats.

I wish you would consider these matters. Send any further instructions by my courier that you may have for me. He will return tonight.
I am, very respectfully, your obedient servant,

LEWIS ZAHM,
Colonel, Commanding Second Cavalry Brigade.

October 4th—We moved up Salt river to Shepherdsville and
remained one day resting in camp.

October 6th—Moved to Taylorsville, and the next day we marched
to Shelbyville.

October 8th—Marched to Frankfort, the state capital, where we
found a small force of the enemy. Had a skirmish; one man of the
Fourth Ohio killed and several wounded; lay on our arms in line of
battle all night. We remained at Frankfort until the 11th, when we
moved to Lawrenceburg, and on the 13th to Harrodsburg.

October 14th—We marched to Danville.

LEXINGTON

October 16th—The Third Battalion, under Major Seidel, and a
detachment of the Fourth Ohio, under Captain Robie, started out in the
afternoon with orders to go to camp Dick Robinson to guard some
commissary stores that had been abandoned by the rebels in their retreat.
Arriving at the camp we found a regiment of Union troops in charge of
the stores. We went into camp and Major Seidel sent out a patrol. When
they returned they brought in two men mounted and in Federal uniform,
who claimed to be Federal officers, but their answers to questions put to
them were not entirely satisfactory, and so they were placed under guard.
The next morning we started for Lexington, arriving early in the afternoon. The Union people gave us an ovation as we entered the town.
Their houses were decorated with the Stars and Stripes, and they were
in their door yards and on the sidewalks waving handkerchiefs and flags
and cheering us as we passed. We had not seen such a demonstration
since leaving Ohio. When we reached Lexington we found another
detachment of the Fourth Ohio camped in Court House square, and
Major Seidel marched his command out on the Richmond pike about two
miles and went into camp at Ashland, the homestead of Henry Clay.

The two prisoners captured at Camp Dick Robinson were left in
charge of the men camped at the court house.

Our camp was in a fine grove of native forest trees on the south side
of the road, and a short distance east of the Clay mansion. A strong post
and rail fence was between the road and the camp ground, and the only
entrance, a gateway through which we marched by two's. Our pickets
were posted about half a mile from camp, and in the evening Major Seidel

sent Lieutenant Hall with Company K out to patrol the road in the direction of Richmond. Soon after midnight Lieutenant Hall sent in under guard two white men and a negro. The men were officers in Morgan's command and for disclosing their identity the negro was shot after we had been captured. As the night passed, Major Seidel became uneasy and anxious, not hearing anything further from his patrol. He realized that we ought to get out, but disliked to abandon his men. Towards morning he sent word to Major Robie to saddle and be ready to move out at a moment's notice. Just as the dawn of day appeared in the east the firing of our pickets alarmed the camp, and as the firing continued we knew that it meant an attack. Major Seidel believed we ought to mount and retreat to Lexington or beyond, but Captain Robie, without consultation, marched his men, dismounted to the east end of the park, formed into line of battle and commenced firing. Major Seidel coming into position with the Third, we opened with our carbines on the enemy who could now be plainly seen just coming over a ridge within easy rifle range, firing as they advanced. It was now plainly evident that we had overwhelming odds to contend with. That long line coming down the slope would soon envelop us and we fell back to our horses, intending to retreat toward Lexington. We had only just reached our horses, however, when we were confronted by another force of Confederate cavalry advancing upon us from the direction of Lexington, and to complete our discomfiture, a regiment came charging down the road from the direction of Richmond, in column of fours. As they came opposite to our position, they fired a volley into our confused and broken ranks, Morgan's battery at the same time coming into position and sending a few shells in our direction. Morgan was there with the goods, and like Davy Crocket's coon, we concluded it was best to come down, so we surrendered. We were marched to the Clay mansion and paroled, Morgan taking our horses, arms and most of our personal belongings. We marched down through Lexington, but there were no Stars and Stripes floating. A few Confederate flags were displayed, however. We marched to Frankfort and there took the cars for Columbus, by the way of Louisville and Indianapolis. We remained at Columbus until we were exchanged, when we returned to the regiment early in 1863.

In regard to the number of men in the engagement at Lexington, the Third had in the fight six officers and 78 men; total, 84. They had four killed and 80 wounded and prisoners.

The Fourth had four officers and 206 men; total, 210—wounded and prisoners. As a part of the Fourth was in Lexington and took no part in the fight, we had not to exceed 250 officers and men in the fight. The Confederates say their force was 1800. It probably exceeded 3000. We do not know what their loss was. Among their killed was Major

Morgan, a cousin of the general. As no record of our wounded was kept in either the Third or Fourth Regiments we have no means of knowing the number of wounded.

On the night of the 18th Major Seidel returned to Danville and reported what he had learned while held a prisoner in Morgan's house, in regard to Morgan's contemplated movements, after which he went to Camp Chase and remained until exchanged.

Report of Major Charles B. Seidel, Third Ohio Cavalry, of Skirmish Near Lexington.

DANVILLE, October 19, 1862.

SIR: In compliance to orders I received from your headquarters to go to Camp Dick Robinson and take charge of the provisions left there by the rebel forces I left camp on the 16th of October at 2 p. m., and arrived at Camp Dick Robinson at 5 p. m., finding Colonel Hoskins in charge of those stores, consisting of 2600 barrels of pork and 2000 bushels of wheat. Went into camp at Dick Robinson with intention to return the following morning to Danville. At 11 o'clock of same night I received a message from Colonel Hoskins of the approach of General Morgan with 500 men strong toward Hickman Bridge with intention to burn said bridge, and recommending one battalion of my forces to be immediately dispatched to Hickman Bridge to prevent it from being burned by General Morgan's forces. This I complied with, by sending one battalion of the Fourth Ohio Volunteer Cavalry under command of Captain Robie.

The next morning (October 17th) at 5 o'clock I started with the balance of my command, consisting of one battalion Third Ohio Volunteer Cavalry, to join Captain Robie at said bridge. On my arrival here I learned that Captain Gotwald, commanding four companies of Fourth Ohio Volunteer Cavalry, had left Nicholasville for Lexington to drive a portion of Morgan's cavalry forces from that vicinity to prevent their pilage and burning of bridges. I then, knowing that Captain Gotwald could not accomplish his object with the force under his command, went with all the force under my command, numbering in all 260 men, to reenforce him, which I accomplished by 3 o'clock of same day. Finding Captain Gotwald with his force stationed in town, I then went into camp one and one-half miles from Lexington on the Richmond pike.

At 1 o'clock the same night two citizens living about seven miles from Lexington came in with the following statement, viz.: Morgan's forces of about 500 or 600 men were advacing on the Richmond pike. I immediately sent out a scouting party of 22 men, under command of Lieutenant Hall, Company K. Third Ohio Volunteer Cavalry, to procure all possible information. At about 3 o'clock one corporal and two privates returned with two rebel prisoners in charge, captured about five miles from Lexington on the Richmond pike. The balance of the scouting party marched on. On questioning said prisoners I became satisfied that a heavy force was coming upon us. I therefore called out my command immediately and formed in line, when we were attacked by General Morgan's forces of about 3000 strong and six pieces of artillery pouring in most deadly volleys of musketry and grape on all sides. My command most manfully and gallantly returned their fire and fought them hand to hand until overpowered by an overwhelming force, when we were compelled to surrender. Our loss was four killed and 24 wounded.

The loss of the enemy I was unable to ascertain, but saw three wagons of killed and wounded leave the battle ground. Major Morgan, of General Morgan's cavalry, was mortally wounded. The scouting party have not been heard from. As a large rebel force left the scene of action in pursuit of them fears are entertained that all have been captured.

Much credit is due to Captain Robie, of the Fourth Ohio Volunteer Cavalry, for his cool and gallant behavior during the fight. Capatain P. H. Warner, Company D; Lieutenant H. Hamilton, Company A, and Lieutenant W. E. Crane, Company C, (Fourth) Ohio Volunteer Cavalry, having left the command on the evening previous without permission and remained in town all night, and have not reported themselves yet.

The greatest credit is due to all officers and men.

Most respectfully, your obedient servant,

CHARLES B. SEIDEL,
Major, Commanding Third Ohio Volunteer Cavalry.
COLONEL ZAHM.

[Indorsement.]

Respectfully forwarded, with the addition that the four companies of the Fourth Ohio Volunteer Cavalry stationed at Lexington, under command of Captain Gotwald, have surrendered likewise. Have had no official reports from him.

LEWIS ZAHM,
Colonel, Commanding Second Cavalry Brigade.

CHAPTER VIII.

MOVEMENTS OF THE FIRST BATTALION
1862

On July 9th, when the Second and Third Battalions left Mooresville, Alabama, to go to Woodville, the First Battalion, in command of Major Foster, moved with Wood's Division northward into Tennessee. Passing through Fayettville, they arrived at Shelbyville with the wagon train July 15th. On the 16th they escorted the wagon train out on the Murfreesboro pike, and left at 10 p. m. for Fayetteville. On the 18th they marched to Wartrace. From there they moved to Winchester, where they went into camp. They were kept busy doing picket duty, scouting and foraging. On July 28th a foraging party captured 87 head of beef cattle that were being driven to Chattanooga for the rebel army.

August 14th they broke camp at Winchester and marched to within six miles of Manchester and camped.

August 15th—Reveille at 4 a. m.; moved out at 5. Marched to Manchester and camped in a piece of woods south of the town.

August 16th—A detachment went out on a scout; went to Beach Grove; returned to camp at 1 a. m.

August 17th—Reveille sounded at 3 a. m. Moved out at 5. Marched about 12 miles towads Vervilla. Camped at noon near some fine springs of water on campmeeting grounds.

August 20th—Moved to Vervilla and camped.

August 21st—A detachment of the Third and Eighth companies of the Fifteenth Indiana Infantry went out in the mountains after guerrillas. They went to Altamont and captured about 20 doubtful citizens. Returning they camped at the foot of the mountain. Company M went with the wagon train to Beech Grove after forage.

August 22d—Returned to camp.

August 24th—Started out at 1 a. m. Marched to McMinnville. Stopped to feed and rest our horses and then started toward Decherd. Camped after dark.

August 26th—Wood's Division moved to Vervilla. Companies B and H went as rear guard.

August 27th—Started out at 5 a. m. Marched to Hickory Creek, two and one-fourth miles south of McMinnville, and camped.

August 29th—Started at 5 a. m. Passed through McMinnville, and left the infantry at the foot of the mountain. The cavalry, under Major Foster, went up and to within five miles of Dunlap. He drove in the rebel pickets, captured five prisoners and five horses, returned to the foot of the mountain and camped with the infantry.

August 30th—On the march early; passed through McMinnville. We went into camp about 5 p. m.

September 2d—Division moved out at 5:30 a. m. Cavalry rear guard camped at Young's tannery.

September 3d—Foraging.

September 4th—Started soon after sunrise. Passed through Bradyville; captured three prisoners; arrived at Readyville at 10 p. m. and went into camp.

September 5th—We were late in getting started, the road being blockaded with wagons. Our column, delayed on that account, arrived at

Murfreesboro a little before noon. We camped near a spring and found the Second and Third Battalions were also there.

September 6th—Started early and passed through Lavergne. Drew up in line and waited for General Wood to come up. Marched to Nashville and camped at the fair grounds.

September 7th—Started at 11 a. m. Crossed the Cumberland river on the railroad bridge, marched out six miles and camped.

September 8th—Moved out at sunrise, passed through Saundersville and camped about four miles from Gallatin. The battalion went about two miles beyond Gallatin on the Lebanon pike; returned to camp late.

September 9th—On the march early, Company L in advance, Company H rear guard for the Division. Found the stockade at Gallatin evacuated. Country rough and water scarce; men and horses suffered from thirst. Camped on a stream of water about twelve miles south of Franklin, Kentucky.

September 10th—Started at 4 a. m. Came up with the wagon train at Mitchelville. We left the pike and got past the train before we reached Franklin. Stopped at Franklin to rest. Camped at Nichols. Company H ordered to Bowling Green; marched at 7 p. m.; passed through Woodburn; arrived at Bowling Green at 10 p. m. and camped on the old camp ground of the spring before.

September 11th—Moved up and camped west of town.

September 17th—Started soon after sunrise, formed in line of battle five miles north of Bowling Green, moved forward, struck the rebel cavalry and commenced driving them before us. At 3 p. m. we camped. Water was very scarce; it commenced to rain about 5 o'clock. The wagons did not come up and we had no supper.

September 18th—The Division marched at sunrise. The First Battalion in advance of the column found the rebels in our front and commenced driving them; drove them a mile north of Cave City, skirmishing constantly as we advanced. We found some seventy wounded in the town and captured 400 prisoners, a number of horses, some arms and equipments.

September 19th—Formed in line of battle the First Battalion on the right of a section of artillery, the cavalry in front sheltered by woods; the woods in our rear occupied by our infantry. The prisoners taken at Mumfordsville passed through our lines on their way to Buell's headquarters. After they had passed through our skirmishers were called in and pickets posted and the troops fell back to draw rations and rest.

September 21st—In the saddle before daylight. General Thomas sent the First Battalion in the advance. We came up with the rebel cavalry a short distance beyond our pickets, and commenced skirmishing with them and drove them before us for about nine miles until they reached

Mumfordsville. Here they took a strong position behind some buildings on a rise of ground south of the river. We dismounted and attempted to dislodge them, but after fighting for an hour, we concluded their position was too strong for us and we waited for the infantry to come up. As soon as they arrived they formed in line and charged, driving the enemy from their position and out of Mumfordsville. The enemy lost three officers and eighteen men killed, and fifty wounded and prisoners. One of the officers killed was Lieutenant Colonel Brown, of the First Alabama Cavalry. We encamped south of the town.

September 22d—Started early, Wolford's cavalry in the advance, crossed Green river and before noon crossed Bacon creek, driving the enemy before us and taking a number of prisoners. Some artillery skirmishing in front. Two of our men killed. Pushed on to Elizabethtown, where we halted and fed our horses then marched about eight miles, towards Louisville, and camped.

September 23d—Marched to West Point and camped at the mouth of Salt river. The enemy had left our front.

September 24th—Moved out in the rear of Crittenden's wagon train. Camped on the bank of the Ohio river. Late in the evening a rumor came that Louisville was attacked and we saddled up and were ready to move in five minutes, but had to wait for Crittenden's Division to pass. Stopped south of the city and lay down to rest.

September 25th—Moved late in the afternoon; camped west of the city.

September 26th—Went out on a reconnaissance seven miles toward Shepherdsville; returned and camped about two miles south of the city.

September 29th—We received some recruits, just arrived from Ohio.

October 1st—Moved out at 8 a. m.; marched southward about ten miles.

October 2d—Advanced five or six miles further south. Skirmishing in front.

October 3d—Companies B and H went off to the left to reconnoiter; found no enemy. Camped on Salt river; found the bridge burned; skirmishing in front.

October 4th—Started out early, without breakfast. Wood's division of infantry and about 350 cavalry, the First Battalion of the Third Ohio, six companies of the First Ohio, and two companies of the Second Kentucky. The cavalry in the advance. We marched through Fairfield, struck the pike near the fair grounds north of Bardstown. Captain Flannagan, in a linen duster and armed with a double barreled shotgun, had command of the advance guard. As we were moving toward the pike the advance came to some rebel pickets and commenced skirmishing with them, capturing two Texan rangers. The command formed into line, advancing toward the pike and opposite to the fair grounds. As we moved forward about 3 p. m. a squad of rebels appeared to the left, moving toward Bardstown. Captain Flannagan and the advance guard gave chase, following them down the pike. As our line moved forward General Wharton's division of cavalry (which was entirely concealed from our view by the high board fence of the fair grounds), moving in column by the left flank, came around north of the fair grounds at a gallop, and charged, overwhelming our small force, breaking our line and throwing it into confusion. Captain Flannagan came charging back much faster than he went, the tails of his linen duster streaming in the air. In the mixup and getaway we lost forty-two of our men, who were captured, while we took thirty-nine of the enemy prisoners. Our infantry was only about half a mile in the rear, but could not assist us in the scrimmage. Our men who were captured were taken to Springfield and paroled about 3 a. m. of the 5th, returning to our lines the same day and going on to the paroled camp at Columbus, Ohio, to await exchange. The division moved on through Bardstown, Springfield and Lebanon, to Perryville, where it was engaged in the battle of the 8th on the right wing of the army. After the battle it moved to Danville. On the night of the 14th it moved out at midnight, and engaged the enemy at Stanford at daylight on the morning of the 15th, following to Crab Orchard. The latter part of October the cavalry was ordered to Lebanon to refit and the infantry was ordered to concentrate at Bowling Green.

October 30th—General Buell was superseded by General Rosecrans, who took command of the army, which was designated by the government as the Fourteenth Army Corps. This designation very soon gave place to the more popular and appropriate one—The Army of the Cumberland.

November 3d—The cavalry arrived at Bowling Green and the next day the infantry was ordered to move to Nashville. The Confederate army concentrated at Murfreesboro. Immediately on assuming command General Rosecrans proceeded to reorganize the army. All the cavalry was placed under the command of General D. S. Stanley, who organized it into brigades. Ours was the Second Brigade, Second Division. It was composed of the First, Third and Fourth Ohio Cavalry Regiments, and was commanded by Colonel Zahm.

November 8th—Zahm's brigade moved on Gallatin, and driving out Morgan's division, captured some twenty prisoners. The cavalry remained in position north of the Cumberland river, occupying Hartsville, Gallatin, Fountain Head, and Franklin, until Nov. 17th, when Colonel Kennett, commanding the division, moved from Hartsville, crossed the Cumberland river and took position south of Nashville.

November 27th—The division under Colonel Kennett went out on the Franklin pike, encountered a force of the enemy and routed them, driving them fifteen miles. He captured a number of prisoners and horses.

December 11th—General Stanley with a strong force of cavalry went out on the Franklin pike, the First division in the advance; marched within four miles of Franklin and bivouacked for the night.

December 12th—Moved forward at daylight, attacked the enemy, driving them. Killed one officer and four men, captured twelve prisoners and a large number of horses, wagons and supplies. Returned to camp at night. The regiment camped on the Nolensville pike about three miles from Nashville.

December 14th—The division reviewed by General Stanley. During the month of December the regiment was constantly engaged scouting, doing picket duty and foraging. We were compelled to get forage for our animals from the country most of the time. While at Nashville we were obliged to go long distances, and take strong guards with the trains. Very frequently the foraging parties were attacked and our men had a number of skirmishes on these occasions.

CHAPTER IX.

THE BATTLE OF STONE RIVER

December 25th—We had received orders to pack up and after we were all ready to move the orders were countermanded, and the brigade wagon train with a strong guard was sent out after forage. The train was attacked by the enemy's cavalry, who captured two wagons and eight men of the Fourth Ohio. The remainder of the wagons were brought in safely, loaded with forage.

December 26th—Orders to send all camp equipage to the city; to take no wagons only such as were necessary to carry rations and ammunition. Zahm's brigade moved out on the Franklin pike. It was a rainy, disagreeable day; skirmishing in front most of the afternoon. The enemy made a stand about half a mile from Franklin. Colonel Zahm formed his lines, threw out skirmishers, and moved forward, driving the enemy, when the Third Ohio was ordered forward, charging through the town and driving the enemy several miles beyond, when darkness stopped the pursuit. A number of the enemy were killed and wounded. We captured some prisoners, also a number of arms, horses and mules. We returned to camp late at night.

December 27th—The brigade advanced toward Triune. One battalion of the Third Ohio sent to Franklin found the enemy in the town;

attacked them, but were unable to drive them out; rejoined command in the evening.

December 28th—The brigade moved forward to Triune; met with no opposition.

December 29th—Moved forward toward Murfreesboro. Found the enemy's pickets; they fell back as we approached. Encountered the rebel cavalry, driving them several miles to the protection of their infantry and artillery supports. At night we fell back some distance and camped.

December 30th—Advanced toward Murfreesboro, skirmishing with the enemy's cavalry all day. Lay on our arms in line of battle all night. Everything indicated that we were in the immediate presence of the main rebel army and that a great battle was imminent, and could not be delayed much longer.

December 31st—We were early astir and in line, waiting for reports from the patrol sent out in our front. It was scarcely daylight when the sound of artillery and infantry firing off to our left and front brought the tidings that the battle had commenced. The roar of cannon and the rattle of musketry was terrific, showing that on one side or the other a desperate assault was being made, and we soon learned that it was the enemy that had commenced the attack, and that the troops on the right of the Union lines were being driven from their position, closely pursued by their victorious enemy. We were compelled to fall back to prevent being cut off by the enemy. At this point the ammunition train of General McCook was in great danger of being captured, when the Third Ohio was raillied for its protection, and repelling the repeated assaults of the enemy, held them at bay until the wagons moved out to a place of safety.

As we came up to the Murfreesboro pike we found the rebels had attacked another of our wagon trains, the regiment driving off the enemy and saving the train. The fighting on this part of the line continued until nightfall, but the enemy was unable to drive us any further, although they made frequent attempts to do so. The day's battle closed with the right of the Union army occupying a position parallel to the railroad and Nashville pike and at right angles to that held when the battle commenced.

January 1st—The brigade started with a large train of wagons for Nashville. A short distance west of La Vergne we were attacked by General Wheeler's division of cavalry, who made several desperate attempts to stampede and capture the train, but were finally driven off with considerable loss. We arrived in Nashville late at night, remaining at Nashville one day, and on the 3d started for Murfreesboro in charge of the train. We were again attacked by Wheeler near La Vergne, who was again repulsed with loss. Arrived at Murfreesboro soon after midnight, Jan. 4th. While we had been absent at Nashville the undecisive battle of the 31st had been renewed. On Jan. 1st, 1863, neither commander was desirous of renewing the conflict. Each was in hopes that the other would retreat. January 2d the conflict was renewed in the afternoon, but this time it was between the left wing of the Union army and the right of the Confederates—the advantage being on the side of the Union army. Bragg thought it prudent to withdraw. This was the first battlefield, in the West at least, where the Union cavalry had been used in large bodies. The Confederates had had the advantage of us in that they had consolidated their cavalry so that they were able to use it with effect, while the Union cavalry had been scattered in small bodies, and never were strong enough to accomplish any great results heretofore. But under the new order of things they proved themselves the equals of the Confederates in this arm of the service. The losses of the brigade, the First, Third and Fourth Ohio Regiments, at Stone's River were killed, 18; wounded, 44; missing, 59; total, 121. Among the killed were Colonel Milliken and Major Moore of the First Ohio.

When General Bragg was forced back out of Kentucky he knew that the Union army would in all probability be concentrated at Nashville, which had been successfully held by the Union troops against the Confederate forces under General Breckenridge during Bragg's invasion. He had therefore selected Murfreesboro as the most available point for the concentration of his army from which to threaten Nashville, and block the way of the advance of the Union army toward Chattanooga. The Battle of Murfreesboro had been the result, and General Bragg had been forced to retire, leaving the Union army in possession of the field. The annals of the war do not record a more stubbornly contested battle, the contesting armies being of nearly equal strength. General Rosecrans marched out from Nashville to give battle. General Bragg selected the ground upon which to fight. Each commander had his own plan of battle, and singularly enough the two plans were entirely similar. The plans involved the massing of troops on the left flank of the battle line of each army; an attack by the left, followed up along the line from left to right, the right holding its position as a pivot while the army made its right wheel, forcing its opponent back and getting possession of his line of communications. On the morning of the 31st of December General Bragg took the initiative and made a fierce attack on the right wing of our army, and it was soon evident that here was the point where Bragg was going to force the fighting. The Confederate left extended far beyond our right, which was compelled to fall back to prevent the enemy from getting in their rear. Slowly and stubbornly contesting every foot of ground, the right wing was driven back until they reached the Nashville pike and railroad, occupying a position at right angles with the one they held in the morning when the battle commenced. The left and center had held their ground.

Two assaults were made by the enemy on our right wing in their new position along the Nashville pike, but they were repulsed. January 1st, 1863, was spent by the Union army in strengthening their position. On the 2d Bragg determined to drive back our left, but his attempt only resulted in the loss of about 2000 of his best troops, therefore he determined it was best to retreat. He fell back to Tullahoma, his right occupying Manchester, and his left strongly posted at Shelbyville with cavalry on his right at McMinnville and on his left at Franklin and Columbia.

———

Reports of Col. Lewis Zahm, Third Ohio Cavalry, commanding Second Brigade, including skirmishes at Franklin, December 26-27, Wilkinson's Cross-Roads, December 29, Overall's Creek, December 31, La Vergne, January 1, Cox's Hill, January 3, and on Shelbyville Pike, January 5.

HDQRS. 2D CAV. BRIG., IN CAMP ON WILSON'S PIKE,

NEAR NOLENSVILLE CROSSING, *December 27*, 1862.

GENERAL: In compliance with orders received, I moved from our old camp at Nashville yesterday morning at 8 o'clock with the First, Third, and Fourth Ohio Cavalry Regiments, 950 strong in all. I crossed over on the Franklin pike, south of General Thomas' headquarters, as I afterward learned. I passed the immense trains and troops on the Franklin pike, beyond Brentwood. I halted my command, as I had not seen General Thomas yet. I supposed he was on the move with the troops in front. I kept inquiring along the column, and was told that he was in the advance. I proceeded myself on the Wilson Creek pike some two miles, almost to the head of the column, but then learning from General Rousseau that General Thomas was in the rear, I immediately started back some six miles; there ascertaining that General Thomas had cut across the country to the Nolensville pike, I thought further pursuit would be useless. I started back to join my command and to carry out the remainder of my instructions. I proceeded to Franklin; encountered the enemy's pickets two and a half miles out; drove them in. Skirmishing continued until within half a mile of Franklin, when a sharp skirmish ensued, we driving the rebels. They then made another halt in town. I dismounted some six companies to act as skirmishers on foot; came round on both flanks with mounted skirmishers, and their reserves finally charged through the river into town, where some considerable firing ensued; drove the rebels out; drove them some two miles beyond town; the lateness of the day prevented further pursuit, for by this time it began to be dark. The enemy was taken by surprise; could not get their forces together before we were upon them; therefore made it rather an easy task to drive them, as they were in several directions, formed several lines, but as we advanced and fired they invariably fled. We took ten prisoners, one of them a lieutenant of General Bragg's escort, who was there on business with sixteen men. We captured a private of the same escort. We captured that number of horses, several mules, some shotguns, from the best information received, I made out the force to have been about 900, consisting of Colonel Smith's regiment and an independent battalion. I shall send the prisoners to Nashville this morning.

I learned that quite a force of infantry and artillery were nine miles out of Franklin, on the road leading to Murfreesboro. I arrived in camp here at nearly 9 o'clock last evening; reported to General Rousseau, in the absence of General Thomas. We learned that the enemy had quite a force at Triune, some ten miles south of this. General Rousseau and myself came to the conclusion to use my brigade today in reconnoitering the front and right, until further orders could be received from you. I shall therefore send some 500 men toward Petersburg and Triune to reconnoiter; shall likewise send a smaller force over toward Franklin, to ascertain whether the enemy has come back again or not. My force will be back in camp toward evening; will remain here and picket Wilson's Creek pike, as instructed, until your further orders are received.

I forgot to mention that we killed three of the enemy; could not ascertain the number of wounded; must have wounded some in proportion to the killed. My command behaved nobly, both officers and men.

The Third Ohio Cavalry had the advance, and did the principal part of the fighting; there was no flinch to them; they moved steadily onward, and finally made the charge through town.

I am, General, your obedient servant,

LEWIS ZAHM,
Colonel, Commanding Second Cavalry Brigade.

GENERAL STANLEY,
Commanding Cavalry.

———

HEADQUARTERS SECOND CAVALRY BRIGADE,
NASHVILLE, TENN., *January* 2, 1863—11 o'clock.

GENERAL: I have the honor to report that, at 9 a. m. yesterday, I proceeded with the Third Ohio Cavalry and the Anderson Troop, as directed, forward to guard the trains in motion on the road to Nashville. I took up every train in front of me which was in motion. At Stewart's Creek I found the Third Division train just putting out. It detained me about one hour; at the same time I learned that a heavy cavalry force was to the left of me. I ordered the train to proceed at a brisk walk. We moved on until we arrived at La Vergne; the train had passed the flats at La Vergne, myself and command resting on the flat, when my flankers discovered the enemy to our left and engaged him. I immediately turned into the field, formed line of battle, and dispatched orderlies to the front to move the train on a trot.

The enemy formed; then ensued skirmishing with the skirmishers. The enemy formed a new line, which I counteracted; kept him at bay ready to receive their charge; they, however, declined to charge—wheeled in column of fours, moved to the left of our train and forward around a hill in front and to the left of the road, with the intention of heading off the train. By this time the rear of the train was half a mile ahead of us. I immediately followed the train; sent flankers at a rapid pace toward the front to watch and engage the enemy if approaching. The enemy did not succeed in heading the train.

After proceeding about two miles further, discovered the enemy charging up the pike on our rear. I met them and repulsed them. They charged again. I repulsed them again, charged them back for two miles, scattered them, killed nine, wounded eleven, and took two prisoners. I had a few men slightly wounded. After this they troubled my train no more. Not a wagon fell into their hands ahead of the escort. Some four or five wagons broke down, which we left and destroyed. The enemy's forces were Wheeler's brigade, with two pieces of artillery, which they played upon us pretty lively. A short time before we were attacked a large number of the Second Tennessee came running by my column, running away from the front, stating that our forces were in full retreat. I placed a company in the road, halted every one of them, but at the breaking out of the skirmish they ran again like sheep. I am sorry to say that the Anderson Troop, with very few exceptions, as the enemy charged us in the rear, scampered off in most every direction; did not stand up to the work at all; the contrary, caused, together with the negroes, Second Tennessee, all running, somewhat of a stampede among the wagons, which caused the few break-downs above mentioned.

I arrived here at 9 p. m. Found no forage for horses. Sent out a train after forage this morning, so it will be 5 o'clock this p. m. before our horses will get a mouthful to eat. Since 3 o'clock yesterday morning they have labored very hard, and consequently are not fit for any service today. Both horses and men are very much used up.

I am awaiting further orders. I have ordered the Anderson Troop to report to me early this morning, but they have not done so up to this time. They are very much demoralized. In any work for me to do, I ask you to please not to count them as being any help to me. I would sooner do without them.

I am, very respectfully, your obedient servant,

LEWIS ZAHM,
Colonel, Commanding Second Cavalry Brigade.

GENERAL STANLEY,
Commanding Cavalry.

Eli Long, a native of Kentucky, was appointed colonel of the Fourth Ohio Cavalry
shortly after the battle of Stones River, Tennessee, where he was wounded in the
arm while serving with the Fourth U.S. Cavalry. Promoted to brigadier general of
volunteers in August 1864, he finished the war commanding a division in J.H.
Wilson's Cavalry Corps, and was badly wounded at Selma, Alabama in April 1865.
Long was awarded every brevet in both the regular and volunteer services up to and
including the grade of major general. He died in 1903.

Colonel Minor Milliken, First Ohio Cavalry, was killed December 31, 1862 in the battle of Stones River, Tennessee.

HEADQUARTERS SECOND CAVALRY BRIGADE,
IN CAMP NEAR MURFREESBORO, TENN., *January* 6, 1863.

LIEUTENANT: I herewith have the honor to report the part taken and the work performed by my brigade since our departure from Nashville until the close of the battle before Murfreesboro.

I left Nashville on the morning of the 26th ultimo, with three regiments of my brigade, viz: the First, Third, and Fourth Ohio Cavalry, the Fifth Kentucky remaining at Nashville. My force numbered 950 men. We marched out on the Franklin pike, the Third Ohio having the advance. When within two miles of Franklin, drove in the rebel pickets, skirmished all the way down to Franklin, drove the enemy out, and pursued him some two miles. From the best information received, the enemy were 900 strong (all cavalry), part of Wharton's brigade. We killed four, wounded several, and took ten prisoners, among them a lieutenant of General Bragg's escort, several horses and mules, and destroyed their camps, with some tents standing thereon. We retired from Franklin, moved over to the Wilson Creek pike, and picketed said pike.

On the 27th, sent the First Ohio and most of the Fourth Ohio, under command of Colonel Milliken, on the Wilson Creek pike, toward Triune, to reconnoiter. They proceeded within two miles of Triune, captured six of the rebel pickets, when the enemy opened on them with shells; threw some fifty without damaging us any; then my force retired to camp. I likewise had sent a battalion of the Third to Franklin to reconnoiter, which drove in the rebel pickets, who had returned in force after my command had left the evening previous. Quite a skirmish ensued, in which three of the rebels were killed and several wounded. After skirmishing some two hours, and the enemy being too strong to drive, the battalion returned to camp in good order without any loss.

On the 28th, moved with the command to Triune without anything occurring worth mentioning.

On the 29th, proceeded toward Murfreesboro, moving between the Franklin road and the road called Bole Jack road, which General McCook's corps moved on. I divided my brigade into three columns, marching parallel with one another and with the main force, the right, (the Fourth Ohio) moving on the Franklin road, the Third in the center, and the First on the left, the columns being from one to one and one-half miles apart, throwing out skirmishers, connecting one column with the other, and connecting on the left with the main column. We thus proceeded for five miles, when the center column encountered the enemy's pickets, which they drove in, the different columns steadily advancing.

Shortly after, both the right and the left encountered pickets, driving them in before them. After proceeding about one mile farther, we came upon the enemy's cavalry (Wharton's brigade), engaged them for three hours, sometimes the right wing, then the left, then the center, receiving several charges, which were repulsed, driving the enemy some two miles, when the brigade concentrated, repelling a heavy charge from the enemy, driving him back under his guns, which were only a short distance from us. We then retired some two miles and went into camp.

Some few casualties occurred this day. The officers and men behaved admirably during the whole day. The Fourth had proceeded until the enemy threw shells into them pretty rapidly, when they retired. We were within four miles of Murfreesboro.

On the morning of the 30th was ordered to proceed on the Franklin road toward Murfreesboro, to push the enemy hard. We had encamped that night near the brick church, on the road leading from General McCook's headquarters to the Franklin road. I proceeded that morning with my command and the Second East Tennessee, (which reported to me that morning), via. that road to the Franklin road, at which crossing we encountered the enemy's pickets and drove them in. Sent a party of the Fourth to reconnoiter on the road leading south to Salem, where they soon came upon a stronger force, and a brisk skirmish ensued. I increased the number of skirmishers, especially to the left, skirmished with the enemy for an hour or more, when a courier arrived, saying that the enemy was approaching with a heavy cavalry force and some artillery.

In the meantime I had ascertained, likewise, that a heavy force of the enemy was encamped some little distance south of the Franklin road, and east of where my column halted. I did not think it prudent to advance, and, owing to the bad grounds (being all timber) where my force halted, I retired to my camping-ground, near which were large open fields, well adapted for cavalry movements. I soon formed a line of battle. The enemy made his appearance. Skirmishers engaged him pretty quickly. The enemy maneuvered with the design to outflank us, but did not succeed. I forestalled him every time. With the exception of severe skirmishing, nothing transpired. The enemy retired, when I concluded to join the main body of our army.

After marching about a mile, met General Stanley, with a brigade of infantry and a battery of artillery, to reinforce me. The General marched the whole command toward the enemy's camp. On reaching its vicinity the enemy drew up in line of battle. Skirmishing ensued. Remained there about half an hour, when the General withdrew, with the remark that we were not ready yet to fight the whole of Hardee's army corps. That night we encamped one and one-half miles from the enemy's camp, and laid on our arms all night.

At daybreak on the morning of the 31st, I had my command drawn up in line of battle in the rear of my camp; sent out two squadrons to the front and to the right to reconnoiter. Had been in the line about half an hour, when I heard heavy firing—cannon and musketry—to my left and a little to the front. Soon after I beheld our infantry scattered all over the fields, running toward my line, when I learned that General Johnson's division was repulsed. At about the same time my skirmishers engaged the enemy, when they were driven in, reporting that the enemy were approaching in heavy force. Sure enough, I soon discovered heavy lines of infantry coming toward my front and on the left, where General Johnson's division had been posted; also to my right the enemy's cavalry were coming round in long columns, with the evident design to outflank us.

I concluded to retire slowly toward the main body of our army, the enemy pressing hard on me; kept him at bay with my skirmishers. I retired in this wise for a mile, when I formed a line of battle with the First and Third, when the enemy charged on them with their cavalry, but were repulsed by my men. About this time the enemy began to throw shells into my lines pretty lively. The first shell that landed mortally wounded Major Moore of the First Ohio. I now fell back, formed a new line, received the enemy's charge, repulsed them, and made many of the rebels bite the dust. Shells coming pretty thick again, I retired farther, when I made another stand, supported by Willich's regiment of infantry; received the enemy's charge, and repulsed him again. I then withdrew my whole command through a large strip of wood to another open lot—shells of the enemy helping us along—passing by a line of rebel infantry, marching parallel with my column, not over 200 yards from us, so that we were nearly surrounded, as the enemy's cavalry were working round our right all the time, and the infantry and artillery following us closely on our rear and to our left. They had cavalry enough to spare to strike, or to take position, whenever required.

When we arrived on the open ground, General McCook's aide told me the whole of General McCook's ammunition train was close by, on a dirt road running by that point, and that I must try to save it. I soon formed my command in line, when the enemy made his appearance in a position occupying two-thirds of a circle. They prepared to charge upon us; likewise commenced throwing shells, at which the Second East Tennessee broke and ran like sheep. The Fourth, after receiving several shells, which killed some of their men and horses, likewise retired from their line, as it became untenable. The First had been ordered to proceed farther on into another lot, to form and to receive a charge from another line of the enemy's cavalry. The Third moved to the left, in the vicinity of a white house. About the time the First was formed, the enemy charged upon the Fourth, which, being on the retreat, owing to the shells coming pretty freely, moved off at a pretty lively gait. The Third moved farther to the left, and, somewhat sheltered by the house and barns, the First charged upon the enemy; did not succeed in driving them back.

On returning from said charge the gallant Colonel Milliken and a lieutenant were killed, and another lieutenant severely wounded.

At this juncture the First and Fourth retired pretty fast, the enemy in close pursuit after them, the Second East Tennessee having the lead of them all. Matters looked pretty blue now; the ammunition train was supposed to be gone up, when the Third charged upon the enemy, driving him back, capturing several prisoners, and recapturing a good many of our men, and saved the train. I was with the three regiments that skedaddled, and among the last to leave the field. Tried hard to rally them, but the panic was so great that I could not do it. I could not get the command together again until I arrived at the north side of the creek; then I found that only about one-third of the First and Fourth Regiments were there, and nearly all of the Second East Tennessee. These I marched back across the creek, when, joined by the Third, we had several skirmishes with the enemy's cavalry all day long; received several charges, and repulsed them.

All the officers and men behaved well through all the fighting up to the stampede, which was not very creditable. All of them that I brought back into action again behaved well during the rest of the day. I must say the Third deserves great credit for this day's fighting—for the coolness and bravery of its officers and men, and for its determination to save the train, which they accomplished. I do not wish to take any credit away from the other regiments, as they all fought nobly and did first-rate, with the exception of the stampede.

On January 1st, after being in line of battle since 3 a. m., I was ordered to take the Third Ohio and the Anderson Troop, proceed to Nashville, and escort the army wagon train through to Nashville. I left about 9 o'clock. A little below La Vergne was attacked by General Wheeler's cavalry brigade; repulsed him twice; killed nine, wounded several, and took two prisoners; saved all the train but two or three wagons, which broke down in the excitement; saved several cannon belonging to a Wisconsin battery going along with the train, which were abandoned by the drivers, horses still hitched to the cannon. Some of my men mounted the horses and took the cannon into Nashville. The enemy threw shells at us, but did not succeed in hurting any of the men. The Anderson Troop, I am sorry to say, were of very little benefit to me, as the majority of them ran as soon as we were attacked. Arrived at Nashville at 9 p. m.; found no forage for my horses.

Next day, January 2d, had to send out a foraging party. They returned at 5 p. m., when my horses were fed for the first time since leaving the front, the day previous at 3 a. m.

At 1 o'clock on the 3d was ordered to leave at 3 o'clock to escort a hospital store train and an ammunition train through to the front. When two miles out, had to wait for Colonel McCook to come up with two and a half regiments of infantry and some 150 of the Third Tennessee Cavalry. Two companies of the Fourth Ohio, under command of Lieutenant White, were with me likewise. It was 11 o'clock before we got started. All of this force combined formed the escort of the train. We proceeded about eight miles, when we were attacked by Wheeler's brigade. We repulsed them, taking twelve prisoners, among them two lieutenants; killed fifteen, and wounded many. They did but little damage to the train, which was done through the cowardice of the teamsters. I had one man killed and one wounded. The enemy tried to attack us the second time, but retired before our forces met. We brought the train through safely, and arrived with it at 1 o'clock the next morning. During my three days' absence the First and Fourth were busily employed reconnoitering, doing picket duty, and skirmishing with the enemy's cavalry.

On the 4th, marched my command to the front, near Murfreesboro, to reconnoiter, the enemy having withdrawn their forces.

On the 5th, marched to the front, some four and one-half miles beyond Murfreesboro, on the Shelbyville road, on a reconnaissance, capturing quite a number of rebel stragglers; pushed a squadron of the Fourth some three miles farther, to a point where they could overlook the pike for five miles ahead, when they discovered that the enemy had entirely disappeared. The skirmishers of the Fourth had some skirmishing with some of the rebel cavalry. By 7 o'clock was back to camp again. You will observe that my command had fought nearly every day from the time we left Nashville up to this time. They worked very hard, and deserve a great deal of credit for what they have done, as both officers and men fought bravely.

Herewith find list of casualties, which are not large, considering the number of engagements we were in.

All respectfully submitted.

I am, very respectfully, your obedient servant,

LEWIS ZAHM,
Colonel, Commanding Second Cavalry Brigade.

LIEUTENANT M. B. CHAMBERLIN,
Actg. Asst. Adjt. Gen., First Cav. Div., Army of the Cumberland.

Return of Casualties in the Second Cavalry Brigade (Zahm's) December 26, 1862—January 6, 1863 (Stone's River).

Command	Killed		Wounded		Missing		Remarks
	Officers	Enlisted men	Officers	Enlisted men	Officers	Enlisted men	
1st Ohio Cavalry	3	2	1	10	1	14	
3d Ohio Cavalry	....	6	....	15	....	10	3 enlisted men prisoners.
4th Ohio Cavalry	....	7	....	18	....	16	15 enlisted men prisoners.
Total	3	15	1	43	1	40	

Report of Lieut. Col. Douglas A. Murray, Third Ohio Cavalry, including skirmishes at Franklin, December 26-27, and Overall's Creek, December 31.

IN CAMP NEAR MURFREESBORO, TENN., *January 6, 1863.*

COLONEL: In compliance with instructions received from your headquarters, I have the honor to report, for your information, the part taken by the Third Ohio Cavalry in the several engagements in which the regiment was engaged since leaving Nashville, Tenn., on December 26th last, on which day we proceeded to Franklin, driving the enemy therefrom and taking possession of the town; took some ten prisoners. Remaining in town some time, we recrossed the river, and marched across the country to Wilson Creek pike, about fourteen miles from Nashville, and encamped, arriving in camp at about 10 p. m.

On the 27th, the Third Battalion of the regiment moved toward Franklin, and found that the enemy had in strong force again taken possession of the town; the battalion drove in their pickets under a heavy fire, killing three of them. Seeing that the enemy were in such force, the commander deemed it prudent to retire, and rejoined the regiment, which picketed the roads, etc., in the vicinity of its camp.

On the 28th ultimo, proceeded to Triune and encamped, leaving early next morning across the country toward Murfreesboro, proceeding about five miles in that direction, when attacked by the enemy's pickets in force, which we drove, skirmishing, they frequently making a stand, which we each time broke, and still drove them about five miles.

The 30th ultimo, ordered to proceed to Stone's River; proceeded but a short distance when attacked by the enemy's pickets; the enemy were in force in our front with artillery. We therefore retired, forming on the high ground in our rear to receive them, their pickets, or patrol, advancing, which we repulsed. In the evening our brigade was reinforced by one battery of artillery and three regiments of infantry, and proceeded in reconnaissance to the left of the enemy's lines, where we found General Hardee's *corps d'armee* ready, in line of battle, to receive us. We retired, and encamped in the woods, about two miles in front of the enemy's lines.

On the morning of the 31st we formed; shortly after the enemy appeared in large force, both on our left, center, and right, evidently endeavoring to cut us off. The brigade of infantry to our left gave way, retreating in confusion through our lines, letting the whole force of the enemy's artillery, cavalry, and infantry fall upon us, which compelled us gradually to retire toward the main body of our army. The regiment covering the entire rear of the brigade, supporting one infantry regiment on our right, drove back, with heavy loss, a large force of cavalry which charged upon us, under cover of a piece of artillery, firing well-directed shells, which passed over us. The enemy being in such force, we had to retire about three-fourths of a mile, when an aid-de-camp of General McCook rode up, informing us that the train close by was General McCook's entire ammunition train, which must be saved at all hazards; on intimation of which the regiment was immediately formed for its protection, holding the enemy in check until the entire train, with the exception of a few disabled wagons that could not be moved, was safely withdrawn. The regiment then moved between the enemy and train as far as the Murfreesboro pike, where we found the enemy making a fierce attack upon General Thomas' train, when we again repulsed them at several points, taking many prisoners and saving that entire portion of the train. The attack of the enemy was furious and desperate, which required the greatest firmness and bravery to resist. Colonel Kennett was an eye-witness to the determined bravery of a portion of the regiment rescuing the train from the enemy, which were in force at the hospital on the Murfreesboro pike. The regiment then formed in the field near the hospital, where the brigade soon assembled and reformed, and advanced toward the enemy's left. Soon came up to the enemy's cavalry, supported by artillery, when several other skirmishes ensued during the evening, the enemy's entire object seeming to be to take the train.

On the 1st instant, received orders to proceed to Nashville in charge of train, consisting of some 200 or 300 wagons. When about two miles on the Nashville side of La Vergne, we were attacked by General Wheeler's brigade of cavalry, which made several dashes on the train, and were repulsed. They then attacked our rear in force. After a well-contested fight, our regiment put them to flight in disorder, killing nine of them and wounding several, and arrived in Nashville at 9 p. m. and encamped.

The 2d instant, remained in Nashville and procured forage for our horses, furnishing working party and escort to forage train.

The 3d instant, left Nashville for Murfreesboro in charge of hospital and ammunition trains. Attacked again in force by Wheeler's brigade of cavalry on the Nashville side of La Vergne, which was repulsed with a loss of fifteen on their side and some eight or nine prisoners taken; among the latter the adjutant of the Third Alabama Cavalry. Two of our non-commissioned officers, I regret to inform you, were severely and dangerously wounded, whom we had to leave in a house on the roadside.

Arrived at camp, near Murfreesboro, at 1 a. m., 4th instant, with the train all safe, with the exception of one wagon of the regiment that was cut off by the enemy, and is now supposed to have returned to Nashville.

On the evening of the 4th, proceeded with brigade to Murfreesboro as far as Stone's River, and returned to camp.

On the 5th instant, proceeded again with brigade to Murfreesboro, and beyond it about four and one-half miles, where we halted, taking several prisoners, and returning to camp about 7 p. m.

I have much pleasure in informing you that the conduct and behavior of both officers, non-commissioned officers, and privates of the regiment have been highly creditable, with not a single instance to the contrary in the regiment.

Inclosed please find list of casualties that have occurred since December 26, 1862, to January 5, 1863.*

I have the honor to be, very respectfully, your obedient servant,

D. A. MURRAY,
Lieutenant-Colonel Third Ohio Cavalry, Comdg. Regiment.

COL. L. ZAHM,
Comdg. Second Cavalry Brigade, First Cavalry Division.

No. 179.

*Report of Maj. James W. Paramore, Third Ohio Cavalry, including skir-
mishes at Overall's Creek, December 31, and at La Vergne, January 1.*

HEADQUARTERS THIRD OHIO CAVALRY,

January 8, 1863.

SIR: There are a few incidents in the recent series of battles in which we were engaged which, not having fallen immediately under your observation or of the regimental commander, have escaped notice; and

---

* Embodied in revised statement.

being under my immediate command, in justice to the brave officers and men engaged, I deem it my duty to make this special report.

In the severe fighting of Wednesday, the 31st ultimo, which fell so heavily upon your brigade, you will recollect, when we had been forced back as far as General McCook's ammunition train, and were drawn up in front of it for its protection, the furious charge of the enemy's cavalry. At that juncture an aide of General McCook came up to me, and informed me that "that was their entire ammunition train, and must be held at all hazards." I gave orders accordingly to the left wing of the Third Ohio Cavalry, under my command, and I am happy to report that they held their position and received the galling fire of the enemy with the firmness of heroes, and maintained their ground till all the wagons, except a few that were disabled or deserted by the teamsters, had safely reached the lines of our infantry.

The enemy, seeing our determination and bold resistance, turned and left us. We pursued them over to the Murfreesboro pike, Captain McClelland commanding Companies E and F, taking the right of the pike, and the balance of the command, with myself, taking the left.

When within a short distance of the hospital we again encountered a large force of the enemy coming back to take possession of the train. We at once engaged them, although at least double our numbers, and after a severe struggle put them to flight, with a loss of several killed, wounded, and prisoners. The bravery and daring of Captains Wood and Colver, and their respective commands on this occasion, challenged my admiration. I also learned that Captain McClelland, with his squadron, engaged the enemy farther up the pike, beyond the hospital, with Colonel Kennett and a portion of the Third Kentucky Cavalry, and, after a fierce contest, repulsed them.

This result is greatly attributable to the coolness and bravery of Captains McClelland, Wood, and Colver, and their lieutenants. It was also this portion of the regiment that repulsed the attack of the enemy on the rear of our train the next day near La Vergne as we were proceeding to Nashville, and brought safely into Nashville two pieces of cannon, three cassions full of ammunition, and a wagon loaded with new carbines and ammunition, which had been abandoned by their teamsters.

All of which is respectfully submitted,

J. W. Paramore,
Major, Commanding Left Wing, Third Ohio Cavalry.

Col. L. Zahm,
Commanding Second Cavalry Brigade.

CHAPTER X.

SIX MONTHS AT MURFREESBORO

Immediately after the Army of the Cumberland took possession of Murfreesboro it commenced to fortify and put it in shape for defense. The troops went into winter quarters and made themselves as comfortable as possible. We were destined to remain at Murfreesboro six months. It seemed a long time to the people of the North, who wanted to see the army move—it seemed long to us, who wanted to see the war ended—but there are so many things to be provided for and looked after in connection with a large army that the average person does not think of—transportation, subsistence, clothing, arms, ammunition, etc. Really the needs of a large army are never completely supplied. It was necessary first of all to open up our line of communication. The enemy had played havoc with the railroad between Louisville and Nashville. It was not opened until February, and it was the middle of the month before the cars got to Stone's River, and March before the bridge was completed and the cars were running into Murfreesboro, when the army was put on full rations, and then before an advance movement could be made it was necessary to accumulate sufficient surplus rations and ammunition for the movement.

Then comes the animals necessary—horses for the cavalry and artillery, and horses or mules for the wagon train. The army is hard on men, but it is terrible on horses. The waste and losses were fearful. We always wanted horses and were always on the lookout for them. The government was buying horses all the time, yet we were always calling for more. To show the difficulty of obtaining horses while we were at Murfreesboro, on April 19th Lieutenant Brown and a detail from the regiment took a lot of worn-out, unserviceable horses to Nashville and put them in a corral there and as there were no horses to be had at Nashville, they got on the cars and went to Louisville. Arrived at Louisville April 21st. On May 27th they got a bunch of horses, loaded them on the cars, and arrived in Murfreesboro May 29th, only to have their horses taken from them and given to a Tennessee Regiment, while they carried their saddles back to camp, having been gone just forty days. The weather was very cold, wet and disagreeable a great part of the time we lay at Murfreesboro, but we were not idle. That is the cavalry were not. We were kept busy scouting, picketing and patroling the roads, gathering forage, drilling, etc. The Second Battalion was stationed at Readyville with Hazen's Brigade of Infantry, the left of the Union Army, while the First and Third Battalions were in Camp Stanley, near Murfreesboro. The Second Kentucky Cavalry was added to our (Second) Brigade; the Chicago Board of Trade Battery to the division. Colonel Zahm resigned,

Lieutenant-Colonel Murray taking command of the regiment, and Colonel Paramore being placed in command of the brigade.

February 3d—The brigade, under command of Lieutenant-Colonel Murray, went out on a scout with five days rations; passed through Auburn, going as far as Prosperity Church; coming back to Auburn to camp.

February 4th—Marched at daylight in the direction of Liberty; found a few small bodies of the enemy. Camped near Alexandria. The next morning went in the direction of Rome; brought in some prisoners; passed through Lebanon and camped at Baird's Mills. The next day forded Stone's river and returned to camp.

February 22d—Preparations were made to celebrate Washington's birthday, but for some reason there was delay in the arrival of some of the supplies, and the festivities were not held until the 24th. There were speeches by Generals Stanley, Garfield, and others, and then there was a feast of roast ox, chickens, ducks, and pigs, followed by beer and cigars. The band of the Fourth United States Cavalry furnished the music. The regiment went on picket at night.

February 28th—The always welcome paymaster visited us.

March 1st—Went on a scout with three days rations. Found the enemy in the afternoon at Bradyville, attacking them. They held their ground for about fifteen minutes, when we charged, driving them several miles and capturing about 100 prisoners and a lot of horses. Three men of the regiment were wounded. Camped near Bradyville, returning to Murfreesboro the next day.

March 4th—Cavalry went out with five days rations. Came onto the enemy's pickets near Unionville; charged them, driving them and following them so closely that the enemy did not have time to form, but got right out, leaving all their camp and garrison equipage, which we destroyed. We captured about fifty prisoners. Marching to Eagleville, we halted for the night. We did not unsaddle our horses, but lay on arms in line of battle to guard against surprise. We remained at Eagleville until afternoon of the 5th, when we marched to Chapel Hill, but finding no enemy we returned to our camp at Eagleville. The next morning we started for Murfreesboro, but after marching a few miles we received orders to go to Franklin, marching by way of Triune. We camped about nine miles from Franklin, which place we reached about noon of the 8th and went into camp.

March 9th—We took up the march southward, the Third Ohio in the advance. Found the enemy strongly posted covering the fords at Spring creek; after some skirmishing, fell back to our camp. The next morning we advanced to the creek and attacked the enemy; dismounted, drove them from the ford, but did not cross at that point. Crossing at another ford, we followed the retreating rebels as far as Columbia, where they crossed to the south side of Duck river. We returned to Spring creek and camped about midnight. The next day we marched to Franklin. On the 13th, marched to Triune and camped.

March 14th—The command returned to Murfreesboro, arriving in the afternoon, having been in the saddle for ten days. The men of the Third Battalion captured at Lexington returned to the regiment after an absence of more than four months. On March 17th, grand review by General Rosecrans.

March 20th—A courier came into Murfreesboro bringing a message from Colonel Hall, commanding a brigade of infantry at Milton, saying that he was attacked and likely to be surrounded by General Morgan with a large force of cavalry, and asking for a reinforcement of cavalry to come at once to his assistance. The First and Second Brigades, under Colonel Minty, left Murfreesboro about 2:30 p. m. and arrived at Milton about 6 o'clock and found that the infantry had repulsed Morgan, who had lost heavily in the fight. We remained at Milton for the night, guarding the infantry camp with a strong line of pickets. The next morning the cavalry went out on the different roads, endeavoring to locate the enemy. The Third Ohio, under Lieutenant-Colonel Murray, went to Auburn, found a small body of the enemy, and chased them for two miles, capturing two prisoners. In the afternoon we started back to Murfreesboro, where we arrived about 8 o'clock p. m. The loss in the infantry was twelve killed and thirty-eight wounded.

March 26th—Delos Ashley of Company I wounded at Bradyville on the 2d, died yesterday, and it was decided to send his body home. The regiment, led by the Fifteenth United States Infantry band, escorted the remains to the train and sent them to his friends at home, his brother Augustus accompanying them.

April 2d—The cavalry started out with five days rations and sixty rounds of cartridges on a scout after Morgan in the direction of Liberty. Came up with the enemy in the afternoon, driving them about two miles. We lay on our arms in line of battle. The next morning we moved forward and found the enemy in position near Liberty. We attacked them, driving them back. The next stand was at Snow Hill, where they had a strong position, their battery being posted at a point where it commanded the pike for half a mile in its ascent up the mountain. After a futile attempt to silence this battery, General Stanley sent the Third and Fourth Ohio Cavalry to their left and rear. After climbing the hill, we formed under cover of the woods on the summit, the Fourth Ohio in front, dismounted, the Third mounted. Our skirmishers found the enemy drawn up in line, and the attack by the dismounted men was made with spirit. In a short time the enemy commenced to give way, and the Third was ordered forward, charging the enemy's line, it gave way and broke. Thus far the fighting had all been under cover of the woods, but we soon came out of the woods and in sight of the pike, which was filled with the demoralized troops of Morgan, rushing madly toward Smithville. As far as we could see the road was packed with horsemen, intent on nothing but getting away. We charged them for about two miles, when the recall was sounded and we returned to the brow of the hill. The enemy's loss was heavy in killed, wounded and prisoners, although many of our prisoners escaped in the woods during the charge. Our loss in the brigade was three wounded.

Mosgrove, one of Morgan's officers, winds up his account of the fight at Snow Hill as follows: "Morgan's command was worse demoralized by the affair at Snow Hill than upon other occasions where it had fought hard battles and sustained serious defeat. Some weeks elapsed before the fugitives returned and reported for duty, none of them being able to satisfactorily explain why they rode away from the battlefield and 'kept a-goin'."

We returned to a point about four miles northwest of Liberty and went into camp. The next morning we took up the line of march, passed through Alexandria and camped about twelve miles from Lebanon.

April 5th—Passed through Lebanon and camped at Baird's Mills, returning to camp at Murfreesboro the afternoon of the 6th.

April 10th—Drew five days rations and started out on a scout. The next day we found the enemy in force at Franklin. After we had crossed the river we received orders to fall back. Just then the enemy charged our line of skirmishers and they were driven back through our lines. We fell back to the ford, which we were ordered to hold. We camped near the river and the next day returned to Murfreesboro.

During the latter part of April the division was formed in a hollow square for the purpose of seeing the sentence of a court martial for desertion carried into effect. The man was marched by his guards into the center of the square and in the presence of the division stripped of his uniform, dressed in citizens clothes, branded on the cheek with the letter "D," and then between two guards and followed by the drum corps playing the "Rogue's March," he was paraded in front of the lines all around the square and then drummed out of camp.

To us the punishment seemed terrible. General Rosecrans no doubt thought the example was needed and would have a tendency to check desertions.

April 20th—We started out with six days rations by the way of Readyville and Woodbury for a raid on the McMinnville & Tullahoma Railroad. After leaving Woodbury, we took cross-country roads, striking the railroad early in the forenoon of the 21st, capturing two trains of cars and a lot of supplies, which were burned, tearing up the railroad and destroying bridges as we moved toward McMinnville, where we formed a junction with the troops under General Reynolds, capturing many prisoners. General Morgan escaped, but it was a close call for him. We started back by the way of Smithville and along the pike where Morgan's troopers went in their wild flight from Snow's Hill. Passing through Alexandria and Milton, we returned to our camp on the 26th. During the raid we had had numerous skirmishes with the enemy and captured a large number of prisoners and suffered no serious loss.

May 3d—We started out with sixty rounds of ammunition and one day's rations. Comparing our ammunition with out rations, we concluded that we were expected to do more fighting than eating. But after marching all day over the highways and by-ways, we returned to camp at night with our ammunition intact, but out of rations. We had one lone prisoner to show for our day's hunt.

About the 10th of May, our leaders believing that Wheeler was about to make another raid on the railroad, the regiment was stationed near La Vergne, from which point we patroled and guarded all the fords and crossings of Stone's river. We remained about a week, but all was quiet—no enemy came, and we were ordered back to Murfreesboro.

May 19th—We moved camp about four miles out on the Lebanon pike, where we had plenty of good water near camp. Our new camp was called "Turchin," in honor of our division commander.

May 21st—We organized a little surprise party, planning to make an early call on the Johnnies encamped at Middleton. We marched nearly all night to get there, for we did not want to be late. We got there in time to catch them before they were up. They did not seem to enjoy our visit, for they lit out without saying good-bye. We captured and destroyed all their camp equipage, took seventy-nine prisoners and a large number of horses. Returning to Murfreesboro the next day, we were followed by the enemy, who attacked the rear guard a number of times, but were repulsed by the Third and Fourth Cavalry. Our regiment lost two men wounded, one man captured.

About the last of May, C. L. Valandigham was sent through our lines. He had been arrested by General Burnside for making speeches, encouraging resistance to the government, in its efforts to raise troops to put down the rebellion, inciting treason, etc. He had been tried by court martial and sentenced to be sent through the lines. President Lincoln approved the sentence, although he would have preferred that no notice had been taken of Mr. Valandigham's treasonable utterances. He was taken through the lines in a carriage. From Tullahoma he was sent to Richmond and wined and dined and feted and hailed everywhere as the friend of the South. He was put on a blockade runner at Wilmington, went around through Canada to Windsor, opposite Detroit. He was nominated by the Democratic party for governor and received over two hundred thousand votes from the Copperheads of Ohio.

June 3d—We started out on a scout over in the direction of Morgan's bailiwick. On the 4th we passed through Liberty and over Snow's Hill. Striking the rebels about three miles from Smithville, driving them for five miles, we returned and went into camp near Liberty. In the afternoon of the 6th ten rebels apparently thinking that we had all gone (as part of the command camped outside of us had moved and our pickets were not posted) came trotting down the pike and almost to our camp before they saw us. They fired their guns, wheeled their horses and started back at a gallop, but some of our men were quickly in the saddle and after them and in an exciting chase of seven miles suceeded in capturing six of them, the remainder leaving their horses and taking to the woods. The next day we returned to Murfreesboro by the way of Milton.

June 10th—Colonel Paramore was superseded by Colonel Eli Long as commander of the brigade. Lieutenant Colonel Murray left the regiment. His farewell address was read at dress parade. Most of the boys were sorry to see him go. The men liked him in spite of his fondness for old Scotch—but he would allow it to get the best of him sometimes.

June 23d—Orders to break camp and be ready to move at a moment's notice. All excess baggage to be sent inside the fortifications. Three days rations in the haversacks and nine in the wagons; it looks like business—guess we are going after Bragg.

OFFICIAL REPORTS OF SCOUTS AND SKIRMISHES OF THE THIRD OHIO CAVALRY DURING THE TIME THAT THE ARMY OCCUPIED MURFREESBORO

JANUARY 19, 1863.—Skirmish near Woodbury, Tenn.

Report of Captain Thomas D. McClelland, Third Ohio Cavalry.

HDQRS. SECOND BATTALION, THIRD OHIO CAVALRY,

CAMP NEAR READYVILLE, TENN., *January 20*, 1863,

SIR: In accordance with instructions, the Second Battalion, consisting of Companies E, F, A, and D, reported to Colonel W. B. Hazen, commanding Second Brigade (January 10, 1863), and were marched to this place, a distance of twelve miles. Our time since has been fully occupied in patrolling and scouting, with an occasional skirmish with the enemy's pickets and scouting parties, until yesterday we had quite a brilliant little affair with a portion of Morgan's command, under Colonel Hutcheson. About noon, picket firing was heard to the front. The colonel commanding ordered me to send out and see what it meant. I made a detail from Companies E. F., and A, consisting of 44 men, under command of Lieutenant Hansey, of Company F, and Lieutenant Clark, of Company E. They found it to be our vedettes firing on some rebel cavalry, who had come within range, and upon receiving their fire retreated. Our party followed them, and, after proceeding within two miles of Woodbury, came upon the enemy's pickets, driving them in. At this time they discovered a party of the enemy charging on them in the rear. Lieutenant Clark, who was in command of the rear, immediately wheeled his men, and poured into them from his carbines, a galling fire, and then drew sabers and charged them in fine style, scattering them in all directions, killing two, wounding one and taking ten prisoners, with no loss on our side except two horses wounded. The enemy was now in force in front and on the flanks. A retreat was ordered, the prisoners being sent forward under a guard; the party was divided equally, each lieutenant taking command of a party. One formed a line and held the enemy in check, while the other fell back, and vice versa, by which means they succeeded in bringing their prisoners in without loss. The enemy followed to the pickets, and quite a skirmish ensued, without loss on our side.

Permit me to offer a suggestion. Morgan's brigade is scattered from McMinnville to Woodbury, one and two regiments in a place. Now, in my opinion, with an adequate force of cavalry, and probably some artillery, his command could be taken in detail and routed completely.

I am, very respectfully, your obedient servant,

T. D. McClelland,
Captain, Commanding Second Battalion, Third Ohio Cavalry.

Lieutenant Colonel D. A. Murray,
Commanding Third Ohio Cavalry.

MARCH 27, 1863. Skirmish on the Woodbury Pike, Tenn.

REPORTS.

No. 1.—Colonel William B. Hazen, Forty-first Ohio Infantry, commanding brigade.

No. 2.—Major Charles B. Seidel, Third Ohio Cavalry.

No. 1.

Report of Colonel William B. Hazen, Forty-first Ohio Infantry, Commanding Brigade.

Headquarters Second Brigade,
March 27, 1863.

General: The cavalry you sent out today have had a fight with two regiments of cavalry near Burton's, on the Woodbury pike. Lost one officer and ten men. Considerable loss to the enemy.

W. B. HAZEN,
Colonel, Commanding Second Brigade.

BRIGADIER GENERAL JAMES A. GARFIELD,
Chief of Staff.

No. 2.

Report of Major Charles B. Seidel, Third Ohio Cavalry.

HDQRS. SECOND BATTALION, THIRD OHIO VOL. CAV.,

READYVILLE, *March* 28, 1863.

DEAR SIR: On the evening of March 27th, I was ordered to take my battalion and advance on the Woodbury Pike, to observe the enemy's movements, who was reported advancing on to our lines, and, if possible, to check his advance. I had advanced but a short distance on the above-named pike when I ran against a squad of rebel cavalry, numbering about fifty men. I at once attacked them, and in a short time had them fleeing before me. I had driven them about one and one-half miles, when they were re-enforced. My advance had already engaged them, when I saw a force advancing on my left. I immediately gave orders to fall back. We had retired but a short distance when my advance gave me intelligence I was cut off. I immediately brought my men in line of battle, and at the same time was vigorously attacked by Colonel [Baxter] Smith, who commanded in person. We returned their fire, and, knowing that I had no time to lose whatever, gave the command to draw saber and charge, which was bravely done by my men. The enemy received our charge with their pistols, but being too vigorously attacked, fled in every direction. I then having accomplished my object, rallied my men and pursued the fleeing foe, when I saw the enemy's reserve charging down the pike on me; but, taking the offensive with a small number of men, I repulsed his charges three times, and, by falling back carefully, took all my men safely into camp, with the exception of ten enlisted men and Lieutenant [S. J.] Hansey, of Company F, whom, I suppose, were captured by the enemy's reserve. We took about the same number of prisoners, including a major, but being too far from camp and not able to get re-enforcements, were obliged to give them up again.

The enemy's loss must have been very heavy, for I saw as many as twenty horses without riders. The rebel force, to the best of my judgment, numbered about 400 men, while I had only sixty-five men. My men deserve much praise for their bravery.

Respectfully, your obedient servant,

CHAS. B. SEIDEL,
Major, Comdg. Second Battalion Third Ohio Volunteer Cavalry.

COL. J. W. PARAMORE,
Commanding Second Cavalry Brigade.

[Indorsement.]

HEADQUARTERS CAVALRY,
April 1, 1863.

Respectfully forwarded.

The gallant conduct of the Major and his little command is commended. The attention of the General commanding is called to it. The question is raised whether these cavalrymen are altogether treated fairly. Could not an infantry support have saved us the loss of a lieutenant and ten good men? It appears to me that cavalry patrols in a country of copse and thicket should be used with more discretion than they have been at the post of Readyville.

D. S. STANLEY,
Major-General.

————

HDQRS. 2D BRIGADE, 2D DIVISION, 21ST ARMY CORPS,
READYVILLE, TENN., *April* 4, 1863.

CAPTAIN: I have the honor to make the following report of the expedition made on the 2d instant, under my command, to Woodbury:

The expedition was to have consisted of Cruft's brigade, which should report to me at this post by 10 p. m. of the 1st, and my own. That would enable me to put two columns in motion at 11 p. m., for the purpose of flanking and getting in the rear of Woodbury by daylight.

The brigade of Cruft's did not report till something after midnight, enabling me to start one column, composed of the Forty-first Ohio Volunteers and Sixth Kentucky, under Lieutenant-Colonel Wilson of the former regiment, at 1 a. m., which went to the right of Woodbury, and a column composed of the Ninth Indiana Volunteers and First Kentucky, under command of Lieutenant-Colonel Suman, of the former regiment, at 1:30 a. m., to proceed to the left of Woodbury. The One Hundred and Tenth Illinois, under Colonel Casey, accompanied this column as far as the point on the map accompanying, marked A, where they were to turn to the right, and proceed cautiously to the Woodbury pike, in rear of the picket post of the enemy, marked B, where sixty men were on picket, and remain concealed till the main column, composed of the

Second Kentucky and Ninetieth Ohio, with Standart's battery and the Second Battalion of Third Ohio Cavalry, all commanded by Colonel Enyart, First Kentucky, which started at 3 a. m., should have driven them on to this regiment, that would capture them. The delay of two hours in this brigade to report made it nearly that length of day before the different columns arrived at the points intended. The One Hundred and Tenth Illinois, in consequence, did not reach the pike in time to be of service. I, however, directed the cavalry to charge this post, which they did in fine style, sabering and capturing a dozen of this picket. We pushed on through the town, and came upon the main body of the enemy. Keeping my main column concealed, I permitted the advance to parry with him for about an hour, giving more time for the columns to get in position. I then pressed him forward, and about four miles from town, upon Wiley's column. Upon seeing troops at this point, they at once scattered through the hills in all directions. The columns all gained their positions promptly, correctly, and unknown to the enemy, marching about sixteen miles to do so. Had I not been delayed two hours, the results of the day would probably have been much more satisfactory, as then my original plan, which was to capture entire their main picket and regulate the speed of all the columns so as to have gathered upon the camp at dawn, would have probably succeeded perfectly. As it is, I have to report three of the enemy killed (his wounded is not known), twenty-five prisoners, fifty horses, four wagons, eight mules, with all their baggage and provisions. Colonel Suman captured one picket post almost entire, as did also Colonel Casey.

I have to speak in the highest terms of the battalion of the Third Ohio Cavalry, commanded by Major Seidel. A brigade of such cavalry, well mounted, armed with revolvers and sabers, would be invaluable. Colonel Suman reports to me that the First Kentucky, in command of Major ———, straggled in going out, so as at one time to be a mile long, and detaining him nearly and hour. We returned to our camp at 12 m. See inclosed map, with routes of the columns.*

I am, very respectfully, your obedient servant,

W. B. HAZEN,
Colonel, Commanding Second Brigade.

Report of Lieut. Col. Douglas A. Murray, Third Ohio Cavalry, command-ing Second Cavalry Brigade.

HEADQUARTERS SECOND CAVALRY BRIGADE,

CAMP STANLEY, TENN., *February* 8, 1863.

GENERAL: I have the honor to report, for your information, the part taken by a portion of the Second Cavalry Brigade, consisting of the Third and Fourth Ohio Cavalry, with detachments of the Third and Fourth Indiana Cavalry, from the 3d to the 7th of February, 1863, while attached to the command of Brigadier-General [J. J.] Reynolds.

Joined the command of the General on the morning of the 3d, and proceeded in rear of the command till about four miles to the front of our pickets on the Liberty pike, when the cavalry, with the exception of the Fourth Indiana, were ordered to the front as advance guard, and to push on to Auburn, and, if possible, to Prosperity Church, about three and one-half miles beyond it. The General learning that the enemy were there in strong force, we moved carefully, with a strong advance and flank guard, without any interruption, as far as ordered. Hearing that about thirty rebel cavalrymen had moved at a rapid pace along the road toward the church half an hour ahead of us, we did not succeed in coming up with them. Therefore, in compliance with instructions, returned to Auburn and encamped one-half mile in front of the command, throwing out pickets on the Liberty pike, both front and rear, Woodbury dirt road, and both flanks, taking almost the entire command to furnish the requisite number. Nothing occurred during the night worthy of mentioning. Next morning, at daylight, moved on in advance toward Liberty, driving in a picket of the enemy, consisting of about fifty or sixty men. About two and one-half miles this side of Liberty, we passed over on the road that led to Alexandria, where also a small body of the enemy were seen, and a report that the enemy were in force to our right, which was without foundation. Passed through Alexandria, and encamped about three miles from it on the Lebanon pike, throwing out strong pickets front and rear. The pickets reported hearing that small bands of rebel cavalry were in the country, consisting of from five to ten in number, plundering and stealing all they could lay their hands on, and committing all manner of depredations. Moved early next morning in the advance. Received orders to send scouting parties both on Rome and Gallatin pikes, to proceed about eight miles on both these roads. The Third Ohio Cavalry, consisting of 100 men, took the former, under command of Major J. W. Paramore, and made several important arrests, viz: General R. Anderson, senator; Colonel W. L. Martin, representative; W. B. Pursley and John Cox, conscript agents, and G. A. Pursley, lieutenant so-called C. S. Army, besides three enlisted men. The Fourth Ohio Cavalry, under command of Major [C. G.] Megrue, consisting of 100 men, took the Gallatin pike, and made several arrests. The entire command, with the balance of the cavalry in advance, proceeded through Lebanon, and took the Murfreesboro pike as far as Baird's Mills, and encamped, throwing out pickets to the front on the road and roads leading from the main road as soon as we arrived in camp. About one-half hour after the arrival of the command, reported currently there that Morgan with his command would to a certainty make a strong attack upon us at Stone's river next day, which turned out to be, like the majority of such reports, without foundation. Received orders from General Reynolds to send fifty men as an escort to an officer and five men, who were to carry a dispatch to General Thomas. The escort had orders to proceed to the river and see the dispatch party across and then return. They met with no interruption, neither saw anything to indicate that any forces were in that vicinity, and arrived at camp about 8 p. m. Left camp next morning in advance, and proceeded to Stone's river without the least interruption of any kind; crossed the river, which was fordable; the water about three or three and one-half feet deep, with a very strong current. Received orders to return to the command, and recrossed the river, the rear portion of the train being fired into by a party of rebels, supposed to number about 120 or 130 men, who, after firing, retreated and fled in every direction, I was told. When we recrossed the river, and met the command advancing, ordered again by the General to proceed in the advance to the river, and not cross over until the entire command did so. I threw out strong pickets to the rear and flanks, which I did not withdraw until the entire command had passed over the river, which they did by means of a bridge formed by wagons. We had two small pieces of mountain howitzers with our brigade, which the lieutenant in charge informed me that General Reynolds said to him might with his sanction remain with us. It appears from all I heard that Colonel Wilder will not allow it, as he claims them as his, and wishes them to accompany his brigade (infantry) when they are mounted, which is the intention, I believe. They would be a great acquisition to us, and, if possible, if I cannot obtain those, I hear that there are several such pieces in Nashville, Tenn. Could I not, on your recommendation, procure a section of such guns? I could easily man them, having a number of old artillerymen in the command.

Our horses had ample forage during the scout; worked very hard, and traveled over a large section of country. The country passed through was principally hilly, the roads good, and, with the exception of the bridge over Stone's river, the different bridges on the road were in good order. Our command returned last evening about 8:30 o'clock.

Our casualties were six enlisted men, one of the Third Ohio Cavalry, five of the Fourth Ohio Cavalry, supposed to be captured by the enemy.

The command picked up some fine-looking horses and mules, ninety-one of the former and nineteen of the latter.

I have the honor to be, very respectfully, your obedient servant,

D. A. MURRAY,

Lieut. Col. Third Ohio Cavalry, Comdg. Second Cav. Brigade.

BRIG. GEN. D. S. STANLEY,

Commanding Cavalry.

REPORTS.

No. 1.—Maj. Gen. William S. Rosecrans, U. S. Army.

No. 3.—Col. James W. Paramore, Third Ohio Cavalry, commanding Second Cavalry Brigade.

No. 4.—Capt. William M. Flanagan, Third Ohio Cavalry.

Report of Maj. Gen. William S. Rosecrans, U. S. Army.

MURFREESBORO, TENN.,
March 2, 1863—2 p. m.

General Stanley reports from his expedition to Bradyville: We fared badly for forage. The rebels of Morgan's and Wharton's commands made a stand in Bradyville. Colonels Paramore and Long went in with sabers drawn, and whipped them in about three minutes. Stokes' cavalry advanced bravely with carbines. We took seventy prisoners, including eight officers, their camp equipage, tents, saddles, and some seventy horses, and Basil [W.] Duke's regimental papers. Major [James] Murphy did good service. We lost one man killed and one captain and seven men wounded. We found four of their dead.

W. S. ROSECRANS,
Major-General.

MAJ. GEN. H. W. HALLECK,
General-in-Chief.

———

Report of Col. James W. Paramore, Third Ohio Cavalry, commanding Second Cavalry Brigade.

CAMP STANLEY, NEAR MURFREESBORO,
March 3, 1863.

SIR: I have the honor to submit the following report of the engagement at Bradyville, Tenn., on the 1st instant, between the cavalry under my command, consisting of a portion of the First [Middle] Tennessee, and a detachment of the Second Brigade, consisting of about 100 men from the Third Ohio Volunteer Cavalry, under command of Captain W. M. Flanagan, and 150 men of the Fourth Ohio, under command of Colonel Eli Long, and the rebel force at that place, consisting of Colonel Duke's Second Kentucky Cavalry, commanded by Lieutenant-Colonel [James W.] Bowles, and the Fourteenth Alabama [Battalion], belonging to Wharton's brigade, and commanded by Major James C. Malone, jr.:

About two miles this side of Bradyville, the First [Middle] Tennessee, under command of Major Murphy, being in advance, encountered the rebel pickets and drove them in. When near the village, they found the enemy strongly posted behind the houses in the village and a high piece of ground. After a short skirmish, they (the First Tennessee) were driven back in some confusion. I then brought up the Third and Fourth Ohio, and formed them in line, the Fourth occupying the right and the Third the left. I also sent a squadron of the Fourth Ohio, under command of Major [P.] Mathews, around to the extreme left of the rebel line, and a portion of the Third around to their right. I then stationed the First [Middle] Tennessee as a reserve, and advanced the remainder of the Third and Fourth Ohio to engage the enemy in front, when we found them strongly posted in a piece of woods, about one-fourth of a mile beyond the village, where they were dismounted and sheltered behind rocks and trees, and gave us stubborn resistance for about fifteen or twenty minutes, when the detachments I had sent around to their right and left flanks arrived in position and opened an enfilading fire on both flanks. The enemy gave way in confusion, when a charge was ordered with sabers and pistols. We pursued them for about three miles, during which we took about 100 prisoners, with their horses, arms, and equipments; wounded from twenty to thirty, and found five dead bodies on the field; also a large quantity of commissary and quarter-master's stores fell into our hands. Their rout was complete, and they fled in great consternation, throwing away their guns, overcoats, blankets, and everything that would impede their progress.

Among the prisoners were eight commissioned officers, including the adjutant of the Second Kentucky Cavalry, with all his books, papers, reports, etc., of the regiment. The enemy's force has been variously estimated at from 600 to 1000, while our force, actually engaged, did not exceed 250, and, considering the disparity of numbers and the advantage of the rebel forces in position, I think it may be considered one of the most daring and brilliant feats of the war.

When all, both officers and men, behaved with such determined bravery, it would be almost an act of injustice to mention any names in particular. I will, therefore, send you the names of all the commissioned officers of the Third and Fourth Ohio Volunteer Cavalry. I do not know the officers of the First [Middle] Tennessee, except Major Murphy. Captains C. W. Skinner and H. H. Hamilton, of my staff, were very vigilant and efficient.

Officers of the Fourth Ohio were Colonel Eli Long, commanding regiment; Major P. Matthews; Captains G. A. Boss, commanding Company F; R. E. Rogers, commanding Company G; R. P. Rifenberrick, commanding Company I; C. A. G. Adae, commanding Company K, and Lieutenants [E. S.] Wood, commanding Company L, and [A. R.] Megrue, commanding Company M.

Officers of the Third Ohio: Captains William M. Flanagan, commanding regiment; H. C. Miner, commanding First Battalion; J. B. Luckey, commanding Squadrons I and K, Third Battalion; Lieutenants E. A. Haines, commanding Company H; Norman Brewster, commanding Company L; [J. W.] Likens, commanding Company M; F. Brainard, commanding Company I, and J. R. Hall, commanding Company K.

Casualties as follows:*

We bivouacked for the night about one mile beyond the village. Nothing occurred during the night worthy of record.

All of which is respectfully submitted.

J. W. PARAMORE,
Colonel, Commanding Second Cavalry Brigade.

CAPT. W. H. SINCLAIR,
Assistant Adjutant-General.

———

Report of Captain William M. Flanagan, Third Ohio Cavalry.

HEADQUARTERS THIRD OHIO CAVALRY,
March 3, 1863.

SIR: I have the honor to report the part sustained by the Third Ohio Cavalry in the recent skirmish of March 1, at Bradyville.

Pursuant to orders from brigade headquarters, the Third Cavalry marched at daylight on the 1st instant. On arriving at the Bradyville pike, which lies but a short distance from our camp, I was ordered by the colonel commanding to place my command in the rear of the Second Brigade. I marched in this order until near the village of Bradyville, and in sight of the enemy, who were in large force and strongly posted in the woods, on advantageous ground, on the south side of town. On forming a line of battle, the colonel commanding the brigade, with promptness and energy, ordered me with my command to take the left of the line. I objected somewhat as to the possibility of forming at that juncture at the left, as it would throw my command upon an impracticable, steep, stony side-hill. The Colonel told me it must be accomplished. The enemy commenced about this time to send showers of leaden hail upon us, doing us, however, but little injury.

As the officers and men of the Third seemed anxious for the affray, I ordered them to ascend the hill, which they did as promptly and quickly as the nature of the ground would admit. After getting my command in line, I noticed at this time that I could gain a strong position on the opposite side of a deep ravine that lay between my command and the

———

* Nominal list, omitted, shows 1 killed and 6 wounded.

edge of town; but to gain this position I would have to pass through an open field about 150 yards wide, and which would have exposed my command more to the enemy's fire. The Colonel about this time ordered me forward. I commanded the "Forward!" and with a yell, as if the infernal regions had broken loose, we gained the desired position. We then opened a brisk and active fire upon the enemy, who returned it with a stubborn and determined spirit, holding us in check some ten minutes; but under our regular fire they were compelled to fall back a short distance to the top of a hill and in the woods, where they dismounted and secreted themselves behind rocks, trees, logs, and every place that would afford them shelter. In this position they awaited our approach. We then left our position in the village, and marched in line of battle to the woods on the south side of town, to the point the enemy had recently occupied. We had hardly reached their former position before we were greeted by a galling fire from the secreted enemy, wounding three men and killing seven horses. This was the trying moment; but the gallant Buckeye boys of the Third never flinched. The enemy held us in check some twenty minutes, but their fire was kept up with spirit and energy. The Colonel commanding brigade was present and in the front rank; ordered us to charge, and charge we did, though a little promiscuously, driving the enemy in utter confusion through the woods, capturing fifteen men before they could mount their horses. The pursuit was continued some time, the enemy flying at breakneck speed over hills, rocks, and hollows, throwing away their arms and every incumbrance that impeded their flight. We were finally ordered to cease pursuit, which we did reluctantly. Bivouacked one and one-half miles south of Bradyville for the night. At 4 o'clock on the following morning we took up the line of march for camp, where we arrived about 4 o'clock p. m. of the 2d instant.

I am highly gratified and pleased with the conduct of both officers and men during the skirmish.

The following is a list of the casualties among men and horses, captures, etc.:

Captured eighteen men and horses fully armed and equipped.

The wounded were at once conveyed to camp, and properly cared for by Surgeon M. C. Cuykendall.

All of which is respectfully submitted.

W. M. FLANAGAN,
Captain, Commanding Regiment.

LIEUT. A. M. HEFLEBOWER,
Acting Assistant Adjutant-General.

Report of Captain William M. Flanagan, Third Ohio Cavalry.

HEADQUARTERS THIRD OHIO VOLUNTEER CAVALRY,
CAMP STANLEY, *March* 15, 1863.

SIR: I have the honor to submit the following report of the recent scout of the Third Ohio Volunteer Cavalry:

Pursuant to orders, we marched on the morning of the 4th instant, at daylight, under command of Colonel Eli Long, of the Fourth Ohio Volunteer Cavalry, commanding Second Cavalry Brigade. Taking the Salem pike, we marched about ten miles in the direction of Unionville, a small village located on the Nashville and Shelbyville turnpike. On arriving within two miles of the village, we encountered the enemy's pickets, driving them in and following close upon their rear.

The enemy, occupying that place in force, fled in haste on hearing of our approach. They did not escape in time, however, to prevent a loss of fifty prisoners and their camp and garrison equipage, consisting of tents, cooking utensils, wagons, etc. Not being prepared to carry any of our captured property with us, we remained in camp just long enough to destroy the same. Thence we were ordered toward Eagleville, on the Nashville and Shelbyville pike, where we bivouacked for the night, our horses under saddle, as we anticipated the enemy might follow in our rear; but they were judicious enough to approach and reconnoiter in small squads, which sufficed, however, to keep us on the alert, with our arms by our side, during the night.

We were called up quietly the next morning at 4 o'clock, and went as silently as possible about our respective duties. After we had breakfasted we fell in line, and, learning the enemy were occupying Chapel Hill, we marched for that point at 12 m.

We reached Chapel Hill about 4 p. m., but only to find vacant camps, as General Steedman, with his brave and hardy soldiers, had routed the enemy, killing and capturing a large number. Weary and disappointed, we then fell back to our encampment at Eagleville.

On the following morning we took up our line of march for Camp Stanley, but when four miles out were ordered to countermarch and proceed to Triune. From Triune we marched in the direction of Franklin, and, notwithstanding the roads were in bad condition from recent rains, we made a very expeditious march, encamping at night about nine miles from Franklin. Resuming our march early next day, we reached Franklin about 12 m., where we encamped and remained over night.

Early next morning, with the First Brigade, we took the Maury County pike, and, traveling about six miles, turned to the left on a road leading up a narrow valley to Thompson's Station, expecting there to find the enemy in force; but, being disappointed in this, we marched five miles farther on, making a junction at Columbia pike with a heavy column of troops under command of General Granger. Taking the advance of the whole column, with the First Cavalry Brigade immediately in our rear, we started for Columbia, passing through Spring Hill, a point which the enemy's cavalry had just left, retiring toward Columbia. We pressed them closely, skirmishing with them along the way without any casualties on our part. On arriving near Spring creek we found the enemy strongly posted, guarding every ford and disputing with spirit and energy our passage. After skirmishing for several hours with the enemy across the stream, we returned to camp for the night, the enemy still holding his position.

On the following day we were ordered to drive the enemy from his position on the opposite side of the stream. The Third Ohio Volunteer Cavalry, by order of the Colonel commanding, was dismounted and ordered to dislodge the enemy at the upper ford. I proceeded with my command to a point within 600 or 700 yards of the ford. I divided my command into three parts. I sent one-third, under Lieutenant [N.] Brewster, to the right of the road; one-third, under Captain [J. B.] Luckey, to the left, and the remaining one-third I placed under command of Lieutenant [E. A.] Haines near the road, under protection of a fence and a piece of woods, to cover the retreat of the right and left flanks in case a retreat should be necessary. I then ordered both flanks to advance cautiously, taking advantage of any natural cover that might be presented them.

On arriving within 100 yards of the ford, my right and left flanks were greeted with a brisk fire from the enemy, posted strongly on the opposite side of the stream, but the brave men of the Third did not falter, but returned the fire with energy and spirit, and finally drove him from his position and gained complete possession of the ford. Finding the ford impracticable, we returned and reported accordingly.

On learning that the enemy had been forced from his position, we were ordered to seek a more practicable fording, which we found a short distance below, and, crossing over, we consolidated with the remounted cavalry under General Granger's command, numbering about 3500, and, being placed in the advance, we marched toward Columbia over a dirt road leading from our place of fording to the Columbia pike. After reaching the pike, one company, under command of Sergeant [James M.] Hipkins, was sent to ascertain the practicability of fording Spring creek in our rear, at the pike crossing, which he reported practicable.

When within one and one-half miles of Columbia the main column was halted, and the Third Ohio was ordered to proceed cautiously forward under cover of nightfall and ascertain, if possible, whether the enemy still remained in force this side of Duck river. We found the enemy had withdrawn his whole force across Duck river, taking the ferry-boats and his pontoons with him, and had planted his artillery on the opposite side of the stream.   After waiting in silence to discover, if possible, any movements the enemy might be making, and finding all within his camp quiet, we returned and joined the main column.   We then led, in the advance of the column, in countermarch to a point this side of Spring creek, where we went into camp about midnight.

At dawn on the following day we took up line of march for Franklin, where we arrived at 2 p. m., and encamped for the night, and prepared ourselves with rations for [a march] to Camp Stanley.

On the morning of the 13th, we left camp and marched to a point within two miles of Triune, a distance of about eleven miles, and again encamped for the night.

We resumed our march next morning before daylight, taking in our course the Nashville and Shelbyville turnpike until we reached Eagleville, when we turned to the left, following a dirt road until we reached the Salem and Eagleville pike, leading to Murfreesboro.

We arrived at Camp Stanley about 4 p. m. on the 14th instant, without any casualties or disasters of any character.

I am proud to say that the officers and men of the Third bravely and heroically endured the toils, fatigues, and dangers of the expedition without the least murmur or complaint.

All of which is respectfully submitted.

W. M. FLANAGAN,
Captain, Commanding Regiment.

LIEUT. HEFLEBOWER, *Act. Asst. Adjt. Gen.*

———

SNOW HILL, APRIL 3rd, 1863

*Report of Colonel James W. Paramore, Third Ohio Cavalry, commanding
Second Cavalry Brigade.*

HEADQUARTERS SECOND CAVALRY BRIGADE,
CAMP STANLEY, *April 7,* 1863.

SIR: I have the honor to forward, for the information of the General commanding cavalry, the following report of the part taken by the Second Cavalry Brigade in the recent scout through Auburn, Liberty, Alexandria, and Lebanon:

We left camp on the morning of the 2d instant, at 6 o'clock, with about 400 men, 150 of the Third Ohio and 250 of the Fourth Ohio, the balance of the brigade being on detached and picket duty or dismounted. The portion of the Third Ohio was under the immediate command of

Lieutenant-Colonel D. A. Murray, and the Fourth was commanded by Colonel Long.

We marched on the Liberty pike, in rear of the First Brigade, till we came to Prosperity Church, three and one-half miles beyond Auburn. There a body of Confederate cavalry was encountered by the First Brigade, and, after a short skirmish, the rebel cavalry moved over to the left of the position occupied by the First Brigade, and crossed the river toward their flank. I was then ordered by Colonel Minty to take my brigade across the river and dislodge them from that position, which I did after a short skirmish, in which we killed one and wounded two or three others. We drove them about one and one-half miles, when darkness closed the pursuit, and we foraged for our horses, and, returning to the vicinity of the church, encamped for the night; furnished three companies for picket.

On the morning of the 3d instant, in accordance with instructions received, I moved on a by-road about one and one-half miles to the left of the Murfreesboro and Liberty pike, and parallel with it (with a line of skirmishers covering the front of my column and connecting with those of the First Brigade), until I reached the Lebanon and McMinnville pike. I then moved down that pike, toward Liberty, coming in the rear of the First Brigade. When we arrived at Liberty, I received orders to cross the river to the right and dislodge the enemy's sharpshooters, that were occupying a high hill to the east of the town, and opposing the advance of the First Brigade. I did so, by dismounting a squadron of my command and sending them up the hill as skirmishers, who soon gained its summit and dispersed the rebels. It was accomplished with difficulty, however, as it was a rough, rugged hill, and almost impassable even for footmen. I moved the column over through a kind of gap through the mountain till I struck a cove leading down to the pike. I followed that down to the pike, where I met the First Brigade moving up, and there I received orders to again move to the right across another mountain and occupy a ravine to the right of Snow hill, where we expected the rebels would make a stand. I accomplished that also in safety by climbing the mountain in single file (there being no road), and leading our horses. After we had gained that position and closed up in line of battle, the First Brigade moved up along the pike and formed in the ravine to our left. During this time skirmishing was going on between the rebels and our infantry and artillery moving up the pike, but with what success I could not learn, as they were then concealed from my view. About this time I learned from Lieutenant [W. L.] Hathaway, of the First Middle Tennessee, that there was a path accessible for horsemen, by which we could gain the summit of the hill and get around to the rear of the rebels and cut off their retreat. Thinking that another dose of flank movements might do them good, I determined to make the trial, and started, which, I am happy to state, proved an entire success. "Bonaparte crossing the Alps" was an insignificant affair to our passage over that mountain. But we gained the summit in safety, and shortly met the advance of the enemy coming to drive us back, as it appears they had observed us ascending the mountain. We drove them steadily before us till we came within about one mile of the pike, where they had concentrated their whole force, consisting of seven regiments, numbering between 2500 and 3000 men, commanded by Colonel Duke, who had just arrived from McMinnville. Colonels Gano and Breckinridge were also present.

Here was a place that required nerve, as well as plenty of ammunition. To have retreated down that mountain would have been exceedingly disastrous, and almost an impossibility. After canvassing the ground, and observing that it was a narrow passage or backbone, with a deep ravine on each side, thus preventing them from getting around to our rear, I determined to attack them vigorously, making as much show of force as I could; also feeling confident that we could whip any force that could get in our front. Accordingly, after consultation with Colonel Long and other officers, we opened the attack by dismounting the Fourth Ohio, and sending them on under shelter of logs, trees, etc., to within easy carbine range, when they opened the most terrific fire upon the enemy for so small a number of men that I ever heard. I then placed the lead horses in rear, and brought up the Third Ohio, and kept them mounted in rear of the dismounted men, ready for pursuit in case they should retreat.

Inch by inch the foe gave ground, stubbornly striving to resist our progress, but our men fought with determined spirit, and never once faltered. So rapid was their firing that in twenty minutes I found many of the Fourth were out of ammunition, having fired some sixty shots in that time. But the rebels had now begun to retreat more rapidly, and many of them dropping their guns and cartridge-boxes, I gave orders to fill the exhausted boxes from these. A concentration of force soon became apparent on the enemy's right, and I extended my left and strengthened it from the center and right. The firing again became fierce on both sides, but the advantage was with us, and after slowly pressing them some 600 yards farther through dense timber and thick chaparral, an exultent shout of victory was carried along our lines, and the enemy wheeled and fled precipitately. I immediately ordered the Third to charge, and they rapidly followed the retreating column, pressing close upon its rear and pouring in rapid volleys from their carbines. The Fourth Ohio was well-nigh exhausted from the severe work they had had, dismounted, but mounted their horses as soon as they were brought up, and followed. The enemy's cavalry had meantime reached the Liberty and McMinnville pike, which runs over Snow hill, and struck to the right toward Smithville. A few hundred yards from where we gained the pike, the latter inclines to the left, and here the rear guard of the pursued party attempted to hold the Third in check, firing one volley and wounding two men, a sergeant and private of the Third Ohio, but they were quickly driven from their position and were then pursued for about one mile. Our horses were much worn or the chase would have been continued farther. As it was, we overtook and captured some twelve of the enemy, belonging to the Second and Third Kentucky Regiments. During the fight and the chase we lost none killed and had but three wounded, the two above referred to and one man of the Fourth, while the rebels lost, in killed and wounded, at least twenty, and my opinion is that the number was greater, though it was almost impossible to obtain accurate information. Several of their wounded were picked up in the road and in the thicket, and carried to neighboring houses by the Tenth Ohio, which had now come up and reported to me through the commanding officer. The consternation of the enemy must have been as great as his flight was rapid, for the route was strewn with arms, and accouterments, and clothing, and I am the more convinced that a large number was wounded from the quantity of saddles we found scattered in every direction.

After halting on the hill for an hour, to rest my horses, and also in expectation of further orders from the General commanding, I returned toward Liberty to join the command, and went into camp this side the intersection of the Auburn road. Picketed my front and left flank with two companies.

On the 4th, I moved forward with the column, passing through Alexandria, where I found and seized a government wagon, which had been captured from the Union forces some time since. From Alexandria, having the right of the column, I moved out the Carthage road, according to orders received, a distance of about three or four miles, when a portion of Colonel Wilder's command was met, coming from Carthage, and orders then reached me to countermarch and return to Alexandria. From the latter place I moved in rear of the First Cavalry Brigade, on the Lebanon pike, and camped, about 5 p. m., one and one-half miles from the village of Cherry Valley, where was found an abundance of forage, belonging to a rebel family. Threw out two companies to my front at the village, and one company on the bluff to my left, as picket.

On the morning of the 5th, I moved my command shortly after daylight, and prepared to scout the country between this pike and the Lebanon and Murfreesboro pike, with the consent and approval of the General commanding, who added to my command for this purpose the Fourth Michigan and Seventh Pennsylvania Regiments. The Seventh

Pennsylvania was then sent across the country to the left to move through Statesville and Painesville [Cainsville?]. They were ordered to throw out a line of skirmishers to their front, to arrest all guerrillas and suspicious parties, and to take serviceable horses and mules wherever found. The Fourth Michigan was ordered to move to the right of the Seventh Pennsylvania, with similar instructions, their line of skirmishers to connect on the left with those on the right of the Seventh Pennsylvania. After moving down the pike about one mile farther, I sent out the Third Ohio, their skirmishers connecting with the Fourth Michigan on the left, and their right to move on a line with the left of the Fourth Ohio, whose column was to move in parallel line about two miles nearer Lebanon. By this disposition of forces my line of skirmishers took in some twelve miles of country, and each column was in supporting distance of the others, in case of trouble. I myself, with staff, accompanied the Third Ohio Regiment, Lieutenant-Colonel Murray commanding. All were instructed to regulate their movements so as to be able to report in the evening at Baird's Mills, nine miles from Lebanon. Not having the official reports of commanding officers of the two regiments of the First Brigade, I am unable to give the result of their expedition. The Third and Fourth Ohio Regiments, of my brigade, succeeded in capturing and seizing 110 horses, most of them known to have belonged to guerrillas or other parties in the Confederate service, thirty-three mules, and twenty-two prisoners. Some of the latter were afterward released, nothing appearing against them, and the remainder were, by the brigade provost-marshal, turned over to the infantry. Encamped near Baird's Mills.

On the 6th instant, we moved with the entire command toward Murfreesboro, crossing Stone's river by easy ford. Arrived at camp at 2 o'clock p. m.

Respectfully submitting the above, I am, Captain, your obedient servant,   J. W. PARAMORE,
Colonel, Commanding Second Cavalry Brigade,
Per WM. E. CRANE,
Lieutenant and Acting Assistant Adjutant-General.
CAPT. W. H. SINCLAIR,
Assistant Adjutant-General and Chief of Staff.

Report of Lieutenant-Colonel Douglas A. Murray, Third Ohio Cavalry.

HEADQUARTERS THIRD OHIO CAVALRY,
CAMP STANLEY, TENN., *April 7,* 1863.

SIR: I have the honor to report, for the information of the Colonel commanding, that, in compliance with instructions received, the regiment left camp on the morning of the 2d instant, with five days rations, and proceeded with the brigade on the Liberty pike as far as Prosperity Church, the advance of the First Brigade driving in the enemy's pickets. When the Third Ohio arrived at the church, they were ordered to the left, throwing out a line of skirmishers the enemy being supposed endeavoring to come around on that flank. I formed the line with the left thrown back advancing obliquely to the front pushing the enemy's pickets on their reserve about a mile distant, drawn up in line of battle to receive us. I ordered the left of my line of skirmishers forward, thereby advancing our entire line and reserve direct upon the enemy, who, I should judge, numbered from 100 to 150. As we advanced they fell back, not attempting to offer fight. The regiment still advancing, I received orders to halt and keep my position, if possible, which we did, till ordered to forage and return to camp.

April 3d, left camp, scouring the country to the left of the pike for about four miles, when we turned to the left, getting upon the Alexandria and Lebanon pike leading into the Liberty pike, on which we proceeded some distance; then turned to the right, and scoured the country on the right of Liberty to within two or three miles of Snow hill. From this point we kept still more to the right availing ourselves of a bridle-path to the summit of a high hill, which, after descending, brought us on a flat to the left and front of Snow hill, where we halted and formed, the enemy firing a few shots from the top of the hill opposite.

From this point we crossed the McMinnville road, mounted another high and steep hill, which really was achieved with difficulty. Now being in rear of Snow hill, we advanced toward Liberty pike to the rear of the enemy, proceeding but a short distance, when our advance was attacked in force. The Fourth Ohio Cavalry, being in advance, was immediately ordered to fight on foot and advance, which it did well. The Third Ohio was ordered to the front as a reserve, mounted. The enemy retiring, we were ordered to the front, charging and pursuing them fully a mile, killing some (number unknown) and taking twelve prisoners.

During the pursuit the enemy made two stands, but of no effect; we drove them as before. They getting behind a very thick cover, in which they were entirely concealed from view, and there being a large field between ourselves and them, with fences between at each end of it, and they, from ambush, keeping up a heavy fire upon us, I withdrew, hoping it would draw them out, which, however, did not succeed as I expected. I left a small rear guard, on which a few of them advanced, who, when they turned upon them, fell back to their former position. The balance of our command then coming up, we formed with them.

During the pursuit two of our men were wounded, one severely, Sergeant [William] Van Wormer, Company C, and Private Saltzgaber, Company I, slightly.

We fell back to Liberty, and encamped about four miles this side of it.

April 4, left camp and proceeded to Alexandria, and from there about one mile on the Carthage road, when we countermarched and returned to Alexandria, and took the Lebanon pike and encamped. Remaining there about three hours, again resumed the line of march, about five miles farther on, where we encamped.

From this place I set out, in compliance with instructions, in pursuit of some guerrillas who had fired at the advance guard and fled. The officer commanding the squadron sent Captain [J. B.] Luckey, who made every search possible for them, but without success, and returned to camp, after four hours hard riding.

April 5, left camp and proceeded on the Lebanon pike but a short distance, when we were ordered to the left, to scour across the country in search of guerrillas, meat, provisions, horses, mules, etc., toward Baird's Mills. I deployed three companies as skirmishers to the right and left, connecting with the Fourth Ohio on their right and the Fourth Michigan on their left. We made several captures; in all twenty-nine prisoners, fifty-three horses, and seventeen mules. The prisoners, on our arrival at camp, I turned over to the brigade provost-marshal, several of whom have been released, whom no charges could be brought against. Encamped on the night of the 5th at Baird's Mills.

April 6, returned to camp. Stone's river fordable, with not over two feet of water at the deepest part of the ford.

During the scout our horses had ample forage, and I am happy to state that the conduct of both officers and men of the regiment was highly creditable to them.　　　　　　　Respectfully submitted,

D. A. Murray,
Lieutenant-Colonel Third Ohio Cavalry, Comdg. Regiment.
Captain W. H. Sinclair,
　　Acting Assistant Adjutant General, Second Cavalry Brigade,
　　Camp Stanley, Tenn.

Report of Lieut. Col. Oliver P. Robie, Fourth Ohio Cavalry, commanding
Second Cavalry Brigade.

Camp Stanley, *April* 16, 1863.

Sir: In obedience to your order, received this morning, I have the honor to submit the following report of the part taken by the Second Brigade in the late engagement at Franklin, Tenn.:

I was ordered on Friday, April 10, to assume command of this brigade, consisting of 190 officers and men of the Third Ohio, 257 of the Fourth Ohio, and also a detachment of the Third Indiana Cavalry.

We left camp at 6 o'clock a. m., and marched to within four miles of Franklin, at which point I received orders from the General commading to move with my command across the Harpeth Fork at a ford three miles to the left of the Murfreesboro pike, and proceed to Franklin, on the Lewisburg pike. Having crossed the ford, and while moving in the direction of the Lewisburg pike, my advance guard captured a surgeon and quartermaster belonging to the Confederate Army; also two negroes, who reported a force of the enemy between us and Franklin, 2000 strong. A company which had been sent down the Lewisburg pike also reported the enemy in force in that direction. At this moment heavy firing was heard on the Lewisburg pike. Knowing that the Fourth Regulars had been sent in that direction, and were probably engaged with the enemy, I immediately prepared my command to move to their support. While advancing in line, and when within a few hundred yards of the enemy, who were plainly visible in strong force, I received orders from the commanding General to fall back and recross the stream. My command returned in good [order] to within a short distance of the ford. The enemy observing our movements, advanced rapidly and opened fire upon our right. I ordered my men to return the fire, which was promptly done, with good effect, repulsing them twice.

At this time I ordered the left to hold the enemy in check while I could retire the right of my line. While endeavoring to execute this movement, the enemy charged in strong force, driving in my skirmishers and causing my line to fall back in confusion. I succeeded in rallying my men and formed another line. The enemy having dismounted, advanced rapidly through the open field, and opened fire upon us, at about 300 yards distance. We returned their fire, and drove them back in confusion. I then withdrew my command across the stream, and took position commanding the ford, which I was ordered to hold. My loss was two killed and six wounded. The enemy undoubtedly [lost] more heavily, but they having possession of the ground, were enabled to remove their killed and wounded.

That night we remained in camp at this point. The next morning I surrendered command of this brigade to Lieutenant-Colonel Murray, who is my superior officer, and took command of my regiment, the Fourth Ohio Volunteer Cavalry.

Very respectfully, your obedient servant,

O. P. ROBIE,
Lieutenant-Colonel Fourth Ohio Volunteer Cavalry.

CAPT. W. H. SINCLAIR,
Assistant Adjutant-General.

MAY 12, 1863.—Reconnaissance from La Vergne, Tenn.

Report of Colonel Eli Long, Fourth Ohio Cavalry.

HDQRS. DETACHMENT SECOND CAVALRY BRIGADE,
CAMP NEAR LA VERGNE, TENN, May 12, 1863.

SIR: Pursuant to instructions, I have the honor to report as follows:

I left camp with my command as soon as the Third Ohio Cavalry joined, about 2:20 a. m. today, arriving at the camp of the First Ohio Cavalry at 5:45 a. m. On arriving there, I placed Colonel Eggleston in command of his regiment, 240 men, as he reported, and seventy of the Third Ohio, with the following instructions: To divide his command into three columns; the right-hand column going to Jefferson, and leaving a guard of forty men in the vicinity of Street's Ford, just south of Jefferson, a point where a major of the First Ohio Cavalry, who is better posted in a knowledge of this country than any one I can find, told me the rebels were most likely to cross. The right-hand column was then to come down Stone's River to the Upper Charlton's Ford, leaving guards at all the fords en route. The center column was to move directly east to Charlton's Ford, and remain there until joined by the other two columns. The left-hand column was to move to Steward's Ferry, communicating with Colonel McCook, and then move up Stone's River to Charlton's Ford, leaving guards at the fords, as in the other case. When the three columns had joined at Charlton's Ford, they were to move together to Rural Hill, under Colonel Eggleston, and from that point throw out small scouting parties in different directions, and, if he encountered the enemy, to resist him sufficiently to make him develop his force. Inclosed please find dispatch from Colonel Eggleston, First Ohio Volunteer Cavalry. As the country is very rough, and his command has quite a long march to make, I doubt if he will be able to accomplish it today. I will relieve him tomorrow at noon with a portion of my command; but as it is impossible to place a force sufficient to offer any resistance at all of the various crossing of the stream, some twenty miles, I will only leave a small picket to give warning at suitable places, and keep the rest of my command as well concentrated as I can consistently with patroling the river, and sending small parties across the river to find out which road the rebels contemplate coming. There are 263 men of my regiment here, and 105 of the Third Ohio. There are quite a number of both regiments remaining in camp who should be made to join their commands. It was impossible for me to get them all out in the dark.

Very respectfully, your obedient servant,

ELI LONG,
Col. Fourth Ohio Vol. Cav., Comdg. Detachment Second Cav. Brig.
CAPTAIN W. B. CURTIS,
Assistant Adjutant-General, First Cavalry Division.

MAY 21-22, 1863.—Expedition from Murfreesborough to Middleton, Tenn., and Skirmish.

Report of Major Horace N. Howland, Third Ohio Cavalry.

HEADQUARTERS THIRD OHIO CAVALRY,
Camp Turchin, Tenn., May 25, 1863.

COLONEL: I have the honor to report, for your information, that, in compliance with instructions received from brigade headquarters, I, with a part of the Third Ohio Cavalry, consisting of 127 enlisted men and nine commissioned officers, reported on the 21st instant, at 7 p. m., at the headquarters of the Fourth Ohio Cavalry, whence we proceeded, pursuant to instructions, to join the First Cavalry Brigade, which was to form on the Salem pike, with the right resting on the bridge across Stone's River, about two miles from Murfreesborough. From this point my command moved with the column out on the Salem pike until we struck the old dirt road leading to Shelbyville through the town of Middleton. The column moved out on this road, and after marching all night, arrived at and surprised the camps of the Eighth Confederate Cavalry and First Alabama Cavalry, in the vicinity of Middleton.

During the skirmishing, and until the camps were destroyed, my command was held in reserve and took no part in either. When the column moved out on the return to Murfreesborough, my command was in the rear of the column. I was ordered to throw out a strong rear guard, which I did, sending out two companies, viz, G and C.

Our rear guard was attacked by small parties of the enemy, and skirmishing was kept up for a distance of two to three miles on our return march, the enemy being checked alternately by the Third and Fourth Ohio Cavalry falling back and securing position. Other regiments also took part in the skirmish, but I am not informed what regiments they were.

My command returned to camp at 2:30 p. m. of the 22d, having sustained a loss of two wounded and one missing.

Wounded: Sergt. John Reynolds, Company K, arm shattered by musket-ball, and Private Casper Smith, Company K, leg shattered by musket-ball.

Missing: Private Thomas H. Horobin, Company G.

I have the honor to be, very respectfully, your obedient servant,

HORACE HOWLAND,
Major Third Ohio Cavalry, Commanding Detachment.

COLONEL ELI LONG,
Comdg. Detachment Second Cav. Brig., Camp Turchin, Tenn.

JUNE 4-5, 1863.—Scout to Smithville, Tenn.*

Extract from "Records of Events," Second Brigade, Second Cavalry Division, Department of the Cumberland, Commanded by Colonel Eli Long.†

June 4th, Colonel Paramore, with the Third, Fourth, and Tenth Ohio Regiments, went on a scout, accompanying Colonel Wilder's brigade of mounted infantry. Skirmished with rebel cavalry at Snow Hill, twenty-five miles from Murfreesborough. Drove them from their position and encamped near Liberty.

June 5th, Colonel Paramore moved with his brigade and two regiments of mounted infantry toward Smithville, twelve miles from Liberty. Just below Liberty, encountered rebel skirmishers. Met no heavy resistance until reaching Smithville, where (Thomas) Harrison's brigade of rebel cavalry was encountered and fought for some hours. Drove them back a mile, when they again formed in the woods and resisted stoutly, but were again defeated and fell back in confusion. Colonel Paramore lost two men of the Third Ohio, wounded. Rebel loss unknown, they carrying off their wounded.

CHAPTER XI.

THE TULLAHOMA CAMPAIGN

June 24th—We left camp at 5:30 a. m. and marched to Readyville, twelve miles east of Murfreesboro. Here we were joined by the Second Battalion under Major Seidel. It had been stationed here with Hazen's Brigade of Infantry since January 10th, covering the left flank of the Union Army, while it lay at Murfreesboro. During that time the battalion had been kept busy picketing, patroling, scouting and foraging, and when not otherwise engaged, there was always drill to keep the men busy. During their stay they had a number of encounters with the enemy, three of which we find reports of in the official records. The first was on January 18th, near Woodbury, the battalion being under the command of Captain McClelland, Major Seidel not having returned to the regiment yet after his capture at Lexington. See Major McClelland's report, which with those of Major Seidel of March 27th and April 2d, we reproduce in full, together with the complimentary reports of General Hazen and General Stanley. We were all glad to have the regiment reunited again, and to know that a general movement of the army was being made and we have no doubt but that Bragg and his army would soon be forced out of Tullahoma and across the Tennessee river. General Turchin commanding, the division marched with the Second Brigade under command of

Colonel Long. Wilder's Third Brigade is also on the left of the army. Colonel Minty's First Brigade is on the right flank and is marching by the way of Shelbyville. There was heavy cannonading off to the right and in our front all day. We camped at Bradyville.

June 25th—Rained hard all night. On the march at 7 a. m. in the direction of Manchester. Passed through Hawes Gap. Heavy cannonading on the right. We passed the artillery and Palmer's Division of Infantry. Heavy work for the artillery climbing the mountains. Stopped early in the afternoon in a piece of woods. Captured some prisoners. Very little forage to be had. Rained all day.

June 26th—Still raining. Saddled up at noon, moved forward about three miles. The brigade went into position in a piece of woodland and waited for the wagons to come up. We were in a wild rough country. Cannonading in the direction of Beech Grove, Hoover and Guy's Gaps.

June 27th—Wagons came up in the afternoon; three days rations issued. Moved up to Pochahontas and camped. Our troops had taken Shelbyville, Beech Grove and Manchester; most of the regiment on picket. Some one stole General Turchin's coffee pot. It was of enough importance to send a staff officer in search of it, but he did not find it; rained.

June 28th—Rained in the morning but cleared up in the afternoon. In from picket early. No time for breakfast. Moved out toward Manchester. Roads blocked with wagons, infantry and artillery. Pioneers repairing roads; camped about one mile north of Manchester; wagons came up late in the afternoon; plenty of good water. We spent the afternoon cleaning arms and drying clothes. Inspection of arms. Bragg's army in Tullahoma.

June 29th—Did not move. Forage very scarce. Companies C and G went out foraging and got some corn which Colonel Long, who was in command of the brigade, took from us and gave to the Fourth Ohio. There had been considerable friction between Colonels Paramore and Long ever since the latter was placed in command of the brigade, and when Long took the corn Paramore told him what he thought of him, and Long ordered him under arrest, but Paramore refused to recognize his authority. The next morning Long sent over to the regiment for a horse that Company K had captured. Colonel Paramore sent word to Lieutenant Brown not to let them have the horse. Then Long came himself with his provost guard. Brown got his Company under arms, and Paramore ordered out Companies C and G to support Company K if it was necessary, and as Long came up Lieutenant Brown ordered him to halt and his company to a "ready," and told Long if he advanced another step he would fire on him. Colonel Long retired from the field and reported the matter to General Rosecrans. Both Paramore and Brown were placed under arrest. Paramore was discharged from the service, but there was nothing further done in Lieutenant Brown's case. Colonel Seidel was now in command of the regiment. The third battalion was ordered out in the evening, marched about eight miles, reported to General Brannan and camped about midnight.

July 1st—Third battalion went out on the Winchester road on picket. Relieved at noon and went out with Negeley's Division on the Decherd road. Considerable fighting all afternoon. Went into camp at 9 p. m., eight miles from Decherd. The first and second battalions remained at Manchester until 10 p. m., and after a march of about ten miles, camped one mile from Hillsboro.

July 2d—Started at sunrise, marched to Morrison's ford on Elk river. The banks were high and the rebels had a strong position defended by artillery. We lost two killed and nine wounded. A crossing was effected by some of our troops, some miles below, and the enemy abandoned the ford, when we crossed, putting our carbines in a dugout and fording the river. In some places the horses had to swim. The Third Battalion moved up to Elk river near Decherd, found the bridge burned and the rebels entrenched on the opposite bank. The artillery was brought up and drove them off. The Pioneers came up and went to work on the bridge and the next morning we crossed and moved up within two miles of Decherd and camped.

July 4th—The Third Battalion moved out about noon, passed to the east of Decherd and went up the mountains about six miles. The rebels had abandoned all their positions. We returned to the foot of the mountain, where the infantry were in camp. About 3 a. m. July 5th a terrific storm just before daylight flooded our camp.

July 6th—Brigade left camp about 8 a. m., passed through Decherd and camped about six miles out on the Huntsville road, where the Third Battalion joined us.

July 8th Salutes were fired from all the batteries in honor of the capture of Vicksburg.

July 9th—Regimental inspection in the afternoon.

July 10th—Ordered out on a scout with two days rations. Marched to Fayetteville and went into camp.

July 11th—Boots and saddles at 4 a. m., but we lay at Fayetteville all day.

July 12th—Boots and saddles at 4 a. m. Moved at 10 a. m. in the direction of Pulaski; camped in the evening about thirteen miles from Pulaski.

July 13th—Reveille at 4, moved out at 8, got to Pulaski about noon; ran a lot of rebels out, captured quite a number of prisoners.

July 15th—Reveille at 4 a. m. Moved at 7, got to Elkton about noon. Could not cross because of high water. Camped about twelve miles from Fayetteville, went out foraging, captured two prisoners, two horses and a mule, got a lot of provisions; we lost two men, captured.

During the remainder of July the brigade was scouting over the country, around Pulaski, Tenn., Huntsville, Ala., and Fayetteville, Tenn., gathering all kinds of army supplies—forage, horses, cattle, mules, negroes—several hundred negroes were brought in. We had a number of skirmishes, but all the bodies of rebel troops were either scattered or were driven south across the Tennessee river.

On the 21st we moved to Salem, where we remained for a week, and on the 27th the paymaster visited us and we received four months pay.

Report of Colonel Eli Long, Fourth Ohio Cavalry, commanding Second Brigade.

HDQRS. SECOND BRIGADE, SECOND CAVALRY DIVISION,

IN THE FIELD, FIVE MILES FROM WINCHESTER, TENN., *July* 8, 1863.

CAPTAIN: In pursuance of instructions received, I have the honor to forward the following as a report of the proceedings of the Second Brigade, Second Cavalry Division, in the forward movement from Murfreesboro, from the time of leaving there until present date. Accompanying the same are submitted the regimental reports and reports of detachments detailed from my command at different times.

The brigade marched out of its camp, on the Lebanon pike, at 6 o'clock, June 24, 1863. Moved out the Woodbury pike, in conjunction with the Chicago Board of Trade Battery and the First Brigade, Second Cavalry Division, the latter being subsequently countermarched and separated from Brigadier-General Turchin's command, of which my brigade formed a part. At Readyville, twelve miles from Murfreesboro, I left the Woodbury pike, taking the Bradyville and Manchester road, having at Readyville joined to my command the Second Battalion of the Third Ohio Volunteer Cavalry. Camped near Bradyville that night, in close proximity to General Palmer's infantry division. Hard rain all day, and road heavy.

On the 25th, I marched out at 6 a. m., going by easy motion toward Manchester. Passed Hollow Springs and halted at Lumley's Stand, junction of Bradyville, of Manchester and Shelbyville, and of McMinnville roads. Three suspicious appearing persons were here taken, one of whom proved a notorious character, and I then sent parties to reconnoiter as far as Noah's Fork, three miles to the west, and Pocahontas, lying six miles eastward. Courier stations were found at each of these points, and one rebel courier captured at each, together with three other prisoners near the latter point. Left the Second Kentucky Cavalry on picket, and retired two and one-half miles to camp. Wet weather all day, and my train not up in consequence of difficult traveling.

Moved at 9 o'clock on the morning of the 26th, having previously sent back to Bradyville nine companies of my command to assist in bringing forward the wagons. Made a halt again at Lumley's Stand, and bivouacked, remaining till 2 p. m. of the 27th, when I received orders to move to Pocahontas and camp.

Early on the morning of the 28th, moved my command, by order, toward Manchester, via. Lumley's, and thence southwardly, over roads made by continued wet weather almost impassable even for cavalry. Arrived at Manchester at 10 a. m. From here sent one company of the Fourth Ohio Volunteer Cavalry back to Murfreesboro for train left there. Subsequently had orders to send two battalions to report to Major-General Thomas for outpost duty. Detail was made from Second Kentucky Regiment, and sent under charge of Colonel Nicholas, this leaving but one company of his regiment with me. On the same day two battalions of the Fourth Ohio were detached for outpost duty on General Brannan's front, Major Mathews commanding.

June 29th, two battalions were detailed from the First Ohio to report to General Brannan for picket duty.

On June 30th, one battalion was detached from the Third Ohio, also for picket duty with General Brannan, this making seven battalions detached from the brigade.

Remained in camp at Manchester till 10 p. m. July 1st, when I marched toward Hillsboro, reaching there at 2 the following morning. Moved on the Pelham road and bivouacked.

In the saddle again at 5 a. m. July 2d. Returned to Hillsboro, and thence taking the Winchester road. When within a mile of Morris' ford of Elk river, my advance discovered a squad of rebel cavalry and gave chase, the remainder of their regiment (Fourth Ohio Volunteer Cavalry) moving up briskly. Pursued them to the river, and drove them into the stream, when sharp musketry firing was opened on the advance from the woods on the opposite shore, and replied to by my men, who found the water too deep to ford readily. The enemy proved to be in considerable force, and additional companies were moved up to support the advance. One officer (Captain Adae) and one man of the Fourth were here wounded, and the firing becoming more heavy, I dismounted the remaining company of the Fourth, and sent them forward as skirmishers on the front and left. I then dismounted a part of the Third Ohio and deployed them in the woods on our right. The numbers of the enemy were augmented by reinforcements from their rear, and they occupied a quite strong position, so that it was found difficult to dislodge them till two pieces of Captain Stokes' battery were brought forward, by order of General Turchin, and opened upon them. This silenced their fire for a while, but meantime they were reinforced by a brigade of infantry and two pieces of artillery, the latter of which opened upon us a fierce fire with six and twelve-pounder shells and canister. My main command (twelve companies altogether) was now forced back from the woods. Sharp firing was now kept up on both sides for some time, the rebel infantry retiring toward Decherd, with the two pieces of artillery. At about 2 p. m. a large force of our cavalry arrived, with Major-General Stanley, and I then, by order, moved forward across the river, the enemy having fallen back from the ford. Soon came up with his skirmishers, however, and immediately engaged them, the force proving to be one brigade of Wheeler's cavalry, under direct command of General [W. T.] Martin. I pressed them back slowly, having a heavy line of skirmishers thrown forward and extending some 300 yards to right and left of the road. My progress was stubbornly resisted till toward sundown, when the enemy were put in full retreat, and we had full possession of the ground for the night.

My entire loss during the day was one officer and ten men wounded. Two of the latter were mortally wounded, and died during the afternoon. The loss of the enemy could not be ascertained, their wounded being mostly carried off. A number of dead bodies were found on the field, and Colonel [James D.] Webb, of the Fifty-first Alabama, was found at a farm-house, mortally wounded.

July 3, I moved at 8:30 a. m., following the brigade of Colonel Minty. Passed through Decherd and went into camp near the town. In the evening, pursuant to orders, sent Colonel Eggleston, First Ohio, with the fragments of the First and Fourth Ohio and Second Kentucky, back to Manchester to bring forward the train of the Second Division.

July 4, two battalions of the First Ohio and one battalion of the Second Kentucky were returned to the command, and on the 5th two battalions of the Fourth Ohio returned.

On the 6th of July, I marched out from camp about 9 a. m., following the First Division, General Mitchell. Passed through Winchester, and proceeded on the Winchester and Huntsville road to a point six miles northeast of Salem, and went into camp.

The battalion of the Third Ohio returned to this camp and rejoined the brigade, this leaving my command short one battalion, Second Kentucky.

Remained at same camp during the 7th, the command being mostly employed in foraging during the day.

Respectfully submitted. Eli Long,
    Colonel, Comdg. Second Brigade, Second Cavalry Division.
Capt. W. B. Curtis,
    Asst. Adjt. Gen., Second Cav. Div., Dept. of the Cumberland.

Report of Major Charles B. Seidel, Third Ohio Cavalry.

HEADQUARTERS THIRD OHIO VOLUNTEER CAVALRY,
CAMP NEAR SALEM, TENN., *July* 8, 1863.

SIR: I have the honor to report to you the part taken by the Third Ohio Cavalry Regiment during the scout of the last ten days.

Colonel [J. W.] Paramore, commanding the First and Third Battalions, left camp at Murfreesboro the 24th of June, passing through Readyville, where the regiment was joined by the Second Battalion, under my command. From here the whole brigade advanced into the Barren country, and after a tedious march of four days the regiment arrived at Manchester, where the brigade encamped until July 1. At Manchester Colonel Paramore was put under arrest, and I was ordered to take charge of the regiment. From here the regiment and a few companies of the Fourth Ohio, Second Kentucky, and First Ohio Cavalry, and two pieces of artillery, started for Elk River ford, on the Hillsboro and Winchester [road], where we encountered the enemy for the first time on our march. Here I was ordered by Colonel Long, commanding Second Brigade, Second Division, to dismount the greater part of my men and fight on foot, the balance of the regiment to support the battery during the fight. Finding the enemy too strong, and my command too much exposed, I was ordered to fall back with the regiment until reinforcement had arrived. At 1 p. m. Major-General Stanley arrived with reinforcements, and, finding that the enemy had abandoned his strong position, my regiment was ordered to cross the river, which was immediately complied with, and encountered the enemy's pickets after a short advance. My regiment, marching on the right, up the road, encountered the Fifty-first Alabama Cavalry. I immediately sent two companies, under command of Major Howland, on the left, and one company, under command of Captain Gates, on the right, to outflank the enemy, which was so successfully done that the enemy, after a fight of ten minutes, fled in confusion, leaving his dead and wounded behind. Colonel Webb, commanding the Fifty-first Alabama, was severely wounded, and has since died. My regiment lost one killed and four severely wounded. I pursued the enemy about one mile farther, when, being very much fatigued, I was ordered to go into camp near the battlefield. The next day the regiment marched to Decherd, where we encamped until the 5th instant. Leaving camp on the 5th instant, we moved near Salem, where the regiment is encamped at the present time.

Very respectfully, your obedient servant,

CHAS. B. SEIDEL,
Major Third Ohio Cavalry.

COL. ELI LONG,
    Commanding Second Brigade, Second Cavalry Division.

Report of Lieutenant Chauncey L. Cook, Third Ohio Cavalry.

CAMP NEAR MANCHESTER, *July* 1, 1863.

SIR: In pursuance to your orders to me, I beg leave to report the following:

Started out on the road leading to Hillsboro. Found the country mostly wooded and quite level. Found only five houses on the road, but found a number of roads leading off; think they are plantation roads. Found one wheat-field of ten or more acres cut and in the shock. Found an old picket post three-fourths of a mile from town. Was informed the rebels had three or four men on post last night. Left two men at picket post; advanced with company to the town; formed men in line, and sent out one sergeant and three men. Found in one building, I should think, 100 bushels of corn, some old guns, some army clothing— Southern. Did not search thoroughly. There is a reported force of rebels below town, but did not learn the number; think not much of a force.

Respectfully, your obedient servant,

C. L. COOK,
Lieutenant.

COL. ELI LONG,
Commanding Second Brigade, Second Cavalry Division.

———

July 28th—We marched to Fayetteville and camped, and on the 30th we had a very heavy thunderstorm, and our camp was flooded, the water in many places being a foot deep.

August 2d—Reveille at 3 a. m. On the march at 6. Returned to Salem and went into camp early in the afternoon.

August 3d—Reveille at 4 a. m. Started out at 6; reached Winchester and went into camp about 2 in the afternoon.

August 5th—Orders to be ready to move at a moment's notice. Dress parade and inspection every day; orders very strict against individual foraging.

August 9th—General Crook, who took command of the division, relieving General Turchin, on the 30th ult., inspected the brigade.

August 10th—Captain Luckey of Company C received an order dated August 9th dismissing him from the service for refusing to give up two men of his company who had been out foraging contrary to orders. The officers and men of the regiment regretted very much to see the Captain go, for he was a universal favorite. The Captain was reinstated, and later returned, and was heartily welcomed to our ranks again.

August 13th—Reveille at 1 a. m., marched out at 3 with three days rations. The Third Battalion went to Fayetteville, Company H to Salem, and the remainder of the regiment to Gum Springs, and during the next three days we were guarding railroad, doing scout and picket duty, etc.

August 15th—Regiment marched to Winchester and went into camp, where we remained until the 19th, when the regiment was again divided, the Second Battalion, under Major Howland, going to Cowan to guard railroad, and the First and Third Battalions starting out on the Chickamauga campaign. On the 22d the Second Battalion moved its camp to Decherd, where Major Howland selected a strong position for his camp and fortified it by building breastworks, and took every precaution to guard against surprise. The battalion was kept busy, on picket and scout; had a number of skirmishes with small bodies of the enemy; took some prisoners, and while rumors of forces that were on their way to attack the camp were numerous, yet they were unmolested until September 24th, when the rebels attempted a surprise, driving in the pickets and charging on the fortifications, where they met with a repulse, losing two officers and eight men killed, our loss being one man wounded.

On October 5th the battalion left Decherd for Shelbyville, joined the Fifth Iowa Cavalry and camped at 10 p. m.

October 6th—Started early, moved up to Elk river; found the bridges burned and a force of the enemy on the opposite bank to dispute our crossing; drove them off. Crossing the river, we pushed on toward Shelbyville. Went into camp late at night.

October 7th—Marched to Shelbyville and rejoined the regiment, which with the division was then in pursuit of and close upon the heels of Wheeler, who was headed for the Tennessee river at Muscle shoals. We will now take up the movement of the First and Third Battalions, under Colonel Seidel, in the Chickamauga campaign.

CHAPTER XII.

THE CHICKAMAUGA CAMPAIGN

In August, 1863, the two armies occupied practically the same positions that they had held in 1862, before Bragg crossed the Tennessee and invaded Kentucky. In the Tullahoma campaign, he chose to abandon the country north of the river without a fight. Fearing to risk a battle with the Tennessee in his rear, he fell back to Chattanooga and awaited the next move of General Rosecrans.

The proposition was a difficult one. Chattanooga was protected on the north and west by mountain ranges in such a manner as to make it almost inaccessible, the railroad and wagon bridges across the Tennessee

River were destroyed, the mountain roads were extremely difficult for wagons and artillery, so that the movement of the army and its necessary supplies was a perplexing problem. The plan of General Rosecrans was to move the left of his army across the mountains north of the river to a point opposite the town, threatening it from that direction, then crossing the river with the main part of his army at Bridgeport, strike for Bragg's communications to the south and compel him to abandon his position.

August 19th—Reveille at 4 a. m., left our camp at Winchester at 7 o'clock, marched in the direction of Stevenson and camped at the foot of the mountains.

August 20th—Started soon after sunrise, crossed the mountains and went into camp at Crow creek early in the afternoon.

August 22d—Wagons came up; they had a hard time getting over the mountains. We started out in the forenoon, passed through Stevenson and camped about a mile from the river and five miles from the town. On the 23d we moved up within three miles of Bridgeport and went into camp late in the evening. August 25th—Inspection of horses in the forenoon, and in the afternoon inspection of arms.

August 28th—A detail of men worked clearing a road to the river in the afternoon. Volunteers were called for, men who could swim, to cross the river at the ford.

August 29th—Three officers and fifty-two non-commissioned officers and men, with a guide, started out about 1 a. m. to cross the river at Island Creek ford. The crossing was a dangerous one, as the ford was crooked, and one and one-fourth miles long, and in many places the water reached to the men's armpits. The object was to surprise and capture the rebel pickets posted on the opposite bank. The men had succeeded in getting safely across, when the revolver of one of the officers was accidentally discharged, wounding one of our own men and giving the alarm to the enemy, so that all except one escaped. Soon after daylight the First and Third Ohio and Second Kentucky Cavalry Regiments crossed at the ford and marched in a southeasterly direction, crossing Sand mountain and Lookout valley, and camped on Lookout range, about two miles from the Georgia line.

August 30th—Reveille at 4 o'clock. Started at sunrise, crossed the state line into Georgia, passed through Trenton and marched within about twelve miles of Chattanooga, but found no force of the enemy. Returned by the way of Trenton and camped about sunset on the mountains. The next day we recrossed the river at the ford and got into camp about noon. Brought a few groceries and some tobacco from Trenton. Pontoon bridge was built across the river at Bridgeport and infantry, artillery and wagons crossed.

September 1st—General muster and inspection in the afternoon.

September 2d—Reveille at 4 o'clock. The brigade received orders to march with twelve days rations. Crossed the river at the ford, marched about four miles and camped. Our wagon train went up to Bridgeport to cross on the pontoon bridge.

September 3d—Crossed Sand mountain and went into camp about 8 o'clock p. m. in Wills valley.

September 4th—Moved about four miles and went into camp in Lookout valley. Inspection in the evening.

September 5th—Started out on a reconnaissance early in the morning. Crossed Lookout mountain; found the enemy in Chattanooga valley, but after a little skirmishing returned to camp; captured a few prisoners.

September 6th—Moved our camp about five miles up the valley.

September 7th—Wagon train came up and the next day we got orders to march at 5 p. m. with three days rations. Camped at 10 p. m. on Lookout mountain.

September 9th—Crossed the mountain and descended into Broomtown valley. Found the roads blockaded with fallen timber. It was a difficult matter to get the artillery over the mountains. Found the enemy in the valley near Alpine. We got the roads cleared and down into the valley about noon. After a sharp fight with the rebels in the afternoon, we drove them, and camped on the field. Our regiment lost one man killed, one officer and three men wounded, and a number of horses killed. The enemy retreated toward Rome.

September 10th—Reveille at 3 o'clock. Started out at sunrise. Went within three miles of Summerville, but found no enemy, and we returned to our camp of the night before.

September 13th—Detachments of the regiment out patroling the roads from 3 a. m. until daylight. At 8 a. m. got orders to move. Went out on the Summerville road in the direction of Lafayette, with General McCook; found the enemy in force; went within four miles of Lafayette; captured a number of pickets, returning at night. The next day we ascended Lookout mountain and marched to Dougherty's gap, camping on the mountain on the 15th, in the afternoon.

September 16th—We moved up the mountain toward Chattanooga about fifteen miles, and descending into McLemore's cove, camped on the mountain side at night.

September 17th—The Third Battalion went on a reconnaissance to another pass, but found no enemy. Returned to McLemore's; remained guarding the pass at McLemore's until the 19th. The view from Lookout mountain was very fine. On the 19th we advanced by way of Catlett gap and took position covering the ford of the Chickamauga at Glass's mill, the extreme right of the Union Army. The Confederates held the ford with infantry, cavalry and artillery. We held our position until about noon of the 20th, when General Crook was ordered to move to Crawfish Springs, where we were attacked by a heavy force of cavalry, infantry and artillery, and forced back about two miles. The ground that we occupied at Crawfish Springs was rough and rocky, covered with logs and underbrush, making it difficult to maneuver cavalry. We held our new position until nightfall, when we fell back and took position covering the Dry Valley road about six miles from Chattanooga, at midnight. We held this position until the afternoon of the 21st, when we moved forward until we came against the line of the enemy's skirmishers. We formed a battle line, threw out skirmishers, and remained in position all night.

September 22d—We fell back toward Chattanooga, our advance regiments taking position in front of the gaps in Mission ridge to hold them and prevent the enemy from coming into Chattanooga valley and cutting off a part of our force. Reaching Chattanooga, we crossed the river and went into camp. We lost twenty-five men killed and wounded in the regiment. From September 23d until October 2d the regiment was on duty at the different fords of the Tennessee above Chattanooga.

September 30th—General Wheeler with a large force of cavalry crossed the Tennessee river at Cottonport, after shelling the pickets, a detachment of the First Ohio, guarding the ford at that point. It was Wheeler's evident purpose to destroy the railroad in our rear.

October 2d—The regiment concentrated on the river some twenty-five miles above Chattanooga, for a chase after the divisions of Wheeler and Wharton, both of whom were reported north of the river.

October 3d—Started at sunrise to go after the brigade. Crossed Walden's ridge and the Sequatchie valley; climbed the Cumberland mountains, and camped on the Cumberland plateau, about fifteen miles from McMinnville; neither forage nor water to be had.

October 4th—Started at daylight, overtook the brigade in the forenoon, passed through McMinnville. The town had been captured by Wharton's Division and a large amount of government stores captured and destroyed. General Crook, with a part of the division, had overtaken Wharton's rear guards at the foot of the Cumberland mountains and defeated them in a sharp engagement. Crook lost in this engagement forty-six men killed and wounded. When we left McMinnville Long's Brigade had the advance. We found the rear guard of the enemy in position about two miles out on the Woodbury pike. The divisions of Wheeler and Wharton had formed a junction and the entire force was headed for Murfreesboro, and in order to hold us back until their columns could get out of the way the rear guard made a stubborn fight, but Wilder's Brigade dismounted and came into line on the right and left of the road, while Long's Brigade charged down the pike, and the enemy were driven from their position. We pursued rapidly, driving them from one position to another for six miles, when Wheeler was compelled to face about and fight. After a sharp engagement, lasting until dark, the enemy were driven from their position and we camped on the field.

October 5th—We were in the saddle early. Passed through Woodbury. At Readyville we found the rebel camp fires still burning. Here we crosed over to the Liberty pike, so as to come into Murfreesboro from the north. Arriving at Murfreesboro, we found that Wheeler had passed to the left, going toward Shelbyville. We halted for the night at Murfreesboro, lying in line of battle near the fortifications. No forage for the horses.

October 6th—General Mitchell came up and assumed command, and after drawing rations and ammunition we started out after Wheeler; passed through Guy's gap at sundown and halted for the night seven miles from Shelbyville.

October 7th—Started early, Wilder's Brigade in the advance, Long's Brigade following Wilder. Halted for a short time at Shelbyville. The Second Battalion rejoined the regiment from Decherd. We moved out from Shelbyville on the Lewisburg pike. A few miles from the town we came upon the enemy in a piece of woods to the right of the road, and after driving them a short distance, Wilder's men dismounted and Colonel Long ordered his brigade, the Third Ohio, in the advance, to draw saber and charge, and himself leading, drove the enemy four or five miles. The rebel loss in this charge was about 300 killed, wounded and prisoners. Colonel Seidel's horse was killed in the charge, and falling on him, pinned him to the ground, holding him fast until extricated by some of his men. As we neared Farmington the country became more rough and broken, and taking advantage of a place where he thought cavalry could not operate, the enemy took position in a dense cedar thicket, built barricades and posted their artillery. Here Long was forced to await the mounted infantry and artillery. Wilder's men dismounted, went into line, the battery came into position and opened on the enemy. Wilder's men charged and carried the enemy's position, capturing the battery of four guns and a large number of prisoners. Night came on and stopped pursuit. In the fight at this point Colonel Monroe of the One Hundred and Twenty-third Illinois was killed while leading his regiment.

October 8th—In the saddle early; passed through Lewisburg and Connersville, taking the Pulaski road and pushing forward rapidly, driving the rear guard of the enemy before us. We reached Pulaski, where we found the rebels had taken position to dispute our further progress, but retreated as our advance came in sight, and we were again stopped by darkness. We camped south of the town.

**Corporal Arthur A. Rogers, Company B.
Image by C. Noel, photographer, J.H. Van Stavoren's Gem Gallery,
Columbia, Tennessee.**

First Lieutenant John Moore, Company C, served earlier
as Company E's commissary sergeant.

Captain Oliver M. Brown, Company C, was promoted to major
in April 1865, but never mustered at that rank.

**Private Richard Lemon, Company D, posed fully armed with saber,
Burnside carbine and Colt's revolver at J.H. Van Stavoren's Gem Gallery,
Columbia, Tennessee.**

First Lieutenant Richard B. Wood (left), Company D, was killed February 23, 1864 in a skirmish near Dalton, Georgia. At right is Surgeon John B. Rice, 72nd O.V.I.

**Quartermaster Sergeant Joseph S. Lutz, Company F, mustered out
November 4, 1864. Image by Tunison & Son, Tiffin, Ohio.**

Second Lieutenant Alfred F. Washburn, Company G, photographed shortly after promotion in November 1864. Note buffalo hide cap.

Sergeant Solomon F. Gambee, Company G, was captured in October 1862 at Lexington, Kentucky, and paroled. Image by Reeve & Watts, Columbus, Ohio.

Private Jacob Sanders, Company G, enlisted in February 1864 at age 19.

Private Alvertus E. Gay, Company H.

First Lieutenant Ervin R. Harris, Company K, was 17 years old at his enlistment in September 1861. He rose steadily through the ranks.

Private Lewis B. Tooker
was promoted to first sergeant of Company A in April 1864.

**Tooker was commissioned first lieutenant of Company K in November 1864.
Note distinctive badge on his hat in this August 1865 portrait
taken at L.M. Benham's Gallery in Norwalk, Ohio.**

Group of regimental officers photographed on the steps of the Ohio Statehouse in Columbus, August 1865.

October 9th—We started out on the Lamb's Ferry road. Our advance came up with the rear guard of the enemy, charging their position. They gave way after a slight resistance. Our men killed four and captured sixty-five. We crossed Sugar and Anderson's creeks, and reached the ford of the Tennessee just after the rear of Wheeler's command had crossed. We went into camp after dark near Rogersville. Here we destroyed a large amount of cotton belonging to the Confederate government.

General Crook estimated Wheeler's losses in the raid at 2000 men and six pieces of artillery. He left on the field at Farmington eighty-six dead and one hundred and thirty-seven wounded. One entire regiment deserted and scattered in the mountains.

The loss in General Crook's Division was fourteen killed and ninety-seven wounded. The only Union troops in the fight at Farmington were Miller's (formerly Wilder's) Brigade of mounted infantry, Long's Brigade of Cavalry and a part of the Chicago Board of Trade Battery.

On this raid, marches were made on several days of from forty to fifty-seven miles, and only three days rations were issued during the entire campaign. Many of the men were badly in need of clothing. A little was issued at Murfreesboro, but most of the men had received none since June, before starting out on the Tullahoma campaign.

The campaign had been a remarkable illustration of what men and horses were capable of performing under conditions of deprivation of food and rest. The weather had been bad, raining a great part of the time. The marching and fighting had continued almost without intermission—yet everything was borne cheerfully.

The following extract is from Colonel Long's official report of the fight at Farmington:

October 7th—"We again overtook the enemy a short distance west of Shelbyville, when I was ordered to charge them, which I did with the Third and Fourth Ohio, and Second Kentucky, the First Ohio having been previously detached. The Third Ohio was in the advance. We drove them three or four miles, capturing 140 prisoners, besides leaving many killed and wounded along the road, and driving some 200 or 300 into the woods, thus cutting them off from their command. Lieutenant Colonel Seidel's horse and my own having been shot in the charge and myself wounded, the column was halted until Colonel Miller's Brigade closed up. I had nothing further to do until near night, when one regiment of my brigade was ordered forward, and I sent the Second Kentucky Cavalry; but on arriving within charging distance the road was found to be blockaded and the fences in the way on the side, the regiment was ordered back. It being now night, the engagement closed.

"The losses in my brigade were very slight compared to the injury inflicted on the enemy—ten wounded, two mortally. I would respectfully commend to the favorable notice of the Brigadier General commanding division, the following named officers and soldiers whose good conduct fell under my immediate observation: Lieutenant-Colonel Seidel, who behaved, as he always does, most gallantly; Captain T. D. McClelland, my inspector, and Lieutenant C. J. Norton, aide on my staff. Sergeant Martin, Third Ohio, my standard bearer, had his flag pierced with bullets and the staff shot in twain while carrying it proudly at the head of the brigade. Bugler Henry Deering, Fourth Ohio, and Private Henry Fisher, who has since died of wounds, behaved admirably. Casualties on the trip from Washington, Tenn., to Rogersville, Ala., as far as known: two killed, fourteen wounded, thirty-six missing.

"(Signed) ELI LONG,
"*Colonel, Commanding.*"

October 10th—The Cavalry Corps under General Mitchell concentrated at Rogersville, but as all the rebel cavalry had crossed the river, there was nothing for us to do but to move out in different directions.

October 11th—Long's Brigade was up before daylight, on the road at 6, marching north. Camped thirteen miles south of Pulaski.

October 12th—Reveille at 4. Started at 6; passed through Pulaski and took the Fayetteville road. Camped in the afternoon eight miles from Pulaski. Rained all night.

October 13th—On the march at the usual time. Some of our men out foraging were fired upon; a number were captured, presumably by stragglers from Wheeler's cavalry. They stripped their prisoners and then let them go. Camped on a hill just south of Fayetteville.

October 14th—Rained; rained incessantly. Remained at Fayetteville until afternoon. Marched through Branchville to Salem, arriving long after dark, and the rain pouring down in torrents. Camped west of town. It was one of those nights that made a fellow think of his "ain fireside."

October 15th—The Second Battalion ordered to Decherd. Rained all night.

October 16th—Still raining. Started out at 7 o'clock on the Huntsville road by the way of New Market; camped on a branch of Flint river, one mile east of New Market.

October 17th—Reveille at 4 o'clock. On the march at 6. Passed through Maysville. Camped one mile east of the railroad bridge across Flint river.

October 22d—Moved camp to Maysville. Scouting parties sent out hunting guerrillas; captured Frank Gurley and his brother.

October 26th—Marched to Woodville. Our wagons ferried over the creek at Paint Rock on rope ferry. Went into camp in the afternoon.

October 27th—Lieutenant Isbell started for Stevenson with dismounted men. He took our prisoners along, including Gurley.

October 28th—The Second Battalion, under Major Howland, went on a scout to Gunter's Landing. Did not find any rebels. Colonel Seidel with a force of men engaged getting a locomotive out of the ditch. Worked until long after dark.

October 31st—Cars arrived from Stevenson with stores.

November 4th—Dismounted men left at Murfreesboro on the Wheeler raid came in, bringing a lot of extra horses.

SPECIAL FIELD ORDERS

HDQRS. DEPT. OF THE CUMBERLAND,
CHATTANOOGA, TENN., *November* 10, 1863.

VIII. The following reorganization of the Second Division, Cavalry command, is announced:

The First Brigade will be commanded by Colonel W. W. Lowe, Fifth Iowa Cavalry, and will be composed of: Seventh Pennsylvania Cavalry, Fourth Michigan Cavalry, Fourth U. S. Cavalry, Fifth Iowa Cavalry, Third Indiana Cavalry Battalion.

The Second Brigade will be commanded by Colonel Eli Long, Fourth Ohio Cavalry, and will consist of: First Ohio Cavalry, Third Ohio Cavalry, Fourth Ohio Cavalry, Tenth Ohio Cavalry, Second Kentucky Cavalry.

The Third Brigade will be commanded by Colonel J. T. Wilder, Seventeenth Indiana Volunteers, and will consist of: Seventeenth Indiana Volunteers, Seventy-second Indiana Volunteers, Ninety-eighth Illinois Volunteers, One Hundred and Twenty-third Illinois Volunteers, Ninety-second Illinois Volunteers.

The commanding officers of the several regiments enumerated will report to their respective brigade commanders herein designated. The brigade commanders will report to Brigadier-General G. Crook, U. S. Volunteers, commanding division.

By command of Major-General Thomas,

WM. MCMICHAEL,
Major and Assistant Adjutant-General.

———

November 13th—Major Howland and six sergeants started for Ohio to recruit for the regiment, Sherman's army passing on its way to Chattanooga. The regiments were very small.

November 15th—A party of our men, out foraging, fired on, one wounded and one captured. The regiment went out in pursuit, and succeeded in capturing one lieutenant and three men. We received four months pay.

November 16th—The telegraph line to Stevenson broken and Lieutenant Howland with Company E sent out to find the break and repair it. They found the break near Stevenson, repaired it, and started back for Woodville, meeting the brigade at Scottsboro on the 18th.

CHAPTER XIII.

FIGHTING FOR CHATTANOOGA

November 17th—Orders received for the brigade to move to the front, all dismounted men to remain with the wagon train.

November 18th—The brigade started out toward Chattanooga. The wagons and dismounted men, under command of Captain Livermore, moved to Paint Rock. All superfluous baggage left with wagon train.

November 19th—The brigade reached Stevenson about noon, drew rations and started on up the river, reaching Bridgeport in the evening, and going into camp.

November 20th—Crossed the Tennessee river in the forenoon and moved up toward Chattanooga. Camped at the foot of Raccoon mountain. November 22d—Marched to Brown's Ferry and crossed the river to the north side, moving up to a point opposite Chattanooga, where we had a fine view of the two armies in battle array. Hooker's forces occupying Lookout valley, the Army of the Cumberland, under General Thomas, in the forts and breastworks south of Chattanooga, Sherman's army on the north side of the river above Chattanooga, while the rebel lines could be traced from the point of Lookout across Chattanooga valley and along the crest of Mission ridge. General Grant had his plans perfected, and was only waiting for Sherman to get his men in position for the final move. Not in all the war was there witnessed a grander spectacle than that which was to be presented at Chattanooga during the next three days. The contending armies being in plain view from the surrounding hills on both sides of the river, afforded an opportunity, not only to the commanding generals, but to thousands of spectators, to witness all the movements of troops on the field in a great battle, and it may be possible that the knowledge of the fact that the eyes of their commanders as well as of thousands of their comrades were upon them in a measure influenced their conduct in the hour of battle. It is certainly true that in all the conflicts of those three days the Union soldiers displayed a courage and daring, vim and dash that were never excelled in any war, or on any field.

When the Union army retreated to Chattanooga after the Battle of Chickamauga, General Bragg invested the place, confident of his ability to starve them out, and compel them to capitulate or make a disastrous retreat. Holding as he did Lookout mountain and valley, he commanded the river and the roads bordering it on both sides, compelling the Union commander to haul his supplies in wagons sixty miles up the Sequatchie valley and across the mountains. While we had been able to neutralize his efforts to destroy our communications with his cavalry, yet it looked gloomy enough until about the first of November for our army in Chattanooga. Cattle were driven from Nashville, but forage was so scarce along the road that when they arrived in Chattanooga they were in extremely poor condition. As one of the men aptly put it, "the army was on half rations of hard bread and beef dried on the hoof." But after the two little steamers were ready to bring rations up the river, Hooker crossed at Bridgeport and moved his army up on the south side, defeating Longstreet at Wauhatchie, taking and holding Lookout valley. Then the cracker line was opened up, the army was put on full rations, and matters began to have a brighter look.

Orchard Knob was an elevation about half way between Chattanooga and Missionary ridge. It was occupied by the enemy, who had built a line of breastworks of logs and rails, and was held as an advanced position between their line of pickets and their line of works, near the base of Missionary ridge. On November 23d, as preliminary to the movements contemplated, General Grant ordered General Thomas to make a reconnaissance in force on the enemy's position at Orchard Knob. The Divisions of Generals Wood, Sheridan, and Baird, were selected to make the assault. They were supported by Howard's Corps. At 2 p. m. the divisions formed in front of the Union defenses in plain view of both armies and at the word of command moved forward with firm and steady step, as if on review. No halting or straggling, but with quickening pace, as they reached the enemy's line of pickets, which gave way before their advance, and as they reached the base of the knob, with bayonets fixed they cheered as they rushed forward over the breastworks, driving the enemy over the crest and down the slope. As a result of this conflict, General Thomas advanced the right of his army along Chattanooga creek, to conform with the position at Orchard Knob, while Howard came into position on the left of Thomas, extending the line to the Tennessee river above Citico creek. During the night General Bragg moved Walker's Division from its position at Lookout, in order to strengthen his right, doubtless believing that there was the place where tomorrow's battle would be fought. During the night 3000 men of Sherman's army embarked in pontoons at North Chickamauga creek, and pushing out into the Tennessee, floated silently down, landing on the south bank just below the mouth of the South Chickamauga, and opposite the north end of Missionary ridge.

The boats were then used to ferry men across, and by daylight of the 24th two divisions were over. The pontoon bridge was completed by 11 a. m., and the troops commenced crossing upon it. Early in the morning cannonading in Lookout valley gave notice to friend and foe alike that Hooker was still there, and was going to be heard from. The enemy held a position at the north end of Lookout which they believed to be impregnable, their line of works extending from the palisades to the river across the northern base of the mountain. It was impossible to get on either flank, but the Union guns on Moccasin point and on the hills northwest of Lookout creek, kept up a fierce cannonade of the enemy's position on the mountain, while the infantry, driving the pickets and taking the advance lines, were getting into position for the final struggle. During the morning a thick fog had hung over the valley, concealing the movements of the Union troops from the enemy, but as they advanced up the mountain, they came into a clearer atmosphere. But the fog still hung over the valley, and the rattle of the musketry was heard down in the valley, while the combatants could not be seen for clouds of fog. By 1 p. m. the Union lines had advanced until they were well up toward the last position. The enemy had disputed every foot of the ground.. The artillery could no longer be used, on account of the proximity of the Union lines to the position of the enemy. The lines were formed in a sheltered position for the final assault, and it was discovered that ammunition was running low, and there was no way of replenishing it. The order was given to fix bayonets, and at the word "Forward!" the line advanced at quick step, and as they came into range of the withering fire of the enemy, the command "Charge!" was given, and the men swept forward with a cheer. Heedless of the leaden storm, they struggled up the rocky steeps, passing one obstruction after another, and at last reaching barricade and breastwork, they went over with a rush, and the enemy, driven from every point, retreated down the eastern slope, and the Battle of Lookout Mountain was won. Hooker's men were out of ammunition, but a brigade from Chattanooga came up carrying a partial supply, which was distributed among the skirmishers. During the night some of Hooker's soldiers scaled the palisades and hoisted the Stars and Stripes upon the point of Lookout, where the next morning it could be seen proudly floating by the men of both armies—a signal of victory.

While Hooker's men on the right had been scaling the rocky steeps of Lookout, Sherman on the left had not been idle. By 1 p. m. enough of his army had crossed the river for him to commence his attack on the right flank of the rebel army posted on Missionary ridge. Forming his line of battle, he advanced, carrying the first two positions of the enemy with little effort; but coming to the vicinity of the tunnel, he met with more serious opposition, and the coming on of night ended the conflict, the men lying on their arms in line of battle. The morning of the 25th revealed the fact that during the night the rebels had abandoned all their positions on the eastern slope of Lookout, and withdrawn their forces to the east side of Chattanooga creek. Hooker followed, driving his opponents, and taking position on Missionary ridge, near Rossville, prepared to attack the left of the enemy's position. A signal station was established on Lookout, from which all the movements of the Confederate forces could be observed, and signaled to General Grant at Orchard Knob.

Bragg's army now occupied a position in two lines along Missionary Ridge—one line at the base and the other at the summit—both lines protected by breastworks. He had massed heavily on his right against Sherman, who commenced the battle early, but was unable to dislodge his enemy. Grant, from Orchard Knob, was anxiously watching the result of Sherman's endeavors, and as one repulse followed after another, and the day was passing, he ordered General Thomas to get ready to move against the enemy's line at the base of the ridge. It was what the Army of the Cumberland had been waiting for, and they were soon in line, outside their works, and ready to advance. The signal—six guns fired in rapid succession from Orchard knob—echoed among the hills, and the line moved grandly forward across the valley. Shot and shell and leaden hail beat against their ranks, but there was no pause, no wavering—only a steady line of marching men, with waving banners, going forward with a power that was resistless. Hooker's men had planted their colors on the summit of Lookout. The Army of the Cumberland went forward with the determination that theirs should wave over the rebel works on the summit of Missionary Ridge. The line of works at the base of the ridge was reached, and springing over, the enemy was driven out and up the hill—and up the hill followed that line of marching men and waving banners, and reaching the summit a fierce hand to hand struggle took place, with the enemy losing ground at all points. Their officers vainly endeavoring to stem the tide of battle, were finally overwhelmed and borne from the field in the panic of their utterly routed army, and our banners were floating in triumph from the crest of Missionary Ridge.

CHAPTER XIV.

THE EAST TENNESSEE CAMPAIGN

Late in the afternoon of the 24th Long's Brigade of Cavalry crossed the river on Sherman's pontoon bridge; crossed Chickamauga creek, moving to the rear of the right of Bragg's army. During the night we captured a wagon train loaded with forage, halted and fed our horses and after parking and burning the wagons started in the direction of Ringold. In the forenoon of the 25th we captured a train of fifty-two wagons, loaded with army supplies, food and clothing. After taking all that we could use of the supplies, we burned the train and then marched to Cleveland.

November 26th—The Third Ohio and two companies of mounted infantry started at 7 a. m. for Charleston. Found the enemy occupied Calhoun with infantry and artillery; had a skirmish; tore up some railroad track, returning to Cleveland in the afternoon.

November 27th—Pickets fired on at 2 a. m. Saddled up and got into line, but were not attacked until daylight. As soon as it was light a general attack was made on our position by a very largely superior force, consisting of infantry and artillery. Seeing that they had us at a disadvantage, as we had no artillery, Colonel Long concluded that discretion was the better part of valor, and retreated in the direction of Chattanooga, going into camp on the river bank, a disagreeable and rainy night. Our loss was two killed and fourteen wounded. We captured about 250 prisoners.

November 29th—In the saddle at 5 a. m. and again on the march for Cleveland. The infantry (General Howard's Corps) with us. It looked as if we were on our way to the relief of Burnside at Knoxville. We camped near Cleveland.

November 30th—Marched to Benton, and the next day we continued the march, reaching Athens.

December 2d—Started on a forced march to Loudon, in an effort to save the bridge across the Holston river. When about six miles from Loudon we came up with the rebel cavalry. Colonel Long with the Second Brigade, the Third Ohio in the advance, charged them with drawn sabers, and in column of fours, driving them the entire distance to Loudon. In their mad race to get away from us, the enemy threw away clothing, blankets, saddle bags, arms, and everything that would impede their flight. Reaching Loudon, we found it occupied by the enemy with infantry and artillery, and being unable to dislodge them, we bivouacked for the night. The enemy evacuated the town during the night, destroying the bridge, a number of locomotives and cars, and a large amount of stores and clothing.

December 3d—Colonel Long received orders to march to Knoxville to open communication with General Burnside. We left Loudon at 8 a. m., marched all day and night. During the night we passed in sight of General Longstreet's camp fires, reaching Knoxville at 3 a. m. December 4th, bringing to Burnside and his beleaguered army the welcome tidings that deliverance was at hand. We found them almost on the verge of starvation. Longstreet did not wait, however, until the infantry came up, but early on the 4th raised the siege and retreated eastward.

Our campaign since leaving Woodville, Alabama, fifteen days ago, has been very severe. We have drawn no rations since leaving Chattanooga, living entirely off the country. Our principal hardship has been that we have no coffee. Coffee is the great luxury of the soldier's life in camp. With him it is certainly the "cup that cheers." The weather has been anything but pleasant and enjoyable, and men and horses have given out under the strain. There are only about 300 men in the regiment for duty. Immediately after Longstreet raised the siege foraging parties went out, and the garrison at Knoxville was on full rations again.

December 6th—We left Knoxville, marching to Marysville and camped for the night.

December 7th—The Second Brigade, under Colonel Long, started out in a southeasterly direction to chase after and if possible capture Longstreet's wagon train. As the country is very rough and mountainous and the roads bad, we were in hopes that we might overtake it. Camped in the hills, where we found plenty of forage.

December 8th—On the march early. Marched all day through a rough, hilly country; camped at night near iron works on the Tellico river.

December 9th—On the march; crossed the big Smoky mountains and came down into the valley in North Carolina. Marched to Murphy; found a few rebels in town, drove them out and went into camp south of the town on the Hiawassee river. We remained at Murphy one day; found that our train was too far ahead for us to overtake it; the country is poor and barren and forage very scarce.

December 11th—We took up the line of march back to East Tennessee, and after a rough, hard journey arrived at Charleston on the 15th and camped. The next day the regiment was sent to Columbus to guard a ford on the Hiawassee river, and to do patrol and picket duty. Here we went into camp, expecting to remain for some time.

December 18th—A detachment of the regiment under Lieutenant Howland sent out in the direction of Tellico plains to hunt up a squad of rebels reported to be in that locality, failed to find them and returned to camp at 5 a. m., December 19th.

December 24th—Two men from Company E were captured near Benton while out foraging.

December 27th—Wheeler attacked one of our wagon trains near Charleston, but was driven off after a sharp fight, Colonel Long with 150 men charging with drawn sabers. Wheeler's loss was nine killed, thirty wounded and 131 prisoners. Our loss was two killed and twelve wounded.

There were twenty-one deserters from the rebel army came into camp today. In fact there is hardly a day passes that some do not come in. Wonder if they are not trying to get home to spend the winter and go back to the army when the spring campaign opens. Its dollars to doughnuts that you'll find most of them in the rebel army next summer.

December 31st—The last day of 1863, and to let us know that they have not forgotten us, some kind-hearted person has sent us some coffee, sugar, salt, soap, and candles the first government supplies we have received in a month. While in East Tennessee we were compelled to subsist on the country, gathering forage for our horses and rations for ourselves. The only rations we received from the government were the kind that I have mentioned so that when we were not busy at something else we were gathering in supplies. Our main living consisted of corn dodgers, fried in pork fat, which were all right once in a while, but became monotonous when we had them week-days and Sundays, too. We had to go out and get the corn, bring it to camp, shell it and take it to the mill and get it ground to make our dodgers. At the mill the farmers were very good to us. They would waive their rights and let our grist go in first, so that we would not have to wait our turn. The mills were run by water power and were slow enough in all conscience. They reminded me of the story of the boy who went to mill once when the water was low and the mill running accordingly. Finally the boy got out of patience and said: "I could eat the meal as fast as that mill grinds it." "Yes," said the miller, "but how long could you eat it." "Until I starved to death," promptly answered the boy. Well we ought not to complain; the old mill kept us from starving to death, at least.

January 1st, 1864—Cold, terrible cold; known all over the United States as the cold New Year's. We were provided with what were popularly known as dog tents, which were a very good protection for summer campaigning, yet were not the best in the world for winter quarters. Some of the messes had built log huts with fireplaces, and were more comfortable, but most of the men did not care to go to the trouble, fearing that if they did we would move the next day. In some respects our winter in East Tennessee was unlike any other part of our service. A large part of the country is very rough and mountainous in that it resembled the country around Woodville, Alabama. The soil in the valleys is fairly fertile and productive, but in the mountains it is poor, yielding but a scant return for the toil of the husbandman. It is traversed by many mountain streams, which find their outlet in the Tennessee river. Most of these streams were without bridges and in crossing them on our numerous scouts and foraging expeditions, we were compelled to ford them, plunging into the icy waters which were often so deep and swift as almost to carry our horses off their feet. These, with the rough mountain roads, made travel very diffcult. The climate during our stay in the winter of 1863 and '4 was anything but pleasant and agreeable; many cold rains and severe mountain storms. The people were kind and hospitable, and the great majority of them were loyal to the Union. Many of them were poor and unlearned, and some of their habits and customs were such as would not recommend them to refined society. Very few of the old women that did not smoke, and in some localities they were inveterate snuff dippers. Having very few slaves, they had no interests in common with the slaveholding aristocracy of the South, and they were true as steel to the Union, and nowhere did people make greater sacrifices for the cause than did they. Most of them were small farmers, making a scant living on their mountain farms. The young and able-bodied men were in the Union Army, while the old men and the women and children were left to cultivate the farms, and take care of the homes. They welcomed the Union army with simple hospitality. The old men always greeted us cordially. Their invariable salutation was, "Howdy; won't you light and take a cheer." The march of Longstreet's army, and the many marauding parties that were roaming about in the mountains filled them with terror, and hundreds of families packed their few household goods into wagons and came and camped inside our pickets, feeling secure if they were only near our camps. Many thousands of these refugees were sent to places of safety, and fed and cared for by the government until the close of the war. And when they returned, in most cases, it was only to find blackened ruins where home had been. And many of the families separated by the war were never again reunited, for father, husband, brother, or son, had fallen in the conflict. They were at peace. The strife with them had ended, but with these the struggle was only just begun. Although hearts were breaking and the burdens of life heavy, they must be borne patiently. Although the future seemed hopeless, it must be faced with courage.

January 8th—Orders came to re-enlist, the government offering a thirty days furlough and $402 bounty to the men who came out with the regiment in '61 if they would enlist for three years more.

January 12th—Lieutenant Oates and four men were captured at Boyd's Mills while out foraging.

January 16th—A detachment under Lieutenant Howland went to Benton in the evening; found a dance in progress; captured one man and six horses; got back to camp at 5 a. m.

January 25th—It was reported in camp that a Federal officer who had escaped from rebel prison, was in the mountains east of us and trying to get to our lines. A detachment was sent out and succeeded in finding him about fifteen miles out. It was Colonel Cliff. There were half a dozen mountaineers with him. He had been a fine specimen of physical manhood, but was now wasted by starvation, his uniform in rags, hair and beard long and unkempt, and altogether a most pitiable object to look at. He was brought into camp, where he was cleaned up and cared for and sent on to Brigade headquarters.

January 27th—We received mail for the first time in two months. The arrival of mail in camp was always an important event, and especially so when we had no direct communication, and days and weeks had passed, and the men were anxious to hear from home. Generally, however, our mails came fairly regular, and a letter mailed anywhere in the United States and addressed to the Third Ohio Cavalry would have found us, no matter where we were, without any other directions. The postoffice department allowed letters to go out from the army without prepayment of postage, and at Nashville the Christian Commission paid all the delinquent postage on mail arriving for the army. While we lay at Columbus, Captain Clock, with a detachment composed of Companies L and M. on one of the numerous raids made on Benton captured two guerrillas.

When the brigade left Woodville for Chattanooga, November 18th, 1863, the dismounted men were left to guard the wagon train under command of Lieutenant-Colonel Robie of the Fourth Ohio. Captain Livermore was in command of the men of the Third Ohio. The same day we moved to Paint Rock bridge, parked the wagons, and put the camp in as good a state of defense as possible. The government was unable to get horses as fast as they were required for the service. We had a large number of worn-out horses in corral, and we were kept busy foraging for them and for the mules belonging to the wagon train. The horses made a great amount of trouble getting out of the corral. The fences were very poor. The men had to go long distances after forage. Many refugee families came into camp to seek protection from the bushwhackers in the hills. On the 25th of November a bushwhacker was shot. December 9th a detachment was sent with the unserviceable horses to Nashville, riding the best of them and driving the others.

December 17th—We received a drove of beef cattle to feed and care for. There are some cows among them from which we get plenty of milk.

December 21st—Bushwhackers were reported in the hills and a detachment went out after them, but, as usual, failed to connect.

December 24th—Saddles, bridles, etc., of dismounted men sent to Maysville on the cars. It looks as if we were to move from here before long.

December 26th—Orders to be ready to march at 8 a. m. tomorrow. During the five weeks we have been at Paint Rock we have been kept busy doing picket duty and guarding forage trains. There are over 200 men here without horses.

December 27th—A rainy, disagreeable morning; we left camp at Paint Rock at 7 o'clock. The roads were in a terrible condition. Many places the mud and water about knee deep. It was difficult to get the wagons through; some of them were upset. We marched in the direction of Huntsville. The rain continued to pour down all day. Camped on Flint river, having marched about fifteen miles. It continued to rain very hard all night.

December 28th—The weather was cool; it stopped raining, and we took up the line of march at 8 a. m.; marched up Flint river as far as Brownsboro, but we were unable to cross on account of high water; continued up the river reaching Maysville, we went into camp about 2 p. m. The roads were very muddy.

December 29th—We left Maysville at 9 a. m. and got across Flint river at noon. The current was very swift; two wagons upset in a ditch, and Company M's wagon upset in the river, but we finally all got across and camped about five miles east of Huntsville in a piece of woods.

December 30th—Started at 7 o'clock and arrived at Huntsville at 10 a. m.; found a lot more dismounted men of the brigade, also a lot from Nashville with fresh horses. We continued north, camping about four miles out on the Athens road; forage and provisions plenty.

December 31st—Rained during the night and most of the day. We set out on the march at 7 a. m.; passed through some good country; crossed Limestone creek on a covered bridge; forded Swan creek, marched within four miles of Athens and went into camp in a piece of woods. It commenced to get colder in the evening, with a falling temperature and a fierce, bitter wind all night.

January 1st, 1864—A bitter cold wind blowing strong from the southwest. Overcoats and horse equipments frozen stiff. Reveille at 4 o'clock, on the march at 6, passed through Athens. Marched about nine miles out on the Prospect road and camped in a piece of woods.

January 2d—Reveille at 6 o'clock; on the march at 8; weather still very cold. Crossed the state line into Tennessee; passed through Prospect; crossed Elk river on pontoon bridge, and went into camp about five miles north of Prospect. The teams did not get in, so we had no tents.

January 3d—The wagons arrived about noon, when we moved up to Pulaski, and went into camp in a beech grove on a hill, one mile south of town. The next day the men who came out in '61 commenced re-enlisting, and on the 5th Captain Miner reported that three-fourths of the men had re-enlisted and made application for thirty days veteran furlough.

January 6th—We received a lot of fresh horses. On the 8th we turned our condemned horses into the government corral.

January 9th—The brigade was ordered out into line and the camp and men searched for $4000 in gold that had been stolen from a citizen. The search failed to reveal anything. The next day one of the men that helped steal the gold came forward and confessed, informing on the others. There were five of them. He gave up his share of the gold—$800—but the others refused to tell where the rest of it was hidden and it could not be found. The men did not belong to the Third Ohio. They were turned over to the civil authorities to be dealt with according to law.

January 12th—The re-enlisted men started home on veteran furlough, arriving at Nashville on the 14th. On the 27th they were mustered out and in again. They left Nashville on the 6th of February, and arrived at Bellevue, Ohio, on the 9th, where they were met by Majors Howland and Skinner and Captains McClelland and Culver, with a brass band, taken to Monroeville and entertained. Speeches were made by Colonel Zahm, Rev. Painter, Captain Culver and Chaplain Warner, and the next day the men left for their homes to enjoy their thirty days furlough.

January 12th—The remainder of the brigade started southward, leading the horses belonging to the re-enlisted men. Crossed Elk river at Elkton, and camped about a mile from the river on the Athens road.

January 13th—Started at 7 a. m.; camped about eleven miles from Huntsville.

January 14th—Marched within about three miles of Huntsville and turned the lead horses into the government corral. We remained at Huntsville until the 23d, when we broke camp and forded Flint river; camped at Maysville late at night.

January 24th—Started early, passed through Woodville and camped about three miles out on the Larkinsville road.

January 25th—Started at daylight, passed through Larkinsville and camped at Scottsboro late at night; the roads simply awful.

January 26th—Started soon after daylight, passed through Bellfonte, forded Mud and Crow creeks and camped on Crow creek, about four miles from Stevenson.

January 27th—Took up the march as usual, passed through Stevenson, crossed the Tennessee river at Bridgeport and camped on the south bank of the river.

January 28th—Started at daylight, left the wagon train and pushed on up the river; crossed Lookout creek and camped at the foot of Lookout mountain on the ground made famous by Hooker's men in their battle two months ago.

January 29th—Crossed over into Chattanooga valley and camped about two miles from Chattanooga. We remained here until the 2d of February, when we broke camp about noon, passed through Chattanooga, crossed Chickamauga creek—had to haul the wagons up by hand—camped late at night. The next day we started at sunrise, passed through Harrison. Camped about three miles from Georgetown.

February 4th—Started early, passed through Georgetown, crossed Hiawassee river at Charleston; camped at Calhoun at Brigade headquarters.

February 5th—Moved up the river to Columbus, where we joined the other part of the regiment.

February 12th—The second detachment of re-enlisted men from the regiment started home on veteran furlough.

February 14th—They arrived at Nashville and on the 26th they were paid off in Louisville, arriving home the next day.

February 12th—A detachment of the Fourth Michigan came up to relieve us and we were ordered to be ready to move at 7 o'clock in the morning, when we marched to Calhoun and went into camp.

February 16th—Brigade mounted inspection by General Elliott at 11 o'clock. We remained at Calhoun until the 2d of March, on duty constantly guarding the fords, picketing the roads, foraging, scouting and patroling. The weather was cold and stormy, and while so many of our boys were home on veteran furlough, the men at the front had to do double duty. Often when a detachment was on scout, there were no men left in camp to relieve the pickets, and they had to remain on post for seventy-two hours at a stretch. At some points the rebel pickets were on one side of the river and ours on the other, and frequently they would arrange a meeting for the exchange of newspapers, or our boys would exchange salt and coffee for tobacco. In fact the pickets generally did not appear to manifest any animosity toward each other.

February 22d—The brigade went out on a scout with three days rations; crossed the Hiawassee river, passed through Cleveland, and passing through Red Clay, advanced on the Spring Place road. There is a general movement against Dalton. We are on the left wing of the army.

February 23d—Passed through Spring Place and advanced toward Dalton; drove in the rebel pickets and charged into a fortified camp of infantry within four miles of Dalton. After driving the enemy a short distance, they were reinforced, and we withdrew to Russell's Mills, and from there to Varnell's Station.   On the 24th we moved down the valley and encountered the enemy along the eastern base of Rocky Face ridge. Advancing down the valley, our infantry drove the enemy from a hill, but reinforcements arriving, they charged and drove our men back.   The fight was kept up until nightfall.   The next morning we moved up on the left of the infantry; had some skirmishing; fell back about three miles, after dark.   We returned to camp at Calhoun on the 28th.   Captain Wood of the Third Ohio was killed in the attack on Dalton on February 24th.

March 2d—We left Calhoun and marched to Cleveland and went into camp.

March 6th—Went out about fifteen miles on a scout, but saw no signs of the enemy, returned to camp.   We remained at Cleveland until March 14th, when we moved camp to Ooltewah, and the next day took up the line of march for Ringold, Georgia, where we went into camp.

March 16th—Moved our camp about three miles in the direction of Chattanooga, crossed Chickamauga creek and camped.   We had ten days of very cold weather, and a great snowstorm on the 22d.   Snow fell to the depth of six to eight inches.   The boys had a great snowball battle in a field that lay between our camp and that of the mounted infantry. Our duties were mainly picket and outpost.   On the 27th we went on a scout, going through Ringold gap and along the east side of Taylor's ridge; drove in the rebel pickets.   We got a few shots at the Johnnies, but not at very close range, and it is not very likely that we did much damage.   We returned to camp in the afternoon.   On the 28th we had a heavy hail and rainstorm.   Weather continued cold and disagreeable up to the middle of April, raining a great part of the time, making a soldier's life anything but pleasant.   On April 5th we went on outpost picket about ten miles out, returning to camp in the afternoon of the 7th.   On the 9th we were ordered out at 3 a. m.   It was intended to surprise and capture some of the enemy's pickets, but we did not get through the gap before daylight.   So we were ordered back, only a small party being sent through the gap to locate the picket post.   The next morning we were out in the wee small hours and succeeded in capturing five of the enemy's pickets and chasing the rest of them to their camp at Tunnel Hill.

OFFICIAL REPORTS, EAST TENNESSEE CAMPAIGN

DECEMBER 28, 1863.—Action at Calhoun and Skirmish at Charleston, Tenn.

REPORTS.

No. 1.—Maj. Gen. George H. Thomas, U. S. Army, commanding Department of the Cumberland, with complimentary letter to Colonel Eli Long.

No. 2.—Colonel Eli Long, Fourth Ohio Cavalry, commanding Second Cavalry Brigade.

Report of Major General George H. Thomas, U. S. Army, commanding Department of the Cumberland, with complimentary letter to Colonel Eli Long.

CHATTANOOGA, TENN., *December* 29, 1863.

(Received 1:45 p. m., 30th.)

SIR: Colonel Eli Long, Fourth Ohio Cavalry, commanding Second Division of Cavalry, reports from Calhoun, Tenn., December 28th, that the rebel General Wheeler, with 1200 or 1500 cavalry and mounted infantry, attacked Colonel Laiboldt, escorting a supply train from Chattanooga to Knoxville, about 10 this a. m., at Charleston, on south bank of the Hiawassee. The train and escort had reached and encamped at Charleston last night, and Colonel Laiboldt's skirmishers were hotly engaged with the enemy this a. m., before Colonel Long was apprised of their approach. He immediately mounted the small force for duty in his camp at the time (150 men) and crossed the river to Colonel Laiboldt's support. The rebels shortly afterward gave way, Long pursuing them closely.

Discovering a portion of their force cut off on the right, he charged them with sabers, completely demoralizing and scattering them in great confusion in every direction. Several of the enemy (number not known) were killed and wounded. One hundred and twenty-one prisoners, including five commissioned officers, were captured. The main rebel column fled, and was pursued for five miles, on the Dalton road, and, when last seen, was fleeing precipitately. Long's loss was one man slightly wounded. For this and many other gallant acts of Colonel Long, since serving in this department, I earnestly recommend him for promotion to brigadier-general of volunteers.

The officer in command of the courier station at Cleveland also reports that he was attacked early this morning, December 28th, by a force of 100 rebels. He drove them off.

GEO. H. THOMAS,
Major-General.

MAJ. GEN. H. W. HALLECK,
General-in-Chief.

HEADQUARTERS DEPARTMENT OF THE CUMBERLAND,
CHATTANOOGA, *January* 1, 1864.

COLONEL ELI LONG,
Commanding Brigade, Calhoun.

COLONEL: Your report of your engagement with the enemy on the morning of the 28th was duly received. It was a very pretty affair indeed.

I have the honor to inform you that there are now *en route* to your station four pieces of artillery, escorted by two regiments of infantry. This artillery is intended as a reinforcement to your post. The infantry will return to this place.

The battery was ordered to Calhoun before we heard of your defeating Wheeler.

I am, Colonel, very respectfully,   WM. D. WHIPPLE,
                                                    Assistant Adjutant-General.

P. S.—The command will probably move from Harrison tomorrow morning. It is reported that Wheeler is at Georgetown preparing for an attack on Harrison.

Report of Colonel Eli Long, Fourth Ohio Cavalry, commanding Second Cavalry Brigade.

HDQRS. SECOND BRIGADE, SECOND DIVISION CAVALRY,
CALHOUN, TENN., *December 28, 1863.*

GENERAL: I have the honor to forward, for the information of the Major-General commanding the department, report of attack made this a. m. upon this place by the rebel General Wheeler. The attack was made at about 10 o'clock by a force of from 1200 to 1500 cavalry and mounted infantry, led by General Wheeler in person. Brigadier-General Kelly, with his brigade, formed part of this force. Their object was evidently the capture of the supply train which arrived here last evening under charge of forces commanded by Colonel Laiboldt.

Colonel L[aibolt] encamped on the Charleston side of the river, and his skirmishers were at work with the enemy before I was apprised of their approach. I immediately mounted the small command which remained in camp not on duty (about 150 men), moved across the bridge, and found the infantry pretty sharply engaged, the enemy occupying position in the woods. The latter shortly afterward gave way, and I then started rapidly after them. Discovering a small portion of their force now cut off on the right, I ordered a saber charge, and followed a retreating column of several hundred which had taken out the Chatata road, running up the Hiawassee.

Our rapid pursuit and vigorous use of the saber completely demoralized this force, which was thrown into great confusion, and scattered in every direction, their men throwing away large numbers of arms, accouterments, etc. Several of the enemy (number not known) were killed and wounded, and we captured 121 prisoners, including five commissioned officers. Drove the remainder till I had arrived at a creek, which was scarcely fordable, and deemed it prudent to follow no farther. The main rebel column had fled out the Dalton road. I sent a small force out that road, who followed some five miles, and the enemy is still retreating toward Cleveland. My own loss is one man seriously wounded.

Since returning to my headquarters, I have received a dispatch from the officer commanding couriers at Cleveland. He was attacked early this morning by a force of about 100 men, and drove them off.

Very respectfully, your obedient servant.

ELI LONG,
Colonel, Commanding Second Cavalry Brigade.

BRIG. GEN. W. D. WHIPPLE,
Chief of Staff, Army of the Cumberland.

————

Report of Colonel Eli Long, Fourth Ohio Cavalry, commanding Second Brigade, Second Cavalry Division, of raid on the East Tennessee and Georgia Railroad, and including operations November 17th, 1863—*January* 3, 1864.

HDQRS. SECOND BRIGADE, SECOND CAVALRY DIVISION,
CALHOUN, TENN., *January* [19], 1864.

GENERAL: I have the honor to submit detailed account, as follows, of the operations of my brigade since marching from Woodville, Ala., pursuant to orders received on the night of November 17, 1863:

Lieutenant-Colonel Kitchell, Ninety-eigthth Illinois Mounted Infantry, and Major Gray, Fourth Michigan Cavalry, having reported to me for orders, with detachments of their regiments, I marched on the morning of the 18th, with a command about 1000 strong. Reaching Bridgeport on the evening of the 19th, I crossed the river next morning near Kelley's Ford.

On the 22d, Major Dobb joined me with a battalion of the Fourth Ohio Volunteer Cavalry, and Lieutenant-Colonel Jordan reported with a part of the Seventeenth Indiana Mounted Infantry, and additional detachments of the Ninety-eighth Illinois Mounted Infantry, and Fourth Michigan Cavalry, increasing my command to 1500 men. Marched that evening to Brown's Ferry and crossed the Tennessee river to north side, opposite Chattanooga.

On the 24th, receiving orders from Major-General Thomas to march to Cleveland, Tenn., and destroy as far as possible the enemy's lines of communication in that direction, I crossed by pontoons above Chattanooga, and struck the Chattanooga and Cleveland dirt road, running along the railroad. A few miles east of Chattanooga I cut the telegraph wire, and at Tyner's Station burned two rebel caissons. At other points between this and Cleveland the telegraph was severed, and the railroad was destroyed in frequent places by burning and tearing up the track.

On the night of the 24th, I bivouacked thirteen miles from Chattanooga and sent a party forward to Ooletwah, who found and destroyed some 4000 pounds of flour. On the following day I burned two freight cars, together with 100 cords of tan bark, belonging to the Confederate States of America. Nearing Cleveland, rebel pickets were encountered and driven in. The advance regiment (First Ohio) then charged into the town and drove out Colonel Woodward, with the Second Kentucky (rebel) Cavalry Regiment.

Next morning I sent a detachment, under Colonel Seidel, Third Ohio Volunteer Cavalry, on the East Tennessee and Georgia Railroad, with directions to go, if possible, to Hiawassee river, and ascertain the enemy's strength at Charleston; also to tear up the railroad. Major Patten, with First Ohio Cavalry, was sent down the Dalton road and Major Dobb, with Fourth Ohio, back on the road we came, each party being directed to damage the railroad. Colonel Seidel went as far as Charleston and found Kelly's brigade stationed at Calhoun with artillery, and drove the cavalry across the river, losing one man wounded. Major Patten destroyed ten miles of the Dalton track, and considerable damage was done on the other road. In Cleveland I found a considerable lot of rockets and shells, large quantities of corn, and several bales of new grain sacks, all belonging to the rebel government. Destroyed all that was not appropriated to use of my own command. Burned several railroad cars found here; also the large copper rolling mill—the only one of the kind in the Confederacy.

Early on the morning of the 27th, I was attacked by General Kelly with a brigade of cavalry and a section of two pieces of artillery. Started my command out the Harrison road, sending forward the prisoners under charge of the Fourth Michigan Cavalry. Retired slowly, the enemy pressing us closely and shelling vigorously. A strong line of skirmishers was kept up till we had passed Candy's creek, keeping in rear of my column and holding him in check, when the enemy retired. My loss during the action was two killed, fourteen wounded, and thirteen missing. Most of the latter have since joined. The enemy's loss was not fully known, but he suffered in killed and wounded more severely than we. I moved on, via. Harrison, to Chattanooga, and reported in person at the headquarters of the Major-General commanding.

During this trip I captured 233 prisoners, including a number of officers; also eighty-five wagons and eleven ambulances, which, together with their contents, were burned. Among this number of wagons was the train of General Wright's brigade.

On the 29th November, I again marched for Cleveland, pursuant to orders received at Chattanooga, and reported to Major-General Sherman. From there took road to Benton, sending my ammunition wagons with the infantry column on Charleston road, striking the Federal road. I came upon a drove of about 300 hogs belonging to the Confederate government. Moved on to B[enton] with the main column, sending the Fourth Michigan on reconnaissance to mouth of Ocoee river, and the Fourth Ohio down the Federal road. The latter party captured another drove of about 500 hogs.

December 1st—I marched to Columbus, on Hiawassee river; then, returning to Benton, detached the Fourth Michigan and Fourth Ohio to go back to Cleveland, with captured hogs and prisoners taken on the 29th and 30th. One regiment was sent to secure the boats at mouth of Ocoee and float them down to Charleston, and, with the remainder of the command, I proceeded to Charleston. Orders from General Sherman directed me to move on immediately to Athens, and I reached there some two hours after midnight. From Athens I sent back 150 dismounted men, under charge of Captain Wade, Ninety-eighth Illinois Mounted Infantry, to garrison the town of Calhoun, and hold the bridge at that place; also twenty-five men, to be joined by twenty-five others from the two regiments then at Cleveland, to take the captured hogs to Chattanooga. Detachments of the Third U. S. Cavalry and Fifth Ohio Cavalry reported to me for orders, and I marched for Loudon in advance of General Sherman's forces. Near Loudon my advance regiment (Third Ohio) was met by a force of rebel cavalry, routed them and took about thirty prisoners, losing one killed and two wounded. General Vaughn, with a force of infantry and some artillery, occupied the fortifications about the town, and opened upon my column with shell. Not being able to dislodge the enemy any other way, I determined to charge the works. I dismounted my command, and moved forward in line, but on approaching his position, I found him stronger than anticipated, the confronting force being fully equal, if not superior, to my own in numbers, besides the advantage of position being greatly in their favor. I then fell back, and, after reporting to General Sherman, bivouacked about a mile from Loudon. During the night Vaughn destroyed his stores, took up his pontoons, and, after running into the river four locomotives and forty-four cars, evacuated the place.

On the 3d December, being ordered to move forward to Knoxville and open communication with General Burnside that night if possible, I crossed the Tennessee river and marched via. Maryville. Traveling from M[aryville] I could get no information as to the position of the forces or condition of affairs at Knoxville. All reports that could be obtained indicated that the town was completely surrounded by Longstreet, but near 2 a. m. I struck Colonel Wolford's cavalry pickets some two miles from K[noxville] and camped within his lines. Reported in person to General Burnside the following day.

On the night of the 6th, pursuant to orders from General Sherman, I marched to Maryville, and was here joined by the two regiments which had been sent back to Cleveland. From this point I was directed to start in pursuit of a train of some 300 wagons which had been cut off at Loudon when we marched on that place, and was now making its way into North Carolina. Crossed Little Tennessee river at Motley's ford, and after crossing Tellico and Unaka mountains and Long ridge, following up the Hiawassee, I arrived at Murphy, N. C., on the 9th of December. Met no force of the enemy except a few of Morgan's men and a company of home guards stationed at Murphy. My advance guard had a slight skirmish with these and drove them from the place. Marched six miles from Murphy and camped.

Up to this time, since leaving Chattanooga, I had taken ninety-five prisoners, including seven officers; also a few horses and mules. Found the road from Maryville to Murphy, for the most part, good. After leaving Tellico Plains the route lies through a mountainous country, but the road over the mountains is well engineered and practicable for wagons. The country is very poor, the fields poorly cultivated, and grain and forage more scarce than any locality previously visited during my entire trip. It is well watered, however, by frequent creeks and mountain streams. Frequent incursions have been made in there by rebel cavalry, and but few cattle of any kind, horses or mules, were found.

From the best information I could obtain along the route, it appeared that the rebel train was some five or six days march ahead of me, and traveling with apprehensions of pursuit, so that it was evident it would be impossible to catch it. My horses were all jaded with hard marching, and many of them already given out, leaving a number of the men dismounted, and from the great scarcity of horses in the country I could not supply their place. Therefore, after sending a force ten miles farther into the country to get all possible information, I determined to halt. The reports of the expedition confirmed previous intelligence. After remaining in camp one day to rest my horses, I started back on the 11th of December, and at Tellico Plains found General M. L. Smith encamped with his division of infantry and awaiting my return.

Through him received instructions from General Sherman to rest my horses as long as necessary, and then proceed to Chattanooga via. Charleston. Remained in camp until the morning of the 14th, Major Smith's Battalion, Fifth Ohio Volunteer Cavalry, being meanwhile relieved and ordered to Athens.

Arriving at Calhoun on the 15th, had orders requiring me to remain at that place, guarding the railroad and river as a line looking toward

Georgia. The detachment of Third U. S. Cavalry was relieved from duty with my brigade, and the Fifth Ohio Volunteer Cavalry, Colonel Heath, temporarily attached. I at once prepared to establish a line of couriers to Loudon and Kingston, communicating with General Elliott, chief of cavalry, and the Fifth Ohio Volunteer Cavalry was assigned to the duty. With the Fourth Michigan, I opened a line of communication to Chattanooga. The Third Ohio Volunteer Cavalry was sent to Columbus, on the Hiawassee, to guard the river there and the adjacent fords.

On the 22d, the courier post at Cleveland was attacked by sixty rebel calvary and driven out, with a loss of a few horses and arms, and one man wounded. The rebels retired shortly afterward, leaving two wounded, and the couriers resumed their post.

On the morning of the 28th, a wagon train which had arrived at Charleston the evening before under escort of convalescents, etc., of General Sheridan's command, and commanded by Colonel Laiboldt, was attacked by General Wheeler with about 1500 rebel cavalry. As soon as I was made aware of the attack, I mounted the small portion of my command not on duty (less than 150 men), and as soon as the train had crossed the bridge, moved over the river. Colonel Laiboldt was now sharply engaged, and soon had the enemy's lines wavering. I then drew sabers and charged, driving before me a force of some 400 or 500; pursued them to Chatata creek, capturing 121 prisoners, including five officers, and many stand of arms. The enemy lost several killed and quite a number wounded, among the latter two colonels. The main rebel column retreated out the Dalton road. A detachment of my command followed them some five miles, and left them in full retreat.

December 30th, the Fifth Ohio, by orders, was relieved from duty with me, and their removal caused the removal of the courier line to Kingston, as my command was too small to renew it.

On the 3d instant, Captain Beebe reported to me with a section of his battery, Tenth Wisconsin, and remains here on duty. On the 6th, the Fourth Michigan returned to this camp, the courier line from Cleveland to Chattanooga having been withdrawn, and I then established a line from Calhoun to the Tennessee river at Cotton Port, connecting with line at Washington.

A great many of my horses were unshod when we started from Alabama, as some of the regiments had not been able to get any horseshoes since Wheeler's raid into Middle Tennessee, and there were no extra shoes in the command, nor could any be obtained at Bridgeport or Chattanooga, or anywhere on the whole march. More than one-half of the horses of my command were old, and not yet recovered from the hard marching after Wheeler. During the three days I was encamped in the vicinity of Kelley's Ford, it was with the utmost difficulty that I could get about half rations of short forage for my animals, and during the two days that I lay at Chattanooga I could not draw a grain. On coming to Chattanooga the second time, I was there thirty-six hours and got one feed of corn. On the march to North Carolina, after marching thirty miles, I had to encamp in the mountains without any forage whatever. Between the time we left Alabama, November 18th, and the time we arrived here, December 15th, we traveled (i. e., the main column) 463 miles, and the day we arrived in Knoxville we had marched on that and the two previous days 115 miles. I have been thus explicit in order to explain to the commanding General the reason why my command decreased with such extraordinary rapidity from dismounted men.

I would respectfully present to the favorable notice of the Major-General commanding, for good conduct under all circumstances and unremitting attention to their duties, all of my staff, viz: Captain William E. Crane, Fourth Ohio Volunteer Cavalry, acting assistant adjutant-general; Lieutenant William H. Scott, First Ohio Volunteer Cavalry, acting ordnance officer and inspector; Lieutenant C. J. Norton, Second Kentucky Cavalry, aide; Lieutenant H. H. Siverd, First Ohio Volunteer Cavalry, acting provost-marshal; Lieutenant J. B. Hayden, Fourth Ohio Volunteer Cavalry, acting quartermaster and commissary of subsistence, and Assistant Surgeon John Cannan, First Ohio Volunteer Cavalry, acting brigade surgeon; also Lieutenant-Colonel Seidel, Third Ohio Volunteer Cavalry, whose regiment was in advance approaching Loudon, and Captain F. P. Gates, Third Ohio Volunteer Cavalary, whose company had the advance of the regiment on approaching Loudon, for the gallant manner in which they drove the rebels on that occasion; also Major T. J. Patten, First Ohio Volunteer Cavalry, whose regiment, being in advance, was led by himself in person in fine style in the fight with Wheeler at this point, and also for good conduct on that occasion, Captains Woodlief and Erwin and Lieutenants Hall, Roush, Riggs, and Brison, of that regiment.

The men all did as well as they could.

Very respectfully, your obedient servant,

ELI LONG,
Colonel, Comdg. Second Brigade, Second Cavalry Division.

BRIG. GEN. WILLIAM D. WHIPPLE,
Assistant Adjutant-General.

Reports of Colonel Eli Long, Fourth Ohio Cavalry, commanding Second Brigade, Second Cavalry Division.

NEAR BURNT MILL, ON CLEVELAND AND SPRING PLACE ROAD,
February 22, 1864—2 :20 p. m.

GENERAL: Please find below copy of dispatch received by me yesterday (21st) evening at 4 p. m.:

CHATTANOOGA, *February 21, 1864.*

"COLONEL ELI LONG:

"Move out upon Spring Place road with 600 men and establish communication with Cruft at Red Clay. Push on as far as possible in direction of Dalton, keeping up communication with Cruft to observe movements of enemy, and prevent or give timely warning of any attack of enemy to turn Cruft's left flank. Should the enemy retire, send word to Cruft that he may advance from Red Clay.

"W. D. WHIPPLE,
"Assistant Adjutant-General."

———

I left Calhoun at 6 a. m. this morning with 600 cavalrymen, with ten wagons with forage, and four ambulances. I hardly think they could have known the location of the roads at department headquarters, for this is the nearest point on this (Cleveland and Spring Place) road to Red Clay, and it (Red Clay) is ten or twelve miles from here. I shall encamp tonight at some mills nearly two miles from here on the Connesauga, where I shall remain until I hear something from you. If not inconsistent, please explain to me as clearly as you can what is expected of my command.

ELI LONG,

BRIGADIER-GENERAL CRUFT,
Comdg. First Division, Fourth Army Corps, Red Clay.

P. S.—I have met or heard of nothing as yet.

———

AT CROSS-ROADS OF BENTON AND DALTON ROAD AND VARNELL'S
STATION AND KING'S LOWER BRIDGE ROAD, SIX MILES
SOUTHEAST OF VARNELL'S STATION AND NINE AND ONE-
HALF MILES FROM DALTON, *February 23, 1864—1 :25 p. m.*

SIR: At 11 :30 this a. m. I attacked and drove out of their camp at least a regiment of rebel infantry, three and one-half miles this side of Dalton. They had winter quarters (log-huts), and as they were completely surprised they had no time to move any plunder out of their huts, and from their appearance and the small amount of plunder in them I believe they were preparing to leave. The cars were whistling furiously while the skirmish was going on. I have not force enough to cope single-handed with all of their cavalry, but I think you may advance with safety if you can still keep your supports, Palmer's troops, etc., within supporting distance. I believe they are leaving the place, and they should not be allowed to do [so] undisturbed. I shall be compelled to go somewhere to get some forage. Please let me hear from you as fully, in detail, as you can. I shall either wait here or move up on the road to Varnell's Station until I hear from you.

Very respectfully, your obedient servant,

ELI LONG,

MAJOR W. H. SINCLAIR,
    Assistant Adjutant-General.

I have twelve prisoners. Can't you send me the Fourth Michigan Cavalry and Second Kentucky and Warner's Company, when I may be able to do something?   ELI LONG.

HDQRS. SECOND BRIGADE, SECOND CAVALRY DIVISION,
VARNELL'S STATION, *February* 24, 1864—8 a. m.

SIR: I have just arrived here. Will push down the dirt road that runs alongside of the railroad as far toward Dalton as practicable. I believe there are some rebel cavalry on the main Cleveland and Dalton road. I will be compelled to go back to the Connesauga or somewhere else tomorrow unless I have better luck in foraging today than I did yesterday. Please to forward a copy of this to General Palmer. A brigade of infantry was encamped where we had the skirmish yesterday. I have met nothing this morning. Let me know your location by the bearer.

Very respectfully, your obedient servant,

ELI LONG,
Colonel Commanding Brigade.

MAJOR W. H. SINCLAIR,
    Assistant Adjutant-General.

P. S.—I have not received the dispatch sent to me at 2 p. m. yesterday, nor heard of the bearer.   E. L.

HDQRS. SECOND BRIGADE, SECOND CAVALRY DIVISION,
ON THE ROAD FROM DALTON TO VARNELL'S STATION, JUST
EAST OF TUNNEL MOUNTAIN, *February* 24, 1864—2 p. m.

SIR: I have just driven in with one squadron the infantry pickets on the dirt and railroads three miles from Dalton, and am now in line with pickets skirmishing in front. Their cavalry ran into their infantry supports, which they seem to have on all of the roads. I am now five miles from Dalton, and do not think it prudent to go any farther until I hear further from you and the result of your reconnaissance.

Very respectfully, your obedient servant,

ELI LONG,
Colonel, Commanding Second Brig., Second Cav. Div.

MAJOR W. H. SINCLAIR,
Assistant Adjutant-General.

P. S.—I send with the bearer one company to remain on picket at Varnell's Station to watch the Cleveland and Dalton road that goes down on the other side of the railroad. E. L.

———

HDQRS. SECOND BRIGADE, SECOND CAVALRY DIVISION,

HENDERSON'S HOUSE, FIVE MILES FROM DALTON, ON RAILROAD,
February 24, 1864—6:30 p. m.

SIR: I have just returned from another reconnaissance toward Dalton. Ran into a large infantry cantonment three miles or less from Dalton, and ran out again. I had several men wounded. Who is intended to command, Colonel Grose or myself? Please give some directions about it. I don't think they have all left Dalton as much as I did.

Very respectfully, your obedient servant,

ELI LONG,
Colonel, Comdg. Second Brigade, Second Division.

MAJOR W. H. SINCLAIR,
Assistant Adjutant-General.

———

FEBRUARY 25, 1864—12:15 p. m.

I have my command near a gap road which runs through the ridge on your left, with pickets down the railroad some quarter of a mile. Nothing can come through the gap without my knowing, and I think this is the only road between here and Dalton through which a force can get on your flank or rear, and as my ammunition is nearly exhausted, I will remain here until further orders.

Respectfully, ELI LONG,
Colonel, Commanding Cavalry.

GENERAL CRUFT.

———

FEBRUARY 25, 1864—4:15 o'clock.

GENERAL: The fire has just driven me out of the woods on the ridge that I was occupying. I still have a picket on the road in the gap, however. A few minutes since about forty infantry skirmishers moved up on our right, advancing toward your lines. The rebel lines, I think, extend farther east than yours. At any rate, they came to the foot of the ridge I have been occupying, and I think there may be some danger of their lapping you on your left unless your lines extend completely across the valley in which your left rested this morning. Please let me know for my guidance where your left now is. Cannot your quartermaster send me some forage? Your commissary would not deliver me any rations on Captain Kniffin's order, which please find enclosed with note of commissary.

Respectfully,   ELI LONG,
Colonel, Comdg. Second Brig., Second Cav. Div.
BRIGADIER-GENERAL CRUFT,
   Commanding Division.

P. S.—The rebel cavalry pickets are in sight in our front. Please indorse Captain Kniffin's order, so that I can get the rations.   E. L.

————

HDQRS. SECOND BRIGADE, SECOND DIVISION CAVALRY,
NEAR LEE'S HOUSE, GA., *February 27*, 1864.

GENERAL: I have the honor to submit the following report:

In compliance with orders received February 21, 1864, from headquarters Department of the Cumberland, I left Calhoun, Tenn., Monday, February 22d, 1864, in command of 600 men (350 mounted infantry and 250 cavalry), and marched out on the Spring Place road. Monday evening I encamped near the house of Mr. Waterhouse, on Connesauga River, about thirty miles south of Calhoun. I met no enemy during the day.

I left my encampment near Waterhouse's Tuesday morning, February 23, at 7 a. m. (having communicated with General Cruft at Red Clay the night before), and marched toward Dalton. My advance guard drove in the enemy's vedettes when within four miles of Dalton. I immediately pushed on my column rapidly and attacked a regiment of rebel infantry, which was encamped within three miles of Dalton, driving them from their camp and capturing twelve prisoners belonging to a Mississippi regiment. The enemy then formed, and I withdrew my command to Russell's Mill, a distance of four miles east of Varnell's Station, and encamped for the night. There I received a communication from Major-General Palmer requesting me to advance in the morning, February 24th, in the direction of Dalton via Varnell's Station.

I left my encampment at Russell's Mill at 6 a. m., February 24th, and reached Varnell's about 7, where I halted until about 10 a. m., in the meantime sending small forces on the different roads leading from Varnell's. They met no enemy, and I pushed on toward Dalton, marching on a road running parallel to the Cleveland and Dalton railroad. When within five miles of Dalton I met with the enemy's pickets. My advance squadron drove them to within three miles of Dalton. I then fell back two miles, and drew my command up in line on a ridge one mile west of the railroad awaiting movements of the enemy. I remained in my position, when I was joined by Colonel Grose, commanding a brigade of the First Division, Fourth Army Corps. Soon after the arrival of Colonel Grose, I dismounted my command and advanced in line against the enemy, driving their skirmishers about a mile in the direction of their camp, but there I was compelled to fall back, being attacked by a brigade of rebel infantry, who were firing at my men from behind log-huts. I fell back to the line of Colonel Grose, and soon afterward (as it was nearly dark) retired about two miles to the rear, where I encamped for the night.

The next morning, February 25th, I took a position on the left of our infantry lines and advanced as they did. I moved up about half a mile, when my men became engaged with the enemy. I was then joined by 100 men of the Fourth Michigan Cavalry, who had been ordered to report to me by Brigadier-General Cruft. I pressed on against the enemy until I had gotten a short distance in advance of the left of our infantry lines. I then halted, and remained in my position during the remainder of the day. At dark I retired about a mile to the rear where I remained until 11 o'clock p. m., when I moved my command back on the Dalton and Varnell's Station road, about three miles from the place where we fought during the day.

On the morning of the 26th, I moved to Lee's house, where our infantry was encamped, and remained there until about 1 p. m., at which time our pickets were fired upon by the enemy's cavalry, when I marched out and drove the rebels off. I followed them about two and one-half miles in the direction of Tunnel Hill, when I returned to my camp of the morning.

My horses had had very little forage, not being able to draw any and there being very little in the country. I could not have pursued the rebel cavalry vigorously if the country had admitted of it, which it did not.

During the night our infantry fell back to a place near Catoosa Platform, and I am now near my camp of yesterday.

The following is the list* of casualties in my command since February 22d.

I had no means of ascertaining the injury done the enemy, but it was reported that eight bodies were left on the field. I took twenty-three prisoners.

Very respectfully, your obedient servant,

ELI LONG,
Colonel, Comdg. Second Brig., Second Div., Cav.
BRIGADIER-GENERAL WHIPPLE,
Assistant Adjutant-General.

---

* Nominal list (omitted) shows 1 officer and 1 man killed, 19 men wounded, and 2 men missing.

HDQRS. SECOND BRIGADE, SECOND DIVISION CAVALRY,
RED HILL VALLEY,
TWELVE MILES FROM CLEVELAND, TENN, Feb. 27, 1864.

SIR: After I had left the vicinity of General Cruft's division and come about twenty miles therefrom, he being at Catoosa Platform, a sergeant of the Fourth Michigan Cavalry brought me word that General Cruft was being attacked by rebel cavalry, but as General Cruft expressed no desire for me to return I did not go back, it being nearly night when I received the word by the sergeant, and my horses had no forage today.

Very respectfully, your obedient servant,

ELI LONG,
Colonel, Comdg. Second Brig., Second Div., Cav.

BRIGADIER-GENERAL WM. D. WHIPPLE,
Chief of Staff, Army of the Cumberland, Cleveland Tenn.

CHAPTER XV.

VETERANS IN '64

SPECIAL FIELD ORDERS No. 93.
HDQRS. DEPT. OF THE CUMBERLAND,
CHATTANOOGA, *April 2, 1864.*

*   *   *   *   *   *   *

Second Division, Brigadier General K. Garrard, commanding:

First Brigade: Fourth U. S. Cavalry, Seventh Pennsylvania Cavalry, Fourth Michigan Cavalry.

Second Brigade: First Ohio Cavalry, Third Ohio Cavalry, Fourth Ohio Cavalry.

Third Brigade: Seventeenth Indiana Mounted Infantry, Seventy-second Indiana Mounted Infantry, Ninety-eighth Illinois Mounted Infantry, One Hundred and Twenty-third Illinois Mounted Infantry.

Chicago Board of Trade Battery.

The required reports and returns will be made to include March 31, 1864, in accordance with former organizations.

All reports and returns will be forwarded to the chief of cavalry.

*   *   *   *   *   *   *

By command of Major-General Thomas:

WM. McMICHAEL,
Major and Assistant Adjutant-General.

April 15th—We broke camp, marched to Chattanooga, turned over our unserviceable horses, and the dismounted men took the cars for Nashville, arriving on the 16th, and the next day rejoined the regiment at Columbia, Tennessee. The first detachment of veteran volunteers and recruits had returned after their thirty day's furlough and went into camp one and a half miles west of Columbia.

April 2d—The second detachment of veterans returning from thirty days furlough arrived at Nashville and went into camp, where they remained until the 13th, having dismounted drill daily.

April 13th—Reveille at 4 a. m., turned over surplus baggage and took up the line of march southward on foot; camped within three miles of Franklin, having marched sixteen or seventeen miles, many of the men suffering with blistered feet.

April 14th—On the march early. Camped near Spring Hill.

April 15th—Passed through Spring Hill, and went into camp on the north side of Duck river, near Columbia. Colonel Seidel was made commander of the post at Columbia; Captain Colver, provost marshal; Companies G and H detailed as provost guards. The provost office was located in the Masonic building and the guards quartered in the county jail. The post commander and provost marshal were kept busy looking after citizens and soldiers, speculators and people wishing to trade, making them take the oath and give bond.

April 25th—A Confederate recruiting officer was captured.

April 27th—The mounted men who marched through from Ringold arrived today, and the regiment is all together again. The regiment is now the Third Ohio Veteran Volunteer Cavalry, and with the recruits we have received its ranks are again full and it is rapidly getting into shape for the campaign of 1864. Drilling, dress parades, inspections, are the order of the day, and as soon as we get our horses, we will be off for the front again.

April 30th—Moved camp out two miles on the Shelbyville pike.

May 1st—General muster and inspection in the forenoon.

May 2d—A detachment went to Nashville after horses, returning on the 11th. In the evening of the tenth two of our men were killed near Spring Hill by bushwhackers.

May 16th—The paymaster came to camp and left a few souvenirs.

May 21st—The brigade marched out five miles to the General Pillow plantation, where we were reviewed by Colonel Long, a tedious day, five hours in the hot sun.

May 22d—Reveille at 3 a. m., broke camp and took up the line of march southward at 6:30; marched twenty-three miles and camped at 3 p. m., eight miles north of Pulaski.

May 23d—Started at 5 a. m., passed through Pulaski; camped at Elkton at 3 p. m.; marched twenty-one miles.

May 24th—Reveille at 2 o'clock, but a very heavy rainstorm kept us from starting until 5 o'clock; forded Elk river; crossed the state line, and camped at Athens, Alabama, at 4 p. m. Marched nineteen miles. Remained at Athens until the 26th. Reveille sounded at 2 o'clock; on the march at 5. Crossed the Tennessee river on a pontoon bridge, and went into camp at Decatur, at 2 p. m. General F. P. Blair's Corps is at Decatur on its way to join Sherman's Army. We had not been in camp over an hour when boots and saddles sounded and we started out on the Courtland road after the Rebel General Roddy's command. We chased him for eight miles, capturing five wagons, one flag and fifteen prisoners. Returning to Decatur, we got in camp about 8 o'clock.

May 27th—We left Decatur at 11 a. m. A brigade of infantry in advance found Roddy about three miles out. After some skirmishing by the infantry, we took the advance, driving them to Courtland, where we arrived about 10 o'clock p. m.

May 28th—Started out at 7 o'clock on the Moulton road leaving the infantry at Courtland. We went by the way of Mountain Home. Passed through Moulton at 2 o'clock p. m.; went into camp two miles east of the town on the Somerville road in a piece of woods on the south of the road. There was considerable firing on the picket line at intervals during the night.

THE FIGHT AT MOULTON, ALABAMA.

Sunday morning, May 29th—After driving General Roddy's forces from Decatur to Courtland on the 27th, he left our front, but no doubt he was watching our movements and noting our strength. And as the command was divided, part taking the road past Swope's Mill on the 28th, he may have been deceived as to our numbers. It is certain, however, that he believed his forces strong enough to clean us up. Coming into Moulton Saturday night and ascertaining where we were encamped, he got his brigade into position, ready to surprise and stampede us at daybreak. Our camp was in a valley. The land was very uneven. In fact, a succession of hills and valleys, covered in many places with timber and underbrush interspersed with cleared fields. Company I of the Third was on picket on the Moulton road, and during the night they erected a barricade of logs and rails across the road. The orders the night before were not to unsaddle, but a shallow creek that ran through the camp separated Company C from the rest of the regiment, and they not getting the order, unsaddled. As soon as it was light Roddy moved forward in line of battle with the Moulton road as his center. Driving in our outposts, he moved forward toward the position occupied by Company I. Here his advance met with a check, our men defending their works so stubbornly that Roddy was forced to order up a piece of artillery to shell them out. Meanwhile our brigade, aroused by the rapid firing on the Moulton road, was busy getting in readiness for the fray. But when the booming of the cannon awoke the echoes amongst the hills, "there was mounting in hot haste," for we knew then that the Johnnies meant business. Simultaneously with the report of that first cannon shot the rebel line on the right of the road came into plain view from our camp as it advanced over the ridge and came charging down the slope half a mile away. Bugle calls followed each other in rapid succession, the regiments were formed and marched into position. In a very few brief moments our lines were formed just back of our camp to receive the oncoming attack. Their artillery had the range of our position and were sending shot and shell into our ranks. Our artillery (not the Chicago Board of Trade Battery) were a little slow in getting into position, but when they did commence they rendered valiant service in helping to check the rebel advance. Our regiment was ordered on the right flank, and just as we were wheeling from line into column a shell from one of the rebel guns killed two horses, passing through the first one and taking a leg off the second, but fortunately the shell did not explode. The advance of the rebel right was checked in our camp, and the Third moving to the right came into line, and advancing over the hills, found the enemy in position in a piece of timber. After we had fired a few volleys from our carbines they commenced to fall back, and in a short time were in full retreat toward Moulton. We followed them for a short distance, but as the country was not a good one to charge over with a large body of cavalry, and Colonel Long was under orders to join Blair's Corps, the bugles sounded the recall, and we returned to our camps and got breakfast. We do not know the exact loss of the enemy, as considerable of the fighting was in places covered with a thick growth of bushes, but their loss was considerable. There were some twenty-five killed in our camps and we took sixteen prisoners, amongst them three officers, one a lieutenant and General Roddy's adjutant. He told us that Roddy was deceived by his scouts, who told him we were green troops going to the front. And he thought in that case he could surprise us in camp, and stampede and capture the whole outfit; but he had hardly got hooked up before he found out his mistake. "It was the same old regiment, only it had got new clothes." Our loss in the brigade was three killed and fourteen wounded. We lost a number of horses, but these were more than made good by captures. Captain Howland relates the following incident: The evening before his darkey cook had captured a chicken, and was up early and had it in the kettle cooking when the rebels charged on us. After the fight when we returned to our camp he found a rebel lying dead by his camp fire with a piece of his chicken in his hand and a rifle ball in his brain. But it didn't get on the Captain's nerves. He had chicken for breakfast, and enjoyed it. After breakfast we started on the march. Passing through Somerville late in the afternoon, we camped fifteen miles out on the Warrenton road at midnight, having marched forty miles and fought a battle.

May 30th—Marched only six miles. We halted for our wagon train and the infantry to come up, when we drew rations, fed our horses, and went into camp at the foot of Sand Mountain, about twelve miles from Warrenton.

May 31st—Reveille at 3:30. Started at daylight; had a rough, hard climb up Sand Mountain. Passed through Warrenton, went into camp on Drum creek, about ten miles east of Warrenton. A detachment went to Guntersville, on the Tennessee river, with our wounded and did not get to camp until midnight.

June 1st—Reveille at 2 a. m., but did not leave camp until noon. Marched all night, halting only to feed our horses and going into camp on a small stream near Van Buren, in the valley between Sand and Lookout Mountains at 10 a. m. of June 2d; rained most of the afternoon and night.

June 3d—Reveille at 3 a. m.; on the march at daylight; passed through Van Buren, crossed the Lookout range, descending at Blue pond; crossed Chattanooga creek, passed through Cedar Bluffs and camped about five miles out; weather rainy.

June 4th—On the march at 7 a. m. Passed through Coosaville, marching over a very hilly but fertile country. Crossed the Oostenaula River and arrived at Rome, Georgia, about 2 o'clock p. m. Rome was a very pretty town, lying between the Oostenaula and Etowah rivers, where they unite and form the Coosa. We went into camp two and a half miles out on the Kingston road, having marched twenty-seven miles in a steady rain. We remained in camp one day, a day of scorching sun and frequent showers; received a little mail, the first we have had since leaving Columbia.

June 6th—On the march at 6 a. m., crossed Conasana creek and camped on a rocky hill near Two Run creek, east of Kingston.

June 7th—Reveille at 2 a. m., on the march at daylight; crossed the Etowah river on a long covered bridge, four miles south of Kingston; camped at the railroad bridge across Etowah river, near Cartersville; the wagon train came up. It was the first time we have seen them for a week.

June 8th—Company A drew Spencer carbines; we left camp at 11 a. m., passing Allatoona furnace; we camped at 3 p. m., between Allatoona and Ackworth. General Sherman's headquarters are at Ackworth; the enemy is in a very strong position in front of Kenesaw mountain. General K. Garrard is in command of the division. We are on the left flank of the army.

June 9th—Did not move today; our mail is coming regularly; company inspection.

June 10th—We drew two days rations and left camp at 11 a. m.; marched about six or eight miles in a southerly direction. General Sherman moved his headquarters to Big Shanty.

June 11th—Moved our lines about three miles to the left. In the afternoon our regiment went out to reconnoiter and came on to the rebel pickets, driving them back on-to their lines of breastworks near Noonday creek. After a sharp engagement we fell back, being compelled to leave two of our men on the field. We brought off ten of our wounded, among them Lieutenant Colonel Howland, whose horse was shot dead under him at the time he was wounded. We fell back to our former position, building breastworks in our front. The orders of the day were to fortify every time we make an advance. We are still getting our regular daily and nightly rains.

June 12th—We did not move out of our works today; some cannonading over on the right; still raining.

June 13th—More rain; the roads are in a terrible condition, almost impassable for wagons and artillery.

June 14th—Some firing on the pickets. Saddled up two or three times, but did not move out. A part of the regiment on picket. The Confederate General Polk was killed on Pine mountain by a shell from one of our batteries. During the night a section of the Chicago Board of Trade Battery was brought out on the picket line and at daylight opened on the rebel position, creating some excitement on both sides.

June 15th—At 1 p. m. the division moved out of its position, mounted. Advancing about a mile, when we found the advance lines of the enemy. The Second Brigade dismounted, attacking the enemy and driving them about two miles back to their entrenchments, but were unable to dislodge them. After expending all our ammunition we fell back about two miles and worked most of the night building breastworks a mile in advance of our old position. The Second Brigade lost three killed and thirteen wounded.

June 16th—The division moved about two miles to the right, where we joined on-to McPherson's left; considerable fighting, McPherson's men capturing the Fortieth Alabama Regiment. Here we went to work and built another line of breastworks.

June 17th—Did not move our lines today. Detachments doing picket duty; picket firing and cannonading all the time. Raining nearly all the time. Our battery got into position and opened up on the rebel works at the foot of Kenesaw, the rebels replied from their batteries on Bushy mountain.

June 18th—Constant cannonading and picket firing. Our horses saddled all day. It rained all day and night.

June 19th—Moved back into the timber about 8 a. m., and at 10 o'clock our batteries opened up, but received no reply. Wilder's guns were also brought into action, supported by the Second Brigade, dismounted. But failing to dislodge the enemy, we withdrew, moving to the left and occupying nearly the same position that we did in the fight on the 15th. We got our usual portion of rain.

June 20th—More rain and plenty of it. Heavy cannonading to the front and left of Kenesaw. We moved in support of Wilder's and Minty's brigades, and in support of the battery, dismounted. Advanced about a mile, but fell back to our old position after nightfall, in the mud and rain. Part of the command on picket.

June 21st—Cannonading continued at Kenesaw. Our pickets are close up to those of the enemy. Much picket firing, and the pickets are compelled to keep under cover. No bugle calls are sounded in camp. In front of our picket lines was an old mill, on Noonday creek, occupied by rebel sharpshooters, who were doing all they could to make life disagreeable for us. The place was covered by the rebel pickets, so that it was not an easy matter to burn it, but the officer in charge of that part of the line determined to do it, and while engaging the enemy in his front, sent a detachment around under cover, which succeeded in capturing the sharpshooters and burning the mill.

June 22d—Moved about a mile to the front and built another breastwork. There is considerable firing all along the line. We had a fine day, for a change.

June 23d—Another fine day. The division moved forward at 2:30 p. m. Advanced to Noonday creek, dismounted and crossed, but before our line was formed the rebels charged us. We repulsed them and drove them back; then recrossed the creek and returned to our breastworks after dark. The problem of getting past Kenesaw is a hard one to solve. Johnson from his position on Kenesaw is able to watch every move that Sherman makes, and while acting on the defensive is ready to take advantage of any false move he may make. But Sherman is moving with caution, has his army well in hand, and is constantly pushing and crowding. The lines are so close together that we can plainly hear the whistles of the locomotives beyond the rebel camps, while they can not only hear ours but can see them as they come from Ackworth into Big Shanty.

On June 24th General Sherman issued orders to his army commanders to make preparations for a general assault on the enemy's works on the 27th. The orders to be kept secret even from their staff officers.

All movements of troops to be made during the night time, and while artillery fighting and skirmishing was to be kept up all along the line, each commander was to select a point of attack and make a vigorous attempt to break through the enemy's lines. General McPherson near the southwest end of Kenesaw, General Thomas about a mile farther south, and General Schofield at a point as near Marietta as seemed to offer the best prospect of success. In the evening of the 26th we moved our lines forward about a mile on the left.

June 27th—No bugle calls in camp, but orders to saddle up. Leaving our horses, we advanced about two miles on foot and came into line on the left of the Third Brigade, built breastworks of logs and rails, supporting the artillery, which is hotly engaged shelling the rebel position on Kenesaw. Further to the right we can hear the roar of battle, where McPherson and Thomas are making a desperate effort to break through the lines of the enemy, and while they gained and held some ground, yet nowhere did they break through. When night came on we had lost 2500 men, and had gained no material advantage. The bombardment of Kenesaw continued, and during the nights the sight was extremely grand, the incessant roar of the artillery interspersed with the flashes of the guns and the bursting shells amongst the trees made a sight never to be forgotten. The same night General Sherman resolved on a movement by the right and commenced preparations for it. In the evening we returned to the place where we had left our horses.

June 28th—Cannonading and some musketry firing on our right. In our front the pickets made a truce, agreeing not to fire unless an advance was ordered. Some of the pickets met between the lines, trading coffee and salt for tobacco. A detachment from the regiment went on a reconnaissance to the left and rear. Two of Company A men captured by rebels in our uniform. We brought in six deserters from the rebel army.

July 1st—Cannonading from our side brought no response from the enemy.

July 2d—We moved out at 9 p. m.; marched to the right, and camped at midnight south of Big Shanty. Rumors that the enemy are falling back.

CHAPTER XVI.

IN FRONT OF ATLANTA

July 3d—Great day. At daylight our men got possession of Kenesaw, and our signal flags are waving from its summit. Sherman's move to the right has compelled Johnston to abandon his position at Kenesaw and retreat toward Atlanta.

We moved out at 9 a. m., following the line of railroad through the gap between Bushy and Kenesaw Mountains and on to Marietta. The rebels had torn up about a mile of the railroad track and taken the rails away with them. Most of the people had left Marietta, abandoning their homes. We came up with the rear guard of the enemy a short distance beyond the town. They fell back with little opposition to our advance. We camped at night in a piece of woods about four miles east from Marietta.

July 4th—Reveille at 2 a. m.; moved out at daylight. The Third Ohio in advance of the division, Company C advance guard. About two miles from camp the rebel skirmishers opened up on us from a piece of woods half a mile in our front. General Garrard sent a staff officer with an order for the advance guard to fall back. The battery was brought into position and commenced shelling the woods, while the division formed, dismounted. A strong skirmish line from the Third Ohio was deployed and advanced on the enemy. The ground in our front was an old abandoned plantation, about a mile across. Our artillery continued to shell the woods over our heads until we were nearly across the clearing. When we reached the timber we found we were on the edge of a swamp, and the only place we could cross was on a corduroy bridge on the road. Rallying on the center, we charged across the bridge, driving the enemy from their position and up the hill on the opposite side. When we reached the top of the hill we were ordered to halt, our line being in a sheltered position behind a fence. In our front was an old clearing grown up with thick brush. About noon the enemy had gathered quietly in the brush in our front, and firing one volley, they gave that old rebel yell and came charging on us over that old fence, driving us back half way down the hill; when we made a counter charge, driving them back again. We continued to skirmish with them until about 4 p. m., when we returned to our horses and moved to our camp of the previous night.

July 5th—Reveille at 2 o'clock. Infantry and artillery firing kept up on the right all night. Hardee's Corps in a strongly fortified position at Smyrna camp ground, is covering the crossings of the Chattahoochee. We started out early in the forenoon, marching in a northeasterly direction to strike the river at Roswell. There is a ford and a bridge at that point, and if possible we were to save the bridge. Minty's Brigade is in the advance and early in the day came up with a small froce of the enemy, the advance driving them. Coming within a mile of the river, Minty drew saber and went in on a charge, capturing some prisoners, but was too late to save the bridge, which was in flames when he got there. Roswell was a pretty little place on the west bank of Vickory creek, just above where it empties into the Chattahoochee. We found there a cotton factory in operation, making cloth for the Confederate government. It was under the management of a Frenchman, who claimed to own it, and had hoisted the French flag over the building, believing that it would protect his property. There were several hundred women employes in the factory, most of them from the North. Mr. Frenchman was very beligerent; claimed to be a citizen of France, and under the protection of the French flag, and told of all the dire calamities that would befall the United States if we dared to touch his property or his flag. Our boys knew only one flag and that was "Old Glory," and in the territory that they occupied all other flags must come down. The Frenchman was made a prisoner, his flag was hauled down, and under orders from General Sherman, the factories were burned. The operatives were sent North. We hauled them to Marietta in the army wagon train, and from there they were furnished transportation on the railroad.

July 6th—On picket along the Chattahoochee. General Wheeler's forces are on the opposite side of the river, and there is considerable picket firing on our front, while from the right our ears are greeted with the sound of booming cannon.

July 9th—Orders came for us to force a crossing at the ford. Our battery got into position, and after shelling the woods on the opposite side, we crossed at the ford, meeting with but little opposition. Wheeler had fallen back. We moved out about two miles; found very few of the enemy; posted pickets and remained all night. The next morning we recrossed the Chattahoochee and returned to our camp. A number of Company H men were captured. They got too far from the main body. It is a wild, rough country, and it is not safe to wander off too far from the command.

July 11th—We moved about one mile south from Roswell and camped in a thick wood.

July 13th—The Third Battalion went to Marietta guarding a wagon train; returned on the 15th with the wagons loaded with supplies.

July 14th—The First and Second Battalions went out on a scout, returning the next day. They had a little skirmishing and captured a number of prisoners.

July 16th—We crossed the Chattahoochee and camped about a mile from the river.

July 17th—Part of the regiment went on a scout in the direction of

Stone mountain; found very few of the enemy; had one horse killed and one man wounded. Returning to camp, found McPherson's troops were crossing the river at Roswell. General Johnston was superseded in the command of the Confederate Army by General Hood. The authorities at Richmond are dissatisfied with General Johnston's management of the campaign. He does not fight enough to suit them.

July 18th—The First and Third Brigades went on a raid on the East Georgia Railroad, intending to strike it near Stone Mountain. The Second Brigade remained to do picket duty and guard the division wagon train. Two deserters from the Confederate army came into camp.

July 19th—The Second Brigade started after the division at 10 a m., marched to Stone Mountain and tore up the railroad for a number of miles, after which we fell back about four miles, where we found the rest of the division and the wagon train.

July 20th—Moved up to Decatur. The roads were blocked with infantry and our progress was slow. It is a part of McPherson's Corps. General Hood, thinking that he saw an opportunity to strike Sherman and beat him in detail, he (Sherman) having divided his army, sending the Army of the Tennesse and the Army of Ohio to Decatur, and General Thomas with the Army of the Cumberland having crossed the Chattahoochee at Pace's Ferry, was moving toward Atlanta. They had crossed Peach Tree creek when they were unexpectedly assailed by the entire rebel army. The Army of the Cumberland, however, repelled every assault that was made upon their lines, and Hood and his army were hurled back with fearful loss. The first blow struck by the new commander under circumstances that gave good hope of success had most signally failed.

Reports of Colonel Eli Long, Fourth Ohio Cavalry, commanding Second Brigade, of Operations May 26-July 15.

HDQRS. SECOND BRIGADE, SECOND CAVALRY DIVISION,
NEAR ROSWELL, GA., *July* 12, 1864.

CAPTAIN: Please find annexed a report of the operations of the Second Brigade, Second Cavalry Division, since leaving Decatur, Ala., on the 26th of May and up to the 1st of the present month, which I have the honor to forward for the information of the Brigadier-General commanding corps:

Leaving Decatur, I proceeded on the Courtland road toward Courtland, Ala., and soon found the enemy, a portion of General Roddey's cavalry command. Attacking them at once, they were thrown into a hasty retreat, and we captured twelve prisoners and two stand of colors, besides wagons, horses, mules, arms, etc.; our loss nothing.

Next day Roddey's entire command was met near Courtland, and, after an engagement of half an hour, I drove him through town, taking three prisoners and killing Major Williams. We had one man wounded. On the 28th we had no fighting, but surprised and captured six of Roddey's men.

May 29, near Moulton, Ala., I was attacked at 4 a. m. by General Roddey with cavalry and four pieces of artillery. After a severe engagement, lasting two hours, the enemy was completely repulsed on all sides, and compelled to retreat in great disorder toward Moulton, leaving his dead and some wounded on the field. Roddey's loss was twelve to fifteen killed; the number of his wounded not known. We took sixteen prisoners, including one lieutenant-colonel and two lieutenantts. Our own casualties were three killed and fourteen wounded. Marched that morning at 8 o'clock, passing through Somerville, Ala., and on the 30th of May overtook the Seventeenth Army Corps, Major-General Blair. Remained with this command until the 6th of June, when we arrived at Kingston, Ga. Crossing Raccoon and Sand Mountains was very severe upon our horses, although the roads by this route were generally good and water abundant. Our supply of forage was very limited, and we depended for the most part upon the grazing.

Crossed Lookout Mountain on the 3d June, and marched toward Rome, Ga., surprising and capturing sixteen rebel soldiers and one lieutenant-colonel. June 6th, marched from Rome to Kingston, and on the following day to Etowah bridge, thence toward Marietta. June 11th, while encamped ten miles from Marietta, I sent out the First Ohio Volunteer Cavalry on a reconnaissance toward that town. They met a force of the enemy, and drove them some four miles. The Third Ohio Volunteer Cavalry was sent on another road, and found the enemy a few miles from camp, attacked them, but found they had largely superior numbers, and the regiment was compelled to fall back. Our loss here was twelve wounded and two missing. The enemy had several wounded, and we took one prisoner. Remained in camp at Noonday creek, having frequent skirmishing with the rebel pickets, until the 15th, when I received marching orders. At 2 p. m. I attacked General Wheeler's cavalry command, and fought him for about an hour, but was at length compelled to fall back, Wheeler being well fortified, and intrenched beyond our power to drive him out. In this engagement we lost two killed, sixteen wounded, and two missing. Rebel loss unknown. On the 16th of June I moved toward the front and encamped near Kenesaw Mountain, remaining here until the 19th, when, upon orders received, I moved my command, and drove the enemy to Noonday creek. Here I formed a junction with the Third Brigade. The enemy made a stand on the farther bank of the creek and fought stubbornly for several hours. June 20th, was ordered to reinforce Colonel Minty's brigade, which had encountered the enemy and been driven back to the creek. June 23d, crossed Noonday creek, and was attacked by the enemy some five miles from Marietta. The attack was handsomely repelled, and the enemy driven back, with a loss of one killed and several wounded; our loss, two wounded and two missing. During the remainder of the month my command rested, for the most part, quietly in camp.

Since leaving Decatur the brigade has marched (the main column) 215 miles, much of this distance being mountainous country. Besides horses, mules, wagons, and arms taken, we captured a total of five officers and fifty-four men, and lost, in killed five; wounded, forty-five; missing, 6.

I have the honor to be, very respectfully, your obedient servant,

ELI LONG,
Colonel, Commanding Brigade.

CAPT. J. E. JACOBS,
Assistant Adjutant-General.

HDQRS. SECOND BRIGADE, SECOND CAVALRY DIVISION,
NEAR ROSWELL, GA., *July* 14, 1864.

SIR: I have the honor to forward, for the information of the division commander, the following report, showing the movements and operations of the Second Brigade from the first of the present month to date:

Being encamped near Noonday creek, north of Marietta, I remained there until the evening of the 3d, then marching to Big Shanty. On the following day I received orders to follow the enemy, who was retreating, and, marching via. Marietta, I pursued him some four miles southeast of that town. At 3 a. m. of the 4th I again had marching orders, and on moving out of camp found the rebels in considerable force a short distance in front of the pickets, with strong breastworks thrown up. This was found to· be Wheeler's cavalry, reinforced, as nearly as could be ascertained, by a division of infantry. Fighting immediately ensued, and was continued at intervals throughout the day with heavy skirmishing, in which my loss was but one killed and one wounded, the men being protected by rail breastworks hastily thrown up. We took two prisoners. Not being able 'to dislodge the enemy or effect any decided result, the command returned in the evening to camp. On the 5th I marched to within one mile and a half of the Chattahoochee river, near the town of Roswell, remaining here until the evening of the 8th, when the brigade moved as advance of the division to Roswell. July 9th, upon orders received, I sent the Fourth Ohio Volunteer Cavalry, at 3 a. m., to McAfee's bridge, across the Chattahoochee, eight miles above Roswell, with instructions to hold it and prevent the enemy from crossing or destroying it. The other regiments of my brigade were held as a reserve, saddled, and in readiness to move at the shortest notice. The enemy held the farther end of the bridge, and skirmishing with them was continued until evening, when they fell back, and the Fourth Ohio held the bridge entire, having no loss except one man wounded. Later in the evening the regiment was ordered back to camp. July 10th, Lieutenant P. B. Lewis, of Third Ohio Volunteer Cavalry, and topographical engineer on my staff, was captured at Alpharetta, Ga., together with four of the brigade scouts, by a company of rebel cavalry. On the same day the Third Ohio lost by capture four men, who constituted the rear guard of wagon train coming from Marietta. On the 11th brigade moved camp to the old Alabama road, where it is intersected by the Roswell and Cumming road, and continue encamped at that place.

During the month six prisoners have been taken and twenty-one deserters from the rebel ranks received.

I am, Captain, very respectfully, your obedient servant,

ELI LONG,
Colonel, Commanding Brigade.

CAPT. R. P. KENNEDY,
Assistant Adjutant-General, Second Cavalry Division.

July 21st—We moved out from our position near Decatur in the evening, in light marching order. Went east along the railroad, passing Stone Mountain. We marched about twenty-five miles and halted to rest and feed our horses at 2 a. m., July 22d. Starting on soon after daylight, we burned a bridge and tore up and destroyed the railroad for five miles, burning the ties and twisting the rails east and west of Covington. We captured two trains of cars loaded with household goods of people who were leaving their homes to get away from the advance of our army. They were allowed to take their goods out of the cars, after which the cars were burned; also a large amount of cotton. Our march had been through the finest and best country we had seen in the whole South. Fine plantations, large mansions, everything indicating wealth and prosperity. The owners little thought in the early years of the war that there was any possibility of the despised Yankee invaders penetrating thus far. They were, however, rudely awakened from their fancied security when Sherman's army passed Kenesaw and forced its way across the Chattahoochee. Many of them in wild alarm, packing up a few of their household treasures, loaded them in wagons, seeking safety in flight. We overtook many of them as we were riding to Covington. Some of the drivers had unhitched their horses, mounted and rode away, leaving women, children and household stuff in the wagons by the wayside. Finding that they were not molested, they soon returned to their homes, satisfied in their minds that the Yankees were not the demons they had been led to believe them to be. The next morning we started back at daylight, burning a lot more cotton on our way back. We camped at sundown, near Stone mountain.

July 24th—Returned to Decatur, turned over our prisoners (about 200), which we had taken on the raid. We also brought in a large number of horses and mules, and learned that General Hood had made his second attempt to destroy Sherman. On the afternoon of the 22d, having succeeded in getting Hardee's Corps on the flank and rear of McPherson's army, which composed Sherman's left flank. They had come in over the ground vacated by our division on the evening of the 21st. For a time our wagon trains parked near Decatur were in danger of capture, but were finally gotten out and moved to a place of safety. In their fierce onslaught the enemy carried everything before them, capturing some prisoners, cannon and battle flags, but the veterans of the Army of the Tennessee rallied and made a counter charge, recapturing most of the guns and many prisoners. The Confederates had made a most desperate assault, but had failed at every point. Both armies had lost heavily. Amongst the killed was the gallant General McPherson. It is said that death loves a shining mark. It certainly found one when it struck down McPherson. Standing in the front rank of Generals, he was beloved by all from the commanding General to the humblest soldier. Ohio gave many noble sons to the cause of the Union, yet of all who fell in battle, none acquired greater fame or was more sincerely mourned than he. He sleeps in the beautiful cemetery at Clyde, his home town. A fine monument erected by his fellow citizens marks his grave. In the defense of the wagon train at Decatur four guns of the Chicago Board of Trade Battery rendered heroic service in checking and holding back the rebel lines until the wagons were moved out on the way to a place of safety.

July 26th—We went out at daylight and worked putting up barricades and defenses. Orders came to get ready to move out in light marching order, pack mules and extra baggage to be left in camp near the infantry lines.

July 27th—Reveille at 4 a. m. Started out at 6 in the direction of Stone Mountain. Encountered very little opposition from the enemy. General Stoneman is in command of the expedition, composed of his own and General Garrard's Division. About eighteen miles east of Atlanta we turned south, while Stoneman with his Division kept on east as far as Covington, when he turned south by the way of Monticello to Macon. General Garrard's orders were to march to Flat Rock and wait for Stoneman. We camped that night at Flat Rock Shoal, on South river. It rained most of the day.

July 28th—Some firing on the pickets during the night. Saddled up at 1 o'clock a. m.; commenced skirmishing at daylight. We built rail barricades. The Second Brigade with the artillery was in position at the bridge across South river. Here the enemy made an attack and our artillery opened on them, the Third Ohio supporting the battery. But for some reason the enemy did not force the fighting and in the evening withdrew. We fell back toward Lithonia and encamped.

July 29th—We did not move our camp. Foragers were sent out, who found forage rather scarce.

July 30th—Reveille at 4 o'clock. On the march at 6. Passed through Lithonia and went into camp three miles south of Cross Keys.

July 31st—We moved to Buckhead and went into camp. Heavy cannonading and some musketry firing in the works in front and to the right.

August 6th—Stoneman's men are coming in. His command was surrounded and many of them captured. Those that escaped came straggling into our lines, ragged, dirty, and nearly starved to death. Our duties during the first half of August were mostly on the picket line. General Sherman was working down on the right, having destroyed the Augusta Railroad in such a manner that it was impossible for the enemy to repair it in any reasonable time. He had abandoned Decatur, drawing in the left of his army and moving to the right and rear of Atlanta, and bombarding the city with heavy artillery nearly all the time.

August 9th—The brigade marched to Decatur; saw only a few of the enemy. Captured some pickets. Remained at Decatur until sundown. Brought in some horses, mules and cattle. We got back to camp about 8:30 p. m.

August 11th—Lieutenant-Colonel Howland returned to the regiment entirely well. He was wounded on the 11th of June, just two months ago. We have been pounding away ever since, and we are not in Atlanta yet.

August 13th—Regiment turned over Burnside and Sharps carbines and drew Spencers. We were inspected by the Brigade Inspector.

August 15—Heavy musketry and artillery firing in front just as day was breaking. Saddled up, but we did not move until noon. Marched to Decatur and found a small force of the enemy, but they cleared out at our approach, refusing to have anything to do with us. A part of the brigade went about seven miles toward Stone Mountain, but found no enemy. Left Decatur at dark and arrived in camp about midnight.

August 17th—Saddled up twice during the day but did not leave camp until 10 o'clock p. m., when we started out on the Kilpatrick raid.

CHAPTER XVII.

KILPATRICK'S RAID

By the middle of August, 1864, Sherman's army occupied a position south of the Chattahoochee river, the left of the army holding the Augusta Railroad east of Atlanta, the right resting on the river at Sandtown. It had been demonstrated that the Confederate works north of Atlanta were too strong to be taken by direct assault, without great sacrifice of life, and General Sherman, preparatory to a flank movement, determined to send a cavalry force and destroy the railroads south of Atlanta.

General Kilpatrick was selected to command the expedition. He with his Third Division of cavalry occupied a position covering the right flank of the army at Sandtown. The Second Division was in position near Cross Keys, covering the left.

On the afternoon of the 17th of August the First and Second Brigades of the Second Division received orders to be ready to march at 10 o'clock p. m., with five days rations. Colonel Minty of the First Brigade was in command, Colonel Long commanding the Second Brigade and Colonel Seidel commanding the Third Ohio.

At 10 o'clock we started out, and after marching all night in the rear of our lines, we arrived at Sandtown and reported to General Kilpatrick at 7 a. m. August 18th.

We went into camp and unsaddled our horses, resting until the afternoon; drew sixty rounds of ammunition, and late in the afternoon General Kilpatrick formed the command in a hollow square. It consisted of his own, the Third Division, and the First and Second Brigades of the Second Division of Cavalry, and four guns of the Chicago Board of Trade Battery, in all about 5000 men. General Kilpatrick made a brief address. He said that we had been selected for a special service, our arms and equipments were the best that the government could furnish, and that he had all confidence in the ability of the command to perform the task to which it had been assigned. He asked and expected the hearty co-operation of the entire command, officers and men, willing obedience to orders, and at all times prompt and energetic action.

At 6 o'clock the column moved out, the Third Division in the advance, the Third Ohio in the advance of the Second Division. We had marched but a few miles before the enemy appeared in our front, and commenced skirmishing with the advance guard. Skirmishing was kept up all through the night, the roads were barricaded and our progress was very slow, and it was daylight, August 19th, before we had reached the West Point Railroad near Red Bank, whereas General Kilpatrick had expected to reach there by 8 or 9 o'clock in the evening and Jonesboro by daylight.

Here General Kilpatrick requested Colonel Minty to take the advance and push on as rapidly as possible to Jonesboro. He said, "Let nothing delay you; we should be there now." Colonel Minty says, "I ordered Colonel Long to dismount his leading regiment, the Third Ohio;" it rapidly deployed, advanced at double-quick, dislodging the enemy. We mounted and pushed forward, but soon encountered more barricades. We dismounted, a section of the battery was brought up and fired a few shells into them, and we went forward, the Third Ohio dismounted, over the works, the First and Fourth Ohio, mounted, around them. And thus we pressed forward all the day, the column keeping well closed up so that very little time was lost at the points where we encountered obstructions.

When we came to Flint river we found the planking had been torn loose and thrown into the river and floated away, but the stringers were left in fairly good shape. The enemy, dismounted, occupied a strong position on the east bank. Our battery was brought into position and soon silenced their guns. We charged, dismounted, across the bottom land, and with our Spencers drove them out of their works. A part of the command crossed on the stringers and deployed as skirmishers. Rails were carried and placed for planking, and the entire Second Division, except the Seventh Pennsylvania, with two guns of the battery, were soon over and we were pushing the enemy, consisting of the cavalry brigades of Armstrong, Ferguson and Ross, into Jonesboro.

The enemy had constructed a fort of cotton bales near the depot; a few shells from the battery set the cotton and buildings on fire. Our line moved forward, driving the enemy through the town. As soon as we reached Jonesboro the telegraph wires were tapped and a message caught saying that Cleburn's Division of Infantry and Martin's Division of Cavalry were on the way to reinforce the men we were now fighting, Jackson's Division of Cavalry.

When Kilpatrick's Division came up they commenced destroying the railroad south of Jonesboro, while the Second Division formed between them and the enemy, to protect them from attack while working.

At about 10 p. m. Kilpatrick sent word to Minty that about two miles of railroad track was destroyed, and he was going to move south, and instructing him to follow and cover his movement. When Kilpatrick attempted to move south he found a large force of Confederate infantry occupying a strong position behind barricades, protecting the railroad. After feeling of their position he decided not to attack, but to move east toward McDonough, and then endeavor to get on the railroad again near Lovejoys Station. Minty's Brigade took the advance, while Long's Brigade formed to hold the enemy's cavalry in check and protect the rear.

By daylight of the 20th the entire force, except Long's Brigade, was on the road for Lovejoys Station, where we expected to resume the work of destroying the railroad. About sunrise Long's Brigade moved out after the command, the Third Ohio as rear guard. The enemy's cavalry, which had been operating in our front all day yesterday, now attacked us in the rear, keeping us busy holding them in check.

About noon the First Ohio formed in line of battle on the north side of a small stream, and we crossed over into a piece of open woodland on the south side, where we halted to feed our horses and make coffee; just as our coffee was ready, the Johnnies made a charge on the First Ohio, driving them back. Our bugles sounded to horse, coffee was too hot to drink, and many of the boys mounted and rode into line holding their cups of coffee until it cooled. We drove the rebels back and then started southward again. As we neared Lovejoys Station we found the fences had been opened up for eighty rods on each side of the road by our skirmishers, and the sound of rapid firing in our front told us that our boys were already hotly engaged, and that we had another foe to reckon with besides the one that had followed us so persistently all the day. We came up with the rest of the command about one mile from Lovejoys, dismounted and went forward at double-quick, coming in with the battery just in time to repulse a charge made by the enemy's infantry on our First Brigade. The Confederate infantry that had checked the advance of the Third Division south of Jonesboro, had moved down the railroad and taken position in a cut some three or four feet deep, and as Minty's Brigade moved forward toward the railroad, coming into line of battle with skirmishers in front, they fired a volley, and with that same old rebel yell rushed forward over the skirmish line, and for a few moments carried everything before them, and it was only the timely arrival of Long's Second Brigade and the battery that saved the First Brigade from being overwhelmed and captured. One of our guns was disabled and could not be hauled off the field. A number of the men of the Third Ohio assisted the battery boys in bringing it off and loading it in a wagon to prevent it from falling into the hands of the enemy.

Kilpatrick now realized that his position was extremely critical, and that he must devote all his energies to getting his command out, and give up all attempts to further destroy the railroad. Confederate forces of infantry, cavalry and artillery had gathered in from all directions, until we were completely surrounded. In our front was the Confederate General Reynolds, with seven regiments of infantry, occupying a strong position on the railroad, from which we were unable to dislodge him. Directly in our rear, on the McDonough road, over which we must retreat, were the cavalry brigades of Ross and Ferguson, dismounted, and in line of battle behind rail breastworks. Occupying a position on a hill was a three-gun battery, supported by Martin's Division of Cavalry.

On the right of the road was a force of State troops, and on the left a brigade of Pat Cleburn's Division of Infantry three lines deep. The field over which we must charge was an old plantation, seamed with water-gullies, many of them very deep, crossing our course at right angles. The prospect was anything but inviting, but it was our only way out. Four brigades were ordered to their horses. The order for the charge was to form by regiments in columns of fours facing the rear. Long's Brigade was formed on the right, Minty's in the center, Kilpatrick's Division on the left. While we were forming, the men who were guarding our rear were fighting desperately to hold the infantry in check, the batteries in our front were sending their messengers of death into our ranks, staff officers and orderlies on foaming steeds were carrying orders to the different commanders, Kilpatrick grim and silent waiting anxiously for the moment to come when he can give the word, and that moment has come in much less time than it has taken me to tell it. He turns to his bugler, who lifts his bugle and sounds the advance, and simultaneously the call is taken up by every brigade and regiment, and the different columns move forward, steadily at first, then at a trot, then at a gallop, and finally the bugles sound the charge, and the earth trembles beneath the beating hoofs of 5000 rushing steeds. The rattle of musketry is drowned in the shouts of the men, who, with flashing sabres and yelling like demons, are riding madly to victory or death. Men and horses go down, but those that are left ride on, the guns of the enemy sweep the field, but they cannot stop the onrushing hosts as they press forward

> "Into the jaws of death,
> Into the mouth of hell."

And now the guns are silenced, and shot and shell no longer sweep the field. And now it is a fierce hand-to-hand encounter for a few brief moments, and the enemy's line, pierced and broken at all points, scatters in every direction in a frantic effort to escape from our victorious battalions. The brigades of Ross and Ferguson were out of the fight so far as being of any use in helping to corner Kilpatrick's men. And now the recall is sounded, and the Second Division is formed in line facing the rear, to cover the retreat to our lines east of Atlanta by way of McDonough. Our artillery came up on a gallop and took position on the line and commenced firing. The ambulances came through loaded with wounded, our ammunition wagons and pack mules were the last to come through and take up the line of march.

Colonel Long was ordered to hold his position until the Third Division was well out of the way, and Minty had formed a new line of defense. As soon as Cleburn found that Kilpatrick was retreating he commenced to press forward, advancing on our line and shelling the road over which our column was moving, and had already gained a position on our left, threatening to cut us off from the McDonough road. Colonel Long was wounded, and Colonel Eggleston, of the First Ohio, took command of the brigade.

An orderly galloped up with instructions for the brigade to fall back, as Minty had the First Brigade in position to hold the enemy if they followed us. The Second Brigade at once took up the retreat by regiments; passing through the lines of the First Brigade we bade Cleburn good-bye just as the sun went down. One of the guns which had rendered such excellent service burst while we were defending this position, and was left on the field. We passed through McDonough, marching most of the night, which was very dark and the rain pouring down in torrents. The Third Division was in the advance, and the frequent halts we were compelled to make made marching tedious in the extreme.

This was our fourth night in the saddle, and the strenuous work of the last two nights and days, during which time the command had been constantly engaged with the enemy, culminating in that last terrific charge at Lovejoys Station, had left men and horses almost completely exhausted, and at the frequent halts many of the men would dismount and lie down on the wet ground by the roadside to rest their weary bodies and get a few moments sleep, and it was with the utmost difficulty that they were aroused by their more alert comrades as the column moved on.

Toward morning we found some corn and halted by the wayside to feed our horses, after which we again took up the line of march. The night's rain had swollen the creeks to rivers, and Cotton Indian creek, which we were obliged to cross, was a roaring torrent, through which the entire command was compelled to swim their horses. The current was so swift that it was necessary to march twelve or fifteen rods above the ford on the south side, slide off the bank into the stream, and as the horses swam across, the current carried them down to the ford on the north side. In crossing one man and about fifty horses and mules were drowned, and for lack of animals some of the wagons had to be destroyed, amongst them the wagon containing the dismantled gun, which was hidden so that it could not be found by the enemy.

Our position, however, was not by any means safe or assured. While we probably had liittle to fear from the enemy, we had fought at Jonesboro and Lovejoys, yet we might at any time meet with troops sent out from Atlanta to intercept us. And wet and tired as we were, we must still march on.

We crossed South river and burned the bridge, and pushing on, reached Lithonia on the Augusta Railroad early in the evening of the 21st, where we bivouacked for the night, unsaddled our horses and lay down to rest. On the morning of the 22d we resumed the march, passed through Decatur and returned to our old camp.

Colonel Minty in his report gave the loss of the Third Ohio as follows: "Eight killed, thirty-three wounded, five wounded and left on the field, three missing." The small number missing speaks volumes for the discipline of the regiment and the able manner in which it was handled. Colonel Minty in his official report further said: "Every officer and soldier in the command acted so well, so nobly, so gallantly, that under ordinary circumstances they would be entitled to special mention. Day and night, from the 18th to the 23d, these gallant men were without sleep, and almost without food. During that time they marched and skirmished incessantly, fought four pitched battles and swam a flooded river, and all without once complaining or murmuring."

Among those severely wounded and left on the field at Lovejoys Station was Lieutenant George Garfield of Company D, who doubtless owed his life to Private John Grabach of his company, who nobly and unselfishly remained with him and nursed him back to life.

Colonel Minty is my authority on the Confederate forces that were opposing us the first day, from the West Point Railroad to Jonesboro. Also for the infantry forces on the railroad at Lovejoys Station.

The following Confederate account of the charge at Lovejoys gives the Confederate forces through which we hewed our way. It was copied from the Memphis-Atlanta Appeal, published at Macon, Ga., early in September, 1864:

"The newspapers have lately been full of accounts of how Martin's Division of Cavalry was run over by the Yankees at Lovejoys on the 20th ultimo. The writer was on the field on that occasion, and in justice to the much-abused cavalry states the facts in the matter.

"Martin's Division, supporting the battery, was formed on the McDonough road; Ross's and Ferguson's Brigades, on foot, were in front and on each side of the battery, behind rail breastworks. A brigade of Cleburn's Division was on the left of the road in three lines, the last one in a piece of woods about 100 yards in the rear of the position of the battery.

"On the right of the road the State troops were formed in line. When the Yankees charged they came in a solid column ten or twelve deep, running their horses and yelling like devils. They did not stop to fire, but each fellow for himself rushed on, swinging his saber over his head. They rode right over Ross's and Ferguson's men in the center, and over through Cleburn's lines, one after the other, on the left. Cleburn's first line tried to use their bayonets, but the Yankees cut them to pieces. After the Yankees had cut through all the other forces, and captured the battery, Martin, seeing the field was lost, retreated in good order. The effort to arouse the people against Martin and his brave division is more disgraceful and demoralizing than the Yankees' charge itself, and should be frowned upon by all who wish well to our cause."

During the charge at Lovejoys Station on the 20th an officer of General Kilpatrick's staff and a small party of our men found themselves cut off from the main body. After making several ineffectual attempts to return, they finally succeeded on the 21st, and reached the command in safety.

Report of Colonel Long, Second Brigade, Second Division Cavalry, Kilpatrick's Raid—August 17th to 22d, 1864.

HDQRS. SECOND BRIGADE, SECOND CAVALRY DIVISION,
BUCK HEAD, GA., *August 23,* 1864.

CAPTAIN: I have the honor to report the part taken by this brigade in the late expedition of General Kilpatrick in the enemy's rear. In pursuance of orders received on the evening of the 17th, I furnished my command with rations for five days, and moved from camp shortly after midnight, reporting to Colonel Minty, of First Brigade, in charge of First and Second Brigades, with an effective force of 72 officers and 1300 men. Lieutenant Bennett's section of Board of Trade Battery reported for duty with me. Marched in rear of First Brigade for Sandtown, arriving there early the next morning. Remained in camp near Sandtown during the day, and reported at headquarters of Brigadier-General Kilpatrick. According to instructions received from him, marched again at sundown, the Third Cavalry Division being in column and Brigadier-General Kilpatrick commanding. My command now reduced about 100 men by the giving out of horses on the previous night's march. Traveling all night, we crossed the Atlanta and West Point Railroad, near Fairburn, at daylight on the 19th. Having orders to destroy the road at this point, I detailed for this work the First Ohio Volunteer Cavalry, who tore up half a mile of the track. Meanwhile, I had moved forward in column with the remainder of the brigade, the First Brigade holding the rear, and had not marched far when artillery was opened by a force of the enemy, who appeared in the woods on our left. I returned to the railroad, mounted the First Ohio, and formed line of battle in the woods. The First Brigade being now already engaged, I advanced my line to co-operate with the other brigade, and the enemy retired, and, after considerable skirmishing, was driven back through his camp, which we temporarily occupied. The column was then moved forward, my brigade taking the advance, and I soon found a force on my front; skirmished with them during the greater part of the day, driving them gradually toward Jonesboro until my advance guard drew near Flint river.

The enemy had taken a strong position on the farther bank and at the town, and engaged us sharply with musketry and artillery. Dismounting my command, I succeeded in pressing them slowly back, aided by the fire from our artillery, which had been directed upon their lines. We charged down to the bridge over the river, and after a few shots the regiments crossed on the bridge, which had been partially torn up. An advance toward the town was then made in two lines on each side of the road, the Fourth U. S. Cavalry and First Ohio forming the first line and the Third and Fourth Ohio the second line, the Fourth Michigan being deployed as skirmishers in front. Some little firing occurred as the lines advanced, and the command moved into Jonesboro without further opposition. I then ordered forward my led horses, meantime employing a portion of the command in destroying the railroad, burning the track at and below the town for half a mile. At dark went into camp, and rested until 11 o'clock, when I was ordered forward to the breastworks on the south side of the town, remaining here till near daylight. I then moved out on the McDonough and Jonesboro road, covering the rear of the column, and, arriving at Pittsburg, marched southwardly toward the railroad again, and at an early hour my rear guard (a battalion of First Ohio Volunteer Cavalry) was attacked by a force of cavalry and driven slowly back upon the column. Upon going to the rear and finding this battalion hard pressed, I brought the remainder of the regiment into position, ordered back the Third and Fourth Ohio Regiments, and succeeded in checking and driving the enemy. A portion of his force now appeared in my front, and between the brigade and the main column, having come in on a right hand road; but the Fourth Ohio repulsed this demonstration, and, being then ordered forward, I marched in rear of First Brigade. Arriving near Lovejoys, on the Atlanta and Macon Railroad, I found the advance brigade engaged with an enemy in their front, and received orders to throw forward a dismounted battalion. Before this could be accomplished the skirmish line was forced back, and I dismounted my entire command, forming a line across the field on my left, and threw up a line of rail breastworks in the rear. The firing now became heavy on both sides. The First Ohio and a portion of the Fourth repulsed the enemy, then, falling back to the breastworks, held him in check until he desisted from firing, and enabled a section of our artillery to be withdrawn from the field. The command was then ordered back to their horses, to mount. Immediately after mounting I was directed to take position in rear of First Brigade, Second Division, and to follow it out (when a general charge was made shortly after), which was done. In this charge Captain William H. Scott, of First Ohio Cavalry, inspector on my staff and a most gallant officer, was severely wounded.

The column was now marched on the road toward McDonough, my brigade covering the rear. The motion of forming and moving out was slow, and the rebel infantry now closed up on my rear, attacking with considerable vigor my line of skirmishers, formed by a battalion of the Third Ohio. The remainder of this regiment was at once dismounted to strengthen this line. The enemy presented a formidable front, extending well to my right, and poured in heavy volleys of musketry, while his artillery opened with excellent precision upon the other regiments in column on the road. Lieutenant Bennett was in position in rear, and worked his one piece with good effect. The enemy still pressed forward with increased numbers. The Third Ohio stood well their ground, pouring repeated volleys into the enemy's ranks, and only fell back from overpowering numbers. Flushed with slight successes, the rebels now made a fierce onset, charging with their main force. In front of the Third Ohio was a declivity descending to marshy ground, and beyond this a creek. The enemy were on the farther side of this creek, and, riding by the side of Colonel Seidel, of the Third, I saw the force advancing to the creek, and directed him to hold the fire of his men, protected somewhat by breastworks, until the enemy should cross, and then to fire rapidly and with precision. Immediately after this I observed Colonel Seidel raise his hand and motion for his regiment to fall back, the cause of this being that the enemy was coming up in heavy force on his right flank and the safety of the regiment being endangered. Just at this moment I was shot in two places, my horse having also been shot a moment before, and I was then forced to retire from the field, turning over the command to Colonel Eggleston, of First Ohio. The Third Ohio fell back, and was soon after relieved by the First Brigade. The command, all now moving forward, marched through McDonough and camped that night near Cotton river. On the morning of the 21st crossed Cotton Indian creek, swimming the horses, and camped at night at Lithonia. Arrived at Buck Head on the evening of the 22d.

During the expedition the loss in my brigade was severe, but not great, when considering the forces it engaged. The loss inflicted upon the enemy is, of course, unknown, but he probably suffered severely.

To Lieutenant Bennett and his very efficient section of artillery much credit is due, as also to the First, Third, and Fourth Ohio for their admirable behavior under all circumstances. Officers and men all did well.

Below will be found a summary of casualties during the expedition, the major part of them occurring on the 20th.

To the officers of my staff who were with me on the expedition are due my thanks for promptitude on all occasions, and for efficient aid in the field and on the march; and I would recommend to the favorable notice of the General commanding the names of Captain William E.

Crane, acting assistant adjutant-general; Captain William H. Scott, acting assistant inspector-general; Lieutenant E. S. Wood, aide-dé-camp; Lieutenant H. H. Siverd, provost marshal; Lieutenant J. N. Squire, ordnance officer; Lieutenant J. B. Hayden, acting commissary of subsistence, and Assistant Surgeon John Cannan, medical director.

I have the honor to be, very respectfully, your obedient servant,

ELI LONG,

Colonel Fourth Ohio Volunteer Cavalry, Comdg. Brigade.

CAPTAIN R. P. KENNEDY,

Assistant Adjutant-General, Second Cavalry Division.

CASUALTIES.

Command	Killed		Wounded		Wounded and missing		Missing	
	Officers	Men	Officers	Men	Officers	Men	Officers	Men
1st Ohio Volunteer Cavalry	....	4	1	13	....	......	....	2
3d Ohio Volunteer Cavalry	1	7	....	30	....	5	....	2
4th Ohio Volunteer Cavalry	....	3	3	16	....	......	2	5
Total	1	14	4	59	....	5	2	9

Immediately after the return of Kilpatrick, General Sherman commenced his movement by the right flank to place his army on the railroad south of Atlanta. Sending all his extra baggage and supplies to the fortifications on the Chattahoochee, with General Slocum's Corps to man the works at that point, and leaving General Schofield's Corps in the works near Atlanta to keep up a constant cannonading of the city. He commenced to develop his plan, which was to move one corps at a time from the extreme left to the extreme right, each corps as it came into position protecting its front with fortifications.

August 25th—The dismounted men and the wagon train under Lieutenant-Colonel Howland sent back to the river, the division moving to Sandtown.

August 26th—Dismounted men and wagon train moved to Sandtown.

August 27th—Division moved toward Red Oak, covering the left flank of the army in its movement against Jonesboro.

September 1st—The division moved on to Rough and Ready and commenced destroying the railroad. Two corps of the Confederate army have entrenched at Jonesboro and Sherman's army is concentrating against them. Stewart's Corps still holds Attlanta, but he can't hold it long. In the afternoon a part of the Fourteenth Corps having gained a position from which an assault of the enemy's works at Jonesboro, could be advantageously made, General Thomas ordered the charge to be made with the bayonet, and about 5 p. m., everything being ready, the line moved forward with the same resistless force that they had manifested at Missionary Ridge, charging up to and over the entrenchments, regardless of the deadly fire of the enemy, many of whom were captured in the breastworks. Our losses in the campaign south of Atlanta were about 1200. The enemy lost upwards of 2000 prisoners, and left more than 300 dead upon the battlefield. The same night Stewart burned locomotives and cars with supplies and ammunition, that they were unable to take with them, and evacuated the city. The noise of exploding shells in the burning trains were plainly heard at Jonesboro, sounding like a fierce battle. The next morning General Slocum sent a force toward the city to reconnoiter. They were met by the mayor and a delegation of citizens, who formally surrendered the place to its victorious conquerors. The rebel army concentrated and fortified at Lovejoy Station, while Sherman, thoroughly destroying the railroads to the south, retired to Atlanta to await developments and get his army in shape for the next move. The night of the 1st the division encamped about five miles south of Rough and Ready.

September 2d—Division moved south; camped in a pine woods near the railroad, two miles north of Jonesboro.

September 3d—The dismounted men and wagon train sent back to Atlanta. On the 4th the division moved to the left, covering the Atlanta and McDonough road, many deserters from the rebel army coming into our lines.

September 7th—Marched at 6 a. m.; encamped eight miles south of Decatur. On the 8th we moved up to Decatur, and on the 11th moved our camp to Cross Keys.

The aggregate casualties of the Army of the Cumberland from May 1st to September 6th were as follows: Killed, 3041; wounded, 15,783; captured, 2707; died of wounds, 1067; died of disease 207; sick sent to rear, 26,184.

The following is a copy of Special Field Orders No. 66:

HDQRS. MILITARY DIVISION OF THE MISSISSIPPI,
IN THE FIELD NEAR JONESBORO, GA., *September* 6, 1864.

I. The General-in-Chief communicates, with a feeling of just pride and satisfaction, the following orders of the President of the United States, and telegram of Lieutenant-General U. S. Grant on hearing of the capture of Atlanta:

EXECUTIVE MANSION, WASHINGTON, D. C., *Sept.* 3, 1864.

The national thanks are rendered by the President to Major-General W. T. Sherman, and the gallant officers and soldiers of his command before Atlanta for the distinguished ability, courage and perseverance displayed in the campaign in Georgia, which under divine favor, has resulted in the capture of the City of Atlanta. The marches, battles, sieges and other military operations that have signalized the campaign must render it famous in the annals of war, and have entitled those who have participated therein to the applause and thanks of the nation.

(Signed) ABRAHAM LINCOLN,
President of the United States.

Second, That on Wednesday, the 9th day of September, commencing at the hour of 12 m., there shall be fired a salute of one hundred (100) guns, at the arsenal at Washington, and at New York, Boston, Philadelphia, Baltimore, Pittsburg, Newport, Ky., St. Louis, New Orleans, Mobile, Pensacola, Hilton Head, and Newbern, or the day after the receipt of this order, for the brilliant achievements of the army under command of Major-General Sherman in the State of Georgia, and the capture of Atlanta. The Secretary of War will issue directions for the execution of this order.

(Signed) ABRAHAM LINCOLN,
President of the United States.

CITY POINT, VA., *Sept.* 4, 1864—9 p. m.

MAJOR-GENERAL SHERMAN: I have just received your dispatch announcing the capture of Atlanta. In honor of your great victory, I have ordered a salute to be fired with shotted guns from every battery bearing upon the enemy. The salute will be fired within an hour, amidst great rejoicing.

(Signed) U. S. GRANT,
Lieutenant-General.

II. All the corps, regiments and batteries composing this army, may, without further orders, inscribe "Atlanta" on their colors.

By order of Major-General W. T. Sherman.

L. M. DAYTON,
Aide-de-Camp.

Report of Colonel Charles B. Seidel, Third Ohio Cavalry.

HDQRS. THIRD OHIO VETERAN VOLUNTEER CAV.,
NEAR CROSS KEYS, GA., *September* 11, 1864.

SIR: I have the honor to submit the following report of operations of Third Ohio Veteran Volunteer Cavalry during the campaign just closed:

The regiment left Columbia, Tenn., on the 22d day of May, 1864, and proceeded to Decatur, Ala., where we arrived on the 26th, and were sent out same day in pursuit of a portion of General Roddey's command (rebel), and skirmished with them, driving them six miles, their wagon train being captured by another portion of the brigade. May 27th, proceeded to Courtland, skirmishing slightly in the advance along the route. On 28th, marched through Moulton, toward Somerville, and camped three miles beyond, and were attacked in our camp at 4 a. m., 29th, by Confederate force under General Roddey. After an hour and a half of fighting we drove them, aiding to capture two field officers, four line officers, and a number of enlisted men. The enemy retired to Moulton, leaving eleven killed on the field. Our loss, one killed and two wounded. Same day marched forty miles, camping ten miles southeast from Somerville, in the rear of the Seventeenth Corps, with which we marched to Rome, Ga., where we arrived on the 4th day of June. From there we proceeded to join the division (Second Cavalry), which we did on the 7th of June, near Etowah, Ga. Marched to the left of the army near Noonday creek, and on the 11th the regiment was sent on a reconnaissance to Noonday creek, and had an engagement with Iverson's Brigade of Cavalry, being repulsed with a loss of fourteen killed, wounded and missing. We fought again on the 15th, without gaining any advantage and with no loss. On the 23d advanced across Noonday creek; had a skirmish with the enemy, and returned with loss of two wounded. No other operations until the 3d of July, when we advanced, following the enemy on their retreat from Kenesaw Mountain. The 4th of July skirmished most of the day; loss one man killed. The 14th of July the regiment left camp near Roswell, and marched to Cumming, Ga., where we arrived at 4 a. m. the 15th, but found no enemy in force; captured a large amount of tobacco and a number of horses and mules, and returned to camp same day. The 16th crossed the Chattahoochee river at McAfee's bridge, and went into camp one mile and a half from it. 19th, marched to the Georgia Railroad, near Stone Mountain, Ga., and assisted in destroying the road for several miles, and returned to camp. 21st, marched to Yellow river; next day to Covington, Ga., on the Georgia Railroad, fifty miles east of Atlanta, where we destroyed the road for a distance of ten miles; met no enemy in force. 23d and 24th, returned to Decatur, having destroyed a large amount of cotton, captured a number of prisoners, contrabands, horses, and mules. 27th, left camp and marched to Flat Rock, where the division was attacked on the 28th by a superior force and nearly surrounded. The enemy was repulsed, and we returned to Latimar's Corners, where we remained two days, then marched around Stone Mountain to the rear of our army in front of Atlanta.

On the 18th of August started, under command of General Kilpatrick,

**Second Lieutenant William Goodnow, Company I,
died of illness May 27, 1862 at Corinth, Mississippi.**

Private Leonard Winkler, Company I, posed at right shortly after his enlistment in December 1863. Seven months later he was wounded in the right arm at the battle of Peachtree Creek, Georgia.

Above, Winkler as he appeared during the summer of 1865.

Leonard Winkler's pocket photograph album struck by a bullet at Peachtree Creek. After glancing off the album's cover the bullet entered Winkler's right arm.

Unidentified member of Company I, photographed by the Nashville firm
of T.M. Schleier. Note damage at left caused by the bullet which hit
Leonard Winkler's album at Peachtree Creek.

Private Solomon Baker, Company I.

Follett House Museum

Private John Beer, Company I.

Follett House Museum

Private Frederick Blum, Company I.

Private Martin L. Bridenstine, Company I.

Private Frederick Burns, Company I.

Private George Gooseman, Company I.

Private Cyrus L. Henney, Company I.

Private Enoch Henney, Company I.
He also served in the company as corporal
and commissary sergeant.

Private Anthony Hoover, Company I.
He was appointed farrier on July 1, 1865.

Bugler Jacob Hummel, Company I.

Follett House Museum

Private George Kryder, Company I.

Follett House Museum

Private Patrick Lauler, Company I.

Corporal Charles Mason, Company I.

Private Thomas W. McCoy, Company I.

Private Edwin W. Niver, Company I.
He was captured November 15, 1863 near Woodville, Alabama,
and died June 19, 1864 in Andersonville prison.

Follett House Museum

Private Francis M. Parks, Company I.

Follett House Museum

First Sergeant Francis Riley, Company I.

Private Gaylord M. Saltzgaber, Company I.

Follett House Museum

Private Isaiah Schwab, Company I.

Corporal Charles J. Smith, Company I.

Corporal Henry Sweetland, Company I.

Saddler Conrad Thoman, Company I.

Follett House Museum

Private Hyatt Travis, Company I.

Corporal Jacob Wies, Company I.

for the expedition to the rear of Atlanta. Left Sandtown at sundown on the 18th, and marched all night, skirmishing most of the time. 19th, fought all day and got possession of the Macon Railroad at Jonesboro, at 4 p. m.; burnt the public buildings and destroyed the railroad for a distance of two miles. Left Jonesboro at 3 a. m. of the 20th, and marched to Lovejoy's Station, having a brisk skirmish in the rear on the route. At Lovejoy's met the enemy in large force, cavalry, artillery, and infantry. After fighting an hour we formed in advance of brigade and charged in column of fours on the enemy in our rear, scattering them badly, and causing them to abandon one piece of artillery, which was brought off the field by our brigade (Second Cavalry); also captured a number of prisoners. The regiment was detailed for rear guard, the column marching toward McDonough, and was attacked by one division of rebel infantry. After fighting them an hour, losing eight men killed, thirty wounded, and four missing, was relieved by a portion of the First Brigade, Second Cavalry Division. 21st, marched to Lithonia, being closely followed by the enemy until we crossed South river, where we burned the bridge, thus stopping their advance. 22d, returned to camp at Buck Head, and remained until the 25th, when we left camp and marched to Vining's Station and bivouacked. 26th, marched to a point on the Chattahoochee river opposite Sandtown. 27th, marched a short distance to the left of the army; regiment placed on picket; had a slight skirmish on the 28th; no loss; relieved at 2:30 p. m. by battalion of mounted infantry. Remained in camp until the 30th. At 3 p. m. left camp and marched to the La Grange Railroad, and camped five miles from East Point and ten from Jonesboro.

September 1st, marched to Macon Railroad, at Rough and Ready, eleven miles from Atlanta. The regiment was sent out reconnoitering, and went five miles in direction of McDonough, but found no large body of the enemy's troops. September 4, moved camp to Mount Zion Church, on the left of the army, where we remained until the 7th, when we came to our present camp, near Cross Keys, Ga., where we arrived September 10th, 1864.

The aggregate loss during the campaign is as follows: Killed, or died of wounds received in action, one commissioned officer, twenty men; wounded, one field officer, sixty men; missing in action, two commissioned officers, twenty men; total loss, four commissioned officers, 100 men.

Total number of miles traveled during the campaign, 1021.

Believing the above to be essentially correct, I am, General, very respectfully, your obedient servant, C. B. SEIDEL,

Colonel, Comdg. Third Ohio Veteran Volunteer Cavalry.

ASSISTANT ADJUTANT-GENERAL,

Military Division of the Mississippi.

BENJAMIN F. W. COSIER, REGIMENTAL CHAPLAIN—AN APPRECIATION.

Amongst the officers and men of the Third Ohio Cavalry with whom the writer became acquainted, he remembers none with greater pleasure than Chaplain Cosier. He came to the regiment in May, 1864, and served with it until the close of the war.

Methinks there is no position in a regiment that is harder to fill satisfactorily than that of chaplain, requiring as it does peculiar qualifications. Men in the army were not inclined to be over religious. The environments were such as to discourage all efforts on that line. The duties of the soldier were practically the same on the Sabbath that they were during the week. All days looked alike in the army, and it needed a man of great influence amongst his fellows to turn men's thoughts to better things. Men cared little for flowery sermons, but they did care for a man who was a lover of his fellow men and who cared for their comfort; who with them was ready and willing to endure the hardships of the campaign; who knew no fear on the battle line, encouraging the men by his presence and words of cheer; bringing water to the thirsty; aid and comfort to the wounded; consolation to the dying; taking their last messages to the loved ones at home, and pointing them in their dying moments to the "Lamb of God, that taketh away the sins of the world."

Such was Chaplain Cosier. Is it any wonder that the men of the regiment loved and respected him as the minister of God; the preacher of righteousness to dying men? He not only preached love to God and love to man, but exemplified it in his life. Like the Apostle James, he showed his faith by his works.

Chaplain Cosier has gone to his reward. He has heard the voice of the Master saying, "Come ye blessed of my Father, inherit the kingdom prepared for you, for I was hungry and ye fed me, thirsty and ye gave me drink, sick and in prison and ye visited me." "For as much as ye did it to one of the least of these my brethren ye did it unto me."

———

The time of many of the men who enlisted in 1861, and had not re-enlisted, having expired, they marched to Atlanta on September 21st, taking the cars to Columbia, Tenn., via. Chattanooga and Nashville. They were mustered out October 3d, and paid off at Columbus, Ohio, October 10th.

September 22d—The division started down the Chattahoochee, camping at Point of Rocks, three miles from Sandtown.

September 24th—Crossed to the west side of the river at Sandtown, formed line and moved down to the Sweetwater. The report that rebs were crossing proved to be a false alarm. We returned to the east side of the river at Sandtown and camped.

September 25th—The wagons came up; we drew five days rations and the wagons went back to Atlanta. The First and Second Brigades crossed the river and marched northward, camping about ten miles southwest of Marietta.

September 26th—Reveille at 4 a. m., on the march at 6, Third Brigade in the advance. Second Brigade halted at Powder Springs. Moved toward Ackworth, camped near the railroad north of Big Shanty.

September 27th—On the march at 7 a. m., moved to Ackworth and took the road to Roswell. Bore to the left to cross Little river at McConnell's Mills; bridge burned. Camped near Benson's Mills.

September 28th—On the march, crossed the Chattahoochee at the Roswell ford; encamped two miles south of the ford.

September 29th—Moved to our old camp at Cross Keys. The next day Lieutenant Lewis returned to the regiment, bringing thirty recruits for the brigade.

October 2d—Moved to the Chattahoochee, near Vining Station; camped on the east side. Heavy rains had raised the river and washed out a number of bridges. The wagon and part of the railroad bridge are gone.

CHAPTER XVIII.

HOOD MARCHES NORTHWARD

October 3d—Crossed the river and marched to Powder Springs. Hood's army at this date is north of us, having crossed the Chattahoochee at points below Campbellton, on the 29th of September, and at this date is west of Lost Mountain. A member of Company I was shot on picket.

October 4th—A part of the Confederate Army captured the garrison at Big Shanty and at Ackworth and broke up a number of miles of railroad. The regiment moved to the west of Kenesaw; had a skirmish with the enemy near Big Shanty.

As soon as General Sherman ascertained to a certainty that General Hood had crossed the Chattahoochee river with his entire army and was marching northward, he at once set to work to checkmate him. Just what the plans of the Confederate commander were, General Sherman could only guess, and he had to plan to meet and counteract him. General Sherman's first move was to send General Thomas to Nashville to take command of all the forces in Tennessee, and along the lines of railroad outside of the points covered by General Sherman's immediate army. He also ordered General Corse to gather what forces he could and concentrate at Allatoona, where General Sherman had all his surplus supplies stored. General Hood, having sent a force on to the railroad north of Kenesaw, cut the telegraph and tore up the railroad from Big Shanty to Ackworth. He also sent General French with his division to capture Allatoona with its garrison and supplies. General French arrived in front of the place on October 5th, and after getting his men into position, sent in a flag of truce, asking an unconditional surrender, as he had the place surrounded and it would prevent a needless effusion of blood.

General Corse replied for him to go ahead with the effusion as soon as he was ready. He at once opened up the attack in what proved to be one of the most desperate small engagements of the war. The Confederates attacked with a spirit of bravery and daring that might have gained the victory if the works had been less valiantly defended. All through the day General Sherman from the top of Kenesaw was anxiously watching the battle, hurrying reinforcements forward to the sorely pressed garrison, and signaling to them messages of encouragement. It was with great satisfaction that he saw the enemy repulsed in every assault and driven from the field.

General Thomas was in Nashville, and General Sherman wishing to send a message to him and also to congratulate General Corse for his gallant defense of Allatoona, ordered General Garrard to send a Squadron of Cavalry, and Captain Luckey was sent with Companies K and L of the Third Ohio, the former under command of Captain Howland, on the perilous mission. Captain Luckey receiving his message late in the afternoon of October 5th, passed through Marietta just at dark, and marching to the south and east of Kenesaw. Soon after starting Luckey halted the command and told the men that they were going on an extra hazardous expedition; that if any of them wanted to go back to camp they could do so; but none of the men volunteered to go back. When the command reached the Roswell and Canton road they turned north. The night was very dark, and it commenced to rain, pouring down in torrents, and so dark it was impossible to find the way. Some time after midnight Luckey was compelled to halt and wait for daylight. As soon as it was light he found some corn, fed the horses, and started on. When the command got to Canton they found something to eat and then went down to the Etowah river to cross; found it swollen by the rains of the night and it looked dangerous to attempt to cross it. Finally a couple of dugouts were found and the men commenced to ferry over. A part was gotten safely across and some one suggested that the rest of the horses would have to be shot, but Davy Cosgrove of Company K swore that if anyone shot Mollie there would be somebody else shot. It was then decided to drive the horses in and give them a chance. A number were drowned in crossing, and it was dark before the command were all across and started on the march down the river to Cartersville. About midnight we struck the pickets of the Fifth Ohio Cavalry and camped with them until morning.

Starting out on the morning of the 7th, we crossed the Etowah again on a pontoon bridge near Cartersville and reached Allatoona in the afternoon. The place bore all the signs of a fierce conflict. Many of the Confederate dead lay unburied on the field. We fed and rested our horses, and then resumed the march by the way of Ackworth and Big Shanty. Reaching Kenesaw, Captain Luckey reported to General Sherman, after which we rejoined the regiment near Marietta.

October 5th—On the march at 6:30. Colonel Eggleston, First Ohio, in command of the brigade since Colonel Long was wounded at Lovejoys Station. Troops crossing the river on three pontoon bridges; detachments of the Third along the road from the river to Marietta.

October 7th—Sherman on Kenesaw directing the movements of the army from signal station; the railroad torn up by the rebels will soon be repaired; artillery firing in the direction of Dallas.

October 9th—On the march at 7 a. m.; passed through Marietta and to the left of Kenesaw Mountain, marching in the direction of New Hope Church. The country is entirely cleaned up of forage. Breastworks and fortifications everywhere. We camped about four miles from Dallas.

October 10th—The division on the move at 6 a. m., the Second Brigade in advance. Crossed Pumpkinvine creek; camped at Stilesboro, south of Etowah river.

October 11th—In the saddle soon after midnight, and after some delays got started, heading towards Rome. We crossed and recrossed the Etowah river; halted for breakfast at 9 a. m. Some skirmishing during the forenoon. Election day in Ohio, and the Second Brigade is voting for member of congress and state officers. The ballot boxes and election officers are in ambulances. The men on the skirmish line were relieved and came in to vote. Fighting a double battle, front and rear; Confederates in front, Copperheads in the rear; bullets for one, ballots for the other. It was a busy day. We marched thirty-five miles, driving the enemy before us, at the same time doing our duty as American citizens at the ballot box. Camped one mile south of Rome.

October 12th—Reveille at 5 a. m., on the march at 8. Crossed the Etowah and Oostenaula rivers; ran into the rebel cavalry, Ross and Armstrong's Brigades, drove them about five miles and camped near the Oostenaula. Skirmishing on picket line all night; one of our pickets wounded.

October 13th—In the saddle early. Found the enemy a short distance from our pickets and commenced driving them; the Third Brigade dismounted and advanced in line, the First and Second Brigades mounted in support of the Third. At the entrance to Chattooga valley the enemy took a strong position and made a stand. The Third Brigade going in dismounted, soon drove them out, when the First Brigade went forward, charging with the saber, killing and capturing more than 100 men, one battle flag and two pieces of artillery.

October 14th—On the march at 6:30. We recrossed the Oostenaula; passed through Rome; took the Kingston road, going into camp six miles south of Adairsville.

October 15th—Marched out at 6:30; road blocked with wagon train of the Twenty-third Army Corps. Passed through Adairsville, marching east of the railroad. At noon we found forage and halted to feed. Encamped two miles south of Resaca.

October 16th—Moved out at 7:30; crossed the Oostenaula river at Resaca; encamped a short distance northwest of the town. No feed for horses. Foragers went out five miles after corn.

October 17th—Marched at 8 a. m.; progress slow. We are headed toward Snake Creek Gap. About noon we turned to the left, crossing Big and Little Snake creeks, marching on the Summerville road. We encamped at dark.

October 18th—Started out at 6:30. Crossed Johns creek at Morris Mills during the forenoon. Passed Floyd's Springs; crossed Armachee creek; camped near Summerville.

October 19th—Marched at 6, Third Ohio in the advance. Passed the Twenty-third Army Corps two miles out. Found the roads blockaded with fallen timber. The pioneers went forward and soon had the road so we could pass. Crossed Chattooga river, passed through Summerville. Found the Fifteenth and Twenty-third Army Corps here. Took the road toward Cedar Bluffs. About five miles out we ran on to Wheeler's Cavalry. The Third Ohio, dismounted, deployed and went forward, driving them about ten miles, when we halted on account of darkness, about twelve miles from Cedar Bluff.

October 20th—In the saddle early, the Third Brigade in the advance, the Third Ohio rear guard. The advance skirmishing with the rebels. Drove them across Little river; marched along Chattooga river and through the valley.

October 21st—The Second Brigade started out at 8 a. m., the Third Ohio in the advance. Marched to Edwards Ferry on the Coosa river by the way of Round Mountain Furnace. Countermarched to the furnace and took the road toward Gadsden, down the Coosa river. Came upon the enemy and drove them for two miles, and camped at 3 p. m. The First and Third Brigades marched in the direction of Blue pond, skirmishing with the enemy.

October 22d—Did not move until 2 p. m. Marched to Blue Pond, and turned towards Gadsden, and went into camp ten miles from Little river camp ground.

October 23d—Moved out at 8 a. m., General Elliott, chief of cavalry, with us, heading towards Gadsden. About one mile from camp we came upon the enemy posted behind entrenchments, with artillery. After feeling of them, we returned to last night's camp ground.

October 24th—Moved one mile beyond our former camp ground on Little river and went into bivouac at 2 p. m. Supply train came up and we received rations and mail.

October 25th—Reveille at 2 a. m.; on the march at 3:30, headed toward Gadsden. Came up with the infantry about 9 a. m., the Fifteenth and Seventeenth Army Corps. The Third Ohio sent forward on the skirmish line. The enemy had entrenched about fourteen miles from Gadsden. The infantry drove them out of their entrenchments and the Third Ohio drove them for seven miles. At one point the rebel cavalry rallied, making a charge on the skirmish line and driving them back on to the main column. We encamped nine miles from Gadsden.

CHAPTER XIX.

SHERMAN GOES TO THE SEA

October 26th—Boots and saddles sounded at 5 a. m. Moved out at 8 o'clock. Camped at our old camp ground on Little river. General Hood's movements now indicating that his objective was Nashville by the way of Decatur and Florence, General Sherman determined to follow him no further, but to cut loose, destroy Atlanta, and march to the sea, leaving General Thomas in command of the troops in Tennessee with which to meet and vanquish Hood. Sherman withdrew from Alabama by the way of Rome to Kingston, where he made preparations for his great march through the heart of Georgia. While General Thomas at Nashville proceeded to gather together his scattered forces and stop Hood's advance. General Wilson was placed in command of all the cavalry, under General Thomas.

October 27th—The Third Brigade and the Third Ohio went out on a scout. Marched out on the Jacksonville road to Terrapin creek and camped. The next morning we started out at 6 o'clock; ran into a strong rebel force about three miles from Ludaga. Their position was too strong for us to force and we moved back in the direction of Cedar Bluff On the 29th we marched within eight miles of Rome, and on the 31st marched to Rome and turned over all our serviceable horses to the Third Division, under General Kilpatrick, which was to go with General Sherman in his march to the sea.

*Report of Brigadier-General Kenner Garrard, U. S. Army, commanding
Second Cavalry Division.*

HEADQUARTERS SECOND CAVALRY DIVISION,
NASHVILLE, TENN., *November* 16, 1864.

GENERAL: Before the new organization of the cavalry, and during
the time General Elliott was chief of cavalry, this division was actively
employed during the operations of the army against Hood. For the
movements of the division during that time, I now have the honor to
make a report.

About the 18th of September, while encamped at Blake's Mill and
Roswell, owing to the suspected movements of the enemy, I was ordered
to the vicinity of Sandtown, and a reconnaissance on the west branch
of the river by a portion of my division ascertained that Jackson's
cavalry had crossed and a portion of the rebel infantry was crossing, and
the rest of Hood's army moving from Jonesboro toward the West Point
Railroad and the river. I was then ordered back to Blake's Mill by
Powder Springs, Acworth, Canton, and Roswell; reached my camp on
the 30th and found orders to move at once to Sweet Water and join
Kilpatrick. On the 3d camped on Sweet Water, crossing the river at the
railroad bridge. On the 4th moved to Kenesaw, passing near Marietta,
and struck the pickets of the rebel infantry near the railroad. At the
time the railroad near Big Shanty was being destroyed, and in view a
long line of the enemy's infantry lay across the road and behind breastworks. On the 5th moved out toward Lost Mountain and skirmished
all day. The Fourth Regulars made a bold advance on the road from
near Lost Mountain toward Allatoona, and drove in the enemy's pickets
and ran the reserves from some works. It was afterward ascertained
from the rebels that the action of the division on this day caused the
enemy to fall back from Allatoona, a report reaching them in the hottest
part of the action there, that they had been cut off from their army and
that a division of cavalry was advancing on their rear. On the 7th was
ordered to gain the cross-roads at New Hope Church to obtain information. Within two miles of the church struck Armstrong's brigade. After
some heavy skirmishing, drove him from the cross-roads and to within
a mile of Dallas. Captured a brigadier-general and a colonel in an ambulance passing from the rear of the infantry to the cavalry. The Fourth
Regiment had the advance and made the capture. On the 8th and 9th
remained near New Hope, but sent strong detachments toward Burnt
Hickory through Dallas and to within five miles of Van Wert, and kept
the major-general commanding fully informed of the movements and
course of the enemy. On the 10th moved to Stilesborough, and at 11 p.
m. moved on again toward Rome, at which place I arrived early on the

afternoon of the 11th. As the route taken approached near the enemy, considerable opposition was met with on the way, but full information concerning the enemy was obtained. He had crossed most of his infantry at Quincy's Ferry, ten miles below Rome, and was moving in the direction of Dalton. On the 13th the enemy's cavalry appeared on the hills west of Rome. The division crossed the Etowah and then the Oostenaula, and drove the enemy away and five miles down the road toward Coosaville. On the 13th received orders to find out if the enemy had taken up his pontoon bridge, and if so, on which side of the river. The Twenty-third Corps was ordered to support me. After advancing some four miles, struck the enemy. The First Ohio was dismounted as skirmishers, and the Third Ohio was sent out on the flanks mounted, and the Third Brigade, Miller's, was at once dismounted and brought up in line, two regiments on each side of the road. The advance was ordered, and the First Brigade (Jennings commanding) was ordered up, passing the led horses.

The enemy, after a little skirmishing, fell back, but our advance continued. Soon the enemy opened artillery. We were moving through woods, and could not see his position, but continued to advance, the Third Brigade and First Ohio in line on both sides of the road, dismounted, the First Brigade mounted in column of fours in the road, the head of column on line with the dismounted men and two companies of the Third Ohio mounted on each flank. When within long rifle range of their position, the woods ended, and large open cornfields lay between us and the enemy, who had formed line beyond a creek on a ridge in the edge of some timber. Just as the line was about to emerge from the woods, the charge was ordered. The enemy stood firing his artillery up to the last moment, and the cannoneers used their pistols in defense of their pieces. The artillery, two pieces, was captured just as it was limbered up. The enemy was routed and pursued on several different roads. Their killed, wounded, and captured, which fell into our hands, was over seventy, but every pursuing party reported large numbers left wounded and killed on the roads and in the woods. The main body was pursued on the Coosaville road fourteen miles below Rome and full and complete information was gained in regard to the pontoon bridge. The rebel cavalry was Allen's division, of Wheeler's Corps. One of the brigades was the Texas Brigade. A set of colors of one of the Texas regiments was captured. The loss on our side was fourteen killed and wounded and between thirty and forty horses. The enemy was completely routed, and I learned afterward it was more than three days before this rebel division of cavalry could be collected together. The 14th, 15th, and 16th were occupied in marching from Rome, via. Woodlands, to Resaca and Snake Creek Gap. On the 18th passed around John's Mountain and through Dirt Town en route to Summerville. On the 19th passed through Gover's Gap and Summerville and followed the road to Gaylesville; struck the enemy a few miles from Summerville and drove him until dark. On the 20th advanced through Gaylesville, skirmishing, and drove the enemy beyond Little river. On the 21st advanced through Blue Pond; took the road to Gadsden; sharp skirmishing, and toward evening engaged a division and a brigade formed behind breastworks; charged the works and took them. On the 22d, 23d, and 24th employed in gaining information and compelled to drive the enemy from point to point. On the 25th the new organization was ordered, but the division was employed as before every day until the order to move to Nashville was issued.

Very respectfully, your obedient servant,

K. GARRARD,
Brigadier-General, Commanding Division.

BRIG. GEN. W. D. WHIPPLE,
Chief of Staff, Department of the Cumberland.

By the following Special Orders No. 3, General Long, who had been promoted on the recommendation of General Thomas, was assigned to the command of the Second Cavalry Division.

HDQRS. CAV. CORPS, MIL. DIV. OF THE MISSISSIPPI,
ROME, GA., *October 29,* 1864.

I. Brigadier-General Garrard will immediately organize his division into two brigades, and after furnishing what horses General Kilpatrick requires, mount the Second Brigade of the new organization. As soon as this duty is accomplished he will proceed to Nashville with the division, taking all horses unfit for field service, and gathering all dismounted men found along its route.

Upon his arrival at Nashville General Garrard will turn over the men and command of his division to Brigadier-General Eli Long.

II. Brigadier-General Eli Long will relieve, at Nashville, Tenn., Brigadier-General K. Garrard from the command of the Second Division, Cavalry Corps, Military Division of the Mississippi.

Upon assuming command General Long will remain in Nashville for the purpose of collecting, remounting, and equipping the dismounted men of his division there.

By command of Brevet Major-General Wilson.

E. B. BEAUMONT,
Captain and Acting Assistant Adjutant-General.

November 1st—We started out at 2 p. m. Some of the men were mounted on mules and unserviceable horses; the balance on foot. Camped about six miles from Rome on the Calhoun road. The next day we arrived at Calhoun about noon, and on the 4th took cars for Nashville, by the way of Dalton and Cleveland. Arriving at Chattanooga on the evening of the 5th, we went into camp, awaiting transportation. All trains being used to carry infantry troops back to Nashville.

Tuesday, November 8th, 1864—Presidential election, and the soldiers by a very large majority cast their ballots for Abraham Lincoln, and a vigorous prosecution of the war. We lay at Chattanooga until the 11th, when we broke up camp and took the train for Nashville. Arriving the next day at 10 o'clock, we put up at the Zollicoffer House for the night. In those days when we stopped in Nashville we always put up at the Zollicoffer, and while there was considerable grumbling amongst the patrons of that famous hotel in regard to the bill of fare and sleeping accommodations, yet it had a steady patronage, and no kicking on the rates. The next morning we moved our baggage out to Camp Smith, where we found a part of our regiment and the First Ohio. The next morning we took train for Louisville, arriving on the morning of the 15th. We went into camp two miles out on the Preston St. pike, to wait for horses. While we lay at Louisville we had drills, dress parades, and inspections, dismounted. There being no prospect of getting any horses, a detail of twenty men from each company, under a commissioned officer, was made on the 8th of December. And mounted on horses borrowed from the Fourth Michigan Cavalry, a cordon of guards was put around the city, and no one allowed to go out. The men gathered up every good saddle horse they could find in the city. About 700 were brought into camp. The citizens came into camp by scores, complaining and pleading for their horses. But it was no use. General Long was inexorable. The government needed the horses, and if the people refused to sell them, we would take them under the law of military necessity, and settle for them afterwards. The impressment of horses continued for several days, many of the citizens hiding them in cellars and out of the way places. The country was scoured for miles in every direction.

The following official correspondence indicates the confidence that General Long had in Colonel Seidel:

HDQRS. CAV. CORPS, MILITARY DIV. OF THE MISSISSIPPI,
NASHVILLE, TENN., *Nov. 29, 1864.*

BRIG. GEN. ELI LONG,
Comdg. Second Division of Cavalry.

GENERAL: General Wilson requested Major Price to ask what two regiments you would prefer having transferred from your division to be replaced by one Indiana regiment to be assigned to it. The strength of the Indiana regiment will probably be as large as that of the two regiments transferred.

I am, General, very respectfully, your obedient servant,

E. B. BEAUMONT,
Major, and Assistant Adjutant-General.

The following was General Long's reply:

CAMP NEAR LOUISVILLE, KY., *November* 29, 1864.

MAJOR E. B. BEAUMONT,
   A. A. G., Cavalry Corps, Mil. Div. of the Miss., Nashville, Tenn.

MAJOR: Please have the order changing the regiments in the division (if the order is to be issued) made out as soon as you can conveniently.

I want Colonel Seidel of the Third Ohio Cavalry, who is a fighting man and will do good work with the brigade, to command it, and the sooner the Fourth Michigan Cavalry and the First Ohio Cavalry, both of whose Colonels rank him, are taken out of the brigade, the greater it will facilitate me in organizing it and rendering it efficient.

Hoping that you will attend to this matter as soon as you can, I am, very truly yours,   ELI LONG.

The only thing that was done in the matter was the transfer of the First Ohio Cavalry to Upton's Division, no other regiment being sent to replace it.

CHAPTER XX.

MARCHING SOUTH AGAIN

We remained at Louisville until Christmas Day, 1864, when we again took up our march southward, full of the hope that the war would be speedily ended. Everything indicated that this was to be the final campaign. Hood's army had received a staggering blow at Franklin and was overwhelmingly defeated at Nashville, and his broken, demoralized forces driven across the Tennessee and scattered in every direction. Sherman had made his famous march to the sea, and was ready to start north through the Carolinas, and if need be, take Richmond from the South. While the veterans of the Army of the Potomac, under General Grant, were crowding Lee and his brave army to the last extremity. Christmas night we camped at Mt. Washington and the next day marched to Bardstown and went into camp near the fair grounds, where the First Battalion had its fight with Wharton in October, 1862. Captain McCormick of Colonel Minty's staff and Surgeon Shirk were shot by some of Munday's band of guerrillas.

On the 29th General Long and the rest of the division came up. The weather was very cold.

December 30th—Weather still cold. On the march early. We camped at New Haven on the Lebanon branch of the L. & N. Railroad.

December 31st—The year 1864 went out as it came in—very cold. Reveille at 4 a. m.; on the road soon after 6. Passed through Hodgensville. It was near here that Lincoln was born; a rough, hilly country; the roads very bad. We camped at Elizabethtown, where we bade the old year, with all its hardships and privations, its marches, bivouacs and battles, good-bye.

January 1st, 1865—A cold, clear day; the thermometer registered 8 degrees below zero in the middle of the forenoon. On the march at 9 o'clock. Roads bad and very rough; camped at Sonora, on Nolin's creek. The Third Ohio had the advance during the day. We marched sixteen miles.

Janury 2d—The morning was cold, but the sun came out bright and the snow melted, making the roads muddy. Reveille at 4 o'clock, but we did not march until 7. The road was rough until we reached the pike, four miles north of Mumfordsville, which place we reached about noon. The First Brigade crossed Green river at the ford; the Second Brigade camped on the north side; forage plenty. The next morning the wagon train and part of the Second Brigade crossed the river, the Third Ohio remaining on the north side.

January 4th—The Third Ohio crossed the river and the division moved forward, the regiment camping at Bells Station.

January 5th—Reveille at 4 o'clock; on the march at 7. The roads good. We arrived at Bowling Green about noon, and camped about three miles south of the town, near Lost river. The 5th was a cold, wet, disagreeable day, the rain turning to snow during the afternoon. We were on the march at the usual hour, camping at night about three miles from Franklin, Ky. Clothing and blankets wet.

January 6th—The weather a duplicate of yesterday, only worse. On the march as usual. Camped about two miles from Franklin. The 7th was an improvement as regards weather. The sun came out warm and the snow soon melted. We were on the road at the usual hour. Passed through Mitchelville, Tenn., and camped twenty-seven miles north of Nashville. The next day we marched to Edgefield, on the north bank of the Cumberland river, opposite Nashville. The regiment lay at Edgefield until the 12th. All excess baggage was loaded on a boat to go to Eastport, Miss. We crossed the Cumberland on the railroad bridge, and went into camp some three miles south of Nashville, on the Franklin pike, on the battle ground where Hood's army was so signally defeated four weeks ago. Signs of a fierce conflict are everywhere visible.

January 13th—On the march at the usual hour; the roads everywhere in bad condition. The country shows the effect produced by the march of armies; very few fences left; the country cleaned up of all forage; many of the inhabitants leaving and going North. This was a very wealthy and fertile section before the war, but the iron heel has been heavy upon it. We went into camp one mile south of Franklin. On the 14th we moved up to Columbia, camping on the north side of Duck river, the water too high to cross. The next day Miller's Brigade came up. On the 16th a pontoon was laid across the river and McCook's and Johnson's Divisions commenced to cross. But the bridge parted before they were all over. They got the bridge repaired, but it broke again on the 17th. Although we succeeded in getting supplies across from Columbia, and on the 18th the water had settled sufficiently for us to ford it. We passed through Columbia, camping about three miles out on the Mt. Pleasant pike, near our old camp ground of last spring. Colonel Seidel was mustered out, bidding the regiment good-bye and starting North, which leaves Colonel H. N. Howland in command.

January 19th—On the march at the usual hour, and as we move over the road how many of the scenes which have now become familiar remind us of the past days. We first marched over this road in the spring of '62, when we were on the way to Shiloh. Again after our reenlistment one year ago, we started out over this same road to join Sherman in his victorious campaign against Atlanta, and now we trust that we are marching on to victory and the final campaign of the war. We passed again the home of Bishop Polk, the reverend General of the Southern Confederacy, who had sealed his devotion to the cause with his life's blood since we passed his home last year, having been killed by a cannon shot on Pine Mountain in June. We passed through Mt. Pleasant and camped at Faust's Springs, which had been a pleasure resort previous to the war.

January 20th—On the march as usual; camped thirteen miles north of Waynesboro; very little forage. The country almost deserted. The next day we arrived at Waynesboro about noon. Forage more plentiful; a better country. The brigade camped on Green river.

January 22d—On the march as usual. We camped on Bear creek, in Pleasant valley. The roads bad, and the wagon train did not come up; it camped five miles back. The next morning at 10:30 train descended the ridge and we moved on at 2 p. m. The roads very bad; we only made about ten miles and camped at 9 p. m.

January 24th—The brigade halted and the wagon train moved on toward Gravelly Springs. Rations getting short, and foragers were sent out; they brought in a supply of grain. On the morning of the 25th we started on after the train, and overtook it about eight miles from Thornton's, where we waited for the mounted infantry to come up; then moved forward and arrived at Gravelly Springs, about two miles north of the Tennessee river, and camped at 4 p. m. We are thirteen miles from East-port, Mississippi; forage plenty, but rations scarce and no foraging allowed. Boats with rations cannot get up the river on account of ice. The men getting some meal ground at the mills, but living mainly on parched corn. On the 28th a small amount of meal and pork was issued. Orders from headquarters were strictly against all foraging. In fact, there was very little to be found on the north side of the river, and as the river was patroled, it was difficult to get over, and there was danger of capture. Yet there were many foraging parties that managed to slip through in the night time, and if they could not get back before daylight, would remain under cover until the next night, when they would come in under the cover of darkness.

January 29th—Sunday, as General Wilson was riding through the camp of the Second Brigade some of the Fourth Ohio men yelled, "Hard tack! Hard tack!" The General became very angry; and declaring that he would give us "hard tack," ordered the brigade under arms and into line and kept them until 11 p. m., some seven or eight hours. We lay in camp at Gravelly Springs until March 13th. After February 1st rations came more regularly. The men were kept busily drilling, having inspec-tions, reviews, dress parades, patrol and picket, unloading transports, etc. etc.; getting supplies and everything in good shape for a campaign. Chap-lain Cosier was with the regiment, and he was an ideal chaplain; had services every Sabbath when possible, and always preaching good, strong sermons. He was loved and respected by all. In time of battle he was always up at the front to render assistance.

In the reorganization of the Cavalry Corps under General James H. Wilson for the campaign of 1865, the Second Division, under the com-mand of General Eli Long, was composed of two brigades. The First Brigade consisted of the Seventeenth and Seventy-second Indiana and the Ninety-eighth and One Hundred and Twenty-third Illinois Mounted Infantry, under command of Colonel Miller, the Second Brigade was composed of the Third and Fourth Ohio, the Fourth Michigan, and the Seventh Pennsylvania Cavalry, under command of Colonel Minty. The entire division was armed with Spencers. The Fourth United States Cavalry had been assigned to General Wilson's headquarters, and the First Ohio to General Upton's Fourth Division. The Chicago Board of Trade Battery was still with the Second Division.

CHAPTER XXI.

THE WILSON RAID

March 13th—The Second Brigade started out at 3 a. m. Marched down the river to Waterloo, and crossed on ferryboats to Eastport, going into camp at Chickasaw. By the 15th the Second Division and wagon train were all across to the south side of the Tennessee, and all is activity and hustle, getting ready to move, disposing of all superfluous baggage, loading wagon trains with rations and ammunition, issuing quartermasters and commissary stores, shoeing horses, etc. Everything indicated an important movement. General Wilson's train of 250 wagons loaded with supplies for the expedition and guarded by 1500 dismounted men under Major Archer, commenced to move out on the 19th. On the 21st the boats came up with forage and rations, which were issued to the command, and the next morning at 5 o'clock the Second Brigade moved out and went into camp four miles south of Buzzards Roost, Alabama. On the 23d we marched to Franklin, Companies I and K of the Third guarding the wagon train and did not reach camp until 9 p. m. On the 24th we passed through Russellville, camping on the Tuscaloosa road, eight miles south of the town. On the 25th the division on the march at usual hour, 5 a. m. A detachment from the Third was sent out with Captain Lewis, topographical engineer on General Long's staff. The brigade in its march crossed Little and Big Bear creeks, the latter at Allen's Factory, which was burned by Colonel Streight when on his raid in 1863. We camped at Underwood's Mill. On the 26th we marched to within five miles of Thornhill, camping on Splunge creek; roads bad. Compelled to repair roads and build bridges, we were late getting into camp. The detachment of the regiment out with Captain Lewis did not get in until after midnight. On the 27th we marched to Jasper and found more swampy country and bad roads, which we were compelled to repair. The Seventh Pennsylvania built a bridge across Clear creek.

March 28th—We remained at Jasper until 3 p. m. Rations and forage issued. The town showed the effects of war, most of the buildings having been burned. We camped late at night at Mulberry Fork of the Black Warrior river. Found the roads very bad. The wagons did not get to camp that night, but came up in the morning of the 29th. We have been having so much rain that the rivers and creeks are both deep and rapid, many of them difficult to cross. In crossing the Mulberry the horses had to swim. One man belonging to the Seventeenth Indiana was drowned. The country through which we marched was rough, pine barrens; the people very poor, very little either forage or rations to be had. Eight and one-half miles from Mulberry fork we came to Locust fork. The stream was deeper than Mulberry, but not so wide or rapid. Upton's Division crossed on the 28th, and on the 29th the First and Second Divisions got over. It was a rainy, disagreeable day. We crossed Cane creek and camped five miles from Locust fork.

March 30th—Another rainy day. Reveille at 3 a. m., on the march at 5. Crossed a branch of Black Warrior river, after which we struck a better country, as we neared Elyton. Here we halted and fed our horses; found a lot of flour, meat, molasses, etc. From Chickasaw to Elyton our course had been in a southeasterly direction. From Elyton to Selma it was nearly due south. At Elyton General Croxton's Brigade of the First Division was detached from the command and ordered to go to Tuscaloosa. Six miles south of Elyton we came to Gilmore's furnace (which was built and equipped at a cost of $3,000,000). It was burned, together with houses of workmen, etc. Camped at night on the north bank of the Cahawba river.

March 31st—It rained in the morning, but cleared up, and the rest of the day was fine. We crossed the Cahawba river on the railroad bridge. Dismounting, we led our horses. Many of them had to be blindfolded. Upton's Division in advance; passed through Montevallo; here another large furnace was destroyed. Upton found the enemy in some force and inclined to dispute his further advance. The Third Iowa charged, scattering them and capturing about twenty prisoners. We left Montevallo about 3 p. m., General Long, with the Second Division, taking the road toward Randolph, to the right of the main Selma road; Upton's Division following the main road. There was continued skirmishing, but the enemy were unable to check our advance; camped twelve miles from Montevallo. Two men killed and a number wounded during the day.

April 1st—On the road early; passed through Randolph, General McCook with his Second Brigade, taking the road to Centerville to co-operate with General Croxton against General Jackson, who was reported to be on the road between Tuscaloosa and Centerville, with 4000 men. Generals Long and Upton, marching toward Selma, encountered General Forrest in position and ready to give battle at Ebenezer Church, about four miles north of Plantersville. The First Brigade of Long's Division had the advance, and coming into line, after a brief contest charged, driving them from their position in confusion toward Plantersville. The losses of the enemy in this engagement were three pieces of artillery, 300 prisoners and a large number killed and wounded. It was reported that General Forrest himself was in command and was wounded. Our loss in the engagement was twelve killed and forty wounded. The enemy was driven beyond Plantersville, and the Divisions of Long and Upton camped near that place. We were now only about twenty miles from Selma, and were looking forward to a fierce struggle before we got possession of the city. It was late at night when the Second Brigade of Long's Division, which had covered the rear during the day, got into camp. General Wilson's order for the march on Selma, issued at 8 p. m. April 1st, was as follows:

1st. The Second Division will move out at 5:30 a. m.

2d. The Fourth Division will follow the Second Division.

3d. Should the enemy show a front requiring more than one division to drive him from his position, General Long will move his division to the right of the Selma road in order to allow the Fourth Division to come up on his left. As the corps approaches the city, General Long will incline toward the Summerfield road, and both divisions will, if practical, march in columns of brigade.

Our sick and wounded were left in hospital at Plantersville.

Sunday, April 2d—A fine, warm spring morning; the troops were up early. Long's Second Brigade were on the march at 5:30, the Third Ohio, Lieutenant-Colonel Howland in command, in the advance. A part of Company A, under Lieutenant Skillman, advance guard. The Third Battalion of the regiment, Companies I, K, L and M, under command of Captain Clock, were detached and sent off to the right on a reconnaissance. Our advance guard met with little opposition during the forenoon. They came up occasionally with small bodies of the enemy; skirmishing with them, but no effort was made by the enemy to delay the march of the column. When within about six miles from the city Long's Division moved over to the right and after getting on the Summerfield road followed it. The advance arriving in front of the works about 2:30 p. m. The Third Ohio were deployed as skirmishers, covering the right flank of the division, while it dismounted and got into position for the assault.

The City of Selma is situated on the northern bank of the Alabama river. It was of vast importance to the Southern Confederacy, because of its great foundries, machine shops, arsenal, and factories. In the early years of the war an elaborate system of defences had been built around it, extending from a point on the river west of the city following a northerly course along the east bank of Valley creek for about one mile, and then taking a circular course to the river above, and east of the city. The outer line of works were about three miles in extent, the north and northeast portions of the city being also protected by an almost impassable swamp.

That part of the line of works assaulted and carried by Long's Division consisted of a parapet eight to twelve feet high and about the same thickness, a ditch five feet deep and four feet in width, partly filled with water, and a stockade of heavy posts, five feet high, sharpened at the top and set into the ground firmly in front of the ditch. Forts had been erected at advantageous points along the line, mounting thirty-two cannon, including one thirty-pound Parrott. Behind these works were more than 7000 Confederate troops, commanded by Forrest and half a dozen other Southern Generals.

General Upton's Fourth Division, marching in the rear of General Long's Second Division, continued on the direct road to Selma. The roads upon which the two columns advanced toward the city were nearly parallel to each other and about one mile apart.

Between General Upton and the works of the enemy was a swamp, impassable for cavalry. General Wilson, after examining the works in Upton's front, rode over to General Long's position on the Summerfield road about 4 o'clock, and after dismounting, the two Generals went forward to the skirmish line of the Second Brigade, and creeping forward to the crest of the ridge in their front, made an examination of the enemy's fortifications and the ground in their front. At this time the Second Division was formed with its right (consisting of the Second Brigade) in line of battle with the Summerfield road as its center, and the First Brigade in line on the left of the Second Brigade.

After looking over the grounds in front of the enemy's works, General Wilson ordered General Long to move his First Brigade from its position on the left of the Second Brigade and place it on the right, thus bringing it into position to charge diagonally across the Summerfield road.

When leaving General Long, General Wilson said, "As soon as General Upton gets into position I will have him push forward on the left at a signal gun from his battery, at which time you (General Long) must also advance with your division."

General Wilson's plan of attack was for General Long to form his division on the Summerfield road, and General Upton forming on the Range Line road, both divisions to attack simultaneously. As Upton had the longest distance to march to get into position, he, when ready, was to give the signal by firing a single cannon.

General Long formed line of battle under cover of a ridge out of range of musketry fire but exposed to the fire of the artillery from the forts, which did little damage, however. The following regiments, dismounted, formed the line of assault: From right to left, Seventeenth Indiana, One Hundred and Twenty-third Illinois, and Ninety-eighth Illinois, of the First Brigade; the Fourth Ohio and Seventh Pennsylvania of the Second Brigade. The Chicago Board of Trade Battery occupied a position on a rise of ground near the Summerfield road about three-fourths of a mile from the enemy's line of works. The Fourth Michigan was posted near the battery. Four Companies of the Seventy-second Indiana, of the First Brigade, were guarding the wagon train. Five Companies were posted at a creek covering the rear, and one Company

was supporting the battery. Soon after reaching its position in front
of the works at Selma, four Companies of the Ninety-eighth Illinois
were sent out on the Summerfield road to guard against any force of the
enemy coming from that direction, leaving only eleven officers and 161
men from that regiment to take part in the assault. General Long, contemplating the strength of the works in his front, and the forces of the
enemy defending them, and then looking at his own small division, only
1550 men in line, thought the work cut out for him was rather a large
job for his small force, and sent a note to General Wilson, asking him
to change his plan of attack, and order General Upton to form the
Fourth Division in the rear of the Second Division and support it in its
assault on the rebel stronghold. General Long was at first led to believe
that General Wilson approved the change, but afterward for some reason
changed his mind and adhered to his original plan. Meanwhile the
afternoon was fast passing and General Long, knowing that the enemy
in his front were being constantly reinforced, and fearing an attack from
the rear, became impatient at the delay, and resolved to attack at once,
without waiting for Upton's signal gun on the left. He sent his orders
to the brigade commanders and to Captain Robinson of the battery,
telling him that he intended to move on the works and that he was to
support the division with the battery. The following extracts are from
General Long's report of the battle:

"I determined to make the assault at once, without waiting for the
signal gun on the left. I moved forward at 5 p. m., my entire line
advancing promptly, and in less than twenty-five minutes after the command to advance had been given the works were ours. The works
carried consisted of a heavy line of earthworks eight or twelve feet in
height, and fifteen feet in thickness at the base, with a ditch in front
partly filled with water, four feet in width and five feet deep, and in front
of this a stockade or picket of heavy posts planted firmly in the ground,
five feet high and sharpened at the top. Four heavy forts with artillery
in position also covered the ground over which the men advanced. The
ground was rough, and a deep ravine had to be passed before the works
could be reached. The men fully understood the difficulties before them.
There was no flinching; all seemed confident of their ability to overcome
them. As soon as we uncovered the hill about 600 yards from the earthworks the enemy opened a rapid and destructive fire of musketry and
artillery on the line. But we moved forward steadily until within short
range, when a rapid fire was opened by our Spencers, and with a cheer
the men started forward for the works on a run, sweeping forward in
solid line over fences and ravine, scaling the stockade and on the works
with resistless force. The enemy fighting stubbornly, many of them
clubbing their guns, but forced to retreat in greatest disorder. Our men

continuing in pursuit through the city, and taking many prisoners.
* * * According to General Forrest's own statement his force exceeded the assaulting force in numbers. My entire force in the charge was 1550 officers and men. The carrying of these works and the town by my division resulted in the capture of over 2000 prisoners.

"We captured no less than twenty pieces of artillery in position, including one thirty-pounder Parrott, and a large number of small arms."

"When within 150 yards of the works on the Summerfield and Selma road I was wounded and carried off the field, a short time after which, General Wilson was riding by and inquired of my aide-de-camp, Lieutenant Deering, if we had carried the works. I had the satisfaction of hearing the answer in the affirmative.

"The Chicago Board of Trade Battery, commanded by Captain Geo. I. Robinson, occupied a position on the hill in the rear of my line. Their rapid and effective firing contributed greatly to the demoralization of the enemy. It was afterward reported to me that this battery did good and efficient service in assisting the driving of the enemy through the town. I have no doubt from the manner in which it had always executed its work hitherto, that it did everything possible to be done. In this affair the entire division did their whole duty, than which no greater praise can be given to a soldier.

"The First Brigade, owing to longer practice and being more accustomed to fighting on foot, probably kept a better line than the Second Brigade, but so far as courage is concerned and the time that different regiments and portions of the division approached the works, no appreciable difference could be seen or was reported to me."

When the division advanced to the assault the Third Ohio was ordered to their horses, and coming up near the Summerfield road received orders to charge into the city. While most of the guns in this part of the rebel works had been captured and were silent, yet the inner line of works were still held by the enemy and one of the forts that covered the Summerfield road was still unsubdued. General Wilson, arriving on this part of the field, sent his escort, the Fourth United States, on a charge against this second line. They coming up against some obstructions under fire from the guns in the fort recoiled and were driven back in some confusion through our ranks. Lieutenant Colonel Howland gave the command forward and charging down the road we went through and over the works, the enemy being in full retreat.

As we charged down the road General Wilson and staff, mounted, were on a rise of ground to our left waving their hats and cheering us on. Before we reached the works the shades of night were falling, and we could see the flashes of the guns after the fort was hidden in darkness.

The regiment was then dismounted, and together with the Fourth Michigan entered the city, capturing some prisoners. After Long's Division had carried the works in their front, Upton charged into the city on the Range Line road, meeting with but little resistance, and the two divisions met in the heart of the city. Forrest and a large part of his command escaped over the Burnsville road, and thus it was that most of the prisoners and battle flags were captured by Upton's men, who intercepted them in their flight from the fierce onslaught of the Second Division. There was little rest in camp that night. With many of the men the one thing most to be desired was a good square meal. One squad of the Third Ohio happened on to the place where a fine turkey had been roasted and a sumptuous dinner prepared for General Forrest and his staff, to be eaten after the fight. But after the fight they had pressing engagements elsewhere. Well, the Third Ohio was equal to an occasion of that kind, and that particular squad enjoyed the dinner, although none of the ladies of the household appeared and bade them welcome.

The Third Battalion of the regiment, under Captain Clock, encountered a force of the enemy and had a narrow escape from capture. In the skirmish that ensued the battalion lost one man killed, three men wounded and one officer and seven men captured. By making a wide detour and returning to the Selma and Plantersville road it escaped. Sending a couple of messengers in advance to report to General Long, Captain Clock followed with his command, reaching Selma late at night, having marched forty miles. Lieutenant D. C. Lewis of Company M and a number of the men captured perished at the time of the explosion on the steamer Sultana.

April 3d—General Long having been wounded in the battle of yesterday, Colonel Minty took command of the division and Lieutenant-Colonel Howland succeeded to the command of the brigade, leaving Major Livermore in command of the regiment. General Wilson having succeeded in taking Selma now wished to get into communication with General McCook, whose division had been detached, the First Brigade, under General Croxton, at Elyton on March 30th, to proceed against Tuscaloosa. At Randolph on April 1st, it having been learned that General Croxton was confronted by a superior force of the enemy at Trion, General McCook was sent to reinforce him. At 7 a. m. April 3d Captain Howland, in command of a battalion of the Third Ohio, was sent with a dispatch to General McCook, notifying him of the capture of Selma and ordering him to rejoin the command. The battalion marched to Summerfield, where they found a small force of the enemy. Following them closely, our men finally charged and drove them through the town, but as they took the road that our men wished to take, there was no other course for them to pursue but to go after them. Noticing that the road looked as if an army had marched over it, the question was asked of some of the citizens, what troops were in our front, and we were answered, Chalmer's Division of Forrest's forces. They continued in front of the battalion for a number of miles, our men charging into their rear and hurrying them along. Finally they turned off on a road leading south, while Howland and his men continued west. The battalion marched to Perryville, where they burned a lot of rebel supplies, and learned that General McCook was on another road marching to Selma. Taking the back track, they came across McCook at Summerfield, delivered their dispatches and returned to Selma.

General Croxton with his brigade did not rejoin the command until May 1st at Macon, having been separated from it one month, during which time they marched over 650 miles in a mountainous country, swimming rivers and fording creeks, destroying iron works, mills, factories, bridges, etc.; having numerous encounters with the enemy, capturing four pieces of artillery, 300 prisoners and a large number of small arms, with a loss to his command of four officers and 168 men killed, wounded, and missing. April 27th General Croxton was met at the Chattahoochee river by a flag of truce from the commanding officer at Newman, informing him of the armistice and claiming protection under it. General Croxton replied that he could not recognize the information as official, but presuming it was true he would trouble nobody who kept out of his way, and would observe the armistice as far as foraging was concerned, but could not consent to discontinue his march.

In the assault and capture of Selma, General Long, commanding the Second Division; Colonel Miller, commanding the First Brigade; Lieutenant-Colonel Biggs, commanding the One Hundred and Twenty-third Illinois; Colonel McCormick, commanding the Seventh Pennsylvania, were wounded. Lieutenant-Colonel Dobb, commading the Fourth Ohio, was killed. The losses in the division were four officers and thirty-eight men killed, twenty-six officers and 245 men wounded, and one officer and seven men missing. Total, 320.

The losses in Upton's (Fourth) Division were small, as the enemy in his front abandoned their works without resistance after Long's Division had carried the works in their front. Immense stores of war material were captured at Selma, but we will not enumerate them here, but leave them for the final summing up at the end of the Wilson raid.

The following is Major Livermore's report of operations April 1st and 2d:

HEADQUARTERS THIRD OHIO VOLUNTEER CAVALRY,
SELMA, ALA., *April* 5th, 1865.

MAJOR: I have the honor to make the following report of operations on the 1st and 2d instant:

On the 1st the regiment marched forty-six miles, but took no part in the engagement. On the 2d instant marched in advance of division toward this place, skirmishing occasionally with the enemy's rear guard until within sight of his works, when two battalions (the Third Battalion having been sent to the right of the road) were deployed as skirmishers (mounted), but did not advance until the first line of the enemy's works were captured, when they were ordered to charge the second line of works on the enemy's left in rear of the Fourth United States Cavalry, which was repulsed. The regiment was then dismounted and marched into town, meeting with but slight resistance, capturing about forty prisoners and several horses and mules. The casualties were six men wounded, none dangerously. The Third Battalion (sent to the right) found the enemey in force, and after a skirmish was forced to return by a circuitous route (to avoid being captured) to the main road and follow the column. The loss sustained was two men wounded, one commissioned officer (Lieutenant D. C. Lewis, Company M), and seven enlisted men captured. Total loss of regiment, eight men wounded, one commissioned officer and seven men captured.

Very respectfully, your obedient servant,

D. E. LIVERMORE,
Major, Commanding Third Ohio Volunteer Cavalry.

MAJOR ROBT. BURNS,
Assistant Adjutant-General, Second Cav. Div.

———

On the 3d of April General Forrest. who had escaped from Selma over the Burnsville road, arrived at Plantersville, and captured the hospital with our sick and wounded. The hospital had been left without a guard. He paroled the nurses and slightly wounded, but did not molest the surgeons and the dangerously wounded.

April 5th—A detachment from the regiment went to Cahawba River; found a small body of the enemy west of the river; skirmished with them and captured a number of horses and mules.

April 6th—The wagon train arrived at Selma. A detachment went on a scout to Burnsville; found a few rebels and had a skirmish with them. The arsenals and government's warehouses in Selma were burned. The negroes in large numbers came in with the wagon train. Orders were issued to organize them into three regiments, one for each division. Major Archer of the Third Ohio was promoted to Colonel in command of one of the regiments. The sick and wounded were brought in ambulances from Plantersville. General Wilson met General Forrest at the Cahawba under a flag of truce, but was unable to come to any agreement with him regarding an exchange of prisoners. During the conversation, however, General Wilson learned that General Croxton had had an engagement with Wirt Adams near Bridgeville, forty miles southwest of Tuscaloosa. General Wilson determined to leave Selma as soon as the bridge across the Alabama river could be completed.

April 8th—Pontoon bridge completed in the afternoon and the Second Division, under command of Colonel Minty, got across, although the bridge was broken a number of times during the crossing. The river is about 500 yards wide, with a very rapid current, and deep enough to navigate by steamers of considerable size. The division marched about five miles in the direction of Benton and went into camp.

April 10th—The entire force having gotten across the river, the march toward Montgomery was begun, the First Division, under General McCook, taking the advance, General Upton with the Fourth Division in the center and Colonel Minty with the Second Division bringing up the rear. Encumbered with a large number of prisoners, and our sick and wounded in ambulances and carriages, our march was delayed so that we did not get started until 1 o'clock p. m. Marched eleven miles and camped near Benton at 11 p. m.

April 11th—On the march; progress slow. The Third Ohio on rear guard. Parked the train at Mt. Gilead Church and fed our horses; were compelled to build corduroy road for half a mile across a swamp. Built pontoon bridge across Big Swamp creek; tore down a barn two miles from the crossing to get material to make floor for the bridge. It was 4:30 a. m. April 12th before the rear of the division was across. Sergeant Hill of Company D was drowned near Benton.

April 12th—The regiment marched fifteen miles and camped about fourteen miles west of Montgomery. The roads were swampy and full of holes, and it was necessary to corduroy them in order to get our train over. The First Division was in the advance all the way from Selma, and had considerable skirmishing with the enemy; but when they arrived in front of Montgomery this a. m., the city was surrendered without opposition. By a singular coincidence we, here in the first capital of the Confederacy, received the news that Richmond had fallen.

April 13th—Passed through Montgomery and moved out on the Columbus road, and the next day the command was put in motion for Columbus, Georgia, General Upton with the Fourth Division taking the direct road while Colonel La Grange with the First Brigade of the First Division took the road to Tuskegee; the Second Division still guarding the wagon train in the rear of La Grange's Brigade.

The following report of the capture of the battle flag of the Twelfth Mississippi Cavalry by a small party of men from the Third Ohio explains itself. Comrade Shoef states that the flag is now in the relic room at Columbus, Ohio:

HEADQUARTERS THIRD OHIO CAVALRY,

MACON, GA., *April* 30th, 1865.

MAJOR ROBERT BURNS, *A. A. G.*

MAJOR: I have the honor to forward herewith the battle flag of the Twelfth Mississippi Cavalry, C. S. Army, which was captured with the commanding officer of the regiment, Major Cox, on the 15th instant, about six miles from Tuskegee, Ala., by John H. Shoef, private, Company H, Third Ohio Volunteer Cavalry. He is very desirous of retaining it if he can be allowed to do so.

I am, very respectfully, your obedient servant,

D. E. LIVERMORE,

Major, Commanding Regiment.

———

Columbus, Georgia, is situated on the east bank of the Chattahoochee river. There were several bridges and it was important that at least one or more if possible should be captured before the enemy had time to destroy them. General Upton's Division arrivd in front of the defences of the city during the afternoon of the 16th and was at once gotten into line for a night attack. At 8 o'clock the order for the assault was given and was executed with the energy and enthusiasm which had character- ized all of the movements of the campaign, and after a stubborn contest of two hours duration our men won a complete victory, driving the enemy in confusion across the bridges and following so closely that they had not time to destroy them, although they had made every preparation for doing so. At one of the bridges the rebels had two twelve-pound howitzers loaded with canister in position, but were unable to fire them without killing their own men, our forces being so close after them. The capture of this bridge left General Wilson in position to move at once against Macon.

There were captured at Columbus 1500 prisoners, twenty-four can- non, eight battle flags and immense quantities of Confederate stores of all descriptions. All public property, including the rebel gunboat Jackson, which was almost ready for sea, was destroyed. On the same day Colonel La Grange captured West Point on the Chattahoochee, securing the bridge at that point.

On April 15th the Second Division was delayed bringing the wagon train across a swamp some 300 yards wide. They marched twenty-two miles, camping about three miles east of Tuskegee. April 16th, marched thirty-nine miles and camped after dark ten miles west of Columbus.

CHAPTER XXII.

OCCUPATION OF MACON

April 17th—On the march at 3 a. m. Arrived at Columbus at 7 o'clock; marched through the town and went into camp three miles out on the Macon road. At 5:30 p. m. the Third Ohio, under command of Major Livermore, and the Fourth Michigan, under command of Major Eldridge, Lieutenant-Colonel Pritchard of the Fourth Michigan in command of the expedition, started out on a forced march to capture if possible the double bridges across Flint river on the road to Macon, forty-five miles distant. The command was in light marching order; all pack stock left in camp. Nothing of interest occurred to break the monotony of the night march. At daylight the command moved forward at a trot and the advance guard was ordered to charge and capture everybody that they came in sight of. At Pleasant Hill, four miles from the river, we overtook a refugee train and some rebel soldiers, who showed fight. They soon changed their minds, however. In the skirmish two were killed, one mortally wounded and three captured. From this point a charge for the bridges was ordered and executed with such precipitancy that the guard at the bridges, consisting of fifty men, under instructions to defend and destroy them, was completely surprised, receiving no knowledge of our approach until the head of our column struck the bridge at a gallop, charging across and sweeping everything before it, not allowing the enemy time to fire a volley. A few scattering shots were fired, but without effect. The whole force then broke and fled, some making good their escape, as their horses were fresh, while ours were worn and jaded from their night march and the final charge for the bridges. We chased them about four miles, and then returning to the bridges took position to defend them against any attempt that the enemy might make to recapture and burn them. In addition to securing the bridges we captured five commissioned officers and forty-four enlisted men, fifteen wagons, 150 horses and mules, and a large quantity of commissary stores. In his report Lieutenant-Colonel Pritchard commended Majors Livermore and Eldridge for the good management of their regiments. The rest of the division came up during the afternoon and camped.

April 19th—Started out at 9 a. m. and marched thirteen miles, camping three miles east of Thomaston. In the afternoon Captain Howland with a detachment of the regiment went into the mountains fourteen miles to the north; captured thirty mules from a refugee train. Lieutenant Keller with a detachment went out in the opposite direction and brought in a bunch of horses and mules.

April 20th—The division started out at 3 a. m., the First Brigade in the advance, moving on the direct road to Macon. When near Spring Hill, twenty-one miles from Macon, the advance, the Seventeenth Indiana, came on to a force of the enemy about 400 strong, behind a rail barricade. Dismounting, our men charged, driving them out from one position to another, capturing a number of prisoners. At Tobosofkee creek a force of the enemy about 300 strong had torn a part of the planking off the bridge, set it on fire and were posted behind rail barricades on the east side, and a small force occupied a stone mill about 100 yards below the bridge. The advance went on the bridge at a gallop, but were compelled to halt where the planking was removed. They quickly dismounted, charged across on the burning stringers, routed the enemy and saved the bridge. Three miles east of the creek and about thirteen miles from Macon the advance were met by Brigadier-General Robertson of the Rebel Army with a flag of truce, bearing a dispatch from General Cobb, stating that an armistice between General Sherman and General Johnston had been agreed upon. The advance was halted and the message taken by an officer to Colonel Minty, who sent it on to General Wilson, who was somewhere in the rear, at the same time sending word to General Robertson to return to Macon, and General Wilson's answer would be delivered to him at that place, and also informing him that the column would move forward five minutes after he received this message and that he must keep out of the way.

Colonel Minty sent orders to Lieutenant-Colonel White, commanding the advance, to give the flag of truce five minutes start, and then to push forward and if General Robertson did not keep out of the way, to take him and his party prisoners. The following is from Lieutenant-Colonel Frank White's official report of the capture of Macon:

"The flag of truce detained us about half an hour. I then received orders from Colonel Minty to give them five minutes to get out of the way, and then to drive everything before me and save the bridge over Rocky creek at Bailey's mill. I placed Adjutant W. E. Doyle in charge of the advance guard of fifteen men, giving him instructions and sending him forward at a trot, supporting him closely with the regiment. After going about two miles he came in sight of the flag of truce party covering the rear of a force of about 250 men, said to be Blount's Battalion. They were moving slowly, and evidently trying to delay us. Seeing this, the adjutant, as I had instructed him, charged them, causing the flag of truce to run into the woods, capturing three of the officers that were with it, and driving the rebel cavalry pell-mell along the road. They kept up a continual fire on us for some time, but with no effect. On getting within sight of Rocky Creek bridge the enemy were discovered on foot attempting to set it on fire. The advance drove them off, and pursued them closely to the palisades in the road. Before getting to the bridge the Adjutant had sent to me for a small reinforcement, and I sent him Major Weiler and Lieutenant McDowell with Company E. The Major caught up before getting to the bridge. On arriving at the palisades the advance got up amongst the rebels and some firing ensued, the enemy breaking off the road through the gardens on the right in confusion. The advance tore down a few of the palisades, passed through and rode up near the rebel works. Here Major Weiler and Adjutant Doyle rode up on the works and demanded their surrender, telling the rebels that we had two divisions of our cavalry in their rear. The colonel commanding not being present, the men believed that they were cut off. Subordinate officers surrendered their commands, and the soldiers threw down their arms as directed and marched down to the road, where Lieutenant McDowell took charge of and formed them. The Major and Adjutant were at this time riding along the line of works, telling the men to throw down their arms and surrender; that they were cut off and were our prisoners; that flight was vain and that fighting would avail nothing; and the rebel soldiers were throwing down their arms and hastening to the road, the officers following the men. I came up at this time with the regiment and found the rebel prisoners in line along the road under Lieutenant McDowell. I ordered Adjutant Doyle to the forts on the right of the road to receive their surrender. As soon as the regiment got inside the line of works the entire line surrendered, finding themselves cut off from the town, and Colonel Cumming, who commanded the forces (one brigade) immediately on the road, came down with about 500 men and surrendered to me. I left two companies in charge of prisoners and moved on toward town with the balance of the regiment. At the edge of town I was met by some officers with a flag of truce from General Cobb, asking what terms I would give him if he surrendered the city and forces. My answer was unconditional surrender, and gave the flag five minutes to get out of my way. After passing into the town the distance of four or five squares, another flag of truce met me, stating that General Cobb submitted to my terms, surrendering the city and everything in it. I marched into town and up to General Cobb's headquarters, thus taking formal possession of the city. I placed patrols on duty at once, and camped the regiment in Courthouse square and adjoining street. We captured in the city and in the works Major-General Howell Cobb, Brigadier-Generals Gus W. Smith, Mackall, and Mercer, 3500 prisoners, including over 300 officers of all grades below brigadier-general, five stand of colors, about sixty pieces of artillery and 3000 stand of arms, besides large quantities of quartermaster's, commissary, medical and ordnance stores; also four two-pounder breech-loading Travis guns intended for General Forrest, and a large number of horses and mules.

"We had in the action during the day twenty-one commissioned officers and 500 enlisted men. We lost one killed and two wounded. The four two-pounder (brass) Travis guns were boxed and buried in the smallpox burying ground."

Camped on Rocky creek, about three miles west of town. In the six days since leaving Montgomery we had marched 215 miles. Since leaving the Tennessee river the command had marched upward of 600 miles. General Wilson arrived at Macon in the evening of the 20th, when General Cobb renewed his protest and insisted that he should acknowledge the existence of the armistice and withdraw his troops to the point where they were met by the flag of truce. General Wilson could not take that view of the situation, however, and informed General Cobb that he would not withdraw from the city; but continue to hold it, and consider the garrison, including the generals, prisoners of war, until his acts were disapproved by competent authority after a full investigation of the case.

The war was virtually over. Richmond evacuated; Lee surrendered; Jefferson Davis a fugitive endeavoring to escape from the country; Johnston and his army ready to give up the fight. The Confederacy was going to pieces, and the dawn of peace was at hand. General Wilson in his report to General Thomas enumerates some of the things accomplished by the troops under his command, which, taking into consideration the number of men engaged and the results accomplished, must give it rank as the greatest cavalry raid of our own or any other war. In that report he says:

"Since leaving the Tennessee river the troops under my command have marched an average of 525 miles in twenty-eight days, captured five fortified cities, 23 stand of colors, 288 pieces of artillery, 6820 prisoners, including five generals; have captured and destroyed two gunboats, 99,000 stand of small arms, seven iron works, seven foundries, seven machine shops, two rolling mills, five collieries, thirteen factories, four nitre works, one military university, three C. S. arsenals and contents, one naval armory and contents, one powder magazine and contents, five steamboats, thirty-five locomotives, 565 cars, three railroad bridges, and immense quantities of quartermaster's, commissary, and ordnance stores, of which no account could be taken, and have paroled 59,878 prisoners, including 6134 commissioned officers. Our total loss was thirteen officers and eighty-six men killed, thirty-nine officers and 559 men wounded, and seven officers and twenty-one men missing. I cannot close this report without calling attention to the remarkable discipline, endurance and enthusiasm displayed throughout the campaign by men, officers and regiments."

GENERAL LONG'S FAREWELL ADDRESS.

On April 23d General Long issued his farewell address to the officers and soldiers of the Second Division Cavalry Corps. He said:

"According to the advice of the surgeon, I leave you for a time. How long I am unable to say. I do not feel like separating myself from you, possibly forever, without a few parting words expressing my heartfelt gratification at your gallant and soldierly conduct since I have had the honor and good fortune to command you, but particularly so in the present campaign. During the first portion of the march unfortunate circumstances placed you in the rear of the corps, thus rendering your labors extremely arduous by having to travel roads originally bad, but rendered miserable by the passage of other troops in your advance. By your untiring energy and hard work you, however, overcame these difficulties and arrived in front of Selma, garrisoned by a strong force under command of General Forrest, in time to administer to him and his command, behind almost impregnable works, one of the most complete and severe castigations received by any command during the war. Of the circumstances and details of this fight, with which you are all familiar, it is unnecessary for me to speak. It was, however, the turning point— the decisive fight of the campaign. The nature of the works assaulted, the character and number of troops behind those works, which numbers, according to the admissions of their commander, General Forrest himself, under a flag of truce, exceeded your own, and the number of pieces of artillery in position, are facts which show beyond controversion that this feat has been equaled by none accomplished by cavalry during the war, and excelled but in a few instances by infantry. Having naturally no love for war, and if it should be my fortune, as I hope it may be, never again to hear the fire of a gun in battle, I shall consider that it is honor enough to last me the remainder of my life to have had the honor to command you on that occasion. Whether or not all or any portion of us may meet again, I shall watch your career with interest, and my prayers shall be for your welfare and happiness. To all and each of you, for the present at least, I bid you an affectionate farewell.

"ELI LONG,
"Brigadier-General, U. S. Volunteers."

Late in the afternoon of the 27th orders were issued for the division to march on the morrow.

April 28th—Marched out about three miles when the command was halted, and searched for private property, gold, silver, watches, and jewelry, which it was supposed the men had appropriated during the campaign. Some was found in the first company searched. The others, being warned in time, succeeded in secreting what they had in the sand under their feet until the search was over. It is not known what was done with what little was found; as far as is known no report was ever made of it; returned to camp at 4:30 p. m. As the armistice is in force and no foraging allowed, an arrangement has been made by General Wilson by which, for the present, we are drawing rations from the Confederate commissary supplies and clothing from the quartermaster's department.

May 4th—In the afternoon a pole was raised in the street in front of the Lanier House, where General Wilson has his headquarters. A salute of 200 guns was fired in honor of the Union victories and the prospect of an end to the war. The people of Macon seem to be willing to be reconciled to the Yankee rule. Business in the city is being resumed, but the storekeepers do not like to take Confederate money. No objection to the United States greenback, however. Men from the armies of Lee and Johnston in large numbers passing through on their way home, glad that the war is over. While we are anxious to return home, we realize that a part of the army will be needed to maintain order in the South for some time until the state governments can be organized and gotten into working order.

After the surrender of Generals Lee and Johnston, Jefferson Davis determined to escape from the country if possible. He started with an escort of four brigades of cavalry; but thinking his chances of escape were better with a small party, he abandoned his escort and, with his family, a few officials of the late Confederacy and a small bodyguard, was making his way south through Georgia. General Wilson having been informed of Davis's flight proceeded to make such disposition of his forces as would best insure his capture. Colonel Minty received orders to picket the Ocmulgee and Flint rivers, and send detachments of his division to pursue and capture him.

He ordered Lieutenant-Colonel Pritchard, commading the Fourth Michigan Cavalry, to march at once with his regiment; move as rapidly as possibe to Spalding and leave pickets at all fords and ferries between that place and Hawkinsville.

Lieutenant-Colonel Pritchard started out from Macon at 6 p. m. May 7th, and Colonel Minty ordered Lieutenant-Colonel Howland to follow him the next morning with the Third Ohio and Seventh Pennsylvania Regiments.

After marching seventy-five miles, the Fourth Michigan reached Abbeville about 3 p. m. May 9th. Here they learned that a party with several wagons and two ambulances had crossed the Ocmulgee river at Brown's Ferry, one and one-half miles above Abbeville, about 12 o'clock the night previous; halted at Abbeville long enough to feed and had gone on in the direction of Irwinville. Lieutenant-Colonel Pritchard here met Lieutenant-Colonel Harnden of the First Wisconsin, who informed him that he had been following the trail of the Davis party on the north side of the river and that his men were ahead of him following the trail toward Irwinville. The two regimental commanders separated without agreeing upon any concerted plan of action. Lieutenant-Colonel Pritchard moved on down the river, leaving one company at Brown's Ferry. Finding that there were two roads to Irwinville, Lieutenant-Colonel Pritchard decided to take the longer one, and selecting 150 of his best mounted men, he started out at 4 p. m. Arriving at Irwinville at 1 o'clock a. m. May 10th, representing themselves as Confederates, they learned that the camp of the fugitives was out one and a half miles on the Abbeville road. Pressing into service a negro guide, Lieutenant-Colonel Pritchard marched out and surrounded the camp, and just as day was dawning closed in upon it, capturing the entire party without firing a shot. Just then, however, the advance guard of the First Wisconsin came down the road from the direction of Abbeville, and not recognizing each other in the dim light, each thinking the other to be the enemy, a sharp skirmish ensued, and before the mistake was discovered two men of the Fourth Michigan were killed and one officer wounded, and three men of the First Wisconsin were wounded. Lieutenant-Colonel Howland with the Third Ohio and the Seventh Pennsylvania arrived at Hawkinsville the same day, and after a few hours rest started for Abbeville at 2 a. m. of the 11th, but before they reached Abbeville they met Lieutenant-Colonel Pritchard and the Fourth Michigan with their prisoners.

May 13th—Jeff Davis and his party arrived in Macon in the afternoon, escorted by their captors, and left at 5 p. m. by rail for the North via. Atlanta, Augusta and the sea, finally landing in Fortress Monroe. Lieutenant-Colonel Howland sent a number of scouting parties in the direction of Milledgeville, returning to Macon with the brigade on the 17th. The regiment received mail for the first time since leaving the Tennessee river, in March. A number of commissions arrived for the Third Ohio, amongst them that of Colonel Howland, Lieutenant-Colonel Livermore and Major O. M. Brown.

The following is Colonel Howland's report of the movements of the Second Brigade:

HEADQUARTERS SECOND BRIGADE, SECOND DIVISION CAV. CORPS,
NEAR HAWKINSVILLE, May 10th, 1865—10 p. m.

CAPTAIN: I have the honor to report that I arrived at this place about an hour since; that Jeff Davis with an escort of forty men and a train of two ambulances and twelve or fifteen wagons crossed the Ocmulgee at Abbeville on the evening of the 8th. And hearing of Colonel

Pritchard, he (Davis) started down the river at 12 the same night.

Colonel Pritchard arrived at Abbeville the afternoon of the 9th and at 4 p. m. started in pursuit with 150 of the best mounted men of his command, leaving the balance in camp at Abbeville or that vicinity. I got this intelligence from a courier.

I have directed Colonel Andress to take 250 of the best mounted men of his regiment (the Seventh Pennsylvania), leaving all baggage except rations in camp, and move rapidly to the support of Colonel Pritchard, taking the road from here to Irwinville, thinking he will strike Davis' trail before reaching that point. In case he does not, to march in the direction of Waresborough and communicate with me opposite Albany on the Flint river. In case I strike his trail I will communicate with him by sending on Davis' back track. I shall move at 2 a. m. tomorrow with 250 or 300 of the best mounted men of the Third Ohio (light as possible) on the road leading from here through Millwood to Cedar Hill and Fort Early and follow down Flint river to a point opposite Albany, unless I strike the trail of Davis before reaching that point.

I have directed Major Livermore to take command of all detachments left back and proceed to picket the ferries on the river as quickly and as far down as possible, so that in case any of the officers who are trying to escape are yet on the east side of the Ocmulgee he may capture them.

I have directed Major Greeno to report to Colonel Andress and go with him. It is reported that Clement C. Clay is with Davis.

I have directed Colonel Andress to keep his command mounted by pressing horses when it becomes absolutely necessary, and receipting for same.

I shall pursue the same course and spare no effort to accomplish the object of the expedition.

In laying the course of the two columns I have gone on the supposition that Davis wishes to go West, and can see no reason why he should go East or South unless forced to do so.

I am, respectfully, your obedient servant,

H. N. HOWLAND,
Colonel Commanding.

CAPTAIN SCOTT,
    A. A. G., Second Cavalry Division.

May 23d—The Second Division commenced to break up, Colonel Minty in command of the division, with the Fourth Michigan, the Fourth Ohio, Seventy-second Indiana, the Ninety-eighth and One Hundred and Twenty-third Illinois Regiments taking up the line of march homeward bound. As they marched through town the Second Brigade band played for them, to the great delight of the darkeys. The Third Ohio, Seventh Pennsylvania and Seventeenth Indiana are the only regiments of the division left at Macon.

May 31st—Company G of the Third Ohio was sent to Thomaston and Company K to Dublin to maintain order and protect property.

June 7th—All the members of the regiment whose terms of enlistment expire before October 1st started home. They were to be discharged under an order from the War Department. This included the recruits who joined the regiment in the summer of 1862. During the month Colonel Howland went on a tour through Southwest Georgia to secure information for the Freedmen's Bureau, regarding the conditions existing between the freedmen and their late masters. He returned to Macon on the 26th and reported that he found efficient agents of the Freedmen's Bureau were everywhere needed to prevent abuse of power over the weak, ignorant and defenseless blacks by their former owners. In localities in any-wise remote from the Union troops, all the oppressions of slavery were in full force. He found the general sentiment of the people who had not been in the Confederate army bitter against the government of the United States, and they would gladly welcome any foreign power that would come and overthrow it, thinking that thereby they would obtain a new lease of slave power. He found some few who were inclined to treat the negro fairly, and adjust themselves to the new order of things. The feeling of hostility toward the government he found mainly amongst the large planters who had formerly been wealthy, but was not participated in by most of the returning Confederate soldiers.

Amongst the men remaining in the regiment camp life became exceedingly tedious and irksome. There was none of the excitements that had characterized our four years of service. The scout, the picket, the bivouac, and the battle, were all done with, we hoped forever. The fierce charge, the cannon's roar, the rattle of musketry, the terrible field of carnage, with its dying and its dead; we had passed through it all. Like a dreadful nightmare, it all seemed. And yet how real it all was! And we were all anxious to leave the scenes of warfare and strife and go back to God's country, to home and friends and loved ones; to lay aside the uniform and the sword and take up the implements and avocations of peace.

General Wilson issued the following farewell order:

HDQRS. CAVALRY CORPS, MILITARY DIVISION OF THE MISSISSIPPI,
MACON, GA., *July 2d*, 1865.

To the Officers and Men of the Cavalry Corps, Military Division of the Mississippi:

Your Corps has ceased to exist. The rebellion has terminated in the establishment of your country upon the basis of nationality and

perpetual unity. Your deeds have contributed a noble part to the glorious
result. They have passed into history and need no recital from me. In
the nine months during which I have commanded you, I have heard no
word of reproach upon your conduct, have had no disaster to chronicle.
The glowing memories of Franklin, Nashville, West Harpeth, Ebeneezer
Church, Selma, Montgomery, Columbus, West Point and Macon, may
well fill your hearts and mine with pride. You have learned to believe
yourselves invincible, and contemplating your honorable deeds may well
justly cherish that belief. You may be proud of your splendid discipline,
no less than your courage, zeal, and endurance. The noble impulses
which have inspired you in the past will be a source of enduring honor
in the future. Peace has her victories no less than war. Do not forget
that clear heads, honest hearts, and stout arms, guided by pure patriotism,
are the surest defense of our country in every peril.

Upon them depend the substantial progress of your race and order
of civilization, as well as the liberty of all mankind. Let your example
in civil life be an incitement to industry, good order, and enlightenment,
while your deeds in war shall live in the grateful remembrance of your
countrymen. Having discharged every military duty honestly and faithfully, return to your homes with the noble sentiment of your Martyr
President deeply impressed on every heart. "With malice toward none,
with charity for all, strive to do the right as God gives you to see the
right."   J. S. WILSON,
                                          Brevet Major-General.

July 5th—Colonel Howland started for Hilton Head on business
connected with the Freedmen's Bureau.

While we lay at Macon, Captain Clock of the Third Ohio, on duty
as officer of the guard, was killed by a drunken soldier of the Fourth
United States Cavalry, while attempting to arrest him.

On July 22d the regiment received orders to turn over all ordnance
and quartermaster's stores preparatory to starting for home. We left
Macon at 8 a. m. on the 23d, going by railroad and arriving at Atlanta
in the evening. We remained at Atlanta until the next afternoon at
2 p. m., when we left for Chattanooga and Nashville, arriving at the latter
city at 8 p. m. of the 25th. We remained in the cars all night, and the
next morning Lieutenant-Colonel Livermore was informed that it had
been the intention to retain the regiment in service, but in view of the
fact that we had turned over all arms, horses and equipments, General
Thomas revoked the order, and the regiment was ordered to camp at
Edgefield to be mustered out. The muster-out rolls were all completed
on August 3d, and in the afternoon the regiment had dress parade.
Colonel Howland made a short address, telling us "this was the last time

that we would be assembled and in ranks as a regiment; on the morrow we would be mustered out of the service, and as soon as transportation could be obtained we would start North on our homeward journey, bearing with us the proud satisfaction of knowing that we had won for the Third Ohio Cavalry an honorable place, an imperishable name in the records of our country."

We were to separate after four years of honorable service, the memory of which service would go with us through life. In the years to come, how dear to our hearts would be the comradeship formed as we camped and marched and fought for the Union and the Flag.

While we rejoiced that the war was over, that peace had again taken up its abode in our land, that the victory had been won by the Union armies, and we believed that secession and treason were forever destroyed; yet our hearts were saddened as we thought of our brave comrades who had fallen. The lines of march of our victorious armies were marked with the graves of our fallen heroes.

We were all glad that the task was finished and we knew that the men who had so faithfully performed their duty to their country in its hour of greatest need as soldiers would also as citizens be just as faithful, just as true, just as loyal, just as patriotic, in the performance of every duty.

August 4th—The regiment was mustered out by Captain Neill, U. S. Army, the same officer who had mustered us into service in 1861; the last company being mustered out by 12:30 p. m. There was no cheering amongst the men; everything quiet and orderly. We remained at Edgefield until the 7th, when we broke camp and marched to the railroad, where we found the U. S. Special waiting for us, box cars with soft pine boards for seats. We left Edgefield at 4 p. m. At daylight the next morning we were at Mumfordsville. Arriving at Louisville at 11 a. m., we went from the train to the wharf, and going on board the steamer General Buell, left Louisville at 4 p. m. and steamed rapidly up the river, homeward bound. The scenery along the river was fine. The men were very quiet, seeming disinclined to be talkative, each occupied with thoughts of home. The morning of the 9th was very foggy on the river and our progress necessarily slow. The Captain stopped the boat for about an hour waiting for it to clear. Arrived at Cincinnati at 7:30 a. m. and two hours later left for Columbus, where we arrived at 5:30 p. m. We marched to Todd Barracks, but most of us did not fancy the quarters, which were alive with bedbugs and gray-backs, living together on the most amicable terms, and ready to unite and attack all returning soldiers who came their way. We remained at Columbus until August 14th, when Major Price, United States paymaster came and commenced paying off the regiment but did not get through until the 16th, when the last man was paid off and received his honorable discharge, and here the men scattered in various directions, going to their homes by the first train to take up the threads of civil life where they had been so rudely sundered in 1861.

We have endeavored in these pages to give to the reader some idea of the work that the cavalry had to do, but we realize that our task has been but poorly performed. One writer has said: "For boldness, effectiveness, and devotion to duty, endurance, celerity of movement and accomplishment of results, the Federal Cavalry in the West made a proud record, and its history when written in detail, will be full of thrilling interest."

But it is not at all likely that it will ever be written in detail. Its service was so varied and so much of it performed where there were none to witness and herald it to the world. The newspaper correspondent did not march with the cavalry, and that innate modesty which everywhere marks the true soldier, be he of the cavalry, infantry or artillery, prevents the cavalryman from blowing his own bugle.

Many of our comrades in the infantry had little conception of the kind and amount of work that the cavalryman had to do. All the time the safety of the camp depended on the vigilance and faithfulness of the cavalry. All the while the camp was sleeping the cavalry was patrolling the high-ways and by-ways between the two armies, that no enemy might creep in and take it by surprise. Who will tell of the many thrilling incidents that happened out on the patrol, for it was not unusual to meet our enemy patroling the same roads, and sometimes (though that did not occur often) we met and exchanged shots with some of our own patrol. The service demanded of the cavalry required the highhest type of courage. It required every nerve kept at its utmost tension; it required the utmost vigilance, every sense keen and alert. If there was an exposed point, the cavalry must go there; if there was country to be explored the cavalry must explore it, although in doing so the chances were favorable for that arm becoming a target for an ambushed foe. Many times the cavalry in the advance would get its orders to march until fired on by the enemy's pickets, then draw saber and charge; saddles might be emptied, but that was to be expected, and those that were left rode on, it might be to victory, it might be to death.

Nearly half a century has passed since our sabers were thrust into the scabbard, and our banners were furled, and the white winged angel of peace settled over our land. Very many of our wild riders have answered the last roll call, and the remnant that are still with us show that the weight of years is upon them. And yet, as we call to memory the things that happened in those days, our pulses quicken and the old fire lights up our eyes, as again we hear the bugle sounding the charge, and see the sabers flash in the sunlight.

Unidentified lieutenant wearing cavalry identification pin on vest.

Unidentified first lieutenant.

Unidentified captain.

Unidentified first lieutenant.

Unidentified officer.

CHAPTER XXIII.

THE THIRD OHIO VETERAN VOLUNTEER CAVALRY MEMORIAL ASSOCIATION

Soon after the close of the war, the survivors of the regiment took steps to perpetuate the ties of comradeship that had been formed during the war and the association named above was organized. It first met in 1866, and has continued to meet in annual reunion from that time to the present. Many of the leading spirits who were the life of our gatherings in the years gone by have passed away and at each succeeding reunion we miss some familiar face, and as the annual death roll is called, we hear the names of near and dear comrades, who have gone from us

> "On fame's eternal camping ground
> There silent tents are spread,
> While glory guards with solemn round
> The bivouac of the dead."

But as the years are passing and our ranks are thinning, the ties of comradeship only bind us closer to each other. We had a grand reunion in Toledo in 1908. Two hundred and thirty members of the regiment met together and under our old commander, Colonel Seidel, marched in the parade of the Grand Army of the Republic. It was a day that none of us will ever forget.

The records of the first eight reunions have been lost.

	PRESIDENT	SECRETARY
The 9th was held at Clyde in 1874....		
The 10th was held at Kelley's Island in 1875	CAPTAIN LUCKEY	J. T. WOODFORD
The 11th was held at Norwalk in 1876	COLONEL ZAHM	M. J. LAWRENCE
The 12th was held at Perrysburg in 1877	COLONEL HOWLAND	M. J. LAWRENCE
The 13th was held at Elmore in 1878..	CAPTAIN COLVER	T. B. TERRY
The 14th was held at Toledo in 1879..	CAPTAIN LUCKEY	T. B. TERRY
The 15th was held at Sandusky in 1880	CAPTAIN PEARL	T. B. TERRY
The 16th was held at Tiffin in 1881....	CAPTAIN COLVER	H. S. STECKEL
The 17th was held at Bellevue in 1882	CAPTAIN LUCKEY	T. B. TERRY
The 18th was held at Pemberville in 1883	MARTIN E. ELLIS	F. VANHORN
The 19th was held at Oak Harbor in 1884	COLONEL PARAMORE	C. FINKBEINER
The 20th was held at Monroeville in 1885	COLONEL PARAMORE	C. FINKBEINER
The 21st was held at Elmore in 1886..	COLONEL ZAHM	C. FINKBEINER
The 22d was held at Lakeside in 1887.	CAPTAIN COLVER	C. FINKBEINER
The 23d was held at Columbus in 1888	CAPTAIN COLVER	C. FINKBEINER
The 24th was held at Sandusky in 1889	CAPTAIN COLVER	C. FINKBEINER
The 25th was held at Chicago, Ohio, in 1890	CAPTAIN LUCKEY	C. FINKBEINER
The 26th was held at Detroit, Mich., in 1891	CAPTAIN LUCKEY	C. FINKBEINER

	PRESIDENT	SECRETARY
The 27th was held at Sandusky in 1892	CAPTAIN LUCKEY	C. FINKBEINER
The 28th was held at Genoa in 1893..	A. F. HOUSE	C. FINKBEINER
The 29th was held at Toledo in 1894..	THOMAS CROFTS	C. FINKBEINER
The 30th was held at Norwalk in 1895	COLONEL SEIDEL	C. FINKBEINER
The 31st was held at Wakeman in 1896	CAPTAIN HOWLAND	C. FINKBEINER
The 32d was held at Bowling Green in 1897....................	T. B. TERRY	C. FINKBEINER
The 33d was held at Toledo in 1898..	CAPTAIN LUCKEY	THOMAS CROFTS
The 34th was held at Toledo in 1899..	MAJOR ADAMS	THOMAS CROFTS
The 35th was held at Toledo in 1900..	CAPTAIN PEARL	THOMAS CROFTS
The 36th was held at Toledo in 1901..	A. J. EYSTER	THOMAS CROFTS
The 37th was held at Clyde in 1902...	H. GRABACH	THOMAS CROFTS
The 38th was held at Genoa in 1903...	LIEUT. GEO. FRENT	THOMAS CROFTS
The 39th was held at Norwalk in 1904	GEO. W. LEE	THOMAS CROFTS
The 40th was held at Bowling Green in 1905....................	THEO. ALEXANDER	THOMAS CROFTS
The 41st was held at Wauseon in 1906	JAS. BIDDLE	THOMAS CROFTS
The 42d was held at Toledo in 1907..	A. J. EYSTER	THOMAS CROFTS
The 43d was held at Toledo in 1908..	COLONEL SEIDEL	THOMAS CROFTS
The 44th was held at Oak Harbor in 1909	C. H. NELSON	THOMAS CROFTS

The Forty-fifth Reunion is to be held at Monroeville on the third Wednesday in August, 1910.

OTTO SCHIMANSKY, President.

THOMAS CROFTS, Secretary and Treasurer.

Reunion Rhymes

OUR OLD FLAG

BY SERGT. TOM CROFTS OF COMPANY C.

Only a few shreds of faded silk,
　Yet their price can never be told;
Only a bent and battered staff,
　That cannot be bought with gold.

It is all that is left of a beautiful flag,
　Presented by the ladies of Norwalk fair,
To the "Third Cavalry Regiment,"
　When it marched away to the war.

That was a proud day when it was placed in our care,
　With its broad stripes and its field of blue,
And its stars shone bright as we made the vow
　Ever to guard it faithful and true.

Of the twelve hundred men who made that vow,
　Only a remnant are left, to tell
The story of four years of war
　And of battlefields where our comrades fell.

And like our "old flag," we bear the marks
   Of "those years" long past and gone.
But dear to our hearts is the comradeship
   That was formed in sixty-one.

And dear to our hearts is our grand old flag,
   For the memories that around it are clustered
Of the camp, and the march, the picket and fight,
   While under its folds we were mustered.

The silent lips of that tattered flag,
   Speak more eloquently than language can,
Of heroic struggle and sacrifice
   For freedom, and the rights of man.

On more than two score of bloody fields,
   With armies marshalled in "battle array,"
Amidst shot and shell, carnage and death,
   It waved triumphant above the fray.

Amidst "Stone River's" cedars dark
   Its blazing stars illumed the night—
In "Chickamauga's" awful storm,
   They shone in splendor, clear and bright.

It led the way to where "Old Kennesaw"
   With its frowning batteries stood,
      Then on to proud Atlanta,
   With its harvest of death and blood.

At Lovejoy's station in that wild charge,
   How our cheers arose to the sky,
As it waved o'er the foeman's cannon,
   And his broken ranks turned to fly.

It was still in the front at Selma,
   At Macon we knew that the end was nigh,
And that our proud banner of freedom
   Forever would float on high.

And so our tattered flag we greet today,
   Greet it with reverence, love and pride,
For beneath its folds brave men have fought—
   Defending it our comrades died.

Then give us a cheer for our honored flag,
   A loud huzza and a three times three,
For of all the flags this wide world holds,
   There is none so dear to me.

MY BUGLE

BY DR. CHARLES O. BROWN.

'Mid the hustle of the office,
   And the jostle of the street,
'Mid the greeting by the wayside,
   Of the friends I daily meet;

Oft' there comes the thrilling echoes
   From the fields of long ago,
And the well remembered music
   Of the calls I used to blow.

There was music in my bugle,
   When it sounded breakfast call,
And it needed no repeating,
   For you knew it one and all;

Pork and beans were in the kettle,
   Hard-bread in the haversack,
Every one could hear the bugle,
   When it sounded for a snack.

I could see you as I blew it,
   Snatch your cups and double-quick,
Every Third Ohio soldier,
   Big and little knew the trick.

Reveille in early morning,
   Say at four o'clock or three,
That was not the same exactly,
   For you comrades, or for me.

Oft' I saw you coatless, hatless,
   Sometimes pantless tumble out,
When the orderly was shouting,
   "Roust about, men; roust about!"

And the bugler, like an umpire
   Of a modern baseball game,
Sometimes had to dodge the missiles,
   And keep sounding just the same.

Oh, the echoes of my bugle!
   I can hear them sounding yet,
And remembrance holds their music,
   Which I never shall forget.

Some were glad notes, and the horses
   Whinnied in the early morn,
When the call said to the stables,
   Clean your horses, give them corn.

Other echoes tell of guard-mount,
  Clean the camp, and doctor's call—
Say, it surely was a caution,
  How the saltz held out for all.

Other bugle echoes mingle,
  With your shouting in the fight,
I can hear their shrill notes calling,
  Calling, in my dreams at night.

Others still of solemn import,
  Sound the taps of former years
O'er the graves of fallen comrades,
  Which we watered with our tears.

Other echoes tell of marches
  Through Kentucky, Tennessee
On the pike through Murfreesboro,
  Then in mud up to the knee.

On to Shiloh and Stone River,
  Chickamauga, Stevenson,
Lookout Mountain where Joe Hooker
  Fought above the clouds and won.

Roddy charged our camp at day-break,
  Breakfast cooking, early day,
Quick we formed and quickly licked him,
  Ate our breakfast, went our way.

On to Ringgold and Resaca,
  Dalton too and Tunnel Hill,
Noonday Creek and then Big Shanty,
  Earlier was Cartersville.

Kenesaw to sky uplifting
  Ragged peak, rock-ribbed for fight
With its thousand circling campfires,
  Gleaming through the solemn night.

And the echoes of the bugles
  Sounding from Joe Wheeler's camps,
With our own were often mingled
  'Mid the evenings dews and damps.

On to Chattahoochee Crossings,
  Peach Tree Creek, and Covington,
Then we joined Kilpatrick's raiders—
  Kept the Johnnies on the run.

We were in that charge at Lovejoy,
  With its cut, and slash, and yell,
We were with our Uncle Billy,
  When Atlanta struck and fell.

Back to Louisville for horses,
  From the barns and parlors, too,
Thought that horses raised on bluegrass,
  For our regiment would do.

South again through old Kentucky,
  Bardstown Pike, and Bowling Green,
On through Nashville to Duck River,
  Camping where we oft' had been.

Gravelly Springs—we'll skip the story,
  Of "Starvation Rendezvous"—
On to Eastport, then to Shelby,
  Ebeneezer, Selma, too.

Oh, the bugle, I can hear it,
  More than forty years away,
As it sounded for the battle
  Of that afternoon in May.

I can hear you cheer our comrades
  As they scaled the parapet—
I can see our charging column
  'Mid the crash of cannon yet!

On to Macon and to Edgefield,
  For the muster-out review,
Onward, homeward, war is over—
  Open arms to welcome you.

❧

Sometimes 'mid the falling shadows,
  We can hear another call,
Clearly from the camp up yonder,
  Sounds assembly for us all.

Oh, ye comrades of the great days,
  When we went two million strong,
Fall in! for the march remaining,
  Now keep step, it won't be long.

Bravely we'll salute the colors,
  Hail the land that gave them birth,
Hail the onward coming morrow,
  When our flag shall rule the earth.

Hail the union that we saved, boys!
  And the glory yet to be,
And rejoice 'twas ours to battle
  For the nation of the free.

Cheer with all the old-time fervor,
  That the sons of worthy sires
Keep alive on sacred altars
  All of Freedom's holy fires.

Oh, how beautiful the flag is!
  Oh, how proudly does it wave
O'er the land of worthy freemen,
  O'er the homes of heroes brave.

Every stripe of fairest color,
  Brightly gleams each fadeless star.
Glory to the God of battles,
  Honor to the men of war.

Once again touch elbows, comrades,
  Bravely hail the last grand round;
Cheerfully salute the trumpet
  When the final taps shall sound.

THE THIRD OHIO V. V. CAVALRY

Written by Thomas Crofts, Sergeant Co. C, Third O. V. V. C.,
and read at the Twelfth Annual Reunion at Perrysburg, August 22, 1877.

Again we meet. Another year
  Is marked by time's unerring pen;
We meet our friendship to renew,
  And grasp each other's hand again.

And as we rally 'round our flag,
  Each squadron in its ranks again,
We will, for this one day at least,
  Be Third Ohio Cavalry men.

But as we gaze along the line,
  Our meager ranks their story tell,
Of camp, and march, and flood, and field,
  Where brave men fought and fell.

And we think of the time when we marched away,
  Our column a mile and a quarter long,
And on the muster rolls the names
  Of a regiment twelve hundred strong.

With waving banners and gleaming steel
  Proudly we marched away,
'Mid deafening cheers of the gathered throng,
  Assembled their tribute to pay.

For four long years we fought for the flag—
  The starry flag of the free,
Till it waved in triumph o'er every state,
  From the mountains unto the sea.

Then we furled our banners and sheathed our swords
  At the welcome call of peace,
Rejoicing that the day had come
  When war and strife might cease.

But where is our regiment today?
  Hundreds sleep 'neath a southern sky,
And from the Ohio to the Gulf,
  In every state, our comrades lie.

Nobly contending for the flag that they loved,
  In the thickest of the fight they fell,
Where steel crossed steel and squadrons met,
  Midst rifle shot and bursting shell.

Our noble dead! In memory dear
  They are enshrined today;
We drop for them the silent tear,
  To them our heart's best tribute pay.

THE STORMING OF SELMA

Reunion Third O. V. Cavalry, Toledo, August 20, 1879.

BY BUGLER C. O. BROWN.

In the dim faded distance of bygone years,
Lie marches and battles, and blood, wounds and tears;
Nor would we lay open with enmity's knife,
These wounds now grown over—the scars of the strife;
But we gather to stir in each other again,
Emotions most sacred of times that have been;
Of times when our hearts in one heart were wrought,
By the hardships we bore—by the battles we fought.
To tell over again the triumphs of yore,
Is to us like the blast of the bugle once more;
And I'm sure, boys,' you'll listen though illy 'tis told,
To a story which never, to us, can grow old.

Toward Selma our march we'd been heading for days;
We paused not for mountains for rivers or frays;

We forded the streams—a dozen or more—
And kept the rebs running—our brave Wilson's corps;
For the order had been to ride through and through
This proud state that sneered at the red, white and blue;
And to give it a taste of the fearful cost
Of revolt for a "Cause" that deserved to be "Lost."
Our leader, brave Wilson (we sing him with pride,
Who led us to vict'ry on many a ride;
Who had learned of the Third that we certainly knew,
When we needed the "hard-tack" and "sow-belly" too);
Had told us to forage for all we were worth,
And teach them respect for the Union henceforth.

We remember them boys—those roosters and hens,
The mules hid in swamps, the pigs in the pens;
The smoked shoulders hanging, so tempting, you see,
Put up by the Johnnies for you and for me!
The darkies all grinning from north to south ear,
And calling out: "Massa, I tells ye, see heah,
Dere's a mighty smart heap ob hosses jes yon
In de woods, dat I'll show ye! so Massa come on!"
Oh, pshaw! boys, you know it all—what is the use
Of my telling again how we "cooked the goose";
How we went to the barn yards and milked the fat bossies,
And then to the stables and just "traded" hosses,
And rode off the chargers of old Alabam,
And to balance the bargain just strapped on a ham!
So with fighting the Johnnies and fording the streams,
We issued at last where the radiant beams
Of Dixie's bright sunshine, fell piercingly down,
On the city of Selma, the reb-guarded town.
Her ramparts were built in the war's early days,
(When "niggers" were plenty as McClellan's delays)
And were made high and strong in the form of a bow,
From the river above to the river below.
We had driven old Forrest the day before,
At the point of the sabre from Boyle's Creek—and more,
We'd kept him a running so scared and so fast,
That he stopped not to breathe, till in Selma at last
He felt himself safe from our sabres that night!
Then he boastfully swore—soon as free from the fright—
That he'd turn the cursed Yankees back northward again,
To starve in the swamps, or be "bagged" for Wirz's pen!
But as true as I tell you—to the last man,
From bugler to general we had our own plan;
And could we've told Forrest—no matter he knew,
'Twas Selma we wanted, with him in it, too!

'Twas April 2d, '65—
The works with gray-coats were alive;
The guns frowned o'er the parapet,

And tried to say to us "Not yet."
As on that afternoon we rode
Into that open field and stood,
A mounted line of eager men,
Expecting every moment, when
The order would be giv'n to make
The very earth around us quake
With loudest shouts of victory!
But you remember readily,
How we were ordered to dismount.
Ere we had fairly time to count
The chances of success that day,
Or sniff the powder of the fray.
But scarcely had we "hugged the ground,"
When booming guns awoke the sound,
And shot and shell were quick to say:
"I'm after you 'right smart' today!"

And you mind boys the ordering of the line,
With Upton's men coming around so fine,
To take their "posish" on the left out of sight,
While we, with old Eli, away on the right,
Had been waiting, impatient, an hour or two,
For the order to charge—for the bugle to blow?
We saw the rebs swarming as thickly as bees,
And could hear them a talking as plain as you please;
While only just yonder, in train after train,
Our boys from their prison were swept south again!
Those boys—how we pitied them with friends in full view,
To be hurried off that way, to where, we all knew.

Stay! Hark! What's that booming back yon in the rear?
"There's some mischief a-brewing my boys, I fear,"
Says Eli—just taking the pipe from his mouth)
"And I'd rather fight Forrest with all of the South,
In a fair open field with our faces to front,
Than to *turn back* for Chalmers—be hanged, boys!) I won't!
We'll wait here no longer—here bugler, I say,
Sound the charge!" Then up from the ground where they lay,
Sprang the Second Division as if 'twere one man.
And were off like clockwork with Long in the van!
Oh, the belching of shot and the screeching of shell,
As though they poured forth from the belly of hell!
But did that line waver or pause in its course?
Not a moment! But swept on, shouting till hoarse:
"Fort Pillow!" "Fort Pillow!" "Remember it well!"
'Twas the battle cry raised and it drowned the rebs yell.
And even when Long fell pierced through the head,
They paused not, but followed as Minty now led,
And shouted: "Who's with me? Ho! Forward my men;
Let's over these works though but two to their ten!"

And o'er the abatis—the high palisade—
He climbed and he vaulted, as though he had played
A fine game of leap-frog; then swinging his hat,
"Come and follow me, boys, to this parapet!"
In a twinkling 'twas done and who can tell how?
The ramparts were won!—a moment, and now
The bugle is sounding the Third to go in,
And charge them on horseback with sabre and din.

"To the Right, and By Fours; now Forward," he said,
And when the "Charge" sounded 'twas our colonel who led,
And there was one by him, a stripling I know,
But he didn't "hold horses" when fight was the show—
No matter; right on with drawn sabres we went,
With our spurs in the hub deep, as if we were sent.
Straight down through the gully—up through the stockade,
'Mid the screeching of shells—'twixt the dying and dead;
And the Johnnies went flying as if for their lives,
To find a new shelter and dodge our long knives!
We charged to the fort which belched forth its shot,
And leaving our horses we formed on the spot,
Where the regulars thought it not healthy to stay,
And *left us* to gather the laurels that day!
Shall we ever forget it—that fearful storm—
Of thick leaden hail—as we paused to form?
Shall we cease to remember how coolly that day,
Our Colonel gave orders and rode midst the fray?
We stayed but an instant—with loudest yell,
'Mid the whizzing of grape and the screeching of shell,
We were off at the word—we charged on a run,
We mounted the breastworks*—the vict'ry was won!
Though the sun had gone down ere we finished the fight,
Yet we slept on our arms *in Selma* that night!

'Twas morning and the sun looked down,
As brightly on the captured town
As though the scenes of yester's strife
Had never vexed its quiet life.
All scattered through our camp there lay,
At dawn when we awoke that day,
Cold forms of men in gray and blue—
The vanquished and the victor, too;
In life divided they were foes,
In death united they repose.
Beneath the ramparts sheltering shade,
A long, deep trench we sadly made;
And in it placed with tend'rest care,
Our boys who died for Country there.
'Tis meet we never should forget

---

*A second line within the city.

Those graves which once our tears have wet;
And they who lived not to return—
They, through the spell of thoughts which burn
On mem'rys altar, in our breast,
Should here be present with the rest.

Oh, comrades, buried far away,
Be in our thought enthroned today!
We'll twine for you with hand unseen,
A chaplet of love's evergreen;
And into it there shall be wrought,
With fadeless lines of grateful thought,
An oath as sacred as your grave,
That what you died for we will save!

WITH SEIDEL "BOOT TO BOOT"

BY E. LEGGETT, CO. H, THIRD O. V. C.

Here's a double health to field and staff
Brave officers were they,
Their chivalry and courage high
No words of mine convey;
Though I no more their orders hear
Nor in their presence stand;
On memory's field I still salute
That fine illustrious band.

TO THE THIRD OHIO CAVALRY.

Come, Third Ohio Cavalry, and pitch your tents with me
Upon historic camping ground along the Tennessee;
The echoes of our bugle notes ring clear as silver bell,
Once more we're riding "boot to boot" with Zahm and with Seidel.

When the dragon red sought to devour sweet Liberty's fair child
Columbia, and when Freedom's shriek rang out with anguish wild,
Then Lincoln called, and then, Old Third, your voices swelled the roar,
"We're coming, Father Abraham, three hundred thousand more."

You blithely joined the dance of death set to the bugle's blast
That government, once crushed to earth, might rise and live and last;
You helped to tear hell's ensign down, secession's impious bars,
To keep thirteen stripes flying high, and thirty-five bright stars.

I've seen your weary ranks drag slow—both famished man and horse—
And seen you burst upon the foe, with more than tempest's force,
At McMinnville and Mumfordsville, Bardstown and Bradyville,
Where you and Stanley charged the slopes of cedar-crowned Snow Hill.

At Lebanon, at Stewart's Creek, Corinth and Lexington,
At Noonday Creek and Kenesaw, Moulton and Middleton,
At Peachtree Creek and Courtland Road, historic Franklin, too.
Where in three different fights the Gray retired before the Blue.

Stone River's dark and bloody field, where horse and rider fell
Before that fearful onslaught—that storm of shot and shell—
You saved the ammunition train and held the foe at bay
'Till victory flung back defeat that dark December day.

On Chickamauga's field were you, where shot and rebel yell
Transformed the lovely southern glades into an earthly hell;
When Thomas slowly marched away, scorning to fly or yield,
The "Old Third" formed the stubborn rear—the last to leave the field.

You braved Old Boreas winter storms in Eastern Tennessee,
To save beleaguered Knoxville and set her inmates free.
Helped drive away the rebel crew and save the town from loot
By riding o'er the mountain trail, with Seidel boot to boot.

And when in front of Selma that final charge you made
When Howland led the regiment against that palisade,
The rebels fled before you, and the victory was won,
As you rode forward, boot to boot, while Wilson cheered you on.

Comrades, my head is white with age; my march is waxing slow;
My bivouac here is almost done; my campfire's burning low;
I soon shall meet the last grand charge of mightiest of foes,
Whose shadowy lance no sabre stroke nor parry may oppose.

I'm proud to think my blood drops flowed with yours on Georgia's plain,
When treason snatched our stars and we helped wrest them back again;
That when Kilpatrick's sharp command five thousand sabres drew,
We drove Pat Cleburne's rebel horde as sunbeams banish dew;

Proud that our swords at Farmington flamed up like wings of light,
And that two hundred captives were our trophies of the fight.
We heard the order from Seidel; we charged them horse and foot;
And the Old Rough Riders did it well, while riding "boot to boot."

I still recall those war-like days of which you've oft heard tell
By Brown and Crofts' whose fluent tongues have told the story well.
I'm glad I mingled in those scenes, of which you've seen and heard;
Proud that I had my comradeship in Ohio's Fighting Third.

But there's a foe armed with a scythe who marches down the years;
The only one who e'er was feared by Seidel's Cavaliers.
Give back, Old Time, our sabres bright; give back each sinewy limb;
Give back the voice that rang with mirth and sang our battle hymn.

Restore the good steeds that we rode; roll back our vanished years;
Give back the hearts that once beat high, nor quaked at coward's fears;
Give back the rifles that we used, and well knew how to shoot,
And let us charge as once we charged with Seidel "boot to boot."

Remember, boys, the "noble dead" who with us wore the blue,
Whose blood gave to our country's flag a purer, richer hue;
Their life, their death, their sacrifice, with your own wounds and scars,
Have made a nobler emblem of "Old Glory's stripes and stars."

In dreams these moving pictures show Old Dixie land to me,
As when with Crook and Long we marched along the Tennessee;
In dreams I hear our bugle note ring clear as silver bell,
Again we're riding "boot to boot" with Howland and Seidel.

Roster of Survivors

Colonel Charles B. Seidel.........................Lyndan, Kentucky
Lieutenant Colonel D. E. Livermore, 5608 Jackson Ave., Chicago, Illinois
Major Oliver M. Brown..........2222 Jackson Bvd., Chicago, Illinois
Battalion Adjutant W. S. Foster............R. D. No. 1, Chicago, Ohio
Hospital Steward James B. Green.................Mishawaka, Indiana
Regimental Quartermaster Sergeant Myron H. Barrett...Belleville, Ohio
Regimental Commissary Sergeant W. O. Johnson.....Wadsworth, Ohio

COMPANY A

Captain W. B. Gates....................R. D. No. 4, Ottawa, Kansas
Lieutenant Isaac Skillman, 213 Mt. Vernon St., Grand Rapids, Michigan
Lieutenant Joe M. Fox....................Soldiers Home, California
Lieutenant Samuel Currie................611 Buffalo St., Toledo, Ohio
Sergeant A. C. Ritter................................Sandusky, Ohio
Sergeant S. B. Liedorff.................R. F. D. No. 1, Collins, Ohio
Sergeant M. V. McCrillis..........................Monroeville, Ohio
Sergeant John Monaghan...........................Sandusky, Ohio
Sergeant Albert McMaster.....................Muskegon, Michigan
Sergeant Enos Griss.................................Perrysburg, Ohio
Sergeant Eugene A. Osborne, Sr..........118 Milan St., Norwalk, Ohio
Corporal S. B. Kies..............................West Toledo, Ohio
Corporal Wm. E. Akers.............................Norwalk, Ohio
Corporal Samuel Lingo.....................Box 137, Rossford, Ohio
Corporal C. A. Shively...........................Monticello, Illinois
Farrier Joel F. Smith................................Norwalk, Ohio
Private Joseph Ball.......................R. F. D. No. 4, Tiffin, Ohio
Private Ira Blackman.............................Roxana, Michigan
Private William Colwell..........................Syracuse, Indiana
Private George W. Clark............................Wauseon, Ohio
Private Samuel L. Ensign...................McLane, Pennsylvania
Private Philip C. Funk...........................Funk, Nebraska
Private Henry Glenn..,...............122 Howard St., Bellevue, Ohio
Private Ervin Hewitt...............................Tontogany, Ohio
Private William H. Horton..................Sandusky Home, Ohio
Private William Himberger........................Norwalk, Ohio
Private Lewis Johnson.................26 Forest St., Norwalk, Ohio
Private C. C. Jewell..........................Kent City, Michigan

Private Chris. J. Kinzel.........................R. D., Pioneer, Ohio
Private J. H. Kendall................................Havana, Ohio
Private C. A. Lakins.....................R. D. No. 1, Ashley, Indiana
Private James L. Lasley................................Carey, Ohio
Private Allan McFerson.........................Rocky Ridge, Ohio
Private James Price...................R. D. No. 2, Labelle, Missouri
Private Theo. Rickey..................................Clyde, Ohio
Private Ezra H. Root.................................Milan, Ohio
Private Frank Slaughter..............................Ellis, Kansas
Private George W. Wright.............................Genoa, Ohio
Private John White.......................Fairmount, West Virginia

COMPANY B

Captain A. H. Pearl.................................Huron, Ohio
Captain John G. Oates........................North Fairfield, Ohio
Sergeant Philip Bangle...............Soldiers and Sailors Home, Ohio
Sergeant Hiram Sexton.....................Breckenridge, Michigan
Corporal Orin Adams.............................Lacey, Michigan
Corporal Alanson Adams.............Soldiers Home, Sandusky, Ohio
Corporal Charles E. Husted..........Box 278, Cripple Creek, Colorado
Corporal M. J. Lawrence............................Cleveland, Ohio
Farrier G E Hawley..................................Wauseon, Ohio
Private T. P. Barber..........National Home, Grand Rapids, Michigan
Private Anson P. Clinger................R. F. D. No. 2, Huron, Ohio
Private D. A. Crippen...............................Republic, Ohio
Private William Fisar........................Sandusky Home, Ohio
Private Joseph Gregory............ 515 Church St., East Toledo, Ohio
Private B. Goodell..................................Norwalk, Ohio
Private Jesse Hollister....................716 First St., Toledo, Ohio
Private Ed. Hollister....................R. F. D. No. 3, Huron, Ohio
Private William H. Houpt..........................Springfield, Ohio
Private H. J. Knapp.............................New London, Ohio
Private William Mire...............................Norwalk, Ohio
Private Thomas W. McKim........................West Unity, Ohio
Private George W. McKim........................West Unity, Ohio
Private Jerome C. Nelson.............................Collins, Ohio
Private C. H. Nelson...........................St. Cloud, Florida
Private F. J. Peck.......................Grand Forks, North Dakota
Private Mark M. Peck............................Fort Scott, Kansas
Private Edwin Sexton...........................St. Louis, Michigan
Private Benjamin Vroman...........R. F. D. No. 3, Monroeville, Ohio
Private Styles Webb.............................New London, Ohio

COMPANY C

Sergeant A. J. Eyster...............919 Oakwood Ave., Toledo, Ohio
Sergeant Thomas Crofts.............R. F. D. No. 6, East Toledo, Ohio
Sergeant George Wertenberger....................West Salem, Ohio
Commissary Sergeant A. B. Conant........857 Nessle St., Toledo, Ohio
Sergeant Harlow Burr.............................Hicksville, Ohio
Sergeant William Van Wormer.........17 Alva St., West Toledo, Ohio
Sergeant George J. Miller............R. F. D. No. 1, East Toledo, Ohio
Corporal C. O. Brown...........2222 Jackson Bvd., Chicago, Illinois
Corporal John Kerman.................1074 Hicks St., Toledo, Ohio
Corporal H. B. Pike.....................116 Tenth St., Toledo, Ohio
Corporal John A. Rice.................R. F. D. No. 5, Norwalk, Ohio
Corporal Wm. Smith........266 Fourth Ave., Grand Rapids, Michigan
Corporal Isaac Whitson............................Lime City, Ohio
Farrier J. E. Thompson.................1067 Hicks St., Toledo, Ohio
Saddler John Redding...........................West Toledo, Ohio
Private H. D. Benedict.....................Fredericktown, Missouri
Private L. A. Brown.................447 Fifth St., East Toledo, Ohio
Private John Broadbeck.................Box 275, Oak Harbor, Ohio
Private E. W. Bradley............................Chino, California
Private Frederick Barnes..............1718 Ontario St., Toledo, Ohio
Private John Cooney...........................Dennison, Michigan
Private B. M. Crandall....................R. F. D., Walbridge, Ohio
Private Peter Eddy.............................Blissfield, Michigan
Private R. B. Gorsuch..........650 South Platt St., East Toledo, Ohio
Private Charles Hatfield...............................Delta, Ohio
Private S. H. Hess....................638 Lynn St., Fostoria, Ohio
Private Bernhard Miller.............R. F. D. No. 6, East Toledo, Ohio
Private William B. Meeker....................Liberty Center, Ohio
Private Nicholas Nellis.............................Bellevue, Ohio
Private George R. Underwood.................Shadeland, Tennessee

COMPANY D

Lieutenant Joe Berry.......208 South Second St., Independence, Kansas
Quartermaster Sergeant David H. Lentz.................Piqua, Ohio
Sergeant R. H. Benfer.................R. F. D. No. 5, Bellevue, Ohio
Sergeant John Clary....................................Osage, Iowa
Sergeant Alex Tittle.................................Bellevue, Ohio
Corporal O C. Russell.......................Bowling Green, Ohio
Bugler Henry G. Stahl.............................Fremont, Ohio
Bugler George W. Myers.........................Carrothers, Ohio
Farrier J. K. White..................411 Division St., Toledo, Ohio

Private E. W. Amsden..........................Ormond, Florida
Private Hezekiah Allbee.....................Sandusky Home, Ohio
Private John Bitzer..............................Cologne, Minnesota
Private Charles Bunsey.............................Sandusky, Ohio
Private Philip Ehman.......R. F. D. No. 1, South Frankfort, Michigan
Private Hezekiah Edwards.............R. F. D. No. 2, Fremont, Ohio
Private William Eno...............................Woodville, Ohio
Private John R. P. Foster..............247 Point View, Dayton, Ohio
Private Henry Grabach................................Clyde, Ohio
Private John Grabach.....................Grand Island, Nebraska
Private Samuel Garnes............................Montpelier, Ohio
Private Marion Hawk................................Fremont, Ohio
Private Samuel Haines...............................Elmore, Ohio
Private Joe A. Hill.........................Powersville, Missouri
Private G. W. Hill................................Warren, Illinois
Private Jacob Helmkee.......................Fort Wayne, Indiana
Private James Kelsey................................Clyde, Ohio
Private William Long..........253 East Pearl St., Coldwater, Michigan
Private O. M. Mallernee.............................Clyde, Ohio
Private H. H. Sloan................................Genoa, Ohio
Private Solomon Shively.......................Hastings, Michigan
Private E. D. Smith.............................Chester, Michigan
Private John Setzler.....................R. F. D. No. 2, Clyde, Ohio
Private G. W. Smith..........................Gibsonburg, Ohio
Private John W. Timmons....................Vicksburg, Michigan
Private Thomas Warren...........................Flint, Michigan
Private George D. Welker.........................Fremont, Ohio

COMPANY E

Quartermaster Sergeant L. W. Severns...............Mansfield, Ohio
Commissary Sergeant Thomas Allen...............Emmittsburg, Iowa
Sergeant William O. Hissong.....................Tulsa, Oklahoma
Corporal Milton Cake................................Ashland, Ohio
Corporal Lewis Deems..............R. F. D. No. 2, Lexington, Ohio
Corporal Nathan Dewitt........................Falmouth, Michigan
Corporal Leander Glenn...........R. F. D. No. 3, West Liberty, Iowa
Corporal Peter Stillwagan......R. F. D. No. 2, West Branch, Michigan
Corporal Johnson Taylor...................R. D. No. 1, Galion, Ohio
Farrier Thomas H. Sefton.....................Lagrange, Indiana
Private Hiram Allen...................................Palo, Iowa
Private William Ash...........................St. Clair, Michigan
Private William A. Bushong.......521 East Fifth St., Ottawa, Kansas

Private John Brown................................Norwalk, Ohio
Private John Cunningham.....................New Lexington, Ohio
Private F. M. Clay...........224 South Logan St., Holdrege, Nebraska
Private Joseph Dufner.............................Norwalk, Ohio
Private Charles Endly.........................San Diego, California
Private William H. Follin..............R. F. D. No. 5, Mansfield, Ohio
Private Abram Gibson.............R. F. D. No. 3, West Liberty, Iowa
Private Leonard Gfell.............................West Toledo, Ohio
Private Henry Greenwalt..1963 West Forty-seventh St., Cleveland, Ohio
Private Henry Grower..............................Belleville, Ohio
Private Levi Hissong.................................Butler, Ohio
Private James L. Kerr...........R. F. D. No. 3, New Lexington, Ohio
Private Jacob Laird.................................Mansfield, Ohio
Private R. C. Miller............260 Manchester Ave., Wabash, Indiana
Private Henry Martin.........609½ North High St., Columbus, Ohio
Private John Martin.....................R. F. D. No. 1, Attica, Ohio
Private Ezra Potter..............13½ North Park St., Mansfield, Ohio
Private F. B. Platt.................................Mansfield, Ohio
Private James Piper...................................Butler, Ohio
Private Henry Princehorn..........289 West Fifth St., Mansfield, Ohio
Private S. S. Pearson..............................Ottawa, Illinois
Private Albert Perry.................................Galion, Ohio
Private Thomas Simmons..............................Butler, Ohio
Private Daniel Spayde................................Butler, Ohio

COMPANY F

Captain George F. Williams.................Eckelson, North Dakota
Captain L. W. French..............................Wakeman, Ohio
Quartermaster Sergeant D. A. Bishop..............Boughtonville, Ohio
Sergeant E. R. Holliday..........................Wellington, Ohio
Sergeant Aaron E. Thompson........................Chicago, Ohio
Corporal George W. Lee.....................West Clarksfield, Ohio
Corporal S. G. Mitchell.........................Avon, South Dakota
Bugler Abe Sinfield....................National Military Home, Ohio
Private Horace Barnes............................Wellington, Ohio
Private J. H. Bailey.....................R. F. D. No. 1, Kipton, Ohio
Private William H. Blair..........................Rochester, Ohio
Private L. D. Fisher..............332 Prairie St., Charlotte, Michigan
Private F. J. Freer...............................Ashland, Ohio
Private James R. Hanley...........................Rochester, Ohio
Private Isaac P. Haskins...........................Wakeman, Ohio
Private Dean Keefer.......................Chicago Junction, Ohio

Private H. King...................................Bucyrus, Ohio
Private Charles L. Lee..................................Polk, Ohio
Private Joseph S. Lutz.........................Jonesville, Michigan
Private James H. Mann............................Rochester, Ohio
Private A. W. Mitchell.............................Rochester, Ohio
Private Thomas McCoy..............R. F. D. No. 1, West Salem, Ohio
Private G. W. Ransom...........................Wellington, Ohio
Private William H. Roberts..................Competition, Missouri
Private Louis Shreck..............................Niles, Michigan
Private William O. Town.............R. F. D. No. 4, Middlefield, Ohio
Private John B. Taylor..........................New London, Ohio
Private William Vanscoy..............National Military Home, Ohio

COMPANY G

First Sergeant J. J. Anderson.........................Urbana, Ohio
Sergeant John M. Bearse.....................Webberville, Michigan
Sergeant J. C. Clayman.................R. F. D. No. 1, Urbana, Ohio
Sergeant R. R. Wilkinson.....................Charlevoix, Michigan
Sergeant D. W. Fisher............................Bettsville, Ohio
Corporal W. R. Dunlap...............................Benton, Ohio
Corporal Ansel Elmes...............................Sheridan, Ohio
Corporal C. J. Hoote.................................Tiffin, Ohio
Corporal James Hyde..........................Bowling Green, Ohio
Corporal H. E. Mandel..............R. F. D., No. 3, Perrysburg, Ohio
Corporal George Porter............................Defiance, Ohio
Saddler J. D. Coleman...........................Bailey, Michigan
Private Henry C. Broka...........................Perrysburg, Ohio
Private William Cowgill..............................McComb, Ohio
Private George F. Crowe..............................Tiffin, Ohio
Private Harmon Cooper.....................Carson City, Michigan
Private N. W. Eichelberry..............R. F. D. No. 2, Republic, Ohio
Private William Finley,..............................Luckey, Ohio
Private Elias Freze...........................Bowling Green, Ohio
Private L. S. Gibson...............................Norwalk, Ohio
Private J. F. Gregg...............................Sycamore, Ohio
Private George Hospelhaum............................Tiffin, Ohio
Private A. F. House...............8926 Euclid Ave., Cleveland, Ohio
Private Isaac Logan................................Elmore, Ohio
Private George D. Mauk.............................Dundee, Ohio
Private Charles J. McDargh...........422 Storms Ave., Urbana, Ohio
Private Martin Marble.................................Tiffin, Ohio
Private James McCallister.......................Hudson, Indiana

Private J. L. Miller ....Jackson, Ohio
Private J. P. Northcutt.............................Urbana, Ohio
Private William Post..................................Salem, Ohio
Private L. H. Palmer...............................Sycamore, Ohio
Private H. L. Steckel..................................Tiffin, Ohio
Private B. F. Sanford..................................Siam, Ohio
Private Joseph Smith.........................St. Charles, Michigan
Private Otto Schimansky..............................Elyria, Ohio
Private Philoman Turner........................Port Clinton, Ohio
Private Henry Tryan...............................Calmus, Iowa
Private James E. Tanner..........................Mt. Victory, Ohio
Private A. J. Van Etten...........................Pemberville, Ohio
Private James K. Webb............................Defiance, Ohio
Private Nelson Wilkins............................Scranton, Kansas
Private Hiram Wurtz....................................Attica, Ohio
Private Ephraim York.................626 Sears St., Bucyrus, Ohio

COMPANY H

Lieutenant A. D. Hawes.........................Blissfield, Michigan
First Sergeant D. W. Weitz.........................Butler, Indiana
Sergeant D. J. Prickitt...........................West Unity, Ohio
Sergeant Isaac Bricker...............................Ladora, Iowa
Sergeant Harmon L. Miller....704 E. Warner Ave., Guthrie, Oklahoma
Sergeant E. S. Frager.............................Wetmore, Kansas
Corporal D. E. Hart...............................Neligh, Nebraska
Corporal Michael Lochard.............R. F. D. No. 3, Osborn, Kansas
Corporal William H. Letcher.........................Fayette, Ohio
Corporal Eustace Leggett...........R. F. D. No. 2, Morenci, Michigan
Private John P. Beard.............................Montpelier, Ohio
Private Fletcher Bishop.........................Morenci, Michigan
Private James M. Biddle............................Wauseon, Ohio
Private Irvin Bates.................................Kinde, Michigan
Private C. S. Bemis..........................Temperance, Michigan
Private D. P. Blosier...............................Augusta, Ohio
Private William M. Castle.........................Millersport, Ohio
Private Josiah Dukes.........................Pleasant Lake, Indiana
Private Nathan Edwards.................................Bryan, Ohio
Private Lafayette Esterline...........................Fayette, Ohio
Private Michael Fickle............................Montpelier, Ohio
Private J. N. Hine...................R. F. D. No. 7, Wauseon, Ohio
Private David Hawkins.............West Fifth St., Pomona, California
Private Joseph Haines.................................Elmore, Ohio

Private W. H. Hartman...........................West Unity, Ohio
Private Burdett Lamson...............722 West High St., Bryan, Ohio
Private Horace W. Platt............................Hamilton, Ohio
Private J. H. Prickitt........896 West Seventh St., Pomona, California
Private W. C. Russell.............................St. Cloud, Florida
Private C. K. Ragan.............................Hanford, California
Private W. P. Rogers.................Box 1048, Raton, New Mexico
Private W. H. Scannell.........................Gary, South Dakota
Private Charles Super...................20 Perry St., Mansfield, Ohio
Private F. B. Sheffield..................Box 382, Morenci, Michigan
Private Josiah Smith..............................West Unity, Ohio
Private John H. Shouf................................Bryan, Ohio
Private R. R. Tunitin.......................Minneapolis, Minnesota
Private George W. Yoder............................Pioneer, Ohio
Private J. B. Frager.............R. F. D. No. 4, Washington, Kansas

COMPANY I

Lieutenant Edward A. Haines.........................Elmore, Ohio
Lieutenant Clark Center...........1143 Central Ave., Sandusky, Ohio
Lieutenant George B. Watson.......................Greenwich, Ohio
Sergeant John W. Blackman.......................Gibsonburg, Ohio
Sergeant J. E. Mitchell........................North Fairfield, Ohio
Sergeant Charles McMaster..............R. F. D. No. 1, Chicago, Ohio
Commissary Sergeant Robert H. Spalding............Marblehead, Ohio
Corporal Adam Fetter.................................Shelby, Ohio
Corporal Henry Sweetland............525 Sandusky St., Toledo, Ohio
Corporal Jacob Weis.................517 Wayne St., Sandusky, Ohio
Corporal Richard Waggoner.......................Beloit, Wisconsin
Farrier Henry A. Libe................................Attica, Ohio
Saddler Conrad Thoman...........................Hicksville, Ohio
Private Jacob F. Artz..............................Norwalk, Ohio
Private Milton J. Bell............................Plymouth, Ohio
Private John Bier..................1006 Hancock St., Sandusky, Ohio
Private Fred Blum..................Soldiers and Sailors Home, Ohio
Private M. L. Bridenstine............................Forest, Ohio
Private Leander Bliss..................R. F. D. No. 1, Chicago, Ohio
Private Urial Bliss............................Oskaloosa, Kansas
Private N. B. Downing.............................Norwalk, Ohio
Private William H. Davis....................West Clarksfield, Ohio
Private Anson P. Green...........................Auburn, Indiana
Private George Goosman.....8-10 E. Grant St., Minneapolis, Minnesota
Private Jacob Hummel..........................Monroeville, Ohio

Private C. L. Henney............................Mitchelville, Iowa
Private George W. Hiberling........................Fremont, Ohio
Private George Kryder..............................McClure, Ohio
Private John Lewis.................................Defiance, Ohio
Private W. D. Leek................................Iowa City, Iowa
Private Mark McMaster...........R. F. D. No. 1, Garden City, Kansas
Private Dexter McMaster....................Box 161, Deshler, Ohio
Private W. W. Parsons.................R. F. D. No. 1, Chicago, Ohio
Private Joseph E. Schwab..........................Sandusky, Ohio
Private G. M. Saltzgaber...........................Van Wert, Ohio
Private Hyatt Travis..............................Greenwich, Ohio
Private Austin E. Taylor..........................Albion, Indiana
Private Mason Varner.........................Liberty Center, Ohio
Private W. S. Van Horn...........211 N. Co. Line St., Fostoria, Ohio

COMPANY K

Captain O. H. Howland.......................San Diego, California
Lieutenant J. R. Hall.....................Cannon Falls, Minnesota
First Sergeant John Maloney........................Sandusky, Ohio
Sergeant James Drury.........................Sandusky Home, Ohio
Sergeant James Fisher........................Sandusky Home, Ohio
Sergeant Francis Shaw..........................Bayfield, Wisconsin
Corporal Charles Brunthaver, 503 Twelfth St., N. W., Washington, D. C.
Corporal D. W. Campbell..........................Kinsley, Kansas
Corporal G. M. Gottshall......................Muskegon, Michigan
Corporal John Toomey................................Huron, Ohio
Wagoner Charles Yance................................Clyde, Ohio
Private Albert Arnold............R. F. D. No. 36, Camden, Michigan
Private Joseph Brightenburg........................Vickery, Ohio
Private J. C. Campbell............................Gibsonburg, Ohio
Private Jeremiah Couts..............................Bucyrus, Ohio
Private Stephen Entsminger..........................Bradner, Ohio
Private William Grow..............1947 Delaware Ave., Toledo, Ohio
Private William Gowitzke..242 Walnut St., Manchester, New Hampshire
Private Samuel Grow................................Lakeside, Ohio
Private Philip Henley..........611 North Anglim St., Cleburne, Texas
Private Lewis Heller...............4108 Muriel Ave., Cleveland, Ohio
Private Charles Hill.................................Tedrow, Ohio
Private Jacob Klever.............1012 West Broadway, Toledo, Ohio
Private George Letherer...........................Perrysburg, Ohio
Private V. Lybarger...............................Hicksville, Ohio
Private Frank McMullen............................Sandusky, Ohio

Private E. K. Roberts..............................Sylvania, Ohio
Private Augustus Sipfle..........................Port Clinton, Ohio
Private John Ward................................Sandusky, Ohio
Private W. H. Withington....................Sandusky Home, Ohio
Private George Welever.........R. F. D. No. 2, Temperance, Michigan

COMPANY L

Lieutenant John Dusing.............R. F. D. No. 3, Monroe, Michigan
Lieutenant G. W. Boggs.............Soldiers and Sailors Home, Ohio
Commissary Sergeant S. A. Shepherd............Kingfisher, Oklahoma
Sergeant Christian R. Hopkins......712 Spruce St., St. Louis, Missouri
Sergeant B. F. Kirtz...................................Carey, Ohio
Sergeant J. G. Miller.................249 Wasaon St., Toledo, Ohio
Sergeant D. W. Wood...............119 Main St., East Toledo, Ohio
Corporal W. W. Brim...............................Millbury, Ohio
Corporal James Boggs.................................Elmore, Ohio
Corporal Michael Hughes.......................Kelley's Island, Ohio
Corporal August Helbing.................North Fort Worth, Texas
Corporal William Huling.........245 West Broad St., Columbus, Ohio
Corporal Doc Van Howton............................Holland, Ohio
Farrier Frank A. Riedy..............1027 Market St., Sandusky, Ohio
Wagoner C. P. Bartram.........................Maitland, Missouri
Private Theodore Alexander....134 N. Church St., Bowling Green, Ohio
Private Ben Aldrich.................................Sylvania, Ohio
Private George W. Benedict........266 West Third St., Mansfield, Ohio
Private J. W. Bradshaw...........2131 Flourney St., Chicago, Illinois
Private H. L. Cook............................Bowling Green, Ohio
Private Amos D. Day.................R. F. D. No. 4, Thayer, Kansas
Private Jacob Eddleman........................Metamora, Indiana
Private Chris Finkbeiner..........................Perrysburg, Ohio
Private James W. Fuller.....................Breckenridge, Michigan
Private Henry Frymire.................410 May St., Fremont, Ohio
Private Jacob E. Fuller.......................Columbus Grove, Ohio
Private G. W. Goodman............................Perrysburg, Ohio
Private Charles Green.............................Graytown, Ohio
Private B. R. Hull.............638 East Broadway, East Toledo, Ohio
Private David Hatcher....................Box 413, Perrysburg, Ohio
Private Henry Hendricks...........................Defiance, Ohio
Private Thomas Hayes..............R. F. D. No. 2, Perrysburg, Ohio
Private John Hecksteden...........402 Sidney St., St. Louis, Missouri
Private B. P. Kimball................................Elmore, Ohio
Private Ira Knull.................................Perrysburg, Ohio

Private Casper Kahl..............................Defiance, Ohio
Private William Luckey......................Box 179, Elmore, Ohio
Private Harvey Long..................................Elmore, Ohio
Private William M. Long............................Elmore, Ohio
Private Louis Lafayette..................712 Dexter St., Lorain, Ohio
Private Charles A. Myers..........................Metamora, Ohio
Private James H. Merrill...............................Marion, Ohio
Private Peter Necher...............................Swanton, Ohio
Private Guy D. Pierce..........Soldiers Home, Los Angeles, California
Private Charles Price.................National Military Home, Ohio
Private Charles H. Robinson.............................Delta, Ohio
Private George B. Scott........................Kirkwood, Nebraska
Private William H. Smith...............Lock Box 116, Lakeside, Ohio
Private W. F. Thatcher..............635 Wilson Bldg., Dallas, Texas
Private James Taylor................................Sylvania, Ohio
Private Baker Woodruff.....................Sandusky Home, Ohio
Private John T. Woodford........................Larned, Kansas

COMPANY M

Lieutenant J. W. Likens............................Fulton, California
First Sergeant J. S. Chapin....1045 East Fifth Ave., Pomona, California
Sergeant William S. Furbay.......................Mt. Gilead, Ohio
Sergeant J. H. Fisher.................118 Lincoln Ave., Canton, Ohio
Sergeant L. R. Miller..........................Dodge City, Kansas
Sergeant Robert Mears..........................Covina, California
Sergeant John M. Ropp.............................Delaware, Ohio
Sergeant H. D. Smith.............................Cardington, Ohio
Corporal Rufus Aurand.............................Bucyrus, Ohio
Corporal E. A. Chapin.....................Box 423, Meade, Kansas
Corporal Daniel Clinger...521 South Eighth St., Upper Sandusky, Ohio
Corporal James S. Dodge...........................Elkhart, Indiana
Corporal Milton P. Martin...........R. F. D. No. 4, Mt. Vernon, Ohio
Corporal John E. Mahaffy..............Ravenden Springs, Arkansas
Corporal F. M. Smith.............................Garrison, Kansas
Bugler Jacob Trott.....................R. F. D. No. 3, Clyde, Ohio
Farrier Math Harrah.................................Larue, Ohio
Wagoner E. O. Morgan.....................Pluna Valley, Nebraska
Private Martin Adams...............................Bellevue, Ohio
Private Henry Beagle.......................Prattsville, Michigan
Private Henry Diefenbacher........................Bucyrus, Ohio
Private William Downard.......................Wapakoneta, Ohio
Private Samuel A. Essex.........................Greencamp, Ohio

Private Samuel Everett.............................Belvue, Kansas
Private L. Hollingsworth.............................Edison, Ohio
Private W. H. Hollenshead.........................Norton, Kansas
Private John T. Jamison.............................Findlay, Ohio
Private Michael Monlett.....................Sandusky Home, Ohio
Private James H. Madden............R. F. D. No. 19, Elsie, Michigan
Private Andrew J. Miller...........................Delaware, Ohio
Private William Pycroft.............................Marion, Ohio
Private Rose J. Parks.................R. F. D. No. 7, Delaware, Ohio
Private G. W. Preston.................................Galena, Ohio
Private Stephen Rucle.........................Seelemonia, Indiana
Private J. A. Simons.............................Greenleaf, Kansas
Private Jerry Wagoner.............................Dupont, Ohio
Private L. F. Webster.........................Ventura, California
Private Frederick Yahn.............................Rockford, Ohio

Third Ohio Volunteer Cavalry

THREE YEARS SERVICE

This Regiment was organized from the State at large, at Monroeville, Huron county, Ohio, from September 4, 1861, to December 11, 1861, to serve three years.

On the expiration of their term of service, the original members (except veterans) were mustered out, and the organization composed of veterans and recruits was retained in service until August 4, 1865, when it was mustered out in accordance with orders from the War Department.

The official list of battles, in which this Regiment bore an honorable part, has not yet been published by the War Department, but the following list has been compiled, after a careful research, during the preparation of this work:

SIEGE OF CORINTH, MISS., beginning . APRIL, 30, 1862.

MUMFORDSVILLE, KY., ... SEPTEMBER, 21, 1862.

BARDSTOWN, KY., ... OCTOBER 4, 1862.

LEXINGTON, KY., ... OCTOBER 17, 1862.

STONE RIVER, TENN., ... DECEMBER, 31, 1862.

STEWART'S CREEK, TENN., . . . JANUARY 1, 1863.

MIDDLETOWN, TENN., ... JANUARY 31, 1863.

CHICKAMAUGA, GA., ... SEPTEMBER 19-20, 1863.

McMINNVILLE, TENN., ... SEPTEMBER 28, 1863.

SHELBYVILLE PIKE (near Farmington, Tenn.), ... OCTOBER 7, 1863.

DECATUR, COURTLAND ROAD, ALA., MAY 26-27, 1864.

MOULTON, ALA., ... MAY 28-29, 1864.

NOONDAY CREEK, GA., ... JUNE 20, 1864.

KENESAW MOUNTAIN, GA., ... JUNE 27, 1864.

VINING STATION, GA., ... JULY 2, 1864.

PEACH TREE CREEK, GA., ... JULY 20, 1864.

JONESBORO, GA., ... AUGUST 19-20, 1864.

LOVEJOY STATION, GA., ... AUGUST 20, 1864.

FRANKLIN, TENN., ... NOVEMBER 30, 1864.

SELMA, ALA., ... APRIL 2, 1865.

COLUMBUS, GA., ... APRIL 16, 1865.

MACON, GA., ... APRIL 20, 1865.

Third Ohio Cavalry Monument at Chickamauga.

3rd Regiment Ohio Volunteer Cavalry

FIELD AND STAFF.

Mustered in December 11, 1861, at Camp Worcester, O., by James P. W. Neill, 1st Lieutenant 18th Infantry, U. S. A., Mustering Officer. Mustered out August 4, 1865, at Edgefield, Tenn., by James P. W. Neill, Captain 18th Infantry, U. S. A., and Acting Commissary of Musters, Cavalry Corps, M. D. T.

Names	Rank	Age	Date of Entering the Service	Period of Service	Remarks
Louis Zahm	Colonel	41	Aug. 6, 1861	3 yrs.	Appointed Aug. 6, 1861; resigned Jan. 5, 1863; brevetted Brig. General to date from March 13, 1865.
James W. Paramore	... do ...	31	Sept. 27, 1861	3 yrs.	Appointed Major Sept. 27, 1861; promoted to Colonel Jan. 5, 1863; honorably discharged to date July 1, 1863.
Charles B. Seidel	... do ...	25	Sept. 7, 1861	3 yrs.	Promoted to Major from Captain Co. E Jan. 16, 1862; captured Oct. 17, 1862, at Lexington, Ky.; paroled ——; promoted to Lieut. Colonel June 17, 1863; to Colonel Aug. 1, 1863; mustered out Jan. 16, 1865, on expiration of term of service.
Horace N. Howland	... do ...	37	Aug. 15, 1861	3 yrs.	Promoted to Major from Captain Co. O Jan. 5, 1863; to Lieut. Colonel Nov. 23, 1863; to Colonel April 8, 1865; brevetted Brig. General to date from March 13, 1865; mustered out with regiment Aug. 4, 1865.
Douglas A. Murray	Lt. Col.	36	Oct. 10, 1861	3 yrs.	Promoted from 2d Regiment U. S. Cavalry Oct. 10, 1861; resigned June 7, 1863.
Darius E. Livermore	... do ...	28	Nov. 1, 1861	3 yrs.	Promoted to Major from Captain Co. B Nov. 30, 1864; to Lieut. Colonel April 8, 1865; mustered out with regiment Aug. 4, 1865.
John H. Foster	Major	47	Sept. 13, 1861	3 yrs.	Appointed Sept. 13, 1861; resigned Feb. 14, 1863.
James S. Brisbin	... do ...				Appointed Dec. 12, 1861; commission declined.
Charles W. Skinner	... do ...	42	Aug. 20, 1861	3 yrs.	Promoted from Captain Co. H Feb. 14, 1863; resigned Sept. 10, 1864.
Leonard Adams	... do ...	28	Aug. 13, 1861	3 yrs.	Promoted from Captain Co. G June 7, 1863; mustered out Nov. 23, 1864, at Louisville, Ky., on expiration of term of service.
Thomas D. McClelland	... do ...	40	Sept. 4, 1861	3 yrs.	Promoted from Captain Co. E Dec. 8, 1863; mustered out Nov. 23, 1864, at Louisville, Ky., on expiration of term of service.
Martin Archer	... do ...	30	Aug. 20, 1861	3 yrs.	Promoted from Captain Co. G Nov. 30, 1864; to Colonel of the 137th Regiment U. S. Colored Troops April 7, 1865; from which he was mustered out as Colonel with the regiment Jan. 15, 1866.
Francis P. Gates	... do ...	26	Sept. 7, 1861	3 yrs.	Promoted from Captain Co. H Nov. 30, 1864; mustered out with regiment Aug. 4, 1865.
Oliver M. Brown	... do ...	35	Aug. 16, 1861	3 yrs.	Promoted from Captain Co. C April 8, 1865, but not mustered out with regiment Aug. 4, 1865.
Marion O. Cuykendall	Surgeon	32	Oct. 28, 1861	3 yrs.	Appointed Oct. 28, 1861; mustered out Nov. 16, 1864, at Columbia, Tenn., on expiration of term of service.
William B. Boyd	... do ...	34	Mch. 30, 1864	3 yrs.	Appointed Asst. Surgeon from civil life March 30, 1864; promoted to Surgeon Dec. 1, 1864; mustered out with regiment Aug. 4, 1865.
Stephen F. Selby	Ast. Sur.	....	Nov. 4, 1861	3 yrs.	Appointed Nov. 4, 1861; resigned Nov 15, 1863.
David K. Moore	... do ...	....	Aug. 19, 1862	3 yrs.	Also borne on rolls as John K. Moore; appointed Aug. 19, 1862; discharged as supernumerary Dec. 9, 1862, by order of War Department.
John G. Bingham	... do ...	....	Nov. 5, 1863	3 yrs	Appointed Nov. 5, 1863; declined commission.
William W. Bickett	... do ...	28	Mch. 31, 1864	3 yrs.	Appointed from civil life March 31, 1864; mustered out with regiment Aug. 4, 1865.
Lewis R. Zahm	Adjutant	17	Sept. 27, 1861	3 yrs.	Appointed Sept. 27, 1861; resigned Dec. 9, 1862.
George O. Probert	... do ...	24	Oct. 26, 1861	3 yrs.	Appointed Battalion Quartermaster Oct. 26, 1861; discharged Sept. 2, 1862, as supernumerary; re-appointed 1st Lieutenant and Adjutant March 31, 1863; resigned March 30, 1864.
Thomas Nunan	... do ...	20	Sept. 6, 1861	3 yrs.	Assigned from 1st Lieuenant Co. F July 22, 1864; promoted to Captain Co. I Nov. 30, 1864.

Names	Rank	Age	Date of Entering the Service	Period of Service	Remarks
David E. Tyler........	Adjutant	20	Sept. 4, 1861	3 yrs.	Promoted to Sergt. Major from Sergeant Co. B April 4, 1864; to 1st Lieutenant and Adjutant Nov. 30, 1864; mustered out with regiment Aug. 4, 1865; veteran.
William S. Foster.....	Bat.Adj.	20	June 29, 1861	3 yrs.	Promoted from private Co. D, 8th Regiment, O. V. I., Nov. 26, 1861; discharged Sept. 2, 1862, as supernumerary, by order of War Department.
Wood Fosdick	... do ...	23	Oct. 25, 1861	3 yrs.	Appointed Oct. 25, 1861; discharged Sept. 2, 1862, as supernumerary, by order of War Department.
Victor J. Zahm..........	... do ...	24	Oct. 26, 1861	3 yrs.	Appointed Oct. 26, 1861; discharged Sept. 2, 1862, as supernumerary, by order of War Department.
Frank S. Sowers.......	R. Q. M.	37	Aug. 30, 1861	3 yrs.	Appointed Aug. 30, 1861; resigned June 2, 1863.
Frank Wilham	... do ...	25	Oct. 6, 1861	3 yrs.	Appointed Batt. Q. M. Sergeant Oct. 6, 1861; promoted to 2d Lieutenant Co. G Jan. 21, 1863; to 1st Lieutenant and Regt. Quartermaster from 2d Lieutenant Co. A May 9, 1864; to Captain Nov. 30, 1864, but not mustered; mustered out Jan. 16, 1865, on expiration of term of service.
Thomas L. McEwen...	... do ...	21	Sept. 7, 1861	3 yrs.	Promoted to Regt. Com. Sergeant from Q. M. Sergeant Co. E Oct. 3, 1864; to 2d Lieutenant Co. F Nov. 30, 1864; to 1st Lieutenant and Regt. Quartermaster from 2d Lieutenant Co. F March 29, 1865; mustered out with regiment Aug. 4, 1865; veteran.
William R. Jackson...	B. Q. M.	38	Nov. 4, 1861	3 yrs.	Appointed Nov. 4, 1861; discharged Sept. 2, 1862, as supernumerary, by order of War Department.
Stiles W. Burr..........	... do ...	44	Oct. 26, 1861	3 yrs.	Appointed Oct. 26, 1861; discharged Sept. 2, 1862, as supernumerary, by order of War Department.
Seymour B. Coe.......	Cm.Sub.	43	Sept. 4, 1861	3 yrs.	Promoted to Batt. Q. M. Sergeant from private Co. I Sept. 7, 1861; to Regt. Q. M. Sergeant ——; to 1st Lieutenant and Commissary of Subsistence Dec. 15, 1862; to Captain Co. E Nov. 30, 1864.
Reed V. Boice	... do ...	29	Dec. 11, 1861	3 yrs.	Promoted to Batt. Hospital Steward from private Co. C Dec. 11, 1861; to Regt. Hospital Steward ——; to 1st Lieutenant and Commissary of Subsistence Nov. 30, 1864; to Captain Aug. 2, 1865, but not mustered; mustered out with regiment Aug. 4, 1865; veteran.
Edward Y. Warner....	Chaplain	28	Sept. 25, 1861	3 yrs.	Appointed Sept. 25, 1861; resigned Aug. 1, 1862.
Benj. F. W. Cozier.....	... do ...	28	May 9, 1864	3 yrs.	Appointed from civil life May 9, 1864; mustered out with regiment Aug. 4, 1865.
Henry M. Miller	Ser.Maj.	23	Sept. 7, 1861	3 yrs.	Promoted from Sergeant Co. E ——; to 1st Lieutenant Co. G March 21, 1863.
Calvin S. Kimball.......	... do ...	26	Sept. 10, 1861	3 yrs.	Promoted from private Co. C Jan. 4, 1864; to 2d Lieutenant Co. G March 31, 1864; veteran.
Joseph Berry	... do ...	38	Aug. 20, 1861	3 yrs.	Promoted from Sergeant Co. H March 1, 1865; to 2d Lieutenant Co. D April 8, 1865; veteran.
James Ransom Hall...	B. S. M.	21	Sept. 4, 1861	3 yrs.	Promoted from 1st Sergeant Co. A Dec. 1, 1861; to 2d Lieutenant Co. K May 21, 1862.
Henry Strieker	... do ...	34	Sept. 7, 1861	3 yrs.	Appointed Sept. 7, 1861; promoted to 2d Lieutenant Co. A May 16, 1862.
Edward A. Haines......	... do ...	22	Sept. 10, 1861	3 yrs.	Promoted from Sergeant Co. D ——; to 2d Lieutenant Co. H Sept. 11, 1862.
Brainard Fish	... do ...	20	Sept. 7, 1861	3 yrs.	Promoted from private Co. E Dec. 1, 1861; to 2d Lieutenant Co. D May 20, 1862.
Edwin Clark	... do ...	25	Sept. 4, 1861	3 yrs.	Promoted from Sergeant Co. A ——; to 2d Lieutenant Co. E May 20, 1862.
Myron H. Barrett.....	R.Q.M.S	20	Sept. 7, 1861	3 yrs.	Promoted from private Co. E ——; mustered out Oct. 3, 1864, on expiration of term of service.
George H. Frent........	... do ...	28	Dec. 3, 1861	3 yrs.	Promoted from Sergeant Co. K Oct. 3, 1864; to 2d Lieutenant Co. C Nov. 30, 1864; veteran.
Robert H. Bliven......	B.Q.M.S	18	Sept. 10, 1861	3 yrs.	Promoted from private Co. C Nov. 1, 1861; mustered out Dec. 15, 1862, at Columbus, O., to date Nov. 12, 1862, by order of War Department.
Jesse N. Squires........	R. C. S.	20	Sept. 3, 1861	3 yrs.	Promoted to Batt. Com. Sergeant from Sergeant Co. B Dec. 1, 1861; to Regt. Com. Sergeant ——; to 1st Lieutenant Co. H June 2, 1863.
William O. Johnson...	... do ...	....	Aug. 20, 1861	3 yrs.	Promoted from private Co. H ——; prisoner of war; mustered out April 7, 1865, at Columbus, O., on expiration of term of service.

Names	Rank	Age	Date of Entering the Service	Period of Service	Remarks
Francis W. Shaw......	R. O. S.	20	Nov. 27, 1861	3 yrs.	Promoted from Q. M. Sergeant Co. K May 1, 1865; mustered out with regiment Aug. 4, 1865; veteran.
James H. Johnson.....	B. O. S.	23	Aug. 29, 1861	3 yrs.	Promoted from Q. M. Sergeant Co. F Nov. 1, 1861; discharged to date Nov. 9, 1862, at Columbus, O., by order of War Department.
Christian R. Hopkins.	... do ...	23	Sept. 4, 1861	3 yrs.	Promoted from private Co. L Nov. 1, 1861; discharged to date Nov. 12, 1862, at Columbus, O., by order of War Department.
Silas M. Adams........	Hos.Std.	26	Sept. 4, 1861	3 yrs.	Promoted from private Co. A ——; mustered out Oct. 3, 1864, on expiration of term of service.
James B. Green..........	... do ...	18	Feb. 26, 1864	3 yrs.	Promoted from private Co. F Nov. 1, 1864; mustered out with regiment Aug. 4, 1865.
Edwin D. Tyler.........	... do ...	44	Sept. 4, 1861	3 yrs.	Promoted from private Co. B Jan. 1, 1865; mustered out with regiment Aug. 4, 1865; veteran.
John C. Grafton......	B. H. S.	22	Sept. 10, 1861	3 yrs.	Promoted from Corporal Co. G Dec. 1, 1861; discharged Jan. 22, 1863, on Surgeon's certificate of disability.
Horace B. White........	... do ...	50	Sept. 8, 1861	3 yrs.	Promoted from private Co. M Dec. 1, 1861; died March 9, 1862, at Cardington, O.
James M. Burg........	Sad. Ser.	24	Sept. 2, 1861	3 yrs.	Promoted to Batt. Sad. Sergeant from private Co. G Dec. 1, 1861; to Reg. Sad. Sergeant ——; mustered out Oct. 3, 1864, on expiration of term of service.
William H. Gardner...	... do ...	32	Sept. 3, 1864	1 yr.	Promoted from private Co. H May 1, 1865; mustered out June 15, 1865, at Nashville, Tenn., by order of War Department.
Andrew J. Noggle.....	B.S.Sgt.	31	Sept. 10, 1861	3 yrs.	Promoted from Saddler Co. D Dec. 1, 1861; discharged to date Nov. 12, 1862, at Columbus, O., by order of War Department.
William Hinman	Chf Bug.	28	Aug. 20, 1861	3 yrs.	Promoted from Bugler Co. H Dec. 1, 1861; discharged Nov. 19, 1862, by order of War Department.
Jerome R. Graham........	... do ...	22	Dec. 11, 1861	3 yrs.	Also borne on rolls as "Jerome R. Graves;" discharged Nov. 1, 1862, on Surgeon's certificate of disability.
Joseph Ott	... do ...	23	Aug. 20, 1861	3 yrs.	Promoted from Corporal Co. O Jan. 4, 1864; transferred to 2d Regiment Veteran Reserve Corps May 2, 1865, as Chief Bugler; died Feb. 15, 1866, from the effect of freezing.
George Doll	Vet. Sur.	45	Nov. 19, 1861	3 yrs.	Promoted from Farrier Co. K March —, 1863; mustered out Dec. 19, 1864, at Nashville, Tenn., on expiration of term of service.
Levi Cook	B. V. S.	38	Aug. 24, 1861	3 yrs.	Promoted from Farrier Co. O Dec. 1, 1861.
Artimus Richards	... do ...	25	Nov. 2, 1861	3 yrs.	Promoted from Farrier Co. F Dec. 1, 1861.
James B. Page........	... do ...	23	Sept. 24, 1861	3 yrs.	Promoted from Corporal Co. I Dec. 1, 1861; discharged Dec. 9, 1862, by order of War Department.

COMPANY A.

Mustered in September 4, 1861, at Camp Worcester, O., by James P. W. Neill, 1st Lieutenant 18th Infantry, U. S. A., Mustering Officer. Mustered out August 4, 1865, at Edgefield, Tenn., by James P. W. Neill, Captain 18th Infantry, U. S. A., Acting Commissary of Musters, Cavalry Corps, M. D. T.

Names	Rank	Age	Date of Entering the Service	Period of Service	Remarks
Dewitt C. Doane.......	Captain	47	Sept. 4, 1861	3 yrs.	Appointed Sept. 4, 1861; resigned Nov. 20, 1862.
Harrison Terry	... do ...	27	Sept. 4, 1861	3 yrs.	Appointed 2d Lieutenant Sept. 4, 1861; promoted to 1st Lieutenant Jan. 16, 1862; to Captain Feb. 14, 1863; resigned Dec. 14, 1864.
William B. Gates........	... do ...	20	Sept. 7, 1861	3 yrs.	Promoted to 1st Lieutenant from 2d Lieutenant Co. E Nov. 30, 1864; to Captain Dec. 14, 1864; on detached duty at Division headquarters since Jan. 11, 1865; mustered out Aug. 4, 1865, at Nashville, Tenn.
Thos. D. McClelland..	1st Lieu.	40	Sept. 4, 1861	3 yrs.	Appointed Sept. 4, 1861; promoted to Captain Co. E Jan. 16, 1862.

Names	Rank	Age	Date of Entering the Service	Period of Service	Remarks
Henry Stricker	1st Lieu.	34	Sept. 7, 1861	3 yrs.	Promoted to 2d Lieutenant from Batt. Serg. Major May 16, 1862; to 1st Lieutenant Feb. 1, 1863; to Captain July 13, 1864, but not mustered; mustered out Nov. 24, 1864, at Louisville, Ky., on expiration of term of service.
Joseph M. Fox	do	21	Sept. 7, 1861	3 yrs.	Promoted from 2d Lieutenant Co. E Jan. 6, 1865; mustered out wih company Aug. 4, 1865; veteran.
Frank J. Wilham	2d Lieu.	25	Oct. 6, 1861	3 yrs.	Transferred from Co. G April 24, 1863; promoted to 1st Lieutenant and Regt. Quartermaster May 9, 1864.
Samuel C. Currie	do	20	Sept. 4, 1861	3 yrs.	Mustered as private; appointed 1st Sergeant ——; promoted to 2d Lieutenant Co. L Nov. 30, 1863; transferred from Co. L Aug. 1, 1864; mustered out Nov. 26, 1864, at Louisville, Ky., on expiration of term of service.
Thomas C. Baker	do	19	Aug. 24, 1861	3 yrs.	Promoted from 1st Sergeant Co. G Nov. 30, 1864; to 1st Lieutenant Co. G Jan. 6, 1865; veteran.
Maylam J. Bassett	do	19	Sept. 4, 1861	3 yrs.	Promoted from 1st Sergeant Co. F Nov. 30, 1864; to 1st Lieutenant Co. O June 16, 1865; veteran.
James Ransom Hall	1st Serg.	21	Sept. 4, 1861	3 yrs.	Appointed Sept. 4, 1861; promoted to Batt. Sergt. Major Dec. 1, 1861.
John G. Oates	do	24	Sept. 4, 1861	3 yrs.	Appointed Corporal Nov. 13, 1861; Sergeant Jan. 2, 1862; 1st Sergeant May 1, 1862; promoted to 2d Lieutenant Co. B June 19, 1863.
Lewis B. Tooker	do	20	Sept. 4, 1861	3 yrs.	Mustered as private; appointed April 4, 1864; promoted to 1st Lieutenant Co. K Nov. 30, 1864; veteran.
Isaac Skillman	do	19	Sept. 4, 1861	3 yrs.	Mustered as private; appointed Dec. 2, 1864; promoted to 2d Lieutenant Co. B April 8, 1865; veteran.
Anson C. Ritter	do	26	Sept. 4, 1861	3 yrs.	Appointed Corporal Sept. 4, 1861; Q. M. Sergeant Jan. 1, 1865; 1st Sergeant June 10, 1865; mustered out with company Aug. 4, 1865; veteran.
George Milliman	Q. M. S.	22	Sept. 4, 1861	3 yrs.	Appointed Sept. 4, 1861; died April 13, 1862.
James B. Howarth	do	24	Jan. 1, 1862	3 yrs.	Mustered as private; appointed ——; mustered out Jan. 11, 1865, at Nashville, Tenn., on expiration of term of service.
Harrison Green	do	21	Sept. 4, 1861	3 yrs.	Mustered as private; appointed Com. Sergeant Jan. 1, 1865; Q. M. Sergeant June 10, 1865; mustered out with company Aug. 4, 1865; veteran.
Pitt Simons	Com Ser.	29	Sept. 4, 1861	3 yrs.	Mustered as private; appointed Sergeant ——; Com. Sergeant June 10, 1865; mustered out with company Aug. 4, 1865; veteran.
Edwin Clark	Sergeant	25	Sept. 4, 1861	3 yrs.	Appointed Sept. 4, 1861; promoted to Batt. Sergt. Major ——.
John W. Ward	do	27	Sept. 4, 1861	3 yrs.	Appointed Sept. 4, 1861; died Jan. 5, 1863, of wounds received ——.
Edward I. Hurlburt	do	21	Sept. 4, 1861	3 yrs.	Appointed Sept. 4, 1861.
Charles B. Bennett	do	18	Sept. 4, 1861	3 yrs.	Appointed Sept. 4, 1861; discharged Feb. 26, 1863, on Surgeon's certificate of disability.
Dailey Bennett	do	18	Sept. 4, 1861	3 yrs.	Mustered as private; appointed ——; mustered out Oct. 3, 1864, at Columbia, Tenn., on expiration of term of service.
Richard Meredith	do	20	Sept. 4, 1861	3 yrs.	Appointed Corporal Dec. 1, 1861; Sergeant May 1, 1863; discharged Feb. 18, 1864, at Richmond, on Surgeon's certificate of disability.
Thomas Tully	do	21	Sept. 4, 1861	3 yrs.	Mustered as private; appointed ——; mustered out Oct. 3, 1864, at Columbia, Tenn., on expiration of term of service.
Eugene A. Osborn	do	18	Sept. 4, 1861	3 yrs.	Appointed Bugler Sept. 4, 1861; Sergeant ——; discharged March 27, 1865, on Surgeon's certificate of disability; veteran.
Martin V. McCrillis	do	27	Sept. 4, 1861	3 yrs.	Appointed Corporal Sept. 4, 1861; Sergeant Dec. 2, 1864; mustered out with company Aug. 4, 1865; veteran.
Boston Lidruff	do	19	Sept. 4, 1861	3 yrs.	Appointed Corporal ——; Sergeant Dec. 2, 1864; mustered out with company Aug. 4, 1865; veteran.
Enos Griss	do	21	Sept. 4, 1861	3 yrs.	Appointed Corporal ——; Sergeant Jan. 11, 1865; mustered out with company Aug. 4, 1865; veteran.
John Monaghan	do	20	Sept. 4, 1861	3 yrs.	Appointed Corporal ——; Sergeant June 10, 1865; mustered out with company Aug. 4, 1865; veteran.
Albert McMaster	do	20	Sept. 4, 1861	3 yrs.	Appointed Corporal ——; Sergeant June 10, 1865; mustered out with company Aug. 4, 1865; veteran.

Names	Rank	Age	Date of Entering the Service	Period of Service	Remarks
Jacob Bauman	Corporal	23	Sept. 4, 1861	3 yrs.	Appointed Sept. 4, 1861; died July 3, 1862, of wounds received from guerrillas.
William E. Akers........	... do ...	26	Sept. 4, 1861	3 yrs.	Appointed Sept. 4, 1861; discharged June 20, 1862, on Surgeon's certificate of disability.
Siberia Kies	... do ...	24	Sept. 4, 1861	3 yrs.	Appointed Sept. 4, 1861; discharged Aug. 18, 1862, at Nashville, Tenn., on Surgeon's certificate of disability.
William McMaster	... do ...	24	Sept. 4, 1861	3 yrs.	Appointed Sept. 4, 1861; discharged April 22, 1863, on Surgeon's certificate of disability.
Henry M. Meachan.....	... do ...	24	Sept. 4, 1861	3 yrs.	Appointed Sept. 4, 1861; discharged May 18, 1862, on Surgeon's certificate of disability.
John Leary	... do ...	23	Dec. 10, 1863	3 yrs.	Appointed ——.
David H. Crippin.......	... do ...	24	Sept. 4, 1861	3 yrs.	Appointed ——; mustered out Oct. 3, 1864, at Columbia, Tenn., on expiration of term of service.
Richard Wilson	... do ...	28	Sept. 4, 1861	3 yrs.	Appointed ——; mustered out Oct. 3, 1864, at Columbia, Tenn., on expiration of term of service.
William Frederick	... do ...	24	June 29, 1862	3 yrs.	Appointed Dec. 1, 1864; mustered out June 17, 1865, at Nashville, Tenn., by order of War Department.
Charles Payne	... do ...	24	Sept. 4, 1861	3 yrs.	Appointed ——; mustered out with company Aug. 4, 1865; veteran.
James O. Grady........	... do ...	19	Dec. 4, 1863	3 yrs.	Appointed ——; mustered out with company Aug. 4, 1865.
William Raney	... do ...	23	Feb. 6, 1864	3 yrs.	Appointed ——; mustered out with company Aug. 4, 1865.
Samuel Lingo	... do ...	18	Sept. 4, 1861	3 yrs.	Appointed June 10, 1865; mustered out with company Aug. 4, 1865; veteran.
Colonel Shively	... do ...	19	Sept. 19, 1863	3 yrs.	Appointed June 10, 1865; mustered out with company Aug. 4, 1865.
Milton H. Straight......	... do ...	22	July 17, 1863	3 yrs.	Transferred from Co. C April 1, 1864; appointed June 10, 1865; mustered out with company Aug. 4, 1865.
Jacob Pye	... do ...	18	Dec. 10, 1863	3 yrs.	Appointed June 10, 1865; mustered out with company Aug. 4, 1865.
Henry Drage	... do ...	26	Sept. 4, 1861	3 yrs.	Appointed June 10, 1865; mustered out with company Aug. 4, 1865; veteran.
Ralph U. H. Osborn..	Bugler	21	Sept. 4, 1861	3 yrs.	Appointed Sept. 4, 1861; discharged March 16, 1864, at Camp Dennison, O., on Surgeon's certificate of disability.
John Nelis	... do ...	18	Sept. 11, 1863	3 yrs.	Appointed ——; mustered out with company Aug. 4, 1865.
Joel F. Smith..........	Farrier	24	Sept. 4, 1861	3 yrs.	Appointed Sept. 4, 1861; mustered out Oct. 3, 1864, at Columbia, Tenn., on expiration of term of service.
John B. McFadden.......	... do ...	43	Sept. 4, 1861	3 yrs.	Appointed Sept. 4, 1861; mustered out to date Aug. 4, 1865, at Columbus, O., by order of War Department; veteran.
William Voltz	... do ...	18	Sept. 11, 1863	3 yrs.	Appointed Feb. 11, 1865; mustered out with company Aug. 4, 1865.
Edward Morton	Saddler	21	Sept. 4, 1861	3 yrs.	Appointed Sept. 4, 1861; discharged Aug. 29, 1862, at Columbus, O., on Surgeon's certificate of disability.
Thos. G. Humphrey ..	... do ...	27	Dec. 4, 1863	3 yrs.	Appointed ——.
Adams, Silas M.	Private	26	Sept. 4, 1861	3 yrs.	Promoted to Hospital Steward ——.
Ames, Harrison	... do ...	21	Sept. 4, 1861	3 yrs.	Discharged Dec. 25, 1862, at Camp Rosecrans, Tenn., on Surgeon's certificate of disability.
Anderson, Isaac	... do ...	34	Aug. 4, 1863	3 yrs.	
Ball, Joseph	... do ...	20	Sept. 4, 1861	3 yrs.	Mustered out with company Aug. 4, 1865.
Bixby, Joseph	... do ...	25	Dec. 2, 1863	3 yrs.	Appointed Corporal ——; reduced April 20, 1865; mustered out with company Aug. 4, 1865.
Blackman, Ira	... do ...	39	Sept. 4, 1861	3 yrs.	Transferred to Co. K, 5th Regiment, Veteran Reserve Corps, Dec. 18, 1863, from which mustered out Sept. 9, 1864, by order of War Department.
Boehn, Peter	... do ...	23	Sept. 18, 1862	3 yrs.	Died June 17, 1863.
Brooks, Homer W......	... do ...	20	Sept. 4, 1861	3 yrs.	Mustered out Oct. 3, 1864, at Columbia, Tenn., on expiration of term of service.
Broughton, Alfred C..	... do ...	32	Sept. 4, 1861	3 yrs.	Discharged Sept. 1, 1862, at Columbus, O., on Surgeon's certificate of disability.
Burch, Hiram C........	... do ...	25	Sept. 4, 1861	3 yrs.	Discharged May 18, 1862, on Surgeon's certificate of disability.
Burch, John U.........	... do ...	20	Sept. 4, 1861	3 yrs.	
Caldwell, William	... do ...	18	Dec. 19, 1863	3 yrs.	Mustered out with company Aug. 4, 1865.
Carlisle, George	... do ...	25	Sept. 4, 1861	3 yrs.	Mustered out with company Aug. 4, 1865; veteran.
Carpenter, John	... do ...	22	Sept. 4, 1861	3 yrs.	Transferred to Co. L Jan. 1, 1862.
Chollar, Charles B....	... do ...	19	Jan. 1, 1862	3 yrs.	Prisoner of war; mustered out Feb. 28, 1865, at Columbus, O., on expiration of term of service.
Clark, George W......	... do ...	18	Aug. 30, 1863	3 yrs.	Mustered out with company Aug. 4, 1865.
Clark, Jacob	... do ...	26	Sept. 13, 1863	3 yrs.	Mustered out with company Aug. 4, 1865.

Names	Rank	Age	Date of Entering the Service	Period of Service	Remarks
Clawson, August	Private	18	Aug. 31, 1863	3 yrs.	Mustered out with company Aug. 4, 1865.
Conley, Thomas	...do...	18	Feb. 29, 1864	3 yrs.	Mustered out with company Aug. 4, 1865.
Conley, William	...do...	24	Sept. 4, 1861	3 yrs.	Captured Aug. 20, 1864, in battle of Lovejoy Station, Ga.; mustered out June 24, 1865, at Camp Chase, O., by order of War Department; veteran.
Crouse, William	...do...	23	Sept. 4, 1861	3 yrs.	Mustered out with company Aug. 4, 1865; veteran.
Deckenhousen, Ernest H.	...do...	42	Jan. 4, 1864	3 yrs.	Mustered out with company Aug. 4, 1865.
Dolph, Joseph	...do...	19	Sept. 4, 1861	3 yrs.	
Ecchard, William V.	...do...	19	Oct. 4, 1862	3 yrs.	Died Jan. 25, 1863.
Engles, Silas	...do...	39	Sept. 4, 1861	3 yrs.	Discharged March 9, 1863, on Surgeon's certificate of disability.
Ensign, Samuel L.	...do...	19	Sept. 7, 1863	3 yrs.	Mustered out with company Aug. 4, 1865.
Filler, Christopher	...do...	24	Dec. 15, 1863	3 yrs.	Mustered out with company Aug. 4, 1865.
Ford, Isaac W.	...do...	23	Sept. 4, 1861	3 yrs.	Mustered out Oct. 3, 1864, at Columbia, Tenn., on expiration of term of service.
Foster, Norman T.	...do...	24	Sept. 4, 1861	3 yrs.	Discharged Jan. 14, 1863, to receive promotion.
French, Stephen	...do...	19	Sept. 4, 1861	3 yrs.	Mustered out Oct. 3, 1864, at Columbia, Tenn., on expiration of term of service.
Frost, Curtis	...do...	19	Sept. 4, 1861	3 yrs.	Mustered out Oct. 3, 1864, at Columbia, Tenn., on expiration of term of service.
Funk, Philip	...do...	18	Feb. 26, 1864	3 yrs.	Mustered out with company Aug. 4, 1865.
Funk, William	...do...	19	Jan. 18, 1864	3 yrs.	Mustered out with company Aug. 4, 1865.
Glenn, Henry	...do...	18	Sept. 4, 1861	3 yrs.	Discharged June 30, 1862, on Surgeon's certificate of disability.
Goss, William	...do...	18	Aug. 1, 1864	3 yrs.	Mustered out with company Aug. 4, 1865.
Granger, Joseph R.	...do...	18	Nov. 19, 1861	3 yrs.	Mustered out with company Aug. 4, 1865; veteran.
Griggs, John	...do...	20	Dec. 1, 1863	3 yrs.	Prisoner of war since April 1, 1865; no further record found.
Hart, Franklin	...do...	19	Sept. 4, 1861	3 yrs.	Transferred to Co. F Jan. 4, 1864; veteran.
Hewitt, Ervin	...do...	33	Sept. 4, 1861	3 yrs.	Discharged March 17, 1863, on Surgeon's certificate of disability.
Hicks, Thomas W.	...do...	23	Sept. 4, 1861	3 yrs.	Discharged Jan. 29, 1863, on Surgeon's certificate of disability.
Himberger, William	...do...	20	Sept. 4, 1861	3 yrs.	Discharged to date Dec. 14, 1862, by order of War Department.
Hopkins, Silas H.	...do...	26	Sept. 4, 1861	3 yrs.	Mustered out Oct. 3, 1864, at Columbia, Tenn., on expiration of term of service.
Horton, Elijah	...do...	32	Sept. 4, 1861	3 yrs.	Transferred to Co. A, 8th Regiment, Veteran Reserve Corps, Sept. 12, 1863; mustered out from same Dec. 9, 1864, on expiration of term of service.
Horton, William H.	...do...	19	Sept. 4, 1861	3 yrs.	Mustered out with company Aug. 4, 1865; veteran.
Howard, Charles	...do...	18	Oct. 18, 1864	1 yr.	
Hughes, Michael	...do...	25	Sept. 4, 1861	3 yrs.	Transferred to Co. L Nov. 13, 1861.
Hunt, Isaac	...do...	42	Sept. 4, 1861	3 yrs.	Discharged Aug. 20, 1862, on Surgeon's certificate of disability.
Jewell, Charles C.	...do...	18	Sept. 4, 1861	3 yrs.	Mustered out Oct. 3, 1864, at Columbia, Tenn., on expiration of term of service.
Johnson, Lewis	...do...	18	Sept. 4, 1861	3 yrs.	Discharged March 16, 1863, at Readyville, Tenn., on Surgeon's certificate of disability.
Keeler, Joseph S.	...do...	24	Sept. 4, 1861	3 yrs.	Discharged April 9, 1863, on Surgeon's certificate of disability.
Kendall, John H.	...do...	18	Feb. 11, 1864	3 yrs.	Discharged May 17, 1865, on Surgeon's certificate of disability.
Kennedy, George W.	...do...	22	June 29, 1862	3 yrs.	Mustered out June 17, 1865, at Nashville, Tenn., by order of War Department.
Kinzel, Christopher J.	...do...	21	Nov. 9, 1861	3 yrs.	Mustered out Nov. 9, 1864, at Columbia, Tenn., on expiration of term of service.
Lakins, Albert C.	...do...	19	Oct. 26, 1861	3 yrs.	Mustered out Oct. 31, 1864, at Columbia, Tenn., on expiration of term of service.
Lamphier, Austin	...do...	18	Dec. 10, 1863	3 yrs.	Also borne on rolls as "Milo A."; mustered out with company Aug. 4, 1865.
Lapier, Joseph	...do...	25	Nov. 25, 1864	1 yr.	Mustered out with company Aug. 4, 1865.
Large, John W.	...do...	22	Sept. 4, 1861	3 yrs.	Mustered out Sept. 20, 1864, at Columbus, O., on expiration of term of service.
Lasley, James D.	...do...	18	Feb. 27, 1865	1 yr.	Mustered out with company Aug. 4, 1865.
Lee, Thomas A.	...do...	22	Aug. 17, 1862	3 yrs.	Discharged Feb. 3, 1863, on Surgeon's certificate of disability.
Letherer, George	...do...	22	Sept. 4, 1861	3 yrs.	Transferred to Co. K Dec. 11, 1861.
Lidkey, John A.	...do...	23	Dec. 23, 1863	3 yrs.	Also borne on rolls as "Leidke"; prisoner of war; mustered out June 19, 1865, at Camp Chase, O., by order of War Department.
McFerson, Allen	...do...	19	Sept. 4, 1861	3 yrs.	Also borne on rolls as "McPherson"; mustered out Oct. 3, 1864, at Columbia, Tenn., on expiration of term of service.
Martin, Henry G.	...do...	19	Jan. 4, 1864	3 yrs.	Mustered out with company Aug. 4, 1865.
Maxwell, James	...do...	25	Jan. 4, 1864	3 yrs.	Mustered out with company Aug. 4, 1865.
Meir, Alois	...do...	22	Dec. 10, 1863	3 yrs.	Mustered out with company Aug. 4, 1865.

Names	Rank	Age	Date of Entering the Service	Period of Service	Remarks
Meier, Xavier	Private	29	Dec. 12, 1863	3 yrs.	Died Oct. 27, 1864, of wounds received in action.
Miller, Levi	... do ...	19	Sept. 4, 1861	3 yrs.	Died May 29, 1862, near Corinth, Miss.
Moler, David E.	... do ...	20	Dec. 10, 1863	3 yrs.	Mustered out with company Aug. 4, 1865.
Morton, Robert E.	... do ...	18	Sept. 4, 1861	3 yrs.	Transferred to Co. K —.
Noggle, George W.	... do ...	22	Sept. 4, 1861	3 yrs.	Discharged Sept. 17, 1862, on Surgeon's certificate of disability.
Parkason, John	... do ...	29	Sept. 4, 1861	3 yrs.	Mustered out Oct. 3, 1864, at Columbia, Tenn., on expiration of term of service.
Parker, Hiram C.	... do ...	27	Oct. 7, 1862	3 yrs.	Discharged Oct. 29, 1863, on Surgeon's certificate of disability.
Pearce, Charles	... do ...	26	Sept. 17, 1863	3 yrs.	Discharged Dec. 21, 1864, on Surgeon's sertificate of disability.
Pearce, James	... do ...	26	Aug. 24, 1863	3 yrs.	Mustered out with company Aug. 4, 1865.
Peterson, Charles	... do ...	27	Dec. 4, 1863	3 yrs.	Mustered out with company Aug. 4, 1865.
Phelps, John D.	... do ...	18	Jan. 4, 1864	3 yrs.	Mustered out with company Aug. 4, 1865.
Polly, Jay	... do ...	19	Sept. 4, 1861	3 yrs.	Also borne on rolls as Jay A. Polley; mustered out Oct. 3, 1864, at Columbia, Tenn., on expiration of term of service.
Price, James	... do ...	19	Aug. 24, 1864	1 yr.	Mustered out June 17, 1865, at Nashville, Tenn., by order of War Department.
Purcil, Patrick	... do ...	20	Sept. 4, 1861	3 yrs.	Mustered out with company Aug. 4, 1865; veteran.
Raabe, August	... do ...	33	Jan. 4, 1864	3 yrs.	Mustered out with company Aug. 4, 1865.
Reed, Henry	... do ...	45	Sept. 15, 1863	3 yrs.	Mustered out with company Aug. 4, 1865.
Repetoy, Peter	... do ...	25	Jan. 4, 1864	3 yrs.	Mustered out with company Aug. 4, 1865.
Reynolds, Horace	... do ...	24	Sept. 4, 1861	3 yrs.	Died Feb. 5, 1864, at Nashville, Tenn.; veteran.
Rickey, Theodore	... do ...	26	Sept. 4, 1861	3 yrs.	Mustered out Oct. 3, 1864, at Columbia, Tenn., on expiration of term of service.
Rinehamer, Frederick	... do ...	21	Dec. 2, 1862	3 yrs.	Mustered out to date Aug. 3, 1865, by order of War Department.
Ritter, Witter	... do ...	31	Dec. 2, 1863	3 yrs.	Also borne on rolls as William; mustered out with company Aug. 4, 1865.
Root, Ezra H.	... do ...	19	Sept. 4, 1861	3 yrs.	Mustered out Oct. 3, 1864, at Columbia, Tenn., on expiration of term of service.
Saam, John W.	... do ...	33	Nov. 28, 1863	3 yrs.	Mustered out with company Aug. 4, 1865.
Satorious, Frank	... do ...	40	Dec. 2, 1863	3 yrs.	Also borne on rolls as Sartories; mustered out with company Aug. 4, 1865.
Seabolt, Jacob E.	... do ...	18	July 10, 1863	3 yrs.	Prisoner of war since April 1, 1865; no further record found.
Sekinger, Joseph	... do ...	38	Sept. 4, 1861	3 yrs.	Died Aug. 16, 1862, at Louisville, Ky.
Slaughterbeck, Charles	... do ...	41	Dec. 26, 1863	3 yrs.	Also borne on rolls as Slatterback; captured Aug. 20, 1864, at battle of Lovejoy Station, Ga.; mustered out June 24, 1865, at Camp Chase, O., by order of War Department.
Slaughter, Frank	... do ...	18	Dec. 27, 1863	3 yrs.	Mustered out with company Aug. 4, 1865.
Smith, George	... do ...	22	Sept. 4, 1861	3 yrs.	Discharged July 7, 1862, on Surgeon's certificate of disability.
Sprang, William	... do ...	22	Dec. 24, 1863	3 yrs.	Mustered out with company Aug. 4, 1865.
Strang, Jasper	... do ...	22	Sept. 4, 1861	3 yrs.	Also borne on rolls as Strong; died March 10, 1865, in hospital at Columbus, O.; veteran.
Sullivan, John	... do ...	19	Jan. 13, 1864	3 yrs.	
Turner, Marshal M.	... do ...	24	Sept. 4, 1861	3 yrs.	
Veader, George U.	... do ...	27	Sept. 4, 1861	3 yrs.	Transferred to Veteran Reserve Corps July 1, 1863; discharged Jan. 6, 1864, on Surgeon's certificate of disability.
Vokle, August	... do ...	42	Sept. 8, 1863	3 yrs.	Also borne on rolls as "Augustine Volk;" captured Nov. 14, 1864, at Marysville, Tenn.; reported May 24, 1865, at Camp Chase, O., as a paroled prisoner; mustered out July 18, 1865, at Camp Chase, O., by order of War Department.
Wait, Charles A.	... do ...	26	Sept. 4, 1861	3 yrs.	Died May 15, 1862, on Hamburg and Corinth road.
Weisonburger, George	... do ...	30	Dec. 12, 1863	3 yrs.	Mustered out with company Aug. 4, 1865.
Welch, Benjamin F.	... do ...	20	Sept. 4, 1861	3 yrs.	Discharged July 23, 1862, at Nashville, Tenn., on Surgeon's certificate of disability.
Weldon, James	... do ...	26	Sept. 4, 1861	3 yrs.	Transferred to Co. K Dec. 11, 1861.
Whidden, James T.	... do ...	18	Sept. 10, 1863	3 yrs.	Mustered out with company Aug. 4, 1865.
White, Henry R.	... do ...	22	Dec. 4, 1863	3 yrs.	Captured Aug. 20, 1864, at battle of Lovejoy Station, Ga.; supposed to have died Sept. 12, 1864, in Polk Hospital at Macon, Ga., of wounds received in action.
White, John	... do ...	19	Jan. 2, 1865	1 yr.	Absent with leave since Jan. 2, 1865; no further record found.
Williams, James O.	... do ...	21	Sept. 4, 1861	3 yrs.	Discharged Oct. 28, 1862, on Surgeon's certificate of disability.
Willoughby, John W.	... do ...	22	Aug. 29, 1861	3 yrs.	Transferred to Co. L Nov. 14, 1861.
Winnegar, William H.	... do ...	18	Sept. 5, 1863	3 yrs.	Died Feb. 29, 1864.
Woodford, John T.	... do ...	21	Sept. 4, 1861	3 yrs.	Appointed Corporal Sept. 4, 1861; transferred to Co. L Nov. 13, 1861; returned to Co. A Sept. 18, 1864; mustered out Oct. 3, 1864, at Columbia, Tenn., on expiration of term of service.

Names	Rank	Age	Date of Entering the Service	Period of Service	Remarks
Wright, George W.	Private	18	Sept. 4, 1861	3 yrs.	Discharged March 16, 1863, at Louisville, Ky., on Surgeon's certificate of disability.
Wright, Thomas C....	... do ...	21	Sept. 4, 1861	3 yrs.	Mustered out Oct. 3, 1864, at Columbia, Tenn., on expiration of term of service.
Young, Henry	... do ...	21	Sept. 4, 1861	3 yrs.	Mustered out with company Aug. 4, 1865; veteran.
Young, Martin	... do ...	26	Dec. 26, 1863	3 yrs.	Transferred to Co. E ——.
Zahmn, Michael	... do ...	38	Oct. 7, 1862	3 yrs.	Prisoner of war; mustered out June 15, 1865, at Camp Chase, O., by order of War Department.
Barrette, Barton	Cook	24	April 29, 1865	3 yrs.	Colored under-cook; mustered out with company Aug. 4, 1865.
Lock, Lewis	... do ...	34	April 7, 1865	3 yrs.	Colored under-cook; mustered out with company Aug. 4, 1865.
Mathews, Noble	... do ...	36	April 7, 1865	3 yrs.	Colored under-cook; mustered out with company Aug. 4, 1865.

COMPANY B.

Mustered in September 4, 1861, at Camp Worcester, O., by James P. W. Neill, 1st Lieutenant 18th Infantry, U. S. A., Mustering Officer. Mustered out August 4, 1865, at Nashville, Tenn., by James P. W. Neill, Captain 18th Infantry, U. S. A., Acting Commissary of Musters, Cavalry Corps, M. D. T.

Names	Rank	Age	Date of Entering the Service	Period of Service	Remarks
Leonard B. Chapin....	Captain	27	Sept. 4, 1861	3 yrs.	Appointed Sept. 4, 1861; resigned March 5, 1863.
Darius E. Livermore ..	... do ...	28	Nov. 1, 1861	3 yrs.	Promoted from 1st Lieutenant Co. K Feb. 1, 1863; to Major Nov. 30, 1864.
Christopher C. Clay....	... do ...	23	Aug. 20, 1861	3 yrs.	Promoted from 1st Lieutenant Co. F Nov. 30, 1864; mustered out with company Aug. 4, 1865.
Elisha M. Colver......	1st Lieu.	27	Sept. 4, 1861	3 yrs.	Appointed Sept. 4, 1861; promoted to Captain Co. K June 16, 1862.
Oliver M. Brown........	... do ...	35	Aug. 16, 1861	3 yrs.	Promoted from 2d Lieutenant Co. C July 20, 1862; captured Oct. 17, 1862, at battle of Lexington, Ky.; paroled ——; transferred to Co. K April 24, 1863.
Addison H. Pearl........	... do ...	31	Sept. 4, 1861	3 yrs.	Appointed Sergeant Sept. 4, 1861; promoted to 2d Lieutenant May 16, 1862; to 1st Lieutenant March 5, 1863; to Captain Nov. 30, 1864, but not mustered; mustered out Dec. 10, 1864, on expiration of term of service.
Thomas Marlin	... do ...	40	Oct. 28, 1861	3 yrs.	Promoted from 2d Lieutenant Co. M Jan, 6, 1865; mustered out with company Aug. 4, 1865; veteran.
Alonzo B. Ennis.......	2d Lieu.	34	Sept. 4, 1861	3 yrs.	Appointed Sept. 4, 1861; promoted to 1st Lieutenant June 16, 1862, but not mustered; resigned July 21, 1862.
Norman Brewster	... do ...	41	Sept. 4, 1861	3 yrs.	Promoted from Sergeant Co. L May 20, 1862; to 1st Lieutenant Co. C June 7, 1863.
John G. Oates...........	... do ...	24	Sept. 4, 1861	3 yrs.	Prisoner of war; promoted from 1st Sergeant Co. A June 19, 1863; to Captain Nov. 30, 1864, but not mustered; mustered out April 17, 1865, at Columbus, O., on expiration of term of service.
James M. Hipkins......	... do ...	29	Sept. 4, 1861	3 yrs.	Transferred from Co. L April 24, 1863.
Isaac Skillman	... do ...	23	Sept. 4, 1861	3 yrs.	Promoted from 1st Sergeant Co. A April 8, 1865; commanded Co. A since June 10, 1865; promoted to 1st Lieutenant Aug. 2, 1865, but not mustered; mustered out with company Aug. 4, 1865; veteran.
Garner Stimson	1st Serg.	25	Sept. 4, 1861	3 yrs.	Mustered as private; appointed Sergeant ——; captured Nov. 15, 1862, in action at Gallatin, Tenn.; paroled ——; appointed 1st Sergeant Feb. 10, 1864; promoted to 1st Lieutenant Co. I Nov. 30, 1864; veteran.
John H. Lawrence......	... do ...	20	Sept. 4, 1861	3 yrs.	Mustered as private; appointed Dec. 2, 1864; promoted to 2d Lieutenant Co. E April 8, 1865; veteran.
Philip B. Bangle........	... do ...	25	Sept. 4, 1861	3 yrs.	Mustered as private; appointed Sergeant Sept. 20, 1864; Com. Sergeant Dec. 2, 1864; 1st Sergeant June 17, 1865; mustered out with company Aug. 4, 1865; veteran.
Martin E. Ellis........	Q.M.Ser.	35	Sept. 4, 1861	3 yrs.	Discharged Sept. 11, 1862, at Columbus, O., on Surgeon's certificate of disability.

Names	Rank	Age	Date of Entering the Service	Period of Service	Remarks
Horace B. Porter......	Q.M.Ser.	35	Sept. 4, 1861	3 yrs.	Appointed Corporal Sept. 4, 1861; Q. M. Sergeant ——; captured Aug. 19, 1864, at battle of Jonesboro, Ga.; paroled ——; mustered out June 19, 1865, at Camp Chase, O., by order of War Department; veteran.
Arthur A. Rogers......	Com Ser.	19	Sept. 4, 1861	3 yrs.	Appointed Corporal April 4, 1864; Sergeant Dec. 2, 1864; Com. Sergeant ——; mustered out with company Aug. 4, 1865; veteran.
Jesse N. Squires	Sergeant	20	Sept. 4, 1861	3 yrs.	Promoted to Battalion Com. Sergeant Dec. 1, 1861.
Judson Willard	... do ...	28	Sept. 4, 1861	3 yrs.	Died Feb. 5, 1864, at Nashville, Tenn.; veteran.
John Bartlet	... do ...	32	Sept. 4, 1861	3 yrs.	Mustered out Oct. 3, 1864, at Columbia, Tenn., on expiration of term of service.
Henry N. Porter..........	... do ...	37	Sept. 4, 1861	3 yrs.	Discharged Dec. 15, 1862, at Cincinnati, O., on Surgeon's certificate of disability.
David E. Tyler..........	... do ...	20	Sept. 4, 1861	3 yrs.	Mustered as private; appointed ——; promoted to Sergt. Major April 4, 1864; veteran.
George W. Cole........	... do ...	26	Sept. 4, 1861	3 yrs.	Mustered as private; appointed ——; mustered out Oct. 3, 1864, at Columbia, Tenn., on expiration of term of service.
Hiram Sexton	... do ...	26	Sept. 4, 1861	3 yrs.	Mustered as private; appointed ——; mustered out Oct. 3, 1864, at Columbia, Tenn., on expiration of term of service.
Cornelius Ellis	... do ...	20	Sept. 3, 1861	3 yrs.	Appointed from Corporal ——; mustered out Oct. 3, 1864, at Columbia, Tenn., on expiration of term of service.
Samuel B. Bassett	... do ...	24	Sept. 4, 1861	3 yrs.	Mustered as private; appointed ——; mustered out Oct. 3, 1864, at Columbia, Tenn., on expiration of term of service.
Ambrose D. Hawes.....	... do ...	18	Sept. 4, 1861	3 yrs.	Mustered as private; appointed ——; promoted to 2d Lieutenant Co. H Nov. 30, 1864; veteran.
Titus B. Terry..........	... do ...	19	Feb. 23, 1864	3 yrs.	Appointed Corporal April 4, 1864; Sergeant Dec. 2, 1864; mustered out July 27, 1865, at Macon, Ga., by order of War Department.
Henry S. Rounds........	... do ...	22	July 16, 1863	3 yrs.	Appointed Corporal Oct. 30, 1864; Sergeant Dec. 2, 1864; mustered out with company Aug. 4, 1865.
William A. Segar........	... do ...	18	Feb. 29, 1864	3 yrs.	Mustered as private; appointed ——; died June 16, 1865, at Macon, Ga.
Franklin Starr	... do ...	18	Oct. 16, 1863	3 yrs.	Mustered as private; appointed ——; died July 7, 1865, at Macon, Ga.
Seneca Ronk	... do ...	23	Feb. 27, 1864	3 yrs.	Appointed Corporal Dec. 2, 1864; Sergeant June 16, 1865; mustered out with company Aug. 4, 1865.
Frederick H. Kellogg..	... do ...	23	Jan. 4, 1864	3 yrs.	Appointed Corporal Dec. 2, 1864; Sergeant June 17, 1865; mustered out with company Aug. 4, 1865.
Thomas C. Bryant.......	... do ...	20	Nov. 22, 1863	3 yrs.	Appointed Corporal Dec. 2, 1864; Sergeant July 6, 1865; mustered out with company Aug. 4, 1865.
Charles Johnson	Corporal	28	Sept. 4, 1861	3 yrs.	Mustered out Oct. 20, 1864, at Columbia, Tenn., on expiration of term of service.
George W. Burgess.....	... do ...	27	Sept. 4, 1861	3 yrs.	Died July 12, 1862, at Nashville, Tenn.
John J. Cowels..........	... do ...	20	Sept. 4, 1861	3 yrs.	Died May 23, 1862.
Morgan J. Carpenter.....	... do ...	30	Sept. 4, 1861	3 yrs.	Died April 28, 1862.
Hiram C. Reed	... do ...	21	Sept. 4, 1861	3 yrs.	Discharged March 15, 1863, at Columbus, O., on Surgeon's certificate of disability.
Byron L. White..........	... do ...	21	Sept. 4, 1861	3 yrs.	Died March 3, 1863, at Murfreesboro, Tenn.
James C. Ronk..........	... do ...	25	Sept. 4, 1861	3 yrs.	Appointed ——; died May 2, 1862, on board hospital boat near Paducah, Ky.
David C. Fields..........	... do ...	20	Sept. 4, 1861	3 yrs.	Appointed ——; died July 4, 1864, near Marietta, Ga., of wounds received in action; veteran.
George Wilson	... do ...	17	Sept. 4, 1861	3 yrs.	Appointed ——; died Aug. 16, 1864, at Buck Head, Ga., of wounds received in action.
Charles E. Heusted......	... do ...	18	Feb. 19, 1864	3 yrs.	Appointed ——; mustered out May 25, 1865, at Louisville, Ky., by order of War Department.
James Vantassel	... do ...	19	Nov. 24, 1863	3 yrs.	Appointed ——; mustered out April 11, 1865, at Camp Dennison, O., by order of War Department.
Charles Lasselle	... do ...	18	Feb. 14, 1864	3 yrs.	Appointed ——; mustered out June 13, 1865, at Camp Dennison, O., by order of War Department.
Henry Thompson	... do ...	29	Aug. 19, 1863	3 yrs.	Appointed April 11, 1865; mustered out with company Aug. 4, 1865.
Royal P. Peck..........	... do ...	19	Feb. 23, 1864	3 yrs.	Appointed April 11, 1865; mustered out with company Aug. 4, 1865.
Mortimer Lawrence	... do ...	18	Sept. 4, 1861	3 yrs.	Appointed May 13, 1865; mustered out with company Aug. 4, 1865; veteran.
John Scott	... do ...	23	Aug. 18, 1863	3 yrs.	Appointed May 25, 1865; mustered out with company Aug. 4, 1865.

Names	Rank	Age	Date of Entering the Service	Period of Service	Remarks
Samuel L. Hillyer.....	Corporal	18	Feb. 24, 1864	3 yrs.	Appointed June 16, 1865; mustered out with company Aug. 4, 1865.
Orin Adams	... do ...	21	Sept. 4, 1861	3 yrs.	Appointed June 17, 1865; mustered out with company Aug. 4, 1865; veteran.
Alansan Adams	... do ...	23	Feb. 2, 1864	3 yrs.	Appointed July 6, 1865; mustered out with company Aug. 4, 1865.
William D. Chaffer....	Farrier	37	Sept. 4, 1861	3 yrs.	
Elisha Jenkins	... do ...	37	Sept. 4, 1861	3 yrs.	Discharged Aug. 6, 1862, on Surgeon's certificate of disability.
Garrett Hawley	... do ...	22	Sept. 4, 1861	3 yrs.	Absent from Nov. 30, 1861, to Nov. 1, 1863; appointed Feb. 28, 1865; mustered out Sept. 7, 1865, at Camp Dennison, O., by order of War Department.
Lawrence Michael	Saddler	23	Sept. 4, 1861	3 yrs.	Appointed ——; mustered out with company Aug. 4, 1865; veteran.
Myron Sweet	Wagoner	42	Sept. 4, 1861	3 yrs.	Appointed ——; mustered out with company Aug. 4, 1865; veteran.
Akeins, Jerome	Private	18	Aug. 6, 1863	3 yrs.	
Ames, Saren	... do ...	19	April 23, 1862	3 yrs.	Mustered out May 18, 1865, at Cleveland, O., on expiration of term of service.
Atkinson, Delmer	... do ...	19	Feb. 24, 1864	3 yrs.	Mustered out with company Aug. 4, 1865.
Avary, George W.	... do ...	24	Feb. 25, 1865	1 yr.	Mustered out with company Aug. 4, 1865.
Barber, Theodore P....	... do ...	24	Sept. 4, 1861	3 yrs.	Mustered out Aug. 1, 1865, at Camp Dennison, O., by order of War Department.
Beckwith, Christ. C...	... do ...	44	Dec. 11, 1863	3 yrs.	Mustered out June 5, 1865, at Louisville, Ky., by order of War Department.
Berg, Cornelius K....	... do ...	18	Feb. 27, 1864	3 yrs.	Also borne on rolls as Cornelius Kburg; mustered out with company Aug. 4, 1865.
Blackman, Simeon	... do ...	18	Sept. 4, 1861	3 yrs.	Discharged Sept. 26, 1862, at Columbus, O., on Surgeon's certificate of disability.
Brooks, James	... do ...	19	Sept. 4, 1861	3 yrs.	Discharged June 17, 1862, on Surgeon's certificate of disability.
Brown, Charles	... do ...	31	Sept. 4, 1861	3 yrs.	Discharged June 4, 1863, on Surgeon's certificate of disability.
Brown, Henry	... do ...	28	Sept. 4, 1861	3 yrs.	
Brown, Isaac	... do ...	21	Sept. 4, 1861	3 yrs.	Mustered out Oct. 3, 1864, at Columbia, Tenn., on expiration of term of service.
Buckley, Frank	... do ...	20	Sept. 4, 1861	3 yrs.	
Camfield, Luther	... do ...	18	Sept. 4, 1861	3 yrs.	Detached as Wardmaster in hospital at Louisville, Ky.; no further record found.
Case, Lester	... do ...	24	Sept. 4, 1861	3 yrs.	Discharged Nov. 1, 1861, at Monroeville, O., on Surgeon's certificate of disability.
Cherrington, John G...	... do ...	32	April 1, 1865	1 yr.	Mustered out with company Aug. 4, 1865.
Church, Elias	... do ...	18	Aug. 30, 1862	3 yrs.	Discharged Sept. 1, 1863, on Surgeon's certificate of disability.
Clinger, Anson	... do ...	19	Sept. 4, 1861	3 yrs.	Discharged Dec. 22, 1862, on Surgeon's certificate of disability.
Collingwood, Ransom .	... do ...	22	Sept. 4, 1861	3 yrs.	Mustered out with company Aug. 4, 1865; veteran.
Colvin, Jerred	... do ...	27	Sept. 4, 1861	3 yrs.	
Corbon, Jude	... do ...	20	Sept. 4, 1861	3 yrs.	Discharged Jan. 19, 1863, on Surgeon's certificate of disability.
Crippin, Daniel A......	... do ...	24	Feb. 23, 1864	3 yrs.	Mustered out July 20, 1865, at Louisville, Ky., by order of War Department.
Dolan, James P........	... do ...	24	Aug. 19, 1863	3 yrs.	
Drake, Benjamin F.....	... do ...	24	Sept. 4, 1861	3 yrs.	Died Sept. 21, 1862.
Drake, Frederick	... do ...	22	Sept. 28, 1861	3 yrs.	Transferred from Co. I April 17, 1865; mustered out with company Aug. 4, 1865; veteran.
Earl, Thomas	... do ...	42	Jan. 1, 1862	3 yrs.	Mustered out Jan. 11, 1865, at Nashville, Tenn., on expiration of term of service.
Eastman, William	... do ...	18	Sept. 4, 1861	3 yrs.	Mustered out Oct. 3, 1864, at Columbia, Tenn., on expiration of term of service.
Edwards, Avery	... do ...	34	Sept. 4, 1861	3 yrs.	Absent from Oct. 20, 1861, to Nov. 1, 1863; mustered out with company Aug. 4, 1865.
Fairfax, James	... do ...	28	Sept. 4, 1861	3 yrs.	Discharged June 2, 1862, at Cincinnati, O., on Surgeon's certificate of disability.
Farr, Martin	... do ...	24	Aug. 19, 1863	3 yrs.	Also borne on rolls as Finn, and Tin.
Fay, Franklin	... do ...	24	Sept. 4, 1861	3 yrs.	Mustered out Oct. 3, 1864, at Columbia, Tenn., on expiration of term of service.
Fay, James W..........	... do ...	25	Sept. 4, 1861	3 yrs.	Died March 1, 1863, at Nashville, Tenn.
Fisar, William	... do ...	28	Sept. 4, 1861	3 yrs.	Also borne on rolls as Fizer; discharged Oct. 25, 1864, on Surgeon's certificate of disability; veteran.
Fonger, William	... do ...	30	Mch. 4, 1864	3 yrs.	Mustered out with company Aug. 4, 1865.
Goodell, Bethel	... do ...	31	Jan. 4, 1864	3 yrs.	Mustered out with company Aug. 4, 1865.
Gray, James M.........	... do ...	40	Oct. 20, 1862	3 yrs.	Discharged June 29, 1863, on Surgeon's certificate of disability.
Green, Albert H........	... do ...	18	Feb. 26, 1864	3 yrs.	Mustered out with company Aug. 4, 1865.
Gregory, Joseph	... do ...	18	Aug. 10, 1863	3 yrs.	Mustered out with company Aug. 4, 1865.
Hamton, Peter	... do ...	21	Mch. 17, 1865	1 yr.	Mustered out to date Aug. 4, 1865, at Columbus, O., by order of War Department.
Harding, Lewis	... do ...	37	Sept. 4, 1861	3 yrs.	Died Dec. 26, 1862, at Nashville, Tenn.

Names	Rank	Age	Date of Entering the Service	Period of Service	Remarks
Hardy, Eli S............	Private	34	Sept. 4, 1861	3 yrs.	Died Sept. 14, 1862.
Haynes, John P........	...do ...	27	April 5, 1865	1 yr.	Mustered out with company Aug. 4, 1865.
Hayes, William	...do ...	32	Sept. 4, 1861	3 yrs.	Discharged to date Nov. 4, 1862, by order of War Department.
Henry, Mendile	...do ...	32	Sept. 4, 1861	3 yrs.	Shot by guerrillas Feb. 6, 1863.
Hernando, George	...do ...	20	Aug. 29, 1863	3 yrs.	Discharged Aug. 24, 1864, at Camp Dennison, O., on Surgeon's certificate of disability.
Hickock, Herman	...do ...	19	Sept. 4, 1861	3 yrs.	Mustered out with company Aug. 4, 1865; veteran.
Hillman, Benjamin B.	....do ...	31	Sept. 4, 1861	3 yrs.	Discharged Aug. 20, 1863, at Columbus, O., on Surgeon's certificate of disability.
Hollister, Edwin	...do ...	22	Sept. 4, 1861	3 yrs.	Mustered out with company Aug. 4, 1865; veteran.
Hollister, Jesse	...do ...	18	Sept. 4, 1861	3 yrs.	Mustered out with company Aug. 4, 1865; veteran.
Horton, Edward W...	....do ...	19	Mch. 28, 1864	3 yrs.	Mustered out with company Aug. 4, 1865.
Houpt, William H.	...do ...	22	Feb. 27, 1864	3 yrs.	Mustered out June 2, 1865, from hospital at Camp Dennison, O., by order of War Department.
Huff, Willard A........	...do ...	40	Feb. 12, 1864	3 yrs.	Mustered out with company Aug. 4, 1865.
Humphery, Truman	...do ...	26	Feb. 6, 1864	3 yrs.	Mustered out with company Aug. 4, 1865.
Ingles, Lorenzo	...do ...	18	Sept. 4, 1861	3 yrs.	Killed Dec. 2, 1863, in action at Philadelphia, Tenn.
Jenkins, William	...do ...	21	Sept. 4, 1861	3 yrs.	Mustered out June 17, 1865, at Nashville, Tenn., on expiration of term of service.
Keim, Conrad	...do ...	19	Sept. 4, 1861	3 yrs.	Discharged Feb. 9, 1863, on Surgeon's certificate of disability.
Kilburn, Flarius	...do ...	24	Sept. 4, 1861	3 yrs.	Discharged to date Nov. 22, 1862, on Surgeon's certificate of disability.
King, Michael	...do ...	19	Sept. 3, 1863	3 yrs.	Prisoner of war; mustered out Sept. 20, 1865, at New York City, by order of War Department.
Knapp, Henry J........	...do ...	18	Oct. 13, 1863	3 yrs.	Mustered out with company Aug. 4, 1865.
Kress, Henry E.........	...do ...	42	Sept. 4, 1861	3 yrs.	Mustered out Oct. 3, 1864, at Columbia, Tenn., on expiration of term of service.
Lane, Henry C. G......	...do ...	25	Sept. 4, 1861	3 yrs.	Transferred to Co. D, 2d Regiment, Veteran Reserve Corps, ——; mustered out from same Sept. 5, 1864, at Detroit, Mich., on expiration of term of service.
Lavin, Bartley	...do ...	24	Feb. 21, 1864	3 yrs.	Mustered out with company Aug. 4, 1865.
Leonard, Henry	...do ...	22	Aug. 19, 1863	3 yrs.	
Lipke, David C.	...do ...	22	Sept. 4, 1861	3 yrs.	
McFall, John G.	...do ...	27	Sept. 4, 1861	3 yrs.	Mustered out with company Aug. 4, 1865; veteran.
McGloon, Charles M...	...do ...	22	Sept. 4, 1861	3 yrs.	Died May 3, 1862, in camp near Corinth, Miss.
McKim, George W......	...do ...	19	Jan. 1, 1862	3 yrs.	Mustered out Jan. 11, 1865, at Nashville, Tenn., on expiration of term of service.
McKim, Thomas W....	...do ...	22	Sept. 4, 1861	3 yrs.	Mustered out with company Aug. 4, 1865; veteran.
Mack, Henry	...do ...	21	April 5, 1865	1 yr.	Mustered out with company Aug. 4, 1865.
Malki, James	...do ...	18	Sept. 4, 1861	3 yrs.	Killed Dec. 31, 1862, in battle of Stone River, Tenn.
Mason, Almon	...do ...	25	Sept. 4, 1861	3 yrs.	Discharged Dec. 18, 1862, on Surgeon's certificate of disability.
Mason, Jeremiah B. ..	...do ...	22	Sept. 4, 1861	3 yrs.	Mustered out with company Aug. 4, 1865; veteran.
Mason, Norman	...do ...	38	Sept. 4, 1861	3 yrs.	Discharged Aug. 20, 1862, at Nashville, Tenn., on Surgeon's certificate of disability.
Menus, John C..........	...do ...	18	Feb. 29, 1864	3 yrs.	Also borne on rolls as Monise; mustered out with company Aug. 4, 1865.
Mire, William	...do ...	19	Feb. 3, 1864	3 yrs.	Also borne on rolls as Myer; mustered out with company Aug. 4, 1865.
Miller, John	...do ...	23	Jan. 5, 1864	3 yrs.	Mustered out with company Aug. 4, 1865.
Miller, Samuel	...do ...	21	Mch. 4, 1864	3 yrs.	
Monday, William	...do ...	....	Sept. 4, 1861	3 yrs.	Discharged Sept. 4, 1863, at Nashville, Tenn., on Surgeon's certificate of disability.
Morris, Amos A........	...do ...	22	Sept. 4, 1861	3 yrs.	Died July 10, 1862.
Nelson, Charles H......	...do ...	20	Feb. 27, 1864	3 yrs.	Mustered out with company Aug. 4, 1865.
Nelson, Jerome C......	...do ...	18	Nov. 23, 1863	3 yrs.	Mustered out with company Aug. 4, 1865.
Parker, John	...do ...	29	Aug. 17, 1863	3 yrs.	Died March 13, 1864, at Nashville, Tenn.
Peck, Flavus J.........	...do ...	18	July 1, 1863	3 yrs.	Mustered out with company Aug. 4, 1865.
Peck, Marcus M.......	...do ...	18	Aug. 31, 1862	3 yrs.	Discharged Jan. 23, 1863, on Surgeon's certificate of disability; re-enlisted Feb. 22, 1864, for 3 years; mustered out with company Aug. 4, 1865.
Peck, Uriah A.........	...do ...	16	Feb. 23, 1864	3 yrs.	Mustered out July 14, 1865, from hospital at Camp Dennison, O., by order of War Department.
Perham, George	...do ...	39	July 16, 1863	3 yrs.	Prisoner of war since Jan. 12, 1864; died Sept. 21, 1864, at Andersonville Prison, Ga.
Rice, Myron	...do ...	18	Sept. 4, 1861	3 yrs.	Died April 13, 1862, at Nashville, Tenn.
Rice, Rodney	...do ...	30	Sept. 4, 1861	3 yrs.	Mustered out Oct. 3, 1864, at Columbia, Tenn., on expiration of term of service.
Roberts, Simon	...do ...	21	Sept. 4, 1861	3 yrs.	
Robinson, John	...do ...	27	Feb. 20, 1864	3 yrs.	

Names	Rank	Age	Date of Entering the Service	Period of Service	Remarks
Robinson, William	Private	19	Feb. 22, 1864	3 yrs.	Mustered out with company Aug. 4, 1865.
Rounds, George R........	do ...	18	July 16, 1863	3 yrs.	Mustered out with company Aug. 4, 1865.
Scott, Henry H..........	do ...	19	Sept. 4, 1861	3 yrs.	Discharged Sept. 11, 1862, at Nashville, Tenn., on Surgeon's certificate of disability.
Sexton, Edwin	do ...	30	Oct. 20, 1862	3 yrs.	Mustered out with company Aug. 4, 1865.
Shellenburger, Conrad.	do ...	25	Sept. 4, 1861	3 yrs.	Mustered out with company Aug. 4, 1865; veteran.
Shunkle, John	do ...	21	Aug. 24, 1863	3 yrs.	Mustered out May 29, 1865, at Louisville, Ky., by order of War Department.
Smith, Albert C.........	do ...	19	Sept. 4, 1861	3 yrs.	Died April 17, 1862.
Smith, John H.	do ...	18	Oct. 16, 1863	3 yrs.	Died July 28, 1865, at Jeffersonville, Ind.
Smith, John Y..........	do ...	38	Sept. 4, 1861	3 yrs.	Died May 23, 1862.
Snyder, Frederick M...	do ...	20	April 6, 1865	1 yr.	Mustered out with company Aug. 4, 1865.
Spurier, Willard	do ...	18	Sept. 4, 1861	3 yrs.	Mustered out April 20, 1865, at Columbus, O., on expiration of term of service.
Stark, Lewis	do ...	28	Feb. 25, 1864	3 yrs.	Mustered out with company Aug. 4, 1865.
Starr, Orlando	do ...	20	Sept. 4, 1861	3 yrs.	Discharged May 18, 1862, at Camp near Corinth, Miss., on Surgeon's certificate of disability.
Staunton, Byron	do ...	....	Dec. 1, 1861	3 yrs.	Also borne on rolls as "Stanton;" killed Dec. 30, 1862, in battle of Stone River, Tenn.
Stewart, John W........	do ...	19	Feb. 24, 1865	1 yr.	Mustered cut with company Aug. 4, 1865.
Squire, George B........	do ...	21	Sept. 4, 1861	3 yrs.	Mustered out with company Aug. 4, 1865; veteran.
Tripp, Edmon	do ...	21	Sept. 4, 1861	3 yrs.	Discharged Sept. 11, 1862, on Surgeon's certificate of disability.
Tracy, Parmer	do ...	25	Sept. 4, 1861	3 yrs.	
Tucker, William	do ...	18	July 16, 1863	3 yrs.	Mustered out with company Aug. 4, 1865.
Tyler, Edwin D.........	do ...	44	Sept. 4, 1861	3 yrs.	Promoted to Hospital Steward Jan. 1, 1865; veteran.
Vorman, Benjamin	do ...	18	Feb. 14, 1864	3 yrs.	Mustered out with company Aug. 4, 1865.
Walker, Henry S........	do ...	18	Feb. 29, 1864	3 yrs.	Mustered out Aug. 1, 1865, from hospital at Camp Dennison, O., by order of War Department.
Webb, Styles	do ...	18	Aug. 11, 1863	3 yrs.	Mustered out May 30, 1865, at Cleveland, O., by order of War Department.
Welch, Robert	do ...	23	Sept. 4, 1861	3 yrs.	Died April 19, 1865; veteran.
Welch, William	do ...	18	Aug. 23, 1863	3 yrs.	
Wetz, Peter	do ...	20	Sept. 4, 1861	3 yrs.	Discharged Aug. 20, 1863, at Nashville, Tenn., on Surgeon's certificate of disability.
Adams, Samuel	Cook	18	April 26, 1865	1 yr.	Colored under-cook; no further record found.
Clark, Charles	do ...	35	June 17, 1863	3 yrs.	Colored under-cook; mustered out with company Aug. 4, 1865.
Jones, Stephen	do ...	....	June 21, 1865	1 yr.	Colored under-cook; mustered out with company Aug. 4, 1865.
McFarlin, Kit	do ...	45	April 26, 1865	1 yr.	Colored under-cook; died May 6, 1865, at Macon, Ga.
Washington, Jerry	do ...	45	Mch. 4, 1863	3 yrs.	Colored under-cook; mustered out with company Aug. 4, 1865.

COMPANY C.

Mustered in October 8, 1861, at Camp Worcester, O., by James P. W. Neill, 1st Lieutenant 18th Infantry, U. S. A., Mustering Officer. Mustered out August 4, 1865, at Nashville, Tenn., by James P. W. Neill, Captain 18th Infantry, U. S. A., Acting Commissary of Musters, Cavalry Corps, M. D. T.

Horace N. Howland...	Captain	37	Aug. 15, 1861	3 yrs.	Appointed Aug. 15, 1861; captured Oct. 17, 1862, at battle of Lexington, Ky.; paroled ——; promoted to Major Jan. 5, 1863.
James B. Luckey........	do ...	18	Sept. 4, 1861	3 yrs.	Promoted from 1st Lieutenant Co. L Jan. 5, 1863; transferred to Co. L April 5, 1864.
Oliver M. Brown........	do ...	35	Aug. 16, 1861	3 yrs.	Appointed 2d Lieutenant Aug. 16, 1861; promoted to 1st Lieutenant Co. B July 20, 1862; to Captain from 1st Lieutenant Co. K Aug. 19, 1863; to Major April 8, 1865, but not mustered; mustered out with company Aug. 4, 1865.
Jonathan B. Blivin....	1st Lieu.	....	Aug. 24, 1861	3 yrs.	Appointed Aug. 24, 1861; honorably discharged Jan. 21, 1863.
Elihu Isbell	do ...	26	Sept. 6, 1861	3 yrs.	Promoted from 2d Lieutenant Co. F Jan. 5, 1863; transferred to Co. F April 24, 1863.
Samuel J. Hansey.......	do ...	26	Aug. 20, 1861	3 yrs.	Promoted from 2d Lieutenant Co. H Sept. 11, 1862; resigned June 19, 1863.

Names	Rank	Age	Date of Entering the Service	Period of Service	Remarks
Norman Brewster	1st Lieu.	41	Sept. 4, 1861	3 yrs.	Promoted from 2d Lieutenant Co. B July 7, 1862; mustered out Dec. 5, 1864, at Louisville, Ky., on expiration of term of service.
John Moore	... do ...	26	Sept. 7, 1861	3 yrs.	Promoted from 2d Lieutenant Co. I Nov. 30, 1864; to Captain Feb. 23, 1865, but not mustered; resigned June 11, 1865; veteran.
Maylam J. Bassett....	... do ...	19	Sept. 4, 1861	3 yrs.	Promoted from 2d Lieutenant Co. A June 16, 1865; mustered out with company Aug. 4, 1865; veteran.
Orange H. Howland...	2d Lieu.	23	Aug. 15, 1861	3 yrs.	Appointed 1st Sergeant Sept. 10, 1861; promoted to 2d Lieutenant July 20, 1862; captured Oct. 17, 1862, at battle of Lexington, Ky.; paroled ——; transferred to Co. E April 24, 1863.
Christopher C. Clay ..	... do ...	23	Aug. 20, 1861	3 yrs.	Appointed Q. M. Sergeant Aug. 31, 1861; 1st Sergeant ——; promoted to 2d Lieutenant Feb. 14, 1863; to 1st Lieutenant Co. F July 13, 1864.
John M. Keller.........	... do ...	33	Sept. 7, 1861	3 yrs.	Promoted from 1st Sergeant Co. G July 13, 1864; to 1st Lieutenant Co. E Nov. 30, 1864; veteran.
George H. Frent........	... do ...	28	Dec. 3, 1861	3 yrs.	Promoted from Regt. Q. M. Sergeant Nov. 30, 1864; to 1st Lieutenant Feb. 23, 1865, but not mustered; resigned June 21, 1865; veteran.
Theodore W. Harlow.	1st Serg.	29	Aug. 23, 1861	3 yrs.	Appointed Corporal Aug. 31, 1861; captured Oct. 17, 1862, at battle of Lexington, Ky., paroled ——; appointed 1st Sergeant ——; mustered out Oct. 3, 1864, at Columbia, Tenn., on expiration of term of service.
Francis C. Dodge.....	... do ...	26	Sept. 15, 1862	3 yrs.	Appointed Corporal ——; 1st Sergeant ——; promoted to 2d Lieutenant Co. I Nov. 30, 1864.
Archibald J. Eyster ...	... do ...	20	Aug. 19, 1862	3 yrs.	Appointed Corporal ——; 1st Sergeant Dec. 7, 1864; mustered out June 17, 1865, at Nashville, Tenn., by order of War Department.
Barnard W. Dolan.....	... do ...	33	Sept. 6, 1861	3 yrs.	Mustered as private; appointed Sergeant ——; Com. Sergeant Jan. 4, 1863; Q. M. Sergeant Dec. 7, 1864; 1st Sergeant June 17, 1865; mustered out with company Aug. 4, 1865; veteran.
John C. Donahue......	Q. M. S.	22	Aug. 26, 1861	3 yrs.	Captured Oct. 17, 1862, at battle of Lexington, Ky.; paroled ——; appointed Corporal ——; Com. Sergeant Dec. 7, 1864; Q. M. Sergeant June 17, 1865; mustered out with company Aug. 4, 1865; veteran.
Austin B. Conant.....	Com Ser.	23	Aug. 24, 1861	3 yrs.	Appointed Sergeant Aug. 31, 1861; discharged Jan. 8, 1863, at Columbus, O., on Surgeon's certificate of disability; re-enlisted Dec. 10, 1863, for 3 years; appointed Corporal April 6, 1864; Sergeant Oct. 3, 1864; Com. Sergeant June 17, 1865; mustered out with company Aug. 4, 1865.
Frank F. Moyer.......	Sergeant	21	Aug. 24, 1861	3 yrs.	Mustered as private; appointed ——; died Oct. 19, 1863, of wounds received Oct. 7, 1863, in battle of Shelbyville Pike, Tenn.
William Van Wormer..	... do ...	28	Aug. 26, 1861	3 yrs.	Appointed Corporal Aug. 31, 1861; Sergeant ——; mustered out Oct. 3, 1864, at Columbia, Tenn., on expiration of term of service.
Francis Allen	... do ...	23	Aug. 26, 1861	3 yrs.	Appointed Corporal Aug. 31, 1861; captured Oct. 17, 1862, at battle of Lexington, Ky.; paroled ——; appointed Sergeant ——; mustered out Oct. 3, 1864, at Columbia, Tenn., on expiration of term of service.
Thomas Crofts	... do ...	21	Aug. 26, 1861	3 yrs.	Appointed Corporal Aug. 31, 1861; captured Oct. 17, 1862, at battle of Lexington, Ky.; paroled ——; appointed Sergeant ——; mustered out Oct. 3, 1864, at Columbia, Tenn., on expiration of term of service.
George Wertemberger..	... do ...	25	Sept. 26, 1861	3 yrs.	Mustered as private; captured Oct. 17, 1862, at battle of Lexington, Ky.; paroled ——; appointed ——; mustered out Oct. 3, 1864, at Columbia, Tenn., on expiration of term of service.
Isaac Wertemberger ...	... do ...	19	Sept. 26, 1861	3 yrs.	Mustered as private; appointed ——; died Nov. 26, 1864, in hospital at Chattanooga, Tenn.; veteran.
George J. Miller.........	... do ...	23	Aug. 23, 1861	3 yrs.	Mustered as private; appointed June 17, 1865; mustered out with company Aug. 4, 1865; veteran.
Lewis Fisher	... do ...	21	Aug. 21, 1861	3 yrs.	Mustered as private; captured Oct. 17, 1862, at battle of Lexington, Ky.; paroled ——; appointed June 17, 1865; mustered out with company Aug. 4, 1865; veteran.

Names	Rank	Age	Date of Entering the Service	Period of Service	Remarks
Harlow Burr	Sergeant	21	Nov. 21, 1861	3 yrs.	Mustered as private; captured Oct. 17, 1862, at battle of Lexington, Ky.; paroled ——; appointed June 17, 1865; mustered out with company Aug. 4, 1865; veteran.
William H. Dustin........	... do ...	18	Aug. 28, 1861	3 yrs.	Mustered as private; appointed June 17, 1865; mustered out with company Aug. 4, 1865; veteran.
Orrin Burr	... do ...	18	Jan. 19, 1864	3 yrs.	Appointed Corporal ——; Sergeant June 17, 1865; mustered out with company Aug. 4, 1865.
Calvin Spangler	Corporal	22	Aug. 24, 1861	3 yrs.	Appointed Aug. 31, 1861; discharged June 28, 1862, at St. Louis, Mo., on Surgeon's certificate of disability.
William F. Bradley.......	... do ...	18	Aug. 28, 1861	3 yrs.	Appointed Jan. 13, 1863; mustered out to date Aug. 3, 1865, at Columbus, O., by order of War Department; veteran.
Levi Genson	... do ...	23	Aug. 17, 1861	3 yrs.	Appointed ——; mustered out Oct. 3, 1864, at Columbia, Tenn., on expiration of term of service.
William Smith	... do ...	19	Aug. 26, 1861	3 yrs.	Captured Oct. 17, 1862, at battle of Lexington, Ky.; paroled ——; appointed ——; mustered out Oct. 3, 1864, at Columbia, Tenn., on expiration of term of service.
Joseph Ott	... do ...	23	Aug. 20, 1861	3 yrs.	Appointed Bugler Aug. 31, 1861; Corporal ——; promoted to Chief Bugler of regiment Jan. 4, 1864; veteran.
John Kerman	... do ...	19	Aug. 16, 1862	3 yrs.	Appointed ——; mustered out June 17, 1865, at Nashville, Tenn., by order of War Department.
Orrin Buzzell	... do ...	35	Dec. 22, 1863	3 yrs.	Wounded Aug. 20, 1864, in battle of Lovejoy Station, Ga.; appointed Oct. 3, 1864; mustered out July 17, 1865, at Columbus, O., by order of War Department.
Adam J. Carter..........	... do ...	33	Dec. 17, 1863	3 yrs.	Appointed ——; mustered out with company Aug. 4, 1865.
John A. Rice.............	... do ...	18	Dec. 16, 1863	3 yrs.	Appointed ——; mustered out with company Aug. 4, 1865.
Isaac T. Whitson........	... do ...	18	Feb. 13, 1864	3 yrs.	Appointed ——; mustered out with company Aug. 4, 1865.
Charles O. Brown.......	... do ...	16	Feb. 18, 1864	3 yrs.	Appointed ——; mustered out with company Aug. 4, 1865.
Hoyt B. Pike............	... do ...	18	Dec. 24, 1863	3 yrs.	Appointed June 17, 1865; mustered out with company Aug. 4, 1865.
Joseph Meirhoffer	... do ...	21	Dec. 21, 1863	3 yrs.	Appointed June 17, 1865; mustered out with company Aug. 4, 1865.
Levi B. Whitlock......	Bugler	42	Aug. 24, 1861	3 yrs.	Appointed Aug. 31, 1861; discharged July 1, 1862, at St. Louis, Mo., on Surgeon's certificate of disability.
Levi Cook	Farrier	38	Aug. 24, 1861	3 yrs.	Appointed Aug. 31, 1861; promoted to Batt. Veterinary Surgeon Dec. 1, 1861.
Edward McDonald	... do ...	36	Aug. 28, 1861	3 yrs.	Appointed Sept. 10, 1861; mustered out Oct. 3, 1864, at Columbia, Tenn., on expiration of term of service.
James E. Thompson..	... do ...	19	Sept. 8, 1861	3 yrs.	Also borne on rolls as Joseph; appointed ——; mustered out Oct. 3, 1864, at Columbia, Tenn., on expiration of term of service.
John Antibus	Saddler	29	Aug. 27, 1861	3 yrs.	Appointed Sept. 7, 1861; discharged June 17, 1862, at St. Louis, Mo., on Surgeon's certificate of disability.
John Redding	... do ...	35	July 16, 1862	3 yrs.	Appointed ——; mustered out June 17, 1865, at Nashville, Tenn., by order of War Department.
John Griner	Wagoner	29	Aug. 10, 1861	3 yrs.	Appointed Sept. 10, 1861; captured Oct. 17, 1862, at battle of Lexington, Ky.; paroled ——; transferred to 87th Co., 2d Battalion, Veteran Reserve Corps, Jan. 5, 1864; mustered out from same as private Oct. 7, 1864, at Cincinnati, O., by order of War Department.
Samuel C. Fry..........	... do ...	34	Aug. 20, 1861	3 yrs.	Appointed ——; died March —, 1865, on march to Selma, Ala.; veteran.
Abbott, John F........	Private	18	Dec. 1, 1863	3 yrs.	Mustered out with company Aug. 4, 1865.
Alden, Albert	... do ...	18	Feb. 20, 1864	3 yrs.	Mustered out with company Aug. 4, 1865.
Allen, John	... do ...	29	Sept. 14, 1861	3 yrs.	
Allkney, Samuel	... do ...	25	Oct. 4, 1862	3 yrs.	Mustered out with company Aug. 4, 1865.
Austin, Daniel	... do ...	23	Aug. 22, 1863	3 yrs.	Mustered out May 31, 1865, from Mound City Hospital at Cairo, Ill., by order of War Department.
Baldwin, John A.......	... do ...	29	Aug. 13, 1861	3 yrs.	Transferred to Co. L Jan. 1, 1862.
Barlow, Thomas	... do ...	28	Dec. 4, 1863	3 yrs.	Mustered out with company Aug. 4, 1865.
Barnes, Frederick	... do ...	19	Dec. 24, 1863	3 yrs.	Mustered out with company Aug. 4, 1865.
Barton, Hiram	... do ...	18	Aug. 19, 1861	3 yrs.	
Battenfield, Daniel S...	... do ...	23	Aug. 28, 1861	3 yrs.	Died April 18, 1863.
Beggs, Thomas C........	... do ...	18	Dec. 26, 1863	3 yrs.	Mustered out with company Aug. 4, 1865.

Names	Rank	Age	Date of Entering the Service	Period of Service	Remarks
Benedict, Horace	Private	18	Aug. 26, 1861	3 yrs.	Mustered out Oct. 3, 1864, at Columbia, Tenn., on expiration of term of service.
Berry, Alexander	... do ...	....	Oct. —, 1861	3 yrs.	Died at Savannah, Tenn., April —, 1862.
Bessell, August E......	... do ...	37	Sept. 3, 1863	3 yrs.	Mustered out with company Aug. 4, 1865.
Blivan, Robert H.......	... do ...	18	Sept. 16, 1861	3 yrs.	Promoted to Battalion Q. M. Sergeant Nov. 1, 1861.
Boice, Henry	... do ...	37	Aug. 16, 1862	3 yrs.	Discharged Jan. 23, 1863, at Nashville, Tenn., on Surgeon's certificate of disability.
Boice, Reed V...........	... do ...	29	Dec. 11, 1861	3 yrs.	Promoted to Battalion Hospital Steward Dec. 11, 1861; veteran.
Bradley, Edward W......	... do ...	19	Dec. 23, 1863	3 yrs.	Mustered out with company Aug. 4, 1865.
Bradley, Henry A........	... do ...	18	Dec. 20, 1863	3 yrs.	Mustered out with company Aug. 4, 1865.
Broadbeck, John	... do ...	25	June 27, 1863	3 yrs.	Also borne on rolls as "Brodbeck;" mustered out with company Aug. 4, 1865.
Brown, Daniel	... do ...	29	Sept. 10, 1861	3 yrs.	Transferred to Co. K Jan. 1, 1862.
Brown, Loren A.........	... do ...	29	Sept. 7, 1861	3 yrs.	Discharged June 28, 1862, on Surgeon's certificate of disability.
Burk, Edward	... do ...	44	Dec. 29, 1863	3 yrs.	Mustered out with company Aug. 4, 1865.
Campbell, James	... do ...	30	Oct. 2, 1863	3 yrs.	
Cannon, John	... do ...	24	Aug. 19, 1861	3 yrs.	Discharged Jan. 31, 1863, on Surgeon's certificate of disability.
Carr, Edward	... do ...	17	Aug. 26, 1861	3 yrs.	Killed Oct. 17, 1862, in battle of Lexington, Ky.
Charter, Samuel	... do ...	20	Dec. 10, 1863	3 yrs.	Mustered out May 24, 1865, from hospital at Columbus, O., by order of War Department.
Chilson, Peter	... do ...	18	Sept. 3, 1861	3 yrs.	Transferred to Co. K Dec. 11, 1861.
Clukey, Peter	... do ...	21	Dec. 14, 1863	3 yrs.	Also borne on rolls as "Cleukey;" mustered out with company Aug. 4, 1865.
Coffee, John	... do ...	20	Feb. 29, 1864	3 yrs.	Mustered out with company Aug. 4, 1865.
Cole, Emanuel	... do ...	21	Aug. 26, 1861	3 yrs.	Captured Oct. 17, 1862, at battle of Lexington, Ky.; paroled ——; mustered out Oct. 3, 1864, at Columbia, Tenn., on expiration of term of service.
Coltrin, Charles H.	... do ...	17	Aug. 17, 1861	3 yrs.	Killed Oct. 18, 1862, in battle of Lexington, Ky.
Conn, Samuel	... do ...	23	Sept. 1, 1861	3 yrs.	Died May 7, 1862.
Conrad, John	... do ...	34	Jan. 8, 1864	3 yrs.	Transferred from Co. M Jan. 4, 1865; mustered out with company Aug. 4, 1865.
Cook, Henry	... do ...	21	Aug. 20, 1861	3 yrs.	Mustered out with company Aug. 4, 1865; veteran.
Cooney, John	... do ...	19	Sept. 4, 1861	3 yrs.	Captured Oct. 17, 1865, at battle of Lexington, Ky.; paroled ——; mustered out Oct. 3, 1864, at Columbia, Tenn., on expiration of term of service.
Cosgrove, David	... do ...	28	Aug. 27, 1861	3 yrs.	Transferred to Co. K April 1, 1864; veteran.
Cowles, William	... do ...	21	Oct. 6, 1862	3 yrs.	Captured Dec. 31, 1862, at Murfreesboro, Tenn.; no further record found.
Crandall, Bradley M.....	... do ...	21	Oct. 1, 1864	1 yr.	Drafted; mustered out with company Aug. 4, 1865.
Cressy, Osgood D.......	... do ...	18	Dec. 10, 1863	3 yrs.	Died March 7, 1864, in U. S. General Hospital at Nashville, Tenn.
Crompton, William	... do ...	34	Sept. 4, 1861	3 yrs.	Captured Oct. 17, 1862, at battle of Lexington, Ky.; paroled ——; mustered out with company Aug. 4, 1865; veteran.
Dalby, David	... do ...	20	Aug. 26, 1861	3 yrs.	Discharged May 20, 1862, on Surgeon's certificate of disability.
Davis, Robert M........	... do ...	40	Aug. 15, 1861	3 yrs.	Discharged Nov. 23, 1862, at Nashville, Tenn., on Surgeon's certificate of disability; re-enlisted Feb. 23, 1864, for 3 years; mustered out with company Aug. 4, 1865.
Dawes, Lewis	... do ...	35	Oct. 27, 1864	1 yr.	Mustered out with company Aug. 4, 1865.
Donahue, William K.....	... do ...	26	Aug. 26, 1861	3 yrs.	Transferred to Co. I, 7th Regiment, Veteran Reserve Corps, Jan. 25, 1864; mustered out from same Nov. 14, 1865, at Washington, D. C., by order of War Department.
Drumond, Alexander.....	... do ...	28	Nov. 5, 1863	3 yrs.	
Drurior, Joseph	... do ...	19	Dec. 14, 1863	3 yrs.	Also borne on rolls as "Drowier;" died Aug. 16, 1864, at Cartersville, Ga.
Dumersy, Alfred P......	... do ...	19	Jan. 18, 1864	3 yrs.	Also borne on rolls as "Dumaresy;" died May 9, 1865, at Jeffersonville, Ind.
Dustin, Benjamin F.....	... do ...	28	Aug. 28, 1861	3 yrs.	Captured Oct. 17, 1862, at battle of Lexington, Ky.; paroled ——; mustered out Oct. 8, 1864, at Columbia, Tenn., on expiration of term of service; re-enlisted Jan. 2, 1865, for 1 year; mustered out with company Aug. 4, 1865.
Dustin, Francis B......	... do ...	31	Aug. 28, 1861	3 yrs.	Captured Oct. 17, 1862, at battle of Lexington, Ky.; paroled ——; mustered out Oct. 3, 1864, at Columbia, Tenn., on expiration of term of service; re-enlisted Jan. 2, 1865, for 1 year; mustered out with company Aug. 4, 1865.
Dustin, Walter	... do ...	19	Aug. 26, 1863	3 yrs.	Mustered out with company Aug. 4, 1865.

Names	Rank	Age	Date of Entering the Service	Period of Service	Remarks
Eddy, Peter	do ...	25	Aug. 24, 1861	3 yrs.	Captured Oct. 17, 1862, at battle of Lexington, Ky.; paroled ——; mustered out Oct. 3, 1864, at Columbia, Tenn., on expiration of term of service.
Eichholt, Jacob	Private	51	Aug. 20, 1861	3 yrs.	
Emch, Benedict	do ...	21	Sept. 24, 1861	3 yrs.	Discharged Jan. 23, 1863, on Surgeon's certificate of disability.
Farner, Wilson	do ...	25	Aug. 20, 1861	3 yrs.	Mustered out Oct. 3, 1864, at Columbia, Tenn., on expiration of term of service.
Fitzpatrick, William....	do ...	28	Aug. 19, 1862	3 yrs.	Mustered out June 12, 1865, at Louisville, Ky., by order of War Department.
Foley, James	do ...	29	Sept. 8, 1863	3 yrs.	Mustered out with company Aug. 4, 1865.
Foster, William H......	do ...	34	Sept. 7, 1861	3 yrs.	Mustered out June 17, 1865, at Nashville, Tenn., by order of War Department.
Fountain, Oliver	do ...	20	Aug. 25, 1861	3 yrs.	Killed Sept. 20, 1863, in battle of Chickamauga, Ga.
Gordanier, Jacob	do ...	24	Nov. 2, 1861	3 yrs.	Captured Oct. 17, 1862, at battle of Lexington, Ky.; paroled ——; mustered out with company Aug. 4, 1865.
Gorsuch, Russell B......	do ...	22	Dec. 18, 1863	3 yrs.	Discharged Feb. 9, 1865, from hospital at Cleveland, O., on Surgeon's certificate of disability.
Green, John R...........	do ...	44	Sept. 3, 1862	3 yrs.	Mustered out June 17, 1865, at Nashville, Tenn., by order of War Department.
Greenwood, John	do ...	27	Dec. 15, 1863	3 yrs.	Mustered out with company Aug. 4, 1865.
Gyor, Eli	do ...	18	Dec. 10, 1863	3 yrs.	Mustered out with company Aug. 4, 1865.
Hallett, Daniel H......	do ...	26	Aug. 26, 1861	3 yrs.	Captured Oct. 17, 1862, at battle of Lexington, Ky.; paroled ——; mustered out Oct. 3, 1864, at Columbia, Tenn., on expiration of term of service.
Hancock, Albert	do ...	29	Mch. 1, 1864	3 yrs.	Mustered out with company Aug. 4, 1865.
Harris, Henry H.......	do ...	18	Feb. 29, 1864	3 yrs.	Mustered out with company Aug. 4, 1865.
Harris, Joseph	do ...	20	Dec. 15, 1864	1 yr.	Mustered out with company Aug. 4, 1865.
Hatfield, Charles	do ...	18	Jan. 9, 1864	3 yrs.	Mustered out with company Aug. 4, 1865.
Hess, Samuel H.......	do ...	25	Sept. 7, 1861	3 yrs.	Wounded April 2, 1865, in battle of Selma, Ala.; mustered out Aug. 3, 1865, by order of War Department; veteran.
Hilton, Martin G.......	do ...	26	Sept. 13, 1862	3 yrs.	Mustered out June 17, 1865, at Nashville, Tenn., by order of War Department.
Holmes, Jesse	do ...	28	Oct. 1, 1861	3 yrs.	Died Oct. 22, 1862, in hospital at Louisville, Ky.
Holt, William	do ...	29	Nov. 6, 1863	3 yrs.	
Howard, James	do ...	26	Jan. 2, 1865	1 yr.	Mustered out with company Aug. 4, 1865.
Johnson, James L......	do ...	26	Oct. 1, 1864	1 yr.	Drafted; mustered out with company Aug. 4, 1865.
Jones, Thomas	do ...	18	Oct. 1, 1861	3 yrs.	
Karr, Joseph S.	do ...	18	Oct. 5, 1864	1 yr.	Mustered out with company Aug. 4, 1865.
Kimball, Calvin S......	do ...	26	Sept. 10, 1861	3 yrs.	Promoted to Sergt. Major Jan. 4, 1864; veteran.
Kreiter, Philip	do ...	41	Aug. 26, 1861	3 yrs.	Mustered out with company Aug. 4, 1865; veteran.
Lawrence, William A....	do ...	44	Aug. 25, 1861	3 yrs.	Captured Oct. 17, 1862, at battle of Lexington, Ky.; paroled ——; mustered out June 17, 1865, at Nashville, Tenn., by order of War Department.
Lee, David	do ...	31	Sept. 26, 1861	3 yrs.	Discharged July 3, 1862, on Surgeon's certificate of disability.
Lenhart, Hiram	do ...	30	Aug. 20, 1861	3 yrs.	Mustered out with company Aug. 4, 1865; veteran.
Lennon, Lawrence	do ...	31	Sept. 8, 1861	3 yrs.	
Longendoroff, Joseph....	do ...	44	Aug. 23, 1861	3 yrs.	Discharged April 7, 1862, on Surgeon's certificate of disability.
Love, Almond	do ...	18	Feb. 9, 1864	3 yrs.	Mustered out with company Aug. 4, 1865.
Lyons, Samuel	do ...	35	Aug. 16, 1862	3 yrs.	Captured Oct. 17, 1862, at battle of Lexington, Ky.; paroled ——; mustered out June 17, 1865, at Nashville, Tenn., by order of War Department.
McCarty, John	do ...	23	Dec. 3, 1863	3 yrs.	Mustered out with company Aug. 4, 1865.
McDougal, James F.....	do ...	18	Dec. 1, 1861	3 yrs.	Transferred from Co. K Jan. 1, 1862; captured Oct. 17, 1862, at battle of Lexington, Ky.; paroled ——; mustered out Dec. 21, 1864, on expiration of term of service.
Marker, Alexander	do ...	45	Aug. 26, 1861	3 yrs.	Captured Oct. 17, 1862, at battle of Lexington, Ky.; paroled ——; mustered out Oct. 3, 1864, at Columbia, Tenn., on expiration of term of service.
Meeker, Benjamin F.....	do ...	18	Aug. 24, 1861	3 yrs.	Died Oct. 6, 1862, at Nashville, Tenn.
Meeker, William B......	do ...	25	Aug. 24, 1861	3 yrs.	Mustered out Oct. 3, 1864, at Columbia, Tenn., on expiration of term of service.
Mix, Samuel	do ...	18	Dec. 16, 1863	3 yrs.	Mustered out with company Aug. 4, 1865.
Miller, Brainerd	do ...	19	Aug. 13, 1863	3 yrs.	Mustered out with company Aug. 4, 1865.
Mills, James	do ...	20	Aug. 24, 1862	3 yrs.	Captured Oct. 17, 1862, at battle of Lexington, Ky.; paroled ——; transferred to Co. K April 1, 1864.

Names	Rank	Age	Date of Entering the Service	Period of Service	Remarks
Mott, Charles	... do ...	24	Dec. 29, 1863	3 yrs.	Died Oct. 5, 1864, at Chattanooga, Tenn., of wounds received in action.
Navarre, Oliver	... do ...	32	Aug. 23, 1861	3 yrs.	Discharged July 23, 1862, on Surgeon's certificate of disability.
Navarre, Peter	Private	30	Aug. 23, 1861	3 yrs.	Discharged March 25, 1863, on Surgeon's certificate of disability.
Nelles, Nicholas	... do ...	38	Dec. 14, 1863	3 yrs.	Mustered out with company Aug. 4, 1865.
Nishwitz, John	... do ...	19	July 2, 1863	3 yrs.	Transferred to Co. K April 1, 1864.
Norton, Henry G.......	... do ...	20	Aug. 24, 1861	3 yrs.	Discharged July 22, 1862, on Surgeon's certificate of disability.
Orton, James C.........	... do ...	28	Oct. 2, 1861	3 yrs.	Died Oct. 24, 1862, at Louisville, Ky.
Pike, Henry D..........	... do ...	19	Dec. 21, 1863	3 yrs.	Died June 25, 1864, at Bartow Iron Works, Ga.
Pinkerton, James	... do ...	21	Aug. 26, 1861	3 yrs.	Captured Oct. 17, 1862, at battle of Lexington, Ky.; paroled ——.
Priame, Bradley L......	... do ...	37	Aug. 18, 1861	3 yrs.	Discharged Nov. 19, 1862, at Cincinnati, O., on Surgeon's certificate of disability.
Price, Charles	... do ...	27	Sept. 10, 1861	3 yrs.	Transferred to Co. K ——.
Ray, John H.............	... do ...	32	Oct. 12, 1863	3 yrs.	Discharged Sept. 19, 1864, on Surgeon's certificate of disability.
Reed, Amos K...........	... do ...	43	Oct. 1, 1861	3 yrs.	Died Oct. 29, 1861.
Richmond, Thomas ...	... do ...	21	Nov. 5, 1863	3 yrs.	
Rottler, Mathias	... do ...	27	Aug. 28, 1861	3 yrs.	Died April 18, 1862.
Sager, George	... do ...	34	Dec. 10, 1863	3 yrs.	Mustered out with company Aug. 4, 1865.
Searles, Jacob	... do ...	25	Nov. 20, 1861	3 yrs.	Transferred to Co. K April 1, 1864.
Shepherd, Thomas	... do ...	22	Aug. 24, 1861	3 yrs.	Captured Oct. 17, 1862, at battle of Lexington, Ky.; paroled ——.
Siren, Thomas	... do ...	27	Nov. 6, 1863	3 yrs.	
Smith, George W.......	... do ...	21	Dec. 1, 1861	3 yrs.	Transferred from Co. K Jan. 1, 1862; died Nov. 19, 1862, at Nashville, Tenn.
Smith, Thomas H.......	... do ...	22	Aug. 26, 1861	3 yrs.	Mustered out Oct. 3, 1864, at Columbia, Tenn., on expiration of term of service.
Snider, Jacob	... do ...	45	Nov. 6, 1861	3 yrs.	Transferred from Co. L Jan. 1, 1862.
Spangler, Harrison	... do ...	22	Sept. 17, 1864	1 yr.	Mustered out June 17, 1865, at Nashville, Tenn., by order of War Department.
Spangler, Henry D......	... do ...	18	Aug. 24, 1861	3 yrs.	Discharged Nov. 11, 1862, on Surgeon's certificate of disability.
Spathe, John	... do ...	38	Dec. 15, 1864	1 yr.	Mustered out with company Aug. 4, 1865.
Straight, Milton H......	... do ...	22	July 17, 1863	3 yrs.	Transferred to Co. A April 1, 1864.
Summerhalter, Fred'k.	... do ...	37	Sept. 10, 1861	3 yrs.	Discharged Feb. 4, 1863, on Surgeon's certificate of disability.
Taft, Frank S..........	... do ...	24	Aug. 30, 1862	3 yrs.	
Trembly, Joseph E......	... do ...	19	Sept. 2, 1861	3 yrs.	Died June 26, 1862.
Underwood, Geo. R.....	... do ...	19	Sept. 17, 1861	3 yrs.	Discharged Dec. 6, 1862, at Louisville, Ky., on Surgeon's certificate of disability.
Van Fleet, Otis........	... do ...	20	Aug. 26, 1861	3 yrs.	
Van Slacke, Richard....	... do ...	41	Sept. 23, 1862	3 yrs.	Mustered out June 17, 1865, at Nashville, Tenn., by order of War Department.
Walton, William A......	... do ...	18	Aug. 18, 1861	3 yrs.	
Webber, Jacob	... do ...	28	Aug. 23, 1861	3 yrs.	Veteran.
Welsh, John	... do ...	19	Aug. 26, 1861	3 yrs.	Discharged Feb. 6, 1863, on Spurgeon's certificate of disability.
Wilcox, William	... do ...	36	Aug. 31, 1861	3 yrs.	Died June 20, 1862, at Tuscumbia, Ala.
Williams, Albert L.....	... do ...	18	Oct. 3, 1861	3 yrs.	Discharged Nov. 1, 1861, on Surgeon's certificate of disability.
Wintermute, James S...	... do ...	18	Dec. 7, 1863	3 yrs.	Mustered out with company Aug. 4, 1865.
Wintermute, Wm. H...	... do ...	27	Dec. 14, 1863	3 yrs.	Mustered out with company Aug. 4, 1865.
Wolcott, Henry C.......	... do ...	31	Jan. 4, 1864	3 yrs.	Mustered out with company Aug. 4, 1865.
Yager, Jonas	... do ...	19	Dec. 19, 1863	3 yrs.	Died Sept. 1, 1864, in hospital at Marietta, Ga.
Zedicker, John H........	... do ...	21	Aug. 20, 1861	3 yrs.	Captured Oct. 17, 1862, at battle of Lexington, Ky.; paroled ——; mustered out Oct. 3, 1864, at Columbia, Tenn., on expiration of term of service.
Coleman, Robert	Cook	21	April 8, 1865	3 yrs.	Colored under-cook; mustered out with company Aug. 4, 1865.
Hurd, Lewis	... do ...	49	April 8, 1865	3 yrs.	Colored under-cook; mustered out with company Aug. 4, 1865.
Mathews, Abednego ...	... do ...	25	April 8, 1865	3 yrs.	Colored under-cook; mustered out with company Aug. 4, 1865.
Mathews, Thomas	... do ...	33	April 8, 1865	3 yrs.	Colored under-cook; mustered out with company Aug. 4, 1865.

COMPANY D.

Mustered in September 10, 1861, at Camp Worcester, O., by James P. W. Neill, 1st Lieutenant 18th Infantry,
U. S. A., Mustering Officer. Mustered out August 4, 1865, at Nashville, Tenn., by James
P. W. Neill, Captain 18th Infantry, U. S. A., Acting Commissary
of Musters, Cavalry Corps, M. D. T.

Names	Rank	Age	Date of Entering the Service	Period of Service	Remarks
William B. Amsden ...	Captain	23	Sept. 10, 1861	3 yrs.	Appointed Sept. 10, 1861; died June 19, 1862, at Fremont, O.
Richard B. Wood........	... do ...	26	Sept. 10, 1861	3 yrs.	Appointed 1st Lieutenant Sept. 10, 1861; promoted to Captain June 20, 1862; killed Feb. 23, 1864, in action at Dalton, Ga.
Elihu Isbell	... do ...	26	Sept. 6, 1861	3 yrs.	Transferred from Co. L April 4, 1864; mustered out Nov. 21, 1864, at Louisville, Ky., on expiration of term of service.
Paul Deal	... do ...	43	Sept. 10, 1861	3 yrs.	Appointed Sergeant Sept. 10, 1861; 1st Sergeant ———; promoted to 2d Lieutenant Co. K Nov. 24, 1863; to 1st Lieutenant from 2d Lieutenant Co. K Nov. 30, 1864; to Captain Jan. 6, 1865; mustered out with company Aug. 4, 1865.
George F. Williams....	1st Lieu.	21	Sept. 10, 1861	3 yrs.	Appointed 2d Lieutenant Sept. 10, 1861; promoted to 1st Lieutenant June 20, 1862; to Captain Co. F April 17, 1863.
Brainard Fish	... do ...	20	Sept. 7, 1861	3 yrs.	Promoted to 2d Lieutenant from Batt. Sergt. Major May 20, 1862; to 1st Lieutenant June 19, 1863; to Captain Nov. 30, 1864, but not mustered; mustered out Jan. 10, 1865, at Nashville, Tenn., on expiration of term of service.
Thomas A. O'Rourke..	... do ...	24	Sept. 8, 1861	3 yrs.	Promoted from 2d Lieutenant Co. L Jan. 6, 1865; mustered out with company Aug. 4, 1865; veteran.
George Garfield	2d Lieu.	31	Aug. 20, 1861	3 yrs.	Promoted from 1st Sergeant Co. H June 7, 1863; to Captain Nov. 30, 1864, but not mustered; mustered out Dec. 21, 1864, at Cleveland, O., on expiration of term of service.
Joseph Berry	... do ...	37	Aug. 20, 1861	3 yrs.	Promoted from Sergt. Major April 8, 1865; to 1st Lieutenant Aug. 2, 1865, but not mustered; mustered out with company Aug. 4, 1865; veteran.
Charles S. Kelsey......	1st Serg.	23	Sept. 10, 1861	3 yrs.	Appointed Corporal Sept. 10, 1861; 1st Sergeant April 4, 1864; promoted to 1st Lieutenant Co. L Nov. 30, 1864; veteran.
William L. Stackhous.	... do ...	29	Sept. 10, 1861	3 yrs.	Appointed Sergeant Sept. 10, 1861; 1st Sergeant Dec. 2, 1864; promoted to 2d Lieutenant April 8, 1865, but not mustered; mustered out with company Aug. 4, 1865; veteran.
Henry H. Sears........	Q. M. S.	35	Sept. 10, 1861	3 yrs.	Appointed Sept. 10, 1861; discharged Jan. 19, 1863, on Surgeon's certificate of disability.
David H. Lentz.........	... do ...	24	Sept. 10, 1861	3 yrs.	Mustered as private; appointed Dec. 2, 1864; mustered out with company Aug. 4, 1865; veteran.
Isaac Parrish	Com Ser.	23	Sept. 10, 1861	3 yrs.	Mustered as private; appointed Dec. 2, 1864; mustered out with company Aug. 4, 1865; veteran.
Edward A. Haines.....	Sergeant	22	Sept. 10, 1861	3 yrs.	Appointed Sept. 10, 1861; promoted to Batt. Sergt. Major ———.
George W. Butler........	... do ...	23	Sept. 10, 1861	3 yrs.	Appointed Sept. 10, 1861; died May 19, 1862.
John Linebaugh	... do ...	37	Sept. 10, 1861	3 yrs.	Appointed Corporal Sept. 10, 1861; Sergeant ———; mustered out Sept. 10, 1864, at Columbia, Tenn., on expiration of term of service.
Robert Benfer	... do ...	19	Sept. 10, 1861	3 yrs.	Mustered as private; appointed ———; mustered out Sept. 10, 1864, at Columbia, Tenn., on expiration of term of service.
George Wolcott	... do ...	32	Sept. 10, 1861	3 yrs.	Appointed Corporal Sept. 10, 1861; Sergeant ———; prisoner of war; mustered out April 8, 1865, at Columbus, O., on expiration of term of service.
Benjamin F. Hill........	... do ...	18	Sept. 10, 1861	3 yrs.	Mustered as private; appointed ———; drowned April 11, 1865, near Benton, Ala.; veteran.
Levi Hair	... do ...	18	Sept. 10, 1861	3 yrs.	Mustered as private; appointed ———; mustered out with company Aug. 4, 1865; veteran.
Joseph P. Linebaugh..	... do ...	20	Sept. 10, 1861	3 yrs.	Mustered as private; appointed ———; mustered out with company Aug. 4, 1865; veteran.
John Clary	... do ...	19	Sept. 10, 1861	3 yrs.	Mustered as private; appointed ———; mustered out with company Aug. 4, 1865; veteran.
Isaiah Stout	... do ...	31	Sept. 10, 1861	3 yrs.	Mustered as private; appointed ———; mustered out with company Aug. 4, 1865; veteran.

Names	Rank	Age	Date of Entering the Service	Period of Service	Remarks
Alexander Tittle	Sergeant	21	Sept. 10, 1861	3 yrs.	Mustered as private; appointed ——; mustered out with company Aug. 4, 1865; veteran.
Jacob Stahl	Corporal	24	Sept. 10, 1861	3 yrs.	Discharged April 1, 1863, on Surgeon's certificate of disability.
William Meredith	... do ...	27	Sept. 10, 1861	3 yrs.	Discharged Dec. 10, 1862, on Surgeon's certificate of disability.
Michael Farmer	... do ...	22	Sept. 10, 1861	3 yrs.	Died May 30, 1862.
Dennis D. Glass	... do ...	18	Sept. 10, 1861	3 yrs.	Mustered out Sept. 14, 1864, at Columbus, O., on expiration of term of service.
William A. Blanden......	... do ...	24	Sept. 10, 1861	3 yrs.	Discharged May 19, 1862, on Surgeon's certificate of disability.
Wheeler Ferguson	... do ...	23	Sept. 10, 1861	3 yrs.	Appointed ——; died Aug. 20, 1864, at Lovejoy Station, Ga., of wounds received in action.
Obed C. Russell..........	... do ...	20	Sept. 10, 1861	3 yrs.	Appointed ——; wounded Aug. 20, 1864, in battle of Lovejoy Station, Ga.; mustered out Nov. 23, 1864, at Louisville, Ky., on expiration of term of service.
Jacob S. Stahl..........	... do ...	20	Feb. 20, 1864	3 yrs.	Appointed ——; mustered out with company Aug. 4, 1865.
John Gould	... do ...	37	Feb. 20, 1864	3 yrs.	Appointed ——; mustered out July 28, 1865, from Tripler Hospital, Columbus, O., by order of War Department.
Philip C. Hoffman......	... do ...	23	Sept. 10, 1861	3 yrs.	Appointed ——; mustered out with company Aug. 4, 1865; veteran.
Edward P. Lehr........	... do ...	22	Sept. 10, 1861	3 yrs.	Appointed ——; mustered out with company Aug. 4, 1865; veteran.
William A. Gregg.......	... do ...	38	Feb. 20, 1864	3 yrs.	Appointed ——; mustered out with company Aug. 4, 1865.
Hiram Arlin	... do ...	22	Oct. 7, 1862	3 yrs.	Appointed ——; mustered out with company Aug. 4, 1865.
John A. Deitz..........	... do ...	37	Sept. 10, 1861	3 yrs.	Appointed ——; mustered out with company Aug. 4. 1865; veteran.
Washington Logan	... do ...	20	Feb. 3, 1864	3 yrs.	Appointed ——; mustered out with company Aug. 4, 1865.
Henry G. Stahl........	Bugler	18	Sept. 10, 1861	3 yrs.	Appointed ——; mustered out Sept. 10, 1864, at Columbia, Tenn., on expiration of term of service.
George W. Myers........	... do ...	18	Sept. 10, 1863	3 yrs.	Appointed ——; mustered out with company Aug. 4, 1865.
Gabriel Bunough	Farrier	29	Sept. 10, 1861	3 yrs.	Died May 17, 1863.
James White	... do ...	18	Sept. 10, 1861	3 yrs.	Appointed ——; mustered out with company Aug. 4, 1865; veteran.
Alonson Grover	... do ...	18	Sept. 10, 1861	3 yrs.	Appointed ——; mustered out with company Aug. 4, 1865; veteran.
Andrew J. Noggle......	Saddler	31	Sept. 10, 1861	3 yrs.	Appointed Sept. 10, 1861; promoted to Batt. Saddler Sergeant Dec. 1, 1861.
Able, George	Private	23	Sept. 10, 1861	3 yrs.	Discharged Dec. 19, 1862, on Surgeon's certificate of disability.
Albee, Hezekiah D.......	... do ...	20	Sept. 10, 1861	3 yrs.	Mustered out with company Aug. 4, 1865; veteran.
Aldridge, Hiram	... do ...	28	Feb. 24, 1864	3 yrs.	Mustered out with company Aug. 4, 1865.
Allbee, William	... do ...	28	Sept. 10, 1861	3 yrs.	Died March 4, 1862, at Fremont, O.
Allen, Martin P.........	... do ...	19	Oct. 6, 1862	3 yrs.	Died Jan. 27, 1863.
Amsden, Edward W......	... do ...	18	Sept. 10, 1861	3 yrs.	Mustered out Sept. 10, 1864, at Columbia, Tenn., on expiration of term of service.
Baker, Daniel	... do ...	19	Feb. 26, 1864	3 yrs.	Mustered out with company Aug. 4, 1865.
Basore, David	... do ...	28	Feb. 6, 1864	3 yrs.	Mustered out with company Aug. 4, 1865.
Beck, Julius	... do ...	23	Sept. 10, 1861	3 yrs.	Discharged Sept. 24, 1862, on Surgeon's certificate of disability.
Bennett, Leonard	... do ...	23	Oct. 12, 1862	3 yrs.	Discharged March 25, 1863, on Surgeon's certificate of disability.
Brice, Stephen	... do ...	25	Sept. 10, 1861	3 yrs.	Transferred to 77th Co., 2d Battalion, Veteran Reserve Corps, as "Stephen Bice," Oct. 10, 1863; mustered out from same Sept. 20, 1864, on expiration of term of service.
Bitzer, John	... do ...	25	Sept. 10, 1861	3 yrs.	Mustered out with company Aug. 4, 1865; veteran.
Boor, Silas C............	... do ...	21	Feb. 23, 1864	3 yrs.	Mustered out with company Aug. 4, 1865.
Boyer, John	... do ...	30	Sept. 10, 1861	3 yrs.	Died Jan. 10, 1865.
Buck, John	... do ...	35	Sept. 1, 1862	3 yrs.	Mustered out June 17, 1865, at Nashville, Tenn., by order of War Department.
Bunscy, Charles	... do ...	20	Dec. 9, 1861	3 yrs.	Mustered out with company Aug. 4, 1865; veteran.
Cavil, Edward	... do ...	28	Sept. 10, 1861	3 yrs.	
Cox, Burgess F..........	... do ...	18	Aug. 27, 1862	3 yrs.	
Curry, John C.;	... do ...	19	Feb. 24, 1864	3 yrs.	Captured May 29, 1864, at battle of Moulton, Ala.; paroled ——; mustered out June 28, 1865, at Camp Chase, O., by order of War Department.
Deitrich, Joseph	... do ...	36	Sept. 10, 1861	3 yrs.	Transferred to Co. E, 7th Regiment, Veteran Reserve Corps, Aug. 14, 1863; mustered out Sept. 10, 1864, on expiration of term of service.
Deleware, Christopher.	... do ...	22	Sept. 10, 1861	3 yrs.	Mustered out to date Aug. 4, 1865, by order of War Department; veteran.

Names	Rank	Age	Date of Entering the Service	Period of Service	Remarks
Dickerson, John	Private	36	Sept. 10, 1861	3 yrs.	Mustered out Sept. 10, 1864, at Columbia, Tenn., on expiration of term of service.
Donnel, James L........	do ...	30	Feb. 24, 1864	3 yrs.	Mustered out with company Aug. 4, 1865.
Edwards, Hezekiah	do ...	19	Sept. 10, 1861	3 yrs.	Discharged Aug. 16, 1862, on Surgeon's certificate of disability.
Ehman, Philip	do ...	24	Sept. 10, 1861	3 yrs.	Mustered out Sept. 10, 1864, at Columbia, Tenn., on expiration of term of service.
Eno, William	do ...	26	Feb. 24, 1864	3 yrs.	Mustered out with company Aug. 4, 1865.
Fawsey, William H......	do ...	18	Feb. 24, 1864	3 yrs.	Mustered out with company Aug. 4, 1865.
Ferguson, Charles	do ...	19	Aug. 25, 1862	3 yrs.	Died April 8, 1864, in hospital at Columbia, Tenn.
Forester, Absalom	do ...	19	Aug. 25, 1862	3 yrs.	
Foster, John R. P......	do ...	17	Sept. 10, 1861	3 yrs.	Discharged June 24, 1864, at Nashville, Tenn., on Surgeon's certificate of disability.
Fought, Aaron	do ...	21	Sept. 10, 1861	3 yrs.	Discharged May 8, 1862, on Surgeon's certificate of disability.
Frazier, Darius N......	do ...	28	Jan. 2, 1864	3 yrs.	
Garnes, Samuel	do ...	20	Feb. 24, 1864	3 yrs.	Mustered out with company Aug. 4, 1865.
Geru, Demas	do ...	18	Feb. 24, 1864	3 yrs.	Mustered out with company Aug. 4, 1865.
Graback, Augustus	do ...	18	Feb. 26, 1864	3 yrs.	Mustered out with company Aug. 4, 1865.
Graback, Henry	do ...	18	Sept. 10, 1861	3 yrs.	Mustered out with company Aug. 4, 1865; veteran.
Graback, John	do ...	19	Nov. 27, 1861	3 yrs.	Captured Aug. 20, 1864, at battle of Lovejoy Station, Ga.; mustered out Jan. 30, 1865, at Gravelly Springs, Ala., on expiration of term of service.
Grigwire, Louis	do ...	25	Sept. 10, 1861	3 yrs.	Discharged May 18, 1862, on Surgeon's certificate of disability; re-enlisted Sept. 30, 1862, for 3 years; discharged Feb. 22, 1864, at Gallatin, Tenn., on Surgeon's certificate of disability.
Grigwire, Peter	do ...	23	Sept. 10, 1861	3 yrs.	Discharged Sept. 2, 1862, at Camp Chase, O., on Surgeon's certificate of disability.
Haines, Samuel	do ...	19	Sept. 10, 1861	3 yrs.	Discharged July 18, 1862, on Surgeon's certificate of disability.
Hare, John	do ...	30	Oct. 1, 1862	3 yrs.	Also borne on rolls as John Hair; captured Aug. 17, 1864, in action at Jonesboro, Ga.; mustered out June 24, 1865, at Camp Chase, O., by order of War Department.
Harrison, George A.....	do ...	23	Feb. 23, 1864	3 yrs.	Mustered out with company Aug. 4, 1865.
Hathaway, Philip	do ...	18	Feb. 22, 1864	3 yrs.	Mustered out with company Aug. 4, 1865.
Hawk, Marion	do ...	17	Sept. 10, 1861	3 yrs.	Prisoner of war; mustered out May 15, 1865, at Columbus, O., on expiration of term of service.
Helmkee, Jacob	do ...	21	Sept. 10, 1861	3 yrs.	Captured Oct. 14, 1863, in action near Fayetteville, Tenn.; mustered out March 21, 1865, at Columbus, O., on expiration of term of service.
Hill, Gilbert W.........	do ...	18	Feb. 24, 1864	3 yrs.	Mustered out with company Aug. 4, 1865.
Hill, Joseph A.........	do ...	22	Sept. 10, 1861	3 yrs.	Mustered out Sept. 10, 1864, at Columbia, Tenn., on expiration of term of service.
Hill, Thomas M........	do ...	20	Feb. 24, 1864	3 yrs.	Mustered out with company Aug. 4, 1865.
Hill, William A........	do ...	23	Feb. 23, 1864	3 yrs.	Discharged Jan. 27, 1865, at Gravelly Springs, Ala., on Surgeon's certificate of disability.
Hill, William O........	do ...	27	Aug. 25, 1862	3 yrs.	Mustered out June 17, 1865, at Nashville, Tenn., by order of War Department.
Holcomb, Allen	do ...	18	Sept. 10, 1861	3 yrs.	
Holland, John	do ...	28	Sept. 10, 1861	3 yrs.	Mustered out with company Aug. 4, 1865; veteran.
Inman, Barzillia	do ...	19	Feb. 23, 1864	3 yrs.	Mustered out with company Aug. 4, 1865.
Jackson, Thomas	do ...	22	Sept. 10, 1861	3 yrs.	Discharged Aug. 30, 1862, on Surgeon's certificate of disability.
James, Milo	do ...	21	Sept. 10, 1861	3 yrs.	Died Nov. 17, 1862, at Nashville, Tenn.
Kelsey, James	do ...	19	Sept. 10, 1861	3 yrs.	Discharged June 24, 1864, at Cleveland, O., on Surgeon's certificate of disability; veteran.
Kerns, Harvey	do ...	25	Aug. 25, 1862	3 yrs.	Mustered out June 17, 1865, at Nashville, Tenn., by order of War Department.
King, Isaac	do ...	26	Aug. 25, 1862	3 yrs.	Captured Oct. 14, 1863; paroled Nov. 30, 1864; mustered out June 17, 1865, at Nashville, Tenn., by order of War Department.
Kisher, Jacob	do ...	20	Sept. 1, 1863	3 yrs.	Died March 22, 1864, in hospital at Nashville, Tenn.
Lemon, Richard	do ...	18	Sept. 10, 1861	3 yrs.	Mustered out with company Aug. 4, 1865; veteran.
Lemon, Williard	do ...	18	Mch. 2, 1864	3 yrs.	Mustered out with company Aug. 4, 1865.
Lockwood, Sardus B....	do ...	18	Sept. 10, 1861	3 yrs.	Discharged Oct. 6, 1862, on Surgeon's certificate of disability.
Long, William M.......	do ...	19	Feb. 20, 1864	3 yrs.	Mustered out with company Aug. 4, 1865.
Lucas, David O........	do ...	26	Sept. 10, 1861	3 yrs.	
McElhaney, Frank	do ...	21	Sept. 10, 1861	3 yrs.	Mustered out Sept. 10, 1864, at Columbia, Tenn., on expiration of term of service.
McFeters, William W....	do ...	24	Feb. 6, 1864	3 yrs.	Mustered out with company Aug. 4, 1865.
Mallenee, Oliver	do ...	25	Sept. 10, 1861	3 yrs.	Mustered out Sept. 10, 1864, at Columbia, Tenn., on expiration of term of service.
Merriman, Frank	do ...	23	Feb. 13, 1864	3 yrs.	Mustered out with company Aug. 4, 1865.

Names	Rank	Age	Date of Entering the Service	Period of Service	Remarks
Michaels, George	Private	21	Feb. 15, 1863	3 yrs.	Mustered out with company Aug. 4, 1865.
Miller, Able	... do ...	18	Sept. 10, 1861	3 yrs.	Died June 8, 1862.
Miller, Gabriel D.	... do ...	34	Sept. 1, 1862	3 yrs.	Discharged March 26, 1863, on Surgeon's certificate of disability.
Miller, Jacob	... do ...	20	Sept. 10, 1861	3 yrs.	Mustered out with company Aug. 4, 1865; veteran.
Miller, Joseph G.	... do ...	24	Jan. 5, 1864	3 yrs.	
Miller, Reuben	... do ...	22	Sept. 10, 1861	3 yrs.	Died Oct. 14, 1863, of wounds received in action.
Minckley, Marion	... do ...	18	Sept. 10, 1861	3 yrs.	Discharged Nov. 22, 1862, on Surgeon's certificate of disability.
Morse, Edward D.	. do ...	19	Sept. 10, 1861	3 yrs.	Mustered out with company Aug. 4, 1865; veteran.
Moyer, Abraham	... do ...	18	Sept. 10, 1861	3 yrs.	Died May 22, 1862, at Nashville, Tenn.
Muney, George W.	... do ...	30	Sept. 10, 1861	3 yrs.	Discharged Aug. 8, 1862, on Surgeon's certificate of disability.
Neepe, Henry	... do ...	19	Feb. 3, 1864	3 yrs.	Mustered out with company Aug. 4, 1865.
Neff, George	... do ...	24	Sept. 10, 1861	3 yrs.	Discharged Jan. 26, 1863, on Surgeon's certificate of disability.
Neff, Samuel	... do ...	26	Sept. 10, 1861	3 yrs.	Died May 14, 1862.
Norton, Henry G.	... do ...	19	Jan. 4, 1864	3 yrs.	Promoted to 1st Lieutenant and Regt. Adjutant 137th Regiment U. S. Colored Troops April 8, 1865; from which mustered out with regiment Jan. 15, 1866.
Oakes, Charles	... do ...	19	Feb. 5, 1864	3 yrs.	Mustered out with company Aug. 4, 1865.
Odell, Thomas	... do ...	18	Sept. 10, 1861	3 yrs.	Mustered out with company Aug. 4, 1865; veteran.
Ora, Francis	... do ...	18	Nov. 8, 1861	3 yrs.	Transferred from Co. M Dec. 10, 1861; mustered out Jan. 11, 1865, at Nashville, Tenn., on expiration of term of service.
Palmer, Frederick	... do ...	26	Sept. 1, 1863	3 yrs.	Mustered out with company Aug. 4, 1865.
Parish, Joseph	... do ...	31	Sept. 10, 1861	3 yrs.	Discharged Feb. 25, 1863, on Surgeon's certificate of disability; re-enlisted Jan. 16, 1864; mustered out to date Aug. 3, 1865, by order of War Department.
Patterson, Franklin	... do ...	26	Jan. 2, 1864	3 yrs.	Mustered out with company Aug. 4, 1865.
Peck, Jefferson	... do ...	27	Sept. 10, 1861	3 yrs.	Mustered out with company Aug. 4, 1865; veteran.
Pickett, John	... do ...	19	Sept. 10, 1861	3 yrs.	Died June 19, 1862, at Tuscumbia, Ala.
Pope, Henry P.	... do ...	25	Sept. 10, 1861	3 yrs.	Mustered out June 17, 1865, at Nashville, Tenn., by order of War Department.
Ream, Franklin	... do ...	20	Aug. 31, 1862	3 yrs.	Died March 17, 1864, in hospital at Nashville, Tenn.
Sanders, John	... do ...	40	Aug. 25, 1862	3 yrs.	Mustered out June 17, 1865, at Nashville, Tenn., by order of War Department.
Seaman, John	... do ...	21	Sept. 10, 1861	3 yrs.	Mustered out with company Aug. 4, 1865; veteran.
Setzler, John	... do ...	18	Feb. 26, 1864	3 yrs.	Mustered out with company Aug. 4, 1865.
Shively, Solomon	... do ...	29	Feb. 24, 1864	3 yrs.	Mustered out with company Aug. 4, 1865.
Sloan, Hilliard H.	... do ...	18	Sept. 10, 1861	3 yrs.	Discharged Sept. 1, 1862, on Surgeon's certificate of disability; re-enlisted Jan. 2, 1864; wounded Aug. 20, 1864, in battle of Lovejoy Station, Ga.; mustered out June 21, 1864, at Camp Dennison, O., by order of War Department.
Smith, Emanuel D.	... do ...	20	Feb. 24, 1864	3 yrs.	Mustered out with company Aug. 4, 1865.
Smith, Francis M.	... do ...	19	July 22, 1863	3 yrs.	Mustered out with company Aug. 4, 1865.
Smith, George W.	... do ...	18	Feb. 23, 1864	3 yrs.	Mustered out with company Aug. 4, 1865.
Spohn, Jonathan	... do ...	44	Mch. 2, 1865	1 yr.	Mustered out with company Aug. 4, 1865.
Stackhouse, Jos. G. M.	... do ...	18	Sept. 10, 1861	3 yrs.	Died June 20, 1862.
Sweet, John	... do ...	23	Feb. 26, 1864	3 yrs.	Mustered out with company Aug. 4, 1865.
Timons, John	... do ...	18	Feb. 23, 1864	3 yrs.	Mustered out with company Aug. 4, 1865.
Trescott, Erastus E.	... do ...	21	Sept. 10, 1861	3 yrs.	Mustered out with company Aug. 4, 1865; veteran.
Warren, Thomas	... do ...	18	Sept. 10, 1861	3 yrs.	Discharged April 1, 1863, on Surgeon's certificate of disability.
Welker, George D.	... do ...	19	Sept. 10, 1861	3 yrs.	Discharged Oct. 26, 1862, on Surgeon's certificate of disability.
West, David	... do ...	31	Sept. 10, 1861	3 yrs.	Mustered out Sept. 10, 1864, at Columbia, Tenn., on expiration of term of service.
Yeasting, Henry	... do ...	20	Sept. 10, 1861	3 yrs.	Mustered out Sept. 10, 1864, at Columbia, Tenn., on expiration of term of service.
Beech, Charles	Cook	28	April 26, 1865	3 yrs.	Colored under-cook; mustered out with company Aug. 4, 1865.
Fleming, George	... do ...	24	Mch. 16, 1865	3 yrs.	Colored under-cook; mustered out with company Aug. 4, 1865.
Moore, Alexander	... do ...	26	April 8, 1865	3 yrs.	Colored under-cook; mustered out with company Aug. 4, 1865.
Reed, James	... do ...	37	April 8, 1865	3 yrs.	Colored under-cook; mustered out with company Aug. 4, 1865.

COMPANY E.

Mustered in November 4, 1861, at Camp Worcester, O., by James P. W. Neill, 1st Lieutenant 18th Infantry, U. S. A., Mustering Officer. Mustered out August 4, 1865, at Nashville, Tenn., by James P. W. Neill, Captain 18th Infantry, U. S. A., Acting Commissary of Musters, Cavalry Corps, M. D. T.

Names	Rank	Age	Date of Entering the Service	Period of Service	Remarks
Charles B. Seidel......	Captain	25	Sept. 7, 1861	3 yrs.	Appointed Sept. 7, 1861; promoted to Major Jan. 16, 1862.
Thomas D. McClelland	... do ...	40	Sept. 4, 1861	3 yrs.	Promoted from 1st Lieutenant Co. A Jan. 16, 1862; to Major Dec. 8, 1863.
Edwin Clark	.. do ...	25	Sept. 4, 1861	3 yrs.	Promoted to 2d Lieutenant from Batt. Sergt. Major May 20, 1862; to 1st Lieutenant Feb. 14, 1863; to Captain Dec. 8, 1863; mustered out Nov. 19, 1864, at Louisville, Ky., on expiration of term of service.
Seymour B. Coe.......	... do ...	43	Sept. 4, 1861	3 yrs.	Promoted from 1st Lieutenant and Regt. Commissary of Subsistence Nov. 30, 1864; brevetted Major to date from March 13, 1865; promoted to Major Aug. 2, 1865, but not mustered; mustered out with company Aug. 4, 1865.
Robert Moore	1st Lieu.	31	Sept. 7, 1861	3 yrs.	Appointed Sept. 7, 1861; resigned June 20, 1862.
Francis P. Gates.......	... do ...	26	Sept. 7, 1861	3 yrs.	Appointed 2d Lieutenant Sept. 7, 1861; promoted to 1st Lieutenant June 20, 1862; to Captain Co. H March 5, 1863.
Orange H. Howland...	... do ...	23	Aug. 15, 1861	3 yrs.	Transferred from Co. C as 2d Lieutenant April 24, 1863; promoted to 1st Lieutenant March 31, 1864; to Captain Co. K Nov. 30, 1864.
John M. Keller..........	... do ...	33	Sept. 7, 1861	3 yrs.	Promoted from 2d Lieutenant Co. C Nov. 30, 1864; to Captain Co. F March 29, 1865; veteran.
William B. Gates......	2d Lieu.	20	Sept. 7, 1861	3 yrs.	Appointed Bugler Sept. 7, 1861; 1st Sergeant ——; promoted to 2d Lieutenant Nov. 24, 1863; to 1st Lieutenant Co. A Nov. 30, 1864.
Joseph M. Fox	... do ...	21	Sept. 7, 1861	3 yrs.	Appointed Sergeant Sept. 7, 1861; 1st Sergeant April 4, 1864; promoted to 2d Lieutenant Nov. 30, 1864; to 1st Lieutenant Co. A Jan. 6, 1865; veteran.
John H. Lawrence......	... do ...	20	Sept. 4, 1861	3 yrs.	Promoted from 1st Sergeant Co. B April 8, 1865; mustered out with company Aug. 4, 1865; veteran.
William B. Kerr.......	1st Serg.	21	Nov. 4, 1861	3 yrs.	Mustered as private; appointed Dec. 2, 1864; promoted to 2d Lieutenant April 8, 1865, but not mustered; to Captain 137th Regiment U. S. Colored Troops April 8, 1865, from which mustered out with regiment Jan. 15, 1866; veteran.
Lycurgus W. Severns..	Q. M. S.	21	Sept. 7, 1861	3 yrs.	Appointed Sept. 7, 1861; mustered out Oct. 3, 1864, at ——, on expiration of term of service.
Thomas L. McEwen......	... do ...	21	Sept. 7, 1861	3 yrs.	Appointed Corporal Sept. 7, 1861; Sergeant ——; Q. M. Sergeant ——; promoted to Regt. Com. Sergeant Oct. 3, 1864; veteran.
James C. Serrels..........	... do ...	23	Sept. 7, 1861	3 yrs.	Also borne on rolls as Clark Serrels; mustered as privat; appointed Dec. 2, 1864; mustered out with company Aug. 4, 1865; veteran.
John Moore	Com Ser.	26	Sept. 7, 1861	3 yrs.	Appointed Sergeant Sept. 7, 1861; Com. Sergeant ——; promoted to 2d Lieutenant Co. I May 9, 1864; veteran.
Thomas Allen	... do ...	23	Nov. 4, 1861	3 yrs.	Mustered as private; appointed ——; mustered out with company Aug. 4, 1865; veteran.
Henry M. Miller........	Sergeant	23	Sept. 7, 1861	3 yrs.	Appointed Sept. 7, 1861; promoted to Sergeant Major ——.
John Delong	... do ...	20	Sept. 7, 1861	3 yrs.	Appointed Sept. 7, 1861; discharged Sept. 23, 1863, on Surgeon's certificate of disability.
Oliver Crouse	... do ...	20	Sept. 7, 1861	3 yrs.	Appointed Sept. 7, 1861; died Nov. 24, 1861.
Milton Askue	... do ...	21	Sept. 7, 1861	3 yrs.	Appointed Corporal Sept. 7, 1861; Sergeant ——; mustered out Oct. 3, 1864, on expiration of term of service.
William A Martain...	... do ...	20	Sept. 7, 1861	3 yrs.	Mustered as private; appointed ——; mustered out Oct. 3, 1864, on expiration of term of service.
Daniel A. Smith	... do ...	21	Sept. 7, 1861	3 yrs.	Mustered as private; appointed ——; mustered out with company Aug. 4, 1865; veteran.
William H. Potter.......	... do ...	22	Sept. 7, 1861	3 yrs.	Mustered as private; appointed ——; captured Nov. 15, 1862, at Gallatin, Tenn.; paroled ——; promoted to Captain 137th Regiment U. S. Colored Troops April 8, 1865; from which mustered out with regiment Jan. 15, 1866; veteran.

Names	Rank	Age	Date of Entering the Service	Period of Service	Remarks
John Mail	Sergeant	20	Sept. 7, 1861	3 yrs.	Mustered as private; appointed ——; mustered out with company Aug. 4, 1865; veteran.
William O. Hissong	... do ...	23	Sept. 7, 1861	3 yrs.	Mustered as private; appointed ——; mustered out with company Aug. 4, 1865; veteran.
John T. McClelland	... do ...	34	Dec. 24, 1863	3 yrs.	Mustered as private; appointed ——; died April 2, 1865, of wounds received in battle of Selma, Ala.
Samuel A. Bell	... do ...	31	Sept. 7, 1861	3 yrs.	Appointed Corporal ——; Sergeant April 2, 1865; mustered out with company Aug. 4, 1865; veteran.
William A. McAtee	Corporal	19	Sept. 7, 1861	3 yrs.	Appointed Sept. 7, 1861; discharged April 22, 1863, on Surgeon's certificate of disability.
George W. Polick	... do ...	25	Sept. 7, 1861	3 yrs.	Also borne on rolls as Pollock; appointed Sept. 7, 1861; mustered out Oct. 3, 1864, on expiration of term of service.
George Desoe	... do ...	22	Sept. 7, 1861	3 yrs.	Appointed Sept. 7, 1861; discharged Nov. 21, 1862, on Surgeon's certificate of disability.
Adam J. Endley	... do ...	21	Sept. 7, 1861	3 yrs.	Appointed Sept. 7, 1861; discharged Dec. 15, 1862, on Surgeon's certificate of disability.
Hugh Thompson	... do ...	32	Sept. 7, 1861	3 yrs.	Appointed Sept. 7, 1861; died May 20, 1863.
Milton Cake	... do ...	21	Sept. 7, 1861	3 yrs.	Appointed ——; mustered out Oct. 3, 1864, on expiration of term of service.
Johnson Taylor	... do ...	18	Sept. 7, 1861	3 yrs.	Appointed ——; mustered out Oct. 3, 1864, on expiration of term of service.
Isaac White	... do ...	25	Sept. 7, 1861	3 yrs.	Appointed ——; mustered out with company Aug. 4, 1865; veteran.
Lewis Deems	... do ...	16	Sept. 7, 1861	3 yrs.	Appointed ——; mustered out with company Aug. 4, 1865; veteran.
Nathan Dewitt	... do ...	18	Jan. 6, 1864	3 yrs.	Appointed ——; mustered out with company Aug. 4, 1865.
Peter Stillwagoner	... do ...	19	Sept. 7, 1861	3 yrs.	Appointed ——; mustered out with company Aug. 4, 1865; veteran.
George Strawhaker	... do ...	21	Aug. 24, 1863	3 yrs.	Appointed ——; mustered out with company Aug. 4, 1865.
John Kohl	... do ...	31	Dec. 7, 1863	3 yrs.	Appointed ——; mustered out with company Aug. 4, 1865.
Everett Stonestreet	... do ...	18	Dec. 8, 1863	3 yrs.	Appointed ——; mustered out with company Aug. 4, 1865.
Leander Glenn	... do ...	21	Sept. 24, 1861	3 yrs.	Appointed April 2, 1865; mustered out with company Aug. 4, 1865; veteran.
Ebenezer Lowery	Bugler	18	Aug. 20, 1863	3 yrs.	Appointed ——; died Aug. 7, 1864, of wounds received at Cartersville, Ga.
Thomas H. Sefton	Farrier	26	Sept. 7, 1861	3 yrs.	Appointed Sept. 7, 1861; discharged Jan. 8, 1863, on Surgeon's certificate of disability.
John Shafer	... do ...	35	Sept. 7, 1861	3 yrs.	Appointed Sept. 7, 1861; mustered out Oct. 3, 1864, on expiration of term of service.
James Burns	... do ...	21	Sept. 7, 1861	3 yrs.	Appointed ——; mustered out Oct. 3, 1864, on expiration of term of service.
Isaac Bicktal	... do ...	44	Nov. 1, 1863	3 yrs.	Appointed ——; mustered out with company Aug. 4, 1865.
John Haywood	... do ...	26	Aug. 4, 1863	3 yrs.	Appointed ——; mustered out with company Aug. 4, 1865.
William Lamley	Wagoner	44	Sept. 7, 1861	3 yrs.	Appointed Sept. 7, 1861; mustered out with company Aug. 4, 1865; veteran.
Thomas P. Miller	Saddler	30	Sept. 7, 1861	3 yrs.	Appointed Sept. 7, 1861; mustered out with company Aug. 4, 1865; veteran.
Allen, Hiram	Private	18	Feb. 24, 1864	3 yrs.	Mustered out with company Aug. 4, 1865.
Allen, Joseph F.	... do ...	24	Aug. 29, 1862	3 yrs.	Mustered out June 17, 1865, at Nashville, Tenn., by order of War Department.
Allen, Socrates	... do ...	21	Sept. 7, 1861	3 yrs.	Discharged July 16, 1862, on Surgeon's certificate of disability.
Ash, William	... do ...	19	Aug. 10, 1863	3 yrs.	Mustered out with company Aug. 4, 1865.
Baker, William C.	... do ...	22	Sept. 7, 1861	3 yrs.	Mustered out to date Aug. 4, 1865, by order of War Department; veteran.
Balliard, David	... do ...	18	Sept. 7, 1861	3 yrs.	Died May 10, 1862.
Barrett, Myron H.	... do ...	20	Sept. 7, 1861	3 yrs.	Promoted to Regt. Q. M. Sergeant ——.
Bishop, Samuel	... do ...	27	Mch. 2, 1865	1 yr.	Mustered out with company Aug. 4, 1865.
Boyer, Jacob	... do ...	25	Sept. 7, 1861	3 yrs.	Died Nov. 19, 1861.
Brown, John	... do ...	28	Sept. 7, 1861	3 yrs.	Mustered out Oct. 3, 1864, on expiration of term of service.
Buckner, Arthur J.	... do ...	26	Feb. 16, 1864	3 yrs.	Discharged Aug. 23, 1865, on Surgeon's certificate of disability.
Bruro, John	... do ...	42	Nov. 25, 1863	3 yrs.	Mustered out with company Aug. 4, 1865.
Burns, John M.	... do ...	25	Aug. 29, 1862	3 yrs.	Mustered out June 17, 1865, at Nashville, Tenn., by order of War Department.
Bushong, William A.	... do ...	19	Sept. 7, 1861	3 yrs.	Mustered out Oct. 3, 1864, on expiration of term of service.
Olay, Francis M.	... do ...	18	Jan. 15, 1864	3 yrs.	Mustered out with company Aug. 4, 1865.
Orowner, Thomas	... do ...	23	Dec. 26, 1863	3 yrs.	Mustered out with company Aug. 4, 1865.
Oulp, Jefferson	... do ...	21	Sept. 7, 1861	3 yrs.	Captured ——, in action at Columbia, Tenn.; paroled ——; died Jan. 31, 1864, at Bowling Green, Ky.
Oulver, Martin V. D.	... do ...	20	Sept. 7, 1861	3 yrs.	Mustered out Oct. 3, 1864, on expiration of term of service.

Names	Rank	Age	Date of Entering the Service	Period of Service	Remarks
Cunningham, John ...	Private	24	Sept. 7, 1861	3 yrs.	Mustered out Oct. 3, 1864, on expiration of term of service.
Curtzwiler, Charles ...	... do ...	18	Feb. 28, 1865	1 yr.	Mustered out July 19, 1865, from hospital at Camp Dennison, O., by order of War Department.
Diddian, Martin	... do ...	21	Jan. 8, 1864	3 yrs.	Also borne on rolls as "Martin Dedon;" mustered out with company Aug. 4, 1865.
Dufner, Joseph	... do ...	22	Dec. 29, 1863	3 yrs.	Mustered out with company Aug. 4, 1865.
Eggleston, James G....	... do ...	22	Sept. 7, 1861	3 yrs.	Mustered out with company Aug. 4, 1865; veteran.
Endly, Charles	... do ...	18	Sept. 7, 1861	3 yrs.	Mustered out Oct. 3, 1864, on expiration of term of service.
Englbreth, Henry	... do ...	26	Sept. 7, 1861	3 yrs.	Mustered out Oct. 3, 1864, on expiration of term of service.
Etswiler, Thomas	... do ...	22	Sept. 7, 1861	3 yrs.	Mustered out Oct. 3, 1864, on expiration of term of service.
Fassett, Hamilton	... do ...	18	Jan. 18, 1864	3 yrs.	Mustered out with company Aug. 4, 1865.
Finley, Thomas	... do ...	29	Oct. 5, 1863	3 yrs.	Mustered out with company Aug. 4, 1865.
Fish, Brainard	... do ...	20	Sept. 7, 1861	3 yrs.	Promoted to Batt. Sergt. Major Dec. 1, 1861.
Fisher, Henry	... do ...	17	Sept. 7, 1861	3 yrs.	Died Oct. 7, 1863, of wounds received in action.
Follin, David F.........	... do ...	21	Sept. 7, 1861	3 yrs.	Died May 25, 1863, at Nashville, Tenn.
Follin, William	... do ...	26	Sept. 24, 1861	3 yrs.	Discharged Aug. 18, 1862, on Surgeon's certificate of disability.
Fox, Stephen	... do ...	22	Aug. 10, 1863	3 yrs.	Left at Cartersville, Ga., dismounted, June 8, 1864; no further record found.
Fry, John	... do ...	26	Sept. 24, 1861	3 yrs.	Discharged Aug. 25, 1862, on Surgeon's certificate of disability.
Gfell, Leonard	... do ...	19	Jan. 5, 1864	3 yrs.	Mustered out with company Aug. 4, 1865.
Gibbs, John	... do ...	21	Sept. 7, 1861	3 yrs.	Mustered out Oct. 3, 1864, on expiration of term of service.
Gibson, William W....	... do ...	24	Sept. 24, 1861	3 yrs.	Mustered out with company Aug. 4, 1865; veteran.
Gibson, Abraham	... do ...	20	Sept. 24, 1861	3 yrs.	Mustered out with company Aug. 4, 1865; veteran.
Godfrey, George	... do ...	21	Sept. 7, 1861	3 yrs.	Discharged Nov. 21, 1862, on Surgeon's certificate of disability.
Godfrey, William	... do ...	26	Sept. 7, 1861	3 yrs.	
Goodman, John	... do ...	46	Sept. 7, 1861	3 yrs.	Discharged July 8, 1862, on Surgeon's certificate of disability; re-enlisted Oct. 7, 1862, for 3 years; died March 7, 1864, in hospital at Louisville, Ky.
Gorman, John	... do ...	29	Oct. 5, 1863	3 yrs.	Mustered out with company Aug. 4, 1865.
Grant, Thomas	... do ...		Nov. 4, 1861	3 yrs.	Mustered out Nov. 5, 1864, on expiration of term of service.
Green, Sherman	... do ...	19	Sept. 7, 1861	3 yrs.	Mustered out Oct. 3, 1864, on expiration of term of service.
Greenwalt, Henry	... do ...	20	Oct. 22, 1863	3 yrs.	Mustered out May 30, 1865, at Camp Dennison, O., by order of War Department.
Griffin, John	... do ...		Sept. 24, 1861	3 yrs.	Discharged Aug. 25, 1863, at Stevenson, Ala., on Surgeon's certificate of disability.
Grower, Henry	... do ...	24	Sept. 7, 1861	3 yrs.	Captured Dec. 31, 1862, at battle of Murfreesboro, Tenn.; paroled ——; mustered out with company Aug. 4. 1865; veteran.
Hafer, Daniel	... do ...	24	Aug. 29, 1862	3 yrs.	Discharged March 30, 1863, on Surgeon's certificate of disability.
Harris, Ervin R.........	... do ...	17	Sept. 7, 1861	3 yrs.	Promoted to 2d Lieutenant Co. M Jan. 21, 1863.
Hartshorn, Alfred	... do ...	27	Aug. 29, 1862	3 yrs.	Also borne on rolls as "Albert Hartshorn;" mustered out June 17, 1865, at Nashville, Tenn., by order of War Department.
Hepp, William	... do ...	22	Sept. 7, 1861	3 yrs.	Mustered out Oct. 3, 1864, on expiration of term of service.
Hettinger, George	... do ...	28	Sept. 7, 1861	3 yrs.	Died May 24, 1862.
Hissong, Levi	... do ...	23	Nov. 4, 1861	3 yrs.	Discharged Oct. 22, 1862, on Surgeon's certificate.
Hooper, Sidney	... do ...	22	Oct. 2, 1863	3 yrs.	Died June 17, 1864, at Louisville, Ky.
Hoy, Cyrus	... do ...	25	Sept. 7, 1861	3 yrs.	Transferred to 42d Co., 2d Battalion Veteran Reserve Corps, Aug. 28, 1863.
Hunt, William	... do ...	18	Jan. 11, 1864	3 yrs.	Mustered out with company Aug. 4, 1865.
Huston, John	... do ...	19	Sept. 7, 1861	3 yrs.	
Ingerson, Daniel	... do ...	33	Dec. 11, 1863	3 yrs.	Mustered out May 31, 1865, at Columbus, O., by order of War Department.
Johnson, Richard M....	... do ...	25	Sept. 7, 1861	3 yrs.	Discharged Sept. 18, 1863, at Camp Dennison, O., on Surgeon's certificate of disability.
Johnston, Thomas	... do ...	27	Oct. 24, 1864	1 yr.	Mustered out with company Aug. 4, 1865.
Jones, George W........	... do ...	20	Aug. 10, 1862	3 yrs.	Mustered out May 30, 1865, at Cleveland, O., by order of War Department.
Jones, James	... do ...	20	Nov. 2, 1863	3 yrs.	
Kannaly, Thomas	... do ...	45	Oct. 14, 1863	3 yrs.	Also borne on rolls as "Thomas Kaneeley;" mustered out with company Aug. 4, 1865.
Kennedy, William	... do ...	43	Oct. 1, 1863	3 yrs.	Prisoner of war; mustered out June 24, 1865, at Camp Chase, O., by order of War Department.
Kennedy, William	... do ...	22	Sept. 7, 1861	3 yrs.	Died June 15, 1862.

Names	Rank	Age	Date of Entering the Service	Period of Service	Remarks
Kerr, James L.........	Private	18	Dec. 16, 1863	3 yrs.	Mustered out with company Aug. 4, 1865.
Kuncy, Norman	... do ...	22	Feb. 27, 1864	3 yrs.	Mustered out with company Aug. 4, 1865.
Laird, Jacob	... do ...	22	Aug. 29, 1862	3 yrs.	Mustered out June 17, 1865, at Nashville, Tenn., by order of War Department.
Lash, Thomas	... do ...	23	Mch. 2, 1865	1 yr.	Mustered out with company Aug. 4, 1865.
Lichty, Amos	... do ...	18	Sept. 7, 1861	3 yrs.	Mustered out Jan. 20, 1865, at Columbus, O., on expiration of term of service.
Lockheart, Henry	... do ...	21	Sept. 7, 1861	3 yrs.	Discharged June 21, 1862, on Surgeon's certificate of disability.
Machel, George	... do ...	22	Sept. 7, 1861	3 yrs.	Mustered out Oct. 3, 1864, on expiration of term of service.
Martin, Henry	... do ...	21	Sept. 7, 1861	3 yrs.	Discharged Aug. 6, 1862, on Surgeon's certificate of disability.
Martin, John	... do ...	19	Dec. 29, 1863	3 yrs.	Mustered out with company Aug. 4, 1865.
Melville, David C.......	... do ...	33	Aug. 9, 1862	3 yrs.	Discharged Feb. 8, 1863, at Camp Stanley, Tenn., on Surgeon's certificate of disability.
Miller, Cantwell	... do ...	18	Feb. 27, 1864	3 yrs.	Mustered out with company Aug. 4, 1865.
Moulett, Michael	... do ...	19	Feb. 28, 1865	1 yr.	Mustered out with company Aug. 4, 1865.
Mulcahy, Cornelius	... do ...	42	Dec. 11, 1863	3 yrs.	Discharged Feb. 2, 1865, on Surgeon's certificate of disability.
Muttersbaugh,Abraham	... do ...	21	Sept. 7, 1861	3 yrs.	Mustered out Oct. 3, 1864, on expiration of term of service.
Murphy, John	... do ...	27	Sept. 6, 1863	3 yrs.	Mustered out with company Aug. 4, 1865.
O'Connor, Edward	... do ...	27	Nov. 2, 1863	3 yrs.	Mustered out with company Aug. 4, 1865.
Pearson, Samuel S......	... do ...	18	Nov. 3, 1863	3 yrs.	Transferred from Co. I ——; mustered out with company Aug. 4, 1865.
Peasley, William T.....	... do ...	24	Aug. 29, 1862	3 yrs.	Discharged March 23, 1863, on Surgeon's certificate of disability.
Peckinpaugh, Sebas. S.	... do ...	18	Feb. 29, 1864	3 yrs.	Mustered out July 27, 1865, at Camp Dennison, O., by order of War Department.
Perry, Albert	... do ...	22	Sept. 7, 1861	3 yrs.	Mustered out with company Aug. 4, 1865; veteran.
Pifer, Nathan J.........	... do ...	22	Sept. 7, 1861	3 yrs.	Mustered out Oct. 3, 1864, on expiration of term of service.
Piper, James	... do ...	21	Nov. 4, 1861	3 yrs.	Mustered out Dec. 30, 1864, at Nashville, Tenn., on expiration of term of service.
Platt, Benjamin F.....	... do ...	21	Sept. 7, 1861	3 yrs.	Mustered out Oct. 3, 1864, on expiration of term of service.
Potter, Ezra	... do ...	17	Sept. 7, 1861	3 yrs.	Mustered out Jan. 24, 1865, at Columbus, O., on expiration of term of service.
Princehorn, Henry	... do ...	20	Sept. 7, 1861	3 yrs.	Transferred to 106th Co. 2d Battalion, Veteran Reserve Corps, Dec. 3, 1863; mustered out from same Oct. 13, 1864, on expiration of term of service.
Schwabley, Urban	... do ...	23	Dec. 26, 1863	3 yrs.	Mustered out with company Aug. 4, 1865.
Seymour, Peter	... do ...	21	Dec. 29, 1863	3 yrs.	Mustered out June 2, 1865, at Louisville, Ky., by order of War Department.
Shann, Henry	... do ...	20	Jan. 6, 1864	3 yrs.	Died July 21, 1864, at Columbia, Tenn.
Shortice, Asbury	... do ...	27	Sept. 7, 1861	3 yrs.	Mustered out with company Aug. 4, 1865; veteran.
Showers, Jeremiah	... do ...	23	Sept. 7, 1861	3 yrs.	Mustered out Oct. 3, 1864, on expiration of term of service.
Simmons, Abraham	... do ...	30	Mch. 2, 1865	1 yr.	Mustered out with company Aug. 4, 1865.
Simmons, Otho	... do ...	24	Feb. 25, 1864	3 yrs.	Died Sept. 15, 1864, at Atlanta, Ga.
Simmons, Thomas	... do ...	21	Mch. 2, 1865	1 yr.	Mustered out with company Aug. 4, 1865.
Singleton, William	... do ...	40	Dec. 18, 1863	3 yrs.	Mustered out May 30, 1865, at Camp Dennison, O., by order of War Department.
Smith, Robert R.........	... do ...	19	Sept. 13, 1863	3 yrs.	Discharged April 20, 1865, on Surgeon's certificate of disability.
Snavely, Jacob R........	... do ...	23	Sept. 7, 1861	3 yrs.	Died April 6, 1863.
Spaide, Daniel	... do ...	24	Sept. 7, 1861	3 yrs.	Mustered out Oct. 3, 1864, on expiration of term of service.
Starrett, William	... do ...	19	Oct. 1, 1863	3 yrs.	Mustered out with company Aug. 4, 1865.
Strayer, Reuben	... do ...	18	Feb. 2, 1864	3 yrs.	Mustered out with company Aug. 4, 1865.
Thornton, A. C...........	... do ...	....	Dec. 21, 1861	3 yrs.	Discharged July 11, 1862, at Columbus, O., on Surgeon's certificate of disability.
Tiaxler, Charles	... do ...	20	Sept. 7, 1861	3 yrs.	Transferred to Co. F ——.
Tindle, Francis	... do ...	15	Dec. 9, 1863	3 yrs.	Mustered out with company Aug. 4, 1865.
Venett, Frank G. E.....	... do ...	27	Oct. 1, 1863	3 yrs.	Mustered out with company Aug. 4, 1865.
Webb, Chester C.........	... do ...	18	Dec. 29, 1863	3 yrs.	Mustered out Aug. 24, 1865, from hospital at Camp Dennison, O., by order of War Department.
Wickireo, Washington.	... do ...	19	Mch. 8, 1865	1 yr.	Mustered out with company Aug. 4, 1865.
Witt, Horatio	... do ...	43	Aug. 29, 1862	3 yrs.	Mustered out June 17, 1865, at Nashville, Tenn., by order of War Department.
Worley, David	... do ...	21	Feb. 15, 1864	3 yrs.	Mustered out with company Aug. 4, 1865.
Wright, William B......	... do ...	19	Mch. 2, 1865	1 yr.	Mustered out with company Aug. 4, 1865.
Wright, William B......	... do ...	17	Sept. 7, 1861	3 yrs.	Mustered out Oct. 3, 1864, on expiration of term of service.
Yeoman, John	... do ...	20	Sept. 7, 1861	3 yrs.	Mustered out Oct. 3, 1864, on expiration of term of service.
Young, Martin	... do ...	26	Dec. 26, 1863	3 yrs.	Also borne on rolls as "Martin You;" transferred from Co. A ——; mustered out May 31, 1865, at Camp Dennison, O., by order of War Department.

Names	Rank	Age	Date of Entering the Service	Period of Service	Remarks
Zimmerman, Lafayette	Private	22	Sept. 7, 1861	3 yrs.	Killed Nov. 15, 1862, in a skirmish.
Ingham, James	Cook	18	Mch. 18, 1865	3 yrs.	Colored under-cook; mustered out with company Aug. 4, 1865.
Walker, Miles	... do ...	35	Oct. 14, 1863	3 yrs.	Colored under-cook; mustered out with company Aug. 4, 1865.
Warton, Mingo	... do ...	20	April 28, 1865	3 yrs.	Colored under-cook; mustered out with company Aug. 4, 1865.
Williams, Jordan	... do ...	30	April 28, 1865	3 yrs.	Colored under-cook; mustered out with company Aug. 4, 1865.

COMPANY F.

Mustered in December 11, 1861, at Camp Worcester, O., by James P. W. Neill, 1st Lieutenant 18th Infantry, U. S. A., Mustering Officer. Mustered out August 4, 1865, at Nashville, Tenn., by James P. W. Neill, Captain 18th Infantry, U. S. A., Acting Commissary of Musters, Cavalry Corps, M. D. T.

Names	Rank	Age	Date	Period	Remarks
Oliver G. Smith........	Captain	33	Aug. 17, 1861	3 yrs.	Appointed Aug. 17, 1861; honorably discharged Oct. 26, 1862.
George P. Roberts.....	... do ...	23	Sept. 2, 1861	3 yrs.	Appointed 1st Lieutenant Sept. 2, 1861; promoted to Captain Sept. 11, 1862; resigned April 17, 1863.
George F. Williams....	... do ...	20	Sept. 10, 1861	3 yrs.	Promoted from 1st Lieutenant Co. D April 17, 1863; mustered out Nov. 23, 1864, at Louisville, Ky., on expiration of term of service.
Philander B. Lewis....	... do ...	28	Dec. 28, 1861	3 yrs.	Promoted to 2d Lieutenant Co. F from 1st Sergeant Co. L Nov. 24, 1863; to 1st Lieutenant Co. G Nov. 30, 1864; to Captain Co. F Jan. 6, 1865; transferred to Co. M Feb. 10, 1865.
John M. Keller..........	... do ...	33	Sept. 7, 1861	3 yrs.	Promoted from 1st Lieutenant Co. E March 29, 1865; mustered out with company Aug. 4, 1865; veteran.
Elihu Isbell	1st Lieu.	26	Sept. 6, 1861	3 yrs.	Appointed 2d Lieutenant Sept. 6, 1861; promoted to 1st Lieutenant Co. C Jan. 5, 1863; transferred from Co. C April 24, 1863; promoted to Captain Co. L Aug. 12, 1863.
Thomas Nunan	... do ...	20	Sept. 6, 1861	3 yrs.	Appointed 1st Sergeant Sept. 10, 1861; promoted to 2d Lieutenant Jan. 5, 1863; to 1st Lieutenant March 31, 1864; assigned to Regt. Adjutant July 22, 1864.
Christopher C. Clay...	... do ...	23	Aug. 20, 1861	3 yrs.	Promoted from 2d Lieutenant Co. C July 13, 1864; to Captain Co. B Nov. 30, 1864.
Thomas J. Coslet.......	... do ...	24	Aug. 20, 1861	3 yrs.	Promoted from 1st Sergeant Co. H Nov. 30, 1864; mustered out with company Aug. 4, 1865; veteran.
Thomas L. McEwen...	2d Lieu.	21	Sept. 7, 1861	3 yrs.	Promoted from Regt. Com. Sergeant Nov. 30, 1864; to 1st Lieutenant and Regt. Quartermaster March 29, 1865; veteran.
Wordon W. Welcher...	1st Serg.	25	Sept. 5, 1861	3 yrs.	Appointed Sergeant Sept. 6, 1861; 1st Sergeant ——; mustered out Nov. 4, 1864, at Columbia, Tenn., on expiration of term of service.
Maylam J. Bassett	... do ...	19	Sept. 4, 1861	3 yrs.	Mustered as private; appointed Oct. 3, 1861; promoted to 2d Lieutenant Co. A Nov. 30, 1864; veteran.
Llewellyn W. French ..	... do ...	20	Sept. 3, 1861	3 yrs.	Mustered as private; appointed Jan. 15, 1865; promoted to Captain 137th Regiment U. S. Colored Troops April 8, 1865; from which mustered out with regiment Jan. 15, 1866; veteran.
James H. Johnson.....	Q. M. S.	23	Aug. 29, 1861	3 yrs.	Appointed Sept. 13, 1861; promoted to Batt. Com. Sergeant Nov. 1, 1861.
Joseph S. Lutz	... do ...	25	Sept. 11, 1861	3 yrs.	Mustered as private; appointed ——; mustered out Nov. 4, 1864, at Columbia, Tenn., on expiration of term of service.
David A. Bishop........	... do ...	24	Sept. 11, 1861	3 yrs.	Mustered as private; appointed Nov. 4, 1864; mustered out with company Aug. 4, 1865; veteran.
Theodore L. Prosser ..	Com.Ser.	20	Sept. 3, 1861	3 yrs.	Mustered as private; appointed Nov. 4, 1864; mustered out with company Aug. 4, 1865; veteran.
William B. Pollinger..	Sergeant	19	Oct. 5, 1861	3 yrs.	Appointed Oct. 28, 1861.
Silas Gould	... do ...	32	Oct. 3, 1861	3 yrs.	Appointed Oct. 28, 1861; died May 12, 1863.

Names	Rank	Age	Date of Entering the Service	Period of Service	Remarks
George G. Holiday.....	Sergeant	21	Sept. 6, 1861	3 yrs.	Appointed Corporal Sept. 6, 1861; captured Dec. 29, 1862, in action at Murfreesboro, Tenn.; paroled ——; appointed Sergeant ——; mustered out Nov. 4, 1864, at Columbia, Tenn., on expiration of term of service.
Dudley W. Post	... do ...	20	Sept. 6, 1861	3 yrs.	Appointed Corporal Sept. 6, 1861; Sergeant ——; mustered out Nov. 4, 1864, at Columbia, Tenn., on expiration of term of service.
Samuel S. Hoyt.........	... do ...	19	Sept. 9, 1861	3 yrs.	Appointed Corporal Sept. 10, 1861; Sergeant ——; mustered out Nov. 4, 1864, at Columbia, Tenn., on expiration of term of service.
William Latham	... do ...	33	Aug. 26, 1862	3 yrs.	Mustered as private; appointed ——; mustered out June 17, 1865, at Nashville, Tenn., by order of War Department.
Alfred F. Washburn......	... do ...	20	Sept. 3, 1861	3 yrs.	Appointed Corporal Sept. 6, 1861; Sergeant ——; promoted to 2d Lieutenant Co. G Nov. 30, 1864; veteran.
William P. Lee...........	... do ...	23	Sept. 2, 1861	3 yrs.	Mustered as private; appointed ——; promoted to 2d Lieutenant Co. H Nov. 24, 1863.
Thomas Martin	... do ...	22	Aug. 31, 1861	3 yrs.	Mustered as private; appointed ——; promoted to 2d Lieutenant Co. K Nov. 30, 1864; veteran.
John B. Young..........	... do ...	19	Sept. 11, 1861	3 yrs.	Mustered as private; appointed ——; drowned July 18, 1865, at Macon, Ga.; veteran.
Edwin R. Holliday.......	... do ...	18	Sept. 6, 1861	3 yrs.	Also borne on rolls as "Edward;" mustered as private; appointed Nov. 4, 1864; mustered out with company Aug. 4, 1865; veteran.
Benjamin F. Shepard..	... do ...	27	Sept. 5, 1861	3 yrs.	Mustered as private; appointed Nov. 4, 1864; mustered out with company Aug. 4, 1865; veteran.
James H. Hart..........	... do ...	18	Sept. 10, 1862	3 yrs.	Appointed Corporal Nov. 4, 1864; Sergeant Jan. 15, 1865; mustered out with company Aug. 4, 1865.
Aaron Thompson	... do ...	18	Sept. 11, 1861	3 yrs.	Appointed Corporal Nov. 4, 1864; Sergeant June 17, 1865; mustered out with company Aug. 4, 1865; veteran.
John T. King...........	... do ...	25	Sept. 3, 1861	3 yrs.	Appointed Corporal Nov. 4, 1864; Sergeant June 17, 1865; mustered out with company Aug. 4, 1865; veteran.
Richard H. Reed.......	Corporal	25	Sept. 9, 1861	3 yrs.	Appointed Sept. 10, 1861; discharged Aug. 26, 1862, on Surgeon's certificate of disability.
Osher W. Coon..........	... do ...	29	Sept. 5, 1861	3 yrs.	Appointed Sept. 6, 1861.
John N. Barnes.........	... do ...	18	Sept. 5, 1861	3 yrs.	Appointed Sept. 6, 1861; died April 19, 1864, at Nashville, Tenn.; veteran.
Hiram Lynn	... do ...	20	Sept. 3, 1861	3 yrs.	Appointed ——; killed Aug. 20, 1864, in battle of Lovejoy Station, Ga.; veteran.
George Mitchell	... do ...	18	Sept. 5, 1861	3 yrs.	Appointed ——; mustered out Nov. 4, 1864, at Columbia, Tenn., on expiration of term of service.
John N. Roberts.........	... do ...	28	Aug. 26, 1862	3 yrs.	Appointed ——; mustered out June 17, 1865, at Nashville, Tenn., by order of War Department.
Albert L. Williams.......	... do ...	18	Oct. 24, 1863	3 yrs.	Appointed Nov. 4, 1864; mustered out with company Aug. 4, 1865.
George W. Lee...........	... do ...	18	Dec. 28, 1863	3 yrs.	Appointed Nov. 4, 1864; mustered out with company Aug. 4, 1865.
Jared Palmer	... do ...	25	Dec. 19, 1861	3 yrs.	Appointed Nov. 4, 1864; mustered out with company Aug. 4, 1865; veteran.
John W. Maxwell.......	... do ...	19	Feb. 5, 1864	3 yrs.	Appointed Nov. 4, 1864; mustered out with company Aug. 4, 1865.
Arthur H. West.........	... do ...	21	Jan. 5, 1864	3 yrs.	Appointed Jan. 15, 1865; mustered out with company Aug. 4, 1865.
Henry S. Barker........	... do ...	42	Oct. 6, 1862	3 yrs.	Appointed June 17, 1865; mustered out with company Aug. 4, 1865.
Henry Van Sickles......	... do ...	18	Nov. 11, 1862	3 yrs.	Appointed June 17, 1865; mustered out with company Aug. 4, 1865.
Sidney G. Mitchell......	... do ...	20	Sept. 5, 1861	3 yrs.	Appointed July 20, 1865; mustered out with company Aug. 4, 1865; veteran.
Joseph A. Locherer....	Bugler	18	Nov. 19, 1861	3 yrs.	Also borne on rolls as "J. A. Locher;" appointed Dec. 11, 1861; discharged Sept. 12, 1862, on Surgeon's certificate of disability.
Abraham Sinfield	... do ...	24	Sept. 10, 1861	3 yrs.	Appointed ——; mustered out with company Aug. 4, 1865; veteran.
Isaac Harbaugh	Farrier	20	Sept. 4, 1861	3 yrs.	Appointed Sept. 4, 1861; mustered out Nov. 4, 1864, at Columbia, Tenn., on expiration of term of service.
Artimus Richards	... do ...	25	Nov. 2, 1861	3 yrs.	Appointed Dec. 11, 1861; promoted to Batt. Veterinary Surgeon Dec. 11, 1861.
John Wall	... do ...	27	Dec. 26, 1863	3 yrs.	Appointed Nov. 4, 1864; mustered out with company Aug. 4, 1865.
Frank Rogers	Wagoner	25	Sept. 6, 1861	3 yrs.	Appointed Sept. 13, 1861; died April 7, 1862.
Adkins, Jackson J.....	Private	39	Aug. 26, 1862	3 yrs.	Mustered out June 17, 1865, at Nashville, Tenn., by order of War Department.

Names	Rank	Age	Date of Entering the Service	Period of Service	Remarks
Adkins, John	Private	20	Aug. 26, 1862	3 yrs.	Mustered out June 17, 1865, at Nashville, Tenn., by order of War Department.
Amerman, Josiah	... do ...	44	Feb. 8, 1864	3 yrs.	Mustered out with company Aug. 4, 1865.
Arnott, Barkdoll	... do ...	18	Sept. 6, 1861	3 yrs.	Died April 14, 1862.
Arnott, James	... do ...	23	Sept. 6, 1861	3 yrs.	Died May 30, 1862.
Bailey, James H........	... do ...	21	Sept. 5, 1861	3 yrs.	Mustered out with company Aug. 4, 1865; veteran.
Bare, Elias	... do ...	21	Sept. 12, 1861	3 yrs.	Died April 29, 1862, at Columbia, Tenn.
Barnes, Harris	... do ...	23	Aug. 22, 1862	3 yrs.	Also borne on rolls as "Horace Barnes;" discharged Feb. 24, 1863, on Surgeon's certificate of disability.
Beardsley, David A.....	... do ...	18	Sept. 12, 1861	3 yrs.	Discharged Aug. 30, 1862, by order of War Department.
Beckerstalk, Jacob ...	... do ...	22	Sept. 9, 1861	3 yrs.	Captured Dec. 29, 1862, in action at Murfreesboro, Tenn.; paroled ——; mustered out with company Aug. 4, 1865; veteran.
Blair, William H........	... do ...	39	Aug. 26, 1862	3 yrs.	Captured Dec. 29, 1862, in action at Murfreesboro, Tenn.; paroled ——; mustered out May 30, 1865, at Camp Dennison, O., by order of War Department.
Bliley, Lawrence	... do ...	43	Sept. 9, 1861	3 yrs.	Mustered out with company Aug. 4, 1865; veteran.
Brady, Jeremiah D.....	... do ...	37	Feb. 15, 1864	3 yrs.	Mustered out with company Aug. 4, 1865.
Breen, Patrick	... do ...	31	Dec. 26, 1863	3 yrs.	Mustered out with company Aug. 4, 1865.
Buckley, Thomas E. ..	... do ...	20	Oct. 24, 1863	3 yrs.	Discharged June 2, 1865, on Surgeon's certificate of disability.
Buxley, Elijah	... do ...	41	Oct. 15, 1861	3 yrs.	Discharged Dec. 22, 1862, on Surgeon's certificate of disability.
Campbell, William	... do ...	34	Sept. 4, 1861	3 yrs.	Transferred to 1st Co., 2d Battalion, Veteran Reserve Corps, Aug. 17, 1863; died Aug. 31, 1863.
Coates, Josiah	... do ...	24	Sept. 5, 1861	3 yrs.	Mustered out Nov. 4, 1864, at Columbia, Tenn., on expiration of term of service.
Coykendall, Wesley ...	... do ...	19	Sept. 3, 1861	3 yrs.	Died May 15, 1862.
Crow, Ira W............	... do ...	19	Sept. 10, 1861	3 yrs.	Mustered out to date Aug. 4, 1865, at Columbus, O., by order of War Department; veteran.
Culver, George W......	... do ...	25	Aug. 26, 1862	3 yrs.	Mustered out June 17, 1865, at Nashville, Tenn., by order of War Department.
Cranwell, Thomas S...	... do ...	26	Nov. 3, 1861	3 yrs.	Also borne on rolls as "Thomas Cromwell;" died April 18, 1864, on board boat en route from Fortress Monroe, Va., to Baltimore, Md.
Dagnon, Peter	... do ...	34	Sept. 5, 1861	3 yrs.	Discharged Feb. 15, 1863, on Surgeon's certificate of disability.
Duxbury, John	... do ...	24	Sept. 9, 1861	3 yrs.	Mustered out Nov. 4, 1864, at Columbia, Tenn., on expiration of term of service.
Engelbeck, Joseph W..	... do ...	19	Feb. 28, 1864	3 yrs.	Mustered out to date Aug. 4, 1865, by order of War Department.
Farley, Albion	... do ...	18	Sept. 9, 1861	3 yrs.	Mustered out Nov. 4, 1864, at Columbia, Tenn., on expiration of term of service.
Fisher, Louis D........	... do ...	20	Oct. 28, 1861	3 yrs.	Mustered out Dec. 30, 1864, at Nashville, Tenn., on expiration of term of service.
Flaven, Thomas	... do ...	21	Aug. 3, 1861	3 yrs.	Absent since Dec. 20, 1864; no further record found.
Fox, Albert S...........	... do ...	21	Sept. 9, 1861	3 yrs.	Mustered out with company Aug. 4, 1865; veteran.
Fox, Thomas	... do ...	34	Nov. 14, 1862	3 yrs.	Mustered out with company Aug. 4, 1865.
Frier, Francis J........	... do ...	18	Sept. 12, 1861	3 yrs.	Also borne on rolls as "Freer;" mustered out Nov. 4, 1864, at Columbia, Tenn., on expiration of term of service.
Gentle, Thomas W......	... do ...	24	Aug. 26, 1862	3 yrs.	Mustered out June 17, 1865, at Nashville, Tenn., by order of War Department.
Gould, Peter H........	... do ...	41	Aug. 26, 1862	3 yrs.	Mustered out June 17, 1865, at Nashville, Tenn., by order of War Department.
Granger, John H.......	... do ...	34	Jan. 1, 1864	3 yrs.	Mustered out with company Aug. 4, 1865.
Green, James B.........	... do ...	18	Feb. 26, 1864	3 yrs.	Promoted to Hospital Steward Nov. 1, 1864.
Grimes, John	... do ...	18	Dec. 14, 1863	3 yrs.	Mustered out with company Aug. 4, 1865.
Hahn, Austin B........	... do ...	18	Mch. 12, 1864	3 yrs.	Mustered out with company Aug. 4, 1865.
Hahn, John	... do ...	19	Mch. 1, 1865	1 yr.	Also borne on rolls as "Houghn;" mustered out with company Aug. 4, 1865.
Hanley, James W......	... do ...	27	Nov. 14, 1861	3 yrs.	Mustered out Dec. 30, 1864, at Nashville, Tenn., on expiration of term of service.
Hanley, John	... do ...	18	Sept. 3, 1861	3 yrs.	Captured Dec. 29, 1862, in action at Murfreesboro, Tenn.; paroled ——; discharged April 21, 1863, to date July 2, 1862, on Surgeon's certificate of disability.
Hart, Franklin	... do ...	19	Sept. 4, 1861	3 yrs.	Transferred from Co. A Jan. 4, 1864; mustered out with company Aug. 4, 1865; veteran.
Haskins, Isaah P.......	... do ...	21	Sept. 10, 1861	3 yrs.	Discharged Sept. 11, 1862, at Columbus, O., on Surgeon's certificate of disability.
Hayne, Charles	... do ...	18	Sept. 3, 1861	3 yrs.	Detached as Orderly in 1862 with General Garfield; supposed to be dead; no further record found.
Heath, Amasa	... do ...	22	Sept. 8, 1861	3 yrs.	Discharged Oct. 29, 1862, on Surgeon's certificate of disability.

Names	Rank	Age	Date of Entering the Service	Period of Service	Remarks
Heath, John L.........	... do ...	18	Feb. 29, 1864	3 yrs.	Mustered out with company Aug. 4, 1865.
Henderson, Frank M..	Private	23	Dec. 5, 1863	3 yrs.	
Hess, William	... do ...	26	Jan. 27, 1864	3 yrs.	Prisoner of war since Sept. 5, 1864; paroled Feb. 26, 1865, at N. E. Ferry, N. C.; no further record found.
Houghton, Alexander..	... do ...	29	Sept. 6, 1861	3 yrs.	Mustered out June 17, 1865, at Nashville, Tenn., by order of War Department.
Houghton, Ncholas	... do ...	18	Sept. 3, 1861	3 yrs.	
Humphries, Parker	... do ...	30	Dec. 8, 1863	3 yrs.	Mustered out with company Aug. 4, 1865.
Kedwell, George	... do ...	18	Sept. 6, 1861	3 yrs.	Died March 24, 1862.
Keefer, Charles H......	... do ...	40	Feb. 13, 1864	3 yrs.	Died March 3, 1865, at Gravelly Springs, Ala.
Keefer, Dean	... do ...	19	Jan. 5, 1864	3 yrs.	Mustered out with company Aug. 4, 1865.
King, Hayburn	... do ...	21	Sept. 3, 1861	3 yrs.	Mustered out with company Aug. 4, 1865; veteran.
King, Henry C........	... do ...	34	Dec. 8, 1863	3 yrs.	Mustered out with company Aug. 4, 1865.
LaDuke, Lewis	... do ...	21	Sept. 10, 1862	3 yrs.	Mustered out to date Aug. 4, 1865, by order of War Department.
LeClear, Daniel	... do ...	....	Sept. 9, 1861	3 yrs.	
Lee, Charles L........	... do ...	21	Sept. 6, 1861	3 yrs.	Discharged Feb. 26, 1863, at Murfreesboro, Tenn., o Surgeon's certificate of disability.
Lee, Frederick S.......	... do ...	30	Feb. 24, 1864	3 yrs.	Mustered out May 22, 1865, at Louisville, Ky., by order of War Department.
Lee, James M.........	... do ...	20	Dec. 10, 1861	3 yrs.	Mustered out Dec. 30, 1864, at Nashville, Tenn., on expiration of term of service.
Lloyd, Lyman G.......	... do ...	22	Sept. 9, 1861	3 yrs.	Mustered out Nov. 25, 1864, at Louisville, Ky., on expiration of term of service.
Long, Alfred H........	... do ...	22	Feb. 23, 1864	3 yrs.	Killed Aug. 20, 1864, in battle of Lovejoy Station, Ga.
Long, John W.........	... do ...	44	Feb. 28, 1865	1 yr.	Mustered out with company Aug. 4, 1865.
Lynn, Melvin S........	... do ...	42	Sept. 3, 1861	3 yrs.	Mustered out Nov. 4, 1864, at Columbia, Tenn., on expiration of term of service.
McCoy, Thomas	... do ...	20	Aug. 19, 1861	3 yrs.	Discharged Aug. 19, 1862, on Surgeon's certificate of disability.
McDannel, Albert	... do ...	19	Dec. 28, 1863	3 yrs.	Died March 23, 1864.
Mann, James H........	... do ...	....	Oct. 22, 1861	3 yrs.	Discharged Feb. 24, 1863, on Surgeon's certificate of disability.
Meddaugh, Randolph...	... do ...	19	Sept. 4, 1861	3 yrs.	Mustered out Nov. 4, 1864, at Columbia, Tenn., on expiration of term of service.
Mitchell, Adelbert	... do ...	18	Feb. 23, 1864	3 yrs.	Mustered out with company Aug. 4, 1865.
Morrison, William	... do ...	20	Sept. 11, 1861	3 yrs.	Died Oct. 19, 1862.
Myers, John	... do ...	22	Sept. 8, 1861	3 yrs.	Mustered out Nov. 4, 1864, at Columbia, Tenn., on expiration of term of service.
Noble, Albert D........	... do ...	19	Sept. 6, 1861	3 yrs.	Shot Aug. 5, 1862, by guerrillas.
O'Brien, Thomas	... do ...	26	Jan. 17, 1864	3 yrs.	Discharged April 18, 1865, at Madison, Ind., on account of wounds received Aug. 20, 1864, in battle of Lovejoy Station, Ga.
Peacock, John	... do ...	18	Nov. 14, 1861	3 yrs.	Died May 30, 1862.
Pierce, Andrew J.......	... do ...	28	Sept. 5, 1861	3 yrs.	Discharged July 22, 1862, on Surgeon's certificate of disability.
Porter, Ira W.........	... do ...	21	Feb. 29, 1864	3 yrs.	Mustered out with company Aug. 4, 1865.
Prosser, Edwin S.......	... do ...	18	Sept. 3, 1861	3 yrs.	Discharged Sept. 8, 1862, on Surgeon's certificate of disability.
Ransom, George	... do ...	18	Dec. 29, 1863	3 yrs.	Discharged June 2, 1865, on Surgeon's certificate of disability.
Redwood, Robert S.....	... do ...	19	Dec. 2, 1862	3 yrs.	Discharged March 11, 1863, on Surgeon's certificate of disability.
Riggs, Samuel	... do ...	28	Sept. 9, 1861	3 yrs.	Discharged Nov. 15, 1862, on Surgeon's certificate of disability.
Roberts, James J.......	... do ...	19	Aug. 26, 1862	3 yrs.	Mustered out June 17, 1865, at Nashville, Tenn., by order of War Department.
Roberts, Hiram M......	... do ...	21	Aug. 26, 1862	3 yrs.	Mustered out June 17, 1865, at Nashville, Tenn., by order of War Department.
Roberts, William H....	... do ...	20	Aug. 26, 1862	3 yrs.	Discharged June 12, 1865, on Surgeon's certificate of disability.
Robinson, John	... do ...	24	Aug. 26, 1862	3 yrs.	Mustered out with company Aug. 4, 1865.
Rounds, Lewis A.......	... do ...	18	Oct. 27, 1861	3 yrs.	Returned to Co. D, 8th Regiment, O. V. I., where he had previously enlisted.
Rowe, Martin	... do ...	20	Sept. 9, 1861	3 yrs.	
Sanford, Victor	... do ...	36	Oct. 31, 1862	3 yrs.	Mustered out with company Aug. 4, 1865.
Setchel, William	... do ...	35	Sept. 6, 1861	3 yrs.	Discharged Aug. 14, 1862, on Surgeon's certificate of disability.
Seymour, Martin E....	... do ...	19	Dec. 28, 1863	3 yrs.	Transferred to Co. I, 17th Regiment, Veteran Reserve Corps, Jan. 16, 1865; mustered out from same Aug. 15, 1865, at Indianapolis, Ind., by order of War Department.
Sheldon, Richard	... do ...	19	Sept. 12, 1861	3 yrs.	Discharged July 29, 1862, on Surgeon's certificate of disability.
Sheldon, William	... do ...	23	Sept. 12, 1861	3 yrs.	Mustered out June 7, 1865, at Columbus, O., on expiration of term of service.
Shepard, Joseph B.....	... do ...	20	Sept. 5, 1861	3 yrs.	Mustered out Nov. 4, 1864, at Columbia, Tenn., on expiration of term of service.
Sherwood, George F...	... do ...	22	Sept. 12, 1861	3 yrs.	Discharged Oct. 22, 1862, on Surgeon's certificate of disability.
Shirley, Job	... do ...	20	Feb. 29, 1864	3 yrs.	Mustered out with company Aug. 4, 1865.

Names	Rank	Age	Date of Entering the Service	Period of Service	Remarks
Shreck, Luis	... do ...	22	Sept. 9, 1861	3 yrs.	Discharged March 13, 1863, on Surgeon's certificate of disability.
Smith, Henry	Private	18	Sept. 6, 1861	3 yrs.	No further record found.
Spencer, George B.	... do ...	18	Sept. 10, 1861	3 yrs.	Also borne on rolls as "Byron Spencer;" mustered out Nov. 4, 1864, at Columbia, Tenn., on expiration of term of service.
Sutton, Andrew J.	... do ...	24	Oct. 5, 1861	3 yrs.	Mustered out Nov. 4, 1864, at Columbia, Tenn., on expiration of term of service.
Sykes, Royal	... do ...	19	Sept. 6, 1861	3 yrs.	Died April 17, 1862.
Tappin, William	... do ...	19	Sept. 3, 1861	3 yrs.	Transferred to Co. L Jan. 1, 1862.
Taylor, Charles	... do ...	18	Dec. 14, 1863	3 yrs.	Died Aug. 28, 1864, at Columbia, Tenn.
Taylor, George	... do ...	18	Jan. 1, 1864	3 yrs.	Mustered out with company Aug. 4, 1865.
Taylor, John B.	... do ...	20	Sept. 5, 1861	3 yrs.	Transferred to Co. B, 8th Regiment, Veteran Reserve Corps, Aug. 31, 1863; mustered out from same Sept. 5, 1864, on expiration of term of service.
Thompson, Fredk. W.	... do ...	43	Sept. 11, 1861	3 yrs.	Discharged Aug. 4, 1862, on Surgeon's certificate of disability.
Tiaxler, Charles	... do ...	20	Sept. 7, 1861	3 yrs.	Transferred from Co. E ——; died Sept. 20, 1862.
Towers, Leo P.	... do ...	44	Dec. 8, 1863	3 yrs.	Died Jan. 4, 1865, in hospital at Louisville, Ky.
Town, William O.	... do ...	18	Jan. 4, 1864	3 yrs.	Mustered out with company Aug. 4, 1865.
Tulian, Joseph	... do ...	33	Feb. 29, 1864	3 yrs.	Mustered out June 5, 1865, at Columbus, O., by order of War Department.
Vanscoy, George	... do ...	18	Mch. 12, 1864	3 yrs.	Mustered out with company Aug. 4, 1865.
Vanscoy, William	... do ...	21	Sept. 3, 1861	3 yrs.	Mustered out Nov. 4, 1864, at Columbia, Tenn., on expiration of term of service.
Vincent, Almond	... do ...	18	Oct. 2, 1861	3 yrs.	Discharged Nov. 28, 1861, by order of War Department.
Watson, James	... do ...	21	Sept. 9, 1861	3 yrs.	Missing in action Aug. 20, 1864; no further record found; veteran.
Weston, George	... do ...	27	Oct. 20, 1863	3 yrs.	Mustered out with company Aug. 4, 1865.
Wininger, Solomon	... do ...	60	Aug. 26, 1862	3 yrs.	Transferred to Co. I, 17th Regiment, Veteran Reserve Corps, Jan. 15, 1865; discharged from same June 24, 1865, at Indianapolis, Ind., on Surgeon's certificate of disability.
Barnes, Robert	Cook	24	June 20, 1865	3 yrs.	Colored under-cook; mustered out with company Aug. 4, 1865.
Caan, Franklin	... do ...	26	June 20, 1865	3 yrs.	Colored under-cook; mustered out with company Aug. 4, 1865.
Perkins, George	... do ...	18	April 7, 1865	3 yrs.	Colored under-cook; mustered out with company Aug. 4, 1865.
Watts, Richard	... do ...	25	April 7, 1865	3 yrs.	Colored under-cook; mustered out with company Aug. 4, 1865.
Walker, Isaac	... do ...	39	Mch. 4, 1863	3 yrs.	Colored under-cook.

COMPANY G.

Mustered in December 11, 1861, at Camp Worcester, O., by James P. W. Neill, 1st Lieutenant 18th Infantry, U. S. A., Mustering Officer. Mustered out August 4, 1865, at Edgefield, Tenn., by James P. W. Neill, Captain 18th Infantry, U. S. A., Acting Commissary of Musters, Cavalry Corps, M. D. T.

Names	Rank	Age	Date	Period	Remarks
Leonard Adams	Captain	28	Aug. 13, 1861	3 yrs.	Appointed Sept. 13, 1861; captured Oct. 17, 1862, at battle of Lexington, Ky.; paroled ——; promoted to Major June 7, 1863.
Martin Archer	... do ...	30	Aug. 20, 1861	3 yrs.	Promoted from 1st Lieutenant Co. H June 7, 1863; to Major Nov. 30, 1864.
Adolph M. Heflebower	1st Lieu.	19	Aug. 20, 1861	3 yrs.	Appointed Sept. 13, 1861; honorably discharged March 20, 1863.
Henry M. Miller	... do ...	23	Sept. 7, 1861	3 yrs.	Promoted from Sergt. Major March 21, 1863; resigned Nov. 20, 1864.
Philander B. Lewis	... do ...	28	Dec. 28, 1861	3 yrs.	Promoted from 2d Lieutenant Co. F Nov. 30, 1864; to Captain Co. F Jan. 6, 1865.
Thomas C. Baker	... do ...	19	Aug. 24, 1861	3 yrs.	Appointed Corporal Oct. 14, 1861; 1st Sergeant Aug. 11, 1864; promoted to 2d Lieutenant Co. A Nov. 30, 1864; to 1st Lieutenant from 2d Lieutenant Co. A Jan. 6, 1865; commanded company from that date until mustered out; mustered out with company Aug. 4, 1865; veteran.
Edwin R. Toll	2d Lieu.	25	Aug. 20, 1861	3 yrs.	Appointed Sept. 13, 1861; promoted to 1st Lieutenant Jan. 21, 1863, but not mustered; honorably discharged March 21, 1863.
Frank J. Wilham	... do ...	25	Oct. 6, 1861	3 yrs.	Promoted from Regt. Q. M. Sergeant Jan. 21, 1863; transferred to Co. A April 24, 1863.

Names	Rank	Age	Date of Entering the Service	Period of Service	Remarks
David E. Golden.......	2d Lieu.	31	Aug. 29, 1861	3 yrs.	Appointed Q. M. Sergeant Oct. 14, 1861; promoted to 2d Lieutenant March 5, 1863; resigned May 16, 1864.
Alfred F. Washburn...	... do ...	20	Sept. 3, 1861	3 yrs.	Promoted from Sergt. Co. F Nov. 30, 1864; veteran.
Calvin S. Kimball.......	... do ...	26	Sept. 10, 1861	3 yrs.	Promoted from Sergt. Major March 31, 1864; prisoner of war; escaped Feb. 21, 1865, near Wilmington, N. C.; promoted to 1st Lieutenant Nov. 30, 1864, but not mustered; to Captain Feb. 23, 1865, but not mustered; mustered out with company Aug. 4, 1865; veteran.
John M. Keller.........	1st Serg.	33	Sept. 7, 1861	3 yrs.	Appointed Sergeant Oct. 14, 1861; 1st Sergeant ——; promoted to 2d Lieutenant Co. C July 13, 1864; veteran.
John J. Anderson.......	... do ...	25	Aug. 29, 1861	3 yrs.	Appointed Sergeant Oct. 14, 1861; 1st Sergeant Dec. 2, 1864; promoted to 2d Lieutenant April 8, 1865, but not mustered; mustered out with company Aug. 4, 1865; veteran.
William Lightcap	Q. M. S.	51	Aug. 20, 1861	3 yrs.	Mustered as private; appointed ——; captured Oct. 17, 1862, at battle of Lexington, Ky.; paroled ——; mustered out Oct. 3, 1864, at Columbia, Tenn., on expiration of term of service.
Miles H. Rice............	... do ...	21	Sept. 8, 1861	3 yrs.	Mustered as private; appointed Jan. 1, 1865; mustered out with company Aug. 4, 1865; veteran.
John J. Miller..........	Com Ser.	20	Sept. 8, 1861	3 yrs.	Appointed Corporal Oct. 14, 1861; Sergeant ——; captured Oct. 17, 1862, at battle of Lexington, Ky.; paroled ——; appointed Com. Sergeant ——; mustered out Oct. 3, 1864, at Columbia, Tenn., on expiration of term of service.
John A. Whitmire......	... do ...	22	Sept. 3, 1861	3 yrs.	Mustered as private; appointed Dec. 2, 1864; wounded March 22, 1865, near Cherokee Station, Ga.; mustered out July 19, 1865, from hospital at Camp Dennison, O., by order of War Department; veteran.
William M. Patrick....	Sergeant	21	Aug. 29, 1861	3 yrs.	Appointed Oct. 14, 1861; killed Aug. 3, 1862, by guerrillas.
Robert R. Wilkinson...	... do ...	26	Aug. 28, 1861	3 yrs.	Appointed Oct. 14, 1861; discharged Jan. 29, 1863, on Surgeon's certificate of disability.
David W. Fisher.........	... do ...	24	Aug. 22, 1861	3 yrs.	Appointed Oct. 14, 1861; discharged Sept. 11, 1862, on Surgeon's certificate of disability.
Nelson Smith	... do ...	36	Sept. 2, 1861	3 yrs.	Appointed Corporal Oct. 14, 1861; captured Oct. 17, 1862, at battle of Lexington, Ky.; paroled ——; appointed Sergeant ——; mustered out with company Aug. 4, 1865; veteran.
Alexander M. Cowgill..	... do ...	26	Sept. 2, 1861	3 yrs.	Appointed Corporal Oct. 14, 1861; Sergeant ——; mustered out with company Aug. 4, 1865; veteran.
Josiah H. Feagles.......	... do ...	24	Aug. 24, 1861	3 yrs.	Appointed Corporal Oct. 14, 1861; Sergeant ——; mustered out Oct. 3, 1864, at Columbia, Tenn., on expiration of term of service.
Henry F. Stross.........	... do ...	30	Sept. 8, 1861	3 yrs.	Appointed Corporal ——; Sergeant ——; mustered out with company Aug. 4, 1865; veteran.
Soloman F. Gambee.....	... do ...	20	Sept. 9, 1861	3 yrs.	Captured Oct. 17, 1862, at battle of Lexington, Ky.; paroled ——; appointed Corporal ——; Sergeant Jan. 1, 1865; mustered out with company Aug. 4, 1865; veteran.
John M. Bearse.........	... do ...	23	Sept. 3, 1862	3 yrs.	Mustered as private; appointed ——; mustered out June 15, 1865, at Nashville, Tenn., by order of War Department.
John C. Clayman.......	... do ...	24	Sept. 10, 1861	3 yrs.	Appointed Corporal ——; Sergeant Jan. 15, 1865; mustered out with company Aug. 4, 1865; veteran.
John C. Grafton......	Corporal	22	Sept. 10, 1861	3 yrs.	Appointed Oct. 14, 1861; promoted to Batt. Hospital Steward Dec. 1, 1861.
Ansel Elemes	... do ...	35	Sept. 12, 1861	3 yrs.	Appointed Oct. 14, 1861; discharged Nov. 10, 1862, at Columbus, O., on Surgeon's certificate of disability.
John Cary	... do ...	22	Aug. 26, 1861	3 yrs.	Appointed ——; mustered out with company Aug. 4, 1865; veteran.
Henry E. Mandal.......	... do ...	22	Dec. 24, 1863	3 yrs.	Appointed ——; mustered out with company Aug. 4, 1865.
Samuel Aldstadt	... do ...	25	Dec. 24, 1863	3 yrs.	Appointed ——; mustered out with company Aug. 4, 1865.
William R. Dunlap....	... do ...	21	Sept. 10, 1861	3 yrs.	Captured Oct. 17, 1862, at battle of Lexington, Ky.; paroled ——; appointed ——; mustered out Oct. 3, 1864, at Columbia, Tenn., on expiration of term of service.
James J. Wolf.........	... do ...	22	Sept. 7, 1861	3 yrs.	Appointed ——; discharged March 5, 1865, on Surgeon's certificate of disability; veteran.

Names	Rank	Age	Date of Entering the Service	Period of Service	Remarks
Conrad J. Hoote......	Corporal	33	Dec. 18, 1861	3 yrs.	Captured Oct. 17, 1862, at battle of Lexington, Ky.; paroled ——; appointed ——; mustered out April 13, 1865, at Columbus, O., on expiration of term of service.
George Sweet	...do ...	18	Jan. 2, 1864	3 yrs.	Appointed ——; mustered out June 16, 1865, at Louisville, Ky., by order of War Department.
James G. Watson........	...do ...	31	Aug. 22, 1862	3 yrs.	Appointed ——; died Aug. 20, 1864, at Buckhead, Ga.
Ephraim York	...do ...	24	Sept. 12, 1861	3 yrs.	Captured Oct. 17, 1862, at battle of Lexington, Ky.; paroled ——; appointed June 1, 1865; mustered out with company Aug. 4, 1865; veteran.
George Porter	...do ...	21	Dec. 16, 1863	3 yrs.	Appointed June 1, 1865; mustered out with company Aug. 4, 1865.
Alexander Musgrave ...	...do ...	18	Mch. 12, 1864	3 yrs.	Appointed June 1, 1865; mustered out with company Aug. 4, 1865.
James Hyde	...do ...	19	Jan. 5, 1864	3 yrs.	Appointed June 1, 1865; mustered out with company Aug. 4, 1865.
Daniel Mogle	...do ...	18	Jan. 4, 1864	3 yrs.	Appointed June 1, 1865; mustered out with company Aug. 4, 1865.
George W. Bigler......	Bugler	35	Sept. 7, 1861	3 yrs.	Also borne on rolls as "Zeigler;" appointed Oct. 14, 1861; discharged Oct. 21, 1862, on Surgeon's certificate of disability.
William Harvey	...do ...	29	Sept. 12, 1861	3 yrs.	Appointed ——; mustered out with company Aug. 4, 1865; veteran.
James T. Leckliter....	Farrier	23	Sept. 12, 1861	3 yrs.	Appointed Oct. 14, 1861; discharged March 13, 1863, on Surgeon's certificate of disability.
Wesley Cranker	...do ...	18	Jan. 1, 1864	3 yrs.	Appointed ——; mustered out with company Aug. 4, 1865.
Uriah Sohn	Wagoner	40	Oct. 21, 1861	3 yrs.	Returned to Co. D, 58th Regiment, O. V. I., where he had previously enlisted, Feb. 7, 1862.
James M. Burg........	Saddler	24	Sept. 2, 1861	3 yrs.	Promoted to Batt. Saddler Sergeant Dec. 1, 1861.
James D. Coleman........	...do ...	32	Sept. 7, 1861	3 yrs.	Appointed ——; mustered out with company Aug. 4, 1865; veteran.
Bearse, William S......	Private	18	Mch. 26, 1864	3 yrs.	Mustered out with company Aug. 4, 1865.
Blue, Samuel	...do ...	36	Sept. 3, 1861	3 yrs.	Discharged July 22, 1862, on Surgeon's certificate of disability.
Boehler, Elias	...do ...	27	Sept. 12, 1861	3 yrs.	Captured Oct. 17, 1862, at battle of Lexington, Ky.; paroled ——; mustered out Oct. 3, 1864, at Columbia, Tenn., on expiration of term of service.
Britton, Milford	...do ...	17	Dec. 1, 1863	3 yrs.	Mustered out with company Aug. 4, 1865.
Briner, Amos	...do ...	30	Aug. 20, 1861	3 yrs.	Transferred from Co. H Dec. 1, 1861; discharged Oct. 1, 1862, on Surgeon's certificate of disability.
Broka, Henry C........	...do ...	21	Feb. 23, 1864	3 yrs.	Mustered out with company Aug. 4, 1865.
Brouse, Henry C........	...do ...	19	Sept. 12, 1861	3 yrs.	
Brown, John A........	...do ...	22	Jan. 4, 1864	3 yrs.	Also borne on rolls as "Joseph A. Brown;" mustered out with company Aug. 4, 1865.
Buffington, Jacob	...do ...	30	Dec. 30, 1863	3 yrs.	Died July 20, 1865, at Louisville, Ky.
Burkhart, William	...do ...	19	Sept. 12, 1861	3 yrs.	Discharged by civil authority.
Caldwell, Andrew J....	...do ...	20	Sept. 12, 1861	3 yrs.	Died Sept. 21, 1864, in Andersonville Prison, Georgia.
Cleveland, Alburtus B.	...do ...	22	Aug. 24, 1861	3 yrs.	Mustered out with company Aug. 4, 1865; veteran.
Coger, Samuel	...do ...	24	Jan. 4, 1864	3 yrs.	Mustered out with company Aug. 4, 1865.
Collins, David	...do ...	23	Aug. 26, 1861	3 yrs.	Transferred to 68th Co., 2d Battalion, Veteran Reserve Corps, Jan. 20, 1864; discharged from same by civil authority.
Cooper, Harmon	...do ...	18	Jan. 4, 1864	3 yrs.	Mustered out with company Aug. 4, 1865.
Cowgill, William	...do ...	23	Sept. 2, 1861	3 yrs.	Captured Oct. 17, 1862, at battle of Lexington, Ky.; paroled ——; mustered out Oct. 3, 1864, at Columbia, Tenn., on expiration of term of service.
Cramer, Joseph	...do ...	39	Sept. 12, 1861	3 yrs.	Died July 2, 1862.
Creglow, Francis M....	...do ...	19	Aug. 24, 1861	3 yrs.	Died June 13, 1862.
Crowe, George F........	...do ...	18	Dec. 20, 1861	3 yrs.	Mustered out Dec. 30, 1864, at Nashville, Tenn., on expiration of term of service.
Davis, Smith	...do ...	26	Aug. 27, 1861	3 yrs.	Prisoner of war; mustered out Oct. 3, 1864, at Columbia, Tenn., on expiration of term of service.
Dellet, James	...do	16	Dec. 4, 1863	3 yrs.	Mustered out with company Aug. 4, 1865.
Diller, Abram	...do ...	21	Sept. 12, 1861	3 yrs.	Captured Oct. 17, 1862, at battle of Lexington, Ky.; paroled ——; discharged May 19, 1863, on Surgeon's certificate of disability.
Doing, David	...do ...	40	Sept. 12, 1861	3 yrs.	Discharged Sept. 20, 1861.
Drain, Jacob	...do ...	18	Jan. 2, 1864	3 yrs.	Mustered out with company Aug. 4, 1865.
Dresander, John C	...do ...	28	Aug. 27, 1861	3 yrs.	Discharged Oct. 6, 1862, on Surgeon's certificate of disability.
Drumhiller, Aaron	...do ...	20	Dec. 4, 1863	3 yrs.	Mustered out with company Aug. 4, 1865.
Duval, Perry	...do ...	21	Nov. 1, 1862	3 yrs.	Mustered out with company Aug. 4, 1865.

Names	Rank	Age	Date of Entering the Service	Period of Service	Remarks
Eichelberry, Miles	Private	18	Sept. 12, 1861	3 yrs.	Captured Oct. 17, 1862, at battle of Lexington, Ky.; paroled ——; mustered out with company Aug. 4, 1865; veteran.
Evans, Walter	... do ...	36	Nov. 20, 1861	3 yrs.	
Eyerly, Joseph	... do ...	18	Dec. 30, 1863	3 yrs.	Mustered out with company Aug. 4, 1865.
Fagar, Nicholas	... do ...	29	Sept. 3, 1861	3 yrs.	Killed Aug. 3, 1862, by guerrillas.
Falkner, John	... do ...	33	Aug. 27, 1861	3 yrs.	Died Oct. 16, 1861.
Finley, William	... do ...	26	Dec. 21, 1863	3 yrs.	Mustered out with company Aug. 4, 1865.
Fisher, Alexander	... do ...	35	Sept. 6, 1861	3 yrs.	Discharged March 10, 1863, on Surgeon's certificate of disability.
Freeman, Charles	... do ...	18	Dec. 28, 1863	3 yrs.	Mustered out with company Aug. 4, 1865.
Freze, Elias	... do ...	25	Aug. 1, 1862	3 yrs.	Discharged Feb. 16, 1863, on Surgeon's certificate of disability.
Gibson, Lewis S........	... do ...	20	Aug. 24, 1861	3 yrs.	Discharged Nov. 10, 1862, on Surgeon's certificate of disability.
Gifford, Homer W......	... do ..	30	Jan. 5, 1864	2 yrs.	Mustered out Aug. 8, 1865, from hospital Cincinnati, O., by order of War Department
Gifford, Jerome	... do ...	20	Mch. 23, 1864	3 yrs.	Mustered out with company Aug. 4, 1865.
Gregg, John F...........	... do ...	27	Feb. 27, 1864	3 yrs.	Mustered out June 2, 1865, from hospital at Camp Dennison, O., by order of War Department.
Grove, Elias	... do ...	18	Aug. 25, 1863	3 yrs.	Died Jan. 1, 1865, in hospital at Knoxville, Tenn.
Hamilton, Charles	... do ...	18	Dec. 30, 1863	3 yrs.	Died Jan. 1, 1865, at home in Benton township, Ottawa county, O.
Horobin, Thomas H. .	... do ...	44	Sept. 3, 1861	3 yrs.	Captured Oct. 17, 1862, at battle of Lexington, Ky.; paroled ——; mustered out Dec. 30, 1864, at Nashville, Tenn., on expiration of term of service.
House, Augustus	... do ...	16	Dec. 30, 1863	3 yrs.	Mustered out with company Aug. 4, 1865.
Hospleham, George	... do ...	19	Aug. 29, 1861	3 yrs.	Discharged July 22, 1865, on Surgeon's certificate of disability; veteran.
Howard, George F.......	... do ...	35	Sept. 12, 1861	3 yrs.	Transferred to Navy ——; veteran.
Hummel, Quintus	... do ...	18	Sept. 10, 1861	3 yrs.	Mustered out Aug. 21, 1865, at Louisville, Ky., by order of War Department; veteran.
Huston, Thomas	... do ...	44	Dec. 7, 1863	3 yrs.	Appointed Corporal ——; reduced May 30, 1865; mustered out with company Aug. 4, 1865.
Jones, George	... do ...	27	Dec. 23, 1863	3 yrs.	Mustered out with company Aug. 4, 1865.
Jones, John	... do ...	20	Jan. 1, 1863	3 yrs.	Mustered out with company Aug. 4, 1865.
Krauss, John	... do ...	54	Sept. 12, 1861	3 yrs.	Captured Oct. 17, 1862, at battle of Lexington, Ky.; paroled ——; discharged March 13, 1863, on Surgeon's certificate of disability.
La Point, Alexander..	... do ...	27	Nov. 4, 1862	3 yrs.	Died Jan. 3, 1863.
Lawrence, James L....	... do ...	19	Aug. 24, 1861	3 yrs.	Discharged June 4, 1863, on Surgeon's certificate of disability.
Lay, Nicholas	... do ...	18	Sept. 12, 1861	3 yrs.	Captured Oct. 17, 1862, at battle of Lexington, Ky.; paroled ——.
Logan, Isaac	... do ...	18	Dec. 23, 1863	3 yrs.	Mustered out with company Aug. 4, 1865.
McCollister, James	... do ...	21	Aug. 28, 1861	3 yrs.	Mustered out with company Aug. 4, 1865; veteran.
McDargh, Charles J.....	... do ...	18	Aug. 13, 1861	3 yrs.	Mustered out Oct. 3, 1864, at Columbia, Tenn., on expiration of term of service.
McDermott, John	... do ...	22	Sept. 8, 1861	3 yrs.	Mustered as private; appointed Sergeant ——; reduced Jan. 1, 1865; mustered out with company Aug. 4, 1865; veteran.
McKibben, James F.....	... do ...	18	Dec. 9, 1861	3 yrs.	Discharged Dec. 15, 1861.
McKinley, Michael R..	... do ...	21	Sept. 9, 1861	3 yrs.	Captured Oct. 17, 1862, at battle of Lexington, Ky.; paroled ——; discharged Nov. 20, 1862, on Surgeon's certificate of disability.
Marble, Martin	... do ...	18	Sept. 2, 1861	3 yrs.	Discharged Nov. 19, 1862, on Surgeon's certificate of disability.
Martin, Robert	... do ...	21	Mch. 3, 1864	3 yrs.	Mustered out with company Aug. 4, 1865.
Mater, Cyrus	... do ...	18	Dec. 21, 1863	3 yrs.	Mustered out with company Aug. 4, 1865.
Mauk, George D........	... do ...	18	Jan. 15, 1864	3 yrs.	Mustered out with company Aug. 4, 1865.
Miller, Gottlieb	... do ...	27	Aug. 30, 1861	3 yrs.	Mustered out Oct. 3, 1864, at Columbia, Tenn., on expiration of term of service.
Miller, Lewis	... do ...	21	Nov. 10, 1862	3 yrs.	Died March 7, 1864.
Miller, John L.........	... do ...	19	Mch. 14, 1864	3 yrs.	Mustered out June 2, 1865, from hospital at Camp Dennison, O., by order of War Department.
Moser, Abram	... do ...	27	Nov. 10, 1861	3 yrs.	Mustered out with company Aug. 4, 1865; veteran.
Mowery, Jacob B.......	... do ...	23	Feb. 4, 1864	3 yrs.	Mustered out with company Aug. 4, 1865.
Myers, Isaiah M.......	... do ...	31	Sept. 10, 1861	3 yrs.	Transferred to Co. I, 12th Regiment, Veteran Reserve Corps, May 20, 1864; mustered out from same Dec. 12, 1864, on expiration of term of service.
Nitchman, DeMarcus L	... do ...	22	Sept. 12, 1861	3 yrs.	Captured Oct. 17, 1862, at battle of Lexington, Ky.; paroled ——; mustered out Oct. 3, 1864, at Columbia, Tenn., on expiration of term of service.
Northcutt, Joseph P..	... do ...	20	Sept. 9, 1861	3 yrs.	Discharged Feb. 20, 1863, on Surgeon's certificate of disability.

Names	Rank	Age	Date of Entering the Service	Period of Service	Remarks
Palmer, Lewis	Private	18	Sept. 7, 1861	3 yrs.	Discharged Jan. 10, 1863, on Surgeon's certificate of disability.
Parkhurst, Abner	... do ...	29	Feb. 1, 1864	3 yrs.	Mustered out with company Aug. 4, 1865.
Post, William	... do ...	21	Nov. 13, 1861	3 yrs.	Captured Oct. 17, 1862, at battle of Lexington, Ky.; paroled ——; discharged April 4, 1863, on Surgeon's certificate of disability.
Randal, Felise	... do ...	26	Dec. 16, 1863	3 yrs.	Mustered out with company Aug. 4, 1865.
Ray, Henry T............	... do ...	21	Sept. 12, 1861	3 yrs.	Captured Oct. 17, 1862, at battle of Lexington, Ky.; paroled ——; transferred to 5th U. S. Cavalry Feb. 3, 1863.
Reed, Reuben	... do ...	22	Dec. 4, 1861	3 yrs.	
St. John, Philo	... do ...	21	Oct. 27, 1861	3 yrs.	Died Oct. 21, 1862, of wounds received in action.
Sanders, George W.....	... do ...	29	Sept. 9, 1861	3 yrs.	Discharged Feb. 18, 1863, on Surgeon's certificate of disability.
Sanders, Jacob	... do ...	19	Feb. 19, 1864	3 yrs.	Mustered out with company Aug. 4, 1865.
Sanford, Benjamin F....	... do ...	21	Sept. 8, 1861	3 yrs.	Discharged March 22, 1862, at Columbus, O., on expiration of term of service.
Schimansky, Otto	... do ...	18	Dec. 2, 1863	3 yrs.	Mustered out with company Aug. 4, 1865.
Scott, John	... do ...	18	Sept. 9, 1861	3 yrs.	Died June 3, 1863, at Murfreesboro, Tenn.
Shephard, John B......	... do ...	22	Nov. 9, 1861	3 yrs.	Died June 5, 1862.
Slaven, Christopher C....	... do ...	20	Sept. 8, 1861	3 yrs.	Captured Oct. 17, 1862, at battle of Lexington, Ky.; paroled ——; killed Aug. 20, 1864, in battle of Jonesboro, Ga.; veteran.
Smith, Frank J..........	... do ...	19	Nov. 14, 1861	3 yrs.	Mustered out Nov. 26, 1864, at Louisville, Ky., on Surgeon's certificate of disability.
Smith, Joseph	... do ...	22	Sept. 6, 1861	3 yrs.	Transferred to Co. D, 2d Regiment, Veteran Reserve Corps, Aug. 19, 1863; mustered out from same Feb. 21, 1865, at Detroit, Mich., on expiration of term of service.
Solenberger, John	... do ...	20	Dec. 29, 1863	3 yrs.	Mustered out with company Aug. 4, 1865.
Steckel, Henry L........	... do ...	25	Oct. 22, 1861	3 yrs.	Mustered out Nov. 5, 1864, on expiration of term of service.
Steckel, Louis P........	... do ...	22	Nov. 14, 1861	3 yrs.	Died July 6, 1865, at Annapolis, Md.
Sullivan, John	... do ...	23	Nov. 11, 1862	3 yrs.	Killed July 20, 1864, in action at Loganville, Georgia.
Tanner, James E........	... do ...	37	Feb. 23, 1864	3 yrs.	Mustered out with company Aug. 4, 1865.
Taylor, John	... do ...	26	Aug. 27, 1861	3 yrs.	Discharged Sept. 20, 1861.
Townsend, James H.....	... do ...	23	Jan. 13, 1864	3 yrs.	Absent, sick, since Jan. 12, 1865; no further record found.
Tryan, Henry	... do ...	18	Dec. 2, 1863	3 yrs.	Mustered out with company Aug. 4, 1865.
Turner, Philoman	... do ...	18	Jan. 1, 1864	3 yrs.	Mustered out with company Aug. 4, 1865.
Vanetton, Aaron	... do ...	20	Jan. 15, 1864	3 yrs.	Mustered out with company Aug. 4, 1865.
Wagner, William P.....	... do ...	40	Dec. 5, 1861	3 yrs.	Discharged July 6, 1863, on Surgeon's certificate of disability.
Walker, Joseph	... do ...	19	Sept. 12, 1861	3 yrs.	Died June 30, 1862, at Tuscumbia, Ala.
Wardell, Lorenzo	... do ...	18	Jan. 15, 1864	3 yrs.	Mustered out with company Aug. 4, 1865.
Warren, Frederick	... do ...	18	Sept. 9, 1861	3 yrs.	Discharged Oct. 1, 1861.
Waterman, John J......	... do ...	19	Sept. 12, 1861	3 yrs.	Captured Oct. 17, 1862, at battle of Lexington, Ky.; paroled ——; mustered out with company Aug. 4, 1865; veteran.
Webb, James K........	... do ...	18	Jan. 2, 1864	3 yrs.	Mustered out with company Aug. 4, 1865.
Webb, Labin	... do ...	33	Jan. 8, 1864	3 yrs.	Mustered out with company Aug. 4, 1865.
Weeks, Myron	... do ...	18	Dec. 2, 1863	3 yrs.	Wounded April 2, 1865, in battle of Selma, Ala.; mustered out Aug. 15, 1865, from hospital at Cincinnati, O., by order of War Department.
Wickham, James W.....	... do ...	23	Sept. 7, 1861	3 yrs.	Mustered out Oct. 3, 1864, at Columbia, Tenn., on expiration of term of service.
Wilkins, Nelson	... do ...	20	Sept. 7, 1861	3 yrs.	Mustered out with company Aug. 4, 1865; veteran.
Winnull, Joseph H......	... do ...	19	Dec. 3, 1863	3 yrs.	Mustered out with company Aug. 4, 1865.
Wise, Lafayette	... do ...	19	Aug. 24, 1861	3 yrs.	Killed Oct. 18, 1862, in action.
Wurts, Hiram	... do ...	22	Nov. 13, 1861	3 yrs.	Transferred to Co. E, 12th Regiment, Veteran Reserve Corps, Aug. 6, 1863; mustered out from same Nov. 16, 1863, on expiration of term of service.
Zachariah, William	... do ...	35	Dec. 3, 1863	3 yrs.	Mustered out with company Aug. 4, 1865.
Bourns, William	Cook	22	April 1, 1863	3 yrs.	Colored under-cook; no further record found.
Heard, Henry	... do ...	....	April 23, 1865	3 yrs.	Colored under-cook; mustered out with company Aug. 4, 1865.
Lared, Artemus	... do ...	....	April 23, 1865	3 yrs.	Colored under-cook; mustered out with company Aug. 4, 1865.
Malen, Jackson	... do ...	....	April 23, 1865	3 yrs.	Colored under-cook; mustered out with company Aug. 4, 1865.
Motley, John	... do ...	25	April 5, 1863	3 yrs.	Colored under-cook; mustered out with company Aug. 4, 1865.

COMPANY H.

Mustered in December 11, 1861, at Camp Worcester, O., by James P. W. Neill, 1st Lieutenant 18th Infantry, U. S. A., Mustering Officer. Mustered out August 4, 1865, at Edgefield, Tenn., by James P. W. Neill, Captain 18th Infantry, U. S. A., Acting Commissary of Musters, Cavalry Corps, M. D. T.

Names	Rank	Age	Date of Entering the Service	Period of Service	Remarks
Charles W. Skinner....	Captain	42	Aug. 20, 1861	3 yrs.	Appointed 1st Lieutenant Sept. 14, 1861; promoted to Captain Oct. 10, 1861; to Major Feb. 14, 1863.
Francis P. Gates........	... do ...	26	Sept. 7, 1861	3 yrs.	Promoted from 1st Lieutenant Co. E March 5, 1863; to Major Nov. 30, 1864.
Jesse N. Squires..........	... do ...	20	Sept. 3, 1861	3 yrs.	Promoted to 1st Lieutenant from Regt. Com. Sergeant June 2, 1863; to Captain Nov. 30, 1864; on detached duty as Act. Inspector General at 2d Division Cavalry Headquarters since April 3, 1865; mustered out Aug. 4, 1865, at Nashville, Tenn.
William Maxwell	1st Lieu.	25	Aug. 20, 1861	3 yrs.	Appointed Oct. 10, 1861; promoted to Captain Nov. 12, 1862, but not mustered; honorably discharged Feb. 1, 1863.
Martin Archer	... do ...	30	Aug. 20, 1861	3 yrs.	Appointed Sergeant Sept. 17, 1861; promoted to 1st Lieutenant Nov. 12, 1862; to Captain Co. G June 17, 1863.
George A. Clark..........	... do ...	31	Sept. 8, 1861	3 yrs.	Promoted from 2d Lieutenant Co. L Nov. 30, 1864; to Captain June 16, 1865, but not mustered; mustered out with company Aug. 4, 1865; veteran.
Samuel J. Hansey.....	2d Lieu.	26	Aug. 20, 1861	3 yrs.	Appointed Sept. 10, 1861; promoted to 1st Lieutenant Co. C Sept. 11, 1862.
Edward A. Haines........	... do ...	22	Sept. 10, 1861	3 yrs.	Promoted from Batt. Sergt. Major Sept. 11, 1862; to 1st Lieutenant Co. I March 31, 1864.
William P. Lee..........	... do ...	23	Sept. 2, 1861	3 yrs.	Promoted from Sergeant Co. F Nov. 24, 1863; mustered out Nov. 23, 1864, at Louisville, Ky., on expiration of term of service.
Ambrose D. Hawes....	... do ...	18	Sept. 4, 1861	3 yrs.	Promoted from Sergeant Co. B Nov. 30, 1864; to 1st Lieutenant Aug. 2, 1865, but not mustered; mustered out with company Aug. 4, 1865; veteran.
George Garfield	1st Serg.	31	Aug. 20, 1861	3 yrs.	Appointed Sergeant Sept. 17, 1861; 1st Sergeant ——; promoted to 2d Lieutenant Co. D June 7, 1863.
Thomas J. Coslet........	... do ...	24	Aug. 20, 1861	3 yrs.	Appointed Sergeant Sept. 17, 1861; 1st Sergeant Jan. 4, 1864; promoted to 1st Lieutenant Co. F Nov. 30, 1864; veteran.
Daniel W. Weitz..........	... do ...	21	Oct. 5, 1861	3 yrs.	Also borne on rolls as "Daniel Wright;" mustered as private; appointed Dec. 2, 1864; mustered out with company Aug. 4, 1865; veteran.
Clinton W. Ely........	Q. M. S.	22	Jan. 14, 1862	3 yrs.	Mustered as private; appointed Oct. 13, 1864; mustered out with company Aug. 4, 1865; veteran.
Orrin Barker	Com Ser.	26	Oct. 5, 1861	3 yrs.	Appointed Corporal Jan. 4, 1864; Com. Sergeant Oct. 3, 1864; mustered out with company Aug. 4, 1865; veteran.
Elias S. Frager........	Sergeant	21	Aug. 20, 1861	3 yrs.	Appointed Sept. 17, 1861; mustered out with company Aug. 4, 1865; veteran.
Joseph Berry	... do ...	38	Aug. 20, 1861	3 yrs.	Appointed Sept. 17, 1861; promoted to Sergt. Major March 1, 1865; veteran.
Isaac Bricker	... do ...	25	Aug. 20, 1861	3 yrs.	Appointed Corporal Sept. 17, 1861; Sergeant ——; mustered out Oct. 3, 1864, at Columbia, Tenn., on expiration of term of service.
Harmon L. Miller........	... do ...	21	Aug. 20, 1861	3 yrs.	Appointed Corporal Sept. 17, 1861; Sergeant ——; mustered out Oct. 3, 1864, at Columbia, Tenn., on expiration of term of service.
Lowell A. Page..........	... do ...	20	Aug. 20, 1861	3 yrs.	Mustered as private; appointed ——; mustered out Oct. 3, 1864, at Columbia, Tenn., on expiration of term of service.
Thomas Stutesman	... do ...	20	Sept. 25, 1861	3 yrs.	Mustered as private; appointed ——; captured ——; died Sept. 16, 1864, in Andersonville Prison, Ga.
Lyman Allgire	... do ...	21	Aug. 20, 1861	3 yrs.	Appointed Corporal Jan. 4, 1864; Sergeant Oct. 3, 1864; mustered out with company Aug. 4, 1865; veteran.
William Brandon	... do ...	34	Oct. 5, 1861	3 yrs.	Appointed Corporal Jan. 4, 1864; Sergeant Oct. 3, 1864; mustered out with company Aug. 4, 1865; veteran.
Henry H. Bunker........	... do ...	21	Oct. 5, 1861	3 yrs.	Appointed Corporal Jan. 4, 1864; Sergeant July 1, 1865; mustered out with company Aug. 4, 1865; veteran.

Names	Rank	Age	Date of Entering the Service	Period of Service	Remarks
Daniel J. Pickitt.......	Sergeant	21	Oct. 5, 1861	3 yrs.	Appointed Q. M. Sergeant Sept. 17, 1861; captured Oct. 4, 1862, at battle of Bardstown, Ky.; paroled ——; appointed from private July 14, 1865; mustered out with company Aug. 4, 1865; veteran.
Marvin R. Sisson......	Corporal	23	Aug. 20, 1861	3 yrs.	Appointed Sept. 17, 1861; killed Jan. 1, 1863, in battle of Stone River, Tenn.
David Hawkins	... do ...	26	Aug. 20, 1861	3 yrs.	Appointed Sept. 17, 1861.
Philip D. Wideman.....	... do ...	43	Aug. 20, 1861	3 yrs.	Appointed Sept. 17, 1861; discharged March 5, 1863, on Surgeon's certificate of disability.
Peter B. Wicoff..........	... do ...	24	Aug. 20, 1861	3 yrs.	Appointed Sept. 17, 1861; discharged July 21, 1864, on Surgeon's certificate of disability.
William Cosslett	... do ...	29	Aug. 20, 1861	3 yrs.	Appointed Oct. 10, 1861; discharged July 16, 1862, on Surgeon's certificate of disability.
Michael Lochard	... do ...	21	Aug. 20, 1861	3 yrs.	Appointed ——; mustered out Oct. 3, 1864, at Columbia, Tenn., on expiration of term of service.
Eustace Leggett	... do ...	20	Sept. 25. 1861	3 yrs.	Appointed ——; mustered out Oct. 3, 1864, at Columbia, Tenn., on expiration of term of service.
John T. Barnes..........	... do ...	24	Sept. 25, 1861	3 yrs.	Appointed ——; captured ——; died March 13, 1865, at Camp Chase, O., of disease contracted in Libby Prison, Va.
Elemuel Alliger	... do ...	20	Aug. 20, 1861	3 yrs.	Appointed Oct. 3, 1864; mustered out with company Aug. 4, 1865; veteran.
James H. Prickitt.......	... do ...	18	Aug. 20, 1861	3 yrs.	Captured Oct. 4, 1862, at battle of Bardstown, Ky.; paroled ——; appointed Oct. 3, 1864; mustered out with company Aug. 4, 1865; veteran.
David E. Hart...........	... do ...	24	Oct. 5, 1861	3 yrs.	Appointed Oct. 3, 1864; mustered out with company Aug. 4, 1865; veteran.
David Poast	... do ...	21	Aug. 5, 1863	3 yrs.	Appointed Oct. 3, 1864; mustered out with company Aug. 4, 1865.
William H. Letcher......	... do ...	19	Mch. 18, 1864	3 yrs.	Appointed Jan. 1, 1865; mustered out with company Aug. 4, 1865.
John S. Lawrence........	... do ...	28	Sept. 25, 1861	3 yrs.	Appointed March 13, 1865; mustered out with company Aug. 4, 1865; veteran.
Franklin Elder	... do ...	20	Aug. 5, 1863	3 yrs.	Appointed Oct. 3, 1864; reduced Feb. 24, 1865; re-appointed July 1, 1865; mustered out with company Aug. 4, 1865.
John N. Johnson........	... do ...	19	Aug. 20, 1861	3 yrs.	Appointed July 1, 1865; mustered out with company Aug. 4, 1865.
William Hinman	Bugler	28	Aug. 20, 1861	3 yrs.	Appointed Sept. 17, 1861; promoted to Chief Bugler Dec. 1, 1861.
Michael Hibbard	Farrier	33	Oct. 28, 1861	3 yrs.	Appointed Nov. 4, 1861; discharged Aug. 6, 1862, on Surgeon's certificate of disability.
William H. Gallup.......	... do ...	36	Nov. 29, 1861	3 yrs.	Appointed Dec. 11, 1861; discharged May 16, 1863, on Surgeon's certificate of disability.
David T. Carpenter......	... do ...	20	Mch. 21, 1864	3 yrs.	Appointed ——; mustered out with company Aug. 4, 1865.
Abanatha, John	Private	23	Aug. 24, 1863	3 yrs.	Mustered out with company Aug. 4, 1865.
Allamen, Jacob	... do ...	33	Dec. 10, 1861	3 yrs.	Mustered out with company Aug. 4, 1865; veteran.
Anderson, Robert	... do ...	21	Aug. 20, 1862	3 yrs.	Mustered out June 17, 1865, at Nashville, Tenn., by order of War Department.
Arling, William H......	... do ...	18	Feb. 5, 1864	3 yrs.	Mustered out with company Aug. 4, 1865.
Arnold, Henry	... do ...	30	Aug. 20, 1862	3 yrs.	Left sick at Columbia, Ky., Oct. 27, 1862; no further record found.
Ayres, Abner	... do ...	18	Mch. 21, 1864	3 yrs.	Mustered out with company Aug. 4, 1865.
Baker, Nathanial	... do ...	39	Aug. 30, 1862	3 yrs.	Died March 16, 1863.
Bates, Irvin	... do ...	18	Mch. 18, 1864	3 yrs.	Mustered out with company Aug. 4, 1865.
Beard, John P...........	... do ...	23	Aug. 7, 1863	3 yrs.	Mustered out with company Aug. 4, 1865.
Becket, Peter	... do ...	27	Mch. 23, 1865	1 yr.	Mustered out with company Aug. 4, 1865.
Bemis, Charles S........	... do ...	20	Mch. 8, 1865	1 yr.	Mustered out with company Aug. 4, 1865.
Bemis, John A...........	... do ...	23	Mch. 21, 1865	1 yr.	Mustered out with company Aug. 4, 1865.
Best, Jesse A............	... do ...	20	Oct. 5, 1861	3 yrs.	Died June 26, 1862, at Tuscumbia, Ala.
Beverage, James	... do ...	21	Mch. 21, 1865	1 yr.	Mustered out with company Aug. 4, 1865.
Biddle, James M........	... do ...	22	Sept. 25, 1861	3 yrs.	Mustered out Oct. 3, 1864, at Columbia, Tenn., on expiration of term of service.
Bishop, Fletcher	... do ...	23	Sept. 25, 1861	3 yrs.	Mustered out Oct. 3, 1864, at Columbia, Tenn., on expiration of term of service.
Blosier, David P........	... do ...	25	Aug. 7, 1863	3 yrs.	Mustered out with company Aug. 4, 1865.
Bohner, William	... do ...	20	Mch. 18, 1864	3 yrs.	Died Oct. 3, 1864, at Chattanooga, Tenn., of wounds received Aug. 19, 1864, in battle of Jonesboro, Ga.
Booth, Marcus D........	... do ...	21	Mch. 21, 1864	3 yrs.	Mustered out May 17, 1865, at Nashville, Tenn., by order of War Department.
Bowman, John	... do ...	25	Sept. 25, 1861	3 yrs.	Mustered out Dec. 30, 1864, at Nashville, Tenn., on expiration of term of service.
Briner, Amos	... do ...	30	Aug. 20, 1861	3 yrs.	Transferred to Co. G Dec. 1, 1861.
Bump, James	... do ...	30	Oct. 5, 1861	3 yrs.	Mustered out July 19, 1865, from hospital at Camp Dennison, O., by order of War Department; veteran.
Bunker, Miles	... do ...	22	Aug. 20, 1861	3 yrs.	Mustered out Oct. 3, 1864, at Columbia, Tenn., on expiration of term of service.

Names	Rank	Age	Date of Entering the Service	Period of Service	Remarks
Burwell, Henry S.	Private	23	Aug. 20, 1861	3 yrs.	Died June 29, 1862.
Campbell, Hosea P.	... do ...	23	Aug. 20, 1861	3 yrs.	Captured Oct. 4, 1862, at battle of Bardstown, Ky.; paroled ——; died Sept. 11, 1863.
Carpenter, David T.	... do ...	18	Aug. 28, 1862	3 yrs.	Discharged Jan. 5, 1863, on Surgeon's certificate of disability.
Carr, Charles	... do ...	44	Mch. 21, 1865	1 yr.	Mustered out with company Aug. 4, 1865.
Carter, Joseph	... do ...	19	Oct. 10, 1861	3 yrs.	Transferred to Co. B, 7th Regiment, Veteran Reserve Corps, Aug. 12, 1863; mustered out from same Nov. 15, 1865, by order of War Department.
Castle, William M.	... do ...	21	July 10, 1863	3 yrs.	Mustered out May 25, 1865, from hospital at Camp Dennison, O., by order of War Department.
Chambers, Asa D.	... do ...	28	Mch. 24, 1865	1 yr.	Mustered out to date Aug. 4, 1865, at Columbus, O., by order of War Department.
Chambers, Samuel C.	... do ...	22	Aug. 20, 1861	3 yrs.	Discharged July 7, 1862, on Surgeon's certificate of disability.
Coon, George L. M.	... do ...	22	Aug. 20, 1861	3 yrs.	Died April 28, 1862.
Cooper, George I.	... do ...	29	Feb. 27, 1865	1 yr.	Mustered out with company Aug. 4, 1865.
Coss, Franklin D.	... do ...	18	Nov. 15, 1861	3 yrs.	Transferred to Co. A, 17th Regiment, Veteran Reserve Corps, Sept. 27, 1863; mustered out from same Nov. 26, 1864, by order of War Department.
Cotton, David	... do ...	18	Jan. 13, 1864	3 yrs.	Mustered out with company Aug. 4, 1865.
Davidson, John F.	... do ...	18	Sept. 25, 1861	3 yrs.	Mustered out Oct. 31, 1864, on expiration of term of service.
Dority, John	... do ...	18	July 25, 1863	3 yrs.	Mustered out with company Aug. 20, 1865.
Doughton, O. Gilbert.	... do ...	24	Aug. 20, 1861	3 yrs.	
Duke, Benjamin F.	... do ...	28	Aug. 26, 1862	3 yrs.	Transferred to Co. O, 23d Regiment, Veteran Reserve Corps, Jan. 15, 1864; mustered out from same July 28, 1865, at St. Paul, Minn., by order of War Department.
Dukes, Josiah	... do ...	28	Feb. 8, 1864	3 yrs.	Mustered out with company Aug. 4, 1865.
Durbin, James L.	... do ...	18	Sept. 25, 1861	3 yrs.	Transferred to Co. M Dec. 1, 1861.
Edwards, Nathan	... do ...	40	Mch. 13, 1864	3 yrs.	Mustered out June 23, 1865, at Louisville, Ky., by order of War Department.
Ely, Columbus G.	... do ...	23	Sept. 3, 1864	1 yr.	Mustered out June 17, 1865, at Nashville, Tenn., by order of War Department.
Ely, Simon B.	... do ...	19	Mch. 13, 1864	3 yrs.	Mustered out with company Aug. 4, 1865.
Esterline, La Fayette.	... do ...	19	Mch. 21, 1864	3 yrs.	Mustered out with company Aug. 4, 1865.
Faukhauser, Christopher	... do ...	24	July 30, 1862	3 yrs.	Mustered out June 17, 1865, at Nashville, Tenn., by order of War Department.
Fennimore, Jordan J.	... do ...	22	Sept. 25, 1861	3 yrs.	Mustered out with company Aug. 4, 1865; veteran.
Fickle, Michael	... do ...	18	Oct. 5, 1861	3 yrs.	Discharged March 25, 1863, on Surgeon's certificate of disability.
Fiddler, David	... do ...	23	Oct. 3, 1861	3 yrs.	Captured Oct. 4, 1862, at battle of Bardstown, Ky.; paroled ——; mustered out Oct. 31, 1864, on expiration of term of service.
Flegel, David	... do ...		Aug. 20, 1861	3 yrs.	Discharged Nov. 7, 1862, at Columbus, O., on Surgeon's certificate of disability.
Fox, Michael	... do ...	20	Aug. 25, 1861	3 yrs.	Discharged July 23, 1862, on Surgeon's certificate of disability.
Frager, Josiah B.	... do ...	18	Aug. 20, 1861	3 yrs.	Mustered out Oct. 3, 1864, at Columbia, Tenn., on expiration of term of service.
Francis, Robert	... do ...	21	Mch. 21, 1865	1 yr.	Mustered out with company Aug. 4, 1865.
Gardner, William H.	... do ...	32	Sept. 3, 1864	1 yr.	Promoted to Regt. Saddler Sergeant May 1, 1865.
Gardner, William W.	... do ...	31	Oct. 5, 1861	3 yrs.	Died April 28, 1862, at Savannah, Tenn.
Gay, Alvertus E.	... do ...	20	Aug. 28, 1862	3 yrs.	Mustered out May 19, 1865, at Nashville, Tenn., by order of War Department.
Gear, Milo	... do ...	24	Sept. 25, 1861	3 yrs.	Transferred to 60th Co., 2d Battalion, Veteran Reserve Corps, Sept. 24, 1863; mustered out from same Sept. 27, 1864, on expiration of term of service.
Gillian, James	... do ...	28	Mch. 24, 1865	1 yr.	Mustered out with company Aug. 4, 1865.
Hager, William M.	... do ...	30	Mch. 30, 1865	1 yr.	Mustered out with company Aug. 4, 1865.
Hager, William M.	... do ...	24	Aug. 20, 1861	3 yrs.	Mustered out Sept. 28, 1864, at Camp Dennison, O., on expiration of term of service.
Haines, Joseph	... do ...	18	July 22, 1863	3 yrs.	Mustered out with company Aug. 4, 1865.
Hambright, William H	... do ...	21	Sept. 26, 1864	1 yr.	Mustered out June 17, 1865, at Nashville, Tenn., by order of War Department.
Hamlin, Seth	... do ...	31	Sept. 25, 1861	3 yrs.	Wounded June 15, 1864, in battle of Noon Day Creek, Ga.; mustered out Oct. 31, 1864, at Columbia, Tenn., by order of War Department.
Hamlin, Woodruff A.	... do ...	17	Aug. 22, 1863	3 yrs.	Mustered out with company Aug. 4, 1865.
Hanna, Ephraim	... do ...	19	Aug. 20, 1861	3 yrs.	Died Jan. 12, 1862.
Harris, William	... do ...	33	Aug. 14, 1863	3 yrs.	Mustered out with company Aug. 4, 1865.
Hart, Able C.	... do ...	18	Mch. 26, 1864	3 yrs.	Mustered out with company Aug. 4, 1865.
Hartman, William H.	... do ...	18	Aug. 20, 1861	3 yrs.	Also borne on rolls as "Henry W.;" captured Oct. 4, 1862, at battle of Bardstown, Ky.; paroled ——; mustered out wth company Aug. 4, 1865; veteran.
Hawkins, Albert	... do ...	22	Oct. 24, 1861	3 yrs.	Died April 17, 1762, at Nashville, Tenn.

Names	Rank	Age	Date of Entering the Service	Period of Service	Remarks
Hawkins, Joseph, Sr..	Private	24	Oct. 24, 1861	3 yrs.	Died Aug. 4, 1862.
Hay, Joshua	... do ...	21	Sept. 25, 1861	3 yrs.	Died May 8, 1862, at Savannah, Tenn.
Hayward, Edgar D...	... do ...	19	Oct. 28, 1861	3 yrs.	Discharged Nov. 19, 1862, on Surgeon's certificate of disability.
Heiser, Philip	... do ...	22	Mch. 22, 1865	1 yr.	Mustered out with company Aug. 4, 1865.
Hine, Joseph N.......	... do ...	18	Aug. 20, 1861	3 yrs.	
Hinman, William C...	... do ...	30	Sept. 3, 1864	1 yr.	Also borne on rolls as "Charles W;" mustered out June 17, 1865, at Nashville, Tenn., by order of War Department.
Hoke, George	... do ...	18	Aug. 7, 1863	3 yrs.	Dscharged Jan. 23, 1864, from hospital at Camp Dennison, O., by order of War Department.
Howard, Veloise J....	... do ...	26	Aug. 29, 1862	3 yrs.	Died Feb. 4, 1863.
Ickes, John B.........	... do ...	27	Oct. 24, 1861	3 yrs.	Discharged Sept. 22, 1862, on Surgeon's certificate of disability.
Jenks, George W.....	... do ...	18	Jan. 4, 1864	3 yrs.	Captured April 16, 1865, at battle of Columbus, Ga.; no further record found.
Jewell, John G........	... do ...	35	Oct. 23, 1861	3 yrs.	Died Feb. 8, 1863, on board hospital boat.
Johnson, William O...	... do ...		Aug. 20, 1861	3 yrs.	Promoted to Regt. Com. Sergeant ——.
Jones, Geoorge W....	... do ...	21	Dec. 10, 1861	3 yrs.	Captured Oct. 4, 1862, at battle of Bardstown, Ky.; paroled ——; mustered out with company Aug. 4, 1865; veteran.
Kelley, Daniel H......	... do ...	39	Feb. 27, 1865	1 yr.	Mustered out with company Aug. 4, 1865.
Kenny, Greenberry ...	... do ...	18	Mch. 21, 1864	3 yrs.	Mustered out with company Aug. 4, 1865.
Kenny, James	... do ...	28	Mch. 23, 1865	1 yr.	Mustered out with company Aug. 4, 1865.
Kent, Chester F.......	... do ...	18	Aug. 5, 1863	3 yrs.	Mustered out with company Aug. 4, 1865.
Kime, George W.......	... do ...	31	Aug. 20, 1861	3 yrs.	Also borne on rolls as "Kinie;" mustered out with company Aug. 4, 1865; veteran.
Kline, Christian	... do ...	21	Dec. 28, 1863	3 yrs.	Also borne on rolls as "Cline;" mustered out June 9, 1865, at Louisville, Ky., by order of War Department.
Lambert, Robert	... do ...	28	July 30, 1862	3 yrs.	Mustered out June 17, 1865, at Nashville, Tenn., by order of War Department.
Lamson, Burdett J....	... do ...	18	Aug. 5, 1863	3 yrs.	Absent since March 20, 1865; no further record found.
Lanoir, Julian	... do ...	19	Jan. 4, 1864	3 yrs.	Also borne on rolls as "John L.;" died Aug. 24, 1864, at Marietta, Ga., of wounds received in action at Flat Rock, Ga.
MaBee, Alphonso	... do ...	23	Aug. 23, 1862	3 yrs.	Discharged Dec. 16, 1862, on Surgeon's certificate of disability.
Marks, David	... do ...	24	Sept. 25, 1861	3 yrs.	Discharged July 17, 1862, on Surgeon's certificate of disability.
Marsh, Edwin P.......	... do ...	33	Aug. 20, 1861	3 yrs.	Mustered out Oct. 3, 1864, at Columbia, Tenn., on expiration of term of service.
Misell, William	... do ...	19	Sept. 25, 1861	3 yrs.	Mustered out with company Aug. 4, 1865; veteran.
Moses, Henry W......	... do ...	25	Feb. 24, 1864	3 yrs.	Mustered out with company Aug. 4, 1865.
Moss, Sanford C......	... do ...	18	Mch. 21, 1864	3 yrs.	Died July 21, 1864, at Big Shanty, Ga., of wounds received June 20, 1864, in battle of Noon Day Creek, Ga.
Munson, William	... do ...	18	Jan. 4, 1864	3 yrs.	Captured April 16, 1865, at battle of Columbus, Ga.; no further record found.
Nutt, John	... do ...	21	Sept. 25, 1861	3 yrs.	Died Aug. 23, 1864, at Lovejoy Station, Ga., of wounds received Aug. 20, 1864, in battle of Lovejoy Station, Ga.
Peach, John	... do ...	33	Mch. 13, 1864	3 yrs.	Mustered out with company Aug. 4, 1865.
Pennington, Joel	... do ...	30	Jan. 4, 1864	3 yrs.	Died April 11, 1864, at Columbia, Tenn.
Pennington, Marion T.	... do ...	21	Aug. 20, 1861	3 yrs.	Died July 16, 1862.
Pew, Thomas S........	... do ...	32	Aug. 20, 1861	3 yrs.	Discharged Jan. 31, 1863, on Surgeon's certificate of disability.
Platt, Horace W......	... do ...	20	Jan. 4, 1864	3 yrs.	Mustered out with company Aug. 4, 1865.
Powers, Henry W.....	... do ...	21	Sept. 25, 1861	3 yrs.	Died Nov. 21, 1862, at Lebanon, Ky.
Radabaugh, John W..	... do ...	27	Aug. 28, 1862	3 yrs.	Mustered out June 17, 1865, at Nashville, Tenn., by order of War Department.
Radabaugh, Milton ...	... do ...	26	Aug. 28, 1862	3 yrs.	Also borne on rolls as "James M.;" mustered out June 17, 1865, at Nashville, Tenn., by order of War Department.
Ragan, Colon K.......	... do ...	24	Aug. 20, 1861	3 yrs.	Mustered out April 26, 1865, at Columbus, O., on expiration of term of service.
Ragan, Henry W......	... do ...	19	Aug. 20, 1861	3 yrs.	Mustered out Oct. 3, 1864, at Columbia, Tenn., on expiration of term of service.
Riggs, Charles W.....	... do ...	35	Jan. 12, 1864	3 yrs.	Mustered out with company Aug. 4, 1865.
Rings, William C.....	... do ...	18	Oct. 5, 1861	3 yrs.	Died April 11, 1863, at Murfreesboro, Tenn.
Robinson, Melvin W..	... do ...	35	Oct. 5, 1861	3 yrs.	Discharged Oct. 25, 1862, on Surgeon's certificate of disability.
Rogers, William T....	... do ...	19	Sept. 25, 1861	3 yrs.	Captured July 10, 1864, in action at Marietta, Ga.; mustered out June 15, 1865, at Camp Chase, O., by order of War Department; veteran.
Ruger, George W.....	... do ...	18	Mch. 23, 1865	1 yr.	Mustered out with company Aug. 4, 1865.
Russell, Richard	... do ...	42	Jan. 4, 1864	3 yrs.	Mustered out with company Aug. 4, 1865.
Russell, William C...	... do ...	18	Aug. 20, 1861	3 yrs.	Mustered out Oct. 3, 1864, at Columbia, Tenn., on expiration of term of service.

Names	Rank	Age	Date of Entering the Service	Period of Service	Remarks
Scannell, William H...	Private	20	Aug. 20, 1861	3 yrs.	Captured Oct. 4, 1862, at battle of Bardstown, Ky.; paroled ——; appointed Corporal Jan. 4, 1864; Sergeant Jan. 1, 1865; reduced July 14, 1865; mustered out with company Aug. 4, 1865; veteran.
Shell, Joseph	do	22	Feb. 24, 1864	3 yrs.	Mustered out with company Aug. 4, 1865.
Sheffield, Frederick B.	do	19	Sept. 25, 1861	3 yrs.	Mustered out Oct. 3, 1864, at Columbia, Tenn., on expiration of term of service.
Shoeff, John H.	do	19	July 5, 1863	3 yrs.	Mustered out with company Aug. 4, 1865.
Smith, Josiah	do	18	Mch. 21, 1864	3 yrs.	Mustered out with company Aug. 4, 1865.
Smith, William C.	do	28	Aug. 20, 1861	3 yrs.	Mustered out Oct. 3, 1864, at Columbia, Tenn., on expiration of term of service.
Smith, William	do	26	Mch. 23, 1865	1 yr.	Mustered out with company Aug. 4, 1865.
Smith, Robert B.	do	30	Mch. 15, 1865	1 yr.	Mustered out with company Aug. 4, 1865.
Snediker, Isaiah F.	do	22	Sept. 3, 1864	1 yr.	Mustered out June 17, 1865, at Nashville, Tenn., by order of War Department.
Spencer, Charles	do	20	Aug. 24, 1863	3 yrs.	Absent since Feb. 25, 1865; no further record found.
Stinchcomb, Christ.	do	35	Nov. 12, 1861	3 yrs.	Mustered out with company Aug. 4, 1865; veteran.
Stout, Alfred	do	18	Oct. 24, 1861	3 yrs.	Captured July 10, 1864, in action at Marietta, Ga.; mustered out June 15, 1865, at Camp Chase, O., by order of War Department; veteran.
Super, Charles	do	18	Jan. 4, 1864	3 yrs.	Mustered out with company Aug. 4, 1865.
Swayne, J. P. K.	do				Mustered out June 21, 1865, at Camp Dennison, O., by order of War Department.
Thomas, Henry	do	19	Aug. 20, 1861	3 yrs.	Mustered out Oct. 3, 1864, at Columbia, Tenn., on expiration of term of service.
Tunetin, Robert R.	do	19	Aug. 20, 1861	3 yrs.	Discharged June 10, 1862, on Surgeon's certificate of disability.
Venande, William C.	do	33	Aug. 20, 1861	3 yrs.	Mustered out with company Aug. 4, 1865; veteran.
Warrington, Henry	do	24	Jan. 5, 1864	3 yrs.	Mustered out with company Aug. 4, 1865.
Whistler, George W.	do	30	Oct. 5, 1861	3 yrs.	Died April 26, 1862.
Whitehead, William H	do	19	Sept. 25, 1861	3 yrs.	Discharged Dec. 2, 1863, on Surgeon's certificate of disability.
Williams, William	do	24	Aug. 20, 1861	3 yrs.	Died May 28, 1862, at Louisville, Ky.
Wilson, George P.	do	18	Aug. 10, 1863	3 yrs.	Died Feb. 10, 1864, at Savannah, Tenn.
Wines, Robert M.	do	36	Oct. 5, 1861	3 yrs.	Died April 18, 1862.
Woodworth, John H.	do	33	Mch. 9, 1865	1 yr.	Mustered out with company Aug. 4, 1865.
Yoder, George W.	do	18	Aug. 7, 1863	3 yrs.	Mustered out with company Aug. 4, 1865.
Preston, Washington	Cook	27	April 25, 1865	3 yrs.	Colored under-cook; mustered out with company Aug. 4, 1865.

COMPANY I.

Mustered in December 11, 1861, at Camp Worcester, O., by James P. W. Neill, 1st Lieutenant 18th Infantry, U. S. A., Mustering Officer. Mustered out August 4, 1865, at Edgefield, Tenn., by James P. W. Neill, Captain 18th Infantry, U. S. A., Acting Commissary of Musters, Cavalry Corps, M. D. T.

Names	Rank	Age	Date of Entering the Service	Period of Service	Remarks
Henry B. Gaylord	Captain	40	Aug. 24, 1861	3 yrs.	Appointed Aug. 24, 1861; captured Oct. 17, 1862, at battle of Lexington, Ky.; paroled ——; resigned May 2, 1864.
Frederick Bernerd	do	25	Aug. 24, 1861	3 yrs.	Appointed 1st Sergeant from Sergeant ——; promoted to 2d Lieutenant May 30, 1862; to 1st Lieutenant Jan. 21, 1863; to Captain July 13, 1864; mustered out Nov. 25, 1864, at Louisville, Ky., on expiration of term of service.
Thomas Nunan	do	20	Sept. 6, 1861	3 yrs.	Promoted from 1st Lieutenant and Regt. Adjutant Nov. 30, 1864; mustered out with company Aug. 4, 1865.
Clark Center	1st Lieu.	28	Sept. 4, 1861	3 yrs.	Appointed Sept. 4, 1861; honorably discharged Jan. 10, 1862.
Edward A. Haines	do	22	Sept. 10, 1861	3 yrs.	Promoted from 2d Lieutenant Co. H March 31, 1864; mustered out Nov. 25, 1864, at Louisville, Ky., on expiration of term of service.
Garner Stimson	do	25	Sept. 4, 1861	3 yrs.	Promoted from 1st Sergeant Co. B Nov. 30, 1864; to Captain Aug. 2, 1865, but not mustered; mustered out with company Aug. 4, 1865; veteran.
William Goodnow	2d Lieu.	22	Aug. 30, 1861	3 yrs.	Appointed Aug. 30, 1861; died May 27, 1862.
George B. Watson	do	27	Oct. 2, 1861	3 yrs.	Mustered as private; appointed Sergeant ——; promoted to 2d Lieutenant Jan. 21, 1863; to 1st Lieutenant Co. M March 31, 1864.

Names	Rank	Age	Date of Entering the Service	Period of Service	Remarks
John Moore	2d Lieu.	26	Sept. 7, 1861	3 yrs.	Promoted from Com. Sergeant Co. E May 9, 1864; to 1st Lieutenant Co. C Nov. 30, 1864; veteran.
Francis C. Dodge.......	... do ...	26	Sept. 15, 1862	3 yrs.	Promoted from 1st Sergeant Co. C Nov. 30, 1864; resigned May 29, 1865.
James Merroe	... do ...	28	Sept. 14, 1861	3 yrs.	Appointed Q. M. Sergeant from Sergeant ——; captured Dec. 29, 1862, at battle of Murfreesboro, Tenn.; paroled ——; appointed 1st Sergeant Dec. 2, 1864; promoted to 2d Lieutenant April 8, 1865; mustered out with company Aug. 4, 1865; veteran.
Daniel C. Lewis........	1st Serg.	36	Sept. 26, 1861	3 yrs.	Captured Oct. 17, 1862, at battle of Lexington, Ky.; paroled ——; appointed from Sergeant Jan. 4, 1864; promoted to 1st Lieutenant Co. M Nov. 30, 1864; veteran.
Francis Riley	... do ...	19	Sept. 4, 1861	3 yrs.	Appointed Q. M. Sergeant from Corporal Dec. 2, 1864; 1st Sergeant June 15, 1865; mustered out with company Aug. 4, 1865; veteran.
Solomon Shoman	Q. M. S.	32	Aug. 24, 1861	3 yrs.	Died April 20, 1862, at Nashville, Tenn.
Charles B. Benham....	... do ...	38	Sept. 25, 1861	3 yrs.	Mustered as private; appointed Com. Sergeant Dec. 2, 1864; Q. M. Sergeant ——; mustered out to date Aug. 3, 1865, by order of War Department; veteran.
Robert H. Spaulding..	Com Ser.	30	Sept. 26, 1861	3 yrs.	Appointed from Sergeant ——; mustered out Oct. 3, 1864, on expiration of term of service.
Enoch Henney	... do ...	23	Dec. 14, 1861	3 yrs.	Appointed Corporal ——; Com. Sergeant ——; mustered out with company Aug. 4, 1865; veteran.
Chauncey B. Wheeler..	Sergeant	41	Sept. 6, 1861	3 yrs.	Discharged Jan. 23, 1863, on Surgeon's certificate of disability.
Cyrus K. Livermore...	... do ...	22	Sept. 6, 1861	3 yrs.	Appointed from Corporal ——; mustered out Oct. 3, 1864, on expiration of term of service.
Thomas Saltzgaber	... do ...	20	Oct. 7, 1861	3 yrs.	Captured Oct. 17, 1862, at battle of Lexington, Ky.; paroled ——; appointed from Corporal ——; wounded Oct. 25, 1864, in action near Gadston, Ala.; mustered out June 21, 1865, at Camp Dennison, O., by order of War Department; veteran.
Thomas E. Hoffmire..	... do ...	27	Sept. 18, 1861	3 yrs.	Appointed from Corporal ——; died Oct. 6, 1864, at Marietta, Ga., of wounds received in action; veteran.
Charles McMaster	... do ...	21	Sept. 14, 1861	3 yrs.	Appointed Corporal ——; captured Oct. 17, 1862, at battle of Lexington, Ky.; appointed Sergeant ——; mustered out with company Aug. 4, 1865; veteran.
John W. Blackman....	... do ...	22	Sept. 17, 1861	3 yrs.	Appointed Corporal ——; Sergeant ——; mustered out with company Aug. 4, 1865; veteran.
Francillo Van Horn...	... do ...	20	Oct. 1, 1861	3 yrs.	Appointed Corporal ——; Sergeant Dec. 2, 1864; mustered out with company Aug. 4, 1865; veteran.
James E. Mitchell.....	... do ...	19	Sept. 30, 1861	3 yrs.	Appointed Corporal ——; Sergeant July 1, 1865; mustered out with company Aug. 4, 1865; veteran.
James D. Benham......	... do ...	27	Sept. 25, 1861	3 yrs.	Appointed Corporal ——; Sergeant July 1, 1865; mustered out with company Aug. 4, 1865; veteran.
James B. Page	Corporal	23	Sept. 24, 1861	3 yrs.	Promoted to Batt. Veterinary Surgeon Dec. 1, 1861.
Albert Sweetland	... do ...	26	Oct. 1, 1861	3 yrs.	Died July 8, 1862.
Amos S. Waltmire......	... do ...	22	Oct. 5, 1861	3 yrs.	Discharged Sept. 11, 1862, on Surgeon's certificate of disability.
Jonas W. Childs.......	... do ...	20	Jan. 15, 1862	3 yrs.	Captured Oct. 17, 1862, at battle of Lexington, Ky.; paroled ——; appointed ——; mustered out with company Aug. 4, 1865; veteran.
Charles J. Smith.......	... do ...	26	Dec. 16, 1861	3 yrs.	Appointed ——; mustered out with company Aug. 4, 1865; veteran.
Christian Sommers	... do ...	21	Oct. 16, 1861	3 yrs.	Appointed ——; mustered out with company Aug. 4, 1865; veteran.
Richard Waggoner.....	... do ...	22	Oct. 5, 1861	3 yrs.	Captured Oct. 17, 1862, at battle of Lexington, Ky.; paroled ——; appointed ——; mustered out with company Aug. 4, 1865; veteran.
Charles Mason	... do ...	21	Sept. 14, 1861	3 yrs.	Appointed Dec. 8, 1864; mustered out with company Aug. 4, 1865; veteran.
Henry Sweetland	... do ...	20	Sept. 23, 1861	3 yrs.	Appointed Dec. 8, 1864; mustered out with company Aug. 4, 1865; veteran.
Adam Fetter	... do ...	26	Sept. 16, 1861	3 yrs.	Appointed July 1, 1865; mustered out with company Aug. 4, 1865; veteran.
Jacob Wise	... do ...	22	Dec. 16, 1861	3 yrs.	Appointed July 1, 1865; mustered out with company Aug. 4, 1865; veteran.
Henry L. Bingham....	Bugler	26	Oct. 15, 1861	3 yrs.	Discharged Sept. 16, 1862, on Surgeon's certificate of disability.

Names	Rank	Age	Date of Entering the Service	Period of Service	Remarks
Jacob Hummel	Bugler	28	Nov. 11, 1861	3 yrs.	Appointed ——; mustered out with company Aug. 4, 1865; veteran.
Jacob Hawk	Farrier	54	Sept. 18, 1861	3 yrs.	Discharged May 18, 1862, on Surgeon's certificate of disability.
Adam M. Rock........	... do ...	27	Sept. 24, 1861	3 yrs.	Mustered out Oct. 3, 1864, on expiration of term of service.
John Hawn	... do ...	27	Aug. 16, 1862	3 yrs.	Apponted ——; mustered out June 17, 1865, at Nashville, Tenn., by order of War Department.
Henry A. Libe..........	... do ...	19	Sept. 17, 1861	3 yrs.	Captured Oct. 17, 1862, at battle of Lexington, Ky.; paroled ——; appointed July 1, 1865; mustered out with company Aug. 4, 1865; veteran.
Anthony Hoover	... do ...	27	Dec. 10, 1863	3 yrs.	Appointed July 1, 1865; mustered out with company Aug. 4, 1865.
Thomas D. Stevenson.	Saddler	....	Sept. 24, 1861	3 yrs.	Discharged Nov. 4, 1862, on Surgeon's certificate of disability.
Conrad Thoman	... do ...	26	Oct. 2, 1861	3 yrs.	Appointed ——; mustered out with company Aug. 4, 1865; veteran.
George W. Skinner	Wagoner	25	Sept. 2, 1861	3 yrs.	Appointed ——; mustered out with company Aug. 4, 1865; veteran.
Allen, Henry H........	Private	29	Sept. 24, 1861	3 yrs.	
Allen, William F.......	... do ...	20	Sept. 24, 1861	3 yrs.	Discharged Dec. 31, 1862, on Surgeon's certificate of disability.
Artz, Jacob F..........	... do ...	21	Dec. 10, 1863	3 yrs.	Mustered out with company Aug. 4, 1865.
Ashley, Augustine	... do ...	22	Aug. 12, 1862	3 yrs.	Mustered out June 17, 1865, at Nashville, Tenn., by order of War Department.
Baker, Thomas	... do ...	28	Sept. 4, 1861	3 yrs.	Captured Dec. 29, 1862, at battle of Murfreesboro, Tenn.; paroled ——; mustered out with company Aug. 4, 1865; veteran.
Baker, Soloman	... do ...	22	Sept. 17, 1861	3 yrs.	Mustered out with company Aug. 4, 1865; veteran.
Banks, John S.........	... do ...	27	Sept. 2, 1861	3 yrs.	Mustered out May 24, 1865, from Tripler Hospital at Columbus, O., by order of War Department.
Barker, Addison	... do ...	20	Feb. 26, 1864	3 yrs.	Mustered out with company Aug. 4, 1865.
Beer, John	... do ...	18	Jan. 1, 1864	3 yrs.	Mustered out with company Aug. 4, 1865.
Bell, Milton J.........	... do ...	22	Feb. 22, 1864	3 yrs.	Mustered out May 20, 1865, at Columbus, O., by order of War Department.
Benson, John H........	... do ...	25	Oct. 26, 1863	3 yrs.	Appointed Corporal ——; reduced Dec. 2, 1864; mustered out with company Aug. 4, 1865.
Berns, Frederick	... do ...	19	Dec. 24, 1863	3 yrs.	Mustered out Aug. 4, 1865.
Bliss, Leander	... do ...	21	Jan. 15, 1862	3 yrs.	Mustered out with company Aug. 4, 1865; veteran.
Bliss, Urial	... do ...	21	Aug. 12, 1862	3 yrs.	Mustered out June 17, 1865, at Nashville, Tenn., by order of War Department.
Bloom, Frederick	... do ...	25	Sept. 9, 1861	3 yrs.	Mustered out with company Aug. 4, 1865; veteran.
Bolster, William	... do ...	21	Sept. 17, 1861	3 yrs.	Died March 18, 1864, at Lagrange, Ind.; veteran.
Boyd, John	... do ...	27	Nov. 3, 1863	3 yrs.	Mustered out with company Aug. 4, 1865.
Bridenstine, Martin L.	... do ...	18	Sept. 17, 1861	3 yrs.	Also borne on rolls as "Louis M. Brightenstine;" mustered out with company Aug. 4, 1865; veteran.
Brinneman, Harmon L	... do ...	19	Sept. 24, 1861	3 yrs.	Killed June 15, 1864, in battle of Kenesaw Mountain, Ga.; veteran.
Broadman, Henry	... do ...	43	Nov. 23, 1861	3 yrs.	Discharged Jan. 23, 1863, on Surgeon's certificate of disability.
Byers, William	... do ...	30	Sept. 4, 1861	3 yrs.	
Camp, Alonzo	... do ...	25	Oct. 2, 1863	3 yrs.	Transferred to Co. K April 1, 1864.
Camp, Edward	... do ...	18	Nov. 3, 1863	3 yrs.	Transferred to Co. K April 1, 1864.
Cobban, Frank	... do ...	18	Sept. 4, 1861	3 yrs.	Died Feb. 4, 1865, at Gravelly Springs, Ala.; veteran.
Coe, Seymour B.......	... do ...	43	Sept. 4, 1861	3 yrs.	Promoted to Batt. Q. M. Sergeant Sept. 7, 1861.
Crawford, Frank M...	... do ...	18	Aug. 20, 1864	3 yrs.	Mustered out with company Aug. 4, 1865.
Davidson, Allen H....	... do ...	23	Feb. 23, 1864	3 yrs.	Mustered out with company Aug. 4, 1865.
Davidson, William H..	... do ...	25	Feb. 23, 1864	3 yrs.	Mustered out with company Aug. 4, 1865.
Davis, Charles	... do ...	19	Dec. 29, 1863	3 yrs.	Mustered out with company Aug. 4, 1865.
Davis, George	... do ...	18	Dec. 29, 1863	3 yrs.	Mustered out with company Aug. 4, 1865.
Davis, William	... do ...	17	Dec. 29, 1863	3 yrs.	Mustered out with company Aug. 4, 1865.
Douglass, William	... do ...	21	Aug. 17, 1862	3 yrs.	Captured Oct. 17, 1862, at battle of Lexington, Ky.; paroled ——; mustered out June 17, 1865, at Nashville, Tenn., by order of War Department.
Downing, Napoleon B.	... do ...	23	Dec. 5, 1861	3 yrs.	Discharged Aug. 7, 1862, on Surgeon's certificate of disability.
Drake, Frederick	... do ...	22	Sept. 28, 1861	3 yrs.	Transferred to Co. B April 17, 1865; veteran.
Frazier, Benjamin F..	... do ...	18	Feb. 27, 1864	3 yrs.	
Frost, Robert B.......	... do ...	18	Dec. 21, 1861	3 yrs.	Captured Oct. 17, 1862, at battle of Lexington, Ky.; paroled ——; died April 2, 1864, at Nashville, Tenn.; veteran.
Gooseman, George ...	... do ...	22	Dec. 16, 1861	3 yrs.	Captured Oct. 17, 1862, at battle of Lexington, Ky.; paroled ——; mustered out with company Aug. 4, 1865; veteran.

Names	Rank	Age	Date of Entering the Service	Period of Service	Remarks
Green, Anson P........	Private	24	Sept. 16, 1861	3 yrs.	Discharged April 7, 1863, on Surgeon's certificate of disability.
Hall, Jeremiah D......	...do ...	29	Oct. 17, 1863	3 yrs.	Mustered out with company Aug. 4, 1865.
Heeps, Thomas	...do ...	28	July 15, 1863	3 yrs.	Captured Oct. 7, 1863, at Farmington, Tenn.; supposed to be dead; no further record found.
Hemminger, Lewis	...do ...	25	Sept. 24, 1861	3 yrs.	
Henney, Cyrus L.......	...do ...	18	Feb. 26, 1864	3 yrs.	Mustered out with company Aug. 4, 1865.
Hobocker, John	...do ...	27	July 13, 1863	3 yrs.	Mustered out with company Aug. 4, 1865.
Hoffman, Frederick	...do ...	20	Oct. 16, 1863	3 yrs.	Mustered out with company Aug. 4, 1865.
Hunter, John E........	...do ...	27	Feb. 26, 1864	3 yrs.	Mustered out with company Aug. 4, 1865.
Johnston, John	...do ...	25	July 24, 1863	3 yrs.	
Johnston, Martin C....	...do ...	41	Sept. 14, 1861	3 yrs.	Captured Oct. 17, 1862, at battle of Lexington, Ky.; paroled ——; mustered out with company Aug. 4, 1865; veteran.
Kappler, Anthony	...do ...	27	Oct. 7, 1863	3 yrs.	Mustered out with company Aug. 4, 1865.
Keith, George W.	...do ...	23	Sept. 4, 1861	3 yrs.	Captured Oct. 17, 1862, at battle of Lexington, Ky.; paroled ——.
Kellogg, Vernon	...do ...	16	Oct. 12, 1861	3 yrs.	Mustered out with company Aug. 4, 1865; veteran.
Kiser, Edmond	...do ...	26	Sept. 4, 1861	3 yrs.	Captured Oct. 17, 1862, at battle of Lexington, Ky.; paroled ——.
Kryder, George	...do ...	27	Nov. 20, 1861	3 yrs.	Mustered out with company Aug. 4, 1865; veteran.
Kyle, William A........	...do ...	18	Nov. 3, 1863	3 yrs.	Mustered out with company Aug. 4, 1865.
Lauler, Patrick	...do ...	20	Sept. 17, 1861	3 yrs.	Mustered out with company Aug. 4, 1865; veteran.
Leek, William D........	...do ...	28	Sept. 25, 1861	3 yrs.	Mustered out with company Aug. 4, 1865; veteran.
Lewis, John	...do ...	21	Oct. 2, 1863	3 yrs.	Mustered out with company Aug. 4, 1865.
Link, Andrew	...do ...	29	Dec. 14, 1863	3 yrs.	Mustered out with company Aug. 4, 1865.
McCoy, Thomas W......	...do ...	23	Feb. 27, 1864	3 yrs.	Mustered out with company Aug. 4, 1865.
McKeehan, David A.....	...do ...	18	Mch. 11, 1864	3 yrs.	Mustered out with company Aug. 4, 1865.
McKelvey, John W......	...do ...	29	Aug. 12, 1862	3 yrs.	Discharged May 24, 1865, on Surgeon's certificate of disability.
McMaster, Dexter	...do ...	19	Nov. 13, 1861	3 yrs.	Captured Oct. 17, 1862, at battle of Lexington, Ky.; paroled ——; mustered out with company Aug. 4, 1865; veteran.
McMaster, Mark	...do ...	18	Aug. 12, 1862	3 yrs.	Captured Oct. 17, 1862, at battle of Lexington, Ky.; paroled ——; mustered out June 17, 1865, at Nashville, Tenn., by order of War Department.
McMillin, Prosser D......	...do ...	18	Sept. 2, 1861	3 yrs.	Discharged Nov. 4, 1862, on Surgeon's certificate of disability.
Magner, Harlan	...do ...	27	April 12, 1863	3 yrs.	Mustered out with company Aug. 4, 1865.
Mahony, James	...do ...	18	Oct. 2, 1863	3 yrs.	Mustered out with company Aug. 4, 1865.
Mann, James A........	...do ...	19	Sept. 14, 1861	3 yrs.	Died Nov. 16, 1863, of wounds received in action.
Meir, James	...do ...	19	Feb. 23, 1864	3 yrs.	Mustered out with company Aug. 4, 1865.
Nagran, Christian	...do ...	37	Sept. 19, 1861	3 yrs.	Captured Oct. 17, 1862, at battle of Lexington, Ky.; paroled ——; mustered out with company Aug. 4, 1865; veteran.
Niven, Edwin	...do ...	17	Oct. 7, 1861	3 yrs.	Captured Nov. 15, 1863, in action at Woodville, Ala.; died June 19, 1864, in prison at Andersonville, Ga.
Owen, Robert T........	...do ...	38	Jan. 4, 1864	3 yrs.	Mustered out with company Aug. 4, 1865.
Parks, Bron P..........	...do ...	24	Sept. 24, 1861	3 yrs.	Discharged April 23, 1862, on Surgeon's certificate of disability.
Parks, Francis M.......	...do ...	19	Dec. 16, 1861	3 yrs.	Mustered out with company Aug. 4, 1865; veteran.
Parksons, Warren W....	...do ...	22	Sept. 24, 1861	3 yrs.	Discharged July 3, 1862, on Surgeon's certificate of disability.
Pearson, Samuel S......	...do ...	18	Nov. 3, 1863	3 yrs.	Transferred to Co. E ——.
Plank, Theopholus S....	...do ...	20	Sept. 2, 1861	3 yrs.	Died June 17, 1862.
Playman, John	...do ...	17	Dec. 14, 1863	3 yrs.	Mustered out with company Aug. 4, 1865.
Robbins, Samuel R....	...do ...	21	Sept. 9, 1861	3 yrs.	Also borne on rolls as "Rosell Robbins;" mustered out with company Aug. 4, 1865; veteran.
Rogers, Henry	...do ...	21	Sept. 24, 1861	3 yrs.	Mustered out Oct. 3, 1864, on expiration of term of service.
Rogers, Otto W.........	...do ...	28	Sept. 24, 1861	3 yrs.	Discharged Jan. 8, 1863, on Surgeon's certificate of disability.
Saltzgaber, Gaylord M	...do ...	16	Sept. 1, 1861	3 yrs.	Mustered out with company Aug. 4, 1865; veteran.
Saltzgaber, William V	do	18	Oct. 7, 1861	3 yrs.	Captured Oct. 17, 1862, at battle of Lexington, Ky.; paroled ——; mustered out July 27, 1865, at Macon, Ga., by order of War Department; veteran.
Sanders, Charles	...do ...	20	Sept. 23, 1861	3 yrs.	Captured Oct. 17, 1862, at battle of Lexington, Ky.; paroled ——; mustered out Oct. 3, 1864, on expiration of term of service.
Schwab, John M........	...do ...	23	Dec. 16, 1861	3 yrs.	Captured Oct. 17, 1862, at battle of Lexington, Ky.; paroled ——; wounded June 11, 1864, at Noonday Creek, Ga.; discharged Feb. 9, 1865, at Cleveland, O., on Surgeon's certificate of disability.

Names	Rank	Age	Date of Entering the Service	Period of Service	Remarks
Schwab, Joseph E.....	Private	18	Jan. 4, 1864	3 yrs.	Mustered out with company Aug. 4, 1865.
Schwab, Isaiah	... do ...	24	Sept. 6, 1864	1 yr.	Mustered out June 17, 1865, at Nashville, Tenn., by order of War Department.
Serier, Jesse	... do ...	18	Sept. 2, 1861	3 yrs.	Captured Oct. 17, 1862, at battle of Lexington, Ky.; paroled.
Silence, David T........	... do ...	24	Oct. 4, 1861	3 yrs.	Died Nov. 12, 1862, at Louisville, Ky.
Smith, Oel T............	... do ...	36	Feb. 25, 1864	3 yrs.	Mustered out with company Aug. 4, 1865.
Spencer, William	... do ...	19	Sept. 10, 1861	3 yrs.	Mustered out July 27, 1865, at Macon, Ga., by order of War Department; veteran.
Stevens, Joseph	... do ...	28	Sept. 2, 1861	3 yrs.	Captured Oct. 20, 1863, at Frog Springs, Ga.; supposed to have been killed; no further record found.
Stuke, Samuel	... do ...	31	Sept. 24, 1861	3 yrs.	Captured Oct. 17, 1862, at battle of Lexington, Ky.; paroled ——; mustered out with company Aug. 4, 1865; veteran.
Taylor, Austin E........	... do ...	23	Jan. 15, 1862	3 yrs.	Captured Oct. 17, 1862, at battle of Lexington, Ky.; paroled ——; mustered out Jan. 15, 1865, on expiration of term of service.
Thomas, Cunrad	... do ...	24	Sept. 26, 1861	3 yrs.	Mustered out with company Aug. 4, 1865; veteran.
Thomas, Henry	... do ...	20	Sept. 16, 1861	3 yrs.	Discharged May 17, 1862, on Surgeon's certificate of disability.
Travis, Hyatt	... do ...	22	Sept. 24, 1861	3 yrs.	Mustered out with company Aug. 4, 1865; veteran.
Van Horn, Wilson S..	... do ...	21	Oct. 7, 1861	3 yrs.	Mustered out with company Aug. 4, 1865; veteran.
Varner, Mason	... do ...	19	Nov. 3, 1863	3 yrs.	Mustered out with company Aug. 4, 1865.
Wall, Michael	... do ...	18	Nov. 3, 1863	3 yrs.	Mustered out with company Aug. 4, 1865.
Wardler, John	... do ...	23	Sept. 2, 1861	3 yrs.	Died Sept. 11, 1862, at Nashville, Tenn.
Wilcox, Charles M......	... do ...	30	Feb. 19, 1864	3 yrs.	Mustered out with company Aug. 4, 1865.
Wilcox, Joseph M......	... do ...	20	Sept. 23, 1861	3 yrs.	Captured Oct. 17, 1862, at battle of Lexington, Ky.; paroled ——; mustered out July 27, 1865, at Macon, Ga., by order of War Department; veteran.
Winkler, Leonard	... do ...	19	Dec. 12, 1863	3 yrs.	Mustered out with company Aug. 4, 1865.
Winteringham, John W	... do ...	21	Sept. 2, 1861	3 yrs.	Mustered out with company Aug. 4, 1865; veteran.
Wise, Nicholas	... do ...	20	July 10, 1863	3 yrs.	Killed Feb. 24, 1864, in action at Ringgold, Ga.
Dunlavy, William	Cook	19	April 27, 1865	3 yrs.	Colored under-cook; mustered out with company Aug. 4, 1865.
Holeton, John	... do ...	25	April 27, 1865	3 yrs.	Colored under-cook; mustered out with company Aug. 4, 1865.
Rogers, Nelson	... do ...	25	April 27, 1865	3 yrs.	Colored under-cook; mustered out with company Aug. 4, 1865.
Thurman, Henry	... do ...	18	April 27, 1865	3 yrs.	Colored under-cook; mustered out with company Aug. 4, 1865.

COMPANY K.

Mustered in December 11, 1861, at Camp Worcester, O., by James P. W. Neill, 1st Lieutenant 18th Infantry, U. S. A., Mustering Officer. Mustered out August 4, 1865, at Nashville, Tenn., by James P. W. Neill, Captain 18th Infantry, U. S. A., Acting Commissary of Musters, Cavalry Corps, M. D. T.

Names	Rank	Age	Date of Entering the Service	Period of Service	Remarks
Daniel Gotshall	Captain	58	Nov. 15, 1861	3 yrs.	Appointed Nov. 15, 1861; died June 17, 1862.
Elisha M. Culver........	... do ...	27	Sept. 4, 1861	3 yrs.	Promoted from 1st Lieutenant Co. B June 16, 1862; resigned Sept. 26, 1864.
Orange H. Howland.....	... do ...	23	Aug. 15, 1861	3 yrs.	Promoted from 1st Lieutenant Co. E Nov. 30, 1864; mustered out with company Aug. 4, 1865.
Darius E. Livermore...	1st Lieu.	28	Sept. 4, 1861	3 yrs.	Appointed Nov. 1, 1861; captured Oct. 17, 1862, at battle of Lexington, Ky.; paroled ——; promoted to Captain Co. B Feb. 1, 1863.
Oliver M. Brown........	... do ...	27	Aug. 16, 1861	3 yrs.	Transferred from Co. A April 24, 1863; promoted to Captain Co. C Aug. 19, 1863.
Ervin R. Harris........	... do ...	17	Sept. 7, 1861	3 yrs.	Promoted from 2d Lieutenant Co. M May 9, 1864; mustered out Nov. 7, 1864, on expiration of term of service.
Lewis B. Tooker........	... do ...	20	Sept. 4, 1861	3 yrs.	Promoted from 1st Sergeant Co. A Nov. 30, 1864; mustered out with company Aug. 4, 1865; veteran.
Oscar W. Treman......	2d Lieu.	36	Oct. 25, 1861	3 yrs.	Appointed Oct. 25, 1861; resigned May 10, 1862.
James Ransom Hall....	... do ...	21	Sept. 4, 1861	3 yrs.	Promoted from Batt. Sergt. Major May 21, 1862; resigned March 18, 1863.

Names	Rank	Age	Date of Entering the Service	Period of Service	Remarks
Chauncey L. Cook....	2d Lieu.	38	Dec. 23, 1861	3 yrs.	Appointed Q. M. Sergeant Dec. 23, 1861; promoted to 2d Lieutenant March 21, 1863; to 1st Lieutenant July 13, 1864, but not mustered; discharged March 28, 1864, on Surgeon's certificate of disability.
Paul Deal	... do ...	43	Sept. 10, 1861	3 yrs.	Promoted from 1st Sergeant Co. D Nov. 24, 1863; to 1st Lieutenant Co. D Nov. 30, 1864.
Thomas Martin	... do ...	22	Aug. 31, 1861	3 yrs.	Promoted from Sergeant Co. F Nov. 30, 1864; detailed to command Co. M May 23, 1865; promoted to 1st Lieutenant Aug. 2, 1865, but not mustered; mustered out with company Aug. 4, 1865; veteran.
John Maloney	1st Serg.	18	Nov. 26, 1861	3 yrs.	Appointed from Sergeant ——; mustered out Dec. 30, 1864, at Nashville, Tenn., on expiration of term of service.
Jesse De Well...........	... do ...	27	Nov. 15, 1861	3 yrs.	Appointed Com. Sergeant from Corporal ——; 1st Sergeant Dec. 11, 1864; mustered out with company Aug. 4, 1865; veteran.
Thomas Marlin	Q. M. S.	40	Oct. 28, 1861	3 yrs.	Appointed from Sergeant July 20, 1864; promoted to 2d Lieutenant Co. M Nov. 30, 1864; veteran.
Francis Shaw	... do ...	20	Nov. 27, 1861	3 yrs.	Appointed Corporal ——; captured Oct. 17, 1862, at battle of Lexington, Ky.; paroled ——; appointed Sergeant ——; Q. M. Sergeant Dec. 11, 1864; promoted to Regt. Com. Sergeant May 1, 1865; veteran.
Philo C. Seager..........	... do ...	25	Dec. 3, 1861	3 yrs.	Appointed Corporal ——; Com. Sergeant Dec. 11, 1864; Q. M. Sergeant May 1, 1865; mustered out with company Aug. 4, 1865; veteran.
William Jones	Com Ser.	39	Nov. 12, 1861	3 yrs.	Appointed Corporal ——; Sergeant Dec. 31, 1864; Com. Sergeant ——; mustered out with company Aug. 4, 1865; veteran.
George H. Frent.......	Sergeant	28	Dec. 3, 1861	3 yrs.	Promoted to Regt. Q. M. Sergeant Oct. 3, 1864; veteran.
Walter T. Burr..........	... do ...	17	Dec. 6, 1861	3 yrs.	Mustered out Dec. 30, 1864, at Nashville, Tenn., on expiration of term of service.
Madison Hesser	... do ...	26	Nov. 29, 1861	3 yrs.	Appointed from Corporal April 25, 1862; discharged Nov. 19, 1862, on Surgeon's certificate of disability.
Daniel Hanley	... do ...	28	Nov. 4, 1861	3 yrs.	Appointed from Corporal Nov. 1, 1862; captured Sept. 19, 1863, at battle of Chickamauga, Ga.; mustered out March 18, 1865, on expiration of term of service.
Silas Genson	... do ...	25	Nov. 21, 1861	3 yrs.	Captured Oct. 17, 1862, at battle of Lexington, Ky.; paroled ——; mustered as private; appointed ——; captured April 2, 1865, at battle of Selma, Ala.; mustered out June 24, 1865, at Camp Chase, O., by order of War Department; veteran.
John Reynolds	... do ...	26	Nov. 26, 1861	3 yrs.	Appointed Corporal ——; captured Oct. 17, 1862, at battle of Lexington, Ky.; paroled ——; appointed Sergeant ——; discharged Feb. 16, 1864, at Nashville, Tenn., on Surgeon's certificate of disability.
James Fisher	... do ...	30	Dec. 4, 1861	3 yrs.	Appointed from Corporal ——; veteran.
James Drurey	... do ...	17	Dec. 6, 1861	3 yrs.	Appointed from private Dec. 31, 1864; mustered out with company Aug. 4, 1865; veteran.
James H. Gidley........	... do ...	24	Aug. 2, 1862	3 yrs.	Appointed Corporal ——; Sergeant Jan. 1, 1865; mustered out June 17, 1865, at Nashville, Tenn., by order of War Department.
Solon Gunn	... do ...	46	Nov. 21, 1861	3 yrs.	Appointed Corporal Dec. 31, 1864; Sergeant May 1, 1865; mustered out with company Aug. 4, 1865; veteran.
David Cosgrove	... do ...	28	Aug. 27, 1861	3 yrs.	Transferred from Co. C April 1, 1864; appointed Corporal Dec. 31, 1864; Sergeant May 1, 1865; mustered out with company Aug. 4, 1865; veteran.
Gottlieb Row	... do ...	23	Dec. 16, 1861	3 yrs.	Appointed Corporal Dec. 31, 1864; Sergeant May 1, 1865; mustered out with company Aug. 4, 1865; veteran.
Jacob Henry	Corporal	32	Nov. 4, 1861	3 yrs.	Killed Dec. 31, 1862, in battle of Stone River, Tenn.
Hiram Barnes	... do ...	20	Nov. 10, 1861	3 yrs.	Discharged Oct. 1, 1862, on Surgeon's certificate of disability.
Gilbert C. Ostrander..	... do ...	27	Nov. 30, 1861	3 yrs.	Discharged to date June 1, 1862, on Surgeon's certificate of disability.
Jacob Rex	... do ...	42	Dec. 12, 1861	3 yrs.	Appointed ——; captured ——; died June 30, 1864, while in prison at Andersonville, Ga.
Howard Bowman	... do ...	18	Dec. 7, 1861	3 yrs.	Appointed Dec. 20, 1864; died April 6, 1865, in hospital at Selma, Ala., of wounds received April 2, 1865, in battle of Selma, Ala.; veteran.

Names	Rank	Age	Date of Entering the Service	Period of Service	Remarks
Augustus Heck	Corporal	22	Dec. 4, 1861	3 yrs.	Appointed ——; mustered out Dec. 30, 1864, at Nashville, Tenn., on expiration of term of service.
George M. Gotshall.......	... do ...	17	Nov. 4, 1861	3 yrs.	Appointed ——; mustered out Dec. 30, 1864, at Nashville, Tenn., on expiration of term of service.
John Toomey	... do ...	18	Dec. 10, 1861	3 yrs.	Appointed ——; mustered out Dec. 30, 1864, at Nashville, Tenn., on expiration of term of service.
James Mills	... do ...	20	Aug. 24, 1862	3 yrs.	Transferred from Co. C April 1, 1864; appointed Dec. 11, 1864.
Robert O. Kennedy....	... do ...	18	Dec. 2, 1861	3 yrs.	Appointed Dec. 31, 1864; mustered out July 27, 1865, at Camp Dennison, O., by order of War Department; veteran.
James McCormick	... do ...	18	Nov. 14, 1861	3 yrs.	Appointed Dec. 31, 1864; mustered out with company Aug. 4, 1865; veteran.
Robert E. Morton	... do ...	18	Sept. 4, 1861	3 yrs.	Transferred from Co. A ——; appointed Dec. 31, 1864; mustered out with company Aug. 4, 1865; veteran.
William Entsminger ...	... do ...	19	Feb. 24, 1864	3 yrs.	Appointed May 1, 1865; mustered out with company Aug. 4, 1865.
Daniel Campbell	... do ...	21	Feb. 3, 1864	3 yrs.	Appointed May 1, 1865; mustered out with company Aug. 4, 1865.
Isaac Blickensdifer	... do ...	39	Dec. 3, 1863	3 yrs.	Appointed May 1, 1865; mustered out with company Aug. 4, 1865.
James K. P. Newell....	... do ...	19	Jan. 15, 1864	3 yrs.	Appointed May 1, 1865; mustered out with company Aug. 4, 1865.
Charles Brunthaver ...	... do ...	18	Feb. 23, 1864	3 yrs.	Appointed May 1, 1865; mustered out with company Aug. 4, 1865.
Henry Trott	Bugler	24	Nov. 11, 1861	3 yrs.	Discharged Feb. 16, 1863, on Surgeon's certificate of disability.
Joseph Tyler	... do ...	26	Nov. 18, 1861	3 yrs.	Died Aug. —, 1862, while at home.
Frederick Sumerhalter.	... do ...	41	Jan. 4, 1864	3 yrs.	Also borne on rolls as "Souholder;" appointed ——; mustered out with company Aug. 4, 1865.
George Doll	Farrier	45	Nov. 19, 1861	3 yrs.	Promoted to Regt. Veterinary Surgeon March —, 1863.
Walter J. Swartz......	... do ...	41	Dec. 6, 1861	3 yrs.	Also borne on rolls as "William G. Swart;" mustered out with company Aug. 4, 1865; veteran.
David W. Forbes.......	... do ...	29	Nov. 22, 1861	3 yrs.	Transferred from Co. L ——; appointed ——; mustered out Dec. 30, 1864, at Nashville, Tenn., on expiration of term of service.
Conrad Kale	... do ...	23	Dec. 12, 1863	3 yrs.	Appointed Dec. 31, 1864; mustered out with company Aug. 4, 1865.
Robert Dutchman	Saddler	35	Nov. 30, 1861	3 yrs.	Discharged March 1, 1863, at Murfreesboro, Tenn., on Surgeon's certificate of disability.
Timothy Goodrich	... do ...	23	Feb. 27, 1864	3 yrs.	Appointed ——; mustered out with company Aug. 4, 1865.
Charles Yance	Wagoner	28	Nov. 22, 1861	3 yrs.	Captured Oct. 17, 1862, at battle of Lexington, Ky.; paroled ——; mustered out Dec. 30, 1864, at Nashville, Tenn., on expiration of term of service.
Ackley, Asa	Private	20	Dec. 17, 1863	3 yrs.	
Allman, Manly	... do ...	31	Oct. 1, 1862	3 yrs.	Discharged Feb. 16, 1863, on Surgeon's certificate of disability.
Arnold, Albert	... do ...	21	Nov. 14, 1861	3 yrs.	Mustered out with company Aug. 4, 1865; veteran.
Bein, Francis	... do ...	18	Mch. 23, 1864	3 yrs.	Also borne on rolls as "Been;" discharged Sept. 20, 1864, at Cross Keys, Ga., on Surgeon's certificate of disability.
Bell, Joseph	... do ...	30	Feb. 28, 1865	1 yr.	Mustered out with company Aug. 4, 1865.
Benson, Mason	... do ...	19	Nov. 14, 1861	3 yrs.	Captured Sept. 20, 1863, at battle of Chickamauga, Ga.; paroled May 8, 1864; mustered out Dec. 14, 1864, at Columbus, O., on expiration of term of service.
Borden, Christopher W	... do ...	31	Nov. 30, 1861	3 yrs.	
Branan, Patrick	... do ...	19	Feb. 29, 1864	3 yrs.	Sick in Louisville, Ky., since Dec. 3, 1864; no further record found.
Brightenburgh, Joseph	... do ...	19	Dec. 14, 1863	3 yrs.	Mustered out with company Aug. 4, 1865.
Brown, Daniel	... do ...	29	Sept. 10, 1861	3 yrs.	Transferred from Co. O Jan. 1, 1862; captured and paroled Aug. 24, 1862, at Lebanon, Tenn.; captured Oct. 17, 1862, at battle of Lexington, Ky.; paroled ——.
Buchanan, William	... do ...	35	Dec. 10, 1863	3 yrs.	Died June 12, 1865, in hospital at Macon, Ga.
Camp, Alonzo	... do ...	25	Oct. 3, 1863	3 yrs.	Transferred from Co. I April 1, 1864; mustered out with company Aug. 4, 1865.
Camp, Edward	... do ...	18	Nov. 3, 1863	3 yrs.	Transferred from Co. I April 1, 1864; mustered out with company Aug. 4, 1865.
Campbell, John C.......	... do ...	26	Feb. 24, 1864	3 yrs.	Mustered out with company Aug. 4, 1865.
Chilson, Peter M.......	... do ...	18	Sept. 3, 1861	3 yrs.	Transferred from Co. O Dec. 11, 1861; captured July 16, 1863, at Pulaski, Tenn., by guerrillas; no further record found.

Names	Rank	Age	Date of Entering the Service	Period of Service	Remarks
Clark, Edmond	Private	28	Feb. 28, 1865	1 yr.	Mustered out with company Aug. 4, 1865.
Clark, John	... do ...	22	Mch. 1, 1865	1 yr.	Mustered out with company Aug. 4, 1865.
Coates, Howard H.	... do ...	24	Nov. 23, 1861	3 yrs.	Discharged to date April 15, 1863, on Surgeon's certificate of disability.
Collins, James	... do ...	32	Sept. 10, 1862	3 yrs.	Mustered out June 17, 1865, at Nashville, Tenn., by order of War Department.
Colwell, Frederick	... do ...	23	Dec. 1, 1863	3 yrs.	Discharged Sept. 6, 1865, at Nashville, Tenn., by order of War Department.
Couts, Jeremiah	... do ...	16	Nov. 18, 1861	3 yrs.	Captured Nov. 15, 1863, in action at Woodville, Ala.; mustered out Jan. 24, 1865, at Columbus, O., on expiration of term of service.
Cummings, George	... do ...	18	Nov. 14, 1861	3 yrs.	Died April 13, 1862, in hospital at Cincinnati, O.
Curtis, Franklin	... do ...	21	Oct. 2, 1863	3 yrs.	
Entsminger, Stephen	... do ...	23	Feb. 24, 1864	3 yrs.	
Fachinger, George	... do ...	28	Nov. 17, 1861	3 yrs.	Discharged March 11, 1863, on Surgeon's certificate of disability.
Fessler, Emanuel	... do ...	25	Jan. 7, 1862	3 yrs.	Mustered out with company Aug. 4, 1865; veteran.
Fitzgerald, John	... do ...	47	Dec. 5, 1861	3 yrs.	Discharged Feb. 16, 1863, on Surgeon's certificate of disability.
Foorman, Aaron	... do ...	43	Feb. 1, 1864	3 yrs.	Mustered out with company Aug. 4, 1865.
Fowler, Carey	... do ...	18	Nov. 30, 1861	3 yrs.	
Frost, Benjamin	... do ...	22	Mch. 4, 1865	1 yr.	Mustered out with company Aug. 4, 1865.
Fry, Joseph	... do ...	22	Jan. 7, 1864	3 yrs.	
Gowitze, William	... do ...	19	Nov. 23, 1861	3 yrs.	Captured Dec. 3, 1864, in action near Nashville, Tenn.; mustered out May 31, 1865, at Columbus, O., on expiration of term of service.
Graves, Daniel G.	... do ...	19	Nov. 21, 1861	3 yrs.	Appointed Sergeant from Corporal ——; reduced Dec. 31, 1864; mustered out with company Aug. 4, 1865; veteran.
Greis, Peter J.	... do ...	25	Nov. 12, 1861	3 yrs.	Discharged Aug. 18, 1862, on Surgeon's certificate of disability.
Grow, Benjamin	... do ...	37	Nov. 27, 1861	3 yrs.	Died April 19, 1862.
Grow, Samuel	... do ...	37	Dec. 10, 1861	3 yrs.	Discharged Sept. 24, 1862, at Cincinnati, O., on Surgeon's certificate of disability.
Grow, William	... do ...	18	Dec. 10, 1861	3 yrs.	Captured Oct. 17, 1862, at battle of Lexington, Ky.; paroled ——; mustered out March 20, 1865, at Columbus, O., on expiration of term of service.
Grube, John K.	... do ...	28	Jan. 7, 1862	3 yrs.	Mustered out Jan. 11, 1865, at Nashville, Tenn., on expiration of term of service.
Gustin, William	... do ...	26	Feb. 24, 1864	3 yrs.	Captured April 2, 1865, at battle of Selma, Ala.; perished by explosion of steamer "Sultana" on Mississippi River near Memphis, Tenn., April 27, 1865.
Harris, William	... do ...	30	Feb. 3, 1864	3 yrs.	Mustered out with company Aug. 4, 1865.
Harvey, Thomas	... do ...	20	Nov. 6, 1861	3 yrs.	Mustered out Dec. 30, 1864, at Nashville, Tenn., on expiration of term of service.
Heller, Lewis	... do ...	20	Nov. 5, 1861	3 yrs.	Transferred to Co. H, 8th Regiment, Veteran Reserve Corps, Oct. 1, 1864; mustered out from same Dec. 12, 1864, on expiration of term of service.
Henderson, Eli	... do ...	22	Dec. 2, 1861	3 yrs.	Mustered out Dec. 30, 1864, at Nashville, Tenn., on expiration of term of service.
Henderson, William	... do ...	19	Dec. 2, 1861	3 yrs.	
Henley, Philip	... do ...	18	Dec. 3, 1863	3 yrs.	Mustered out with company Aug. 4, 1865.
Heslet, George W.	... do ...	17	Dec. 2, 1861	3 yrs.	Mustered out Dec. 30, 1864, at Nashville, Tenn., on expiration of term of service.
Heslet, William	... do ...	20	Dec. 10, 1861	3 yrs.	Died Aug. 30, 1862.
Hess, David	... do ...	19	Nov. 4, 1861	3 yrs.	Captured Sept. 19, 1863, at battle of Chickamauga, Ga.; no further record found.
Hewitt, George	... do ...	24	Dec. 1, 1861	3 yrs.	Mustered out June 17, 1865, at Nashville, Tenn., by order of War Department.
Hewitt, Nathan R.	... do ...	21	June 13, 1863	3 yrs.	
Hill, Charles	... do ...	18	Dec. 17, 1863	3 yrs.	Mustered out Aug. 1, 1865, from hospital at Camp Dennison, O., by order of War Department.
Houghton, Ephriam	... do ...	18	Jan. 12, 1864	3 yrs.	Mustered out with company Aug. 4, 1865.
Ireling, Levi	... do ...	24	Dec. 15, 1863	3 yrs.	Mustered out May 27, 1865, from Tripler Hospital, Columbus, O., by order of War Department.
Kailey, Frederick	... do ...	22	Oct. 4, 1862	3 yrs.	Discharged March 16, 1863, on Surgeon's certificate of disability.
Keen, John	... do ...	25	Nov. 2, 1861	3 yrs.	Died Sept. 28, 1864, in hospital at Atlanta, Ga.
Keller, Harrison	... do ...	19	Nov. 18, 1861	3 yrs.	Discharged March 3, 1863, to enlist in Co. A, 1st Battalion Cavalry, Mississippi Marine Brigade.
Kelly, John	... do ...	26	Nov. 26, 1861	3 yrs.	Discharged to date July 14, 1862, by order of War Department.
Kennedy, Theodore	... do ...	18	Aug. 13, 1862	3 yrs.	Discharged April 10, 1863, on Surgeon's certificate of disability.
King, Francis	... do ...	26	Nov. 26, 1861	3 yrs.	

Names	Rank	Age	Date of Entering the Service	Period of Service	Remarks
Kliber, Jacob	Private	23	Jan. 8, 1864	3 yrs.	Mustered out with company Aug. 4, 1865.
Krebs, Frederick	... do ...	44	Dec. 18, 1863	3 yrs.	Mustered out with company Aug. 4, 1865.
Letherer, George	... do ...	22	Sept. 4, 1861	3 yrs.	Transferred from Co. A Dec. 11, 1861; discharged Nov. 21, 1862, at Nashville, Tenn., on Surgeon's certificate of disability.
Lybarger, Porter	... do ...	28	Oct. 30, 1861	3 yrs.	Mustered out Dec. 30, 1864, at Nashville, Tenn., on expiration of term of service.
McDougal, James F.	... do ...	18	Dec. 1, 1861	3 yrs.	Transferred to Co. O Jan. 1, 1862.
McGravy, Patrick	... do ...	18	Dec. 12, 1863	3 yrs.	Mustered out with company Aug. 4, 1865.
McMullen, Francis	... do ...	32	Dec. 2, 1863	3 yrs.	Mustered out with company Aug. 4, 1865.
Melon, Francis	... do ...	21	Dec. 16, 1863	3 yrs.	Mustered out with company Aug. 4, 1865.
Montle, Joseph	... do ...	36	Dec. 30, 1861	3 yrs.	Mustered out Dec. 31, 1864, at Nashville, Tenn., on expiration of term of service.
Morris, James	... do ...	30	Dec. 2, 1861	3 yrs.	Mustered out Dec. 30, 1864, at Nashville, Tenn., on expiration of term of service.
Mott, Albert	... do ...	....	Dec. 16, 1861	3 yrs.	Died June 15, 1862, at Corinth, Miss.
Nearing, Isaac	... do ...	26	Nov. 21, 1861	3 yrs.	Discharged to date July 30, 1862, on Surgeon's certificate of disability.
Neff, William B.	... do ...	28	Oct. 28, 1861	3 yrs.	Discharged July 2, 1862, at Columbus, O., on Surgeon's certificate of disability.
Nichols, Albert R.	... do ...	20	Feb. 2, 1864	3 yrs.	Mustered out with company Aug. 4, 1865.
Nishwitz, John	... do ...	19	July 2, 1863	3 yrs.	Transferred from Co. A April 1, 1864; mustered out with company Aug. 4, 1865.
Parker, Horace C.	... do ...	22	Jan. 5, 1864	3 yrs.	Discharged to date Sept. 30, 1864, by order of War Department.
Peckins, Ira	... do ...	22	Dec. 11, 1863	3 yrs.	Prisoner of war; mustered out June 19, 1865, at Camp Chase, O., by order of War Department.
Poff, John	... do ...	18	Dec. 30, 1863	3 yrs.	Mustered out with company Aug. 4, 1865.
Pouch, Asa	... do ...	....	Dec. 16, 1861	3 yrs.	Captured April 2, 1865, at battle of Selma, Ala.; perished by explosion of steamer "Sultana" on Mississippi River near Memphis, Tenn., April 27, 1865.
Price, Charles	... do ...	27	Sept. 10, 1861	3 yrs.	Transferred from Co. C ——; captured Oct. 18, 1862, at battle of Lexington, Ky.; paroled ——.
Reed, Jonathan R.	... do ...	43	Nov. 25, 1861	3 yrs.	Died Jan. 3, 1863.
Reel, David G.	... do ...	27	Nov. 17, 1861	3 yrs.	Discharged Feb. 24, 1864, at Camp Dennison, O., by order of War Department.
Reynolds, Charles	... do ...	24	May 10, 1862	3 yrs.	Mustered out June 17, 1865, at Nashville, Tenn., by order of War Department.
Richardson, George W.	... do ...	18	Jan. 15, 1864	3 yrs.	Mustered out with company Aug. 4, 1865.
Riddle, John	... do ...	20	Dec. 14, 1863	3 yrs.	
Ritter, Joseph	... do ...	26	Dec. 3, 1863	3 yrs.	Mustered out with company Aug. 4, 1865.
Roberts, Charles S.	... do ...	32	Dec. 3, 1861	3 yrs.	Discharged Nov. 29, 1862, on Surgeon's certificate of disability.
Roberts, Ebenezer H.	... do ...	19	Dec. 10, 1861	3 yrs.	Mustered out Dec. 30, 1864, at Nashville, Tenn., on expiration of term of service.
Roloff, Lewis	... do ...	40	Dec. 30, 1863	3 yrs.	Mustered out with company Aug. 4, 1865.
Rose, William	... do ...	51	Nov. 15, 1861	3 yrs.	Discharged June 3, 1862, on Surgeon's certificate of disability.
Rowse, James	... do ...	18	Oct. 28, 1861	3 yrs.	Died Jan. 22, 1863, at New Albany, Ind.
Ryan, Rodger	... do ...	20	Dec. 15, 1863	3 yrs.	Mustered out with company Aug. 4, 1865.
Searles, Jacob	... do ...	25	Nov. 20, 1861	3 yrs.	Transferred from Co. C April 1, 1864; mustered out Nov. 25, 1864, at Louisville, Ky., on expiration of term of service.
Sherwood, Charles	... do ...	18	Mch. 17, 1864	3 yrs.	Died April 22, 1864, in hospital at Columbia, Tenn.
Sherwood, John W.	... do ...	20	Mch. 23, 1864	3 yrs.	Mustered out July 25, 1865, from Cumberland Hospital at Nashville, Tenn., by order of War Department.
Showers, George	... do ...	44	Nov. 4, 1861	3 yrs.	Mustered out Jan. 20, 1863, at Benton Barracks, Mo., to enlist in Co. B, Mississippi Marine Brigade Cavalry; transferred to Co. I, Mississippi Marine Brigade Infantry ——; mustered out from same with company Jan. 24, 1865, at Vicksburg, Miss.
Simpkins, Milton M.	... do ...	19	Dec. 15, 1863	3 yrs.	
Sipfle, Augustus	... do ...	20	Mch. 3, 1864	3 yrs.	Mustered out with company Aug. 4, 1865.
Smith, George W.	... do ...	21	Dec. 1, 1861	3 yrs.	Transferred to Co. O Jan. 1, 1862.
Snow, William	... do ...	36	Mch. 10, 1864	3 yrs.	Mustered out with company Aug. 4, 1865.
Thorp, Thomas J.	... do ...	37	Oct. 1, 1862	3 yrs.	Discharged May 22, 1863, on Surgeon's certificate of disability.
Toomey, Michael	... do ...	24	Nov. 4, 1863	3 yrs.	Mustered out with company Aug. 4, 1865.
Tracy, Edward	... do ...	25	Feb. 8, 1864	3 yrs.	Mustered out with company Aug. 4, 1865.
Trott, Jacob	... do ...	22	Nov. 11, 1861	3 yrs.	Transferred to Co. M Jan. 1, 1862.
Vandenburgh, Cornelieus	... do ...	22	Dec. 10, 1861	3 yrs.	Mustered out Dec. 30, 1864, at Nashville, Tenn., on expiration of term of service.
Wadkins, James	... do ...	21	Sept. 10, 1862	3 yrs.	Died Jan. 22, 1865, in hospital at Louisville, Ky.
Ward, John	... do ...	22	Dec. 8, 1863	3 yrs.	
Wells, William H.	... do ...	21	Dec. 9, 1863	8 yrs.	Captured April 2, 1865, at battle of Selma, Ala.; no further record found.
Welsh, James	... do ...	21	Oct. 8, 1863	3 yrs.	Mustered out with company Aug. 4, 1865.

Names	Rank	Age	Date of Entering the Service	Period of Service	Remarks
Weldon, James	Private	26	Sept. 4, 1861	3 yrs.	Transferred from Co. A Dec. 11, 1861; died Aug. 15, 1862, at Woodville, Ala.
Welever, Geo. D.........	... do ...	18	Feb. 17, 1864	3 yrs.	Mustered out with company Aug. 4, 1865.
Wilson, J. W.............	... do ...	....	Dec. 11, 1861	3 yrs.	
Withington, William H	... do ...	31	Dec. 18, 1863	3 yrs.	Mustered cut with company Aug. 4, 1865.
Wright, Lewis	... do ...	23	Dec. 6, 1861	3 yrs.	Mustered out, Dec. 30, 1864, at Nashville, Tenn., on expiration of term of service.
Edwards, Archey	Cook	26	April 28, 1865	3 yrs.	Colored under-cook; mustered out with company Aug. 4, 1865.
Martin, Robert	... do ...	26	April 28, 1865	3 yrs.	Colored under-cook; mustered out with company Aug. 4, 1865.
Maxwell, Daniel	... do ...	19	June 22, 1865	3 yrs.	Colored under-cook; mustered out with company Aug. 4, 1865.

COMPANY L.

Mustered in December 11, 1861, at Camp Worcester, O., by James P. W. Neill, 1st Lieutenant 18th Infantry, U. S. A., Mustering Officer. Mustered out August 4, 1865, at Edgefield, Tenn., by James P. W. Neill, Captain 18th Infantry, U. S. A., Acting Commissary of Musters, Cavalry Corps, M. D. T.

Names	Rank	Age	Date of Entering the Service	Period of Service	Remarks
William Flanagan	Captain	28	Nov. 9, 1861	3 yrs.	Appointed Nov. 9, 1861.
Elihu Isbell	... do ...	26	Sept. 6, 1861	3 yrs.	Promoted from 1st Lieutenant Co. F Aug. 12, 1863; transferred to Co. D April 4, 1864.
James B. Luckey.......	... do ...	18	Sept. 4, 1861	3 yrs.	Appointed 1st Lieutenant Sept. 4, 1861; promoted to Captain Co. C Jan. 5, 1863; transferred from Co. C April 5, 1864; mustered out Nov. 22, 1864, at Louisville, Ky., on expiration of term of service.
James S. Clock..........	... do ...	25	Mch. 20, 1863	3 yrs.	Appointed 1st Lieutenant from civil life March 20, 1863; promoted to Captain Nov. 30, 1864; died July 2, 1865, at Macon, Ga., of wounds received while in discharge of his duty.
Charles S. Kelsey	1st Lieu.	23	Sept. 10, 1861	3 yrs.	Promoted from 1st Sergeant Co. D Nov. 30, 1864; mustered out with company Aug. 4, 1865; veteran.
Ralph Devereaux	2d Lieu.	26	Nov. 2, 1861	3 yrs.	Appointed Nov. 2, 1861; died June 21, 1862, at Iuka, Miss.
James M. Hipkins.......	... do ...	29	Sept. 4, 1861	3 yrs.	Promoted from 1st Sergeant Feb. 1, 1863; transferred to Co. B April 24, 1863.
Samuel C. Currie........	... do ...	20	Sept. 4, 1861	3 yrs.	Promoted from 1st Sergeant Co. A Nov. 24, 1863; transferred to Co. A Aug. 1, 1864.
George A. Clark........	... do ...	31	Sept. 8, 1861	3 yrs.	Promoted from 1st Sergeant Co. M July 13, 1864; to 1st Lieutenant Co. H Nov. 30, 1864; veteran.
Thomas A. O'Rourke..	... do ...	24	Sept. 8, 1861	3 yrs.	Promoted from 1st Sergeant Co. M Nov. 30, 1864; to 1st Lieutenant Co. D Jan. 6, 1865; veteran.
John Dusing	... do ...	21	Sept. 4, 1861	3 yrs.	Mustered as private; appointed 1st Sergeant Sept. 4, 1864; promoted to 2d Lieutenant Nov. 30, 1864; to 1st Lieutenant Feb. 23, 1865, but not mustered; mustered out with company Aug. 4, 1865; veteran.
Philander B. Lewis....	1st Serg.	26	Dec. 28, 1861	3 yrs.	Mustered as private; appointed May 1, 1863; promoted to 2d Lieutenant Co. F Nov. 24, 1863.
Robert G. Clark	... do ...	26	Dec. 29, 1863	3 yrs.	Mustered as private; appointed April 7, 1865; mustered out with company Aug. 4, 1865.
Roswell Perry	Q. M. S.	42	Oct. 3, 1861	3 yrs.	Discharged Feb. 23, 1864, on Surgeon's certificate of disability.
Charles M. Bennett......	... do ...	23	Sept. 12, 1861	3 yrs.	Mustered as private; appointed Com. Sergeant ——; Q. M. Sergeant Dec. 11, 1864; mustered out with company Aug. 4, 1865; veteran.
John F. Russell	Com Ser.	29	Aug. 30, 1862	3 yrs.	Mustered as private; appointed Dec. 2, 1864; mustered out June 24, 1865, at Columbus, O., by order of War Department.
Sheldon A. Shepherd...	... do ...	18	Oct. 2, 1861	3 yrs.	Captured Nov. 13, 1862, in action at Silver Springs, Tenn.; paroled ——; mustered as private; appointed Sergeant ——; Com. Sergeant June 24, 1865; mustered out with company Aug. 4, 1865; veteran.
George W. Boggs.......	Sergeant	23	Sept. 4, 1861	3 yrs.	Promoted to 2d Lieutenant Co. G, 10th Regiment, O. V. C., Oct. 7, 1862.
Norman Brewster	... do ...	41	Sept. 4, 1861	3 yrs.	Promoted to 2d Lieutenant Co. B May 20, 1862.

Names	Rank	Age	Date of Entering the Service	Period of Service	Remarks
Richard F. Blinn......	Sergeant	21	Sept. 5, 1861	3 yrs.	Discharged Jan. 9, 1863, on Surgeon's certificate of disability.
Benjamin F. Kirtz.....	... do ...	25	Sept. 22, 1861	3 yrs.	Also borne on rolls as "Frank Kurtz;" appointed from Corporal ——; mustered out Oct. 3, 1864, at Columbia, Tenn., on expiration of term of service.
John Muir	... do ...	35	Sept. 4, 1861	3 yrs.	Appointed from Corporal ——; mustered out Oct. 3, 1864, at Columbia, Tenn., on expiration of term of service.
Levi Refsnider	... do ...	21	Sept. 5, 1861	3 yrs.	Captured Oct. 4, 1862, at battle of Bardstown, Ky.; paroled ——; appointed from Corporal ——; mustered out Oct. 3, 1864, at Columbia, Tenn., on expiration of term of service.
De Wilton Wood	... do ...	19	Aug. 23, 1862	3 yrs.	Mustered as private; appointed ——; mustered out June 24, 1865, at Columbus, O., by order of War Department.
John G. Miller..........	... do ...	21	Nov. 26, 1861	3 yrs.	Mustered as private; appointed June 24, 1865; mustered out with company Aug. 4, 1865; veteran.
Conrad Guth	... do ...	24	Nov. 11, 1861	3 yrs.	Mustered as private; appointed June 24, 1865; mustered out with company Aug. 4, 1865; veteran.
John A. Baldwin........	... do ...	29	Aug. 13, 1861	3 yrs.	Transferred from Co. O Jan. 1, 1862; appointed Corporal ——; Sergeant June 24, 1865; mustered out with company Aug. 4, 1865; veteran.
Henry W. Adams........	... do ...	21	Feb. 24, 1864	3 yrs.	Appointed Corporal ——; Sergeant June 24, 1865; mustered out with company Aug. 4, 1865.
John T. Sivalls.........	... do ...	25	Dec. 30, 1863	3 yrs.	Appointed from private June 24, 1865; mustered out with company Aug. 4, 1865.
Henry Cross	Corporal	27	Sept. 4, 1861	3 yrs.	Died June 25, 1862, at Tuscumbia, Ala.
Charles Benton	... do ...	38	Sept. 7, 1861	3 yrs.	Captured Oct. 4, 1862, at battle of Bardstown, Ky.; paroled ——; discharged to date Oct. 5, 1862, by order of War Department.
David L. Tremain	... do ...	21	Sept. 5, 1861	3 yrs.	Captured Oct. 4, 1862, at battle of Bardstown, Ky.; paroled ——; mustered out Oct. 3, 1864, at Columbia, Tenn., on expiration of term of service.
Michael Hughes	... do ...	25	Sept. 6, 1861	3 yrs.	Transferred from Co. A Nov. 13, 1861; appointed ——; discharged Aug. 27, 1862, on Surgeon's certificate of disability.
William Huling	... do ...	24	Sept. 27, 1861	3 yrs.	Appointed ——; mustered out Oct. 3, 1864, at Columbia, Tenn., on expiration of term of service.
Gustavus Helbing	... do ...	19	Aug. 4, 1862	3 yrs.	Appointed ——; mustered out June 26, 1865, at Columbus, O., by order of War Department.
Frank A. Shaw..........	... do ...	24	Aug. 26, 1862	3 yrs.	Appointed ——; mustered out June 26, 1865, at Columbus, O., by order of War Department.
Freeman Bellville	... do ...	19	Sept. 17, 1863	3 yrs.	Appointed ——; died May 13, 1864, at Chattanooga, Tenn.
Walter W. Brim........	... do ...	19	Aug. 24, 1863	3 yrs.	Appointed ——; mustered out with company Aug. 4, 1865.
James Boggs	... do ...	24	Dec. 24, 1863	3 yrs.	Appointed ——; mustered out with company Aug. 4, 1865.
William C. Church.......	... do ...	29	Oct. 6, 1863	3 yrs.	Appointed ——; mustered out with company Aug. 4, 1865.
George W. Russell.......	... do ...	36	Dec. 30, 1863	3 yrs.	Appointed June 24, 1865; mustered out with company Aug. 4, 1865.
Doctor Van Howtan......	... do ...	19	Aug. 17, 1863	3 yrs.	Appointed June 24, 1865; mustered out with company Aug. 4, 1865.
Sardis M. Harnes.......	... do ...	20	Dec. 30, 1863	3 yrs.	Appointed June 24, 1865; mustered out with company Aug. 4, 1865.
Andrew Seifielt	... do ...	21	Dec. 13, 1863	3 yrs.	Appointed June 24, 1865; mustered out with company Aug. 4, 1865.
Henry L. Clifford......	... do ...	26	Dec. 30, 1863	3 yrs.	Appointed June 24, 1865; mustered out with company Aug. 4, 1865.
Andrew Nigh	Bugler	43	Oct. 13, 1861	3 yrs.	Discharged Aug. 1, 1862, on Surgeon's certificate of disability.
William Basown	Farrier	26	Sept. 5, 1861	3 yrs.	Died April 16, 1864, at Nashville, Tenn.
Samuel Saltzgaber	... do ...	37	Aug. 28, 1861	3 yrs.	Mustered out Oct. 3, 1864, at Columbia, Tenn., on expiration of term of service.
Frank A. Reidy..........	... do ...	19	Aug. 12, 1862	3 yrs.	Appointed ——; mustered out June 24, 1865, at Columbus, O., by order of War Department.
Sylvester Stump	... do ...	24	Sept. 29, 1863	3 yrs.	Appointed ——; died March 24, 1865, at Russellville, Ala., from injuries received by a falling tree.
George Greinor	... do ...	37	Feb. 23, 1864	3 yrs.	Appointed March 26, 1865; mustered out with company Aug. 4, 1865.
Michael Amend	Saddler	35	Nov. 19, 1861	3 yrs.	Discharged to date May 16, 1862, on Surgeon's certificate of disability.
Corydon P. Bartram..	Wagoner	34	Sept. 23, 1861	3 yrs.	Appointed ——; discharged July 8, 1865, on Surgeon's certificate of disability; veteran.

Names	Rank	Age	Date of Entering the Service	Period of Service	Remarks
Aldrich, Benjamin	Private	19	Jan. 7, 1862	3 yrs.	Captured Nov. 13, 1862, in action at Silver Spring, Tenn.; paroled —; mustered out Jan. 7, 1865, at Nashville, Tenn., on expiration of term of service.
Alexander, Theodore ..	do ...	18	Aug. 24, 1863	3 yrs.	Mustered out with company Aug. 4, 1865.
Arquette, Gilbert	do ...	36	Sept. 6, 1863	3 yrs.	Died Dec. 25, 1862, at Nashville, Tenn.
Bard, William H.......	do ...	19	Sept. 16, 1861	3 yrs.	Died Nov. 19, 1862.
Benedict, George W....	do ...	20	Dec. 30, 1863	3 yrs.	Mustered out Aug. 1, 1865, from hospital at Camp Dennison, O., by order of War Department.
Biddle, Sidney	do ...	24	Sept. 4, 1861	3 yrs.	Mustered out Oct. 3, 1864, at Columbia, Tenn., on expiration of term of service.
Bixby, Ashley	do ...	20	Sept. 27, 1861	3 yrs.	Died Jan. 19, 1863, at Nashville, Tenn.
Bradshaw, James W..	do ...	19	Dec. 24, 1861	3 yrs.	Also borne on rolls as "Bradshall;" mustered out with company Aug. 4, 1865.
Brown, Jacob W.......	do ...	46	Nov. 27, 1861	3 yrs.	Discharged, date not known; no further record found.
Burkhalter, William ..	do ...	45	Oct. 13, 1861	3 yrs.	Died July 18, 1862, at Nashville, Tenn.
Camfield, William	do ...	22	Aug. 25, 1861	3 yrs.	Mustered out with company Aug. 4, 1865.
Carpenter, John	do ...	22	Sept. 4, 1861	3 yrs.	Transferred from Co. A Jan. 1, 1862.
Clock, George H.......	do ...	31	Feb. 24, 1865	1 yr.	Mustered out with company Aug. 4, 1865.
Cole, William	do ...	36	Sept. 6, 1861	3 yrs.	Discharged Feb. 18, 1863, at Gallatin, Tenn., on Surgeon's certificate of disability.
Collins, David	do ...	23	Aug. 14, 1863	3 yrs.	
Collins, Oscar	do ...	27	Nov. 22, 1861	3 yrs.	Discharged Aug. 27, 1862, on Surgeon's certificate of disability.
Cook, Henry L.........	do ...	18	Dec. 26, 1863	3 yrs.	Mustered out with company Aug. 4, 1865.
Cooper, Henry	do ...	27	Mch. 19, 1864	3 yrs.	Mustered out with company Aug. 4, 1865.
Cone, Lester S........	do ...	19	Dec. 26, 1863	3 yrs.	Mustered out to date Aug. 4, 1865, at Columbus, O., by order of War Department.
Cox, Thomas J........	do ...	18	Sept. 25, 1863	3 yrs.	Mustered out with company Aug. 4, 1865.
Cutler, Joseph B.......	do ...	28	Aug. 28, 1862	3 yrs.	Also borne on rolls as "Cotton;" transferred to Co. B, 7th Regiment, Veteran Reserve Corps, Sept. 1, 1863; mustered out from same June 29, 1865, at Washington, D. C., by order of War Department.
Darcy, Henry	do ...	28	Nov. 20, 1861	3 yrs.	
Day, Amos	do ...	18	Dec. 23, 1863	3 yrs.	Mustered out with company Aug. 4, 1865.
Deverna, Edward	do ...	32	Sept. 24, 1863	3 yrs.	Mustered out with company Aug. 4, 1865.
Dewit, Richard	do ...	41	Nov. 6, 1861	3 yrs.	
Dixey, Theodore	do ...	26	Dec. 24, 1863	3 yrs.	Mustered out with company Aug. 4, 1865.
Easterly, Ezra	do ...	18	Dec. 23, 1863	3 yrs.	Mustered out with company Aug. 4, 1865.
Eddleman, Jacob	do ...	18	Sept. 24, 1863	3 yrs.	Mustered out with company Aug. 4, 1865.
Ely, Sebastian	do ...	18	Sept. 10, 1861	3 yrs.	Discharged, date not known; no further record found.
Eoff, James	do ...	18	Dec. 19, 1863	3 yrs.	Died Aug. 24, 1864, of wounds received about July 5, 1864, in battle of Vining Station, Ga.
Erne, Gottfried	do ...	27	Oct. 11, 1862	3 yrs.	Transferred from Co. H, 10th Regiment, O. V. C., —; returned to same —.
Evans, John D.........	do ...	35	Aug. 20, 1862	3 yrs.	
Farran, Alphens	do ...	41	Nov. 12, 1861	3 yrs.	Discharged May 19, 1864, on Surgeon's certificate of disability.
Finkbeiner, Christopher	do ...	19	July 18, 1863	3 yrs.	Discharged March 16, 1865, at St. Louis, Mo., on account of wounds received in action.
Folk, John	do ...	17	Oct. 6, 1861	3 yrs.	Transferred to Co. K —.
Forbes, David W.......	do ...	29	Nov. 22, 1861	3 yrs.	Mustered out Dec. 27, 1864, at Nashville, Tenn., on expiration of term of service.
Freeman, John E.......	do ...	32	Oct. 14, 1861	3 yrs.	Mustered out with company Aug. 4, 1865.
Frymire, Henry	do ...	18	Jan. 14, 1864	3 yrs.	Mustered out with company Aug. 4, 1865; veteran.
Fuller, Jacob E.......	do ...	25	Sept. 4, 1861	3 yrs.	Mustered out with company Aug. 4, 1865.
Fuller, James W.......	do ...	29	Mch. 26, 1864	3 yrs.	Mustered out with company Aug. 4, 1865.
Gathergood, William S	do ...	18	Feb. 18, 1864	3 yrs.	Mustered out with company Aug. 4, 1865.
Goodman, George W..	do ...	18	Aug. 14, 1863	3 yrs.	Captured Oct. 23, 1863, in action at Lookout Mountain, Tenn.; reported at Camp Chase May 3, 1865; mustered out July 11, 1865, at Camp Chase, O., by order of War Department.
Green, Charles	do ...	18	Dec. 30, 1863	3 yrs.	
Griffith, John	do ...	29	Oct. 14, 1861	3 yrs.	Died May 4, 1862, in Fourth Street Hospital, Cincinnati, O.
Groundwater, Lane	do ...	23	Mch. 28, 1864	3 yrs.	Mustered out with company Aug. 4, 1865.
Guth, Jacob	do ...	26	Nov. 11, 1861	3 yrs.	Mustered out May 2, 1865, at Columbus, O., by order of War Department.
Gwinn, Ezra	do ...	26	Nov. 26, 1861	3 yrs.	
Gwinn, William T.....	do ...	48	Nov. 28, 1861	3 yrs.	Discharged Dec. 5, 1862, at Cincinnati, O., on Surgeon's certificate of disability.
Hains, Joseph	do ...	18	Oct. 10, 1861	3 yrs.	Discharged Dec. 4, 1862, on Surgeon's certificate of disability.
Hamlin, Joseph	do ...	25	July 4, 1862	3 yrs.	Mustered out July 13, 1865, at Columbus, O., on expiration of term of service.
Hans, John	do ...	45	Nov. 12, 1861	3 yrs.	Transferred to Invalid Corps Sept. 10, 1863.
Harnes, Ira	do ...	18	Aug. 24, 1863	3 yrs.	Also borne on rolls as "Ira S. Harris;" mustered out with company Aug. 4, 1865.

Names	Rank	Age	Date of Entering the Service	Period of Service	Remarks
Hatcher, David	Private	18	Sept. 25, 1863	3 yrs.	Mustered out with company Aug. 4, 1865.
Hayes, Thomas	... do ...	19	Jan. 4, 1864	3 yrs.	Mustered out with company Aug. 4, 1865.
Heath, Alonzo	... do ...	18	Dec. 29, 1863	3 yrs.	Mustered out with company Aug. 4, 1865.
Hendricks, Henry	... do ...	24	Sept. 22, 1861	3 yrs.	Mustered out Dec. 27, 1864, at Nashville, Tenn., on expiration of term of service.
Hexterdine, John	... do ...	19	Nov. 22, 1861	3 yrs.	Transferred to Invalid Corps Sept. 10, 1863.
Hinman, Samuel	... do ...	36	Aug. 30, 1862	3 yrs.	Discharged Jan. 5, 1863, on Surgeon's certificate of disability.
Hopkins, Christian R.	... do ...	23	Sept. 4, 1861	3 yrs.	Promoted to Batt. Com. Sergeant Nov. 1, 1861.
Hull, Bridwell R........	... do ...	18	Nov. 6, 1861	3 yrs.	Mustered out Dec. 27, 1864, at Nashville, Tenn., on expiration of term of service.
Hurlburt, Edward I....	... do ...	....	Jan. 1, 1862	3 yrs.	
Hutton, John H........	... do ...	45	Oct. 15, 1863	3 yrs.	Mustered out June 2, 1865, from hospital at Camp Dennison, O., by order of War Department.
Jacobs, William	... do ...	29	Nov. 25, 1861	3 yrs.	Died April 30, 1862, at Savannah, Tenn.
Johnson, Ezra	... do ...	36	Aug. 24, 1862	3 yrs.	Mustered out June 24, 1865, at Columbus, O., by order of War Department.
Kahl, Casper	do ...	25	Nov. 27, 1861	3 yrs.	Mustered out Dec. 27, 1864, at Nashville, Tenn., on expiration of term of service.
Kenoc, Adam	... do ...	38	Aug. 25, 1862	3 yrs.	Died Feb. 19, 1863.
Kimball, Benjamin ...	... do ...	24	Sept. 5, 1864	1 yr.	Also borne on rolls as "Perry Kimball;" mustered out June 26, 1865, at Columbus, O., by order of War Department.
Knull, Ira	... do ...	17	July 23, 1863	3 yrs.	Mustered out with company Aug. 4, 1865.
Lafayette, Louis	... do ...	18	Oct. 3, 1861	3 yrs.	Mustered out with company Aug. 4, 1865.
Little, Aaron W........	... do ...	33	Nov. 12, 1861	3 yrs.	Wounded Dec. 31, 1862, in battle of Stone River, Tenn.; transferred to 105th Co., 2d Battalion, Veteran Reserve Corps, ——; mustered out Jan. 4, 1865, by order of War Department.
Long, Harvey	... do ...	29	Aug. 23, 1862	3 yrs.	Mustered out June 24, 1865, at Columbus, O., by order of War Department.
Long, William M.......	... do ...	25	Aug. 23, 1862	3 yrs.	Also borne on rolls as "Manoah Long;" mustered out June 24, 1865, at Columbus, O., by order of War Department.
Luckey, William	... do ...	18	Aug. 23, 1862	3 yrs.	Mustered out June 24, 1865, at Columbus, O., by order of War Department.
McDowell, John	... do ...	22	Sept. 27, 1861	3 yrs.	Mustered out Oct. 3, 1864, at Columbia, Tenn., on expiration of term of service.
McGowen, Charles	... do ...	25	Dec. 23, 1863	3 yrs.	Mustered out with company Aug. 4, 1865.
McGinnis, James	... do ...	22	Aug. 31, 1862	3 yrs.	Died Feb. 7, 1863, at Lebanon, Tenn.
McNuen, John	... do ...	38	Sept. 5, 1861	3 yrs.	Captured Oct. 4, 1862, at battle of Bardstown, Ky.; paroled ——; died May 9, 1863.
Martin, David F.......	... do ...	23	Oct. 13, 1861	3 yrs.	Died Aug. 5, 1864, in Andersonville Prison, Ga.
Merrill, James H.......	... do ...	18	Sept. 5, 1861	3 yrs.	Mustered out Oct. 3, 1864, at Columbia, Tenn., on expiration of term of service.
Miller, John	... do ...	32	Nov. 15, 1861	3 yrs.	Died April 20, 1862, at Savannah, Tenn.
Moore, Charles W......	... do ...	41	Nov. 12, 1861	3 yrs.	Discharged Dec. 16, 1862, on Surgeon's certificate of disability.
Morse, Lewis	... do ...	27	Aug. 30, 1862	3 yrs.	Died April 15, 1863.
Myers, Charles A.......	... do ...	20	Feb. 24, 1865	1 yr.	Mustered out with company Aug. 4, 1865.
Myers, Simeon	... do ...	35	Nov. 20, 1861	3 yrs.	Returned to Co. D. 67th Regiment, O. V. I., Dec. 18, 1861, where he had previously enlisted.
Nachtrieb, John	... do ...	18	Feb. 24, 1865	1 yr.	Mustered out with company Aug. 4, 1865.
Nemyer, Frederick	... do ...	28	Sept. 4, 1861	3 yrs.	Mustered out with company Aug. 4, 1865; veteran.
Netcher, Peter	... do ...	24	Sept. 5, 1864	1 yr.	Mustered out June 26, 1865, at Columbus, O., by order of War Department.
Nigh, Edwin A..........	... do ...	18	Oct. 13, 1861	3 yrs.	Mustered out Oct. 31, 1864, on expiration of term of service.
Olds, Chancey	... do ...	20	Sept. 4, 1861	3 yrs.	Died Nov. 9, 1862.
Olds, Henry	... do ...	42	Sept. 6, 1861	3 yrs.	Discharged May 18, 1862, on Surgeon's certificate of disability.
Partlon, Israel	... do ...	19	Dec. 18, 1863	3 yrs.	Died March 27, 1864.
Peirce, Guy D...........	... do ...	32	Sept. 4, 1861	3 yrs.	Mustered out Oct. 3, 1864, at Columbia, Tenn., on expiration of term of service.
Peterson, Claus	... do ...	....	Aug. 26, 1862	3 yrs.	Died Oct. 30, 1862, at Columbia, Ky.
Plum, Linnaeus T......	... do ...	23	Aug. 30, 1862	3 yrs.	Died May 7, 1864, in hospital at Columbia, Tenn.
Price, Charles	... do ...	20	July 4, 1863	3 yrs.	Mustered out with company Aug. 4, 1865.
Price, John B...........	... do ...	19	Sept. 4, 1861	3 yrs.	Discharged Sept. 19, 1862, on Surgeon's certificate of disability.
Rearick, William F.....	... do ...	19	Sept. 9, 1861	3 yrs.	Captured Nov. 25, 1863, near Cleveland, Tenn.; paroled Feb. 24, 1865; no further record found.
Rice, Ephraim	... do ...	26	Aug. 23, 1862	3 yrs.	Mustered out June 24, 1865, at Columbus, O., by order of War Department.
Robinson, Charles H..	... do ...	21	Sept. 4, 1861	3 yrs.	Mustered out Oct. 3, 1864, at Columbia, Tenn., on expiration of term of service.

Names	Rank	Age	Date of Entering the Service	Period of Service	Remarks
Rush, Jacob	Private	17	Nov. 4, 1861	3 yrs.	Prisoner of war; mustered out May 18, 1865, at Columbus, O., on expiration of term of service.
Scott, George B...........	do ...	26	Dec. 21, 1863	3 yrs.	Mustered out with company Aug. 4, 1865.
Scott, William	do ...	21	Nov. 4, 1861	3 yrs.	Died July 31, 1863, in Confederate Prison hospital at Macon, Ga.
Sconton, Charles J.......	do ...	18	Dec. 26, 1863	3 yrs.	Mustered out with company Aug. 4, 1865.
Sipley, Jacob	do ...	21	Nov. 4, 1861	3 yrs.	Died May 15, 1862, at Camp Dennison, O.
Smith, David	do ...	22	Sept. 4, 1861	3 yrs.	Captured Oct. 4, 1862, at battle of Bardstown, Ky.; paroled ——; mustered out with company Aug. 4, 1865; veteran.
Smith, Henry S...........	do ...	24	Oct. 23, 1861	3 yrs.	Discharged May 18, 1862, on Surgeon's certificate of disability.
Smith, Joshua V.......	do ...	43	July 22, 1863	3 yrs.	Mustered out with company Aug. 4, 1865.
Smith, William	do ...	18	Aug. 24, 1862	3 yrs.	Mustered out June 24, 1865, at Columbus, O., by order of War Department.
Snider, Jacob	do ...	45	Nov. 6, 1861	3 yrs.	Transferred to Co. C Jan. 1, 1862.
Stewart, Henry	do ...	....	Jan. 1, 1862	3 yrs.	Discharged July 17, 1864, on Surgeon's certificate of disability.
Sweet, James M...........	do ...	21	Sept. 4, 1861	3 yrs.	Mustered out Oct. 3, 1864, at Columbia, Tenn., on expiration of term of service.
Tappin, William	do ...	19	Sept. 3, 1861	3 yrs.	Transferred from Co. F Jan. 1, 1862.
Taylor, James	do ...	26	Jan. 26, 1864	3 yrs.	Mustered out with company Aug. 4, 1865.
Thatcher, Wilbur F....	do ...	18	July 11, 1863	3 yrs.	Mustered out with company Aug. 4, 1865.
Thatcher, William E....	do ...	18	Dec. 6, 1861	3 yrs.	Captured Nov. 13, 1862, in action at Silver Spring, Tenn.; paroled ——; appointed Sergeant ——; reduced May 11, 1865; mustered out with company Aug. 4, 1865; veteran.
Trask, Mitchell G........	do ...	25	Sept. 4, 1861	3 yrs.	Killed May 10, 1864, near Columbia, Tenn.
Wallace, James W.......	do ...	18	Sept. 18, 1861	3 yrs.	Mustered out with company Aug. 4, 1865; veteran.
Westcott, Charles A.....	do ...	18	Dec. 26, 1861	3 yrs.	Mustered out with company Aug. 4, 1865.
Wheeler, George C.......	do ...	....	Feb. 28, 1862	3 yrs.	Mustered out Feb. 28, 1865, on expiration of term of service.
Willoughby, John W..	do ...	22	Aug. 29, 1861	3 yrs.	Transferred from Co. A Nov. 14, 1861; captured Oct. 4, 1862, at battle of Bardstown, Ky.; paroled ——; discharged Dec. 19, 1862, to enlist in Co. C, 3d Battalion, 18th Regiment, U. S. Infantry.
Wilson, Moses	do ...	35	Dec. 24, 1863	3 yrs.	Mustered out with company Aug. 4, 1865.
Wilson, Welles	do ...	27	Sept. 19, 1861	3 yrs.	Died July 4, 1862, at Tuscumbia, Ala.
Wisner, George M.......	do ...	22	Sept. 27, 1861	3 yrs.	Died July 2, 1863.
Wolf, Henry J...........	do ...	25	Sept. 4, 1861	3 yrs.	Discharged Oct. 27, 1861.
Woodford, John T....	do ...	21	Sept. 4, 1861	3 yrs.	Transferred from Co. A Nov. 13, 1861; appointed Sergeant Nov. 13, 1861; captured Oct. 4, 1862, at battle of Bardstown, Ky.; paroled ——; reduced from Sergeant Sept. 17, 1864; returned to Co. A Sept. 18, 1864.
Zorn, Louis G...........	do ...	22	Feb. 28, 1865	1 yr.	Mustered out with company Aug. 4, 1865.
James, Henry	Cook	....	April 25, 1865	3 yrs.	Colored under-cook; mustered out with company Aug. 4, 1865.
Milton, Richard	do ...	....	April 25, 1865	3 yrs.	Colored under-cook; mustered out with company Aug. 4, 1865.
Russell, Monroe	do ...	....	April 25, 1865	3 yrs.	Colored under-cook; mustered out with company Aug. 4, 1865.
Webb, Terrill	do ...	....	April 25, 1865	3 yrs.	Colored under-cook; sent to hospital at Macon, Ga., July 18, 1865; no further record found.

COMPANY M.

Mustered in December 11, 1861, at Camp Worcester, O., by James P. W. Neill, 1st Lieutenant 18th Infantry, U. S. A., Mustering Officer. Mustered out August 4, 1865, at Nashville, Tenn., by James P. W. Neill, Captain 18th Infantry, U. S. A., Acting Commissary of Musters, Cavalry Corps, M. D. T.

Names	Rank	Age	Date of Entering the Service	Period of Service	Remarks
John W. Marvin........	Captain	....	Sept. 8, 1861	3 yrs.	Appointed Sept. 8, 1861.
Henry C. Miner........	do ...	25	Sept. 8, 1861	3 yrs.	Appointed 1st Lieutenant Sept. 8, 1861; promoted to Captain Jan. 21, 1863; mustered out Nov. 22, 1864, at Louisville, Ky., on expiration of term of service.
Philander B. Lewis....	do ...	28	Dec. 28, 1861	3 yrs.	Transferred from Co. F Feb. 10, 1865; resigned July 1, 1865.
James W. Likens......	1st Lieu.	36	Sept. 8, 1861	3 yrs.	Appointed 2d Lieutenant Sept. 8, 1861; promoted to 1st Lieutenant Jan. 21, 1863; resigned May 16, 1864.

Names	Rank	Age	Date of Entering the Service	Period of Service	Remarks
George B. Watson.....	1st Lieu.	27	Oct. 2, 1861	3 yrs.	Promoted from 2d Lieutenant Co. I March 31, 1864; mustered out Nov. 24, 1864, at Louisville, Ky., on expiration of term of service.
Daniel C. Lewis..........	... do ...	36	Sept. 26, 1861	3 yrs.	Promoted from 1st Sergeant Co. I Nov. 30, 1864; captured April 2, 1865, at battle of Selma, Ala.; paroled ——; promoted to Captain, but died before receiving commission; perished by explosion of steamer Sultana on Mississippi River, near Memphis, Tenn., April 27, 1865; veteran.
Ervin R. Harris.......	2d Lieu.	17	Sept. 7, 1861	3 yrs.	Promoted from private Co. E Jan. 21, 1863; to 1st Lieutenant Co. K May 9, 1864.
Thomas Marlin	... do ...	40	Oct. 28, 1861	3 yrs.	Promoted from Q. M. Sergeant Co. K Nov. 30, 1864; to 1st Lieutenant Co. B Jan. 6, 1865; veteran.
William S. Burbay....	1st Serg.	32	Sept. 8, 1861	3 yrs.	Appointed Oct. 8, 1861; promoted to 2d Lieutenant Jan. 2, 1863, but not mustered; discharged Jan. 23, 1863, at Camp Stanley, Tenn., on Surgeon's certificate of disability.
George A. Clark	... do ...	31	Sept. 8, 1861	3 yrs.	Appointed Sergeant Oct. 8, 1861; 1st Sergeant ——; promoted to 2d Lieutenant Co. L July 13, 1864; veteran.
Thomas A. O'Rourke..	... do ...	24	Sept. 8, 1861	3 yrs.	Appointed Q. M. Sergeant Oct. 8, 1861; 1st Sergeant Aug. 11, 1864; promoted to 2d Lieutenant Co. L Nov. 30, 1864; veteran.
John S. Chapin..........	... do ...	22	Sept. 8, 1861	3 yrs.	Appointed Sergeant Oct. 8, 1861; Q. M. Sergeant ——; 1st Sergeant Dec. 2, 1864; mustered out with company Aug. 4, 1865; veteran.
William H. Smith.....	Q. M. S.	24	Sept. 8, 1861	3 yrs.	Appointed Corporal Oct. 8, 1861; Com. Sergeant ——; Q. M. Sergeant Dec. 2, 1864; mustered out with company Aug. 4, 1865; veteran.
Owen Gray	Com Ser.	36	Sept. 8, 1861	3 yrs.	Appointed Wagoner Oct. 8, 1861; Sergeant ——; Com. Sergeant Dec. 2, 1864; mustered out with company Aug. 4, 1865; veteran.
John H. Fisher........	Sergeant	20	Sept. 8, 1861	3 yrs.	Appointed Oct. 8, 1861; mustered out Oct. 13, 1864, at Franklin, Tenn., on expiration of term of service.
Henry D. Smith..........	... do ...	29	Sept. 8, 1861	3 yrs.	Appointed Oct. 8, 1861; discharged Aug. 12, 1862, on Surgeon's certificate of disability.
Arthur Black	... do ...	21	Sept. 8, 1861	3 yrs.	Mustered as private; appointed ——; killed Aug. 20, 1864, in battle of Jonesboro, Ga.
Marion Eldred	... do ...	32	Sept. 8, 1861	3 yrs.	Appointed Corporal Oct. 8, 1861; Sergeant ——; mustered out Oct. 13, 1864, at Franklin, Tenn., on expiration of term of service.
Robert Mears	... do ...	23	Sept. 8, 1861	3 yrs.	Appointed Corporal Oct. 8, 1861; Sergeant ——; mustered out Oct. 13, 1864, at Franklin, Tenn., on expiration of term of service.
John A. Brown..........	... do ...	26	Aug. 19, 1862	3 yrs.	Mustered as private; appointed ——; mustered out June 17, 1865, at Nashville, Tenn., by order of War Department.
John M. Ropp...........	... do ...	25	Aug. 19, 1862	3 yrs.	Mustered as private; appointed ——; mustered out June 17, 1865, at Nashville, Tenn., by order of War Department.
Lewis R. Miller..........	... do ...	21	Sept. 8, 1861	3 yrs.	Appointed Corporal Oct. 8, 1861; Sergeant ——; on detached duty at Columbus, O., since June 23, 1863; mustered out Aug. 10, 1865, at Columbus, O., by order of War Department; veteran.
William Young	... do ...	18	Sept. 8, 1861	3 yrs.	Appointed Corporal ——; Sergeant Dec. 2, 1864; mustered out with company Aug. 4, 1865; veteran.
John B. Velie..........	... do ...	41	Oct. 2, 1861	3 yrs.	Appointed Corporal ——; Sergeant Dec. 2, 1864; mustered out with company Aug. 4, 1865; veteran.
William Kneule	... do ...	31	Jan. 2, 1864	3 yrs.	Appointed Corporal ——; Sergeant July 1, 1864; mustered out with company Aug. 4, 1865.
James Dodge	... do ...	18	July 14, 1863	3 yrs.	Appointed Corporal ——; Sergeant July 1, 1865; mustered out with company Aug. 4, 1865.
Findley M. Smith......	Corporal	24	Sept. 8, 1861	3 yrs.	Appointed Nov. 28, 1861; discharged July 2, 1862, on Surgeon's certificate of disability.
Melville R. Benson.......	... do ...	22	Sept. 8, 1861	3 yrs.	Appointed Nov. 28, 1861; missing Dec. 31, 1862, in battle of Stone River, Tenn.; no further record found.
David Taylor	... do ...	29	Sept. 8, 1861	3 yrs.	Appointed Nov. 28, 1861; died May 21, 1862, on Hamburg and Corinth road.
Julius Straw	... do ...	27	Nov. 9, 1861	3 yrs.	Appointed Nov. 28, 1861; captured Sept. 20, 1863, at battle of Chickamauga, Ga.; paroled May 8, 1864; mustered out Nov. 21, 1864, at Columbus, O., on expiration of term of service.

Names	Rank	Age	Date of Entering the Service	Period of Service	Remarks
James K. P. Harris...	Corporal	18	Sept. 8, 1861	3 yrs.	Appointed Feb. —, 1863; mustered out Oct. 13, 1864, at Franklin, Tenn., on expiration of term of service.
Daniel Clinger	... do ...	23	Nov. 30, 1861	3 yrs.	Appointed ——; mustered out Dec. 30, 1864, at Nashville, Tenn., on expiration of term of service.
John E. Mahaffey........	... do ...	21	Sept. 8, 1861	3 yrs.	Appointed ——; mustered out Oct. 13, 1864, at Franklin, Tenn., on expiration of term of service.
Solomon Barcus	... do ...	28	Aug. 19, 1862	3 yrs.	Appointed ——; mustered out June 17, 1865, at Nashville, Tenn., by order of War Department.
Jacob Halderman	... do ...	27	Jan. 25, 1864	3 yrs.	Appointed Dec. 2, 1864; mustered out with company Aug. 4, 1865.
Edward A. Chapin........	... do ...	19	Jan. 4, 1864	3 yrs.	Appointed Dec. 2, 1864; mustered out with company Aug. 4, 1865.
Milton P. Martin........	... do ...	19	Jan. 15, 1864	3 yrs.	Appointed Dec. 2, 1864; mustered out with company Aug. 4, 1865.
Rufus Aurand	... do ...	26	Feb. 24, 1864	3 yrs.	Appointed Dec. 2, 1864; mustered out with company Aug. 4, 1865.
Charles Riley	... do ...	19	Oct. 7, 1863	3 yrs.	Appointed Dec. 2, 1864; mustered out with company Aug. 4, 1865.
Frederick Reidle	... do ...	18	Nov. 24, 1861	3 yrs.	Appointed July 1, 1865; mustered out with company Aug. 4, 1865.
William B. Marshall...	... do ...	38	Feb. 20, 1864	3 yrs.	Appointed July 1, 1865; mustered out with company Aug. 4, 1865.
William Hoy	... do ...	30	Dec. 23, 1863	3 yrs.	Appointed July 1, 1865; mustered out with company Aug. 4, 1865.
Hiram Martin	Bugler	30	Sept. 8, 1861	3 yrs.	Appointed ——; discharged July 18, 1865, at Columbus, O., on Surgeon's certificate of disability; veteran.
Jacob Trott	... do ...	22	Nov. 11, 1861	3 yrs.	Transferred from Co. K Jan. 1, 1862; appointed ——; mustered out Dec. 30, 1864, at Nashville, Tenn., on expiration of term of service.
Mathew Harrah	Farrier	23	Nov. 9, 1861	3 yrs.	Mustered out Nov. 25, 1864, at Louisville, Ky., on expiration of term of service.
Andrew Maxwell	... do ...	41	Nov. 18, 1861	3 yrs.	
Joseph Adams	... do ...	39	Sept. 8, 1861	3 yrs.	Appointed ——; mustered out with company Aug. 4, 1865; veteran.
David Dale	... do ...	36	Jan. 15, 1864	3 yrs.	Appointed ——; mustered out with company Aug. 4, 1865.
Benjamin Kerstetter ..	Saddler	42	Sept. 8, 1861	3 yrs.	Captured April 2, 1865, at battle of Selma, Ala.; paroled ——; perished by explosion of steamer Sultana on Mississippi River near Memphis, Tenn., April 27, 1865; veteran.
Edward O. Morgan...	Wagoner	22	Sept. 8, 1861	3 yrs.	Appointed ——; mustered out July 14, 1865, from hospital at Camp Dennison, O., by order of War Department; veteran.
Adams, John	Private	18	Nov. 8, 1861	3 yrs.	Transferred to Co. K, 11th Regiment, Veteran Reserve Corps, ——; died June 18, 1864.
Adams, Martin	... do ...	18	Dec. 26, 1863	3 yrs.	Mustered out with company Aug. 4, 1865.
Anderson, Charles	... do ...	18	Sept. 8, 1861	3 yrs.	Mustered out Oct. 12, 1864, at Franklin, Tenn., on expiration of term of service.
Barnard, Selah	... do ...	37	Dec. 14, 1863	3 yrs.	Mustered out with company Aug. 4, 1865.
Beagle, Henry	... do ...	18	Feb. 24, 1864	3 yrs.	Mustered out with company Aug. 4, 1865.
Benedict, Napoleon B.	... do ...	19	Nov. 8, 1861	3 yrs.	Died Sept. 3, 1864, in hospital at Vining Station, Ga., of wounds received in action.
Berdine, Abram	... do ...	27	Sept. 8, 1861	3 yrs.	Died July 23, 1863, at Louisville, Ky.
Brown, Samuel S........	... do ...	18	Jan. 4, 1864	3 yrs.	Discharged Feb. 20, 1865, at Columbus, O., on Surgeon's certificate of disability.
Bulger, Benjamin	... do ...	44	Jan. 2, 1864	3 yrs.	Mustered out with company Aug. 4, 1865.
Bundiger, Jacob	... do ...	31	Feb. 11, 1864	3 yrs.	Died June 2, 1865, in General Hospital at Louisville, Ky.
Catlin, Murray B.......	... do ...	19	Mch. 21, 1864	3 yrs.	Mustered out with company Aug. 4, 1865.
Chandler, Smith	... do ...	20	Sept. 23, 1862	3 yrs.	Died March 31, 1864, in General Hospital No. 11 at Nashville, Tenn.
Chapin, Luther C.......	... do ...	18	Sept. 8, 1861	3 yrs.	Died Dec. 31, 1862.
Cherry, Peter	... do ...	25	Feb. 26, 1864	3 yrs.	Left sick at Nashville, Tenn., May 12, 1864; no further record found.
Childers, Valentine	... do ...	18	Sept. 8, 1861	3 yrs.	Mustered out with company Aug. 4, 1865; veteran.
Clagett, James W.......	... do ...	33	Sept. 8, 1861	3 yrs.	Died Dec. 11, 1862, at Nashville, Tenn.
Conrad, John	... do ...	34	Jan. 8, 1864	3 yrs.	Transferred to Co. C Jan. 4, 1865.
Cooper, Orlando G......	... do ...	26	Feb. 25, 1864	3 yrs.	Mustered out with company Aug. 4, 1865.
Culler, Abram	... do ...	22	Sept. 8, 1861	3 yrs.	Discharged Aug. 8, 1862, on Surgeon's certificate of disability.
Culler, Hiram	... do ...	20	Sept. 8, 1861	3 yrs.	Discharged July 30, 1862, at Columbus, O., on Surgeon's certificate of disability.
Dean, William	... do ...	39	Sept. 8, 1861	3 yrs.	Discharged Dec. 4, 1862, on Surgeon's certificate of disability.
Defenbaugher, Henry..	... do ...	18	Oct. 19, 1864	1 yr.	Mustered out June 12, 1865, at Louisville, Ky., by order of War Department.
Delpert, Abram	... do ...	20	Nov. 18, 1861	3 yrs.	Died March 28, 1863, at Nashville, Tenn.
Downard, William J...	... do ...	18	Jan. 4, 1864	3 yrs.	Mustered out with company Aug. 4, 1865.

Names	Rank	Age	Date of Entering the Service	Period of Service	Remarks
Durbin, James L......	Private	18	Sept. 25, 1861	3 yrs.	Transferred from Co. H Dec. 1, 1861; died Aug. —, 1862, while at home.
Dutchman, Robert	... do ...	31	Dec. 26, 1863	3 yrs.	Also borne on rolls as "Randolph R. Derchstman;" mustered out with company Aug. 4, 1865.
Engle, Peter	... do ...	34	Nov. 18, 1863	3 yrs.	Mustered out with company Aug. 4, 1865.
Engleman, David J......	... do ...	19	Feb. 27, 1864	3 yrs.	Mustered out with company Aug. 4, 1865.
Essex, Samuel A........	... do ...	21	Sept. 8, 1861	3 yrs.	Discharged March 25, 1863, on Surgeon's certificate of disability.
Everett, Alexander W.	... do ...	35	Aug. 19, 1862	3 yrs.	Mustered out June 17, 1865, at Nashville, Tenn., by order of War Department.
Everett, Samuel	... do ...	29	Sept. 8, 1861	3 yrs.	Mustered out Oct. 8, 1864, at Columbus, O., on expiration of term of service.
Fickes, Maybery	... do ...	18	Feb. 16, 1864	3 yrs.	Mustered out with company Aug. 4, 1865.
Geary, William	... do ...	51	Sept. 8, 1861	3 yrs.	Discharged July 14, 1862, on Surgeon's certificate of disability.
Goe, William	... do ...	27	Nov. 6, 1863	3 yrs.	Mustered out with company Aug. 4, 1865.
Gray, John W............	... do ...	18	Mch. 7, 1864	3 yrs.	Mustered out with company Aug. 4, 1865.
Harness, George B......	... do ...	30	Sept. 8, 1861	3 yrs.	Discharged Jan. 14, 1863, on Surgeon's certificate of disability.
Harris, Jefferson	... do ...	23	Aug. 24, 1864	1 yr.	Mustered out May 5, 1865, at Tod Barracks, Columbus, O., by order of War Department.
Hart, James J..........	... do ...	36	Jan. 25, 1864	3 yrs.	Transferred to Co. D, 4th Regiment, Veteran Reserve Corps, April 21, 1865; mustered out from same Aug. 19, 1865, at Springfield, Ill., by order of War Department.
Hartrung, Frederick ...	... do ...	18	Sept. 8, 1861	3 yrs.	Died April 2, 1862, at Nashville, Tenn.
Harvey, Albert	... do ...	18	Nov. 19, 1861	3 yrs.	Mustered out Nov. 25, 1864, at Louisville, Ky., on expiration of term of service.
Hebberly, John F.......	... do ...	19	Mch. 1, 1864	3 yrs.	Mustered out June 12, 1865, at Louisville, Ky., by order of War Department.
Held, George	... do ...	40	Dec. 14, 1863	3 yrs.	Mustered out with company Aug. 4, 1865.
Hennie, William	... do ...	18	Sept. 8, 1861	3 yrs.	Mustered out Oct. 12, 1864, at Franklin, Tenn., on expiration of term of service.
Herod, James	... do ...	45	Sept. 8, 1861	3 yrs.	Discharged Nov. 21, 1862, on Surgeon's certificate of disability.
Hodge, Norman	... do ...	23	Sept. 8, 1861	3 yrs.	Mustered out Oct. 12, 1864, at Franklin, Tenn., on expiration of term of service.
Holingshead, William .	... do ...	19	Sept. 8, 1861	3 yrs.	Mustered out Oct. 12, 1864, at Franklin, Tenn., on expiration of term of service.
Hollingsworth, Lafayette.	do ...	19	July 14, 1863	3 yrs.	Mustered out with company Aug. 4, 1865.
Hunter, William R......	... do ...	19	Feb. 18, 1864	3 yrs.	Mustered out with company Aug. 4, 1865.
Irwin, Sims W..........	... do ...	18	Sept. 8, 1861	3 yrs.	Mustered out Oct. 12, 1864, at Franklin, Tenn., on expiration of term of service.
Jacobs, Silas	... do ...	18	Nov. 24, 1861	3 yrs.	Mustered out Dec. 30, 1864, at Nashville, Tenn., on expiration of term of service.
Jamison, John T........	... do ...	21	Sept. 8, 1861	3 yrs.	Mustered out Oct. 12, 1864, at Franklin, Tenn., on expiration of term of service.
Jones, Cornelius	... do ...	18	Sept. 8, 1861	3 yrs.	Died July 3, 1862, at Tuscumbia, Ala.
Kennedy, Daniel	... do ...	18	Sept. 8, 1861	3 yrs.	Mustered out with company Aug. 4, 1865; veteran.
Kile, David	... do ...	23	Nov. 8, 1862	3 yrs.	Mustered out with company Aug. 4, 1865.
Krise, Jacob	... do ...	22	Sept. 8, 1861	3 yrs.	Mustered out Oct. 12, 1864, at Franklin, Tenn., on expiration of term of service.
Lindsey, John	... do ...	22	Sept. 8, 1861	3 yrs.	Killed May 29, 1864, in battle of Moulton, Ala.; veteran.
Luckey, John	... do ...	20	Sept. 8, 1861	3 yrs.	Mustered out Oct. 12, 1864, at Franklin, Tenn., on expiration of term of service.
McCleade, Daniel	... do ...	48	Sept. 8, 1861	3 yrs.	Discharged July 30, 1862, at Columbus, O., on Surgeon's certificate of disability.
McWethy, Charles H..	... do ...	18	Sept. 8, 1861	3 yrs.	Also borne on rolls as "McWelty" and "McWeathey;" captured July 23, 1864, in action near Decatur, Ga.; mustered out June 19, 1865, at Camp Chase, O., by order of War Department; veteran.
Madden, James H......	... do ...	18	Feb. 20, 1864	3 yrs.	Mustered out with company Aug. 4, 1865.
Maxwell, James	... do ...	18	Nov. 18, 1861	3 yrs.	
Merchant, Lemual B...	... do ...	23	Nov. 5, 1861	3 yrs.	Discharged Aug. 21, 1862, on Surgeon's certificate of disability.
Miers, John	... do ...	45	Sept. 8, 1861	3 yrs.	Discharged July 22, 1862, on Surgeon's certificate of disability.
Miller, Andrew J........	... do ...	24	Aug. 23, 1862	3 yrs.	Mustered out June 17, 1865, at Nashville, Tenn., by order of War Department.
Miller, Ira C...........	... do ...	18	July 14, 1863	3 yrs.	Mustered out with company Aug. 4, 1865.
Miller, Levi F..........	... do ...	20	Sept. 8, 1861	3 yrs.	Discharged May 18, 1862, on Surgeon's certificate of disability.
Monlet, Michael	... do ...	18	Nov. 3, 1861	3 yrs.	Mustered out Nov. 25, 1864, at Louisville, Ky., on expiration of term of service.
Morgan, Thomas	... do ...	19	Feb. 1, 1864	3 yrs.	Mustered out with company Aug. 4, 1865.
Mouser, Robert J.......	... do ...	19	Feb. 23, 1864	3 yrs.	Captured July 23, 1864, in action near Decatur, Ga.; mustered out June 19, 1865, at Camp Chase, O., by order of War Department.
Norris, Hiram J........	... do ...	19	Jan. 4, 1864	3 yrs.	Mustered out with company Aug. 4, 1865.
O'Grady, Michael	... do ...	18	Sept. 3, 1863	3 yrs.	Mustered out with company Aug. 4, 1865.

Names	Rank	Age	Date of Entering the Service	Period of Service	Remarks
Ora, Francis	Private	18	Nov. 8, 1861	3 yrs.	Transferred to Co. D Dec. 10, 1861.
Parks, Rose J.	... do ...	22	Sept. 8, 1861	3 yrs.	Discharged March 25, 1863, on Surgeon's certificate of disability.
Payne, Jacob	... do ...	18	April 7, 1865	1 yr.	Mustered out with company Aug. 4, 1865.
Payne, William	... do ...	18	Feb. 29, 1864	3 yrs.	Mustered out with company Aug. 4, 1865.
Preston, George W.	... do ...	25	Nov. 19, 1861	3 yrs.	Mustered out Nov. 25, 1864, at Louisville, Ky., on expiration of term of service.
Pugh, William R.	... do ...	21	Sept. 8, 1861	3 yrs.	Discharged March 19, 1863, on Surgeon's certificate of disability.
Pycroft, William	... do ...	49	Nov. 19, 1861	3 yrs.	
Rigby, Thomas H.	... do ...	18	Dec. 29, 1863	3 yrs.	Mustered out with company Aug. 4, 1865.
Rogers, Joseph	... do ...	23	Sept. 8, 1861	3 yrs.	Mustered out Oct. 12, 1864, at Franklin, Tenn., on expiration of term of service.
Rucle, Stephen	... do ...	23	Sept. 1, 1863	3 yrs.	Also borne on rolls as "Runkle;" mustered out with company Aug. 4, 1865.
Savard, Nelson	... do ...	30	Feb. 13, 1864	3 yrs.	Mustered out with company Aug. 4, 1865.
Scott, Andrew J.	... do ...	21	Sept. 8, 1861	3 yrs.	
Shaw, Henry	... do ...	18	April 7, 1865	1 yr.	Mustered out with company Aug. 4, 1865.
Sheets, Theodore	... do ...	18	Nov. 7, 1863	3 yrs.	Mustered out with company Aug. 4, 1865.
Shreck, August	... do ...	18	Sept. 8, 1861	3 yrs.	Died April 1, 1862, at Nashville, Tenn.
Sidel, Arthur	... do ...	18	Feb. 26, 1864	3 yrs.	Mustered out with company Aug. 4, 1865.
Simons, John A.	... do ...	23	Sept. 8, 1861	3 yrs.	Mustered out Oct. 12, 1864, at Franklin, Tenn., on expiration of term of service.
Simons, Samuel	... do ...	18	Nov. 19, 1861	3 yrs.	Died Oct. 17, 1862, at Nashville, Tenn.
Stanton, Louis	... do ...	18	July 14, 1863	3 yrs.	Died Feb. 3, 1864.
Stormont, William	... do ...	27	Oct. 7, 1863	3 yrs.	
Van Sickle, Selah	... do ...	18	Jan. 4, 1864	3 yrs.	Mustered out with company Aug. 4, 1865.
Wagner, Jeremiah	... do ...	19	Mch. 2, 1864	3 yrs.	Mustered out June 30, 1865, at Louisville, Ky., by order of War Department.
Walkup, Josiah G.	... do ...	23	Feb. 24, 1864	3 yrs.	Mustered out with company Aug. 4, 1865.
Ward, William	... do ...	18	Nov. 16, 1863	3 yrs.	Died March 31, 1864, in General Hospital No. 11 at Nashville, Tenn.
Warner, John	... do ...	18	Sept. 8, 1861	3 yrs.	Mustered out Oct. 12, 1864, at Franklin, Tenn., on expiration of term of service.
Webster, La Fever	... do ...	20	Oct. 22, 1863	3 yrs.	Captured July 23, 1864, in action near Decatur, Ga.; mustered out June 19, 1865, at Camp Chase, O., by order of War Department.
White, Adelbert B.	... do ...	18	Sept. 8, 1861	3 yrs.	Mustered out Nov. 23, 1864, at Louisville, Ky., on expiration of term of service.
White, Horace B.	... do ...	50	Sept. 8, 1861	3 yrs.	Promoted to Batt. Hospital Stewart Dec. 1, 1861.
White, William A.	... do ...	19	Sept. 8, 1861	3 yrs.	Mustered out Oct. 12, 1864, at Franklin, Tenn., on expiration of term of service.
Williams, Charles	... do ...	26	Nov. 14, 1863	3 yrs.	
Wilson, Isaac C.	... do ...	18	Dec. 24, 1863	3 yrs.	Mustered out with company Aug. 4, 1865.
Winn, Barney	... do ...	20	Feb. 23, 1864	3 yrs.	Mustered out with company Aug. 4, 1865.
Winslow, Holden	... do ...	20	Sept. 8, 1861	3 yrs.	Died Dec. 31, 1862.
Yahn, Frederick	... do ...	22	Sept. 8, 1861	3 yrs.	Mustered out Oct. 12, 1864, at Franklin, Tenn., on expiration of term of service.
Yeager, Joseph	... do ...	19	Dec. 23, 1863	3 yrs.	Mustered out with company Aug. 4, 1865.
Davis, George	Cook	....	April 26, 1865	3 yrs.	Colored under-cook; mustered out with company Aug. 4, 1865.
Johnson, Alexander	... do ...	....	April 26, 1865	3 yrs.	Colored under-cook; mustered out with company Aug. 4, 1865.
Sneede, William	... do ...	18	Mch. 3, 1863	3 yrs.	Colored under-cook; mustered out with company Aug. 4, 1865.

UNASSIGNED RECRUITS.

Names	Rank	Age	Date of Entering the Service	Period of Service	Remarks
Adams, John	Private	21	Nov. 8, 1863	3 yrs.	
Anderson, Amos B.	... do ...	20	Aug. 28, 1862	3 yrs.	No further record found.
Antana, Stephen	... do ...	19	Dec. 14, 1863	3 yrs.	No further record found.
Arnold, John C.	... do ...	19	Nov. 17, 1863	3 yrs.	
Atwood, John	... do ...	24	Dec. 10, 1863	3 yrs.	Killed by the kick of a horse, date not given.
Bacon, Worlin B.	... do ...	19	Oct. 6, 1862	3 yrs.	Transferred to 67th Co., 2d Battalion, Veteran Reserve Corps ——; discharged Sept. 16, 1864, on Surgeon's certificate of disability.
Barks, Henry S.	... do ...	42	Dec. 10, 1862	3 yrs.	No further record found.
Beercraft, Charles	... do ...	19	Nov. 27, 1863	3 yrs.	No further record found.
Blackman, Almanzo	... do ...	18	Feb. 25, 1864	3 yrs.	No further record found.
Blaine, Henry	... do ...	28	Dec. 26, 1863	3 yrs.	No further record found.
Boyle, John	... do ...	32	Dec. 22, 1863	3 yrs.	No further record found.
Brister, John H.	... do ...	18	Aug. 29, 1862	3 yrs.	No further record found.
Burt, George	... do ...	26	Dec. 10, 1862	3 yrs.	No further record found.
Butke, William	... do ...	22	Dec. 15, 1864	1 yr.	No further record found.
Butler, John	... do ...	21	Dec. 29, 1863	3 yrs.	No further record found.

Names	Rank	Age	Date of Entering the Service	Period of Service	Remarks
Carleton, James	Private	19	Nov. 17, 1863	3 yrs.	No further record found.
Clapp, Augustus M....	... do ...	18	Sept. 30, 1862	3 yrs.	Died March 9, 1863.
Cliber, Jacob	... do ...	23	Jan. 8, 1864	3 yrs.	No further record found.
Collins, William	... do ...	19	April 6, 1865	1 yr.	Mustered out May 9, 1865, at Tod Barracks, Columbus, O., by order of War Department.
Connell, Charles	... do ...	27	Sept. 23, 1863	3 yrs.	Discharged Nov. 11, 1863, on Surgeon's certificate of disability.
Cooper, William	... do ...	32	Mch. 22, 1864	3 yrs.	No further record found.
Cooper, William	... do ...	26	Mch. 30, 1865	1 yr.	No further record found.
Corey, Stephen C.......	... do ...	32	Dec. 19, 1862	3 yrs.	Transferred to 187th Co., 1st Battalion, Veteran Reserve Corps, ——; discharged May 31, 1865, on Surgeon's certificate of disability.
Cutler, Joseph B.......	... do ...	28	Aug. 26, 1862	3 yrs.	Transferred to Co. B, 7th Regiment, Veteran Reserve Corps. ——; mustered out June 29, 1865, by order of War Department.
Crider, Miles	... do ...	18	Nov. 30, 1864	1 yr.	No further record found.
Cyrus, Henry	... do ...	18	Feb. 26, 1864	3 yrs.	No further record found.
Davidson, Greenbury J	... do ...	19	Feb. 28, 1864	3 yrs.	No further record found.
Dickson, Edward	... do ...	23	Mch. 26, 1864	3 yrs.	No further record found.
Dunn, William	... do ...	33	Jan. 13, 1864	3 yrs.	
Eichor, Henry	... do ...	22	Feb. 27, 1864	3 yrs.	No further record found.
Ewing, Charles	... do ...	27	Feb. 26, 1864	3 yrs.	No further record found.
Farinash, George	... do ...	26	Aug. 22, 1862	3 yrs.	Forwarded to regiment Nov. 15, 1862; no further record found.
Farnsworth, Curtis F.	... do ...	26	Dec. 8, 1863	3 yrs.	Forwarded to regiment Dec. 16, 1863; no further record found.
Ferdinand, Gabriel ...	... do ...	32	April 1, 1864	3 yrs.	No further record found.
Fielding, Joshua	... do ...	20	Dec. 9, 1863	3 yrs.	No further record found.
Finck, John	... do ...	28	Nov. 20, 1862	3 yrs.	Mustered out Dec. 10, 1862, by order of War Department.
Finierty, William	... do ...	18	Mch. 11, 1864	3 yrs.	Forwarded to general rendezvous March 16, 1864; no further record found.
Fix, Jackson	... do ...	44	Mch. 8, 1865	1 yr.	Discharged June 12, 1865, on Surgeon's certificate of disability.
Foutz, Sebastian	... do ...	42	Aug. 31, 1863	3 yrs.	Forwarded to regiment Sept. 21, 1863; no further record found.
Freeman, John	... do ...	21	Mch. 25, 1864	3 yrs.	Forwarded to regiment April 15, 1864; no further record found.
Fry, Henry	... do ...	27	Mch. 22, 1865	1 yr.	Forwarded to regiment March 29, 1865; no further record found.
Gabriel, Ferdinand ...	... do ...	32	April 1, 1864	3 yrs.	No further record found.
Garvy, John	... do ...	30	Jan. 13, 1864	3 yrs.	No further record found.
Gilhart, Charles	... do ...	....	July —, 1862	....	No further record found.
Graham, William	... do ...	28	Aug. 19, 1863	3 yrs.	
Greek, William H.......	... do ...	22	Mch. 18, 1865	1 yr.	No further record found.
Hartz, Jacob	... do ...	21	Dec. 10, 1863	3 yrs.	Forwarded to regiment Dec. 19, 1863; no further record found.
Handley, Michael	... do ...	43	Dec. 30, 1863	3 yrs.	No further record found.
Hayden, William	... do ...	18	Dec. 21, 1863	3 yrs.	Forwarded to Columbus, O., Dec. 23, 1863; no further record found.
Henderson, Thomas ..	... do ...	19	Oct. 19, 1864	1 yr.	No further record found.
Hessner, John	... do ...	28	Nov. 5, 1863	3 yrs.	No further record found.
Hiberling, George W...	... do ...	21	Sept. 12, 1862	3 yrs.	Assigned to Co. I March 8, 1864, but not taken up on rolls of company; no further record found.
Hickey, Thomas	... do ...	27	Dec. 15, 1863	3 yrs.	No further record found.
Hoff, Jacob	... do ...	21	Feb. 9, 1864	3 yrs.	Died Feb. 26, 1864, in General Hospital at Nashville, Tenn.
Hoffman, John G.......	... do ...	19	Nov. 16, 1863	3 yrs.	Forwarded to regiment Nov. 18, 1863; no further record found.
Hogan, John	... do ...	18	July 24, 1863	3 yrs.	No further record found.
Holman, Thomas C....	... do ...	23	Mch. 22, 1865	1 yr.	Forwarded to regiment March 29, 1865; no further record found.
Howard, William	... do ...	26	Nov. 17, 1863	3 yrs.	Forwarded to regiment March 18, 1863; no further record found.
Hutchins, Clinton R...	... do ...	18	Dec. 9, 1863	3 yrs.	Forwarded to regiment Dec. 16, 1863; no further record found.
Hutton, Horace K.....	... do ...	19	Feb. 26, 1864	3 yrs.	Forwarded to regiment March 10, 1864; no further record found.
Iaper, Charles	... do ...	18	Jan. 4, 1864	3 yrs.	No further record found.
James, Charles	... do ...	25	Mch. 20, 1865	1 yr.	Forwarded to regiment March 29, 1865; no further record found.
Johnson, William	... do ...	23	Dec. 17, 1863	3 yrs.	Forwarded to regiment Dec. 25, 1863; no further record found.
Kellogg, Henry H.....	... do ...	23	Jan. 4, 1864	3 yrs.	No further record found.
Kenneally, Edward H.	... do ...	19	Mch. 28, 1865	1 yr.	Mustered out Aug. 1, 1865, at Nashville, Tenn., by order of War Department.
Kennedy, John	... do ...	25	Nov. 5, 1863	3 yrs.	No further record found.
Kennedy, Joseph	... do ...	19	Dec. 8, 1863	3 yrs.	Forwarded to regiment Dec. 16, 1863; no further record found.
Kinney, David	... do ...	18	Mch. 21, 1864	3 yrs.	Forwarded to regiment March 21, 1864; no further record found.
Leach, Pleasant	... do ...	42	Sept. 20, 1862	3 yrs.	Forwarded to regiment Sept. 25, 1862; no further record found.

Names	Rank	Age	Date of Entering the Service	Period of Service	Remarks
Lemon, Jacob	Private	18	Mch. 21, 1864	3 yrs.	Forwarded to regiment March 26, 1864; no further record found.
Lemon, William H.	..do...	21	Feb. 26, 1864	3 yrs.	Forwarded to regiment March 10, 1864; no further record found.
Leonard, Kelley R.	..do...	22	July 16, 1863	3 yrs.	Forwarded to regiment Sept. 21, 1863; no further record found.
Lindall, Marquis E.	..do...	18	Dec. 29, 1863	3 yrs.	Forwarded to regiment Jan. 4, 1864; no further record found.
Long, James L.	..do...	21	Aug. 27, 1862	3 yrs.	Forwarded to regiment Sept. 12, 1862; no further record found.
Long, James E.	..do...	18	Jan. 2, 1864	3 yrs.	No further record found.
Lorn, Lewis G.	..do...	22	Feb. 28, 1865	1 yr.	No further record found.
Louis, Albert	..do...	29	Mch. 29, 1864	3 yrs.	Forwarded to regiment March 31, 1864; no further record found.
McKehiser, Washington	..do...	19	Mch. 8, 1865	1 yr.	No further record found.
Mack, John	..do...	23	Feb. 26, 1864	3 yrs.	Forwarded to regiment March 10, 1864; no further record found.
Madill, Benjamin	..do...	22	Dec. 17, 1863	3 yrs.	Forwarded to Columbus, O., Dec. 23, 1863; no further record found.
Marshall, James	..do...	38	Jan. 13, 1864	3 yrs.	
Martin, Albert	..do...	19	Nov. 21, 1863	3 yrs.	No further record found.
Martin, Frederick	..do...	18	Jan. 5, 1864	3 yrs.	Forwarded to regiment Jan. 14, 1864; no further record found.
Merton, John	..do...	25	Dec. 15, 1863	3 yrs.	Forwarded to Columbus, O., Dec. 15, 1863; no further record found.
Michael, George	..do...	25	Sept. 26, 1863	3 yrs.	Forwarded to regiment Oct. 17, 1863; no further record found.
Miller, John	..do...	20	Mch. 22, 1864	3 yrs.	Forwarded to regiment March 24, 1864; no further record found.
Morrison, William	..do...	18	Jan. 4, 1864	3 yrs.	No further record found.
Monson, James	..do...	27	Feb. 26, 1864	3 yrs.	Forwarded to regiment March 10, 1864; no further record found.
Montgomery, Eli	..do...	19	Mch. 23, 1864	3 yrs.	Forwarded to regiment March 29, 1864; no further record found.
Pennell, William	..do...	22	Aug. 16, 1864	1 yr.	
Perry, John	..do...	28	Mch. 4, 1864	3 yrs.	Forwarded to regiment March 10, 1864; no further record found.
Pew, Joseph A.	..do...	18	Jan. 4, 1864	3 yrs.	Died Feb. 13, 1864.
Phelps, George C.	..do...	18	Mch. 8, 1864	3 yrs.	Discharged May 10, 1864, on Surgeon's certificate of disability.
Porter, William L.	..do...	43	Dec. 14, 1863	3 yrs.	Transferred to 187th Co., 1st Battalion, Veteran Reserve Corps, ——; discharged May 12, 1865, on Surgeon's certificate of disability.
Quirk, William	..do...	37	Dec. 7, 1863	3 yrs.	Died Dec. 14, 1863.
Randoll, Fritz	..do...	18	Dec. 29, 1863	3 yrs.	Forwarded from Columbus, O., Jan. 12, 1864; no further record found.
Raneely, Thomas	..do...	44	Dec. 23, 1863	3 yrs.	No further record found.
Rice, George	..do...	19	Aug. 23, 1862	3 yrs.	Forwarded from Columbus, O., Sept. 12, 1862; no further record found.
Riley, John	..do...	25	Mch. 15, 1865	1 yr.	Mustered out May 9, 1865, from Tod Barracks, Columbus, O., by order of War Department.
Riley, Patrick	..do...	22	July 24, 1863	3 yrs.	No further record found.
Ryan, Rodger	..do...	32	Dec. 22, 1863	3 yrs.	No further record found.
Sampson, Burdett	..do...	18	Aug. 5, 1863	3 yrs.	Forwarded from Columbus, O., Aug. 24, 1863; no further record found.
Sayers, James A.	..do...	24	Feb. 29, 1864	3 yrs.	Forwarded to regiment March 10, 1864; no further record found.
Smith, Charles	..do...	21	Dec. 16, 1863	3 yrs.	Forwarded to regiment Dec. 17, 1863; no further record found.
Smith, Daniel A.	..do...	18	Nov. 25, 1863	3 yrs.	No further record found.
Smith, Hugh	..do...	28	Dec. 18, 1863	3 yrs.	Forwarded from Columbus, O., Dec. 28, 1863; no further record found.
Smith, John	..do...	18	April 5, 1865	1 yr.	Forwarded from Columbus, O., April 24, 1865; no further record found.
Thomas, John B.	..do...	25	Mch. 21, 1865	1 yr.	Forwarded from Columbus, O., March 29, 1865; no further record found.
Tyler, George	..do...	25	Dec. 2, 1863	3 yrs.	Forwarded to regiment Dec. 14, 1863; no further record found.
Valentine, Aaron	..do...	20	Jan. 15, 1864	3 yrs.	No further record found.
Wallace, Hiram W.	..do...	33	Dec. 18, 1863	3 yrs.	Forwarded from Columbus, O., Dec. 28, 1863; no further record found.
Wappert, Charles	..do...	26	Sept. 8, 1862	3 yrs.	Forwarded to regiment Sept. 25, 1862; no further record found.
Wells, Charles	..do...	19	Feb. 20, 1864	3 yrs.	Forwarded to regiment Feb. 20, 1864; no further record found.
Wells, Lemuel H.	..do...	21	Mch. 27, 1865	1 yr.	Mustered out Aug. 1, 1865, at Nashville, Tenn.
Willis, John F.	..do...	18	Sept. 11, 1863	3 yrs.	No further record found.
Woodruff, Baker	..do...	20	Aug. 28, 1862	3 yrs.	Forwarded from Columbus, O., Sept. 12, 1862; no further record found.
Wooley, Gilbert H.	..do...	21	Dec. 21, 1863	3 yrs.	
Wycoff, Merritt	..do...	22	Feb. 23, 1864	3 yrs.	Forwarded to regiment March 10, 1864; no further record found.
Young, Gilbert	..do...	26	Dec. 4, 1863	3 yrs.	Forwarded from Columbus, O., Dec. 28, 1863; no further record found.

A Narrative of Military Service
The Civil War Through the Eyes of a Controversial Fighting General
William B. Hazen

William Babcock Hazen began the Civil War as a first lieutenant and ended it as a major general commanding the 15th Army Corps. Two decades later he wrote this insightful, controversial memoir — an exceedingly rare book to find in its 1885 edition. Hazen's wartime record included command of the 41st Ohio Infantry Regiment, as well as brigade and division command in three different Federal armies. A strict disciplinarian who demanded the best from his men, he fought at Shiloh, Stones River, Chickamauga, Brown's Ferry, Missionary Ridge, the Atlanta Campaign, Fort McAllister and the Carolinas Campaign. General William T. Sherman called Hazen "an officer of the highest professional attainments and of the best possible habits."

Hardcover with dust jacket, 576 pages, 71 photographs, maps, index. $35

With the Western Sharpshooters
Michigan Boys of Company D, 66th Illinois
Lorenzo A. Barker

Of all the regiments serving in Federal armies during the Civil War, the 66th Illinois, known as the Western Sharpshooters, was among the most unusual. Containing volunteers from eight Midwestern states, the Sharpshooters were organized specifically for skirmish duty and may be considered the western-theater counterpart to Berdan's Sharpshooters of the Army of the Potomac. Sergeant Barker's book concentrates on the regiment's Michigan company, which was armed early in the war with Dimick American deer and target rifles, and later with magazine-fed, 16-shot Henry rifles.. It participated in such engagements as Fort Donelson, Shiloh, Corinth, the Atlanta Campaign and the march through the Carolinas. Also included is a newly compiled brief history of the 66th Illinois, highlighted by excerpts from Barker's unpublished diaries.

Hardcover with dust jacket, 192 pages, 68 photographs and engravings. $22.95

History of the 72nd Indiana
Wilder's Lightning Brigade
Benjamin F. Magee

Based on his wartime diary plus dozens of his comrades, B.F. Magee's history of the 72nd Indiana Mounted Infantry is one of the best chronicles of a Civil War regiment. A sergeant in Company I, Magee describes in meticulous detail literally hundreds of events which marked the three-year service of this distinctive Hoosier regiment. His sharp focus on the war's common soldier offers an unusually vivid and often humorous picture of those who bore the brunt of the fighting, suffering and dying. As part of Colonel John T. Wilder's famous Lightning Brigade, the 72nd Indiana used mobility and rapid firepower from its Spencer rifles to awesome effect, and forged an indelible reputation through battles and campaigns in Tennessee, Georgia and Alabama.

Hardcover with dust jacket, 800 pages, 61 photographs, full regimental roster. $40

BLUE ACORN PRESS
P.O. Box 2684 • Huntington, West Virginia 25726 • (304) 733-3917